BALDWIN AND THE CONSERVATIVE PARTY

BALDWIN AND THE CONSERVATIVE PARTY
The Crisis of 1929-1931

Stuart Ball

Yale University Press
New Haven and London
1988

To my parents
in gratitude for their love and support

The publication of this book has been kindly assisted by a grant
from the Twenty-Seven Foundation

Set in 11/12 Bembo by Textflow Services Limited, Belfast, and printed and bound in
Great Britain at the University Printing House, Oxford by David Stanford, printer to
the University of Oxford.

Library of Congress CIP Data

Ball, Stuart, 1956–
    Baldwin and the Conservative Party: the crisis of 1929-1931 / Stuart Ball
        p.   cm.
    Bibliography: p.
    ISBN 0-300-03961-1
    1. Baldwin, Stanley Baldwin, Earl, 1867-1947. 2. Conservative
Party (Great Britain) 3. Great Britain — Politics and
government — 1910-1936. 4. Depressions — 1929 — Great Britain
    I. Title
    DA566.9.B15B34 1988   87-22504

CONTENTS

ACKNOWLEDGEMENTS

It is a pleasure to acknowledge the many people who have helped with the research and writing of this book. In particular, I would like to thank the many officers and agents of constituency Conservative Associations across the country who, with unfailing helpfulness and hospitality, permitted me to consult the records in their care. I am also grateful to those other constituency Associations who have deposited their archives in their local Record Offices and who made them available to me there. The staff of the various Area offices were equally generous in their assistance. Miss Ann Hay kindly allowed me to consult the important collection of records of the Scottish Unionist Association, which she has taken great care to preserve at Scottish Conservative Central Office, Edinburgh. Miss Joan West gave considerable help with the materials still held at Conservative Central Office in London. I would also like to thank Mr. Geoffrey Block O.B.E. and Miss Hay for letters of introduction to the local Associations in England and Scotland respectively.

The archivists and librarians of numerous institutions also gave freely of their time and knowledge. In particular, I would like to thank Dr. Sarah Street of the Bodleian Library for assistance with documents deposited in the Conservative Party Archive, Dr. B.S. Benedikz of Birmingham University Library for sharing his encyclopediac knowledge of the Chamberlain papers, and Mr. R.H. Harcourt Williams for assistance with the documents held at Hatfield House. The staff of the Western Manuscripts Reading Room at Cambridge University Library, of Churchill College Archives Centre, of the Bodleian Library Manuscripts Reading Room, and of the House of Lords Record Office were most helpful, and made my lengthy researches in the many collections in their care pleasurable as well as profitable. I am also grateful for the help and guidance of the staff of the many Record Offices and other institutions, listed in full in the Bibliography, where my visits were more fleeting but no less worthwhile.

Documents in the Royal Archives are quoted by the gracious permission of Her Majesty the Queen. I would like to thank the following for access to and permission to quote from copyright material the Rt. Hon. Julian Amery, MP; Earl Baldwin of Bewdley; Lord Brentford; Mr. W. Bell; Lord Croft; the Earl of Derby; Lord Elibank; the Earl of Halifax; Mr. T.R. Hartman; Vice-Admiral Sir Ian Hogg; Lord Kennet; Prof. A.K.S. Lambton; Mr. W. Maclean; Mrs.

Verity Paget; Mr. J. Peto; the Marquess of Salisbury; Sir David Smithers; Mrs. A Stacey; the Earl of Swinton; and Lord Wraxall. I am most grateful to Mr. A.J.P. Taylor for allowing me to quote from the Beaverbrook Archive; Birmingham University Library for permission to make quotations from the Chamberlain papers; the Master and Fellows of Trinity College Cambridge for extracts from the Butler papers; and the owner of the copyright to the Headlam diary. Passages from documents in the House of Lords Record Office are reproduced by permission of the Clerk of the Records. I acknowledge with thanks the permission of the Master, Fellows, and Scholars of Churchill College in the University of Cambridge, and also of the Syndics of Cambridge University Library, to publish extracts from records in their care. The Conservative Party kindly allowed material in the Conservative Party Archive at the Bodleian Library to be quoted; in this respect I am also grateful to the Scottish Conservative Central Office and to the several local Associations, who have given similar permission. Every effort has been made to trace the copyright holder of unpublished documents from which quotations have been made; I hope that those whom it was not possible to locate will accept my apologies. Finally, I would like to thank the editors of the *Historical Journal* for permission to reproduce material previously published in that journal.

Generous financial assistance towards the costs involved in research was made in awards from the British Academy and the Research Board of the University of Leicester. The publication of this book has been kindly assisted by a grant from the Twenty-Seven Foundation.

I am most grateful for the encouragement and advice of several scholars. I owe a very great debt to Ruddock Mackay and John Ramsden for their constructive help on many occasions. John Turner and Phillip Williamson have saved me from a number of errors of both fact and judgement. Richard Bonney, Aubrey Newman, John Oldfield, and John Young, past and present colleagues at the University of Leicester, gave great assistance by commenting on drafts of this work.

I would also like to thank Richard Mobbs, Jan Simpson, and Sue Williams of the Leicester University Computer Centre for their help in preparing the text.

My parents have unstintingly given their encouragement and support over many years; to dedicate this book to them is only a small token of my gratitude and appreciation for all that they have done. I cannot even begin to adequately acknowledge the debt of thanks which I owe to my wife, Gillian, and our son, Alastair; though they come last in this preface, they are and always will be first in my thoughts.

Stuart Ball
University of Leicester

INTRODUCTION

The development of the party system has been the dominant feature of British politics since the passage of the first Reform Act in 1832. As the most effective means of organising political activity, party has become the most important element in the unwritten constitution. During the last century and a half, major changes have taken place in the composition and nature of the party system. These have often resulted not from the difficulties within one party, but from a period of general crisis which has affected all parties, shifting in the process all the landmarks on the political horizon. However, once established, the individual parties developed considerable powers of survival, acquired a claim on loyalties, and achieved durability simply through longevity. As a result, changes have mainly occurred within the framework of the existing parties, though straining them to the point of fracture. Such crises were apparent in the nineteenth-century, in the mid-1840s and again in the mid-1880s. In the twentieth century, the most significant period of discontinuity has been that which followed from the First World War.

The rearrangement of forces which resulted from this occurred in two stages. The first of these, from 1916 to 1924, has already received its due share of historical attention.[1] The two most visible consequences of the events of this period, the decline of the Liberal Party and the rise of the Labour Party, have also been explored.[2] However, the second stage of the reconstruction of modern British politics, which took place between 1929 and 1931, has not been so fully investigated. This is in spite of the importance of its consequences, for it brought about a reshaping of the party system, and a new basis in the pattern of issues, which was to hold sway for the following fifty years. The system established in 1931 clearly dominated British politics for three decades, thereafter passing into a decline which led towards the next catharsis in the early 1980s.

Not only was each of the three main parties racked by internal dissension between 1929 and 1931; anxiety about their future image and intentions exacerbated their problems. These were also the product of the pressures of the time, resulting from the decline of Britain's economic position, which was combined with the perpetuation of her role as an imperial power on a world scale, with commitments and pretensions beyond her means or will. These problems were apparent throughout the inter-war era, but they came to a head between 1929 and 1931 as a result of the confluence of other factors: the global economic recession; a hung Parliament; and the rise to the brink of power of the generation which had borne the brunt of the fighting in the First World War. Political reappraisal at this time was not limited to disputes within the parties, and it linked them as much as it distinguished them. The air was full of initiatives for mergers and coalitions, centre groups and new parties, all of whose programmes would have required shifting the basic ground of political activity away from the concerns of the immediate past into entirely new pastures. There were loud demands for a government of businessmen, or a non-partisan national government to be created from the best talents of all the parties. Such proposals entailed the submergence of the issues upon which the existing divides had formed, in favour of a new consensus. Although less clearly perceived by the advocates of 'reconstruction', inevitably this would have meant drawing new lines of division.

The period between 1929 and 1931 was a crucial stage in the transition from the political issues which had their roots in the late-Victorian and Edwardian eras and which characterised the 1920s, to those which were the central concerns of the 1930s, and which underlay British politics until the 1960s, if not later. The 1930s were a dramatic decade, but in terms of the party system they had attained the stability which had been so conspicuously lacking since 1914. Because of the danger of another world war, the problems of the slump, and the threats from domestic extremism, it has been customary to categorise the 1930s as a period of instability. But it was the 1920s which had the character of a period preceding a cathartic reconstruction, with the political and economic consequences of the First World War, the after-effects of coalition, the lottery of three-party rivalry, the frequent elections, the emergence of a socialist government, and the general strike. One of the most important direct results of the events of 1929 to 1931 was the re-establishment of the two-party system, which was to remain in force for the next fifty years. The general election of 1929 was the height of equal three-party competition between Liberals, Labour, and Conservatives. Every election thereafter until 1983 consisted of a straight choice between a Labour or a Conservative administration, though in the 1930s this was somewhat disguised by the existence of a 'National' coalition in which the Conservatives formed the dominant element.

Between 1929 and 1931 all three parties passed through changes in fortune, composition, and outlook. The Liberal Party was torn apart by the dilemmas which it faced, first in supporting the minority Labour government, and later in adhering to the National Government formed in August 1931. The consequences of these options led to the division of the Liberals in the period up to 1935, and their disappearance as a significant force in national politics.[3] The Labour

Party suffered a cataclysmic division as a result of the pressures it faced in office between 1929 and 1931, shedding in the process the late-Victorian leadership which had nursed it from birth. The short term result was Labour's exclusion from power for the foreseeable future; the long term result the domination of the parliamentary Party by the Trades Union Congress and a legacy of suspicion of its own leaders and a fear of betrayals, real or imagined. The history of the Labour Party has always been the most thoroughly tilled field in modern British political historiography, and the traumas of the second Labour Government have already been analysed in depth.[4] As a result, the roles of both the Liberal and Labour parties during this crucial period have been fully mapped out. However, the picture is far from complete, for the serious and important parallel crisis within the Conservative Party between 1929 and 1931 has been neglected. A similar position exists so far as analyses of the critical event of the period, the formation of the National Government in August 1931, are concerned. Here, historical attention has been focused upon the problems within the Cabinet, the decisions of Ramsay Macdonald, and the role of King George V.[5] Although the Conservative Party has been described as the sole benefactor from the events of August 1931, its role has been either neglected for its supposed passivity or misunderstood in mood and intention.[6] So long as these two crucial gaps remain, no satisfactory explanation can be provided for the origins of the party system which was to dominate British politics for the next fifty years.

This neglect is even more remarkable in view of the fact that the history of British politics in the century since 1886 has been one of Conservative dominance. Over that period, the Conservative Party, either standing alone or as the predominant partner in an alliance, has provided the government of the country for a total of almost seventy years. There were two periods in which the forces of Conservatism found themselves rejected by the electorate and simultaneously prey to disunity on a scale sufficient to arouse fears for the collapse of the Party: the prolonged bitter exclusion between 1906 and 1914, and the shorter spell in opposition between 1929 and 1931. The brief duration of the latter should not belie its importance. Periods in opposition are more significant in the development of a party than its tenures of office, and reveal more about its nature. This was certainly so for the Liberals from 1895 to 1906, the Conservatives again in 1945 to 1951 and 1974 to 1979, and most demonstrably in the case of Labour from 1979 to 1983. The period from 1929 to 1931 was the only interval of any importance in which the Conservative Party was out of power between the two World Wars. Defeat produced a major internal crisis. There was not only an extremely bitter revolt from below against the leader, but also a reassessment of the Conservative stance in all important policies, and a groundswell of restless disaffection mixed with jaundiced apathy amongst the rank and file. The fundamental crisis which emerged from this explosive situation took the form of a running battle for control of the Party, and therefore a struggle over its leadership.

Although some general surveys exist, the Conservative Party has rarely been investigated in depth. Lord Blake's account of the history of the Conservatives from Peel to Churchill is fluently written, but does not delve deeply into the inter-war period.[7] John Ramsden's more recent study of the Party between 1902 and 1940 has other strengths, but his account of the crisis of 1929–1931 has followed the conventional path.[8] Detailed historical investigation has concentrated upon the earlier series of crises in the Edwardian era.[9] For all its central importance, the history of the Conservative Party after 1914 is one of the darkest areas of modern historiography, into which intermittent beams of light have been cast only by the biographies of a few individuals.[10]

The historiographical context of this study is therefore not so much one of a debate as a vacuum. The present work is intended to fill this gap, and in the process not only to survey a crucial period of crisis in recent British politics, but also to cast a wider illumination over the nature of the Conservative Party in the first half of the twentieth century. The structure of the Party, the way in which it operates, and the influences upon its policies can be thus exposed. The period from 1929 to 1931 saw the finale to the long struggle over tariff reform within the Party. That policy had been the prime cause of its loss of power from 1906 to 1914, and dominates the history of Conservatism in the early twentieth century. The Conservative Party had always regarded itself as the party of empire, and in this period vital decisions concerning the future development of the British Empire were taken. These affected both the economic relationship with the self-governing dominions, and the political evolution of the other important unit within the empire: India. Between 1929 and 1931 the attitude of the Conservative Party to the relationship between home and empire passed through a decisive phase. The consequence of the options taken was, consciously or not, to turn Britain away from world status and towards insularity. Controversy over fiscal policy and the debate over the future devolution of government in India were both subordinated to domestic social and economic concerns. By the time of the formation of the National Government in August 1931, it was apparent that, despite the vocal disagreement of a minority, the Party would put domestic political unity before imperial anxieties. This developing primacy is fundamental to any explanation of the progress of the Conservative Party to the position where after the Second World War it could accept and even preside over the dismantling of empire and the process of decolonisation.

The central themes of this study are the role of the leader and the relationship between the leader and his followers, the rank and file of the Party. The period in opposition between 1929 and 1931 was a crucial phase in the leadership of Stanley Baldwin, and a close study of the crisis within the Conservative Party reveals much about the character and methods of this complex and significant figure. The period between the wars is often seen as 'the Baldwin age', but his tenure was nearly cut short in 1930 after only seven years. Baldwin's survival of this revolt secured his position until he chose to stand down of his own accord in 1937. The succession to Baldwin was also decided by the events of 1929–1931, for this was the most important stage in the rise of Neville Chamberlain. In May 1929 he was only one amongst several significant members of the Cabinet; by October 1931 he had established himself as undisputed crown prince and heir apparent. This period was also a turning point in the career of another major figure in twentieth-century British politics: Winston Churchill. As a result of political developments between 1929 and 1931, he was to spend the rest of the decade in the wilderness, discredited in the eyes of the bulk of the Party. These changes of policy and personnel had matured by August 1931; the unexpected formation of the National Government in that month fixed them into permanent form. The political crisis of August 1931 was the most important and serious in this century, and the role of the Conservative Party in the formation of the emergency coalition was crucial. However, it can only be understood against the background of the divisions which had riven the Conservative Party during the previous two years.

In addition to these themes, another important historical debate is woven into the fabric of this study: the question of the power of the press. The crisis within Conservatism at this time was presented as being the result of the attempt of the proprietors of mass circulation newspapers to wield unconstitutional influence—in Baldwin's famous phrase of March 1931, to exercise power without responsibility, 'the prerogative of the harlot throughout the ages'. Here, the question has been approached from the standpoint of party politics, rather than an analysis of the role of the press in British society. This is more than just a question of methodology. Notwithstanding the claims and fears of newspaper domination held by contemporaries, the power of the press as such was of little moment, unless it could vocalise and organise a substantial body of opinion alienated from, or unrepresented by, the existing parties or leaders. The power of the press barons was conditional upon this, and when they lacked support beyond their Fleet Street premises, their inability to affect the larger issues was revealed. By the 1920s politicians had ceased to be sure that the press reflected public opinion, let alone creating it. However, when the newspapers became the mouthpiece of rank and file disaffection, their apparent strength was given substance. Yet to mobilise such feeling, the establishment of a pressure group, the raising of funds, the enlisting of supporters, and the contesting of elections were necessary features. Once operating in this arena, the press lords had become party politicians, albeit of a novel kind, and thus their role can be better analysed from that perspective.

Concentration upon the figures at the pinnacles of power provides only a part of the picture. One of the most important, and most constructive, developments in the writing of modern British political history has been the approach adopted by the school of 'high politics'. Their surgical examinations of the intricate manoeuvres and stratagems of the leading figures on the political stage almost hour by hour, and their sceptical analyses of the gap between rhetoric and reality, have sent breaths of fresh air through many topics.[11] However, such an exclusive concentration upon a handful of Westminster politicians is appropriate to eighteenth- and nineteenth- rather than twentieth-century British politics. With the growth not only of a mass electorate but also of the mass media, and the concomitant development of party organisation, modern politicians cannot be understood if they are depicted as operating in such a closed environment. Public opinion was always a matter of vital concern, though they could reach it only in an impressionistic or piecemeal fashion. As a result, the formalised expression of the views of the politically active members of the public, transmitted through the party structures upon which the leadership depended for their power, were a crucially important part of their calculations. Yet this element has not been drawn upon either as a source or as a subject for scholarly attention, a fact true not just of works which have taken a conventional Westmister perspective, but even of analyses of party development or general elections.[12] 'Low politics', the examination of the role and attitudes of the party rank and file, must be fully integrated into 'high politics' in order to secure a balanced picture. This has sometimes been attempted through the medium of the local or regional case-study, an approach which affords the opportunity to examine in greater depth the interaction between economic, social, and political formations, by narrowing the focus geographically.[13] However, because these factors varied enormously from one region to another, it is impossible to draw from these limited explorations any valid deductions about popular or party feeling across the country as a whole. For that reason, it has been an essential element in this study that research into the political attitudes of the activist element in the Conservative Party has been made on the most comprehensive basis possible, across the length and breadth of the country. Newspapers cannot shed light into this area, for the most revealing discussions took place in the private forum of the local committees. The minute books of the regional and constituency organisations have cumulatively proved to be a crucial source. These records are even more important than usual for, by chance, no Party Conference was held in either 1930 or 1931. Every known surviving collection of local Conservative Party documents has been traced and examined. This large random sample, covering more than one hundred and twenty constituencies, has enabled new and conclusive information to be brought forward concerning the views and role of the rank and file, and is the foundation for an analysis of the relationship between leaders and followers of a fullness and complexity not previously possible. It is not surprising that, as a result, a different picture has emerged.

The commonly held view that the parliamentary Conservative Party is the decisive force in the removal of unpopular leaders has led to an excessively narrow concentration on the mood and temper of MPs. This is to confuse the knife which strikes the fatal blow, with the hand that wields it. Furthermore, such an approach begs the question as to why the parliamentary party should turn against its leader. The simple answer is the pressure of public or party opinion. For Conservative MPs of the inter-war period, that opinion was composed of four elements. The first of these was the social circle in which they moved, which included county society, the world of business and the City, and the London clubs and season, as well as the gossip of the lobby of the House of Commons. Beyond this immediate circle were the second element, the opinions conveyed by the press, and the third, the views of their local constituency associations. Whilst these came into play throughout the political year, the fourth and final element, though the most direct, was also the most intermittent: the response of audiences addressed at public meetings. By the end of the 1920s politicians turned less and less to the popular press for a reading of public or party opinion; too much of the national press was concentrated in the hands of powerful owners, known for the idiosyncrasy of their editorial control. The result was that, increasingly, the local constituency officials and agents became the eyes and ears of MPs. Through them the temperature was taken of the mood of the voters, and of the morale of the local workers. Between the wars the latter was a crucial consideration in the winning or holding of any seat, even the safest. An apathetic collapse or an angry revolt amongst the rank and file, therefore, would rapidly communicate itself to the parliamentary party, where it would not be taken lightly. The greatest upset within the Party in this period was the overthrow of the Coalition in 1922; which swept away not only the leader, Austen Chamberlain, but most of his leading colleagues. Whilst this came about as the direct result of a vote of the parliamentary party at the Carlton Club meeting, it is clear that the motivating force amongst the middle ranking MPs, the key group of rebels, was the unrest in the constituencies, which reached such alarming proportions that it created the political crisis of 1922.[14]

During this period there was no formal mechanism in the Conservative Party for the deposition of a leader. Baldwin could, however, have been effectively required to resign by either of two quite different methods. The first would have been a request to withdraw from the overwhelming majority of his immediate front-bench colleagues; an event which almost came to pass twice, in October 1930 and March 1931. The front-benchers would have been influenced by their perception of the capacity of the leader, of the state of health of the Party, of its electoral chances, and of public opinion. Fear of disunity and the suspicion of personal ambition were factors restraining any stab in the back. If the knife was wielded at all, it was with reluctance and a hesitation fuelled by the reflection that change might not be for the better. Both in 1922 and between 1929 and 1931 the leaders' colleagues were propelled into action from the ranks below, and only acted when continued drifting seemed to be the greater danger. The second automatic cause of Baldwin's retirement would have been defeat at either of the two Party meetings, summoned in June and October 1930. These gatherings, of Conservative peers, MPs, and prospective candidates, were even more open to pressure from the constituency associations. No single element within the Conservative Party was paramount, but the relative importance of the back-benchers was less, and that of the constituency activists greater, than has hitherto been allowed.

Previous accounts have also tended to conflate the series of separate crises which took place between 1929 and 1931, and at the same time to accept at face value Baldwin's denunciations of his critics. The result has been a lopsided treatment, which A.J.P.Taylor's biography of Beaverbrook, using no other source than Beaverbrook's own papers, hardly even attempted to correct.[15] As the political hobgoblin of the day Beaverbrook has become almost a caricature, whilst the wide range of support he attracted has been forgotten. The slow emergence of the crisis within the Party in 1929 and the existence of a deal between Baldwin and Beaverbrook in early 1930, has been passed over, resulting in a distorted picture. The present study examines the causes and development of the rifts which opened up so acutely in 1930. This is more than just an exercise in narrative, for it reveals the nature of the forces at work within the Party, and provides the context without which later developments are meaningless. Above all, analysis of the evidence from the local constituencies undermines the model of events previously held. The crisis of March 1931 and the St. George's by-election have been given a pride of place which they do not deserve. In fact, the most serious stage of internal revolt occurred months before, with the peak of the crisis coming in September and

October 1930. New interpretations are offered to explain the actions of Baldwin and the leadership, as well as the reactions of their followers. The failure of the revolt within the Party over the issue of India is also reassessed. In the past, primacy of attention has been given to the final stages of the fight over the passage of the India Bill between 1933 and 1935.[16] Here it is argued that the decisive phase of the revolt over India occurred before the formation of the National Government in August 1931; thereafter the rebels were to have no opportunity for changing the leadership's chosen policy.

Conservative politics in this period were curiously insular, and until the midsummer of 1931 they ruled out of court any idea of approaches to either of the other parties. The principal political divide was still, as it had been since 1903, between the protectionist Conservatives on the one hand, and the two free trade parties, Liberals and Labour, on the other. Faith in the tariff reform ideal was still strongly held at every level of the party. In addition, the Conservative leadership of the late 1920s had risen to prominence through the destruction of a coalition with the Liberals. Only a few years before they had denounced as lacking in principle a front based on nothing more than anti-Socialism. So long as the feared and detested Lloyd George remained Liberal leader, Baldwin and his circle would not look at any pact or agreement, however limited. They had no intention of ever allowing that particular cuckoo to climb back into the nest. After the general election defeat of 1929 most Conservatives felt more bitterly towards the Liberal Party than they did towards Labour. However, whilst the lone voice of Winston Churchill could be found preaching a revival of Conservative-Liberal coalitionism, no-one seriously talked of arrangements with Labour. The real political deal of the 1929–1931 parliament was that between the Liberal and Labour parties.[17] Though never formalised, its existence was well known, and it inevitably had the effect of still further accentuating the gulf between the Conservatives and the other two parties.

Although the Conservative leadership, and the vast majority of their followers, were content that such a gulf should exist, there was no lack of others offering to build bridges across it. These were nearly all figures on the fringes of political life, tied loosely to party or not at all. They included the editors of some of the quality newspapers, businessmen of various kinds, journalists, fixers, pundits, and retired politicians or senior civil servants. Though not quite the great and the good, nor the most respectable face of the 'establishment' either, their parallel voices could give the misleading impression of an emerging consensus. Their favoured solution was not a revival of the old Coalition, but a 'national government'. Advocacy of this increased noticeably with the impact of the slump in the winter of 1930–1931, as the mood of national crisis grew. The model that was drawn upon was that of the wartime combination. For some of its enthusiasts, the 'national government' would have consisted of the leading men from all the parties. Others, more radical or less closely linked to party, favoured a ministry composed of business magnates and other 'experts'. The talk of 'national government' fed on itself, and its propagandists publicised each other. Such talk was certainly a symptom of crisis, both political and economic. It was also vague, conflicting, and ultimately divorced from reality. It held no attractions for the Conservatives. However, it required an answer, which was given as a resounding negative not once but many times. As Baldwin remarked as late as July 1931, there was 'nothing doing'.[18] However, talk, and in particular idle talk, is impossible to suppress, and the speculation was constantly fed by rumours, and by the chance remarks of the Labour Prime Minister, Ramsay Macdonald. The sudden crash of August 1931, which swept the Conservatives into just such a combination against their will, has invested the discussions of 'national government' with a seriousness, purpose, and degree of historical importance that they simply did not possess.

Instead of such a stratagem, the Conservatives put their faith in the incapacity of Labour to govern, the swing of the electoral pendulum, and the normal party struggle. In this, the Houses of Parliament were not the most important arena of battle, for throughout this period the opposition were unable to make any impact on the solidarity of the Labour vote in the lobbies, or wean the Liberals away from maintaining the government in office. The result was that the parliamentary stage was reduced to being merely a side-show, to which little attention was being paid by either the leading politicians or the general public.[19] Both were well aware that the fate of parties rested outside, and not inside, the Palace of Westminster. Although the Liberal and Labour parties had their own problems in this period, the Conservatives were unable to profit from them. All their energies during the first two years in opposition were focused inwardly upon their own concerns, and to suggest otherwise would be to distort the world within which they were operating. This is not an uncommon feature of parties in opposition, and a similar point could be made about the pre-occupations of the Labour Party between 1979 and 1983.

The predominant concern of this study is the question of power and authority in Conservative politics. In this period, Baldwin deliberately refused to lead the Party in the direction it instinctively desired to go, and as a result set up a constant tension between the pragmatism of the leadership on the one hand, and the idealism of the back-benchers and the constituency activists on the other. This problem had originated before the general election of 1929, but defeat and the loss of power increased the unrest. Baldwin's continued refusal to give ground stoked the flames, producing a dangerous and explosive situation by September 1930. Crises in the Conservative Party have always focused upon the question of leadership, for in order to change the policy of the Party it is necessary to change the leader. Thus, even fundamental crises within the Party were expressed in such personal terms, rather than in philosophical or ideological critiques. This did not make them any less serious. The issue at stake remained the control and direction of the most enduring force in modern British politics.

CHAPTER 1

Baldwin and the Conservative Party

The problems experienced in acute form within the Conservative Party during the crisis of 1929–1931 did not emerge overnight. To trace their roots, it is necessary to explore the principal themes in the history of the Party over the preceding three decades. In the last years of the nineteenth century, the Conservative Party had enjoyed a long period of power under the leadership of the third Marquis of Salisbury. However, the fortunes of the Party changed abruptly for the worse after the succession of his nephew, Arthur Balfour, in 1902. The aftermath of the Boer War, and the unpopularity in some quarters of Balfour's Education Act of 1902, weakened the Party's position. However, the most important development in Conservative politics in the Edwardian era did not result from any initiative of Balfour's. In 1903 Joseph Chamberlain, the second figure in the government, turned the political world on its head by opening a campaign for tariff reform.[1] His aim was ambitious; he sought to unite the British Empire into an effectire global power through economic links, by offering the dominions reciprocal imperial preference in trading relations. At the same time, these protective duties would shelter British industry from the increasing competition from other advancing industrialised nations such as Germany and the United States, and could thus be presented to working class electors as the cure for unemployment. It was not only a policy for prosperity, but could also be depicted as the only possible counter to the appeal of Socialism. Britain was almost alone in retaining a free trade system. Once imposed, tariffs could be used as a retaliatory weapon with which better terms for British exports could be secured. Another aspect of tariff reform was that it offered a chance to break out of the restraints facing British governments in raising revenue; the money produced by the duties would finance social reforms such

1

as old age pensions through indirect, and not increased direct, taxation.

Tariff reform was intended to be a radical proposal, and some Conservatives found it an anathema. For many others, it was the only living thing in politics, and from 1903 onwards tariff reform was to make a powerful appeal to the enthusiasm of the Conservative activists. In the short term, the Party was wracked with division, and Balfour's government slid into decay. The problem with fiscal reform was that an essential part of the programme was the imposition of duties on imports of food and raw materials. This raised the spectre of food taxes, and a rise in the cost of living for the urban working class. Liberal and Labour politicians sprang to the defence of free trade, and the 'dear food' cry was their most effective card. The Conservatives went down to a landslide defeat in the general election of 1906 for a number of reasons, but the food taxes clearly did the greatest damage. Despite this, tariff reformers were in an overwhelming majority amongst the Conservative MPs who survived the debacle. Balfour, who had so long and so skilfully eluded commitment by clinging to a median position, was forced to accept fiscal reform as the foremost plank in the Conservative platform.[2] Problems persisted during the remainder of Balfour's leadership and, after two further election defeats in 1910, he resigned in the following year. The succession was itself the cause of still further disunity between factions supporting the two leading claimants, Austen Chamberlain and Walter Long, until Andrew Bonar Law was accepted as a compromise candidate. Even so, within little over a year, he was brought to the brink of resignation by another crisis within the Party over the food tax policy. So long as it remained unpopular with the public, tariff reform would continue to provoke powerful passions and dangerous divisions. The contrast between the priorities of the idealists and the pragmatists, and the struggle between them which was fought over the commitment to introduce food taxes, dominated the history of the Conservative Party from 1903 to 1931.

The immediate consequence of the defeats of 1910 was the passage of the Parliament Act, which drastically reduced the power of the Conservative-dominated House of Lords to block legislation passed by the lower chamber. Inevitably, this was followed by the introduction of a Home Rule Bill for Ireland. Opposition to such a measure had been the basis of the Party's existence since 1886. The years from 1912 to 1914 saw the Conservatives united in their vehement hostility to the bill, but reduced to bitter futility, unable to do more than delay its passage. This period saw the deepest antagonism between the parties, with the Conservatives moving to dangerously extreme, even unconstitutional, positions in their support for the claims of Ulster to be excluded from the operation of Home Rule. The outbreak of war in

1914 transformed the political situation, pushing the Irish problem into the background. For the first part of the war the Party was in the frustrating position of acting as a patriotic, and hence uncritical, opposition to a ministry in which it lacked confidence. As the war progressed unsuccessfully, Asquith reconstructed his government in May 1915, bringing the Conservatives into coalition, but simultaneously ensuring that they remained very much junior partners, excluded from the most important offices. By December 1916 Asquith no longer seemed best fitted to lead a wartime government, and with some reluctance the Conservative leadership lent their support to Lloyd George's plan to reform the cumbersome machinery of war direction. The result was Asquith's resignation, and in the coalition formed under Lloyd George the Conservatives were given a larger slice of the cake.

The second coalition was a more genuine fusion of forces, and the Conservatives worked effectively with Lloyd George in an atmosphere of national unity in a time of crisis. This outlook had considerable appeal not only in the darkest days of the war, but also when looking forward to the peace settlement. When the war ended in November 1918, the Conservative leaders had no hesitation in taking their party into the long overdue general election held in December as the larger wing of the coalition forces, under the premiership of Lloyd George, and standing on a moderate and progressive programme.[3] However, the lower ranks of the Conservative Party became increasingly alienated from the coalition, and eventually from their own leaders, when they refused to distance the Party from Lloyd George. Between 1920 and 1922 the coalition outraged Conservative sentiment in its foreign policy, its imperial policy, and above all, in the negotiations which led up to the Irish Treaty of 1921. To this was added the whiff of corruption, in the scandals over the sale of honours on behalf of Lloyd George's political fund. Where the coalition did not provoke anger, it disappointed the lower ranks of the Conservative Party by failing to deliver on any of the issues close to their hearts: restoration of the powers of the House of Lords, reform of the laws governing the trade unions, economy in government expenditure, and the reduction of taxation. The coalition was always presented as the barrier to the advance of Socialism, but by October 1922 many Conservative MPs were convinced that the Party had a better chance of resisting Labour if it stood independently of Lloyd George and his coalition Liberals at the next election. Austen Chamberlain, leader of the Party after Law's retirement due to ill-health in 1921, refused to follow this tactic, and called a party meeting at the Carlton Club in order to overwhelm his critics. In this he was supported by every Conservative Cabinet minister, with the exception of the insignificant figure of the President of the Board of Trade, Stanley Baldwin. The government's apparent lack of principle aroused serious antagonism in the constituencies and amongst backbenchers, and led also to a revolt by the junior ministerial cadre. After many hesitations, Bonar Law emerged from retirement and appeared at the party meeting at the head of the dissidents, who carried the day.[4]

The fall of the coalition and the legacy of coalitionism were of crucial importance in Conservative politics for the remainder of the inter-war years. More important than the division between leaders and followers was the continual and irremovable suspicion with which the pro-coalition ministers were regarded. This sentiment pervaded Conservative politics into the next decade, and was paralleled by a deep hostility towards any dealings with Lloyd George. In November 1922, with the senior Conservative figures going grimly into the wilderness with the ousted premier, Law constructed his government of the second eleven, with Baldwin at the Exchequer. He immediately dissolved parliament, and won a majority in the ensuing general election. Only months later, in May 1923, the final collapse of his health forced his retirement. All the obvious successors in the House of Commons were ruled out because of their coalitionist sympathies, and the leader in the Lords, Curzon, was regarded as impossible on personal as well as political grounds. As a result of this series of chances the glittering prize fell into Baldwin's lap. He became leader of the Conservative Party and Prime Minister, with a secure majority in the Commons and four years of a parliament still to run. Incredibly, before the year was out, he had staked everything on the gamble of an appeal to the country for a mandate to introduce tariff reform, and lost. Nevertheless, Baldwin survived as leader. After the new parliament met in January 1924, Labour took office for the first time under Ramsay Macdonald, as a minority administration relying upon Liberal forbearance. When this first Labour Government fell in October 1924, the Conservatives entered the resulting election with a studiously moderate fiscal programme, advocating only the safeguarding of selected industries from unfair foreign subsidised competition. This stance, together with assiduous playing of the red card, returned Baldwin to Downing Street with a majority of 221 over Liberals and Labour combined—the greatest victory ever achieved by any party.[5] But it was not put to use in a way that satisfied the Party rank and file. Instead, Baldwin went out of his way to emphasise the centrism, rather than the Conservatism, of his government, startling many by appointing the former coalition Liberal Winston Churchill as Chancellor of the Exchequer. The construction of the new Cabinet ended the rift of 1922, at least on the surface, with almost all of the other displaced leaders returning to serve in senior offices under Baldwin.

The Baldwin government of 1924 to 1929 saw a determined attempt by the Conservative leadership to present themselves as the party of moderation. Expensive measures of social reform were passed, and Neville Chamberlain began to make a reputation at the Ministry of Health in reforming local government. The government can be divided into two phases: a relatively successful first half, in which the high points were the treaties of Locarno in 1925 and the defeat of the general strike in 1926; and decline thereafter. In 1927 the government was forced by pressure from below to pass a punitive measure reforming trade union law. Baldwin strained his credibility with his followers by resisting such action for as long as possible. The Trades Disputes Bill, and the breach of diplomatic relations with Russia which followed from the Arcos raid in 1927, were the last things the government did that were popular with its supporters. From that point onwards disillusion with what many saw as no better than 'the least Socialistic party of the three' grew apace.[6] Granting the franchise to women under 30, the so-called 'flapper' vote, was doubly resented in view of the leadership's failure to use their massive majority to bring about a defensive restoration of powers to the second chamber. Another crucial grievance of the constituency associations was the government's failure to reduce its expenditure, and thereby to reduce the levels of local and national taxation. 'We must pull the Party together this year', wrote the Home Secretary to the Prime Minister in 1928.[7] However, the means chosen to do so backfired. The government embarked on a complicated programme designed to reduce unemployment by de-rating productive industry. The result was a measure which the Party found difficult to understand, and with which it was impossible to arouse enthusiasm amongst either the activists or the public.[8] Instead, the constituency parties lapsed further and further into apathy. The failure to help agriculture was one important cause of this.[9] However, the greatest area of disappointment was the rigid adherence to the pledges of 1924 in respect of protection. The Party clamoured for at least the extension of safeguarding to the iron and steel industries. Baldwin rejected such a massive inclusion as being dishonest, amounting to the introduction of protection by the back door. He went further, by once more deliberately imposing a moderate strategy on the Party for the forthcoming election, from which any hint of tariff reform was explicitly ruled out.[10]

Whilst there is little doubt that considerations of domestic politics governed the pace and extent of the Party's commitment to fiscal change, these concerns were a secondary factor for the committed protagonists of imperial preference. Tariff reform was above all a great imperial ideology, originating in concern over the future development of the empire. In this spirit it captured the imagination of its most fervent advocates. The prize for which domestic political risks were to be run was imperial consolidation and unity, and the debate over tariff reform can only be integrated properly with Conservative politics by placing it within the imperial dimension. In this context imperial preference was only one aspect of a wider series of questions concerning the future of the British Empire which faced Conservative politicians in an especially acute form by the end of the 1920s. There was a growing sense that the future of the empire was at the crossroads. The internal crises affecting the empire, the external threats endangering it, and the degeneracy of the home country's will to lead, provided the imperial dimension of the peril facing the nation as perceived by many Conservatives. The problems of empire included the question of imperial defence, bound up in the negoti-ations for naval disarmament, and the difficulties facing imperial policy in East Africa, Rhodesia, Palestine, and Egypt. Above all, the future relationship of the two most important constituent elements in the empire to the mother country clearly would be fundamental issues in the next parliament. India was rightly described as the jewel in the imperial crown, and the debate orer its future political evolution assumed cardinal importance in Conservative politics, together with the question of imperial preference for the dominions. Given the range and significance of these concerns, it was possible to react in terms not of a series of localised questions, but of a general imperial crisis.[11]

After four and a half years in office, Baldwin went to the country in May 1929. The Conservative platform was based more on extolling the achievements of the previous term than in specific proposals for the future. Combined with this posture of relying on proven worth were warnings about the quack nature of the opposition parties' remedies for unemployment, the foremost issue of the day. These themes were linked by the centre-piece of the Conservative campaign, which concentrated on the personal virtues and popularity of the Prime Minister, with posters showing Baldwin smoking his famous pipe and captioned with the slogans 'Trust Baldwin' and 'Safety First'. As the polls closed on the evening of 30 May, most Conservative politicians expected that their party would be returned for another term in office, though perhaps with a reduced majority. However, not only were the Conservatives defeated, but for the only time during the inter-war period they ceased to be the largest single party in the House of Commons. One hundred and fifty-nine seats were lost, and only two hundred and sixty Conservative MPs were returned. Lloyd George's attempt during the previous three years to revitalise the Liberal Party was one of the principal causes of this defeat. The large number of three-sided contests split the anti-Socialist vote, usually to the disadvantage of the defending Conservative MP. This combined with the public disaffection with a ministry which is often seen after a long spell of office to produce the Conservative reverse. The election campaign, which was without any particular alarms, confirmed rather than distorted the prevailing trends. The result was a hung parliament. Neither Labour nor the Conservatives possessed an overall majority, and the small group of Liberals held the balance. The circumstances differed very little from those of 1923, except that on this occasion Labour was the largest of the three parties.

In any study of the history of the Conservative Party, the leader must be the point of first departure. His position is paramount, his influence pervasive, his powers almost absolute. The character, methods, and aims of the leader of the Party illuminate the context within which it operates, and go far to explain the course of events, of action and reaction. Stanley Baldwin's rise to the leadership was one of the most unexpected developments of the twentieth century. His tenure from 1923 to 1937 was one of the longest and most important in the history of his Party, and of his country. Baldwin only entered parliament in middle age, when in February 1908 at the age of forty-one, he inherited his father's Worcestershire seat of Bewdley, as well as a directorship in the family ironworks. He made no particular public mark before 1914, but built up a certain reputation as one of the more reliable Conservative backbenchers, with expertise and moderate views on a range of economic and industrial matters. In December 1916 Bonar Law, then the leader of the Party, became Chancellor of the Exchequer in Lloyd George's coalition government. Baldwin, too old to be taken for military service, received his first and most junior office as Law's parliamentary private secretary. Within a few months he was promoted to be joint Financial Secretary to the Treasury, a crucial step in his career. This was one of the most prestigious and demanding of the junior ministerial posts, and Baldwin filled it steadily, if unspectacularly, for four years. In the reshuffle of March 1921, when Austen Chamberlain succeeded Law as leader of the Party, Baldwin entered the Cabinet as President of the Board of Trade.[12] Almost alone amongst his colleagues, Baldwin shared in the growing revulsion of the rank and file of the Conservative Party against the continuation of the coalition. When the Party revolted in October 1922, the result was a slice off the top of the Conservative leadership, with the weighty names following Lloyd George's star into eclipse. The decline and fall of the coalition was Baldwin's formative political experience. Instead of going into the wilderness, as he had expected, his stand against the coalition led him to the Chancellorship of the Exchequer in Bonar Law's government. When the renewed deterioration of his health forced Bonar Law to resign from the premiership only a few months later, the previous generation of leading figures were still holding themselves aloof, and were still unacceptable to the rest of the Party. Through this series of accidents, Baldwin had become the inevitable successor.

If Baldwin came to the premiership with any aim in mind, it was to clean up British politics after Lloyd George. This amounted to more than just keeping Lloyd George in the wilderness; it meant restoring and maintaining standards in public life, and regaining the trust and respect of the people. For Baldwin, politicians were divided into two classes, good or bad. His prejudices were mainly formed by the events of 1922, and they were strong and persistent. His detestation of Lloyd George was vehement, and this antipathy was to remain one of the cardinal features of his career and his character. Also suspect were Lord Birkenhead, Winston Churchill, Sir Robert Horne, and the barons of the popular press, Lords Beaverbrook and Rothermere. This was not a party matter, nor one of policies. Baldwin was not interested in policy as such, but in character and personality.[13] He did not think that political actions could cure human miseries, and this was one reason for his lack of attention to the detailed formulation of programmes. Nor did he believe that issues could be made; they grew of themselves, from the twin forces of the realities of the situation and the needs or expectations of the public. The politician's role was not to create popular feeling, and certainly not to exploit it in a demagogic or cynical fashion, as Lloyd George had sought to do during the confrontation with the Turks at Chanak in October 1922. Rather, responsible statesmen should react to the mood of the people, often to moderate it.

Baldwin was inclined to think of politics in terms of duty and obligation. The sacrifice of the First World War had profoundly affected him. This sentiment found one expression in his anonymous gift of a substantial portion of his private wealth for the cancellation of war debt. His outlook was also based on a religious conception of the purpose of public life. Baldwin's premiss was that good works could not come from tainted vessels, and it was this attitude which made him set his face against any dealings with Lloyd George. It was not just the fear that he might be supplanted, but a deeper horror of the consequences of allowing the morally corrupt to return to power. Baldwin felt that the virtues of honesty and trustworthiness were the essential prerequisites for creating any lasting achievement in public life. For this reason, when he considered tackling the problem of unemployment in 1923, he went out of his way to honour a promise made by his predecessor, Bonar Law, not to introduce protection without another election, although he had a parliamentary majority willing to pass such a measure without a dissolution. In October 1923, addressing the Conservative Party Conference for the first time as leader, he insisted: 'I am not a man to play with a pledge', adding deliberately: 'I am not a clever man. I know nothing of political tactics'. His point was that, having come to the conclusion that protective measures were necessary, he felt that 'the only honest and right thing' was to make his conviction public.[14] No policy launched in a hole in the corner manner could expect to receive the respect of the Conservative Party or the British people. To Baldwin, this emphasis on character was far more relevant to the needs of British society after the strains of the Great War than the cleverness exhibited by the high priests of the Coalition. Second-class brains were better than second-class characters. Baldwin was always more concerned with reliability, and a certain solidity, which was not the product of stupidity but of consistency based on clear principles and standards, consciously held. As a result, he often found it easier to understand the outlook of Labour politicians, whilst distrusting the erratic and expedient man-oeuvres of the Liberals. The volatile and inconsistent policies of the Lloyd George coalition between 1920 and 1922 were a complete anathema to him, redolent of a shiftless desire to remain in power regardless of purpose.

These attitudes were a part of Baldwin's traditionalism, of his conception of what the true English character was and should be like, and of the responsibilities rather than the privileges of being a gentleman. Like other Conservatives, Baldwin was motivated by a desire to preserve what he believed to be the virtues of the past, looking back with pride through history to Britain's achievements and her hallowed institutions. He found these traditional values more strongly exemplified in rural than in urban life, and for that reason drew his imagery and inspiration from the English countryside, often clothing it in a glow of romantic patriotism. 'To me England is the country, and the country is England', he declared, and few would have contradicted his equation.[15] All these concerns were an important and successful part of Baldwin's public image, but they became magnified in the public eye at the expense of other traits in his complex character.[16] They were nevertheless a genuine part of Baldwin's view of the world, and in that sense were a natural if exaggerated manifestation of his private persona. It can be argued that such an evocation of the mythical side of rural England was an inappropriate diversion from the problems of an industrial and mainly urban society, but this begs the issue of the demands and constraints of the contemporary public mood.[17] Nostalgia for the half-remembered past was something Baldwin reflected rather than created. Furthermore, he did so not from calculation, but because these themes struck a chord in him just as much as in anyone else. An important point about Baldwin's love of the countryside was that his family background, though semi-rural, was not agricultural but industrial. His emotional identification with the shires did not simply spring from his upbringing. His love of the countryside was an example of that same heartfelt longing so often found in the inhabitants of British cities and suburbs, all the stronger for the contrast between the idealisation of something largely unknown and the alienation from an urban existence which seemed to be dehumanising. Baldwin's image of the proper structure of society was appropriate in another sense, for he placed himself in the Disraelian tradition of one-nation Toryism. Together with family ties and the identification of Victorian Liberalism with the urban middle class and with hostility to the Church, this made Baldwin a Conservative in his early politics despite the possession of many centrist attitudes. The evocation of an idealised past, the rejection of class politics, and thus in part of industrialisation itself, and the conviction that politics were concerned not with economic materialism but with the defence of church and constitution, were hardly novel features in the Conservative Party.

Neither were other cardinal traits in Baldwin's character. These were common to most other Conservative politicians, and were a product of the attitudes and ideals of the public school, and to a lesser degree university, education through which they had all passed. Although Baldwin had not been happy at Harrow, he had still passively and unquestioningly absorbed these cultural influences. So completely did he find security in the team-game spirit of collective endeavour and mutual loyalty that the demands of striving for excellence through individual competition proved beyond him at Cambridge. Equally, he found little satisfaction in the adversarial side of politics. In this he differed from his colleagues only in degree. Many likened the party system to a cricket match, with loyalty to your own team and its captain going hand-in-hand with respect for good bowling, or defensive batting, by an opponent. In such a context there was no place for a third and unreliable team: the Liberal Party of the 1920s. On many occasions, especially during general elections, Baldwin shared this perspective. On others, in the clubbish atmosphere of the Commons, he sometimes saw all the trustworthy leading men as part of the same team of statesmen, kept apart by petty prejudices; sometimes in league against their own misguided supporters, more often playing on the world pitch as the representatives of Britain. Though Baldwin did not plot or plan for the formation of a 'national government', suspicious critics were right to detect that he had no deep loyalty to the party system. Once convinced that the new combination was based upon honest common ground, he had no real objection to the arrangement. This does not imply a reversal of his condemnation of coalition in 1922, for, as was shown by his acceptance of promotions within that government, Baldwin did not reject the appeals of national unity. His disgust was aroused by the way in which, after entering Lloyd George's cabinet, he discovered such noble sentiments were being cynically abused for personal ends.[18]

Baldwin's public reputation as the straight and honest man was thrust upon him by the events surrounding the fall of the coalition. It reflected his inexperience in the world of high politics. However, the fact that between 1922 and 1929 his conduct had not lessened but augmented his reputation in this respect, to the point where the Conservative election strategy of 1929 was largely founded upon it, is highly revealing of Baldwin's order of priorities. This image of Baldwin had been purveyed through the length and breadth of the country by both newsreels and newspapers. Ironically, it was to prove a resource of inestimable value when, during the Party crisis of 1929 to 1931, Baldwin cast himself in the role of the honest man maligned by an irresponsible and vindictive press. The part was all the more convincing in that to the public eye Baldwin personified the plain, simple, slow, but straightforward man in politics.[19] Baldwin's position was always stronger in the country as a whole than it was within his own party, and much of his value as leader lay in his ability to attract 'middle opinion' in a way that potential successors could not have done.

Despite the advantages it brought, Baldwin's mixture of honesty and loyalty cannot be dismissed as being merely a politician's rhetoric, even if it was the strongest card to play against Lloyd George and his former coalition cronies. For Baldwin made himself vulnerable by defending two figures to whom he felt personally committed: J.C.C. Davidson, the Chairman of the Conservative Party since November 1926, and Lord Irwin, Viceroy of India from April 1926. This tendency to adhere to pledges or personal loyalties led Baldwin into political danger. Not the least effective cry against him during the Party crisis was the continued dominance of the 'Old Gang' of ex-cabinet ministers in the leadership. Despite pressure to drop some of the more elderly or less able, and his own often-announced, though rarely practised, desire to bring on younger talent, Baldwin proved strangely reluctant to appease these demands. This is partly explicable in terms of another aspect of Baldwin's character: his preference to allow events to take a natural course in the hope of avoiding difficult decisions, a policy he was later to adopt in the abdication crisis in 1936. It may also point to a certain laziness, or hesitancy to act. Baldwin was always reluctant to commit himself to any particular course, not least because of the difficulty of later pulling back. His cautious attitude was to prove a major disappointment to the advocates of tariff reform, for they sought the fervour of the convert, not the pragmatism of the political strategist. Baldwin's failure to drop the 'Old Gang' despite the prolonged agitation against them also reflected the personal conservatism of a shy man, who had become accustomed to certain colleagues, and was not eager to repeat the process with a new and more remote generation. But more than any of these things, his attitude on this question was of a piece with his political character. Despite frequent advice to reconstruct his cabinet before the 1929 election, Baldwin did not do so. It was not simply that he was not a good cabinet butcher; the feeling that restrained him from carrying through such a move, despite its political advantages, was that it offended against common loyalty.

Only one area of politics consistently aroused Baldwin's close interest: those questions which broadly came under the heading of the constitution. This was evident in small things as much as large, in his care over patronage appointments and caution over the granting of honours, and in his conception of the proper role of the Prime Minister. Though hardly a naive idealist, he nonetheless saw the premiership as being to some extent a post above party. Hence the attention he gave to fulfilling non-political roles and providing leadership in fields outside conventional politics. Many of his best speeches were delivered at ceremonial or celebratory occasions, or given as anniversary or rectorial addresses. Whilst Premier he devoted much time to this area of national life, prizing it above political squabble. This characteristic was apparent on a larger scale. Baldwin feared the emergence of class antagonism as the principal political divide. For that reason throughout the 1920s his interest focused upon the parallel themes of industrial harmony and the political education of the democratic electorate which had been created in 1918, as he sought to reconcile these potential dangers to constitutional government.[20] The threat of war was a still greater threat to the fabric of society. In both areas he chose to appease, using that word in the sense of reconciliation rather than concession. The appeasement of labour was the other side of the coin of negotiation with the European dictators. Both policies were pursued in the interests of stability, peace, and tranquillity. All of Baldwin's great political battles were fought over constitutional issues, from the unconstitutional nature of Lloyd George's presidential government, through the general strike, the question of the proper role of the press, and the issue of Indian constitutional advance, to the abdication crisis at the end of his career. It is no coincidence that the most silent phase of Baldwin's career, as a backbench MP between 1909 and 1914, occurred during a period when his instincts of party loyalty must have been in conflict with his reverence for the constitution.

Baldwin's speeches contain many remarks denigrating intellectuals and intellectualism, and it was against these that he continually contrasted the 'simple' virtues. He saw many dangers in systems of political thought, and his anti-intellectualism was a rejection of such rigid ideologies rather than of ability itself. To Baldwin, the possession of intelligence was a God-given talent to be used, but with becoming modesty. Once again, this was a reflection of the conformist ethos of the middle years at public school, rather than the atmosphere of the university. A glorification of intellectual power was either a cover for shallow opportunism, such as he perceived in Birkenhead, or for the dangers of the inhumanity of the theoreticians, be they economists or philosophers. Baldwin himself was shrewd, rather than clever. Like Churchill, by education and by nature he pursued the politics of instinct. In this he was not much removed from many Labour figures, whose Socialism was founded in Christianity and their cultural background of co-operation and collective endeavour. Baldwin's concerns were different, but not necessarily incompatible. This did not imply shallowness, for as his confidant Tom Jones wrote, 'he felt things deeply, and his conscience was more active than his intellect'.[21]

Sometimes Baldwin created his own difficulties. Several of these were the product of defects in his character. Amery considered him to be 'a disconnectedly divided personality', whose outward appearance of phlegmatic tolerance overlay a contrasting strain, 'emotional, impulsive, secretive, and intensely personal in its likes, dislikes, and moral judgements'.[22] The consequent unpredictability and weakness were a frequent source of despair to his colleagues. Baldwin's tendency to inertia was exacerbated by indecision, whilst a setback could produce a mood of apathetic gloom. Lord Irwin, a close friend, commented that Baldwin's temperament led him 'into encouraging himself to sit in the front row of the stalls while the play is being performed'.[23] After serving in his Cabinet between 1924 and 1929, Bridgeman singled out for comment Baldwin's reluctance to commit himself to one side or the other in a dispute, until it became absolutely unavoidable.[24] This vacillation extended to his methods of doing business with his colleagues on a day-to-day basis. Austen Chamberlain complained:[25]

> I have never known so blunt a spearhead as S. B., or a man who left so large a gap between the recognition that he must act and action. Whenever you have settled something with him one day, you must seek him out the next to ask if he has yet done it or even put it in train . . . Too late and in the wrong way sum up my criticism of his leadership.

Baldwin's complacency was often based on an excessively optimistic appreciation of his personal political position. This buoyed him up through the early phases of the Party crisis, but could not hide for ever the signs of his growing unpopularity. When Baldwin was forced in October 1930 to recognise how low his stock had fallen, the effect was 'rather to cow and stupify him, than to inspire him with any sort of determination or capacity to take a decision'.[26]

At the same time, Baldwin was a prey to insecurity and nervousness. This manifested itself in several ways, one of which was his mannerism of licking the edges of his order papers whilst listening to the speeches in the House of Commons. By the time Baldwin became leader of the Party in 1923 he had come to base his decisions upon his feel for the political atmosphere, rather than immersing himself in heavy administrative work or in attention to detail. His preference was always for the broader strokes on the canvas. It was not so much that he wanted to capture public attention, but that he quickly became bored and fractious under the demands of routine. This nervous tension was a severe drain, and he was dependent on the annual institution of a lengthy summer holiday at Aix-les-Bains, where to recoup his energies he cut himself off from British politics and refused to look at the newspapers. However, operating by instinct did not result in certainty or self-confidence. It took Baldwin much time and mental effort to come to any major decision, a habit which on occasion had its own dangers, of actions taken half-heartedly or too late. Neville Chamberlain likened the Party leader to a spinning top, concluding: 'you must keep whipping him or he falls over'.[27] On the other hand, when Baldwin arrived at his decision, his cares often seemed to fall away from his shoulders, and he could be devastating on the rebound, catching his opponents off their guard and recovering from seemingly impossible positions.

Another serious defect was his tactlessness in handling his colleagues. Baldwin was a clumsy operator in his personal relations, often gratuitously offending such admittedly prickly colleagues as Austen Chamberlain. On several occasions he allowed his confidants to quit posts held at his request without sending any words of gratitude or condolence. This happened with both Stanley Jackson and J.C.C. Davidson when they resigned from the Chairmanship of the Party, an office very close to the leader. One explanation offered was that Baldwin seemed to 'distrust or actively dislike most of his colleagues and to be afraid of all his opponents and of himself'.[28] When Neville Chamberlain stood down from the same position in March 1931 'nothing could have been less gracious' than Baldwin's conduct. Austen Chamberlain put this down to simple selfishness: it was 'more inability than purpose', and sprang from 'his being so self-centred that he receives all we give him as a matter of course and takes offence at the least sign that we are not completely at his service for whatever use he likes to make of us'.[29] Allowances might be made for Austen's wounded pride as a former leader of the Party, but similar evidence comes from too many other sources to be so easily dismissed.

Baldwin was an erratic performer on the platform, and his efforts were directly related to the interest they aroused in him, rather than to their political significance. Thus a rectorial address received considerable thought and polishing, but the speech to the 1929 Party Conference, a critical utterance, did not. It contained 'no argument to speak of, no building up to a climax'. Baldwin was 'incorrigibly slovenly' over speeches which did not arouse his interest.[30] There is a pervasive myth of Baldwin as the quintessential House of Commons man; a constant attendant, genial fixture of the Smoking Room, possessing the ear of the House, and exerting an assured dominance over its moods unparalleled by any other figure of the inter-war years.[31] Parts of this image have a semblance of reality, but the period between 1929 and 1931 did not reveal Baldwin at his best. He was frequently absent from the chamber, often on seemingly unproductive speaking tours of northern towns. To the younger members he could appear aloof and indifferent.[32] When he was present, Baldwin was not always an effective force. It was charged that he lacked parliamentary gifts, being unable to debate, or to think and act quickly enough; on another occasion he was categorised as 'useless in the House'.[33] These defects were the result of being out of office, for as Baldwin himself recognised, he did not shine as a leader in opposition. This was a question of temperament, and a sign of Baldwin's failure to fulfil some of the more partisan and adversarial roles incumbent in the party system. He was, on the contrary, noted for his generosity to his opponents; 'he never attacked them when they were down, and always treated them with a remarkable considerateness'.[34] However, this virtue carried with it the compensating vice of not being strong in the attack. Baldwin derived no pleasure from the partisanship of party strife for its own sake, and his lack of enthusiasm for the conventional strategems of opposition was all too obvious. 'He neither makes nor seizes parliamentary opportunities', complained one backbencher.[35] Nor had Baldwin much aptitude for the set-piece attacking speech. His tendency was still to view questions from the position of the ministry, to appreciate their difficulties, and to favour bi-partisan policies. His lack of drive and assertiveness led naturally to the belief that the best tactic in opposition was simply to wait upon events. It was said that he 'never moves of his own motion, but he can sometimes be set in motion by others'.[36]

Despite these failings, Baldwin lasted for almost fifteen years as Party leader, retiring at a moment of his own choice, and he succeeded in riding out the most serious crisis of his career between 1929 and 1931 if not unscathed, at least not unseated. In the end, his strengths were to outweigh his weaknesses. Principal amongst these was the extraordinary power he could summon up on a theme about which he felt deeply, a gift which made some of his parliamentary speeches so effective. This ability suddenly to translate himself and his audience onto a higher plane was critically important in an assembly where the power of oratory was esteemed above all else, and can hardly be over-emphasised. Although Baldwin had not risen to lead his Party because of his skills in debate, after he became leader he established his authority in part due to an ability to produce on the occasions that really mattered speeches of the first quality. These, however, were not the product of practice and preparation, but were stimulated by questions which involved high moral issues, and frequently consisted of an appeal to his own followers to moderate their views. The first such effort, made in March 1925 during the debate on the bill introduced by the Conservative MP for Argyll, F.A. Macquisten, to amend the trade union laws, stamped his authority upon his second administration. With the introduction of full-blooded Socialism out of the question, the matters that divided opposition and government between 1929–1931 did not strike such a chord in the Conservative leader. It is no accident that in this period Baldwin's most successful speeches were produced in criticism of the unconstitutional pretensions of the press lords or against the opponents of further constitutional development in India. His approach usually consisted of an appeal to the best instincts of his audience, to their reasonableness and native good sense. Baldwin spoke to the heart, rather than the mind; not in a sentimental manner, but as a practical man to his fellows. He had an intuitive understanding of the mood of his audience, and in his role of the plain man was able to employ on occasion a 'staggering candour'.[37] In fact, Baldwin had a gift for words rare even amongst political leaders. He ensnared his audience with 'plain discourse, apparently of great moderation, which gradually bound them up in a web, unwilling not to fulfill the purpose of such a straight-forward leader'.[38] His style was 'not in the least oratorical, but intensly human'; the delivery 'slow, steady, uneloquent, but convincing'.[39] Baldwin was often a more effective speaker in public than in parliament, and this, together with his masterly exploitation of the new media of radio broadcasting and the cinema newsreels, was one of the reasons why his standing was consistently higher outside the precincts of the Palace of Westminster than it was within them.[40]

There is no doubt that Baldwin had great personal charm and attractiveness. He was a good listener, always accessible for a discursive chat. As with his reading, he preferred to skim over matters, taking the feel and texture of them, rather than to delve deeply. The complimentary descriptions of his character, from friend and foe alike, are too frequent to be mere polite convention. His admirers were not blinded to his defects, but rather cherished him in spite of them. 'I always find myself agreeing with all his general views', remarked Geoffrey Dawson, the editor of The Times.[41] His most important ability was his capacity to inspire trust. Lloyd George and Churchill might be more fun, have greater gifts for administration, and demonstrate consummate skills in debate, but neither was ever trusted in the way in which Baldwin was. There seems little evidence to discount Bridgeman's assertion that 'of his honesty and sincerity I think nobody ever had any doubts'.[42] The combination of these attributes allowed Baldwin to survive whilst exasperating or disappointing one colleague after another. One such was Amery, who later wrote that 'Baldwin was a personality, with a breadth of outlook, a tolerance and a warm humanity which commanded the admiration, as well as the affection, of those who chafed under the weakness of his leadership'.[43] Baldwin was able to retain the loyalty of his colleagues, and use this reserve of goodwill to contain potential disunity amongst the leadership. One of his fondest boasts was that he had only lost one member from the cabinet between 1924 and 1929 through disagreement. To many in the rank and file of the Conservative Party, in the constituencies and on the back benches, Baldwin came to personify the traditional virtues. To Waldron Smithers, the Member for Chislehurst, Baldwin stood for 'all that is vital, fundamental, and true for the progress and development of Civilisation not only in the Empire but all over the world'.[44]

In a similar fashion, Baldwin could appeal across conventional party boundaries to erstwhile opponents and to the floating voter. He was acknowledged to be the Conservative Party's greatest electoral asset. Though he was not always the favourite of the constituency activists, he was able to attract and reassure uncommitted opinion, especially in the north of England and in Scotland. It was this appeal which the Party determined to exploit by making Baldwin's personality the centre-piece of their campaign in the 1929 election. Although that stratagem failed, this did not revise the estimates of his value at the head of the Party. Baldwin was a better political tactician than has sometimes been allowed, although the excessive attribution of cunning and political guile by such defeated opponents as Beaverbrook and Churchill was more an unconscious saving of their own faces than a true portrait of his abilities. However, he possessed one attribute sufficiently rare in a political leader to be worthy of comment, and that was patience. He could also be stubborn, and refused to be pushed out of office, ignoring attacks from within the Party that were more humiliating than those which had driven Balfour to resign in 1911. This combination gave his approach the character of the 'waiting game', which was often confused, due to his inactivity, with playing a 'deep game'. In reality it was the politics of drift, a result of his inclination to sit back and wait and see. Baldwin was rarely an assertive leader, becoming even less so with advancing age. Whilst premier, he allowed his colleagues a loose rein in their own spheres, and he did not seek to dominate cabinet discussion. Even so, he was always quietly but definitely in control.

Baldwin's position during the Party crisis of 1929–1931 was

buttressed by two external sources of strength, which he exploited to the full. The first of these was the problem of the lack of a suitable successor, or indeed of anyone who was both acceptable and willing to take up what appeared at that time to be a crown of thorns. 'Though far from ideal as a galvanic leader, he is a way ahead of most possible successors', thought Dawson.[45] The second point was even more important. The events of 1929–1931 were a classic example of the powerful position, especially in defence, of the leader of the Conservative Party, under anything short of all-out revolt. There existed no mechanism for the deposition of a Party leader, and the constraints of the deeply ingrained tradition of veneration of the leader and loyalty to his person made rebellion difficult indeed. This was even more the case if the leader made efforts to divide the opposition, to appease at least some of the sections of it, and to give ground without losing face. A high-minded leader, committed unswervingly to a principle or policy, or rigidly obsessed like Austen Chamberlain with his personal honour, was more likely to decide to resign when under pressure. Baldwin came close to doing so, but chose instead a careful mixture of concession and principled stubbornness, which saw him through a series of holding operations against a rising tide of dissatisfaction. If appeasement was a theme of Baldwin's political career, then perhaps its most successful application was in dealing with the troubles in his own Party between 1929 and 1931.

The issues which aroused the greatest passions within the Conservative Party between 1929 and 1931 were inextricably interwoven with the regional, social, and economic background from which the parliamentary Party was drawn. Parties are not abstract forces: they are the combination of individuals, and an analysis of the composition of the Party is an essential element in elucidating the background to the crisis. This is all the more important in the case of the Conservative Party, for it was these influences, rather than clashes of ideology or political theory, which provided the most important divisions amongst its members. Conservative parliamentarians did not define themselves in relation to doctrines of Conservatism, though they did have responses to the principal issues of the day: unemployment, protection, and empire. Above all, they prided themselves on being pragmatists, with the virtues ascribed to the level-headed businessman. Not least for that reason, the sense of what was acceptable to their market was a constant element in their calculations.

The Conservative Party as represented in parliament was never a truly national institution, but drew its support from distinct areas and social groupings. The main strength of the Party lay in the English seats, and even in defeat in 1929 they still held almost half of these. There were marked regional disparities. One striking feature was the strength of the Party in the county constituencies. In 1929 the Conservatives had lost ground heavily in the borough divisions, especially in the midland and northern towns, and it was in these areas that Labour gained its parliamentary lead. However, it was not the case that the Conservatives were more popular in the countryside than in the towns. Although the De-Rating Act passed by the government near the end of its life went some way to appease the anger of the agriculturalists, many were still profoundly disillusioned with the amount of assistance that they had actually received from Baldwin's second administration.[46] The difference in distribution of MPs was the product of electoral factors. The urban seats held by the Conservatives in 1929 can be broadly placed in two categories. The residential middle class areas, mainly a phenomenon found near the largest conurbations, in particular in the Home Counties, were almost invariably safe Conservative territory. The Party was also defending many seats won in 1924 in the socially mixed urban constituencies, often the smaller towns, which had a substantial element of working class population. It was here, and in the semi-rural northern counties, that most of the Conservative casualties were concentrated. The Party also did badly in three other areas of England. Not surprisingly, in view of the events of 1926, the mining seats were barren ground. Equally, Labour did well in central and east London. Although the middle class districts continued to display an almost immovable Conservatism, the Party's candidates went down to defeat in the more socially-mixed boroughs of Islington, Hackney, Hammersmith, Fulham, and St. Pancras, where all three seats went to Labour. The final area of poor performance was in the most depressed rural regions. Many of these had a strong Liberal tradition and were vulnerable to the appeal of a revitalised Liberal Party. The Conservatives lost every seat in Cornwall, and a substantial slice of the East Midlands.

A more significant indicator of the nature of the Conservative Party in 1929 emerges from a regional, rather than typological, breakdown of the seats held in the principal areas, taking borough and county divisions together. The Conservatives retained only 1 of the 35 Welsh seats and 20 of the 71 seats in Scotland. They also returned members for 51 of the 171 northern English constituencies, 44 of the 105 in the Midlands, and 125 of the 209 divisions in southern England. In addition, they returned 10 members from Ulster and 8 from the university seats. More noticeable even than the number of County members is the preponderance of the Conservative MPs who sat for southern English seats—very close to half of the parliamentary Party. In the Midlands the Conservative success rate was considerably lower, and in the North it was even less. Indeed, the geographic alignment of the Conservative Party goes some way towards supporting the 'two nations' interpretation of British society, north versus south. If the

Conservative constituencies can be categorised at all, it would be firstly as English and southern, and only secondly as heavily biased towards the agricultural.

However, this rural base was not carried through to the composition of the parliamentary Party. On the contrary, many successful men from the business world sat for the safer county seats, rather than their own urban environments. A local connection, although important and useful, especially in an area under the influence of a socially prestigious family or local elite, was not essential to selection for even the safest of rural strongholds. The general attitudes and character of the candidate were equally important. His ability to finance himself, his election expenses, and as much as half the running costs of the local Association, was an even more important consideration in the eyes of selection committees. The Deputy Chairman of the Party admitted in 1930 that the consequence was that the good seats were on sale to the highest bidder.[47] Men tended to stick to their own home county, though not necessarily to the constituency in which they made their living. Even this parochialism was not completely uniform: forty Members sitting for English counties had had no prior connection with the area at all.[48] As the balance of wealth shifted from the landed to the business element in society, so the occupational background of the parliamentary Conservative Party adjusted to and reflected this. Men with backgrounds in law or business were increasing their predominance over the landed element throughout the inter-war period. In part this was a result of the disintegration of the Liberal Party, which had formerly drawn much support from the professions and from business. An analysis of the occupational background of the Conservatives returned in 1929 breaks down as follows:[49]

Occupational Background of Conservative MPs 1929–1931

Landed	14%	33%
Diplomatic & Service	19%	
Business: Industry	16%	32%
Business: Commerce	16%	
Legal	21%	35%
Professional	14%	

To simplify further, whilst only one-third of the parliamentary Party came from the traditional backgrounds of land and services, two-thirds came into political life from the commercial, industrial, or professional worlds—from the business sector. This transformation from the landed party of the late nineteenth century was further underlined by the fact that only forty MPs had parliamentary experience stretching back before 1914.

This is certainly not to suggest that the social class of Conservative MPs was changing; rather, it illustrates the ability of the upper classes to accommodate newer sources of wealth within their ranks. After the 1929 election the Conservative Party in the Commons amounted to 260 MPs, of whom 59 were related to the peerage, including 13 heirs to seats in the Lords. All three of the women MPs were the wives of peers. The educational background of the Conservative members of the House of Commons in 1929 demonstrates that they continued to be drawn exclusively from the wealthy upper and upper-middle classes. 134 had attended one of the major public schools, with Eton and Harrow between them providing 93 MPs. Equally, 117 had graduated from either Oxford or Cambridge Universities. Within this group the dominance of the most aristocratically prestigious colleges was marked. At Oxford, 20 MPs had been Christ Church men and 12 had attended New College, whilst of the Cambridge contingent Trinity alone accounted for 29. Many others had passed through the naval colleges or Sandhurst.[50] The majority of the business element were not self-made men but, like Baldwin himself, were building on the economic and social achievements of previous generations of their families.

If the changes in the occupational composition of the Party were continuing as an undercurrent throughout the inter-war period, the defeat of 1929 had had a more direct impact in changing the political complexion of the Party. Broadly speaking, the Diehard, or right-wing, element sat for the safer southern seats. These by their nature tended to be more vigorous and insular in their visceral Conservatism, having no need to make concessions towards other powerful groups of local opinion. Thus the Diehards were on the one hand insulated from the changing social and political nature of the country, and yet on the other hand were protected from the direct electoral consequences of these.[51] The Diehards are a much misunderstood element within the Conservative ranks. Their name had its origins in the group who resisted to the end the passage of the Parliament Act in 1911, but few of the inter-war Diehards were themselves veterans of that battle. Since the First World War the name had come to be given to a small, but distinct, group of inarticulate back-benchers, who held grimly to the social and political attitudes of a previous generation. The Diehards were not intellectually right-wing, but they were utterly out of sympathy with the modern world. Their response was to adopt a position of total hostility to the slightest change; their catchwords were strength and firmness, and they confused these with inflexibility. The Diehards were not so much concerned with policy, or even with specific principles, but with the maintenance of standards. These encompassed the personal behaviour expected of a gentleman, the straightforwardness expected of an Englishman, and the sense of duty combined with authority expected of the white man in Africa and Asia. On these pillars they believed rested the survival of the empire, the prestige of the nation, and the preservation of the social order of their parents' generation of mid-Victorian supremacy and isolation. These personal certainties were combined with a lack of confidence in their political leaders and in the future of the nation and the empire. The equations of the Diehard mind were simple and direct. They looked for straight talk and bold measures, firmness when in opposition and resolution when in government, and found all of these to be lacking between 1927 and 1931. Though their outlook hardly rose to the level of concrete policies, their howls of anguish were sincere. 'Losing their heads with childish vigour', they touched a chord in the hearts of many ordinary Conservatives through the very simplicity of their message.[52]

Diehard attitudes were entrenched in the Conservative psyche, and have never been so acutely summarised as by the cartoonist David Low's later invention of Colonel Blimp. With his inarticulate, choleric, but direct opinions, Blimp was such a successful caricature because he came within a whisker of reality. The Diehards were the least impressive group within the parliamentary Party, and they were almost bereft of skill in tactics or debate. Many of them exemplified the old Conservative Party: landed gentry with military backgrounds, devoted to field and blood sports. Others, however, were more disreputable, coming from the shady side of business, and were known by the epithet of 'the forty thieves'. The leader among the Diehards was Colonel John Gretton, described by a former Chief Whip as 'one of the best-hearted fellows one ever met, kind, generous, self-effacing; ugly as possible, blinking at one through gold-rimmed spectacles; inarticulate, for it is almost impossible to hear a word he says'.[53] Gretton was the chairman of the brewing conglomerate of Bass, Ratcliffe, and Gretton, and had sat in parliament almost continously since 1895. He had been a prime mover in the Diehard rebellion against the Coalition between 1920 and 1922, and had continued to act as their spokesman and focal point for the rest of the 1920s. The other leading figure amongst the right-wing backbenchers was Sir Henry Page Croft, a tireless enthusiast for tariff reform who had been involved in protectionist campaigns and cabals from the 'Confederates' of the Edwardian era onwards.

The Diehards and the tariff reformers were not synonymous, but the majority of the right-wing were protectionists of varying degrees of ardour. Protection was a popular policy in many regions of southern England, where the farmers were in competition with continental growers of fruit and vegetables, with Argentine beef, and with North American grain. It was also attractive to the elderly living on fixed investments in the solidly Conservative seaside resorts: both were areas of strong Diehard support. After the 1929 election the Diehards numbered between 45 and 50 MPs, loosely organised in the 'Conservative Group', of which Gretton was both chairman and convener.[54] One of the first to have joined him in this was Sir Basil Peto, best known as the last MP customarily to wear a top hat in the chamber of the House of Commons. Other leading Diehards included Sir Henry Cautley, Arthur Heneage, Major Guy Kindersley, Major-General Sir Alfred Knox, and Colonel W.G. Nicholson, one of the few privy councillors amongst them.[55] Lieutenant-Colonel Grant Morden and J.R.Remer were prominent amongst the 'forty thieves'. Some of the Diehards were regarded by other Conservative MPs almost with affection, as the predictable touchstones of backwoods feeling, but others were personally unimpressive, such as the abrasive W.G.Howard Gritten or the pompous Sir Herbert Nield. Not all the Diehards were elderly, for their ranks included a number of newly-elected MPs who combined a reactionary mentality with youthful vigour and vehemence, such as Edward Marjoribanks and Viscount Lymington, the heir to the Earl of Portsmouth.

The extent of Diehard influence on the rest of the Party is a complex question, but they clearly typified fundamental Conservative attitudes. It was always understood that the Party could not lightly consider their alienation or defection, without also losing a part of its own essential being. Even so, the Diehards alone could not overthrow the Party leader, or dictate his policy. It was only if events should confirm their constant complaints, or if their outlook on any major issue should come to be widely shared within the parliamentary Party, that a crisis would emerge. This was what had happened in 1922, and was to do so again in 1930 over protection and in 1931 over India. The Diehards would need to persuade not just right-of-centre Conservative MPs, such as Earl Winterton, Viscount Wolmer, Sir Charles Oman, or Sir Martin Conway, but the moderate centre as well. It was the latter who provided the crucial element of ballast in the Party, for the large majority of Conservative MPs fell into this comfortable category. Amongst the centre, three distinct groups provided different but important touchstones of moderate opinion. The first of these were the respected senior members, of whom influential examples were George Lane-Fox, John Wardlaw-Milne, Herbert Spender-Clay, Francis Fremantle, Sir Patrick Ford, Edward Ruggles-Brise, and the chairman of the Conservative Private Members '1922' Committee, Sir Gervais Rentoul. The second group were the rising men clearly destined for Cabinet office in the near future, such as Sir Henry Betterton, Walter Elliot, Douglas Hacking, Sir Thomas Inskip, William Ormsby-Gore, George Tryon, and Sir

Howard Kingsley Wood. These figures were a little apart from the group of young MPs who remained staunchly loyal to Baldwin, though to many contemporary observers the two overlapped. Examples of this last group who had survived the 1929 defeat were Victor Cazalet, Anthony Eden, R.A.Butler, W.S. Morrison, and Noel Skelton. Whilst the Chief Whip, Sir Bolton Eyres-Monsell, and his assistants, might take the grumbles of the Diehards for granted, they constantly monitored the moods of the moderates.

The centre and left wings of the Party, who might have tempered their convictions with electoral expediency, suffered especially badly in the 1929 defeat. Many of the 'YMCA' group of younger left-wing MPs were not returned to the new parliament. Several of them, including Harold Macmillan, Duff Cooper, Terence O'Connor, and Robert Hudson, had represented northern marginal seats, amongst which the losses had been most highly concentrated. Thus, while the balance of British politics moved to the left with the return of a popular Labour government, at the same time the parliamentary representation of the Conservative Party shifted rightward, a potentially dangerous situation for its future prospects. It has been estimated that the Diehard wing, through suffering proportionately fewer losses, rose in composition in the House of Commons from one-seventh of the Party to one-fifth.[56] In addition, their views gained influence both from the absence of the vocal rising moderates, and from the fact that the circumstances of the defeat seemed to confirm their opinions. The tradition of local autonomy of constituencies from outside interference, coupled often with a financial dependence of the same associations upon the Member or his family, and the personal wealth and social eminence of many Diehards, prevented the imposition of effective party discipline. Neither the Central Office nor the Whips had any meaningful sanctions with which they could threaten the safer constituencies and so prevent the return of Diehard MPs. Their opinion was only of significance to those seeking office or honours, and it was a part of the world view of most Diehards that they eschewed any such ambitions. Most were concerned only to do what they considered to be their duty as diligent backbenchers, and were often rounding off a career of achievement in another sphere of life. The average age of the Conservative Members was exactly 50 years, although as always the leadership was drawn from an older political generation.[57]

As an alternative method of control to formal discipline, Conservative leaders had always relied upon the ingrained loyalty that was given by the Party to the leader. However, this loyalty was conditional upon there existing a minimum of trust and confidence in the leadership, and the experience of Austen Chamberlain in 1922 had demonstrated that it could be stretched to breaking point. However, whilst continually aware of the need to carry his existing party with him, Baldwin could not afford simply to pander to their prejudices if the Party was to hope to return to power. Whilst he had one eye on the level of tolerance of the Diehards, he had to have the other on the political temperature of the northern and marginal seats lost in 1929, and which must be regained if the Conservatives were again to win a governing majority. Balancing these two conflicting forces produced many of the problems of the following two years. By the time of the general election defeat of May 1929 pressures were building up within the Party, barely below the surface. It was the inadequacy of the leadership's responses which over the following twelve months was to turn the simmering unrest into an open revolt.

CHAPTER 2

The Shock of Defeat

It is popularly believed that, almost as a law of nature, the Conservative Party in defeat turns on its leader, a view confirmed by the fall of Edward Heath in 1975. The experience of Baldwin after the election of 1929 appears to be the classic illustration of this model. In fact, there is no inevitability about any such process. Both Balfour and Churchill were able to survive landslide defeats in 1906 and 1945. When a revolt has occurred, it has built up over a period of months, and has originated from a wider range of factors than merely electoral disappointment. If anything, the immediate aftermath of defeat produces a lull, even if that turns out to be the calm before the storm. This was the reason why Baldwin was able to survive the short interval spent out of power in 1924. On that occasion his leadership did not come under the sort of sustained pressure which produced a crisis after 1929. The model of Conservative political action revealed by the events of 1929 to 1931 provides a truer and more typical insight into the consequences of defeat. In this second spell in opposition the passage of time had an eroding effect upon his prestige, and upon the obedience and patience of his followers. The course of these early stages of the Party crisis has never been properly explored, and as a result there are many gaps in our understanding of the political scene at the end of the 1920s, and many misconceptions as to what was taking place within the Conservative Party in this period. The essential point is that the crises over policy and leadership built up slowly and inexorably over nearly fourteen months, before they burst forth, threatening to overturn the established hierarchies and sweep away the leader. At the beginning, the Party leadership seemed to hold all the cards. However, within a matter of weeks the situation began to slide out of their control.

The general election held on 30 May 1929 had produced a clear

Conservative defeat, but no overall majority for any party. This result was quite unexpected to the Conservative leadership, for they had been convinced that their strategy was going to secure them a comfortable victory and a further term of office.[1] Because of this confidence, they had no contingency plans with which to face the shock of defeat. The immediate decision that confronted Baldwin, still technically Prime Minister, was what response he should make in the light of the uncertain parliamentary position. It was a measure of the adaptability of the active politician that Labour's success did not produce a panic akin to that seen after the general election of 1923. The absence of revolutionary peril sharply reduced the attraction of any return to coalitionism. Amongst backbench Conservatives in both Houses, hostility to such a combination was vociferous and vehement. An alternative possibility was for the Conservative cabinet to repeat the strategy of 1923, by meeting parliament as a government. This would force the Liberals to choose sides. It was expected that once again they would opt for Labour, and in the process alienate many anti-Socialist Liberal voters. A gloss was put on this plan by Neville Chamberlain and L.S. Amery, who wanted to ride for a fall on a strong protectionist platform, in order to raise the morale of the Conservative rank and file.

Baldwin's first instinct, before anyone other than perhaps his wife influenced him, was to resign immediately.[2] This was not inconsistent with the tenor of the advice he was receiving, for it all assumed that the government would leave office. Only the method of its doing so was a matter of debate. On 2 June Baldwin consulted two of his most valued advisors; the fourth Marquess of Salisbury, leader of the Party in the House of Lords, and Geoffrey Dawson, editor of *The Times*. However, they gave contradictory counsel. Salisbury, while taking no strong line, did not disagree with Baldwin; but Dawson was for holding on and meeting parliament. Despite the doubts this caused him, Baldwin still held to his original intention. He revealed the basis of his reasoning in typical imagery, walking on the afternoon of the 2nd with the King's private secretary. Lord Stamfordham recorded that 'in the true English spirit he accepts his defeat and, if he resigns, the Democracy in an equally British spirit will take off their hats to him as a good sportsman, who has had his run, been beaten, and takes his beating like a man'. This was not pure naivety; Baldwin was convinced that it would count in his favour at the next general election.[3]

Two events on 3 June swept away the last of Baldwin's hesitations. Influenced by the Astors, Dawson's leader in *The Times* swung round to advocating resignation before parliament met. This was reinforced by a letter from the Earl of Derby, who was not only a powerful Conservative magnate in Lancashire, but was also unkindly, though

accurately, characterised as a political weather-vane. Derby was
unequivocal that there must be no question of hanging on to office; the
country had given its decision and this must be accepted without
further protest.[4] At the cabinet meeting held later the same day
Baldwin took the initiative by firmly stating his personal preference
for resignation at once. He was strongly supported by Winston
Churchill, the Chancellor of the Exchequer, and their combined
weight carried the day against a small group who favoured repeating
the 1923 strategy. The King was recovering from a serious illness, and
so Baldwin travelled to Windsor on 4 June to place the resignation of
the government in his hands. The next day Ramsay Macdonald
accepted the royal commission to form a second, minority, Labour
administration. However, as in 1924, Labour took office without
coming to any arrangement with the Liberal Party. Macdonald, as
much as Baldwin, set his face against deals with Lloyd George: the
Liberals must either support Labour, or turn them out if they dared.
With Labour riding on the crest of a wave, and the Liberal organisation strapped for funds and deeply disappointed by its handful of
gains in the election, this was a safe tactical gamble.[5]

Tired and glad to escape from office, Baldwin seemed to be bored
and to lack any clear conception as to what line the Conservatives
should take now that they had unexpectedly found themselves in
opposition.[6] His character naturally led him, through caution and an
odd element of complacency, into doing nothing at all. Baldwin had
always been particularly concerned with larger questions of political
mood: of educating democracy, of the constitution, and of the
appeasement of labour. Testing the air in the first few weeks of the
Labour government's tenure, he was even more than usually concerned with politics in the broadest sense. Baldwin insisted that 'it is
not sufficiently realised that what we were at present fighting was not
a programme, but an atmosphere, which no amount of promulgation
of counter-programmes could affect'.[7] He sought to conform with
this analysis as far as possible, by avoiding giving any hostages to
fortune in the form of new definitions of policy, and by resolving that
Labour should be seen to get a decent run. Meeting Macdonald by
chance in the Athenaeum on 4 June, Baldwin assured him that he
would not indulge in petty opposition tactics, but would give the
ministry fair play. He was receptive to the appeal that Macdonald
made when opening the debate on the King's speech on 2 July, that
matters should be dealt with in the constructive manner of a Council
of State, rather than by the usual adversarial combat between government and opposition. This not only accorded with his own unaggres-
sive instincts, but also logically followed from the decision for
immediate resignation. Baldwin's straightforward approach was his
catchword, and he had a vested interest in ensuring that his reputation

was not marred through pulling the rug too swiftly from under the infant Labour government. Baldwin tolerated Churchill's exploration of the terms of a deal with Lloyd George in July, not because he had any desire to put the government out then, but because he envisaged a replay of the circumstances that had brought about the fall of the first Labour ministry in 1924. He considered it likely that before the year was out he might need Liberal votes in the lobbies to eject the government after it had either blundered badly, or revealed its true Socialist colours in despoliatory legislation. It was highly unlikely that either Baldwin or his fellow anti-coalitionists of 1922 would have gone through with a plot with Lloyd George. However, Baldwin accepted that, whatever the fate of parliamentary Liberalism, Liberal voters in the country must not be stampeded into the Labour camp by the hasty adoption of a tariff programme. Churchill believed that such a tactic would have only one result, a Lib-Lab bloc which would exclude the Conservatives from office for the remainder of his political lifetime.[8]

The prestige of the Labour government continued to rise during the summer and autumn of 1929, principally because of successes in the field of foreign affairs. Macdonald made a triumphal visit to the United States to deal with the tangled question of naval disarmament, and Philip Snowden, the Chancellor of the Exchequer, won much praise for his dogged defence of British interests at the Hague Conference on German reparations. Unemployment continued to fall slightly over the summer months of 1929. This led to the fear that Macdonald might capitalise on the situation by calling a second general election in order to get a working majority. The political indications suggested that, at least until December 1929, such a tactic might well have paid dividends. For this reason above all others Baldwin clung to his centrist image, and the limitations of the safeguarding policy. His political antennae were focused on the seats he needed to win back to regain a parliamentary majority, mainly urban constituencies in the midlands and north of England, and in Scotland. Baldwin was unwilling to progress rapidly in the direction of tariff reform, for his strategy depended on raising no unnecessary obstacles to the return of these decisive marginals to the Tory fold. Nevertheless, no party leader can afford to ignore for long his partisan stalwarts. In the safer seats, especially in the southern half of the country, protectionist sentiment was deeply entrenched in the local Associations. The need to find a formula that would appease the activists in these strongholds without alienating other regions was to remain Baldwin's major problem throughout the period in opposition. This question became acute in the aftermath of the election, with the emergence of debate over the causes of the debacle.

The leadership's analysis had involved remarkably little retrospective soul-searching, and was characterised by an air of complacency more appropriate to the victors than the vanquished. There was a clear preference for blaming the setback on events beyond the cabinet's control. Sir Samuel Hoare, Sir Laming Worthington-Evans, and William Bridgeman all settled for the swing of the pendulum, fatalistically elevating its effects into an axiomatic law of nature.[9] Neville Chamberlain linked with this the insidious workings of Socialist propaganda. Even so, he could contemplate with detached calm the prospect that the new ministry might make such a mess of affairs that within two years the country would be glad to see them go. In a similar fashion, his half-brother Austen pinned the blame for the alienation of working class voters on the trade depression of the late 1920s.[10] The only Cabinet Minister to lose his seat, Sir Arthur Steel-Maitland, found nothing more significant to blame than the enforced absences from his constituency that resulted from his duties as Minister of Labour.[11] As an adjunct to this 'act of God' syndrome, Baldwin and other anti-Coalitionist ministers bitterly blamed another entirely external factor, the activities of Lloyd George and the intervention of Liberal candidates. Within the leadership, the only notes of criticism heard were sounded over the role of two of the leading ex-Coalitionists. Austen Chamberlain had offended by announcing that he had been invited to continue as Foreign Secretary after the election, despite infirmity and the considerable unpopularity of his policies. Winston Churchill was attacked for the whole slant of his fiscal policy at the Exchequer. Amery was the only member of the ousted Cabinet who dissented from these comforting conclusions. He had been deeply disappointed at the eschewal in the manifesto of anything that might savour of tariff reform, such as positive proposals for extending safeguarding, but for the moment he kept his conclusions to himself. After the last meeting of the Cabinet on 3 June he sardonically noted in his diary: 'we all parted very happily, voting ourselves the best government there has ever been'.[12]

This complacent atmosphere contrasted strongly with the aftermath of the 1923 election. On that occasion, the constituencies, on the whole favourable to protection, did not blame the leadership for the defeat, although the circumstances surrounding its formulation produced a bitter debate in the upper echelons of the Party. Now, with an election lost on the moderate policy imposed from above, the roles were reversed with a vengeance. Initially the rank and file adopted an explanation which could be summed up as 'Liberals and lies'. This took the form of blaming the intervention of Liberal candidates for letting the Socialists in, together with the accusation that both Liberals and Labour had swayed voters through employing foul tactics.[13] These had consisted of misrepresentations of the policies and record of the Conservatives, as well as a corrupt political auction conducted by both opposing parties. In Labour's case, this meant bribery with offers of remunerative social welfare legislation; in Lloyd George's, the promise to conquer unemployment. To the Conservatives, both were cynically fraudulent strategies in view of the practical difficulties which were being brushed aside by their promoters. At first, the Party clearly needed to believe that it had been beaten by unfair means, rather than through any deficiency on its own part. The constituency activists were simply blunter than their leaders in fixing the cause on visible opponents rather than vague trends. This allowed the consoling view that the Conservatives had at least preserved their honour, and that political honesty operated even at the price of defeat. In northern constituencies, where for pragmatic electoral reasons demands for a positive protectionist policy were rare, this explanation continued to serve late into 1929.[14]

As the condition of shock wore off during the summer, this initial simplistic explanation underwent a gradual transformation into a position that was not only more complex, but also radically critical of the leadership. One contribution to the developing tendency to find fault with the actions of the late administration was the enquiry held into the views of the local Associations. On 2 July the Central Council of the National Union, responding to grumblings voiced in the backbenchers' 1922 Committee and at the meeting itself, unanimously decided to send to each constituency in England and Wales a request for their analysis of the causes of defeat. The execution of this was a typical piece of clumsiness on the part of J.C.C. Davidson, the Chairman of the Party organisation. His transparent reluctance to pursue the matter and his later desire to sweep the results under the carpet backfired, alienating influential constituency representatives on the Executive Committee of the National Union. While there is no proof that Davidson took advantage of his office in the interests of his leader, it is not unlikely, for he was known to have done so on previous occasions. His institutional position gave him every opportunity to put a spanner in the works, for he was also the Chairman of the Executive Committee of the National Union, as well as being a member of the sub-committee in question. Furthermore, the enquiry was transmitted via his own Central Office, and it is hard to believe that he could not have gathered a better response had he wished. One constituency minuted a complaint that they had not even been sent a copy of the questionnaire: it is unlikely that they were a unique case.[15] By the end of October only 255 Associations had replied, with sixty more trickling in after this. The credibility of the exercise was therefore undermined, for any conclusions were founded on the views of only just over sixty per cent of the English and Welsh constituencies which contested the election.

At the national level, the enquiry simply faded away. The sub-

committee met fruitlessly on several occasions in the winter of
1929–1930, but never produced a formal report.[16] However, a copy of
a draft does survive. This was written by two members of the
sub-committee: the recently retired long-serving London MP Sir
William Bull, and the Hon. Mary Pickford. Neither of these were
Diehards; rather they were moderate Conservatives who were customarily loyal to the leader, although Bull had found himself drifting
out of harmony with the government's approach between 1927 and
1929. Their draft was a bland and vague document, which defended
the Central Office from its critics, but could not conceal the range and
importance of the policies which the responding constituencies had
attacked. Many had blamed the granting of the 'flapper' vote, and felt
that reforms in local government and de-rating had neither been
understood nor aroused enthusiasm. There was 'considerable
complaint that the policy of Safeguarding was not carried out with
greater vigour', and 'it was felt that the leaders had relied on their
record rather than on a definite and constructive policy', which would
have 'offered a positive alternative to Socialism'. The slogan of 'Safety
First' was deemed to typify this: 'the leaders had been irresolute in
action'. The role of a hostile popular press was also singled out as a
cause of the defeat. The conclusion of the draft report gave a clear
portent of the attitude of the rank and file: 'elections are won and lost
on questions of policy, which should be definite and constructive'.[17]
For Conservatives, this was a code which had only one possible
meaning: protection.

   In fact, Bull and Pickford's draft only hinted at the depth of the
dissatisfaction. The comments and resolutions which the enquiry
produced, recorded in the minute books of some local associations,
casts light on a uniquely wide scale into their state of mind (see
Appendix 1). Although several constituencies acknowledged local
deficiencies, nearly all placed the emphasis on errors of policy and
tactics at the national level, if only on the principle of shifting the
blame.[18] Examination of the extant responses produces a strikingly
cohesive picture. An indictment emerges not only of individual
measures but also of the basic political flavour of Baldwin's second
government. The measures of social reform received a unanimous
thumbs-down: de-rating, the 'flapper' vote, widows' pensions, and
the Local Government Act. In addition, there were deep grievances in
three areas close to the hearts of local activists: the failure of the
ministry to grasp the nettle of reconstituting the House of Lords; to
economise on government expenditure; and to advance towards tariff
reform. All these issues had been the constant subject of resolutions
from the constituencies in the past few years.[19] The caution over fiscal
policy in the general election was very unpopular. Defeat confirmed
for many the folly of the lack of a 'clear' policy, which was another

code-word for protection. This played into the hands of those who asserted that Baldwin was not a true Conservative at all. He had taken considerable risks with his 'New Departure' of 1924, and only success at the polls could have secured invulnerability from reaction. It now seemed as if the chickens were coming home to roost. The North Oxfordshire association spoke for many in crisply replying to the questionnaire that the primary cause of defeat was 'the actions of the Cabinet in riding roughshod over public and party opinion in the country, as expressed locally and at conferences of the Party'.[20]

It was only a small step from verdicts like this to claims for a greater role in the formulation of policy for the local Associations. It speaks volumes for the dissatisfaction of the activists that such a demand should be openly voiced in the hierarchical and authoritarian Conservative Party. The usual tactic for the leadership was to take the steam out of any unrest by adopting one or more of the favoured policies of their followers, and then using it as a rallying cry. The question of intra-party democracy could be shelved at this limited price, without allowing the constituencies any more power in practice. This had been the motive force behind the junior Ministers in 1922, when they placed themselves at the head of the revolt from below. If the grumbling was not defused in this way, it was likely to grow rather than diminish, and pose a serious problem for the leadership. The possibility of a total disintegration was not so far removed as might be supposed, for appeals of loyalty could only hold the Party together for a limited period in the face of a fundamental divergence of attitude. This was the experience both of 1903–1906 and 1920–1922, and was again to be demonstrated in the summer of 1930.

The progression of disillusionment with the distribution of power in the Party can be seen in the case of one example, the developing attitudes of Ealing Conservative Association during 1929. They responded to the questionnaire along orthodox lines in September, blaming the defeat on the uninspiring slogan 'Safety First', the hostile press, the de-rating policy, and the lack of emphasis on safeguarding. The absence of any strong lead from above in the period before the Party Conference resulted in the passage of a resolution in October calling for assurances that in future the opinions of the Party would be sought to a greater extent than they had been in the past. The Conference did not resolve the problems, but rather stoked the flames. By December the loss of faith in the leadership had progressed so far that the Ealing Executive were commenting critically on the gagging of speakers and the biased selection of motions at the Conference, although the procedure had been no different from any previous occasion.[21] The zenith of the demands for popular control was reached in October, when the National Union Executive debated an even more explicit resolution sent in from Lowestoft. This insisted that 'important questions of policy, before embodiment in the Party programme, shall be submitted to the consideration of Constituency Associations'. In the end the Executive rejected such a bold inno-vation, which would have amounted to a mutiny, and held fast to the traditional view of the role and prerogatives of the Party leader.[22] However, as the traumas of the following year were to show, so long as the constituencies were alienated from the official policy, demands for popular control were bound to recur, and with increasing vehemence.

Unrest from below was apparent in two other respects. The first, and less serious, was the attempt by one of the junior Ministers in the late government who had lost his seat to organise a Defeated Candi-dates Association. The plan was for this to be represented in all the Party's institutions, and specifically on the Committee of Enquiry into the defeat. However, the founder, J.T.C. Moore-Brabazon, was still fully imbued with the attitudes of party loyalty, and felt unable to establish his group without his leader's approval. Over the crucial months from July to November Baldwin was able to exploit this reluctance, preserving a sphinx-like silence on the question. Signifi-cantly, he only thawed to the idea after the Party Conference, though still ambiguously.[23] Baldwin needed yet further prodding before he approved the new body in December, by which time the candidates were looking forward to the prospects of the next election rather than looking back in anger to the last. They had a vested interest in moderation as the approach most likely to help them regain their marginal seats, and as a group tended thereafter to weigh in on Baldwin's side. The second and more serious development was the attack on Davidson, Baldwin's crony and nominee as Chairman. Although he had done some useful work, he had alienated many important figures by becoming involved in unnecessary and acrimo-nious controversies. Some of the onslaughts on Davidson were directly personal, while others took the form of criticism of the constitutional functions of his office, and these came to be severely reduced under rank and file pressure by reforms in the rules of the National Union passed in the following year.

The reaction of the constituency parties and the backbench MPs to the loss of the election had important consequences in shaping the mood of the Party in the period before the annual Conference in November. One noticeable feature was the bitter hostility to the Liberals, who were far more disliked than Labour. Above all, the circumstances of the election played into the hands of the tariff reformers, affording visible proof of their frequently-aired critique of Baldwin's moderate line.[24] If defeat was bound to discredit the leaders who had chosen the strategy on which it had occurred, it was also bound to strengthen the hands of those who had opposed that programme. Even the distribution of the losses could be used to reinforce these views. As protection was always presented as a policy to bring about prosperity in industry and thus provide the solution to unemployment, a strong line on safeguarding would have held the industrial seats. This argument found a receptive audience in the local Associations, and was the third most frequently cited cause of the reverse. In turn this produced a groundswell of resolutions from below demanding a new and stronger platform. One of the first examples of this foreshadowed the widening rift between north and south. At the Central Council on 2 July a resolution calling for the adoption of extensive safeguarding for all the principal trades of the country, particularly naming iron and steel, was carried in the face of strong opposition from Sir John Haslam, who represented the Westhoughton division of Lancashire, one of the poorest Conservative prospects in the land.

The balance of power in the parliamentary Party had shifted decisively in favour of the southern areas, and the brake of the northern moderates had been removed by the defeat of many of them in the election. The lead came from the south, where it was widely held that the Conservatives could only hope to return to power by advocating a sweeping policy of the extension of safeguarding and the development of the empire. This made for a popular and potentially dangerous combination when linked by the Diehards to criticism of the lack of vigour in the attacks on the government made from the front bench. If Baldwin had been a more determined, more aggressive, or more effective leader of the opposition in the summer months of 1929, it is possible that these disappointments could have been assuaged without paying the price in terms of a change of policy or personality. However, his colourless stance served only to redouble dissatisfaction. Baldwin's failure to give a lead during the months of June and July undermined the confidence of his colleagues, and led to a slump in his personal prestige. By the beginning of July Lord Beaverbrook, admittedly an unfriendly source, was able to claim after having seen almost every member of the former Cabinet that he did not believe the leader had a single sincere supporter.[25]

Other leading Conservatives, frustrated by the lack of movement, sought to grasp the initiative. The first two ex-Cabinet Ministers to break silence were Amery and Neville Chamberlain. Amery had been frustrated by the absence of any systematic approach to fiscal or imparial policy throughout the 1924–1929 government. He contemplated resignation several times, claiming to stay his hand only because of personal loyalty and affection for Baldwin. Defeat confirmed his belief that the Party must have 'a positive political creed' if it was ever to win over 'the industrialised masses'. He was certain that the Conservatives had such a weapon to hand in the appeal of empire, if only they would take it up in a positive fighting spirit.[26] Amery resolved to use his freedom from the restraints of Cabinet collective responsibility at the first opportunity, in the debate on the King's speech after parliament reconvened in the first week of July. Rising on the 9th to speak on economic links within the empire, he acknowledged the divisions amongst the Conservative leaders, and openly confessed his belief that the election had been lost through the lack of a bold fiscal and imperial policy. The message was clear that in the new parliament the important distinction was to be between the rival schools of fiscal opinion, rather than the ostensible party labels. Amery's renowned obsession with the imperialist theme and poor sense of timing and tactics undermined the impact of his advocacy on his colleagues.[27] What made his outburst on this occasion so striking was the fact that he no longer seemed to be hunting alone. At the same time Neville Chamberlain publicly asserted that the Party was no longer bound by the restrictive pledges given before the election. On 4 July he told the Empire Industries Association that the slate had been wiped clean. Amid cheers from the audience of Conservative backbenchers, he declared that the time was ripe for the production of a new imperial policy.

Neither Chamberlain nor Amery indicated more than the outline of the programme that they would like to see adopted. They were trying to provoke discussion, not pre-empt it. They were seeking to change the outlook of the Party at a more general level—an advance of rhetoric rather than substance. Both considered it to be essential that the Party should have a clear and distinctive imperial stance. So far as electoral common sense would allow, this should enthuse the ordinary Conservative. Chamberlain and Amery were contributing to the continual debate within the Conservative Party as to what constituted 'practical politics'. The contention of the committed protectionists had always been that a bold policy fed on itself. It would create its own momentum by inspiring the party activists, who would then carry the banner triumphantly to the wider public. It was for these reasons that Amery and Chamberlain talked in striking terms about an advance of policy that was in fact quite small. At most they were intending an extension of the provisions of the safeguarding legislation to more sections of British industry. This might include the iron and steel trades, but would not extend beyond the manufacturing sector. Certainly, neither wished to go so far as the food tax. To cloak these ambiguities, their declarations were deliberately couched in strong but vague language.

Amery and Neville Chamberlain were the most advanced protectionists amongst the fallen cabinet. Others were more sceptical about the connection between the opinions of the Party faithful and the attitudes of the floating, possibly ex-Liberal, voter. The barometer of policy responded to the debate between the two schools of opinion, and their changing perceptions of the attitudes of the general public. With the possible exception of Churchill, no Conservative leader was opposed to protection on theoretical grounds, and most paid it lip service as an ideal. The debate revolved around the questions of timing and electoral practicability. The efforts of Amery and Neville Chamberlain to commit the leadership to a change of course seriously alarmed both the small free trade element and the moderate centre of the Party. These now proceeded to mount their counter attack. On 13 July Salisbury wrote to Baldwin, expressing his alarm. Ominously, he reported receiving protests from a large number of MPs.[28] In parallel with this, Derby requested that Baldwin publicly affirm that the policy enshrined in his open letter of August 1928 to the Chief Whip, Eyres-Monsell, was still in force.[29] There is no doubt that the alarm was motivated by fear of the electoral consequences. Even the hint of a protectionist programme would enable opponents to raise the cry of 'stomach taxes' against Conservative candidates. This would be a heavy albatross for the Party to hang around its neck, in view of the fact that another general election might come at any time, and that nothing had occurred in the political or economic spheres in the past two months to alter the attitude of the general public. In this context it was hardly surprising that dissent within the parliamentary Party was not limited merely to the neo-free traders; the centre also would not hold. Their fearful entreaties were echoed by a rising ex-Cabinet minister, Sir Samuel Hoare, who usually took care not to deviate from a median position.[30]

Baldwin himself was always slow to change his views once he had settled into them. Having opted for a policy of caution in the general election, and still having lost, he was unreceptive to the gamble involved in the protectionist strategy. The conclusions he had arrived at in considering the verdict of May placed a premium on moderation. He had also been swayed by the arguments of Austen Chamberlain and Churchill that the Conservatives must avoid alienating Liberal voters in the country, though he did not share their desire to negotiate a deal with Lloyd George. Above all, Baldwin was concerned to preserve unity. There could be no doubt in the summer of 1929 that any sudden lurch towards tariff reform would produce division and upheaval on the scale of that witnessed between 1903 and 1906, the Party's worst period in living memory. The alliance of free traders and moderates, together with the need to nurse the marginal constituencies, carried the day with Baldwin. He acceded to the demand for a showdown and summoned a Shadow Cabinet for the purpose. All those present, apart from Amery and Neville Chamberlain, declared their determination to have nothing whatever to do with food taxes. Nor did they wish to propound any new formulations of policy, for these would be likely to put off as many people as they attracted.[31] The opening round had gone to the preservers of the status quo. Loyalty to the leadership precluded Amery and Neville Chamberlain from any further dissension. Baldwin could offer Derby mixed reassurance: the 1928 policy stood until the Party had to draw up its position for the next election, an event to be put off for as long as possible.[32] However, should the national mood show signs of becoming more receptive, the protectionists were likely to find themselves pushing at an open door, for most of the opposition within the Party was based on electoral expediency and not on fundamental beliefs. Even in the moment of defeat at the Shadow Cabinet, Neville Chamberlain noted that his colleagues 'were not averse to the idea that we should make Empire the starting point when we did come to consider the future'.[33]

The uneasy relationship between public opinion and the demands of the activists was to be continually complicated during the next two years by the intervention of Lord Beaverbrook's campaign, which first emerged in the political vacuum following the election defeat. Aged 50 in 1929, Beaverbrook was the son of a Presbyterian minister, and had been christened Max Aitken. He was born and brought up in Canada, where in early life he acquired a large fortune from business ventures and mergers. Domiciled in England since 1910, Beaverbrook had built up a considerable press empire, which was also his abiding interest. Centred upon the *Daily Express*, which had a circulation of 1,693,000 in 1930, his other titles included the *Sunday Express* and the *Evening Standard*. Although he did not receive his peerage simply because of his newspaper interests, as had Lord Rothermere before him, the two men tended to be grouped together under the generic epithet of the 'press lords'. However, no analysis of Beaverbrook's position could be complete that did not acknowledge his background in Conservative politics. The attraction of Joseph Chamberlain's vision of imperial economic union had fired Beaverbrook's enthusiasm, and brought him to Britain in the first place. He soon became the intimate friend of a leading tariff reformer and Conservative front bencher: Bonar Law. Through the latter's good offices, and some lavish expenditure, he was found a parliamentary seat at Ashton-under-Lyne, which he represented from December 1910 until he accepted a peerage in December 1916. In this period Beaverbrook made a wide range of contacts and friends at all levels in the Party, many of whom respected his motives, and always looked upon him, even in aberrant moments, as essentially a good Conservative. Bonar Law's accession to the leadership of the Party in 1911, and his prominent role in the world of high politics as a major figure in the Lloyd George Coalition during and after the war, brought Beaverbrook close to the centre of power, albeit as an observer rather than a participant.[34]

In the immediate post-war period Beaverbrook oscillated between being an intimate member of Lloyd George's inner circle, and making attacks upon government policies. In 1921 he had waged war against the Coalition over a popular imperial issue close to his own heart – the failure to lift an embargo on Canadian cattle. He went beyond simply using his newspapers to attack the government, and, in the same manner as Rothermere's contemporary Anti-Waste League, intervened in by-elections. Beaverbrook was instrumental in defeating the newly-appointed Minister of Agriculture, Sir Arthur Griffith-Boscawen, when he stood for re-election. A second episode encouraged Beaverbrook to supplement these guerilla tactics with personal advocacy from the public platform, when in the general election of 1922 he backed the independent Conservative candidate Hall Caine at East Dorset against F.E. Guest, the former Coalition Liberal Chief Whip. These ventures foreshadowed his activities between 1929 and 1931. After the succession of Baldwin to the premiership when Law retired in 1923, Beaverbrook found himself excluded from the corridors of power. Baldwin had always thought that the undue and unconstitutional influence accorded to the press was one of the most sordid and corrupting features of Lloyd George's regime, and a series of unfortunate incidents during his first two administrations only served to redouble his hostility to the press lords. Baldwin did not view all newspaper proprietors with equal hostility. The Berry brothers, later Lords Camrose and Kemsley, were acceptable because they generally held to a line of party loyalty. It was the wayward and unprincipled potentates Rothermere and Beaverbrook who were beyond the pale. By 1929 a personal animus was well known to exist between these two newspaper barons, and in particular Lord Rothermere, and the Party leader. The hostile publicity which the Party believed it had received as a result figured prominently on their list of causes of the defeat.

Though not a participant in the debates of the House of Lords, Beaverbrook was active in political life, mainly but not entirely through his newspapers. Essentially he was seen as a maverick but sincere advocate of imperial unity through the means of tariff reform. An essential part of his programme was the offer of preferential duties that would favour the importation of food and raw materials from the empire, in return for similar preference for British industry in dominion markets. Beaverbrook was alienated from the Baldwin government on grounds of personality and policy by the time of the 1929 election, and was elated at the failure of 'Safety First'.[35] He did not run imperial preference in his papers during the campaign, for he saw little prospect of capturing the existing Conservative leadership for a programme that they had explicitly ruled out as electorally impossible. Instead, he allowed his papers to drift, filling the empty space with a lightweight discussion of the problems of railway freight. However, he admitted to his aide and confidant Robert Bruce Lockhart that he was merely biding his time.[36] The situation was transformed by the changed balance of power after the election. The visible search of many Conservatives for a clear policy provided Beaverbrook with a tempting opportunity to promote his own vision of imperial unity. An article in the *Morning Post* at the end of June, criticising Beaverbrook for his low profile during the election, provided the stimulus to action. Beaverbrook responded with two articles in the *Sunday Express*, the first a call to arms for an imperial policy, the second unfolding his new initiative.

Beaverbrook's idea was simple: the creation of an economic bloc consisting of Britain, the Dominions, and the Crown Colonies. These would join together in a free trade zone by reducing their tariffs in favour of each other, whilst raising in common a high protective fiscal barrier against competition from outside. Beaverbrook believed this policy would fulfil three distinct aims. Firstly, it would encourage imperial solidarity through economic links, as Joseph Chamberlain had originally proposed. Secondly, it would keep British industry alive by providing it with an assured market, thus reducing unemployment and the challenge of Socialism at home. Finally, it would protect the British farmer from the dumping of cheap foreign surpluses of agricultural produce. Beaverbrook adopted the slogan 'Empire Free Trade' to describe his plan, and claimed that it was a new departure.[37] This was hair-splitting, for he was simply refurbishing the old tariff reform banner of 1903. This was clear from his insistence that a tax on foodstuffs imported from outside the empire was essential.[38] During the course of the next two years Beaverbrook's opinions and policies occasionally altered, sometimes in a contradictory manner. However, the insistence on facing up to the food tax was the most consistent and distinguishing feature of his campaign, and it was not negotiable. Typically, Beaverbrook justified it by citing two conflicting reasons. The first was the fact that a tariff which would give Dominion food exporters a protected market for their produce was essential as a bargaining counter with which reciprocal advantage for British industrial exports could be negotiated. On the other hand, Beaverbrook wooed the disgruntled British farmers, assuring them that his programme would bring prosperity to their depressed industry.[39] Such claims were incompatible at a time when British agriculture was suffering severely from competition from the Dominions themselves. As a result, Beaverbrook tended to place the emphasis upon the aspects of obvious benefit, in the shape of insular protection.[40] This was in any case a necessary first step. The problem for tariff reformers had always been that Britain, with a free trade system, would first have to set up tariff walls before they could be preferentially lowered for the empire. In the battle to persuade the public to abandon free trade, the Conservative Party had lost four elections in the previous three decades, tearing itself apart in the process.

There was a fundamental flaw in the Empire Free Trade programme. The nature of the Dominion economies had developed since Joseph Chamberlain's initiative of 1903, and they now possessed infant but potentially vital industrial bases which their tariff walls were designed to nurture. Many experienced Conservative politicians had serious doubts as to whether the Dominions would be willing to open their home markets to the full blast of British industrial competition. As it went without saying that the Dominions could not be coerced, any such reluctance effectively negated the idea. Beaverbrook never successfully confronted this problem. Instead, he preferred to concentrate his energies on securing the first step in his programme. He aimed to win the mother country for his policy, for in his view 'Great Britain still has the hegemony of the empire'.[41] This was one reason for his almost fanatical insistence on the food tax as the acid test of the new policy. He believed that as the 'dear food' cry would in any case be used by opponents of the scheme, it would be easier to overcome if directly faced. Even here Beaverbrook often wished to have his cake and eat it, in this case almost literally by claiming that the food tax need not raise the cost of living in Britain:[42]

> As the empire produces more wheat than it consumes, it is absurd to suppose that the price of the loaf in this country will be raised when an import duty is levied on foreign wheat. The British housewife will not raise prices against herself by transferring her purchases of loaves from one shop to another, for that is all the change I propose amounts to.

Throughout, the economic arguments for Empire Free Trade were deployed on this crude and simplistic level. These justifications were purely adjuncts to a political propaganda campaign, in which slogans mattered more than the fine points of theory. The assertion of originality, modernity, and vitality was all-important. Beaverbrook's campaign was not without idealism, but it was of a hardheaded and practical kind, concerned with achieving results. His enthusiasm and commitment showed itself in his pursuit of the chimera of Empire Free Trade. Whilst Beaverbrook privately admitted that it might take years to accomplish his goal, he always acted as if one more effort would secure total victory.[43] Beaverbrook was a formidable propagandist, with an obsessional commitment to his policy. 'The only goal that I accept is Empire Free Trade', he declared; 'anything else is only a means to that end'.[44] His religious upbringing reinforced his political instincts, and the slogan became an article of faith that could not be qualified. 'It is as well to fail in a righteous cause', he believed.[45]

At first Beaverbrook's plan was merely to run a propaganda campaign, perhaps along non-party lines, angled to secure Liberal as well as Conservative support.[46] This quickly evolved into an effort to capture the Conservative Party by the traditional pressure-group techniques of propaganda on the one hand, and the establishment of an independent political machine in threatening competition on the other. Initially, Beaverbrook sought to convert Members of Parliament, but before long his tactics changed from pressure through persuasion to pressure by coercion. This transition was encouraged by the fact that it struck a resounding chord in the hearts of the constituency membership in southern England. However, the campaign failed to capture the parliamentary Party, for despite many private assurances of support hardly any MPs came out publicly for Empire Free Trade. The reaction of the Party leaders varied in accordance with their fiscal outlook, but even leading protectionists such as Amery and Sir Robert Horne, Chancellor of the Exchequer betwen 1921 and 1922, could not swallow the food tax as a practical policy. Lord Derby warned from Lancashire that 'everybody is afraid of even breathing such a proposal in our part of the world'.[47] Others more hostile to Beaverbrook viewed his manifesto as being no more than a stunt, designed to boost the circulation of his newspapers. In addition, there was considerable suspicion, not limited to Baldwin's inner circle, that Beaverbrook's motivation was in reality the less elevated one of personal hostility to the Party leader. Neville Chamberlain was typical of the majority of the Party in giving Empire Free Trade a mixed reception. He acknowledged the press magnate's sincerity, whilst condemning his policy as 'obsolete, impracticable, and mischievous'.[48] However, the emergence of the militantly protectionist Empire Free Trade campaign, occurring simultaneously with the initiatives of Amery and Neville Chamberlain, caused considerable alarm in the parliamentary Party.[49]

The tension was increased by the events surrounding the by-election held in Twickenham. A vacancy had been created there by the elevation of Baldwin's former Home Secretary, Sir William Joynson-Hicks, to the peerage as Viscount Brentford. Twickenham was an ideal opportunity for the Empire Free Trade movement to flex its potential muscle at constituency level. Joynson-Hicks had been a traditionalist Tory of the old school, almost Diehard in outlook, and his seat was typical of the safely Conservative commuter belt which encircled London. The real influence of the mass circulation London daily newspapers was metropolitan rather than national, for in this period the vitality of the provincial press militated against the exclusive dominance of Fleet Street in the rest of the country. For that reason, the constituencies in which the influence of the *Daily Express* and *Daily Mail* was most effective were to be found in the middle-class suburbs of the Home Counties, of which Twickenham was a prime example. Not surprisingly, the candidate chosen to succeed Joynson-Hicks was a right-wing Conservative of strong imperialist views, and as such sympathetic to Beaverbrook's programme. Even before the formal announcement of his nomination, Sir John Ferguson asked Beaverbrook for support. Beaverbrook proceeded to apply pressure in order to force Ferguson to come out as openly as possible under the new banner. He candidly replied to Ferguson's request by informing him that he was considering bringing out an independent candidate in the by-election, not pledged to the Conservative Party but fighting simply on Empire Free Trade.[50] For reasons of electoral tactics Ferguson was reluctant to burn too many bridges. However, in view of the considerable support for Beaverbrook among the active element in local Conservative Associations in seats like Twickenham, even more than the supposed impact of his press propaganda, he could not afford to ignore the danger. Ferguson was faced with little option but to pre-empt the threat by proving that he also was not bound in allegiance to the official policy. At the same time, he tried to hedge his bets and, while paying lip service to Empire Free Trade, continually reiterated his loyalty to the leader. He was reluctant to jump from the frying pan into the fire, especially in view of the fact that the swing of the electoral pendulum still seemed to be travelling in Labour's direction.[51] But the pressure was too strong, and the break came when, after a series of lurches in Beaverbrook's direction, Ferguson came out for food taxes in a speech on 16 July.

Baldwin, already under pressure from alarmed colleagues such as Salisbury and Derby, could not afford to ignore this in the same way that he had brushed aside Amery's peroration in the Commons the week before. He had no alternative but to distance the Party as much as possible from identification with Ferguson's views. Baldwin withheld official recognition of Ferguson and withdrew the assistance of Central Office. This was made public in an open letter from Baldwin despatched on 22 July, written more in the tone of sorrow than anger.[52] The move backfired, partly because Davidson, the maladroit Party Chairman, was thought to be the motivating force behind what some MPs considered to be an excessive reaction to Ferguson's offence. It produced considerable resentment amongst the right wing of the Party, sympathetic by nature to Ferguson's politics, many of whom had promised to assist in his contest.[53] The ineffectiveness of party discipline was revealed when a deputation, including such respected long-serving backbenchers as Croft and Peto, informed the Chief Whip on the 24th that they had no intention of breaking their word. In the face of this, the Whips backed down. The Twickenham campaign threw the Party into further disarray, and the by-election provided a parade of Conservative disunity. Dissatisfaction with Davidson's handling of events was so great that Baldwin received a request for the convening of a party meeting, signed by John Gretton, the veteran Diehard spokesman, and twenty-eight backbenchers.[54] However, the Diehards were far from being alienated from Baldwin personally, and it is clear that they wished to debate the policy of the Party and the management of the Central Office, rather than the person of the leader. With the summer recess approaching, and buoyed up by his customary complacency, Baldwin countered by agreeing to see a deputation, but declining to call a meeting. In the event he also succeeded in postponing the deputation until late October, by which time the approach of the annual Conference ruled out the need for a party meeting.

The result at Twickenham on 8 August proved a severe disappointment to Beaverbrook, and confirmed the drawbacks inherent in a protectionist platform in the political climate of summer 1929. Ferguson came close to losing this safe seat; he faced the same Liberal and Labour opponents as had Joynson-Hicks in May, but his majority plummeted from his predecessors' 5966 to a mere 503. Although the Liberal vote had been squeezed, little consolation could be drawn from this in view of the fact that while Labour's share of the poll had risen from 35% in May to 46% in August, the Conservative percentage had marginally declined. It was clear that many Conservative voters had stayed at home, refusing to turn out for the protectionists. Beaverbrook's methods and policy at Twickenham, and their result, caused Amery and Chamberlain to back away. They still considered that food taxes, whilst essential in the long term, could only be carried after a lengthy programme of public education. Furthermore, both were committed to the belief that the Conservative Party was the only institution through which their ideas could come to fruition, and they recoiled from anything that might damage that Party's electoral prospects. So, with critical results for the future, Beaverbrook was left unshackled. He failed to persuade any senior Conservative politician to dilute the leadership of his campaign, despite repeated attempts to secure a respectable figurehead, and he nursed a sense of grievance and betrayal. Beaverbrook was left to operate outside the Party, for the simple reason that his politics would have been more dangerous from within than without.

The first phase of the Party crisis had ended with what appeared to be a complete success for the supporters of the status quo. However, this position was swiftly eroded during the second half of 1929. Its defenders failed to take any further action, and remained passive in the face of the emerging critique from below of the causes of the defeat.

This inactivity was exacerbated by the combination of post-election exhaustion and the widespread state of apathy which resulted from the uninspiring nature of the Party's policies.[55] During the hiatus in Conservative Party activity customarily brought on by the summer recess, neither the national nor the local political elites were exercising their usual firm grip upon the development of rank and file opinion. Of course, it was normal for party activity to die down during the holiday season. What was unusual was that this coincided not with a period of political repose, but with an important stage in the evolution of constituency attitudes. In the absence of contradiction, the criticisms voiced in the popular press took root in the minds of many ordinary supporters of the Party. These people did not withdraw their attention from politics or the newspapers over the summer holiday. Rather, they had more leisure to absorb their daily choice. By the end of the recess it became clear that the concept of Empire Free Trade was attracting a groundswell of approval from the constituency parties. The split in the Conservative Party had already begun to take on an ominous shape. In Beaverbrook the protectionist dissidents would find a leader of national stature, prepared to go the full distance in pursuit of their ends, whatever the political cost.

CHAPTER 3

The Empire Crusade

It is a perennial problem of political management that the local voluntary workers of any party always hold more extreme views than those which would be acceptable to the general public. It is, after all, the possession of these opinions which has often been the motivation for their activism in the first place. The Conservative Party is different in nature from the other parties in the diversity of reasons for which people have joined it. There can be no doubt that both social functions and social climbing attracted their fair share of recruits at constituency level. Bars and bazaars not only provided much of the local parties' funds, but also sometimes seemed to be an end in themselves. Certainly, the role of the Conservative Party as a social institution, rather than a political one, should not be under-estimated. The Party also attracted adherents for the more usual reasons: the influence of family background, regional and religious traditions, and the tendency to innate conservatism often associated with advancing age. Economic factors also played a part, but not one which can be simplistically treated in class terms. The constituency associations were dominated by an upper-class or upper-middle-class local elite, who provided their honorary presidents, office-bearers, executive committees, and often their candidates; but they were also mass bodies, frequently numbering a membership of several thousand, many of whom were lower-middle and working-class. Conservatism was more than anything else a question of temperament. It was not necessary to have a great deal of property to fear despoliation by Bolshevism or its kin, and for many supporters Conservatism wore a defensive face. Nevertheless, it should never be forgotten that, just as with any other political group, it was idealism which evoked the energy and enthusiasm of the voluntary workers who made up the human constitution of the Party. However, the issues upon which an

46

appeal to a Conservative idealism could be made were too dangerously unpopular with the indifferent mass of voters, committed to supporting no particular party, for the leadership to dare to take them up. This left a window of opportunity for Beaverbrook and his emotive Crusade for imperial economic unity.

Beaverbrook had withdrawn from public view after the setback at Twickenham, intending to recommence his campaign in October.[1] During the summer he relied solely upon newspaper propaganda to arouse popular opinion. However, his sudden reappearance on the political stage in the autumn, far from having been carefully calculated, was the result of a sudden fear that he was about to be superseded as the orchestrator of Conservative imperial sentiment. For Beaverbrook was not the only prominent figure from the business fringes of Conservatism at this time to advocate an advance in imperial economic policy. Lord Nuffield, Sir Abe Bailey, and the influential Lord Melchett, former Cabinet minister and chairman of Imperial Chemicals, were also thinking along lines parallel to the original Empire Free Trade proposals of July. Urged on by Amery, this group now seemed likely not only to capture the lead from Beaverbrook, but even more seriously to water down his policy. Melchett wrote to Beaverbrook on 8 October inviting him to a dinner organised by Bailey for the 22nd at which a committee would be appointed to run their campaign, and enclosed a draft of their manifesto. At once Beaverbrook moved to outflank them, selecting both on tactical grounds and from genuine conviction the acceptance of the food tax as the line of demarcation. In his reply, he objected strongly to the omission of any reference to tariffs on food imports. During the following fortnight Beaverbrook prepared the next stage of his campaign, which was designed in both style and timing to recapture the limelight. On 22 October Bailey held his dinner, which was attended by Amery, Croft, Lord Lloyd, and Melchett; Beaverbrook was a noted absentee. His counterblast appeared two days later, when he produced his pamphlet manifesto of the Empire Crusade, entitled simply *Empire Free Trade*. This was to be the opening fanfare in the progress of the campaign from the realms of a newspaper stunt to an active propagandist organisation, though not, as yet, a political party.

Beaverbrook was determined to try to capture the public in person.[2] As the food tax was to become his distinctive cry, he began with an appeal to the agricultural interest. The first stage was the circulation of two proposals through the National Farmers' Union local branches. The first of these set out the policy as being 'in a sentence' that of 'Protection for the Farmers', and the second requested that supportive resolutions be sent to the NFU Executive.[3] The next more critical stage was to take the campaign to the public platform. From now on,

Beaverbrook would not be content with newspaper propaganda alone—he was out to make the news itself. His first public appearance set the keynote. On 28 October he addressed an audience of farmers at the West Sussex county town of Lewes, and nailed his colours to the mast on the food tax issue. Neither Melchett nor Amery could follow this lead, and thus the torch passed back into Beaverbrook's hands. The latter's renewed activity afforded a vivid contrast with the apathy evident throughout the Conservative Party. At the end of October Garvin commented in the *Observer* that Beaverbrook's campaign was 'the only vivid, living thing that is now going on in the Conservative Party'.[4]

At the same time the settlement of July was challenged from within the Party leadership. Sensing that the balance of Conservative opinion was beginning to move towards protection, the pro-tariff element in the leadership sought to give both covert encouragement and restraining direction, to as large a degree as they felt to be consistent with personal loyalty to Baldwin. In public this boiled down to the assertion that some consideration of policy advance was inevitable, together with hints that it would take the form of a policy on imperial trade parallel to Beaverbrook's. Although the contents of such speeches were not in themselves remarkable, taken together with the moves of Beaverbrook and Melchett, they indicated that the solution arrived at by the shadow cabinet had been only a very temporary one. That consensus proved incapable of holding up under sustained pressure. As a result the Party began to divide in a pattern which many thought was ominously similar to that of the initial tariff reform campaign of 1903–1906.[5] It became clear to Baldwin that continued adherence to the position of no advance on the general election policy was no longer preserving unity, but was actively provoking dissension. There were dangerous signs of the likelihood of a lead emerging from below on the model of 1922, if the development of the empire was not placed in the forefront of the Party's programme.[6] The Kent Provincial Division typified rank and file unhappiness that the Party had 'no constructive programme which can be offered to the electorate as an alternative to Socialism'.[7] Even the Chairman of the Party was pressed by his own local committee to formulate a 'definite and strong policy', the perennial euphemism for tariff reform.[8]

Baldwin's leadership was also being called into question on other grounds. The press statement that he had issued at the start of the new session fell flat, not simply because of the absence of a fiscal policy, but also for its muted attack on the Labour government. A crucial problem was Baldwin's lack of drive and his weaknesses as a leader in opposition. This was provoking criticism not only from the lower echelons of the Party, but also from the friendly press, and rising younger figures in the leadership. Baldwin's position at this time was further undermined by his actions over the Irwin declaration, and he badly needed to refurbish his Conservative credentials. This he was partly able to accomplish under the cover of a successful onslaught on the *Daily Mail*, which had overreached itself in its criticism of Baldwin's approval of the Irwin declaration. Nevertheless, it was becoming increasingly apparent that Baldwin could only reassert his position and restore unity by means of some advance in fiscal policy. By the end of October 1929 the Party was clearly rattled: Neville Chamberlain noted an atmosphere of 'depression, distrust, and despair'.[9] In particular, the annual Conference on 21–22 November was likely to produce difficulties unless the leadership pre-empted the position. Failing some movement in the direction demanded by the resolutions on the agenda sent in from many localities, the constituency activists might follow the lead of Beaverbrook instead.[10]

By the middle of November 1929 pressure was mounting from several quarters, propelling the leadership reluctantly forward. Churchill had carried the day in July on the grounds that a tariff policy would force a Lib-Lab alliance in defence of free trade, but by early November this fear was no longer paramount. The parliamentary Liberals had clearly already taken sides with the Labour government and against the Conservative opposition. This not only made a deal unlikely, but also considerably reduced the likelihood of a snap election. At the same time popular approval of the Labour administration diminished as the inadequacy of its remedies for unemployment began to become apparent.[11] Whilst public opinion had ceased to move in Labour's direction, it was not yet swinging back towards their opponents. However, the danger of a bid by Labour to achieve an outright majority receded. These changing circumstances removed the force of Churchill's arguments for conciliating Liberal opinion, and by December 1929 his line was overruled in the shadow cabinet. Like other experienced professional politicians, Churchill was conscious of the changing temperature. He determined to swallow the inevitable, and offered no objection to Baldwin's proposed statement to the Conference. It was the combination of all these factors, as much as the actual emergence of the Empire Crusade itself, which destroyed the assumptions of the July consensus and made it necessary for the leader to respond before the Party Conference. Baldwin was therefore ready to make a limited advance of the kind he had ruled out before the recess. Discussing the situation with Neville Chamberlain at the end of October, he revealed that this would take the form of further extension of the safeguarding legislation, but remained vague on details.[12] This was not expected to cut the ground completely from under Beaverbrook's feet, as Baldwin could not run the risk of espousing agricultural protection. He still had one eye on the urban seats that he would need to win back before forming another administration. As in July, Baldwin's principal aim was the preservation of unity in the collective leadership, and once again his line was that which would hold the support of the largest majority, without driving the minority to despair. Amery and both Chamberlains preferred a bolder stance, and Steel-Maitland and Hoare leaned in their direction. Davidson, Cunliffe-Lister, and Bridgeman favoured Baldwin's electoral caution; Churchill, Worthington-Evans, and Salisbury were reluctant to move at all. Thus Baldwin adopted the median position, in an attempt to keep the leadership united behind him. He assumed that any policy which achieved this could therefore be imposed upon the lower ranks of the Party. In the short term this might be possible, but in the longer term it was to prove an almost fatal miscalculation.

Baldwin did not wish to leave the success of his Conference initiative to chance, and had prepared the ground by putting out feelers in Beaverbrook's direction earlier in November. He accepted that Beaverbrook's campaign, whilst not the root problem, had enormously complicated the situation. Aware that he could only offer an advance that fell far short of Beaverbrook's platform, Baldwin did not expect to be able to negotiate a cessation of the Crusaders' activities. By clothing his moderate advance in deceptively vigorous rhetoric, he sought to induce Beaverbrook into a more constitutional mode of activity. In this respect Baldwin was successful, for in response to his approaches Beaverbrook's campaign passed through a moderated phase in the Conference period. This considerably eased the pressures upon the leadership. The timing of the initiative was no coincidence, coming hard on the heels of Beaverbrook's most divisive move: the open appeal to dissatisfied agriculturalists. The intermediaries were carefully chosen. With Baldwin's approval contact was made by Hoare, a personal friend of Beaverbrook's and a senior figure thought to lean towards protection. Beaverbrook was invited to a confidential discussion over dinner, with Neville Chamberlain making a third. He accepted, and the three men met on the evening of 4 November. At first it seemed that the dinner had been a failure, despite hints from Chamberlain heralding 'a great advance' in the Party's policy on imperial trade.[13] However, on reflection Beaverbrook opted for compromise. By temperament he preferred mergers or partnerships to direct confrontations. The following morning he telephoned Hoare, and enquired if the Conservatives had meant business; if they did, he was prepared to do a deal.[14]

Beaverbrook matched this by translating his campaign onto more orthodox lines. He ceased appearing on the public platform, and assumed the posture of a loyal Conservative respectfully submitting his views to his leader. On 7 November he addressed eighty backbench members of the Conservative Imperial Affairs Committee, where he made a good impression by the moderate and carefully reasoned way he presented the case for Empire Free Trade. Next Beaverbrook published a conciliatory article in the press on the 10th, appealing to Baldwin to take up his policy, and offering to efface himself if necessary. This olive branch, though the product of contacts previously initiated by Baldwin, now gave the leader an opportunity to respond openly. Next day he sent a short but cordial note to Beaverbrook, inviting him to a meeting on the 12th. Here Beaverbrook expounded his policy to Baldwin and Neville Chamberlain for two and a half hours. The meeting showed Baldwin at his most successfully sphinx-like, giving the impression that on the whole he was convinced, and was merely considering political expediencies.[15] This meeting was followed by contacts with several other figures in the Party leadership during the vital pre-Conference period, all of which aimed to encourage Beaverbrook to remain on the constitutional tack.[16] The most significant event of the week before the Conference provided further evidence that Beaverbrook had been tamed. He moved further into the conventional arena by making a rare venture into the House of Lords on 19 November to initiate a debate on Empire Free Trade. The speech he delivered on this occasion was one of the most considered expositions that the Crusade manifesto ever received, but it was the forum rather than the content that attracted the approval of the Conservative leadership.

The stage had been set for the 1929 Party Conference, although the gathering was not without some tension between the leaders and their followers. The delegates directed their criticisms towards two areas: the matter of intra-party democracy and organisation, and the demands for a bolder policy. Many of the resolutions on the agenda dealt with safeguarding, tariffs, and the empire. All urged some kind of definition of intent, but those sent in from the northern divisions were considerably less precise and advanced than those from the south. One indication of the depth of feeling over the way in which the leadership had ignored resolutions passed by previous conferences was the decision of Walsall Conservative Association to instruct its delegation to support 'the deposition of the Leader'.[17] However, criticism was turned aside by concessions which did not actually infringe on the leader's power of absolute discretion. The appeal to let bygones be bygones, and a determined use of the platform's command of the microphone, resulted in comparatively smooth progress. On the evening of 21 November Baldwin addressed the assembled delegates at the Albert Hall. He commenced with a moderately successful attack on the government's record. Having reassured his audience on the matter of his fighting spirit, he then announced his acceptance of a resolution on empire trade which had been passed earlier in the day. This had been proposed by Croft, but was an undefined commitment well suited to Baldwin's tactical needs.

Although progress was promised, caution remained the keynote. A compliment to Beaverbrook and the acceptance of Croft's moderate motion served as a unifying gloss; a substitute for a policy rather than the introduction to one. For the immediate moment Baldwin's oration produced a favourable response from as wide a spectrum as possible, by balancing between the instincts of the eager south and the cautious north.[18] Unknown to those leaving the Albert Hall, this was to be the last Party Conference for more than two years. Instead of the normal session, the Conference held on 1 July 1930 was a purely formal meeting, summoned to ratify rule changes in the National Union; whilst the political crisis of August 1931 and the resulting general election caused the last minute cancellation of the 1931 Conference.

The essential difference between the Albert Hall speech and the compromise of July 1929 was the fact that whilst the latter had attempted to neutralise a dangerous topic for the foreseeable future, the Conference speech was much less ambitious. Its success lay not in what was laid down in concrete terms, for that was next to nothing, but rested on the fact that the speech promised serious attention to imperial economic policy, and therefore implied the unveiling of some detailed programme in the near future. The achievement of a precarious unity did not last because this promissory note was not redeemed with any hard cash. In spite of the keen hopes of the constituencies, it was neither followed up nor further defined.[19] Whatever good effect the Albert Hall speech had hardly outlasted the Conference itself, and certainly had ebbed away by Christmas. With the benefit of hindsight, the defects of Baldwin's speech became more obvious than its merits, and it was exposed as lacking in any substance underneath the rhetorical parade of imperial sentiment. By the end of January 1930 the same demands for a clear lead that had surfaced in October emerged again and with renewed force.[20] Not only had the Albert Hall exercise been merely a question of buying time, but the breathing space had been frittered away. The entente with Beaverbrook proved shortlived, not least because the efforts of the leadership to maintain close personal contact lapsed as the Conference dispersed. Beaverbrook was left to his own devices. By nature restive and tempted to positive action, he came to feel that once again he would have to crusade for Empire Free Trade himself.

Between November 1929 and February 1930 Beaverbrook's conception of the Empire Crusade oscillated between a propagandist pressure group and a fully fledged political party. However, when he talked about a party, what Beaverbrook had in mind was pressure group tactics taken a stage further. This meant setting up local branches and the classic technique of threatening to run divisive candidatures at suitable by-elections. His party would remain a single-issue party, which never seriously aspired to provide a government. Despite occasional outbursts to the contrary, it was always his intention to capture the Conservative Party for his policy, not to replace it. This was the reason for the preoccupation with the equivocations of leading Conservatives which was the despair of those sympathisers who hoped to turn his fire onto Liberal and Labour free-traders. This concern was not excessive hairsplitting, but sound tactics. Beaverbrook felt that it was crucial to secure the Conservative bastion first. The evolution of the Crusade from a propaganda committee to a mass political movement can be traced through these three months, although the process was erratic and sometimes even contradictory. At the beginning of December, Beaverbrook saw the role of the Crusade as that of a section within the Conservative Party. By February 1930 membership and subscriptions were being solicited across the length and breadth of the land. A Crusade committee was formed. The principal members of this were Patrick Hannon, the Conservative member for Birmingham Moseley; the second Viscount Elibank, formerly a Conservative MP and a prominent businessman; R.D. Blumenfeld, editor of the *Daily Express* since 1902; C.A. McCurdy, once Lloyd George's Coalition Liberal Chief Whip; and Sir Hugo Cunliffe-Owen, millionaire chairman of British American Tobacco, who acted as the Crusade's treasurer.[21] In reality the functions of this committee were purely advisory; Beaverbrook remained the kingpin. At the same time he returned to the public platform, and threatened to put up candidates at by-elections against the official line.[22] Beaverbrook viewed politics from the perspective of Fleet Street, and translated circulation figures simplistically into political influence. For this reason he sought the partnership of the Rothermere press in his campaign, although identification with the bitterly antagonistic *Daily Mail* carried with it the implication of a fight to the finish with the Conservative Party and its leader. The alliance with Lord Rothermere was to bring Beaverbrook many problems, but superficially the combined press campaign that emerged at the end of January was double jeopardy indeed for the Party leaders.

The challenge from the Crusade was not the fundamental problem that the official leadership faced between December 1929 and February 1930. It was only a symptom of the real difficulty, which was Baldwin's inaction and his failure to provide effective opposition leadership. This was the direct product of the dilemma which faced Baldwin in attempting to balance between forces which were in fact irreconcilable. The pressure to advance further came primarily from below, but it was echoed in private by Hoare and Neville Chamberlain and in public by Amery and Croft. Many local Associations, especially in traditionally Conservative areas, were swept up by enthusiasm for the Crusade policy as the most attractive option available.[23] Others were stirred into action through the negative stimulus of alarm at the prospect of a split and awareness of the low state of local morale.[24] Opposition to advance was the product of two divergent schools of thought. The first of these were the traditional free-fooders, a declining force in the Party during 1930. Churchill and Salisbury, the leaders of this group, clearly accepted some extension of safeguarding to be inevitable, though they were not happy at the prospect.[25] If resistance from this element wobbled under pressure, that of the second element was even more likely to do so. These were the politicians concerned on pragmatic electoral grounds about what they feared would be a suicidal policy: 'on any proposal involving food taxes no seat in the country is safe'.[26] Whilst their anxiety was more representative of the majority feeling in parliament than the opposition of the free-fooders, it was even more sensitive to changing circumstances and the nuances of public opinion.

Baldwin's lethargy, and the optimism which was often allied with complacency, led him to rest for too long on the laurels of his success at the Albert Hall.[27] He had never found it easy to come to decisions, especially when the issues were difficult but important, and the advice on them unclear. Neville Chamberlain noted that Baldwin 'wavers backwards and forwards on the expediency according to the last person who has talked to him'.[28] Typically, the only thing Baldwin could decide upon was inaction. On 20 December he instructed Central Office to tell constituency agents that no official discussion of the Empire Free Trade policy should take place until further notice. However, the decision to take no decision was in fact the most dangerous of all. In particular, it gave the widespread impression that, far from going forward from the Albert Hall position, Baldwin was drifting backwards from it. This was all the more serious when it was combined with his continued failure to attack the government with sufficient vigour or conviction. The re-emergence of Beaverbrook's pressure group, the divisions of opinion within the Party, and the failure of Baldwin to provide a focal point, produced a serious slump in morale. This was evident in the apathy at constituency level, and even more so in the poor attendance of Conservative Members in the House of Commons. The malaise was consequent upon their loss of confidence as an opposition, and in its turn provoked further alarm in the constituencies. Dissatisfaction with the parliamentary Party made it all the easier for Beaverbrook to make headway. The real strength of the Empire Crusade was always that it reflected the disgruntled element in the Conservative rank and file. In several typical consti-tuencies in southern England and in the agricultural east midlands the Crusade was able to attract more than a thousand members (see Appendix 2). While these elements remained alienated from the parliamentary elite the Crusade provided a suitable vehicle for their resentments. Beaverbrook himself recognised clearly that his strength came from this as much as from enthusiasm for his fiscal policy.[29] However, he still tended to overrate the part played in this by his newspapers and his personal platform oratory, and to underrate the part played by the negativism and weakness of Baldwin's lead. There was a direct relationship between the latter and the appeal of the Crusade, and the first two months of 1930 saw not only the emergence of the Crusade as a political force, but also the first serious stirrings of doubt over Baldwin's suitability as leader.

In the latter half of January 1930 the Party seemed poised on the brink of a crisis. Gretton's Diehard 'Conservative Group', meeting on the 23rd, were agreed that the Party was 'stagnant and distracted, both in the House and the country'.[30] Once again, the groundswell of national opinion was moving, slowly but perceptibly, away from orthodox free trade as unemployment continued to rise.[31] Although this increased the pressure on Baldwin, it also meant that it was easier for him to give ground, once he accepted the need to do so. This was urged on him not only by the speeches of committed protectionists, but also in similar advice from his own inner circle. On New Year's Day Davidson had written to Baldwin suggesting that his forthcoming speech to MPs and candidates at the London Coliseum on 5 February would provide a suitable opportunity to steal the thunder of the press barons. Whilst food taxes were still ruled out as politically impossible, the Party Chairman was firm that 'without going into too much detail the lead must be definite'.[32] The need for this was reinforced by the indications of a crisis of confidence within the Conservative ranks. As opinion evolved, so the Party's public position was left vulnerably exposed to Beaverbrook's sallies. By giving expression to normally inarticulate constituency sentiment, he seemed likely to capture the Party from the grass-roots upwards. The vitality of Beaverbrook's campaign was also making a strong appeal to the younger generation.[33] Gwynne, editor of the staunchly Tory *Morning Post*, told Baldwin frankly that Beaverbrook's strength was the fact that his policy was 'endorsed secretly or openly by 85% of the Conservative Party'.[34]

Faced with this, it was hardly surprising that MPs and their local Association elites became rattled. In addition, like corks swept away on a tide, some of the leading protectionists came close to fusing with, if not actually seceding to, Beaverbrook's camp. Sir Robert Horne, a former Conservative Chancellor of the Exchequer and highly respected in City circles, Croft, Hannon, and Amery advised the press magnate closely. An even more serious symptom was the re-emergence of the Diehards, mobilised by Gretton.[35] Forty MPs signed a letter addressed by him to Baldwin on 27 January. Aware of the danger of being outflanked by the Crusaders, they demanded a clear statement of policy. This was not a declaration of war on Baldwin; they did not aim to remove him, but rather to prod him into coming up to the mark. More precisely, the Diehards sought a return to Baldwin's own 1923 programme of insular protection, which they held to represent the true Conservative policy. By the end of January it had become vital for Baldwin to reassert his authority, and to do so before the lower ranks of the Party stampeded.[36] At the same time, Baldwin was convinced that any suggestion that the Conservatives might go beyond a tariff on manufactured imports to one on foodstuffs would be fatal to the Party's electoral prospects. His opinion was only confirmed by the cautionary advice he was receiving almost simultaneously from several figures of considerable political stature and experience in the assessment of public opinion in their own regions.[37]

This was a matter of immediate concern in view of the uncertain parliamentary situation. The Liberal Party was beginning to show signs of disunity, with Lord Grey and the Liberal Council launching public attacks on Lloyd George's political fund. Even more important, the Liberals were balking at supporting vital clauses of the government's Coal Bill. Throughout February it seemed likely that the Labour ministry might fall at any moment over this measure. On 27 February a Liberal amendment on the quota provisions, to which they particularly objected, was only barely defeated: the government scraped home by 280 votes to 271, but only because four Liberals voted with Labour and a further eight abstained.[38] Baldwin framed his speech for the Coliseum meeting in the context of these limitations. Nevertheless, he was aware that 'the press agitation has made a definite fiscal policy necessary'.[39] The gap would be bridged by a proposal to extend safeguarding to the steel and textile industries. This was the clearest token he could give of his desire for advance without straying into the minefield of foodstuffs. His offer was the product of the political situation, not the economic one.

These tensions came out clearly in the substance of the speech when delivered at the Coliseum on 5 February. Once again, Baldwin attempted to meet criticism of his lack of vigour as opposition leader by making a sharp assault on the government. On the ideal of imperial economic union, his rhetoric effectively overlaid the mild reality of the safeguarding proposal. The latter amounted almost to de-politicising the question by putting the onus for producing a definite plan upon the industrialists of the empire, rather than the governments. However, two elements in the speech could not be glossed over so easily. Baldwin deliberately postponed the thorny question of agriculture to another day, and took out insurance with a specific pledge against food taxes in any form. The speech was merely a holding operation, designed to buy time. In the political context it also went hand in hand with a renewed phase of appeasement of Beaver-brook, with linked concessions and negotiations. The tactics of November 1929 were dusted off and re-used. Offers of mediation in late January 1930 from concerned and respected figures such as Gwynne and John Buchan were given some encouragement. Appearing to be thawed by these intercessions, Baldwin had invited Beaverbrook to a preview of the Coliseum address. Although at this stage there was no suggestion of concluding a deal, the channels of communication had been re-opened.[40]

The policy advance conceded was in the nature of a payment on account only, and it was in this light that it was judged. The considerable relief with which the speech was received was not an indicator of the real value of its contents, but a reflection of the easing of the strains within the Party. The approach adopted by Baldwin in these early months of 1930 was intended to bring along northern Conservative free-food sentiment by moving in easily assimilated stages, without losing the toleration of the protectionist lobby. Two days before delivering the speech, Baldwin had 'whimsically and wistfully' revealed the pragmatic basis of his strategy in conversation with Peto in the lobby of the House, remarking 'I must try and keep as many of my people with me as I can!'[41] The Coliseum speech was a first step in this direction. Whilst welcomed by the Empire Industries Association and acceptable to Gretton, it offered an escape route to free traders such as the Member for Clitheroe, Sir William Brass.[42] However, despite the general atmosphere of relieved gratification, the reaction from the constituencies remained ambivalent. In the south and in agricultural areas the Coliseum speech received only a qualified welcome. It would be of use if expanded into a proper agricultural policy, but on its own it was insufficient. 'Opinion has moved so fast in our Party that a speech which would have been rapturously welcomed a year ago is now felt to be inadequate', noted Amery.[43] The Party's Agents in Kent bluntly declared that 'something much more definite, expressed in the simplest possible language, must be given to us'.[44] On the other hand, the approval expressed by the industrial constituencies of the midlands and the north implicitly assumed that the matter was now settled, and would progress no further.[45]

The initial response of welcome from the Crusaders was purely tactical, and did not represent genuine agreement. The warm and friendly letter of congratulations which Beaverbrook sent to Baldwin immediately after the speech was designed to encourage him to make further concessions. It was in order to speed this up that Beaverbrook took the apparently contradictory step of re-opening his public campaign. In fact, such a move was implicit in his letter to Baldwin.[46] Beaverbrook's aim was to achieve a compromise through increasing the pressure, but not a fight to the finish. Throughout February 1930 the most significant element in political discourse was the language of negotiation. This formed the background to tactical counters designed to promote a settlement. Beaverbrook had been correctly assured that Baldwin's opposition was rooted in pragmatism, not principle. Thus a show of Empire Free Trade strength in the country would actually assist in bringing the two sides together by demonstrating that public opinion was, or could be made to be, ready for a fully fledged tariff programme. Beaverbrook made the running during the first half of February by stumping the agricultural constituencies, pitching his message to the disgruntled farming community. In the absence of any alternative Conservative plan for agriculture, Empire Free Trade took on 'like wild-fire in the agricultural districts'.[47] The success of Beaverbrook's appeal was due to the fact that his view that the Coliseum pledge had been too blunt and final a barrier to any further evolution of policy was shared by a substantial element on the backbenches and in the constituencies. There was no inconsistency between the renewal of the Crusade and Beaverbrook's desire to make a pact with Baldwin. He continued to be well disposed towards him, and believed that the Conservative leader was sympathetic to his aims.

However, the area of divergence between the two men widened instead into an open breach. This was a consequence of their next meeting, arranged for the morning of 12 February. At this Beaverbrook put forward sweeping claims to proselytise the parliamentary Party, presumably by the intimidation of Members and their constituency executives.[48] As it is unlikely that he could have expected Baldwin to agree to such a proposal, this move could only have been intended as another stage in the parallel strategy of pressure reinforcing negotiations. In a threatening manner Beaverbrook had made clear the potential for disruption that his movement could cause, but this provoked Baldwin towards resistance rather than concession. What was doubly unfortunate was that the last part of the interview produced a serious misunderstanding between the two men. Beaverbrook believed that he had secured Baldwin's approval for forming a 'party', but Baldwin afterwards maintained that Beaverbrook had used the word 'league'.[49] This was significant because Baldwin was still thinking of the Crusade as a propagandist pressure group, and hoped to confine its role simply to publicity. The difference was more than mere word-splitting, for the misunderstanding complicated their personal relationship with an element of distrust. It also, perhaps even by design on Baldwin's part, encouraged Beaverbrook to go out on a limb, for the immediate result was the launching of the Crusade as a party. At 3:00 p.m. on the same day Beaverbrook called together the Provisional Committee of the Crusade, and secured their agreement to its transformation. Public announcement of this was delayed for a few days during which Beaverbrook secured his last essential requirement – the alliance with Rothermere. The Empire Crusade with its existing membership was then transformed into the United Empire Party by a proclamation in the press on 18 February. Even this bold step did not represent the throwing over of negotiation, for it was designed to produce quicker results. The United Empire Party was not a party in the genuine sense of the word, for, whatever its methods, its purpose remained that of a single-issue pressure group – as Beaverbrook himself freely admitted.[50] Forming the party had undeniably assisted in capturing Rothermere's support, but this was only secondary to the primary aim, which remained progress through agreement.[51]

Whilst the establishment of the United Empire Party created a new dimension to the picture, the immediate result was an atmosphere in which both sides came under increasing pressure to close the breach. Conservative opinion demonstrated its desire for an end to internecine warfare in an unequivocal fashion. Amery and Horne pressed Baldwin to give more ground on tariffs, and were echoed by two influential deputations received by the leader on the day that the new party was unveiled. The first of these was a representative group of the Diehard wing led by Gretton, and the second a delegation from the Empire Industries Association. Both demurred at the rigidity of the Coliseum platform. This predictable chorus was reinforced by similar expressions from a much wider spectrum, and a further brake on progress was removed by Derby's speech at Macclesfield, where that political weathercock came out for some further advance. In the light of these manifestations, Baldwin rejected the confrontational tactics urged by Churchill, of putting the matter to the test in a series of specially staged by-elections, as too divisive and too risky, clearly preferring to opt for the path of conciliation. In this he may have been influenced by indications that failure to compromise might threaten the position of the entire leadership. There were renewed signs of the tendency of the grass-roots to take the initiative, in the absence of a lead from above.[52] Re-opening the post-election demands for a greater say for the rank and file, the president of the Grantham Association publicly demanded the convening of an emergency conference to decide the Party's fiscal policy. These pressures from below were disturbing parallels with the unrest that had existed during the last period of the Lloyd George coalition government in 1922.

Simultaneously Beaverbrook was also coming under pressure to climb down from the dangerously exposed position which he had assumed on forming the new party. For the alarm which that had caused at all levels of the Conservative Party also found clear expression in a backlash of revulsion against the United Empire Party itself.[53] Despite two decades experience in British politics, Beaverbrook did not seem to have anticipated the universally hostile response which his move provoked. He was shaken, all the more so because it contrasted so strongly with the general approval in which he had basked hitherto. In transforming his propagandist campaign into a party, Beaverbrook came into conflict not just with short-term fears based on electoral expediency, but also with the instinctive solidarity of Conservatism. The antagonism which resulted was partly the normal condemnation of factional strife, but to a marked degree. That this critical response included even the tariff reformers and Diehards weighed heavily with Beaverbrook. When he had proposed the creation of a new party, the active Conservatives on the Crusade Committee had been 'rather staggered at this proposal, as we did not quite see where it was going to lead us, or lead the Conservative Party'.[54] Recognising Beaverbrook's determination, they watered down his manifesto in an unsuccessful attempt to avoid it appearing as an attack on either Baldwin or the Party. This inauspicious start was followed by the rejection of public association with Beaverbrook by even such apparently dissident backbenchers as Ferguson and Gretton. Nor was Croft attracted to the idea of a breakaway movement; he had personal experience, from the National Party of 1917–1921, of the problems inherent in any such venture. The mediatory figures and advisors, Horne, Gwynne, and Amery, were unanimous in their disapproval of the formation of the United Empire Party. It provoked them into reaffirming their loyalty to a Conservative Party lacking the desired imperial programme, in preference to the disruption of the only pro-imperial force.[55] Beaverbrook's manifesto also produced Baldwin's strongest counterblast yet. This took the form of an interview published on 25 February in the new Conservative journal *Home and Empire*. The forthright language in which it was couched had the effect of a shot across the Crusaders' bow; the aim was to capture Baldwin, not drive him into open enmity. Beaverbrook was also having difficulties in keeping the United Empire Party firmly on the rails of his policy. Rothermere was already absorbing Empire Free Trade into a wide-ranging Diehard programme. Beaverbrook began to fear that his movement had been captured by an anti-Baldwin cave of Adullamites, which might produce a result he did not desire—the disintegration of the Conservative Party.[56]

The creation of the United Empire Party produced an atmosphere in which both sides desired to find a road back from the abyss. One symptom of this was the re-emergence of the mediators, with the encouragement of both camps. Several influential figures from the group thought to be loyal to the Conservative Party but sympathetic to Beaverbrook's policy were involved. Horne, Amery, Gwynne, and Elibank were pulling the same way in the sense that they all believed that with some concessions from each side a middle ground could be reached. They were a force for common sense, attempting firstly to keep the lines of communication open during a period of disruptive confrontation, and secondly to defuse the explosive difficulties over policy. After the misinterpretations of 12 February and the announcement of the formation of the United Empire Party, only such intervention could make another meeting between the two principals once again practical politics. At an interview on 19 February Gwynne persuaded Beaverbrook to set out on paper his minimum conditions. These boiled down to the demand that Baldwin must throw off the negative pledge of the Coliseum speech. Gwynne then shuttled backwards and forwards between Baldwin and Beaverbrook in the next four days. During this process the crucial policy aspects of the deal were negotiated, it being agreed that the Conservative leader would no longer rule out a duty on foreign foodstuffs.[57] Baldwin did not find this imprecise declaration impossible to swallow. However, he was motivated by different considerations, and interpreted this commitment in a spirit quite contrary to the revivalist enthusiasm hoped for by Beaverbrook. His pledge no longer to rule out a policy that might at some future date involve a proposal for tariff duties on imported foodstuffs fell far short of any undertaking to actively advocate them.

Thus by 25 February the essential, although artificial, common ground for a deal had been staked out. Having sensed Beaverbrook's loss of nerve, Baldwin did not hesitate to reject an overture from Elibank four days later offering a much less favourable agreement. His suggestion was that the United Empire Party should nominate the holders of three Cabinet posts with prime responsibility in the areas of imperial and economic policy in the next Conservative government. Baldwin immediately played the constitutional card by refusing to allow any infringement of the Prime Minister's prerogatives; the proposal provided Baldwin with ammunition which in the future he was to use with deadly effect. His response to Elibank was an attempt to divide the two press lords. By indicating that he would be prepared to come to an agreement only with Beaverbrook, he was setting him up in the role of Rothermere's keeper.[58] Only two necessary steps remained after these exchanges. The first was that a display of conciliatory public rhetoric would have to be made to prepare the ground and remove the atmosphere of hostility. Though accomplished with remarkable speed, this was inevitably a slower process than the private settlement. The second consideration was that, once the preliminary negotiations and public rapprochement were achieved, the two principals would need to meet face-to-face again, in order to hammer out the details of Baldwin's next pronouncement.

Given the desire in all quarters for a truce, it was not difficult to mould public and Party opinion in its favour. Appropriately enough, the process began with a speech by Amery on 21 February in which he depicted Empire Free Trade as part of the accepted canon of tariff reform. Whilst deprecating the formation of a separate party, he acknowledged that this had been the product of frustration at the laggardly and cautious official line. This theme was taken up by Horne, who made a plea for a broad church spirit to prevail, in an address at the Constitutional Club on 26 February. His closely argued text pointed to the common acceptance of the fallacy of free trade and the need for imperial economic unity. In the meantime he did not see why Conservatives should be herded off into separate pens. This speech was a deliberate attempt at conciliation, for Horne had sounded Beaverbrook in advance over its contents.[59] Elibank acknowledged that it had a 'remarkable effect' on the adherents of both factions.[60] Beaverbrook now felt able to respond with a public gesture of reconciliation, and used for this a meeting he was to address at Gloucester on the following day. Casting himself in the role of supplicant, he begged Baldwin to ignore any counsels of expediency, and withdraw the negative Coliseum pledge which he claimed had driven him out. Ironically, the truth was that for the Conservative leadership the path of expediency now dictated a compromise, to include just sufficient policy advances to entice Beaverbrook back into the fold. The Gloucester speech opened the way to direct negotiation. On Sunday, 2 March, Beaverbrook drafted a note to Baldwin, requesting an interview. Before this could be sent, a telephone message arrived from the Conservative leader, inviting Beaverbrook to call on him the next morning.

At this meeting on 3 March Baldwin started the bidding low by offering the traditional double-election strategy to avoid the food tax bogey. This consisted of a pledge that Baldwin would convene an imperial conference immediately after his next election victory, and would then ratify its results by submitting concrete fiscal proposals to the people in a second general election. According to the version he gave Elibank, Beaverbrook rejected this, but indicated that he would 'accept a Referendum as a second string instead'.[61] This was consistent with the policy advocated by Horne on 26 February, which had met with such general approval. After having considered the idea, Baldwin summoned Beaverbrook back for another interview the same evening, and intimated his acceptance. Beaverbrook hastened to complete the arrangements before Baldwin's address to the Central Council of the National Union, scheduled to take place at the Hotel Cecil on the following morning. After leaving the Party leader late on the evening of the 3rd, he consulted with Rothermere, Hannon, and Horne, and together they drafted an outline of their terms for Baldwin's private use. Horne delivered this personally on the morning of the 4th, before Baldwin left to give his speech. The letter by no means suggested an end to the Empire Crusade, promising only not to oppose any member of the Conservative Party who 'declares for the policy of Empire Free Trade subject to a referendum on food taxes'.[62] Although Beaverbrook was privately convinced that the practical result of this would be to turn the first general election into the referendum, on the surface it appeared to give Baldwin everything he wanted, by postponing to the future any pledge to fight on food taxes.

In another sense, it was a victory for Beaverbrook. On the previous occasion that the idea of a referendum had been proposed, in 1910, it had incurred opposition as a retreat from tariff reform. However, the crucial point about Baldwin's adoption of the referendum was that it represented a further step on his part towards an outright protectionist platform. And it was in this sense that Beaverbrook had made the proposal; not as a final resting place, but as an umbrella under which he could run his Empire Free Trade campaign within the Conservative Party. He could now claim that it did not contradict official policy, but would educate the people in its favour. Nevertheless, in the short term Beaverbrook was clearly willing for tactical reasons to slacken the pressure and wind up his separate party. To Baldwin this, even if it did not last long, was an advantage sufficiently desirable for him swiftly to overcome his constitutional reservations about the referendum. Given the fact that the government had almost fallen as a result of Liberal opposition on the Coal Bill only days before, and a dissolution was a possibility at any time, there was much to be said for a plan that would allow him to take the food tax bogey out of the immediate political debate. In such a context it is hardly surprising that, despite the tensions in his own party, Baldwin was 'afraid of committing himself to anything definite' in the way of fiscal reform.[63] The truce with Beaverbrook did not come anywhere near either to solving the question of the Party's long-term outlook, or to securing a permanent cessation of press attacks, but it did buy Baldwin much-needed time with which to consolidate his position. In reality, the truce was the worst of compromises, for it contained within it the seeds of its own failure. Essentially each side believed that it had achieved directly contradictory results by the agreement. Beaverbrook believed that food taxes were now to be part of the Party programme, but Baldwin held that the referendum had shelved them for the foreseeable future. Certainly before long one, or both, would be disappointed.

CHAPTER 4

The Uneasy Truce

The truce between Baldwin and his supposed arch-enemies, the wicked barons of the press, has been passed over with little comment, almost with embarrassment, by his various biographers. Yet the events of the interlude between March and June 1930 were both complex and important. They reveal much about Baldwin's political aims, and afford an unusual insight into his political methods. It is necessary to unravel them, in order to understand the context from which the serious crisis of the late summer of 1930 was to emerge. The dynamic of the truce period artificially papered over the cracks that were opening up in the Party. It disguised the widening chasm which, by the time the truce collapsed from its own inherent contradictions in June, separated the leadership from too many of their followers.

Peace was declared after Baldwin's speech at the Hotel Cecil on 4 March 1930. The Party leader took care to follow a line calculated to soothe the anxieties of the manufacturing districts and secure the support of candidates nursing marginal seats. He placed most emphasis on the selective safeguarding of industries as a more efficient protective weapon than a general tariff. The key passage was that in which the referendum was unveiled, and here the posture was entirely defensive. The new proposal was presented as little more than a tactical device to avoid the millstone of food taxes being hung around the Party's neck at the next election. Baldwin only went beyond the Coliseum speech when he declared that he had not ruled out any topic from future economic negotiations with the Dominions. He closed with a rousing finale, a mixture of imperialist sentiment and Conservative cliche. In reality signifying nothing, this peroration imparted to the whole speech a flavour acceptable to the palates of the protectionist lobby, even though the promised details of the agricultural policy were once again postponed.

Despite that disappointment, signs of approval began to appear at the Central Council meeting itself, as soon as Baldwin had sat down. Although there had been nothing in his speech to substantiate such a response, so great was the instinctive pressure to demonstrate unity and loyalty that potentially critical resolutions which had been placed on the agenda were withdrawn in the light of his remarks. This was a reflection of the political result of the Hotel Cecil speech, in securing the much-desired concord with the Crusaders, not its slim contribution to the development of the bold programme so frequently desired by the rank and file. In the same way few Conservatives cared for the referendum as a constitutional innovation. They were, however, prepared to embrace it as the means of preventing a fratricidal war in the imperial camp and a political blood-letting in the home counties.[1] The unusually large volume of congratulatory resolutions passed by constituency associations in the following days was a symptom of their relief after a period of considerable anxiety over the establishment of the United Empire Party. The new force had made the greatest inroads among ordinary Conservatives in the suburban and rural southern half of the nation. Accordingly, here the Hotel Cecil policy was interpreted as a signal that Baldwin was moving to support a policy of freer trade within the empire, in which a tariff on agricultural as well as manufactured imports was implicit.[2] An unbridgeable gulf separated this from the conclusions drawn in the midlands and the north. The attitude there was spelled out by Colonel Gadie, Chairman of the divisional associations in Bradford, who took Baldwin to be foreshadowing nothing more than wider safeguarding legislation to shield the declining staple industries. The assumption here was that food taxes were well beyond the edge of the political map.[3] Relief at the end of dissension and division obscured these divergent viewpoints, but only temporarily.

Beaverbrook had become the prisoner of his own tactics. Having urged the referendum on Baldwin, he had little choice but to react favourably, notwithstanding the negative tone of the Hotel Cecil speech. The logic of the position forced him to advise his followers to welcome Baldwin's statement and accept the assurances given in it. Waving a magic wand, Beaverbrook turned the United Empire Party back into the Empire Crusade, making it plain in the process that the latter still had a valuable role in educational and propaganda work. The campaign for Empire Free Trade would go on, he told his supporters, but in conjunction with the Conservatives.[4] Inevitably, with the withdrawal of Beaverbrook, the remnant of the new party was captured by Rothermere for his own purposes. On 7 March he sent Beaverbrook a copy of the five-point Diehard manifesto which he intended to publish the next day. Beaverbrook could not accept the contention that the United Empire Party had ever been anything more than a single-issue pressure group; hence its supersession under the new circumstances. He had little choice but to counter with a press statement of his own, denouncing Rothermere for instituting a complete departure from the aims for which the United Empire Party had been formed.[5] To drive the point home, a further announcement appeared on the same day, to the effect that the new party's fund, having fulfilled its purpose, was to be returned to its donors. The first dividend from the truce was a public division between the former allies.

The split caused Beaverbrook more anxiety than it did Rothermere. Beaverbrook had always rated the power of the press highly, and he both cherished and feared the influence of rival newspapers.[6] He had not expected that Rothermere would continue the fight after the truce was arranged, and now began to feel outflanked by a potentially disruptive rival. As a result, Beaverbrook came to question the wisdom of having suggested the referendum in the first place. In this mood he became increasingly obsessive over signs of caution amongst his Conservative allies. Part of this pattern was Beaverbrook's touchiness over the way in which his acceptance of a deal had been portrayed as a victory for Baldwin by many commentators. This was only a straw in the wind, but it indicated the fragility of the agreement. Beaverbrook in any case saw the truce as a temporary expedient designed to further his idea, and not as a final consummation. 'My principle is—take a trick when you can and go on with the game', he wrote; 'our policy has gained much from recent events'.[7] So long as Beaverbrook felt that the referendum and the truce were helping rather than hindering the progress of Empire Free Trade, he would maintain them as worthwhile advances. Everything depended upon the way in which Baldwin operated the truce.[8] For the moment Beaverbrook proclaimed his belief in Baldwin's sincerity, but he was aware of the danger of having placed the future of his ideal in the hands of someone else less exclusively committed to it. He oscillated between his natural caution and the fear of relinquishing his place to Rothermere on the one hand, and a genuine desire to make the truce work if he could on the other. Although from day to day his course appeared erratic and inconsistent, he blew hot and cold in direct relation to the latest manifestations of Conservative Party opinion. Beaverbrook's greatest anxiety was the sapping effect of timidity and doubt in high places. His dilemma was whether it was better to work within or without the formal structure of the party system. Events were increasingly to confirm his fear that the main obstacle to progress lay firstly in the influence of Free Traders such as Salisbury and Churchill and faint-hearts like Davidson, and finally in Baldwin himself. The progress of the truce towards dissolution, though obscured by initiatives of partnership and consultation from both sides, can be discerned from the middle of March.

The first phase, spanning the period from 4 to 25 March, saw several attempts at genuine co-operation. Davidson made efforts to draw Beaverbrook into a closer formal relationship as co-director of the forthcoming propaganda campaign, involving him in the hope of both appeasing his suspicions, and sharing the responsibility as insurance against criticism.[9] Personal contacts continued to be the favoured method of the leadership for conciliating Beaverbrook. One olive branch proffered in the drive for fusion was an invitation to Beaverbrook to attend either the newly established Business Committee, an informal Shadow Cabinet, or a Committee which would be set up to direct the Party's imperial and fiscal campaign. But this idea also typified the problems of the truce period. It was extended to Beaverbrook in a confused and equivocal fashion, rather than openly and formally, and as a result was declined. Beaverbrook continued to waver between support and antagonism. He was a politician who had lost a party, but not yet found a role. On 12 March Davidson asked him what he proposed to do in the future. Beaverbrook replied that he did not know, but would wait and see. He outlined three possibilities:[10]

> (1) to revive the Crusade with increased intensity . . . This would require at times criticism of the Conservative Party. He could only re-start the Crusade, say, a month hence, by criticising the apathy and the lethargy of the Conservative Party, and probably while accepting the Referendum, explaining quite definitely that food taxes were the only thing to save British agriculture. (2) To turn over the Crusade to the Tory Party and let us run it, and (3) to say I have finished my work. The Conservative Party has come into line: the *raison d'être* of the Crusade has gone.

In the meantime, he told Davidson when they met again two days later, he proposed to continue the Crusade, spending a great deal of money. This was to be raised in small subscriptions, which could only mean a public appeal of some sort. Curiously, Davidson drew from these encounters the comforting conclusion that 'provided we stand pat on the Hotel Cecil policy, we shall get his full support'.[11] However, Beaverbrook had little confidence in Davidson, and if anything their conversations reinforced his doubts. Baldwin kept up the pretence of gratitude for Beaverbrook's initial efforts in opening up the imperial issue in the next speech he made after the Hotel Cecil, on 12 March. Whilst this was a useful exercise in flattery, it contained no signs of the further advances after which Beaverbrook was beginning to hanker.[12]

In these circumstances the public hesitancies of several leading Conservatives of free-trade sympathies took on a significance beyond their real import. Beaverbrook did not understand the loose rein which Baldwin allowed his colleagues, or his reluctance to proscribe deviance in either direction, unless it became unavoidable. To some extent this was a tactical decision on Baldwin's part; some observers thought that he did not exercise discipline because he wished to remain as vague and elusive as possible.[13] A number of events in late March and early April fed the flames of Beaverbrook's paranoia about Conservative apathy. Two senior ex-Ministers, Winston Churchill and Lord Eustace Percy, and a rising former junior, William Ormsby-Gore, placed the most negative interpretation possible upon the Party's position in a series of public speeches. The implication was that the Party would make no real attempt to persuade the electorate to choose in favour of food taxes, now or in the future. The cautious platform of Terence O'Connor, adopted as the Conservative candidate for the Nottingham Central by-election, seemed to be further proof that defeatism was not only rampant, but was being tacitly condoned by the leadership.

The most serious occurrence of all, therefore, was the publication in *The Times* on 25 March of an equally hesitant letter from Salisbury, the leader of the Conservative Party in the House of Lords. Although paying lip service to the ideal of imperial economic unity, Salisbury clearly considered it quite impracticable for the foreseeable future. In Elibank's words, this 'upset the whole applecart'.[14] Beaverbrook was outraged, but the real source of his strength was the similar reaction which the letter provoked in the ranks of the Conservative Party.[15] Because the Free Traders now seemed to be the ones endangering the fragile atmosphere of unity, they received absolutely no support from quarters in which they might have expected to strike a sympathetic chord. Yet they had provoked the wrath of the protectionist right, who for once could portray themselves in the role of defending the official line against faction and division. Great pressure was put on Baldwin to denounce the letter, and on Salisbury to withdraw it. Gretton got up a petition against it on the backbenches; but even more serious was the threat from Croft to use the Empire Industries Association as a potential kangaroo court. As one hundred and eighty-seven Conservative MPs were members, a general meeting of the Association would be tantamount to a party meeting called by an alternative and unofficial leadership. The Empire Industries Association Executive threatened the Chief Whip that such a gathering would be called the following week, unless strong action was taken to repudiate Salisbury's letter. Croft communicated this mutinous resolve to Salisbury directly.[16] Under this barrage, the miscreants were forced to retreat. To save Baldwin from the necessity of pronouncing on the issue, Salisbury wrote a second letter to *The Times*, which appeared on 8 April. Ostensibly a clarification, to all practical purposes it renounced his previous message. Beaverbrook considered that it was 'a regular crawl'.[17] Under similar pressure from within the Party and from the threat of independent Crusade challengers being run in their seats, the other Free Traders also compromised, announcing a facesaving adherence to the Hotel Cecil line. Salisbury's humiliation served to expose the weakness of the Conservative Free Traders even when occupying powerful positions in the hierarchy. They were unable even to put a brake on the Party's progress towards protectionism, never mind actually to recover lost ground. But their outbursts had had a considerable impact on Beaverbrook, and the corollary was his declaration to a meeting of Empire Crusaders at the Savoy Hotel that they must go on with 'renewed energy and redoubled vigour'.[18] Beaverbrook was moving towards the first of the three alternatives that he had outlined to Davidson on 12 March—revival of the Crusade as an independent force.

The strains which these events caused eroded but did not destroy the truce. The obvious rout of the Free Trade counter-attack removed some of the tension. Most important was the fact that Beaverbrook continued to trust in Baldwin's sincerity.[19] Should that prop fall, then the others would not prove strong enough to support the truce. The efforts of several leading figures from both sides to hold the precarious pact together also had a restraining effect on Beaverbrook. These conciliators represented a strand of Party opinion that wanted to adopt Beaverbrook's policy, or a fair approximation to it, whilst at the same time they feared the possible consequences on both policy and Party of wasting energy on factional strife. In the greater or lesser degrees to which they were prepared to support an extra-party pressure group to achieve their aims, these figures were placed along a political spectrum ranging from the Crusade Executive to the wing of the Conservative Party which wanted an advanced imperial programme. Elibank, Horne, Croft, Amery, and Neville Chamberlain sought for the same reasons to make truce work. Their initiatives certainly gave it added strength, and probably made it last longer than it otherwise might have done. However, the power of decision lay with the principals on either side and was beyond their reach.

Neville Chamberlain deliberately set out to maintain the truce as the best means of progress. Until the end of April, he remained optimistic about the possibility of a genuine working relationship.[20] He was not alone in offering Beaverbrook an unofficial alliance in this period, with the intention half of pulling his teeth, and half of using him to frighten the Party on: Amery and Croft also adopted similar tactics. The latter attempted to channel Beaverbrook's energies into more constructive and controlled use by inviting him on 12 March to take a leading part in the Empire Industries Association. A fortnight later he deliberately encouraged Beaverbrook to open a special campaign in Cornwall. The point of this was that the Conservatives had lost every

seat in Cornwall to the Liberals in the 1929 election. Whilst such a
campaign would reap great benefits for the Party, Croft pointed out,
'you will be raising enthusiasm without coming into any definite clash
with sitting Conservative members'.[21] In this period Croft and
Amery came near to open identification with Beaverbrook, a process
which the flexibility of the truce rendered compatible with party
loyalty. From his position on the Crusade Committee Elibank also
tried to bring the two sides closer together in a congenial atmosphere.
On 3 April he arranged a dinner, held in a private room at the Savoy
Hotel, at which Beaverbrook, Horne, Neville Chamberlain,
Hailsham, Cunliffe-lister and Amery were present. Elibank's aim was
to pour oil on troubled waters, by suggesting that Beaverbrook
should put more trust in the imperialist wing of the leadership.
However, the dinner was a failure. If anything, by creating a misunderstanding between Chamberlain and Beaverbrook, it made matters
worse rather than better. From this point onwards the situation
continued to drift without improvement. Over the following month
experience was to demonstrate the lack of room for manoeuvre open
to the loyal moderate protectionists. They were being ground
between the upper and nether millstones. There was no middle way
between either outright revolt against Baldwin or supporting him on
constitutional grounds against the pretensions of the press lords.

The cracks apparent in the middle phase of the truce were papered
over by the co-operation of both sides in the West Fulham by-election.
The seat fell vacant on 12 April, and polling was fixed for 6 May. The
contest appeared to show the truce at its best, with the combination of
the Crusade, Beaverbrook's influential London press, and the Conservative Central Office, behind a mutually acceptable local candidate,
Sir Cyril Cobb. The latter's political outlook was such that Beaverbrook, even had he wished, could hardly have done otherwise than
throw all his weight behind him. Cobb was an influential figure in the
Navy League, and agreed with much of Rothermere's diehard position. Above all, he was a sincere supporter of imperial preference and
of Empire Free Trade, and known to Beaverbrook as such.[22] Beaverbrook determined to secure as substantial a victory for Cobb as
possible, as proof of the electoral value of his policy. In reality, the role
of the Crusade was kept to a minimum by Central Office, which
controlled the direction and organisation of the fight through its
Metropolitan Area agent, Edwards. Beaverbrook made the best of
this, not wishing to rock the boat, and claimed that Edwards was in
any case the most efficient man available. The calculated result was
that the Crusade effort was limited to those parts of its appeal that the
Conservative Party wished to exploit—Beaverbrook's London daily
papers, and his charisma as a platform speaker. Beaverbrook
immersed himself completely in the by-election for three weeks,

giving the party leadership a much-needed breathing space. He had been adroitly outmanoeuvred: any failure could be placed at the doorstep of his policy, while any success could be credibly claimed for the official machine.

The result was a very narrow Conservative victory. Although Cobb did gain the seat from Labour, it was only by a margin of 240 votes. This was interpreted quite differently by the Crusaders and by the party leadership. Whilst stumping the streets, Beaverbrook had become aware of how much the social character of Fulham was changing, turning it into an area with a preponderance of Socialist voters. Under such circumstances, he wrote to Gwynne, even a narrow victory should be taken as a considerable achievement.[23] Whilst Beaverbrook therefore thought West Fulham was encouraging, the Party leadership, expecting a much bigger margin of victory, looked on a gain by only two hundred votes as tantamount to defeat, and a signal of the dangers of a full-blown Crusade policy. The seat had been won back, but the result could not give rise to much confidence about the prospects across the nation as a whole should parliament suddenly be dissolved. This dichotomy was to be a feature of the ambiguous results of most of the by-election fights of 1930, and was to prove an important contributory factor in widening the gulf between the Crusaders and the Baldwinites, encouraging each to progress a stage further down their diverging paths. Even so, West Fulham seemed to demonstrate the success of the truce, with Baldwin sending after the declaration perhaps the friendliest communication he was ever to pen to Beaverbrook, addressed to 'My dear Max', and offering congratulations on his 'gallant conduct in the arena'.[24]

The excitement of fighting West Fulham held the alliance together during April 1930, and obscured the growing divergence between the two sides. Baldwin's strategy was partly unveiled in the only public speech he made in April, at Manchester on the 7th. In this he dwelt at length on the value of safeguarding as the principal remedy available. Trade within the empire was mentioned in the context of its future possibilities, and the function of the referendum in postponing the food tax issue was made quite clear. The negativism of this portion of the speech was balanced by a finale which sounded the trumpet of imperial unity. Beaverbrook's faith in Baldwin survived this diminished but not destroyed. However, it was evident that if Baldwin was to continue speaking in this vein Beaverbrook would consider it to be a breach of their agreement. In the meantime, Beaverbrook attributed the lack of vigour in the speech to the influence of Davidson, Salisbury, and Churchill. Thus for a crucial period he turned his fire against the Free Traders, when in fact their influence was small and dwindling daily. So long as Beaverbrook concentrated upon the symptoms, rather than the cause, of the failure of the Conservative

Party to fall into line behind the Empire Free Trade policy, his course was bound to be erratic. On the day after the Manchester speech, whilst addressing the Conservative association in Salisbury's own backyard of Hertford, he said that he was being driven to the task of addressing meetings up and down the country because his policy was languishing for lack of exponents. Yet at Nottingham three days later he was proclaiming his faith in Baldwin and pinning the blame on the Conservative Free Traders. They were not only castigated for causing the present dissent, but also accused of having repeatedly thrown spanners into the protectionist works throughout the past decade. He affirmed that he believed Baldwin intended to 'plough a straight furrow through the General Election—through a Referendum—and that he would not look back until he had given them their keystone—a tax on foreign foodstuffs'.[25] It was difficult to square such a hope with the Manchester speech; it was to prove impossible to reconcile it with Baldwin's next public foray, at Sheffield on 8 May.

In the month between those two declarations the foundations of trust upon which the truce depended were undermined by a series of incidents. It was Baldwin's good fortune that only one of these directly identified him with a negative approach. This was the troubled candidacy of O'Connor at Nottingham Central. The attempts of the latter to square the circle of satisfying both the demands of Beaverbrook from London and the mood of his by-election audiences in Nottingham Central caused periodic strains. The electors of Nottingham were receptive to a defence of the safeguarding duties, which had been imposed by the previous Conservative government to help the local lace industry, and which were now under threat from the free trade dogmatism of the Chancellor of the Exchequer, Philip Snowden. However, it was equally clear that anything which smacked of tariff reform, even in the mildest sense, was looked on as political poison by this urban electorate. Originally, O'Connor had veered considerably from the official line in order to placate this sentiment, but threats from Beaverbrook brought him back from that exposed position. Instead, he took shelter behind the Hotel Cecil policy, interpreted in its most defensive sense. However, the damage had been done. Suspiciously receiving the reports of O'Connor's speeches, Beaverbrook began to claim that he had forfeited the right to the party label, the approval of the leader, and the support of the Central Office.[26] Baldwin could not allow Beaverbrook to become the arbiter of political acceptability. Now that O'Connor had shaped up to at least an appearance of orthodoxy, Baldwin determined to block Beaverbrook's pretensions by resisting attacks upon him. This Baldwin did partly through the medium of Davidson, the Party Chairman, and partly by sending O'Connor a public letter of support. In the tactical short term this saved O'Connor's bacon, as Beaverbrook acknowledged by coming to a private bargain with him on 8 May. But this had been achieved at the price of more clearly identifying Baldwin himself as the main impediment to progress. This was not a conclusion Beaverbrook wished to draw, with its implication of a return to internecine warfare, but it was becoming unavoidable.[27]

The other events which directly contributed to the collapse of the truce were all linked to the beleaguered position of Davidson. His situation was already precarious, partly as a result of his poor management of the Party before and during the 1929 election campaign. The Party Chairman was also ex officio Chairman of the uppermost tier of rank and file representation, the Executive Committee of the National Union. In this post he had failed to represent adequately the views of the Party in the country, and much of the clamour for intra-party democracy was the product of this. So great had resentment become, that it was resolved at the 1929 Conference to end this position forthwith, and Davidson's successor as Chairman of the Party organisation was no longer to have the same powers.[28] This much-resented facet of Davidson's chairmanship was exacerbated by the second cause of his unpopularity: his unfortunate personal manner, at once tactless, prickly, and offensive. The examples of the important figures in the Party hierarchy outside the charmed circle of Baldwinites whom Davidson alienated by his methods of business were numerous enough by themselves to provide a powerful coalition of unrest. He had also made many enemies amongst the right wing backbenchers.[29] More importantly, his shortcomings were beginning to be recognised as a liability by some of the leadership. Lord Derby wrote bluntly that 'we must get rid of Davidson—he is useless'.[30] Neville Chamberlain, thinking along similar lines and convinced of the need to cut away the deadwood at Central Office, was already preparing to oust Davidson and replace him with a nominee of his own.

The need to jettison Davidson was confirmed by two failures of political management on his part in April 1930. The first of these was the disastrous 'Home and Empire' public campaign promoted by Davidson for the month of May. The stimulus for such a campaign originally came from some of the northern constituencies, and it was only in these urban seats in Scotland, Lancashire, and the west midlands, that it aroused any enthusiasm at all.[31] May was not considered a good month for propaganda work, and the launching of such an effort then was transparently a tactic of desperation on Davidson's part. The centre-piece of the campaign was to be the securing through canvassing work by the local activists of signatures in support of Baldwin's pledge on fiscal policy. One cause of non-participation was the distrust felt at this time by many local executives for any leadership from Central Office. However, the main reason for the failure of the idea to catch on was the negativism of the pledge itself, which, despite repeated interventions by Neville Chamberlain at the drafting stage, reeked of pragmatism and caution.[32] Such an interpretation of the Party's attitude went down well in seats with a large industrial working class population, or where free trade sentiment was still strong.[33] However, this process of satisfying the prejudices of the north alienated the south from the campaign. Once again this demonstrated the problem of the north-south divide which plagued Conservative Party politics throughout the era of tariff reform. The refusal of the south to take up the 'Home and Empire' campaign was clearly linked to grievances concerning the uninspiring nature of Party policy, dislike of the referendum, the lack of an agricultural pledge, and hostility to Central Office.[34] The vocal hostility of a substantial number of associations was only the tip of the iceberg; many others voted with their feet by ignoring the campaign altogether. Analysis of the surviving local records suggests that at the most generous estimate only about a quarter of the English constituencies participated seriously. On any criteria such a response was in itself a dismal failure, and was clear evidence of mismanagement by, and loss of confidence in, the Party chiefs.

If the debacle of 'Home and Empire' damaged Davidson's position, a second blunder sealed his fate. This was the publication by Central Office on his instructions of a publicity handout in which the official position was phrased in a way which suggested a further retreat from the Hotel Cecil policy. Leaflet number 3153 seemed to water down the policy to merely an exercise in limited imperial bartering, more akin to the activities of the Empire Marketing Board than to the grand conception of Joseph Chamberlain. Once again, a breakdown in communication and mutual confidence was revealed. Davidson had sent Beaverbrook a copy of the leaflet in its final printed form on the day before its release, for information and as a courtesy. This hardly accorded with Beaverbrook's understanding that he would see such items at the drafting stage, and that his role would be that of a participant, not just a spectator. During the three weeks following the release of Leaflet 3153 the chorus of disapproval grew stronger. Not suprisingly, several of the more advanced southern constituency associations reacted strongly, calling it 'inaccurate and misleading', and demanding that it should be withdrawn immediately.[35] Beaverbrook's own reaction became progressively stronger with the passage of time. Writing to Amery he described his sense of trust betrayed; he felt it to be 'a startling case of bad faith'.[36] The leader of the Crusade indicted the offending document in a press release on 16 April, ominously declaring that its publication was 'one in a chain of events which have gradually made the present position extremely difficult'.[37] However, Beaverbrook had not yet come to the point of a final breach, for he wanted to work with Baldwin rather than against him, and still hoped that the Party leader would move towards his position.

By the end of May 1930 politicians were sensing that the beginning of a change in public opinion was under way. Rising unemployment was undermining free trade sentiments; Austen Chamberlain thought that 'we are not far from a landslide on protection'.[38] But public opinion did not evolve either quickly or uniformly, and thus the founding of policy on considerations of popular acceptability alone was as likely to succeed as building a house on shifting sands. As was so often the case, if public opinion had advanced one step, the Conservative enthusiasts, having sensed this, were themselves stimulated into another leap forward.[39] The gap did not narrow, and for a while Baldwin's dilemma of reconciling electoral pragmatism with the demands of his followers became if anything even more difficult. For it was quite clear that, even within the dichotomy of the north-south contradiction, the general trend of grass-roots opinion was consistently moving away from the referendum and towards seeking a mandate at the next election for complete freedom to impose any necessary import duties immediately: the policy known as the 'free hand'.[40] The difference between north and south was mainly one of pace. Though the evolution of fiscal opinion in the north was not static, it did not relinquish the shelter of the referendum as promptly as had the south. In part this was the consequence of the different degrees of pressure exerted by the Empire Crusaders amongst the local membership. Essentially their impact was only effective in the southern seats; in areas of traditional agricultural Toryism, in the suburbs, and in the seaside resort towns. Apart from some support in the farming divisions of the east midlands, north of the Trent the Crusade was weak to the point of non-existence (see Appendix 2). Thus, the natural division between the 'two nations' was exacerbated by the unequal distribution of the Crusade itself. The widening gulf that resulted was clearly visible.[41] The political geography of Conservative opinion is nowhere more apparent than in the chorus of demands emerging at this time from the south for a strong, clear, more advanced, definition of policy.[42] However, in view of the wider situation, the Party leadership felt that it would be political suicide to accede to these demands.

The Labour government had begun to run into serious difficulties, and its morale was in tatters: rumours abounded that it might collapse at any time. This would not have been caused by Conservative pressure in the House of Commons, for this was having no effect at all upon either the cabinet or the mass of Labour backbenchers. Indeed, Conservative opposition, by providing a clear focal point, probably shored up government morale, and motivated it to carry on. The threat from the Liberals had also receded. By the end of March the

Labour government had been pressed to the point where they gave in to the Liberals' key demand: they would bring in an Electoral Reform Bill which would include some form of proportional representation.[43] The Liberal onslaught on the final stages of the Coal Bill then failed to materialise, and the two parties began to draw closer together. This was to give the government greater external stability for the rest of its life. However, this was not so apparent at the time, for two reasons. Firstly, the Liberal-Labour relationship continued to blow hot and cold, with occasional stormy upsets. No conclusive pact was arrived at between the two parties, because the Labour cabinet continued to try to keep Lloyd George as far as possible at arm's length.[44] Secondly, the Liberal leader was himself anxious to close none of his options, and kept open his channels of communication with sympathetic Conservatives, constantly hinting that in return for the right package, which always included electoral reform, he would be willing to combine with them to throw Labour out. This was not an attractive option for the Conservative leadership, although a few of the ex-coalitionists still dallied with the idea of some such arrangement. Not only was Lloyd George's price too high but there were also doubts as to whether he could deliver the goods, for his small band of Liberals were becoming fragmented. Above all, however, the anti-coalitionists of 1922 were adamantly set against making common cause with Lloyd George: the events of 1920–1922 were still strong in their memories.

In fact, the problems facing the Labour government were internal. They all revolved around its failure, by now becoming transparent, to deliver on its election promises of reducing unemployment. By the spring of 1930 the worst trade depression in living memory was clearly under way, and by July the 'intractable million' of unemployed which had existed throughout the 1920s had been doubled, with the trend still sharply rising. Achievements elsewhere could not compensate for this, though by the summer of 1930 there were precious few of these. The results of these difficulties were soon apparent. In April the Independent Labour Party, one of the most important founding constituent elements of the Labour Party, voted at its annual conference to set up as an independent faction. Although only eighteen Labour MPs followed the leader of the I.L.P., James Maxton, down this cul-de-sac, it was a clear sign that the cabinet's credit was beginning to run out even amongst its own supporters. More serious was the resignation from the government of Sir Oswald Mosley on 20 May, after his bold plans to grapple with the unemployment problem through programmes of public works and a form of protection were rejected by the Cabinet. Only Mosley's personal unpopularity and his mishandling of the meeting of the Parliamentary Labour Party convened two days later allowed the government to escape without grave damage.[45] In the end, only 29 votes were cast at the meeting for

Mosley's censure of the Labour leaders. The Labour Party in the House of Commons continued to display an almost unshakeable solidarity. Despite Mosley's powerful resignation speech, and the great disquiet over the failure of J.H. Thomas, the Cabinet overlord responsible, to deal with the unemployment problem, only five Labour members abstained on the Conservative censure motion of 28 May, and none voted against the government. At the same time, the inferiority of the Labour front bench team in debate when compared to the Liberals was sapping the government's credibility. Macdonald moved on 5 June to stem the rot. In a cabinet reshuffle, Thomas was shunted out to the Dominions Office, and the Prime Minister announced that from now on he would oversee the battle against unemployment himself.

However, the Conservatives could draw little pleasure from Labour's trials, in view of the appalling combination of apathy and disunity in their own party. The Conservative leaders still considered that the government might fall at any moment. In that situation an advanced tariff policy could only be a liability, affording their opponents an easy target in the ensuing general election. As a result, Baldwin was forced to rely upon vagueness as a deliberate tactic, in an attempt to paper over both the rift between the different sections of his party and the widening gap between the forward elements and the mass of the electorate. This was hardly a respectable or inspiring position, and it brought with it its own problems, for the confusion over policy in the constituencies was considerable. A number of leading figures in the Party attempted to solve this problem by offering their own versions of the policy. These were ignored and, in the case of the Earl of Derby, even tactlessly snubbed by Baldwin for their pains; the last thing he wanted was any restrictions on his freedom to manoeuvre. By the beginning of May it had become apparent that this attempt both to have his cake and eat it, by preserving the truce without paying the price in fiscal policy, was not a solution. The unsettling effects prompted the Principal Agent to write a warning memorandum to Davidson, and Baldwin finally had to come off the fence with the series of speeches he was to make during May in support of the flagging 'Home and Empire' campaign. It was the first of these, at Sheffield, which forced Beaverbrook to face up to the fact that Baldwin would always opt for caution.

These problems were linked with the failures of Baldwin himself as leader of the Party and of the opposition. First and foremost was his lack of grip on policy, which, whether deliberate or not, by the end of April was having counter-productive effects. By avoiding defining his position too closely, and thereby giving hostages to fortune, Baldwin had given a widespread impression of backpedalling furiously, although it would be more accurate to describe his tactics as an attempt simply to rest on the *status quo* of the Hotel Cecil policy. The reason for this was that Baldwin had to take into account wider circumstances. Faced with the determined assaults of the Labour government's free trade Chancellor of the Exchequer on the limited safeguarding duties that were already in existence, Baldwin instinctively adopted a defensive position in which the accent was on the immediate preservation of these tariffs, rather than their possible future extension. A commitment to restore any duties removed was the keynote of his 'Home and Empire' campaign, relegating Empire Free Trade to the indefinite future. This strategy, perhaps acceptable in the atmosphere of late 1929 with the fear of being caught by a snap election, now seemed weak and inadequate. Between February and October 1930 Baldwin was to adopt in slow stages policies demanded by the protectionist section of his party, only to find that the latter had discarded their previous positions in favour of ones yet further advanced. This produced widespread dissatisfaction with his leadership because, although his views evolved, they seemed to be formed by outside pressure, not inner conviction. Rather than his leading the Party towards tariff reform and imperial preference, to many it seemed to have led him, willy-nilly, to that goal.

There were, of course, strong reasons for Baldwin's reluctance: he remembered how in 1906 and 1923 the food tax issue had cost the Party the election. He was loath to take up such a cross again until he was convinced that if he did not do so, an even worse fate would befall the Conservative Party—its fragmentation into impotent splinters. The first duty of a Conservative leader was often defined as preserving the unity of the Party. Certainly, it was only when Baldwin became convinced that such an upheaval was the alternative would he countenance full protection. He did so with extreme reluctance, for the electoral straws in the wind were by no means clear during 1930. Despite accumulating evidence by the end of the summer of a drift of public opinion away from free trade, Baldwin still believed that in a general election, when the chips were down, working class urban voters would vote for the safeguarding of their industries, but not for duties on their food. The result of the Nottingham Central by-election on 27 May seemed to be a confirmation of this. O'Connor's caution was vindicated. In a triangular contest, he increased the Conservative majority from 2998 to 7023 votes. This contrasted favourably with the West Fulham poll three weeks earlier, when Cobb had only barely turned a Labour majority of 2211 into a Conservative one of 240. In percentage terms the difference was not so great; whilst at West Fulham the Conservative poll rose by 11.7%, at Nottingham Central it increased by 12.5%. However, piles of ballot papers and sizes of majorities, rather than such psephological sophistications, made the greatest impact on politicians in this era. Even more important, while the West Fulham by-election was fought only against a Labour opponent, Nottingham Central was a three-corned fight. This had been the norm in 1929, and was expected to be so in the next election as well.

Baldwin shaped his 'Home and Empire' texts against this background, at the price of disappointing many of his supporters and alienating Beaverbrook. Baldwin's position during the first half of 1930 was that of a man performing a balancing trick whilst walking a tightrope, and it is understandable that whenever possible he took refuge in vagueness and confusion. On too many occasions, however, this tactic appeared to his followers and colleagues as a failure of leadership. The deterioration of confidence in Baldwin's leadership was only partly caused by his failure to provide the much-demanded 'clear lead' on policy. It was also the result of his general weakness as a Parliamentarian. He cut a poor figure in opposition, and on no occasion succeeded in throwing off the immediate post-election attitude of giving the government the benefit of the doubt, an impression that was dampening the spirits of a Party which was beginning to sense the Labour government's growing vulnerability. Baldwin's inability to lead a strongly partisan assault on the government was a principal cause of complaint against him by the right wing. By the middle of May dissatisfaction was widespread amongst the backbench MPs. Inskip commented that 'everybody appears to be at sixes and sevens'.[46] The problem was exacerbated by Baldwin's aloofness from many of the younger MPs, and his frequent absences from the House. This remoteness was further emphasised by his spending much time and energy during 1930 in stumping the country. This may have been a subconscious withdrawal from the Commons as an arena in which he was doing badly, but in retrospect Bridgeman considered it to have been a tactical misjudgement: he believed the centre of discontent to be at Westminster.[47]

Baldwin's lack of partisanship was revealed in the debate over the provisions for disarmament negotiated by the government at the London Naval Conference in May 1930. Further reductions in the Navy were regarded with misgivings by most of the Conservative Party. The proposals in the treaty, whilst arousing little criticism from the public at large, were an anathema to the Conservative right. Churchill adopted a position of intransigent opposition, and his concern was underlined by the critical resolutions forwarded from the constituencies.[48] Sensing that on this issue the Party was out of touch with public opinion, Baldwin remained non-committal, but this, combined with the growing unrest on other grounds, came near to causing a rebellion on the backbenches. Significantly, the opinions of the Diehards were echoed across an unusually wide spectrum of Party opinion. They found expression in the forum of the Conservative

Private Members '1922' Committee, where it was decided to urge a strong protest against the proposals.[49] The absence of central direction was exposed when eighty-eight Conservative MPs put their names to a strong motion rejecting the crucial Part III of the treaty, to find on 26 May that their leader would only make the milder criticism of asking for a Select Committee on the issue. A week earlier Neville Chamberlain had noted that the backbenchers were thoroughly dissatisfied with what they considered to be want of leadership by Baldwin. Chamberlain took 'a serious view of their action, which looks to me like the first beginnings of a revolt'.[50]

This was the setting for the disintegration of the truce in early June 1930. The increasing tensions of this last phase first emerged over the Crystal Palace debacle. This incident illustrated Beaverbrook's powerful appeal to the Party grassroots, Davidson's incompetence, and the mounting anger over leaflet 3153. Empire Day had become as much a Party as a national festival, and was a common occasion for the organisation of political mass meetings. Baldwin was due to address such a rally of south London Conservatism at the Crystal Palace on Empire Day, 24 May 1930. When this was being organised in early April the London Associations had insisted that Beaverbrook should be asked to chair the meeting, in order to give it the Empire Crusade seal of approval and thus personify the truce. Davidson wrote to Beaverbrook on 14 April, extending an invitation to preside at the Crystal Palace, only three days after he had forwarded to him the first copies of leaflet 3153. At this point Neville Chamberlain learned of the plan, and was horrified at the tactical blunder Davidson had made by placing Baldwin and the Party in the role of suppliants. He sent Davidson to Beaverbrook to ask him to decline the embarrassing honour. Beaverbrook obliged, indicating that he was committed to attend the Empire Industries Association's Empire Day rally in Hyde Park.[51] At this point the question of the Crystal Palace rally become entangled with the controversy raging around leaflet 3153, about which Beaverbrook's displeasure was by now public property. The south London constituencies were not only generally sympathetic to the Empire Free Trade policy, but were also more concerned than other areas not to antagonise the press lords. The power of the Beaverbrook-Rothermere press was predominantly based in London and the Home Counties, where the high degree of penetration of the *Daily Express* and *Daily Mail* was reinforced by their control of the two London evening daily papers, the *Evening Standard* and *Evening News*. London was Beaverbrook's stamping ground. Consistently, it was the region most responsive to the beat of his drum. At a preliminary meeting on 23 April the London divisions blamed Beaverbrook's refusal on the Central Office, and determined that they must secure his presence if the rally was to be worth staging at all.[52]

The Party leadership seemed dangerously close to losing control altogether. By the time this request reached Beaverbrook, however, his opposition to leaflet 3153 had hardened to such a point that now he did make it the pretext for a second refusal.[53] When this was communicated to the next meeting of the Association chairmen and MPs of the Metropolitan Area on the 29th, they decided by a large majority to cancel the event. This was more than a storm in a teacup, as the party's Principal Agent, Robert Topping, acknowledged on 2 May when reviewing the 'extremely disturbing' and 'most serious' events which had been developing at the local level during April.[54]

It is clear, however, that the decisive factor in the breakdown of the truce was the content and tone of Baldwin's speeches in support of the 'Home and Empire' campaign. In these the negativism implicit in Baldwin's last platform address at Manchester a month previously became explicit. The most damaging of these orations was the first, given at Sheffield on 8 May 1930. This opened with the very mildest criticism of Labour's election promises of 1929, acknowledging that these were made in good faith, although they had been based on ignorance. The bulk of the speech was a defence of the threatened safeguarding duties, but Baldwin did take one step forward by indicating that a future Conservative government would extend them to cover the iron and steel industries. He paid lip service to the concept of Empire Free Trade, but qualified it in three significant ways. The Conservative leader insisted that the extension of safeguarding at home was an essential preliminary to negotiations with the Dominions. In practice this would postpone such discussions to the end, rather than the beginning, of the next administration. Secondly, mention of agriculture was conspicuous by its absence. Baldwin's third reservation was to indicate that the referendum was not, as Beaverbrook had intended, a staging post on the road to adopting the 'free hand'. Instead Baldwin spoke of the referendum as if it were the definitive and final stage of policy, promising not to ask for a mandate at the next election for any tax on imports of foreign foods. In the series of speeches which followed he gave even more emphasis to safeguarding, and less and less prominence to imperial economic unity. Speaking at Bury on 27 May, he dressed up safeguarding as a weapon along the lines of Balfour's retaliation policy of 1903, and explicitly warned that achieving the economic unity of the empire might take a generation or more. In the final speech of the campaign, at Leeds on the 31st, Baldwin failed to make any reference to imperial trading relations. On this occasion he began with a passage which revealed the basis of his strategy, declaring that 'no party can attain power in our country today that cannot make an appeal to the north and to Scotland'.[55] This fear governed Baldwin's thinking, for he revealed at the same time privately that he was 'very convinced that

Beaverbrook cuts no ice in the north, and that any policy of taxing food would not go down there'.[56]

The 'Home and Empire' speeches finally brought into the open the essential flaw of the truce, that peace had only been achieved because of each principal's misconceptions about the aims and intentions of the other. Baldwin believed he had satisfied Beaverbrook by his commitment to summon an Imperial Conference. Through the device of the referendum, the Conservatives had fulfilled their side of the bargain by dropping all the inhibiting promises which had hitherto ruled out most of the recommendations such a Conference would be likely to make. However, Beaverbrook had always understood the Hotel Cecil speech to be the first step towards a stronger and more definite policy. He was dismayed by the transformation of the referendum into yet another negative pledge. Beaverbrook's uneasiness had grown with the increasing intimations that the Conservative leader did not intend any further progress. In parallel with this his frustration mounted at the way in which he seemed to have painted himself into a corner by suggesting the referendum. Baldwin now appeared to be using this, Beaverbrook complained, as a shield instead of a sword.[57] Disillusionment with the Hotel Cecil policy grew slowly in Beaverbrook's mind, a process further delayed by the frenzied activity in West Fulham. His restlessness was at first apparent in private conversation and correspondence, and not made public until the end of May. Despite all the hard things he sometimes said of the Party leader, it took time for Beaverbrook to arrive at the reluctant conclusion that it would be necessary to attack, and perhaps even destroy, his position in order to carry the spirit, as well as the letter, of imperial unity.

Beaverbrook saw the 'Home and Empire' speeches as a betrayal of the truce, and after Sheffield he lost faith in Baldwin.[58] On 19 May he discussed his future plans with Elibank, who noted that the referendum had been 'only a bridge for getting his policy adopted'.[59] The conclusion that it had failed as an instrument led Beaverbrook logically into going all out for the full Crusade policy, without qualifications. On 21 May he publicly tore up the referendum, and with it the truce, in a speech at Enfield. He asserted that 'Empire Free Trade carried with it essentially and necessarily a tax on foreign foodstuffs', and bluntly added that anyone who said otherwise should be dismissed as 'either a fool or a liar'.[60] This only served to confirm the widespread suspicions of Beaverbrook's unreliability and untrustworthiness. Baldwin, believing his own conduct to have been perfectly consistent with his pledges at the Hotel Cecil, saw Beaverbrook as the aggressor in returning to open warfare. The breakdown of the truce set the two men further apart, politically and personally, than ever before. Baldwin reverted to the view that the press lords 'were a couple of crooks'.[61] Meanwhile, Beaverbrook turned his back on the strategy of negotiation with the Party leaders. He was aware of the popularity of his policy with the mass of Conservative supporters, and the consequent vulnerability of the leadership's position. 'The Conservative Party is hopelessly divided', he wrote; 'the rank and file is on the side of Empire Free Trade. Otherwise, the leaders, who march off in the other direction, would smash me at once'.[62] In April he had looked to a backbench revolt for support, but after Salisbury's climbdown this seemed unlikely to materialise without aid from below. By the end of May, therefore, he had decided to appeal directly to the most likely base of popular support, the constituency Associations. 'The truth is I don't care what view Members of the Commons or Lords take of the issue', he told Horne, 'it is to the Constituencies that I lift up mine eyes'.[63] The logic of this plan of campaign included the revival of the Crusade in all its manifestations as a separate party. The organisation of branches now went ahead; funds were again appealed for; and future by-elections were to be contested either by an independent Crusader, or by the official nominee on Beaverbrook's unofficial platform.

At the same time as Beaverbrook was moving towards open confrontation, the Party leadership reduced the target for attack by ditching Davidson, the detested Party Chairman. The reason for this was not that he was a proxy target for assaults on Baldwin, but the reverse. Davidson's unpopularity, compounded by his blunders of the previous two months, was such that Baldwin's continued loyalty was in danger of dragging the Leader down with his Chairman. Even so, Davidson's departure did not occur at Baldwin's instigation. It was Neville Chamberlain who determined to take an initiative himself which his leader might never have taken at all, in order to remove a man he considered not only useless but also a dangerous liability to the entire leadership.[64] Chamberlain was becoming more involved and interested in the workings of the Party's central organisations. On his return from East Africa in March he took over the Conservative Research Department from Lord Eustace Percy, who had acted as its caretaker since its creation in November 1929.[65] Chamberlain had swiftly become aware that Davidson's position—and incompetence—were frustrating all his plans, and almost immediately resolved to secure his removal. Before this could be done, the inevitable problem of who was to replace Davidson had to be solved. At first Neville Chamberlain did not consider himself for the position, preferring instead to secure it for some nominee of his own, as a front through whom he could control the details of day-to-day organisation. He found such a person in Geoffrey Ellis, an influential figure in the Yorkshire Provincial Area who had lost his seat in 1929. Chamberlain kept this part of his plan secret, and in the first week of April he bluntly told Davidson that he had better go before he was forced out. Although the hapless Chairman agreed, he began to use the question of his successor as an excuse for delaying any announcement, and finally suggested in late May that in view of the deteriorating situation it might be better not to change horses in mid-stream. In fact, so far as Neville Chamberlain was concerned, this made it all the more urgent that Davidson should go. At the end of May, determined to put an end to the agony, he sought Davidson out again, and demanded to know when he would resign. Under this hectoring, unsustained by any sign from Baldwin that he should stay, Davidson collapsed, promising that the announcement would be made before the end of the week.[66] Davidson's departure was intended to appease the unrest within the Party. However, with the question of his successor unresolved, and the suspicions that it would probably be another Balwinite yes-man, the Party was still in a highly disturbed state. Nonetheless, the fall of Davidson was the first stage in the process whereby the initiative passed from Beaverbrook to the Party leadership. As the truce disintegrated in the first three weeks of June, they prepared their counterattack. But even the limited success which this was to achieve did no more than postpone their difficulties, whilst the pressures from below were pushing the Party towards a major crisis with growing rapidity.

CHAPTER 5

The Brink of Collapse

Although the truce had bought time, this was not enough to stave off a serious crisis within the Conservative Party in the late summer of 1930. No ground had been gained by June on either of the fundamental problems facing the Conservative leadership: the rift between themselves and their most active supporters over protection on the one hand, and the lack of significant indications that public opinion was moving away from the government and towards their cautious platform on the other. Their position in the summer of 1930 was not only sterile, it was a classic example of having the worst of both worlds. The Party leaders were locked into their commitment to the referendum proposal. This had only been a worthwhile expedient so long as it secured at least the appearance of unity. Once Beaverbrook publicly abandoned it, they were left stranded, exposed to his every sally, yet ironically unable to drop it themselves, for fear of the ultimate humiliation: giving the appearance of being subservient to the press lords. The latter sought to coerce Baldwin, believing that he would give ground under pressure, by attacking the influence of pessimists amongst his colleagues and by capturing from beneath his feet the support of the Party rank and file. Yet, despite the success of both pincers of this strategy in the spring of 1930, the Empire Crusade had failed in its ultimate aim of changing the official line.

Beaverbrook was wont to complain that any previous Conservative leader would not have been so prickly about clinching a deal with the press. This totally missed the point. Whilst Baldwin was rarely concerned about the exact emphasis of any particular policy, he was utterly opposed to making concessions to what he considered to be unconstitutional pressure. To do so would have negated everything that he had stood for in political life. Yet, whilst his followers could and did respect their leader all the more for this, in the summer of 1930 the majority of them did not share his hostility to Beaverbrook. On the contrary, they spoke often of their debt of gratitude to him for having revitalised the cause of empire, bringing it to the forefront of the political stage. Over large parts of the country the constituency activists wanted to take over Beaverbrook's policy, lock, stock and barrel. By June 1930 the situation within the Party was explosive enough. Over the following four months the balance of opinion in the constituency parties began to shift away from the half-way house of the referendum. Like an ice-bound sledge, once free it moved with astonishing rapidity. At the same time, Baldwin held to a posture of rigidity which became increasingly untenable. The inevitable result was that by September 1930 the Party was on the verge of one of the most serious crises in its history, in danger of rending from top to bottom.

Baldwin invested all the capital of his leadership in his attempt to fight off the challenge from the barons of the press. His position was not without its strengths. The Conservative Party was not organised on democratic lines in terms of decision-making, but had evolved as a deferential structure. Policy was handed down from above, not made from below by the Conference. The Executive Committee and Central Council of the National Union were forums for the deliverance and acclamation of policy, not its formulation. Although the decision-making process could be influenced on occasion by the parliamentary Party, it could not be captured from outside or from below without completely restructuring the hierarchy and reallocating the roles of leaders and led. The constituency activists held a potentially destructive power, the threat that if driven too far they would revolt and smash the Party. Strong pressure from below would have an effect on the leadership, but unless it was representative, nation-wide, and consistent it would not alone ensure success for the policy advocated by Beaverbrook. The tradition of party loyalty was extremely strong, and dislike of factionalism could prove stronger than the desire for the 'free hand'. A campaign to oust the leader, particularly if conducted by the press, was likely to alienate more people than it attracted. In the end it could produce a backlash in Baldwin's favour which would shore up his crumbling credibility. Recognition of this possibility caused some uncertainty in the Crusade camp as the truce collapsed. Their dilemma was all the greater in that they sought not to fight the Conservative Party, but to work with it and through it. After June the press barons veered between hopes that Baldwin could still be forced to co-operate against his will and attempts to destroy his position altogether. That lack of consistency was to prove one of the fundamental weaknesses of Baldwin's opponents. It revealed the inhibitions of loyalty that to a greater or lesser degree held back Amery, Croft, and Elibank from the unrestricted hostility displayed by Beaverbrook and Rothermere. For with the end of the truce conciliation was not simplistically transformed into hostilities. Bouts of negotiations, though fruitless until March 1931, indicated that the press lords had not resolved their tactical problems.

During the first half of June both camps drifted further apart. The truce had been tacitly scrapped, but not yet replaced by open confrontation. Typically, it was the impatient Beaverbrook who took the initiative, a decision which was to put him in a poor light. He lost much credit by dropping the referendum, partly because he was seen to be the destroyer of the unity which it had represented, and partly due to his apparent inconsistency in having initiated the referendum proposal himself. The result was a polarisation of Conservative opinion around the two protagonists in the second half of June. This was stimulated by three events which combined to place Baldwin for the first time in an advantageous position from which to launch a counter-attack. The first of these was the much-heralded official policy on agriculture, unveiled in a speech given by Baldwin at a mass open-air rally at Glemham Park on 9 June. Under the cover of a blanket statement that protection must be ruled out as a solution, Baldwin moved a considerable distance in the farmers' direction on specific matters. Once again calling his plan safeguarding, he proffered a guaranteed price system for cereal growers, and appeased their principal grievance by claiming a free hand to stop the dumping of foreign subsidised foodstuffs either by prohibition or a countervailing duty. The importance of this speech, coming at the time it did, can hardly be over-emphasised. At a stroke it closed much of the gap in the most important area where Party policy was well out of step with Conservative supporters: in the agricultural areas of south, midland, and eastern England. The new declaration was very favourably received by the National Farmers Union, which was a power in many constituency associations. At the same time Baldwin side-stepped the issue of Empire Free Trade and avoided the appearance of a concession to Beaverbrook. In fact, the latter seized upon Baldwin's explicit disavowal of food taxes at Glemham Park as a suitable pretext for recommencing hostilities. On 17 June he proclaimed the renewal of the Crusade as a separate party. In doing so he struck a blow at the Conservative Party as a whole, by appealing to his supporters to divert their subscriptions from their local Associations to the Crusade. Tactically this was mistaken, for it provoked resentment in the waverers amongst the local activists, and counteracted the gradual slide of many southern constituencies towards the Crusade camp. Beaverbrook's move left the high ground of party loyalty to the Baldwinites. By pushing moderate protectionists behind the official banner, he isolated rather than assisted the 'whole-hoggers'. This was evident in the reactions of the Executive Committee of the National

Union, which was meeting that very day. Despite the opposition of two right-wing members, who failed to find backing, a resolution was passed in condemnation of Beaverbrook's statement.[1] This reaction from the highest elected body on the voluntary side of the Party was the second signal to Baldwin that the Crusaders might now be caught on the wrong foot.

The resolution of the problem of the vacant Chairmanship in a manner satisfactory to most of the Party was the third important event of mid-June. The long delay in the announcement of a successor to Davidson was itself becoming a destabilising factor. Several names were canvassed, including the former junior ministers Walter Elliot and Kingsley Wood, and the chief whip, Eyres-Monsell. Even more alarming was the growing demand for the appointment of Lord Lloyd of Dolobran, a former Conservative MP with a long record of imperial service, who had been a Diehard hero since his removal from the post of High Commisioner in Egypt and Sudan by the Labour government in 1929. Petitions were circulating among MPs, one in favour of Lloyd and another in favour of Leslie Wilson, a former Chief Whip. In this atmosphere Chamberlain came to the conclusion that Ellis was no longer a sufficiently heavyweight contender, and that he should take the post himself for a limited period.[2] Baldwin preferred to ask Bridgeman, who was also of ex-Cabinet rank, widely respected, and personally much closer to him. As the position was in the leader's gift, Chamberlain could only console himself with the thought that Bridgeman would keep out worse possibilities. However, Bridgeman refused the post, leaving Baldwin in a dilemma from which the acceptance of Neville Chamberlain as Chairman seemed by far the easiest escape. Baldwin appreciated that the selection of Chamberlain would be generally popular and would pull the Party together again.[3] This was precisely the effect Baldwin wanted. His apparent reluctance to appoint Chamberlain has been often misinterpreted. It had nothing to do with fear of a potential rival, but was merely his characteristic difficulty in arriving at decisions on important matters. Since April the newly-established Conservative Research Department, of which Chamberlain was Chairman, had lived under the same roof as the leader and his personal staff, at 24 Old Queen Street, thus bringing the two men into an even closer political relationship. Baldwin needed a loyal lieutenant whom he could trust in the important position of Party Chairman, and Chamberlain fitted this bill as well as anyone after Davidson and Bridgeman. Baldwin could not fail to be aware of the community of feeling they shared both over the detested Lloyd George coalition, which was still a crucial political litmus test, and Irwin's policy in India. Nor had Chamberlain shown any desire in six years of Cabinet office to take up his father's mantle by splitting the Party over tariff reform. Above all,

Baldwin was secure in his reliance on Chamberlain's emotive, as well as merely pragmatic, loyalty to the leader and distaste for intrigue. 'S.B. is my friend as well as my leader', declared Chamberlain, 'and I would not on any account play L.G. to his Asquith'.[4] Unlike Davidson, Chamberlain was not regarded as a mere personal crony of Baldwin; he was a front-rank politician in his own right. His appointment, together with the concession that under its new rules the National Union would select the Chairman of its own Executive, and no longer have the Chairman of the Party organisation thrust upon it, went some way to appease the resentments voiced since the election defeat.

At the same time there was a swelling chorus of disapproval from all levels of the Party against the pretensions and methods of the press lords. Waldron Smithers was far from unusual in condemning the 'un-English methods' of the press, and appealing to the spirit of fair play.[5] The belief that they were usurping the role of parliament encouraged a rally to Baldwin. Whatever his other defects, he could be trusted to defend the constitution. These feelings became the foundation on which Baldwin was to rest his efforts in the propaganda battle for the heart and soul of the Party. He was able to present the debate in terms favourable to himself. Instead of being a dispute over fiscal policy, he portrayed his opponents as challenging the very basis of the parliamentary constitution. Baldwin ignored the support within the Conservative ranks for Empire Free Trade, side-stepping it completely by focusing his attention on the press lords' political ambitions. He exploited Beaverbrook and Rothermere's failure to persuade any significant parliamentary figure to act as the nominal leader of their campaign. From being a battle over political programmes, where Baldwin was of necessity on the defensive if he was to retain a policy acceptable to northern electors, it became a battle over political methods, where Baldwin was on the offensive.

The initiative had now passed to the Conservative leadership. Sensing the opportunity provided by the change of mood, they decided on 19 June to summon a party meeting for the 24th, to be held at the Caxton Hall in Westminster. Furthermore, the announcement of Chamberlain's acceptance of the Chairmanship was carefully timed for the eve of the meeting.[6] The leadership were now confident that the critics could be defeated by appeals to party loyalty, by attacks on methods of the press, and by mobilising the anxieties over food duties still felt by many MPs and almost all the prospective candidates. For them the referendum, whatever its defects, represented a shield against electoral unpopularity. The idea of summoning a conclave of the parliamentary Party had been in the air for some time, as a move to pre-empt Beaverbrook's rumoured intention to agitate for the calling of a special conference of the National Union.[7] In fact, the annual

Conference was due to be held within a few days, on 1 July, although
it was to be different in nature from the normal form of conferences.
Lasting only one day, instead of the usual two, it was being
summoned to ratify a number of rule changes in the National Union
relating to representation at the Conference, and similar organisational questions. The agenda was strictly limited to these matters,
and political issues were to be excluded. However, there was the
danger that, unless some lead was given from the top, the conference
might mutiny, and demand a debate on the Party's fiscal policy and
even on its leadership. A meeting of MPs and candidates would be a
much more favourable forum for the leaders. As a result of the
decision that it should consist only of MPs and candidates, and not
peers, by longstanding precedent it was effectively limited to deliber-
ating on policy and precluded from any discussion of the leadership.[8]

Baldwin produced at this first Caxton Hall meeting on 24 June one
of his periodic oratorical triumphs. His speech was succint but highly
effective; every passage hit its target. The style was set by his opening
words, which came directly to the point. 'We are met here today
because we are told there is a crisis in the Party', he began; 'there will
be a crisis if you cannot make up your minds what you are going to
do'.[9] He was equally candid on the vexed question of the referendum,
which 'was not, and is not, a principle. It is a piece of machinery
adopted to secure the unity of the Party'. It had been Beaverbrook's
idea, but now the press baron was demanding that it must be dropped.
Such fickleness was all very well for a newspaper magnate, 'but great
parties cannot swing from to and fro from week to week without
losing all credit and all confidence'. Even so, Baldwin was willing to
reconsider the position, 'if it can be proved to me that it is a bar to
unity, and that unity can be achieved in any other way'. He remained
cautious and pragmatic about the wisdom of a 'free hand' policy: 'I
have no fresh evidence yet to make me alter the decision to which I
came some months ago, and that is that such a policy at the present day
would lead to our defeat at the polls'.

Having dealt with policy, he rounded on his critics. In a devastating
onslaught, he switched the issue from the press lords' message to the
medium itself, and out-trumped them by playing the constitutional
card. 'There is nothing more curious in modern evolution than the
effect of an enormous fortune rapidly made and the control of
newspapers of your own', he remarked acidly. Grouping together by
name Beaverbrook, Rothermere, and the American newspaper millionaire William Hearst, Baldwin elevated the matter at stake onto an
altogether different plane from the referendum. Power of this kind

> goes to the head like wine, and in all these cases attempts have been
> made outside the province of journalism to dictate, to domineer, to
> blackmail . . . you cannot take your politics from men like that.

The desire to dictate the policy to a big party, the desire to choose the leader, the desire to impose Ministers on the Crown; the only parallel to that was the action of the T.U.C. in 1926.

Baldwin had defeated the General Strike; he would fight this challenge too. Ironically, he was assisted by the maladroit manoeuvres of Beaverbrook's ally, Lord Rothermere. By focusing his specific criticisms on the latter as the most vulnerable and least popular of the press barons, Baldwin was able to damn Beaverbrook by dint of association. The Conservative leader referred in passing to Elibank's proposed terms of late February, and then produced a letter which Rothermere had sent to the protectionist MP, Hannon, in mid-June. Acting as an intermediary, Hannon had shown this missive to David-son, who informed Baldwin of its contents. Realising its potential use, Baldwin had summoned Hannon on 21 June and asked for the letter.[10] Although Rothermere had written this in order to define his position as a prelude to negotiation, it was truculent and dictatorial in tone, and, as a result of incautious phraseology, was potentially damning in content. It gave the impression that Rothermere demanded not merely to know the names of future members of any Baldwin cabinet, but also implied a right of approval over its policy and of veto over its personnel.

The effect of this document when read to the party meeting was dramatic, producing 'a white heat of indignation'.[11] 'A more prepos-terous and insolent demand was never made on the leader of any political Party', Baldwin concluded; 'I repudiate it with contempt'.[12] In the light of this, a rally around the leader was predictable. The motion in support of Baldwin was moved by Rentoul, the Chairman of the '1922' Committee. His resolution was lukewarm on the referendum, but his speech was a vigorous attack on the press lords; which by this point had become the main theme of the meeting. As a result, an amendment proposed by Gretton and Croft to drop the referendum and go instead for the free hand was rejected by a large majority, even though it had carefully avoided the question of the leadership. The decisive speech in Baldwin's favour was made by Horne, who had had a blazing row with Beaverbrook at a private dinner organised by Hannon less than a week before. Horne dismissed the policy distinctions as academic to the main issue. While indicating his personal desire to drop the referendum, he stated firmly that to even appear to do so at the dictation of the press was utterly impos-sible.

Baldwin scored a triumph on 24 June, and in its wake the special conference of the National Union passed off without incident a week later. The party meeting accepted the logic of Baldwin's argument that the constitutional issue transcended the policy one. In political terms, the result of the meeting was much more ambiguous. This was especially the case so far as the referendum was concerned. It remained the official definition of Party policy, and was still looked on as the only practical course in many northern associations.[13] On the other hand, it was increasingly regarded as discredited in metropolitan circles.[14] Amery informed his leader a few days later that the general view was that it had to be dropped at the first opportunity.[15] The party meeting had not provided a solution to the problems facing Baldwin. One reason for this was that its verdict had been written off in advance by his challengers, who denounced it as a packed and stage-managed affair. Austen Chamberlain commented that though the meeting had been necessary and useful, it had settled nothing.[16] Baldwin had won a battle, but not the war. The meeting served as a successful holding action, intended to last until the Imperial Conference that was due to convene in the autumn. This was widely expected to provide a suitable pretext for changing policy.[17] However, the erosion of the limited success achieved on 24 June occurred much more rapidly than this plan allowed for, with the result that the height of the crisis was reached in September 1930, before the Imperial Conference opened.

After the Caxton Hall meeting Baldwin seemed once again to relapse into a mood in which lethargy and complacency were combined. At the same time, his weakness as leader of the opposition was giving rise to despair amongst even the most loyal backbenchers. This was in spite of the fact that on 9 July the Conservatives had scored a rare parliamentary success. By hiding a number of MPs around the Palace of Westminster, the Conservative whips were able to catch their government counterparts off guard, and in a snap division reduce its majority to only three. This sort of stunt could only be pulled once, and was politically meaningless, for the rigidity of party loyalties ensured that the government could reverse any such trick defeat. Nevertheless, a coup of this type might have been expected to raise backbench Conservative morale. Instead, by the end of the session in July there was 'very grave discontent'.[18] The continual sniping of the Beaverbrook and Rothermere press was also slowly affecting the parliamentary Party, causing 'a terrible demoralisation'.[19] This inevitably filtered down to the rank and file, and rendered the seemingly more vigorous approach of the Crusaders all the more attractive by comparison. Baldwin failed to recognise the genuine appeal that the ideal of Empire Free Trade had for his supporters. Instead, bending over backwards in his efforts to satisfy the prejudices of the electorate in the industrial boroughs, he seemed to be retreating from the referendum position, rather than preparing to advance beyond it. The ambiguities of Baldwin's speeches in July and August reflected the contemporary belief that the government might fall before the summer recess. In any ensuing election the 'dear food' cry could provide a weapon with which Liberal and Labour candidates might successfully defend the seats that they had gained in 1929. But, viewed from the angle of internal Conservative tensions, these pronouncements were yet another element adding fuel to the flames of disenchantment. Amongst the inevitable consequences of the failure of leadership was a tendency to factionalism in the Party. In July Croft took the initiative by forming the Imperial Economic Unity group, a new body intended to be more assertive than the Empire Industries Association, and sixty-three MPs from the right of the Party attended the inaugural meeting.

That the situation did not deteriorate faster during July and August 1930 was the result of the cautious approach adopted by Beaverbrook, at the urging of Amery and Croft. He was still torn by the tactical dilemma: wishing to capture Baldwin, yet fearful of being caught by him instead; reluctant to separate himself from Rothermere, yet reluctant also to commence full-scale warfare. Beaverbrook spent the summer casting about from one line of approach to another, swinging from co-operation through neutrality to eventual hostility. In the period immediately after the June party meeting he followed the tactic of working in parallel with the Conservative Party, whilst continuing to advocate an unrestricted food tax policy. This position was partly forced upon him by the circumstances of the North Norfolk by-election, which was in progress during July. The local Conservative association attempted to preserve a precarious unity, declaring that their candidate should fight on the official policy and loyally support the leader, but at the same time welcoming Beaverbrook's assistance. In practice, the candidate, Thomas Cook, fought on the pure gospel of Empire Free Trade, a tactic to which the Party leadership turned a blind eye. Beaverbrook threw all his energies into the fight, campaigning on behalf of the official candidate. His methods were always spectacularly modern; during this contest they included hiring aeroplanes to bombard the scattered hamlets with leaflets dropped from chimmney-pot height.[20] However, North Norfolk was not promising territory for the Crusade; the seat had never been held by a Conservative in its forty-five-year existence. Despite the vocal support of the local branch of the National Farmers Union, Beaverbrook could not sway the longstanding Radical allegiance of the farm labourers. Significantly, the Labour candidate won on a platform of constant denunciations of Conservative food taxes. In fact, this was to be the best result ever achieved by the Conservative Party in North Norfolk, but Beaverbrook had set his sights on capturing it, and his failure to do so was a severe blow to his confidence. 'I went in in the expectation of winning it, but we were beaten', he wrote; 'I was under the impression that our policy would sweep the constituency'.[21]

This setback took the wind out of the Crusaders' sails, and encouraged a return to the negotiating table. Neville Chamberlain, anxious to build on his position as Party Chairman, extended an invitation to talk, which was accepted. Beaverbrook's attitude that despite differing tactics there was a common purpose, and that reconciliation was possible, encouraged Chamberlain in the early stages of these discussions to build up high hopes of a satisfactory outcome. The terms offered, however, became increasingly unattractive to Beaverbrook as his moods shifted during the last week of July.[22] These changes were the product of two complicating factors. The first was the advent of a by-election in Bromley. This was a safe Conservative constituency in the south London suburbs, and thus ideal Crusading territory. The second was the pressure exerted by Rothermere to abandon negotiation for an all-out trial of strength. He wanted to put the matter to the proof by running an independent challenger against the Conservative nominee for the vacant seat. Beaverbrook was reluctant to follow this course, but believed that any settlement which did not include and satisfy Rothermere would be worthless. He sought a middle way between these two positions, and believed he had found it in the suggestion that Rothermere's son, Esmond Harmsworth, should be adopted as the official candidate for Bromley, presumably advocating a highly unofficial policy. Upon these contradictions the negotiations foundered in an atmosphere of mutual suspicion. Beaverbrook could not understand that to accept Esmond would be a humiliation impossible for the Party leadership to swallow. He infuriated Neville Chamberlain by his continual refusal to take no for an answer, and by further maladroit attempts to foist Esmond upon him. These culminated in a disastrous meeting between Rothermere and the Party Chairman on 26 July. However, from this nadir the negotiations recovered sufficiently that by 30 July Chamberlain believed he had reached an informal agreement.[23] Unfortunately, Beaverbrook lost his nerve. Unable to restrain his partner from running his own candidate, he decided that he could not afford to separate himself from his only powerful ally. The manner and timing of this sudden decision left Neville Chamberlain bitterly resentful, convinced that Beaverbrook had abused his trust. The resulting alienation of Chamberlain, who concluded that 'the man is a crook after all', was a serious error on Beaverbrook's part. It provoked a swift and hostile response. Bitter and angry, Chamberlain made it clear to the Executive Committee of the Bromley association the next day that Esmond Harmsworth would be totally unacceptable, and adroitly turned them against Beaverbrook.[24]

The nomination of a loyal candidate, E.T. Campbell, who was known to be almost an Empire Free Trader on policy, was the cornerstone of this response. The running of Campbell provided Beaverbrook with an insoluble dilemma. Rothermere in reply had brought forward under the banner of his United Empire Party an

Independent, Redwood, who was not only a stranger to the division, but also a paid employee of Rothermere's, and of dubious political background. Beaverbrook was hesitant to nail the Empire Crusade's colours to the mast of such an unattractive vessel, fearing the consequences of another disappointing showing in the ballot boxes. He was encouraged to stand aside from the Bromley fight by Amery, Croft, and Hannon, all of whom urged that Campbell was so close to the desired position in both private sympathy and public statements that he should not be opposed. Beaverbrook resolved the difficulty by withdrawing from any active role in the contest, and physically distanced himself by leaving for the south of France. This inactivity lasted into September, for on his return Beaverbrook fell ill, and was confined to bed for several weeks. Redwood fought on a wide-ranging Diehard platform of industrial protection, subsidies for farmers, economy in government spending, firm rule in India and Egypt, and no relations with Soviet Russia, as well as Empire Free Trade. Although Campbell held the seat, Redwood was only three thousand votes behind. Indeed, Campbell only fended off his challenger by the expedient of going a good deal further than the official policy.[25] In doing so he reflected not merely the opinions of insulated southern suburbia, but the evolution of opinion across the whole Party during the late summer of 1930. Ormsby-Gore detected 'a general swing to the right throughout the Tory Party, not merely in a protectionist direction, but all along the line'.[26]

The referendum had never been popular in the south. The new factor was the advance of protectionist views in the north. The stimulus for this was the impact of the economic depression and the consequent steep rise in unemployment and not the onslaughts of the Crusade, which carried little weight north of the Trent (see Appendix 2). By June 1930 opinion here, despite having moved a considerable distance away from free trade during the previous year under the cover of the ambiguous strategy of extended safeguarding, still remained firmly against any food tax. But this barrier was to fall swiftly in the late summer, under the increasing pressure of the slump. As the economic picture darkened in the second half of 1930, the attractiveness of insular protection accordingly increased. This movement of public opinion found a pale reflection in the parallel evolution of Macdonald and Sir John Simon away from the free trade views they had formerly espoused. But such politicians to the left of centre, bound by the free trade orthodoxy of their colleagues and supporters, could never aspire to outbid the Conservatives in any protectionist auction.[27] Even so, it was the constant fear of the more eager Conservative leaders that either Lloyd George or the bolder figures in the Labour cabinet, such as J.H. Thomas, might try to seize the reins of the protectionist chariot, let slacken by Baldwin's feeble grasp.

By September 1930, for perhaps the first time, the sentiments of southern Conservatives were finding an echo, rather than a contradiction, in the north. Though still possessing a residual and instinctive unease over food taxes, the shift in opinion was very marked, and it was also very rapid, catching the leadership completely off balance. It was visible in the resolutions debated at both area and constituency level over these summer months, which began to call for an end to qualifications and reservations, and accepted imperial preference 'with all its implications', including 'import duties in this country on foodstuffs produced outside the empire'.[28] The transformation in Conservative opinion was both paralleled and symbolised by Lord Derby's public endorsement of food taxes in the early autumn. With these changes, the referendum policy became politically redundant. A substantial and serious rift was now opening between the policy to which the leadership was committed, and that which the Party as a whole desired to see advocated; 'a free hand to foster and build up empire trade'.[29] This sentiment was typical of the insistant chorus of similar demands across the length and breadth of the country.[30] Such uniform pressure would be not only difficult but dangerous to resist for a long period. The situation was not the creation of Beaverbrook's Crusade, except in a marginal sense, but it was a situation which the Crusade could readily exploit.[31] Feeling amongst both businessmen and farmers was running feverishly high. One Conservative supporter, a Lincolnshire paper manufacturer, put it in a nutshell. 'What we want is guts and common sense', he complained; 'it is about time our Party did something for us and said damn the foreignor'.[32]

The tensions which had developed within the Conservative Party since the election defeat combined in September 1930 to produce a crisis of an explosive nature. For several years Baldwin had denied his followers strongest desires, thwarting their ideals, and suffocating their enthusiasm. Instead of acting as their leader, he seemed to be a barrier. The genuine respect with which he was personally held, and his powerful position as leader of the Party, enabled him to contain the fermenting unrest until September 1930. But, finally, the dam of loyalty and deference seemed ready to burst. If it should, the forces so long pent up behind it would tear away anything which stood in their path. This was to be the nadir of the leadership's fortunes, and the period in which its support amongst the mass of the Party slumped to the lowest ebb. Despite the more superficially spectacular challenges to Baldwin mounted in the spring of 1931, his position was never again to be as weak as it was in September and early October 1930. In this period the Party came to the very brink of internal collapse, a far greater danger than the buffetings it was to receive from the press lords in February and March 1931. Indeed, the crisis of September 1930 was as threatening as the rebellion that had overthrown Austen

Chamberlain and the Lloyd George Coalition in 1922, and far more so than the running battles over India between 1933 and 1935. Although disaster was averted, the force and range of feeling behind this revolt came from a much larger proportion of the Party than in any other crisis.

Despair affected all levels, high and low. There were alarming signs of disintegration in the local Associations, on an unparalleled scale.[33] The evidence of the local constituency records reveals rifts which were deeper and wider than even those of 1922 over the continuation of the Coalition. Unrest then had been limited to specific areas, and was concentrated in the safest seats, above all those in the southern counties: hostility to the leadership was conspicuously absent in the north and in Scotland. However, in the summer of 1930 it was clear that the leaders' position was becoming unacceptable across the whole length and breadth of the country. Quite simply, the local bedrock of support upon which the Party depended for existence had lost all patience with the official line, had lost faith in its leaders, and was at the breaking point. In parallel with the events of 1922, constituency opinion seemed rapidly to reach the most volatile state during the summer parliamentary recess, when the groups who would normally give it direction were dispersed and disengaged from active politics. By the end of September 1930 the grass-roots of the Party were within a hair's breadth of breaking out in open revolt, and the control of the leader and Central Office was on the brink of 'complete collapse'.[34]

The chaos prevalent in the councils of the local associations was exemplified by the open assaults on the Party leadership debated by several constituencies, a feature unique to this period. In the case of St. Albans this was all the more remarkable for the fact that the attack was delivered in the presence of Lord Salisbury, who was not only the President of the association but also the leader of the Party in the House of Lords. None of the usual deference was displayed.[35] Elsewhere the solidarity of local Conservatism was falling apart. In Blackpool three local councillors and the former MP Sir Lindsay Parkinson seceded to establish a Crusade branch. Official policy was 'absolutely beyond comprehension and we are rapidly losing support', complained the Chairman of the Whitstable Conservative Association.[36] The gravity of the position was illustrated by the widespread demand for an emergency Conference of the National Union.[37] This was tantamount to asserting the right of the localities to make policy and choose or set aside leaders. The crisis was not confined to the seats held by Diehards, or even to the south; whole regions of the Baldwinite north were now equally close to rebellion. Even in Birmingham, the Chamberlain citadel, there was vehement hostility. Lord Derby sounded the alarm after the North West Area Council meeting on 4 October was only balked of making a critical onslaught on both policy and leader by the firmness of their Chairman, Sir Alan Sykes, and his insistence on the fine points of procedure. Not to be thwarted, the delegates insisted on the calling of an untramelled special session in the near future. Their antagonism to Baldwin's leadership was clear. There was little doubt that when they reconvened they would pass a resolution which would in effect be a humiliating and unprecedented vote of censure on their leader.[38]

At the same time, discontent amongst the parliamentary Party was reaching fever pitch. 'The Party is simply rotting before our eyes', Ormsby-Gore warned Salisbury.[39] After taking soundings in the Carlton Club, Croft told Neville Chamberlain that MPs of every shade of opinion confirmed 'the appalling change of feeling in the country in the last two months'.[40] Several of the most promising younger men were becoming mutinous. Most serious of all, this mood was matched amongst the former cabinet. Hoare, not easily rattled, confessed his apprehension that disaffection was 'moving so fast that unless something happens quickly, everything and everybody will collapse like a pack of cards'.[41] Austen Chamberlain intimated his willingness to bell the cat, and head a deputation of front-benchers which would tell Baldwin that it was time for him to go.[42]

To this seething cauldron was added a new initiative by Beaverbrook, who had decided finally on a complete break with Baldwin. The opportunity to strike a blow in the metropolitan territory so favourable to the Crusade was provided when Commodore Henry King, member for the safe seat of South Paddington, was drowned in a yachting accident in Cornwall at the end of August. In the ensuing by-election the reluctant official candidate was Sir Herbert Lidiard, chairman of the local Association for the past eighteen years. Bullied alternately by Beaverbrook and Neville Chamberlain, he veered erratically between endorsement of the Crusade and loyalty to Baldwin's leadership. The struggle for Lidiard's body, if not his soul, was won by Chamberlain in the last week of September, but the prize was a candidate fatally damaged by his own inconsistency, and now at odds with the fervent Crusaders within his own Association. The opportunity was irresistible, and, having secured Rothermere's support, Beaverbrook for the first time brought out a nominee of his own under the Crusade's banner.

Paradoxically, this attack strengthened Baldwin's crumbling position, for those in the Party who desired his departure did not wish to bend their knees to the press lords. Nevertheless, by the time Baldwin returned from his holiday at Aix on 28 September, the position had become so serious that Central Office was driven to the desperate straits of issuing a press release denying that he was about to resign. This statement also promised that the party leader would make a pro-

noucement on policy in the near future, and certainly before parliament reconvened on 28 October.[43] Clearly, a major initiative
would be required if Baldwin was to succeed in holding his party
together. There were many who feared that it was already too late,
and that even the boldest steps could not save his leadership.

Neville Chamberlain, whose position was almost as much at risk as
Baldwin's, had attempted to stem the tide in his leader's absence by
revealing his own advanced 'Unauthorised Programme'. The title
was a deliberate echo of his father's famous campaign of 1885, when
ironically he too had chafed under the leadership of a more popular
figure who was interested in political atmosphere and the broad sweep
of policy rather than in detailed formulations. In fact, Neville Chamberlain's policies were 'unauthorised' only in the sense that he had not
the power formally to commit the Party on any matter. The meat in
them came directly from the work done under his direction by the
Conservative Research Department over the summer months, and in
particular from the report on protection drawn up by Henry Brooke
of the new department's staff.[44] This document was to provide the
foundation of the policy which Chamberlain sought over the next few
weeks to get his colleagues to adopt. In mid-September he publicly
advocated an emergency tariff, a ten per cent import duty across the
board, in the belief that it would be heartily welcomed by the Party.[45]
Well placed as Party Chairman to gauge the seriousness of the
situation, he wanted to announce a major advance towards full
protection as soon as possible. Various methods were considered. The
idea of calling a meeting at which Baldwin would unveil the new
proposals was discarded as too risky given the present state of the
Party. Once the discussion began, there was no knowing where it
might stop. Eventually Chamberlain decided to draft an exchange of
letters between Baldwin and himself, in which the referendum would
be dropped. The emergency tariff would become the main plank of
the new platform, together with a quota system, rather than a tax, for
grain imports.

However, three potential stumbling blocks remained. Of these the
least important was the possibility of renewed opposition from the
Free Trade element, led by Winston Churchill. In view of the shift in
Party opinion, such a protest could if necessary be ignored. Two other
problems posed a more acute dilemma. On the one hand there was
anxiety that if Baldwin remained as leader, the new policy would turn
out to be a damp squib.[46] On the other hand, axing Baldwin and
replacing him with a more acceptable figure was impossible whilst the
fight raged at South Paddington. Such a move would not only be
hailed as a triumph for themselves by the press lords, but, even worse,
would be accepted as such by the public at large. Revulsion against
such subservience would also cause a further split in the Party. The

Business Committee met on 7 October to consider Neville Chamberlain's draft letters, but failed to resolve the problem. The mood of the meeting was 'profoundly uneasy', and the leadership were 'racking our brains to find some method of escape from a dangerous situation'.[47] Partly as a result of Churchill's objections, it was eventually decided to adjourn the discussion for a week. The pressures building up within the Party were so serious that they seemed, paradoxically, to have produced a state of paralysis, in which every option seemed likely only to cause further division. As the leadership were stuck with Baldwin and all his defects, they desperately needed some *deus ex machina* to transform the political picture.

The Business Committee would have clutched at straws; they were doubly fortunate to be thrown a lifebelt from outside the domestic British political arena. In the interval before they met again, a solution was providentially provided, as had earlier been hoped, by events at the Imperial Conference. On 8 October the Canadian Prime Minister, R.B. Bennett, declared that his country would be willing to operate a system of preferential tariffs throughout the empire, if only the mother country would meet them half way. The Labour Government, wedded to free trade, could not respond; but to Neville Chamberlain, it came as 'a truly Heaven-sent opportunity'.[48] It provided the pretext by which Party policy could leap-frog over all objections in a manner best fitting the Conservative Party's imperialist tradition. Furthermore, it avoided any appearance of being a result of, or surrender to, the attacks of the press barons, and bolstered Baldwin's dwindling prestige by appearing to be a great stroke of constructive leadership.[49] The very speed and efficiency with which the response to Bennett's offer was announced restored morale, renewed confidence, and pre-empted the counterstrokes of Beaverbrook and his allies. That the opportunity was seized so swiftly was largely the work of Neville Chamberlain, who reacted promptly on hearing of Bennett's declaration on the morning of 9 October. At once he threw all his energies into preparing a bold response, and bullied Baldwin into assenting to the statement, which was in the hands of the press by six o'clock that afternoon. Caution was put out of mind; the Party accepted the principle of imperial preference and at the next election would seek a mandate for a free hand to impose the necessary duties. The referendum was dead and buried.[50] This was to be the first of two stages on the road to rehabilitation. The press release of 9 October included the definite promise that Baldwin would announce full details of his response the following week. By this stratagem Chamberlain effectively pre-empted the discussions at the Business Committee's meeting of the 14th. On this occasion his draft was rubber stamped, and the effect of this second manifesto was further to restore the prestige of the leadership and the morale of their followers.

This was hardly surprising, for it gave them everything they wanted. Chamberlain himself acknowledged that 'nothing remains between us and the fullest possible policy of protection'. It was 'an amazing advance', even though it had been made at the eleventh hour.[51]

The broad centre of the Party was reassured, and the prospect of a serious split and the collapse of the Party receded even more quickly in October than it had materialised in September. The transformation was especially evident in those associations where dissent had been at boiling point. In all of these there was a retreat from the brink, and a turnover of majority opinion against the mood of September. Outspoken critics on local Executive Committees lapsed into silent acquiescence, or were reduced to an irrelevant minority.[52] Unity had been restored; the new policy was seen to be 'clear, definite, and acceptable'.[53] Most significant of all was the fact that this sentiment was echoed in a chorus of approval across the length and breadth of the nation, and from all types of constituency.[54] This was mirrored in the columns of the loyal Conservative press, even in the north, and amongst the parliamentary Party. The Chairman of the Party noted that 'all the information that comes to me indicates that the whole Party has been bolstered up and feels that it has a policy once more, while SB's personal position has been greatly strengthened'.[55] Indeed, for perhaps the first time since the passage of the Trades Disputes Act in 1927, Baldwin was firmly in tune with the views of his followers, rather than—as had been more usually the case during the last three years—lagging behind or directly contravening them.

In the light of this, the normal centripetal forces of solidarity and loyalty began to operate, producing a rally round the beleaguered leader in the second half of October. In the first instance, the free trade element in the Party swallowed the new policy with varying degrees of acquiescence.[56] The claims of Churchill's free food past took him to the brink of resignation from the Business Committee over the new departure, but he allowed himself to be prevailed upon not to rock the boat. Shaken by what had happened in Lancashire, Lord Derby still considered that the loss of confidence had become so great that Baldwin should retire. When the party leader summoned him to London and sought his opinion on 27 October, Derby told him so with unusual bluntness. However, Baldwin's nervous energy had been converted into a rediscovered self-confidence, which enabled him to shrug aside this unwelcome advice. The tariff reformers, having been at perhaps the nearest point they would ever come to throwing in their lot with Beaverbrook in despair, hastened back into line. Announcing that the main object had been achieved, Croft came out in support of the official candidate at South Paddington. Amery considered that now Baldwin had swallowed the essential point it was only fair that those who believed in the policy should back him.

Similar sentiments were felt by Beaverbrook's allies in the Crusade, Elibank and Melchett, and the effect was to take the wind out of its sails. Beaverbrook did not appreciate this, and became more and more outspokenly hostile in his speeches at South Paddington. The difference between the official line and that of the Crusade was now minimal, but Beaverbrook had no faith in the ability or willingness of the Conservative leadership to fight for their policy, and thus refused to disband his campaign. The inevitable consequence, astutely highlighted by Baldwin in an exchange of published letters, was to make it seem as if Beaverbrook was doing no more than satisfying a personal grudge. This appearance of vendetta became an advantage for Baldwin. The essential justification for Beaverbrook's factionalism had been removed by the leadership's adoption of a popular imperial policy. Continued hostility from the press lords could now be portrayed as a serious threat to the Party's chances of putting that policy into operation. Furthermore, their intransigence served to prove Baldwin's thesis at the June party meeting, and to reinforce his theme of hostility to supposed attempts at press dictatorship.

In this situation, the thoughts of the Party leaders naturally turned to capitalising on the improvement in their standing. Rumours of a demand from Gretton and the Diehards for another meeting of the Party had been in the air before Bennett's declaration. The leadership took the opportunity to turn this attack on its head, feeling strong enough to accede to the request, in the knowledge that in the changed mood of late October such a gathering would confirm, not destroy, Baldwin's position. Instead of isolating the leadership, the Diehards would isolate themselves. Bridgeman was the foremost advocate of calling a meeting as soon as possible, declaring 'while we are in the ascendant we ought to challenge any opposition in the Party', for he was convinced that 'the policy now produced will be endorsed by a large majority'.[57] Neville Chamberlain agreed with this strategy. He replied that a meeting, even one empowered to discuss the leadership, might be granted 'without any serious danger just now'.[58] Unaware of the extent to which they were playing into Baldwin's hands, the Gretton group made two false moves. A memorial sent by forty-seven MPs in the last week of October provided a peg upon which to hang the calling of the meeting, once again to be held at the Caxton Hall, for 30 October. The second tactical error made by the Diehards was to convene a pre-meeting cabal of some forty backbenchers on 28 October at the St. Stephen's Club, where a resolution critical of Baldwin was passed and leaked to the press. Even more embarassingly, its publication was accompanied by a highly inaccurate list of signatories, which included some loyal moderates who had not even been present, and who now hastened to make public their disavowals and condemnations.[59] The Diehards 'U-Boat tactics', seeking to pre-empt the Party's deliberations, produced a further revulsion of feeling in Baldwin's favour as the honest man under assault by devious and disreputable enemies.[60]

This was reflected by the tone of the meeting itself. On his entrance to the Caxton Hall on 30 October Baldwin received an immense ovation. He followed the carefully prepared strategy, confining himself to an exposition of the new policy and avoiding personalities. 'The position was quite different from what it was in the spring. The whole Party, wherever they find themselves—north, midlands, and south—have now got a basis to fight upon', declared Baldwin; 'our fiscal policy, in a word, is the policy of what has always been called throughout this year the policy of the free hand, and I ask this meeting to endorse that policy'.[61] It was an effective speech, and though not as great an oratorical effort as that delivered to the previous party meeting, it had more substance in policy, and therefore relied less on rhetoric and emotion. Above all, 'his manner was strong and his final words impressive'.[62] Inevitably, the motion approving his policy secured almost unanimous assent; only Beaverbrook, sitting alone in the body of the hall, raised his hand against. Having made his point, Baldwin then withdrew and the meeting turned to discuss the leadership question under the chairmanship of Salisbury.

Hailsham delivered the only effective speech during this debate, decisively exploiting the vulnerable role of the press in order to secure support for Baldwin. In contrast, the speeches made on the other side were of very poor quality. Gretton moved the resolution against Baldwin's leadership, but was 'extremely ineffective',[63] whilst the seconder, Kindersley, made 'a complete hash of his speech'.[64] The efforts of their supporters were even worse, culminating in a 'very queer' and 'quite wild' performance by Marjoribanks. One of the handful of young Diehards, he had been first elected to parliament the previous year as member for Eastbourne at the age of twenty-nine, partly through the local patronage of Hailsham, who was his step-father. Marjoribanks was brilliant but arrogant, and his outburst on this occasion was a symptom of the instability which led him finally to commit suicide in April 1932. Beaverbrook, spotted amongst the crowd, was greeted with hoots when he tried to speak, and could make no impression. The best speech from the rebels came from Croft, but characteristically he was 'too egotistical altogether'.[65] It was evident that, deprived of a clear justification over policy matters, the irreconcilable element was incapable of making a convincing case. Although the result of the final vote, with 462 votes for Baldwin and 116 against, revealed a larger hostile element than had been expected, even this was to some extent discounted because of the low personal or political standing of many of those who made up the minority. In Austen Chamberlain's analysis, it included 'the group habitually described as the Forty Thieves, hangers-on of business, not of the best type', as well as 'a good many old and disgruntled peers'.[66]

Victory produced a further bonus. The advances in policy proved sufficient to detach from Beaverbrook all the significant Conservative fellow-travellers, leaving him only the alliance with Rothermere. Amery was the first to respond, but when Baldwin clarified his policy a week later, he also met the requirements of both Melchett and Elibank. The latter was quite clear that any minor differences should now be discussed beneath the Conservative umbrella. To continue warfare in the new mood of Party unity would only alienate the very people who had hitherto looked favourably on the Crusade. Indeed, the more the press lords attacked Baldwin, the more firmly he was being established in the saddle. Distancing themselves publicly from Beaverbrook, Melchett and Elibank issued a press statement accepting the new policy. Croft also joined the chorus of appeals from the protectionist right, urging Beaverbrook to work within the Party for the success of its new platform. Even Hannon wavered, suggesting that the Crusade should adopt the Baldwin line, but continue as a separate campaigning machine. The convening of the party meeting for 30 October provided a solution to the dilemma faced by these Conservatives. The former dissidents responded to the Party's tradition of loyalty, by stating publicly that they would accept the verdict reached at the Caxton Hall. The divisions amongst the protectionists were made absolute by Beaverbrook's decision not to be bound by the result, despite attending the meeting. This only added further credence to Baldwin's denunciations of his political impossibility. The links between Beaverbrook and his allies were severed after October 1930. Correspondence with them ceased abruptly, and personal contacts also dwindled. In tactical terms, Beaverbrook was from now on beyond the pale, paying the price of rejecting the irksome, moderating advice of his Conservative sympathisers in favour of the intransigent admonitions of Rothermere. The victory of Beaverbrook's candidate, Vice-Admiral Taylor, at South Paddington on the day after the second Caxton Hall meeting was completely overshadowed by Baldwin's success. The peak of the Party crisis had passed, leaving the leadership shaken but unscathed.

It has been said that Baldwin was compelled to call both the party meetings of 1930 by the strength and force of the opposition to him.[67] In fact, the contrary is the case. When Gretton and the Diehards had demanded a meeting in November 1929, they were fobbed off. In reality, the party meetings were called by Baldwin to impose his will on the Party, and to bring dissent into the open at a time when it was at a temporarily low ebb.[68] The tactic was to make the hard core of irreconcilables reveal their limited support in the Party at large, and appear as the witting or unwitting dupes of the press lords. They were forced by the order and selection of motions to present themselves in a factious light, by seeming to be separated from the rest of the Party on the dubious grounds of the leader's personal characteristics, not the respectable grounds of policy.[69] Once the meetings are seen as the chosen weapon of the leadership, taking place on their timing, it is not surprising on the one hand that Baldwin triumphed at them, and on the other that such victories had little lasting value. The meetings were an artificial forum, and they failed to have a long-term impact because they were only effective in disguising the extent of anxiety in the Party. The voting figures did not show the large element of unsettled but not yet openly disloyal Conservatives, who felt both exposed to the pressure of the Crusade and uneasy about Baldwin's capacity as leader. Many such MPs and candidates, including some of the rising younger men, voted for Baldwin at the party meetings despite serious misgivings.[70] After each meeting the mood of confidence and consensus proved shortlived, not because of the activities of Beaverbrook, but because Baldwin failed to sustain the momentum of improvement by being more partisan and forceful in either the Commons or the country. Thus the doubts, dutifully suppressed in the face of the unacceptable press dictation highlighted at the meetings, were afterwards confirmed. On both occasions within a few months the situation reverted to being almost as dismal as it had been before. This factor was the reason why even the second Caxton Hall meeting was not the conclusive confrontation that the leadership had looked for, though it was the more productive of the two exercises in achieving some permanent reduction in the range and quantity of criticism.

The first meeting had been less successful, partly because on that occasion the official policy afforded little satisfaction south of the Trent, and partly because the meeting itself was turned by a more temporary appeal to the audience's emotions. Baldwin's trick of tarring Beaverbrook with Rothermere's brush, and playing the constitutional card, succeeded in the heat of the momentary anger over Rothermere's letter. However, it was not as effective in the long run as his own detestation of the press magnates may have led him to believe. Unlike Baldwin, many Conservatives made a distinction between the two men. Rothermere was loathed on grounds of personality and policy by almost all; but many Conservatives sympathised with Beaverbrook, and until the South Paddington by-election hoped to work with him. Furthermore, the first meeting was kept too much under the leadership's thumb. As a result, the dissidents were not convinced that the result was a genuine index of Party feeling, and they therefore refused to accept its verdict as final.

In this sense the second conclave was much more effective from the leadership's point of view. Baldwin was aided by Beaverbrook's

unrestrained antics in the South Paddington campaign, which provoked figures such as Hailsham, who was held in particular respect on
the right, to denounce the press lords with unusual vehemence.[71] The
direct effect of Beaverbrook's attack was to shore up Baldwin's
position and make it all the more difficult for figures such as Derby to
desert him.[72] The crucial achievement of the second Caxton Hall
meeting lay in convincing the most influential dissident leaders, such as
Croft and Elibank, that they should accept its decision as binding; the
minority promised to accede to the majority verdict. This was secured
by an appeal to the spirit of public school fair play, and by allowing the
contest to take place according to the dissidents' own rules. They were
assured a fair opportunity to make their case, and they were to be
allowed all the procedural advantages in terms of speaking order, and
secret ballot, that could reasonably be claimed.[73] However, the
leadership did cover their bets on both occasions by including the
prospective candidates amongst those entitled to attend. These men
and women, mainly from the marginal seats of the midlands, the
industrial areas of the north, and the Celtic fringe, had a greater vested
interest in avoiding electorally extreme positions. The areas which
they sought to represent were those where Baldwin's personal appeal
and the instinctive dislike of food taxes were both more considerable
forces amongst the ordinary voters than elsewhere.[74]

Baldwin was also on firmer ground on the second occasion in
securing acceptance of the policy first, seemingly to concede that the
question of leadership was a separate matter and not bound up in the
policy decision. Of course, by divorcing the objection to his policy
from that to his person, Baldwin actually made the task of his critics
much more difficult.[75] It became impossible because of the careful
timing of the gathering, which was fixed for the day before the poll at
South Paddington. This was not because of any analogy with the
effects of the Newport by-election on the Carlton Club meeting of
1922, but in order to drive home the point that to remove Baldwin
whilst he was actually under the most overt press attack would lay the
Party open to the charge of being subservient to the press.[76] It was this
appeal to their communal self-respect, even more than for sympathy
with Baldwin, which produced the marked reaction of personal
hostility to Beaverbrook from the floor of the meeting. As the decision
of the second Caxton Hall meeting was a foregone conclusion under
these circumstances, the manoeuvre of calling it involved few risks and
offered significant gains. Beaverbrook himself had no doubts before
the meeting that Baldwin would get his vote of confidence.[77]
Baldwin's procedural concessions did not reflect any weakness in his
position; on the contrary, they reflected its strength and his confidence
in the aftermath of the favourable reaction to his having finally grasped
the 'free hand'.

The verdict of the party meetings also settled another issue in dispute—the very distribution of power in the Party. On several occasions between the defeat of May 1929 and November 1930 dissatisfaction at the grass-roots with Party policy past, present, and future, had led inevitably to demands for a dominant voice in the formulation of that policy. These were moving from the implicit to the dangerously explicit. If unsatisfied, they might have led either to a pre-emptive coup by the backbenchers along the lines of 1922, or to open demands for executive power to rest with the National Union and not the front bench, or even both. The decisiveness of the response to Bennett's offer in October 1930 defused this danger as it was becoming most serious, whilst at the same time satisfying the rank and file on policy. There is no doubt that the leaders conceded a good deal to retain control, but at the end of the day their position was preserved. Neville Chamberlain's greatest relief was reserved for the fact that after all the October meeting showed no disposition to question 'that decisions on policy are made by the Leader, after taking such advice as he chooses'; and that these 'require no endorsement from any body representing the Party in any way before becoming binding'.[78] Autocratic oligarchic control remained, and was deferentially received. This was to prove a factor of considerable importance in the very different problems that were to be faced by Baldwin in 1931: in dealing with the emerging revolt over India in January and February; in defeating the final assault on his position in March; and in responding to the national crisis of August. It is to the first of these themes, the India question, that attention must now be turned.

CHAPTER 6

Churchill and India

Protection was not the only great issue to cause serious divisions within the Conservative Party. Though the battle over Empire Free Trade dominated the foreground of Conservative politics from July 1929 to November 1930, it did not completely relegate to the background another crucial question concerning the continuance of Britain as a great power in both political and economic terms. This was the future of the British Raj in India, and degree of power to be accorded to the native population. The fate of the British Empire revolved around the relationship of the mother country with the two most important constituent elements within the empire. These were firstly the Dominions, colonies settled by a white immigrant population and now essentially self-governing, and secondly the jewel in the crown of empire: India. Apart from these two, the remainder of the British Empire consisted of places important only for their role in protecting the routes to India, of which Egypt was by far the most significant; the former German colonies and the mandates; territories of little value acquired in the nineteenth century more by accident than design in the footsteps of missionaries or trading companies; and a rag-bag of trophies from the mercantilist wars of the eighteenth century which since then had sunk into economic decay. At this time politicians were acutely aware of being at a vital crossroads for the future of both nation and empire. Decisions of far-reaching significance affecting both the essential components of the empire could no longer be avoided.

Pride and concern about the empire was the motive force behind the involvement of many, if not most, Conservatives in active politics at every level. But this common ground obscured a wide range of different attitudes and priorities. Conservative parliamentarians ranged from those at one extreme, like Amery and Neville Chamberlain, keen on the development of Africa and the white Dominions, to those such as Churchill who had a romantic attachment to the mystique of the Indian empire but who doubted the practicality of their colleagues emphasis on 'constructive imperialism'. The issue of protection, in its guise of imperial preference, mattered to this imperialist sentiment within the Conservative Party because it was the lynch-pin of their aspirations for uniting the empire on an economic basis, from which would follow a strengthening of political and sentimental ties. Joseph Chamberlain had first promoted tariff reform in 1903 as the antidote to the fissiparous tendencies of the dominions. Partly, if not exclusively, because of this protection had become the fervently-held talisman of many Conservative activists, despite all the ensuing electoral setbacks. The battle over tariff reform has already been examined. Attention must now be directed to the other great question, the future constitutional development of India, for dissension over the best response to this was to cause bitter divisions within the Conservative ranks. This was briefly demonstrated in the furore over the Irwin Declaration in November 1929, but India then took a back seat to the struggle over protection throughout the following year. However, at the same time as the wind was taken out of Beaverbrook's sails by the events of October 1930, divisions over India re-emerged in a new and more acute form. In the early months of 1931, both the imperial themes running in tandem were to be the source of further internal crises.

The existing legislation on the internal government of India, the Montagu-Chelmsford Act of 1921, was due for review at the end of the 1920s. Under its provisions a Statutory Commission, chaired by the leading Liberal MP Sir John Simon, had been set up in 1928 to investigate and recommend the next stages of constitutional development. Since the First World War a considerable agitation had developed in India for 'swaraj', or self-rule. Gandhi had emerged as one of the most prominent leaders of this campaign, which culminated in not only civil disobedience and boycotting but also violence and disorder during the visit of Simon's Commission to the subcontinent. Tensions continued to mount after the Commission's members returned home. Before they could present their report, the question was suddenly thrust to the forefront of British politics as a result of the Irwin Declaration. This was a formal statement made on 31 October 1929 by Lord Irwin, later first Earl of Halifax, a widely respected Conservative Cabinet Minister whom Baldwin had appointed to the Viceroyalty in 1925. The Declaration was not, of course, Irwin's alone; but he was working in such close harmony and sympathy with the Labour government that some Conservatives were beginning to regard him with suspicion and despair. The pronouncement was intended to pacify native opinion by accepting that India should evolve towards eventual Dominion status.

Irwin had come to the conclusion that this move was the minimum necessary to avoid serious civil disturbance, and had discussed his ideas with leading Conservatives whilst home on leave in the summer of 1929. He laid much emphasis on the need for securing domestic unanimity. Even before the 1929 election Baldwin had foreseen that India would be a crucial issue in the next parliament, and had privately indicated his support. He was in any case sympathetic to the proposal: he admired Irwin personally, and trusted his motives as well as his judgment.[1] But the matter was complicated by the fact that the Simon Commission had not yet reported. Furthermore, the crucial decisions on the Declaration were taken in October 1929 during the parliamentary recess with the principals out of close contact with each other: MacDonald was in the United States, and Baldwin as usual was holidaying at Aix-les-Bains. On his journey home Baldwin was met at Bourges by an emissary from the India Office with a copy of the proposed statement. A series of misunderstandings resulted from this meeting. While supporting Irwin, Baldwin pointed out that in the absence of his colleagues his approval could only be given in a personal capacity. There was confusion over the extent to which Simon had been consulted and whether his attitude was favourable. Baldwin's assent was conditional on the approval of Simon and the Commission, and technically did not commit his party.[2] However, the government did not appreciate these reservations. At the same time Baldwin either misunderstood, or was misinformed of, the views of the Simon Commission, and as a result thought that they had acquiesced in the new initiative.

After Baldwin's return, rumours based on the government's interpretation of his promise resulted in a stormy session of the shadow cabinet in the last week of October. Few of those present were content either with Irwin's proposed statement or with the fact that the Party's hands were largely tied by Baldwin's commitment, even if it had been only personal. In this sense the incident is a clear indication of the enormous personal power of the Party leader, for Baldwin's decision gave his followers little room for manoeuvre by making the issue as much one of confidence in himself as leader as of support for Irwin. At the same time Baldwin's caveat allowed him an avenue for retreat should he be unable to carry his party, for he could fall back on the defence that his views had been private ones, and drop them for a more cautious policy. In fact, he executed a combination of both manoeuvres. Having taken the temperature of his colleagues at the shadow cabinet meeting, he allowed Austen Chamberlain to draft a letter to the government which underlined the qualifications he had made at Bourges.[3] This appeased his colleagues, and preserved a facade of Party unity over India, which was Baldwin's real desire. The misunderstandings at Bourges undermined confidence in Baldwin's capacity, and the policy accepted there produced a period of strain within the Party. Nevertheless, Baldwin succeeded in holding the Conservatives to a line of policy that would have been almost unthinkable six months previously.

There can be no doubt that the Declaration caused the greatest misgivings in Conservative circles. Hoare, one of the few on the front bench to support Irwin's policy, admitted that 'scarcely anyone in the Party liked it' and 'the Diehards were much upset'.[4] However, the initial onslaught came from other quarters. The first of these was a group within the leadership with some experience of Indian affairs, who were by coincidence the same personalities identified with the heyday of the Lloyd George coalition: Austen Chamberlain, Winston Churchill, and Lord Birkenhead. The fact that the second source of criticism came from Lloyd George and from the liberal leader in the upper house and Irwin's predecessor as Viceroy, Lord Reading, lent substance to fears of a coalitionist intrigue. The most serious attack of all came from the *Daily Mail*, which exposed the events at Bourges in an article entitled 'Baldwin's Crowning Blunder'. This shook the Party's confidence with its specific, and presumably leaked, allegations that Baldwin had committed the Party without consultations or reservations to the Irwinite line. The action of the *Daily Mail* in making the central issue the manner of Baldwin's commitment, more than the validity or otherwise of the policy he had supported, was a grave tactical error. These dramatic charges cut across the more weighty criticisms of Reading, Birkenhead, and the rest of the Conservative press.[5] The attack from Rothermere had the effect of pushing the Party together in a reflex reaction of solidarity against outsiders.[6] In fact, the *Daily Mail*'s charges were refutable by Baldwin in the letter, if not in spirit. Thus the assault was blocked at the outset.

The Commons debate on the Irwin Declaration was a success for Baldwin, who produced one of his occasional flights of oratory for the occasion, translating the debate to 'an unusually high level'.[7] Despite this, there was almost a serious split, for the dissident ex-coalitionists appeared to be preparing to lead the Diehards into the same hostile lobby as Lloyd George if a division had been called. In the event this was avoided, partly because the Party instinctively shrank back from open disunity. There was also widespread suspicion among MPs that the manoeuvre was designed to bring back the old coalitionist alliance and reverse the verdict of 1922.[8] From this high point the crisis over the Irwin Declaration receded, leaving the Conservative Party committed to the Labour government's policy of summoning a Round Table Conference to discuss Indian devolution, yet without there being 'any permanent effect' upon the Party.[9] Baldwin succeeded in keeping discontent under control by exploiting the loyalty owed to the Party leader, the fear of coalitionist intrigue, and the instinctive aversion to disunity. Underlying this, however, was evidence that the anxieties over India were both real and widespread, with 'considerable unrest among the Diehard element', and even the moderate backbenchers were in an uneasy frame of mind.[10] Baldwin had secured his position, but only in the first engagement of a long campaign.

Baldwin had resisted the pressure from within his party for protection for obvious reasons of pragmatism, but it is less clear why he should have allowed rifts to open up over India. The problems which wracked the Conservative Party on this issue during the next six years could have been avoided if Baldwin had not actively wished to follow the spirit, if not always the letter, of Irwin's calculatedly generous approach. Baldwin personalised politics, and no doubt a good deal of his receptiveness to Irwin's ideas stemmed from his regard for Irwin himself. But Baldwin had never been hostile to imperial reform; though he certainly never intended imperial dismantlement. Together with many of his generation, the example of Ireland was constantly in his mind. Nor should it be forgotten that Baldwin was not alone among Conservative leaders in supporting Irwin's policy. As with protection, he sought always to maintain consensus in the leadership. If any colleagues were lost overboard, they were to be as few in number as possible. This not only reduced the damage, it also kept the dissidents, Amery on tariffs or Churchill on India, effectively isolated. Apart from Churchill, and to a much lesser extent Salisbury and Austen Chamberlain, none of the Conservative front bench saw any future in simple resistance. Baldwin came to feel this strongly, and it is clear that the line he took on India was the result of views he sincerely and deeply held, and went far beyond mere calculations of political or electoral advantage. It was the issue upon which he was willing to stake his reputation and sacrifice his career. But, being a cautious politician, he preferred to carry his followers for the best approximation to his views that he could, rather than to exit in high but futile drama.

Baldwin felt his duty as Conservative leader strongly, and wanted to preserve unity whilst, in almost patronising fashion, he sought to educate his party. He feared that the Party might become fossilised in a posture of sterile reaction, from which it might take years to recover. Thus Baldwin was also concerned in the debate over India to maintain the credibility of Conservatism as an alternative government for the empire which could be trusted to be forward-looking but not foolishly idealistic. At the same time, he saw the consensus between the parties on India to be highly desirable in the higher imperial interest; once again, the warning of the Irish question was before him. Baldwin's aim of maintaining public unity at home was not without support. It appealed to the Party's own self-image that it 'would approach the position solely from the point of view of the good of the empire as a whole, and in particular India'.[11] Of course, one section of the Party fundamentally disagreed that the bipartisan approach was ultimately in the interests of the empire—but there was enough solid evidence to suggest otherwise to convince not only the Irwinites but also the uncertain but crucial moderates. Hailsham, who carried much weight with the Party's right-of-centre, accepted the need to keep public opinion at home united, and was realistically aware of the dangers of striking out on a hard-line policy. For him, as for most Conservatives, the crucial questions concerned the necessary safeguards, in the areas of foreign and defence policy in particular, which would have to be built into any Indian constitution.[12] Thus the debates of the next five years revolved around this issue of safeguards, leaving those who resisted any discussion of further advance for India as an excluded and powerless fringe.

The moderate Conservative line on India became synonymous with Sir Samuel Hoare. Hoare is often wrongly considered to have been a liberal or radical figure in Conservative terms over India, but in fact this crucial step in his career was based upon a careful enunciation of the median position within the Party. He aimed to carry the right with him in a policy of cautious advance. As early as December 1929 Hoare was determined to carve out a niche for himself as the future Conservative Secretary of State for India. In his public utterances he was careful to admit to 'doubts and fears' over India, and to seeking to put 'a brake on demands for ill-considered advance'.[13] At the same time it is clear that he sincerely respected Irwin's viewpoint, even if he did not think it completely practical politics, and sought to keep in close contact with the Viceroy. Between 1929 and 1931 Hoare gradually took over the front bench spokesmanship on India, a position which both enhanced and reflected his growing stature within the Party.[14] Significantly, together with other ambitious younger figures, he chose to follow the path of promotion by adhering to orthodoxy, rather than rebelling against it. If in this strategy there was a strong element of ambition, it was a drive that was to prove of inestimable value in assisting Baldwin to maintain his hold on the Party.

India was pushed from the centre of the political stage after the Irwin Declaration by other issues—for the Conservative Party in particular by Beaverbrook's campaign—until the convening in London of the Round Table Conference almost a year later. In between there was a minor crisis over Gandhi's salt campaign in March 1930 but the combination of firm action by the Indian authorities with a carefully-managed debate in the Commons, in which backbench MPs were able to express their concern, ensured acceptance of Hoare's argument that this event should not deflect the agreed programme. This incident underlined the trend of the intervening year, during which the balance of forces within the Party tilted slowly but decisively in favour of the Baldwin–Irwin line. The cause of this change was the gradual commitment of the Party to a bipartisan policy on India. The Labour government were firmly behind the Viceroy's approach, and this policy was also consistently to receive the support of Lloyd George and the Liberals, despite a flurry of uncertainty in the debate on the Irwin Declaration itself. During the summer months of 1930 the Conservative leaders acted as a brake on Irwin's desire to step up the pace of political development in India, but they would not repudiate him.[15] This consensus had the effect of removing India from the arena of normal party strife. In as far as it could be a political question at all, it became from November 1929 a question within the Conservative Party, in which a numerically small and poorly led Diehard group challenged the wisdom of the front bench. The consequence was to press the centre of the Party into supporting Baldwin's line. He retained this crucial support during the following six years of dissension within the Conservative ranks over India, although on occasion he came close to losing it. Decisions over Indian policy were taken in an atmosphere of co-operation between the front benches. Lord Hugh Cecil commented:[16]

> The main reality is that the decision about Indian Government will be taken here in England; and that the real sovereignty of India lies here . . . I suppose if ten persons or thereabouts on Front Benches come to any decision about India, that decision will in fact operate. No doubt public opinion on some questions greatly influences and sometimes overbears Front Benchdom: but at present, at any rate, public opinion is not excited.

No major politician questioned this analysis, for it was the aim and intention of Winston Churchill, the only important front bench rebel against the bipartisan line, to arouse the sleeping lion of British imperial sentiment, as the only available means of breaking the solidarity of the parliamentary consensus over India.

In the year between the Irwin Declaration and the Round Table Conference, Churchill was a politician in decline, looking for an issue with which to revive his career. He was unpopular with both his colleagues in the shadow cabinet and with the backbenchers. Nor had his term as Chancellor of the Exchequer in the previous Conservative government endeared him to the rank and file. That government had failed to produce the cuts in expenditure expected of it, and the derating scheme with which Churchill was strongly identified had been an electoral disaster. Above all, the presence at the Treasury of a committed free trader was believed to have blocked all initiatives for protection.[17] Throughout 1929 and 1930 Churchill was still considered to be acting as a barrier to imperial preference. Thus he was blamed both for the election defeat, and for splitting the Party over tariffs in 1930.[18] In addition to his anomalous position as a Conservative free-trader whilst tariff reform sentiment was once again enjoying a heyday in the Party, Churchill was widely mistrusted for other reasons. His desertion of the Conservative Party over tariff reform in the Edwardian era, and his transmutation into a combative leading figure in Asquith's Liberal cabinet, could never be forgotten, and barely forgiven, by loyal Conservatives. Combined with this legacy from the bitter heights of pre-war politics were the doubts over his impetuosity and judgement raised by his conduct in the early years of the war, and in particular by the seige of Antwerp and the Dardanelles campaign. His coalitionist past was another sore spot which he exacerbated by pushing the idea of alliance with Lloyd George after the 1929 election. Churchill was incapable of discretion, and was widely thought to be working hand-in-glove with Lloyd George, 'obsessed with the idea of another Coalition', even by some who knew him well personally.[19] Whatever Churchill's motivation, the concept was hardly practical politics in light of the backbenchers' attitude towards Lloyd George. A further cause of Churchill's unpopularity was the widely-held—indeed almost synonymous—view that he was ambitious to reach the top of the greasy pole regardless of the cost to consistency or loyalty. Thus was Churchill discredited, with 'very little following' in the House, and 'most unpopular in the country', a political giant thought to be nearing the end of his career.[20] On top of this, he performed unsatisfactorily in the Commons in the summer of 1929, revealing himself to be surprisingly poor at opposition as well as being frequently absent from the chamber. Churchill also suffered from being one of the most prominent targets of the campaign against the continued presence of the 'Old Gang' of Party leaders during 1930. Thus, despite having been Chancellor—though not second man in the leadership—for the previous five years, the period of opposition saw Churchill at one of the lowest points of his career, depressed about his position, and searching for something new to bring him back into the limelight.[21]

The emergence of the tariff issue as the dominant theme in Conservative politics between October 1929 and October 1930 was a further problem for Churchill, for it was the one issue which he could not take up with credibility. At the height of the tariff crisis in September 1930 Churchill himself acknowledged that the growth of Beaverbrook's influence was 'almost exactly proportionate to the diminution of mine'.[22] The anti-tariff fight did not attract him, for it cast him in the role of a rebel not only against the leadership—which alone would not have prevented him—but also against the deeply expressed instincts of the Party grassroots. It would have been a futile gesture, and Churchill had little desire to go into the political wilderness. His heart had gone out of the defence of free trade, and he reluctantly acquiesced in each step on the road back to a 'whole-hog' tariff policy. Under pressure from the Crusade in his own Essex constituency he only attempted to retain some appearance of consistency with the young free trader of 1903.[23] At the same time he also relinquished his aspirations for an alliance with the Liberals, accepting that coalitionism was truly dead when Lloyd George aligned his party in support of the Labour administration in 1930.

Churchill occupied from 1924 to 1930 a political half-way house between his radical past and his imperial instincts, a position in which the traditional role of the Chancellor as a critic rather than an initiator had fixed him for the duration of the Baldwin government. Only after 1930 did Churchill begin to concentrate his attention on the threats to the position of Britain and her empire in the world. He sought a great imperial issue upon which he could rouse not merely the Party, but also the nation, from decadence. In this the strongest influence was his relationship with Birkenhead, who brought out the Diehard in him on India in particular. Birkenhead's sudden death in 1930 left his friend fixed upon a course of confrontation, yet without a steadying influence. Churchill developed from this point the Diehard theme that dominated his career through the 1930s. The revolt over India, the campaign for rearmament, and the support of Edward VIII in the abdication crisis were all of a piece with this. The first ventures Churchill made down this path were his opposition to the official line on Egypt in 1929 and to the London Naval Treaty in the spring of 1930. These prologues were swiftly overshadowed by the question of India.

Winston Churchill, was a curious and complex political character. It is too simple to say that he took up the India question in order to restore his personal fortunes, or that he did so only out of concern for the future of the British people. Both factors influenced his actions, and the truth lies in between. The area of debate concerns how large a part each played in making up the whole.[24] There is no doubt that, tactically, Churchill had much to gain and little to lose from rebellion—he expected to be dropped from the next Conservative cabinet.[25] His only defence was to improve his support within the Party, and in mid-1930 the Diehards, alienated from Baldwin's leadership and in tune with Churchill's imperialism, seemed to be natural allies. This does not mean that he plotted to oust Baldwin as leader—his position was far too weak for such pretensions. It only meant that the ties which had bound him to the leadership had now all fallen away. Equally it is evident that the prospects of empire, and above all of India, stirred his blood. Far from being a cunning patient intriguer, he was an impulsive romantic enthusiast, and thus reacted to the imperial peril almost by instinct. Although his imperialism did not as with other Conservatives find its expression through advocacy of preferential tariffs, it was as ardently felt. Furthermore, Churchill had a deep personal sense of history and of destiny. Not only had his revered father, Lord Randolph Churchill, once held office as Secretary of State for India, but he himself had many stirring memories of his service as a young subaltern on the North West frontier in the 1890s. It was this vision of India which remained fixed in his mind. The British imperial mission struck a chord in the heart of his being, with the result that any apparent attempts to reduce this role offended against all his patriotic pride. In fact, Churchill had been unhappy over the Montagu-Chelmsford reforms in 1921, feeling strongly that self-government for India was a dangerous delusion. He accepted the rhetoric of the imperial dimension of the national crisis in 1929–1931, and was one of the few first-rank politicians to place it above the domestic sphere in importance. Churchill's political stance was clear: he was talking the language of national revivalism.[26] All that can be said with regard to motivation is to recognise the genuine element of concern over Indian policy, and the fact that on this occasion Churchill was vulnerable and had little to lose. He was no longer confined by any claims of collective responsibility or by the attractions and preoccupations of high office, but instead was a man searching for a political *raison d'etre*.

His fears over British policy in India thus claimed his full attention and his crusading spirit, coinciding with his self-image as a man of destiny who would save the empire. Tactical reasons alone are not sufficient explanation of his conduct, for he had always previously risen through the approval of his leader—Asquith in 1908–1914, Lloyd George in 1917–1922, and finally Baldwin in 1924. Furthermore his previous experience at rebellion, against Balfour in 1902–1903, was not a happy augury of success. But Churchill had never regarded Baldwin as his better, either in experience or in ability. Churchill believed himself to be better fitted to provide leadership in an era of national crisis, and Baldwin was all the more irksome as the barrier to this natural ambition. It was hardly surprising that Churchill came to the position of regarding Baldwin and his close circle of colleagues as weak and small men who must be swept away before their muddled stewardship should bring irretrievable ruin.[27] Like Beaverbrook, however, to do this was to personalise the issues in a way few Conservatives cared for. Furthermore, however sincere the impulse or wholehearted the execution, there were too many sceptics unconvinced by Churchill's Diehard stand to enlist under his banner.

Churchill was only the most vocal figure in a spectrum of dissent over India which spanned the whole Party. Within the leadership, protests came originally from three previous Conservative Secretaries of State for India: the Earl of Birkenhead, Earl Peel, and Austen Chamberlain. Of these, the former's attack at the time of the Irwin declaration was the most outspoken, but even before his early death in 1930 Birkenhead was a discredited and declining force. Austen Chamberlain carried more weight, and although more temperate in his criticism, was equally pessimistic in outlook.[28] Ironically, he was himself barred from leading the Conservative delegation to the Round Table Conference. The reason for this was not that he was too rigid on India, but fears (dating from the Irish negotiations of 1921) that he would concede too much. This veto was applied by Salisbury, who was the most important amongst those in the leadership wishing to maintain the *status quo* in India. Salisbury's resignation in 1931 as leader in the Lords resulted more from the conflict between his loyalty to Baldwin and his views over India, than the publicly announced reason of poor health.[29] The Party leadership fell into three camps: the first of which was the small but politically significant group strongly opposed to Irwin's policy, and only restrained by friendship for Irwin and loyalty to the Party and its leader. The uncommitted middle group was the most numerous, comprising individuals ranging from the sceptical Hailsham and Derby to those such as Cunliffe-Lister and Neville Chamberlain who were mainly immersed in domestic matters. The final element were the supporters of Irwin's line, such as Davidson, Amery, and Hoare, to whose small number was added the compensating weight of Baldwin himself.

There was also considerable anxiety on the backbenches. This found a forum in the Party's own India Committee, despite the fact that such backbench bodies were aimed more at containing criticism than expressing it. The chairman, Wardlaw-Milne, was a loyalist who sought to minimise divisions by taking a middle line between Irwinism and the Diehards. It was from the latter that the most consistent rebellion came, though the danger could only become serious if this group of some fifty MPs could swing the centre of the Party to their way of thinking. The logic of the Diehard mind was expressed by the Member for Lewes, Admiral Beamish, who confessed to 'an innate and strong feeling of racial difference and superiority' after meeting with Gandhi. In his opinion India if left to itself would 'dissolve into anarchy, bloodshed, and degradation'. The British had conquered India and developed it, introducing peace, contentment, and progress. The conclusion drawn from this was held with a simple but fervent faith: 'we have a right and duty to remain and to rule wisely and firmly. Let us do so, come what may'.[30] However, many Diehards, prominent amongst whom was Croft, placed the tariff issue foremost on their political agenda in 1929–1931, and only turned their full energies to the question of India after the achievement of protection at the Imperial Conference held in Ottawa in 1932. This was one reason for the severity of the struggle between 1933 and 1935, despite the fact that the decisive phase had occurred earlier, during this period in opposition. The Diehards lost their chance to capture the hearts and minds of the majority in the Party before the National Government was formed in August 1931. Thereafter they formed a perpetual minority, whose bitterness reflected their isolation and still further diminished the likelihood of securing wider support.

Parallel but not identical with the Diehard opposition were the fears expressed by many of those connected with the Indian services. Retired Indian civil servants and army or police officers were often active figures in their local Conservative associations.[31] This was particularly the case in the seaside resort towns, the London suburbs, and the rural south of England. The former governors of the Indian provinces were the most prominent examples of this type, and they provided the detailed critique upon which the Diehard counter-attack was based. Amongst these the most important figure was Lord Lloyd of Dolobran, a former governor of Bengal, and a Diehard martyr since the incoming Labour government had forced his resignation from the High Commissionership in Egypt in the summer of 1929. Lloyd was not a Diehard as such, and accepted that 'one must face realities'. His concern centred on the crucial question of safeguards, and that nothing should further weaken the central authority.[32] Irwin's declaration seemed to him to imperil this crucial need for security, and Lloyd began a campaign to build up the forces of resistance, though remaining under the umbrella of the Conservative Party. As Dawson noted, the consequence by March 1931 was 'a real cleavage in the Conservative Party on the subject of India'.[33] The critics were supported by influential right-of-centre newspapers and found an echo in certain elements among the Party activists. Rothermere's *Daily Mail* was giving priority to the India issue over Empire Free Trade from the end of 1930, and had some influence amongst Conservative voters in the home counties. Both the *Daily Telegraph* and the *Morning Post* wavered towards the Diehard stance. Only *The Times*, under the editorship of Geoffrey Dawson, another friend and admirer of Irwin, could be said to have been remotely enthusiastic for Baldwin's line. Equally anxious and equally hostile were two important economic interest-groups identified with the Conservative Party: the textile industry of Lancashire and the commercial concerns of the City.[34] The Diehard strategy was focused upon capturing these key regions of Conservative support, as the means of stampeding the Party.[35] The India rebels did not amount to a majority in any section of the Party. Nor yet were the issues clear upon which such a division might be taken one way or the other by the crucial silent majority of uncommitted moderates in the local Associations and on the backbenches. Taken as a whole, the India revolt was a potentially formidable combination of forces, but it remained to be seen if the dissidents could overcome their loyalties and their differences and overturn the bipartisan approach. To do so they would have both to retain their own conviction, as well as convincing others, that in the crises facing the nation, the imperial danger took precedence over domestic anxieties.

The alarm over the Irwin declaration had subsided by the middle of 1930 into a period of calm before the expected storms of the Round Table Conference. In this atmosphere the Simon Report was looked upon as the potential foundation for a reasoned opposition to dominion status. The report was published at the end of June and at first appeared to fulfil this function. However, the acceptance of the report by Conservative opinion transformed it from the maximum forward position into the minimum. Instead of focusing the energies of resistance against the considerable advances advocated by the Commission, the right wing seized gratefully on the fact that it stopped well short of Irwin's statement, and thus swallowed it whole.[36] This unconscious advance was to leave the Diehards in a poor tactical position when the Round Table Conference opened. Their resistance was further undermined by the involvement of a Conservative delegation in the Conference itself. Originally this had been welcomed by those uneasy over the sudden quickening of the pace, as a potential brake on the progress of the Conference and upon the government's policy. Party feeling expressed through the backbench India Committee was overwhelmingly in favour of insisting upon all-party membership of the Conference. Indeed, fears of exclusion had put the Party into a mood of nervous suspicion.[37]

The inevitable result of attending was to involve the Conservative Party in the decisions taken at the Conference, thus effectively curtailing its freedom to adopt any position of outright dissent. This was not surprising, given the careful composition of the Conservative delegation. It reflected the range of opinion in the Party, but excluded any out-and-out Diehard, and was dominated by Hoare. The latter, although representative of the left of centre, conducted himself deliberately in such a way as to contain the anxieties of the Diehards for as long as possible. The policy Hoare backed to ensure that this need not be incompatible with support for Irwin was federalism. This would give responsible government in the provinces, but the Viceroy would retain important safeguards over 'imperial' matters: in particular, the judiciary and police, and foreign and defence policy. Here was an essential difference from the precedent of Irish Home Rule. The merits of this cautious forward policy became apparent soon after the Conference discussions began on 17 November 1930. The decision of the most naturally conservative native element, the Indian princely states, to favour a federal constitution for all India, produced a new situation but did not alarm the mass of Conservatives. However, by knocking away one of the main props of the Diehard case, this rapid progress first took them unawares, and then stampeded them into the conclusion that open resistance was now imperative on the part of British Conservatism, in the light of the collapse of Indian conservatism. For this reason dissension in the Party was at the same time reduced in extent by the Round Table Conference and yet amongst the Diehards increased in intensity to the point of becoming an open rift. The outbreak of the India revolt was a direct result of the success of the bipartisan policy at the Round Table Conference.

Expressions of unrest had been appearing throughout the second half of 1930. In July Lord Lloyd made his first public speech against the official policy, and not long afterwards the Indian Empire Society was established to act as a pressure group, and to co-ordinate the campaign. Churchill converged with this movement during the late summer, symbolically delivering a critical oration at Carson's home in Thanet on 20 August. Churchill's reluctance to come to an open break was eroded by his growing conviction that India was being abandoned as a result of a mistaken policy of appeasement, and his unhappiness with the forward moves on tariff policy. On 14 October, the same day that he almost resigned from the shadow cabinet over protection, Churchill also formally joined the Indian Empire Society. The pace of events at the Round Table Conference stoked the fires of a campaign against further devolution. Thus on 12 December 1930 Churchill spoke at the first public meeting organised by the Indian Empire Society, setting the keynote of their campaign by ascribing the present difficulties to a loss of British will to rule. His audience was left to draw the conclusion that the remedy lay as much in assertiveness at Westminster as in New Delhi. By the end of the first session of the Round Table Conference on 19 January 1931, Churchill had established his credentials as the leading critic of Irwinism.

The period following the adjournment of the Conference in January was regarded on all sides as being of crucial importance. The opponents of devolution sought to convert parliament to their viewpoint before the Conference reconvened for its second session, and thus block any further progress. The first stage of this effort came when the House of Commons debated the Conference on 26 January 1931. Churchill opened with a vigorous speech, which for the first time attracted the approval of many doubtful backbenchers for a position which was essentially 'an indictment of all advance in India'.[38] But it was Baldwin's response that provoked a crisis in the Party over India. Baldwin abandoned the cautious line in which Hoare had been assiduously coaching him, and spoke instead on the spur of the moment, casting aside his notes. In distancing himself from

Churchill's views Baldwin veered dangerously to the left, and his speech, though cheered by the Labour members, met with an ominous silence from the Conservative benches.[39] The immediate result of this was Churchill's resignation from the shadow cabinet on the following day; a decision which took him into the wilderness for the rest of the decade.

The peak of the crisis over India came in the month after 9 February, when Baldwin capped the damage done in the previous debate with an unconvincing address to the Party's India Committee. The traumas of February were exacerbated by the decision of the Viceroy to release Gandhi from jail and negotiate with him—an action which crystallised fears of British degeneracy. Baldwin himself acknowledged that these talks had caused great anxiety in the Party.[40] Support for Irwin in the National Union briefly crumbled. On 24 February for the first time ever Churchill attended a meeting of the Party's Central Council. He was favourably received by the delegates and seconded an Emergency Resolution which was carried unanimously. However, this was only because it was a resolution of much apparent bark and little practical bite, clearly aimed at the Labour Party, and thus accepted as non-divisive by the meeting.[41] This proved to be the high water mark of Churchillian influence in the Party's representative institutions. During the ensuing five years' struggle over India the Diehards never again succeeded in identifying themselves with the majority. They were subsequently always resisted and defeated, even if only by narrow margins.

Even in the spring of 1931 the danger was more apparent than real. The tensions were not caused by approval of Churchill, but by the reaction against Baldwin's line in the debate of 26 January. In fact, the Party had not veered to the right, but had held fast to the central ground which Baldwin himself seemed to have abandoned. Gwynne calculated that 85% of the Party favoured the policy enunciated by Hoare.[42] To ease the position, all that was required was for Baldwin to eradicate this unfortunate impression and for Irwin's tactics to produce some tangible success. When these needs were met, opposition from the Party centre melted away during and after March 1931. Baldwin's meeting with the India Committee on 9 February had marked the painful beginnings of this attempt at reassurance, for he had declared then that the Party was not committed to any specific plans, and endorsed the approach identified with Hoare. Support for Irwin became a more tenable position with the news received on 4 March that his talks with Gandhi had proved successful. Still further soothing balm was applied by Baldwin in a public speech at Newton Abbot two days later. Negatively he promised that he had no intention of supporting a policy of scuttle, and told his audience that far from being ignored, the Simon Report had been the basis of every discussion at the Round Table Conference. He pointed out that as no detailed constitutional plan for India had been proposed, it was impossible to come to any final verdict, and that therefore the Party was uncommitted in any direction. This was backed up by more positive assurances: the rights of British traders with India would be safeguarded, and law and order in that country upheld. A highly contentious issue was the claim of the nationalists for an enquiry into the conduct of the Indian police. If conceded, this demand would not only have outraged Conservative opinion but also have undermined the morale of the police service. This was a mark of the anxiety over the Irwin-Gandhi talks, for it was feared that the Viceroy would give in to the demand. One of the elements in Baldwin's reassertion of Conservatism-without-reaction at Newton Abbot was his firm repudiation of any such enquiry, whilst he welcomed the talks themselves as the first fruit of the co-operation of moderate men over India. Baldwin's success could be gauged from the fact that, without retreating from the spirit of his January declaration, he was able to present his position in such a manner as to find approval even from the Executive Committee of the Indian Empire Society.[43]

Debating skill on the floor of the House of Commons was the foundation of any politician's success, and counted for almost everything in the making of a reputation or the struggle for promotion. Churchill's success in January had set everyone talking and had raised his prestige to a higher level, while Baldwin's ineffectiveness was a major cause of the Party crisis of spring 1931.[44] The next India debate on 12 March decisively reversed this position, for it was Baldwin who produced an oratorical triumph, elevating the discussion to a lofty moral plane whilst at the same time providing a rare exhibition of knock-about debating skill. Churchill was the target for this, and, much discomfited by Baldwin's quotations from his pro-devolution speeches of 1920, produced a weak riposte which bored the House.[45] Churchill persistently overstated his case. The policy of his opponents was presented as being one of immediate scuttle. Baldwin therefore had freedom of manoeuvre in which both to repudiate Churchill and simultaneously strike a sufficiently Conservative note to carry the bulk of his Party with him. Whereas in January Churchill's successful speech had stranded Baldwin on the left of his party, now it was Churchill who was isolated on the right—an isolation from which he was unable to escape.

Characteristically, Churchill would not accept this defeat as conclusive. 'It is not yet too late', he had declared on the day after the Round Table Conference adjourned: 'The key to Indian government is still in our hands'.[46] The dissidents sought to rouse and mobilise public opinion against concessions in the interval before the Conference was due to reconvene in September 1931. They concentrated on resistance to further progress during the life of the Labour government, for that was the period during which they feared that the pass might be sold. Their unquestioned belief in the return of a Conservative government at the next election was supported by the assumption that a Conservative majority in the House would be by definition extremely cautious on the question of India, and would give more emphasis to the matter of safeguards and less to dominion status. In this they were to be fatally mistaken; the line that was followed after August 1931 bore the appearance of Hoare's moderate policy in the letter, but not in the spirit. The error was the product of having overlooked Baldwin's genuine commitment to the Irwinite policy, as a result of confusing this with his temporary need to keep in harmony with the attitudes of the other parties in order to preserve unity at home. The Diehards miscalculated the extent to which Baldwin could carry the centre of the Party with him. They equally failed to anticipate the considerable augmentation of the left and centre proportionately at the expense of the right within the Conservative Party after the recovery of the marginal seats lost in 1929; an essential element of any future electoral victory. Thus the vulnerable period for Baldwin's line on India was in fact between January and August 1931. The Diehards continued the struggle after their setback in the debate of 12 March, despite the odds against them, for they were convinced that they could strike a chord in the very heart of Conservatism in the country. In fact, their campaign failed to make sufficient impact during these decisive months.

The reasons for this were partly structural. The rebel position was weak in a number of crucial areas, the first of which was in the matter of leadership. The Diehards by their very nature tended to be a collection of long-serving but largely inarticulate backbenchers, of no ministerial experience and little debating or platform skill; hence their need to look outside their own ranks for sympathetic leadership from some more prominent figures in the Party. They had found such leaders and allies in 1922, but were not to do so between 1931 and 1935. Churchill was not an acceptable standard-bearer, for his past political record rendered him a highly suspect figure to many in the Conservative Party. Beaverbrook observed that 'he has disclosed too many shifting phases to expect to be regarded as immovable now'.[47] However, the other potential leaders for a Diehard campaign over India were all unwilling to head a Party revolt. Hailsham and Austen Chamberlain swallowed their doubts in the belief that they could wield more influence from within the Party elite. Salisbury, who resigned from the leadership of the Lords mainly over India, allowed his departure to cause no ripples on grounds of party and personal loyalty. Neither were those who placed resistance to Irwinism first able to unite with any other section of Conservatism alienated from

Baldwin. The India rebels and the Empire Crusaders were distinct and separate groups, and did not co-ordinate their strategies. Beaverbrook was hostile to Churchill on protection and at best ambivalent towards his outlook on India, and was strongly resentful of the way in which Rothermere kicked over Empire Free Trade and ran India as the principal issue instead. Many of the Diehards were strong tariff reformers, and they did not find the free trader Churchill an attractive comrade-in-arms. The two campaigns were completely unsynchronised. The battle over protection reached its highest peak between June and October 1930, and unrest on this front was largely appeased by the concessions made in the latter month. India, on the other hand, had briefly flared up in November 1929, but then it remained relatively in the background until December 1930 and only became a serious source of unease after the adjournment of the Round Table Conference in January 1931. It was true that this last stage coincided with Beaverbrook's forays in the East Islington and St. George's by-elections, but these final challenges from the press baron lacked the support of the grassroots, and were in truth the self-defeating rampages of a political rogue elephant. The Diehards were thus left largely leaderless, and proved unable to appeal to the moderates within the Party. Indeed, the latter tended to see the rebels, rather than the leader, as the cause of factional division.

Baldwin still had considerable latent strengths even at the lowest point of his position over India in February 1931. The most important of these were the prestige and power of his position as Party leader, and the trust and loyalty to which he could appeal. He could count on the hesitant support of the Party centre, whom Churchill noted 'are all afraid of being labelled disloyal'.[48] This mood was reflected in the meeting of the parliamentary India Committee held after the Commons debate of 12 March, where of the one hundred MPs present, only five irreconcilable Diehards voted against a resolution approving Baldwin's position. Most significant of all was the fact that the rank and file of the Party were not yet disturbed over India. The low level of concern in the constituency associations was in marked contrast to the considerable energy expended on the question of Empire Free Trade. Only one resolution critical of the India policy was sent up to the National Union Executive.[49] Such concern as was expressed concentrated on the constitutional safeguards, and was felt most acutely in Lancashire due to the potential threat to the cotton trade from future Indian tariffs.[50]

Diehard opinion over India was voiced in the meetings of only five constituencies in the sample of more than one hundred and twenty associations for whom records survive. Significantly, one was in Lancashire and the other four were all safe seats in southern England. The Lancashire constituency of Clitheroe was the only one to pass a resolution, and this was no more than a simple declaration of their concern over the current situation in India. At Chichester the Executive Committee rejected a hostile motion by forty-two votes to twenty, in favour of an alternative which actually supported the Irwinite line, whilst at Aldershot a resolution which went no further than a request to their Member to oppose any premature grant of dominion status was defeated despite its anodyne nature. In the last two examples criticism was weaker still: at Wells the proposer of a critical resolution on India could not even find a seconder, whilst at Winchester the only member of the Executive to raise the topic of India was promptly and easily persuaded to let it drop.[51] Elsewhere the topic was either simply not raised at all, or the comments were pro-Baldwin and aroused no opposition.

One reason for this was the fact that although the discussion between 1929 and 1931 firmly settled the crucial principles, it did not immediately give rise to any specific legislation. The Diehards had nothing of detail or substance to chip away at; policy still appeared to be as yet unformed, and thus the question was for many not yet at the forefront of politics. In fact, the boundaries of debate had enormous implications for the future. It had become quantitative over the safeguards, rather than the outright question of whether there should be significant change. From this advance there could be no retreat, if only because of the importance attached to honouring British pledges. When the National Government began the process of legislation in 1933, the reaction from the Conservative constituencies was much greater, although it was by no means unanimously hostile.[52] But by then it was too late. The basis of policy on India had been firmly established, and had already acquired irresistible momentum. So long as the Party leaders held to their line, it was clear that it could only be altered by their repudiation. The consequence of that would be the destruction of the National Government, a price that few were prepared to pay.[53]

Over and above the appeal of keeping India out of party politics was the fact that the princes themselves had opted for federalism, making that policy both more attractive and more respectable.[54] Support for Irwin himself was a far from negligible factor. This was due in part to his standing and character, and even more to the general Conservative tendency to accept the wisdom of the man on the spot.[55] The approval expressed by the currently serving governors of the Indian provinces, several of whom had been prominent in the middle ranks of the Conservative Party before going to India, reinforced this. Above all, by placing the emphasis at Newton Abbot on the necessity for safeguards, Baldwin first aligned himself with the sentiments of the majority of his party, and then swept them forward when he spoke in the Commons six days later. The two pronouncements taken together are the true expression of Conservative policy on India in the early 1930s. The spirit of the Round Table Conference was to be balanced by safeguards, in acknowledgement 'that the empire, if it is anything, is a living organism' in a 'constant process of evolution'.[56]

Political factors also undermined the Diehard effort to maintain the primacy of the imperial dimension in the rhetoric of concern over national decline. Irwin was succeeded as Vicreoy in 1931 by Lord Willingdon, who had made a lifetime career of imperial administration, having just completed a term as Governor General in Canada. Willingdon, once a Liberal Imperialist MP at the turn of the century, was acceptable to most shades of opinion in the Conservative Party. He appeared to restore stern government after the potentially demoralising spectacle of Irwin and Gandhi meeting on equal terms, but on matters of substance he did not try to put the clock back to the position before 1929. Distractions from the question of India abounded, and due to the relative calm in that country after the Irwin–Gandhi pact, it slipped from the forefront of the public mind. The first diversion was, ironically, the Party's differences with the press lords in February and March 1931. This was compounded by the fact that, in order to regain the confidence of the parliamentary Party in his leadership, Baldwin reasserted himself on 12 March with perhaps the greatest effort of his parliamentary career.[57] This served the dual function of defeating both of the challenges against him. Baldwin overcame the despair of his colleagues by the success of the speech, and flattened the India dissidents both by delivery and content. Paradoxically, the restoration of order in Conservative politics in April 1931 did not provide any opportunity for the India agitation to take the centre of the stage. The emphasis was now placed squarely on the need to get the Labour government out for reasons of domestic policy—and the call for 'economy' held the ring from April to August 1931. The long struggle over tariffs and the Empire Crusade had worn down any toleration of further intra-party faction. Of more significance was the accepted priority of the need to restore an orthodox budgetary policy; thus the forces working for sound government at home were not to be weakened either by disputes of degree over sound government for India, or disagreements over the details of domestic affairs. In the last resort, these were seen as sectional interests, whilst the 'economy' question was a national peril.

By August 1931 the pattern of Conservative policy over India was set. The rebels had missed their opportunity to turn feeling in the Party against the Round Table Conference whilst it was still in a malleable form. All that was left to them after the general election of 1931 swept into the Commons a flood of new moderate supporters of the National Government, was to turn to the last shot in their locker.

They could only try to capture the Party from below through the National Union, turning it into an engine that would force Conservative MPs to break with their leader's policy.[58] This was a herculean task indeed, swimming against the tide of ingrained party loyalties and traditions, and requiring ultimately that the normally deferential National Union adopt a role to which it had never previously aspired. As the experience of Beaverbrook's similar attempt to capture the local associations demonstrated, such a tactic was difficult enough in times when the Party had been defeated and was restless under ineffective leadership. Against a party successful beyond precedent at the polls, and no longer prey to demoralisation, it was to prove impossible. The substantial votes achieved by the Diehards in the conferences and Council of the National Union between 1933 and 1935 should not obscure these realities.[59] There would always be a vocal element of Diehards in the safer southern seats, but they remained a minority within the Party as a whole. Even when Lancashire became more hesitant, it still remained beyond the powers of the rebels to obtain a majority so long as the Cabinet remained united. It was quite clear that in the final analysis the Party would not smash up the National Government over India.

The failure of the right to defeat Baldwin in the spring of 1931 was the decisive moment in British politics so far as the future of India was concerned. Baldwin was never again to be in such a vulnerable position, and the verdict of March 1931 settled the issue against the rebels, despite all their efforts during the subsequent four years to appeal to a higher court. In concluding the matter in this way, the primacy of the domestic over the imperial dimension in practice—if not in rhetoric—was established. Baldwin, Irwin, and their supporters within the Party believed that their policy would strengthen the empire and safeguard its future: decolonisation and withdrawal were not their intentions. But, unlike the Diehards, their policy was based on recognising the realities of the changing position of both the mother country and the dependent populations. In so doing, they accepted that Britain could not, as Churchill wished, arrest or reverse these developments. In that sense, Churchill's stricture that there was no logical stopping point for their policy before full independence was true. The events of 1929 to 1931 were the first but most crucial stage of the evolution of the Conservatives to a position where, within thirty years, they could preside over the dissolution of the empire through its transformation into a loose association of self-governing units, without breaking up the Party. Churchill and the Diehards were aptly categorised as imperialists of Queen Victoria's second jubilee, but, as Irwin acknowledged in March 1931, 'that conception of Imperialism is finished'.[60] Of course, other factors, principal amongst which was the economic exhaustion caused by the Second World War, were more immediate causes of decolonisation. However, the choice of political priorities made by the ostensible party of empire between November 1929 and March 1931 must be a crucial landmark.

CHAPTER 7

The Ides of March

The future of India was only one of three major themes in Conservative politics between October 1930 and March 1931. It was inextricably interwoven with two others; Baldwin's recurrent weakness as opposition leader, and the renewed onslaughts of the press lords. The result was that by March 1931, despite the gains made in the previous October, another crisis over the leadership seemed to be about to break. The origins, the seriousness, and the course of this crisis have been misunderstood by previous commentators. In addition, there is considerable confusion over the roles of the principal figures involved, Baldwin and Neville Chamberlain. It is now necessary to pass on to both a clarification and a reassessment of the Conservative crisis of March 1931.

Baldwin's position in November and December 1930 was stronger than it had been at any time since the 1929 election. Approval for the new platform of a free hand on tariffs continued to be widely evidenced in the constituencies. In late November the backbench '1922' Committee recorded its impression that the steam had gone out of the Crusade campaign, and that the Party was rallying towards unity.[1] The new mood was visibly underlined by two gatherings representative of the rank and file: the Central Council of the National Union on 25 November, and the Annual Conference of the Scottish Unionist Association on 12 December. The tenor of both of these meetings indicated the extent to which opinion was now flowing in Baldwin's direction.[2] The Empire Crusade was like a beached galleon, stranded high and dry by the ebb of that tide, but still firing every possible broadside towards the enemy. The verdict of the party meeting of 30 October 1930 had isolated Beaverbrook from his Conservative allies, and placed him beyond the pale of respectable politics. The basis of his power had been seriously diminished, even if his campaign had not yet been completely destroyed. Placed against this, the victory of the Crusader over the official candidate at South Paddington on 31 October 1930 was hardly a consolation. Contemporary political opinion was quite clear that the by-election result did not signify in comparison to the party meeting of the previous day.[3] South Paddington did not herald a new phase in the struggle, but was rather the last manifestation of the unrest that had been visible throughout the Party in September 1930. By the time the result was announced, this was largely a thing of the past.

Beaverbrook's response to the changed atmosphere was to slacken his activities, returning once again to the path of negotiation. On this occasion the intermediary was tbe City financier Sir Abe Bailey, who approached Neville Chamberlain on 4 November at Beaverbrook's suggestion and arranged a meeting. Chamberlain was still resentful over the breakup of the last round of talks at the time of the Bromley by-election. With the situation now running more strongly in his favour, he had little need to unbend, feeling that there was no particular urgency about clinching a deal. Once again, the problem of the Rothermere connection proved to be a stumbling block. Beaverbrook re-opened the topic of a seat for Esmond Harmsworth, as the bait with which to attract his father. Chamberlain could not and would not consider any such concession, although he did not rule out a seat for Esmond as an eventual by-product of peace. He declared that the press barons must make the first move by lowering the temperature in their papers. Lessening hostilities would itself lead to an arrangement, rather than the other way around. Although it proved impossible to conclude a settlement so soon after the bitter squabbling at South Paddington, an informal neutrality operated successfully during November and December. In further negotiations at the beginning of December, Chamberlain and Beaverbrook explored the possibility of drafting some agreed exchange of letters, but at that stage it was not possible to devise a formula satisfactory to both and humiliating to neither. At Beaverbrook's suggestion, it was decided just to let matters drift.[4] This was acceptable to Chamberlain, for the level of press criticism had indeed been reduced; he had already gained almost all that he could look for from a formal pact.

Ironically, this promising position was undermined by events in the constituency of South Paddington. Friction between Taylor, the Empire Crusade MP, and the local Conservative Association gradually embroiled the principals on both sides in another confrontation. The crunch came in mid-December when the local Conservatives insisted on selecting a new candidate to run against Taylor at the next election. In his position as Chairman of the Party, Neville Chamberlain had no option but to support their right to do so, hoping nonetheless that this would not destroy the entente. By Christmas,

however, the mood created by the October party meeting was
dissipating. Beaverbrook, sensing renewed opportunities, and restless
in his inactivity, seized on this affair as a pretext for once again
reverting to open hostility.[5] But South Paddington was merely the
final straw in a series of factors which had been undermining Beaverbrook's inclination to compromise. Firstly, he remained acutely
suspicious of Baldwin's intentions on fiscal policy, and saw his
continued dampening presence at the head of the Conservative Party
as the most important potential barrier to success. The logical result,
seemingly confirmed by Baldwin's repeated failure to put his policy
across forcefully enough, was the conclusion that 'in order to achieve
Empire Free Trade, we have got to defeat Baldwin'.[6] The second area
of difference concerned the thorny topic of agricultural protection.
From the very beginning the Crusade had been pitched to the farmers,
and this trend increased in the winter of 1930, for they remained the
only important section of Conservative sentiment not entirely
appeased by the recent advances in the Party's policy. Beaverbrook's
growing identification with their interests continued throughout
1931, and was eventually to lead him to replace the Crusade with an
avowed Agricultural Party. This was still in the future, but in January
1931 he recommenced his campaign with a manifesto to farmers
which offered a simple policy of protection for the home producer.[7] In
this, and in the mood of intransigent hostility which he adopted at this
time, Beaverbrook was encouraged and supported by Rothermere,
his only remaining ally. By mid-January the prospect of a truce,
instead of drifting closer, had been washed out of sight by changes in
the political currents. The press lords were once again on the lookout
for a suitable constituency, preferably metropolitan, in which to
declare war on Baldwinism.[8]

This threat from without would have been of little significance,
considering the vastly stronger position of the Party leadership when
compared with September 1930, had not the confidence, so noticeable
throughout the Party in November, been significantly diminished.
The parliamentary session which had opened on 28 October was
becoming an increasingly frustrating one for the Conservatives.
Although weakened by their failure to deal with unemployment, the
Labour government was sustained in office by its exploration during
the winter months of a deal with the Liberals, involving concessions
on electoral reform. At the same time, public opinion seemed to be
moving in the Conservatives' direction, though in many northern
areas this was a slow process, and often difficult yet to detect.[9]
Ironically, this trend made most Liberals more, rather than less,
inclined to support the Labour administration. They feared the resulting general election if they did not. Not only would they lose seats
themselves, but it now looked likely that the Conservatives would

secure a mandate for their 'free hand' policy. The Liberals and Labour were partners in common misery, but the Conservatives were no nearer to the elusive goal of getting the discredited government out of office.

The shape of things to come during the session of 1930–1931 was seen in the debate on the King's speech in early November. In accordance with his Party's new programme, Neville Chamberlain devoted his speech in the debate on the economic situation to a protectionist critique of government policy. As a result, despite their own reservations, the Liberals voted with the Labour Party on the common ground of the defence of free trade.[10] For as long as party politics remained on this fiscal basis, the Conservatives would remain locked into a minority position. The debates on the King's speech were marked by bitter denunciations of the government's weakness by its own backbenchers, but this was not translated into hostile votes in the lobby. The solidarity of the Labour forces remained firm, though their loyalty was under great pressure as the economic picture continued to darken throughout the year. For the Liberal Party, the dilemma of their position was to prove too much. Not all the Liberals were happy under Lloyd George's leadership, or agreed with him that the continuation of Labour in office was the lesser of the two evils before them. In the crucial division on the hostile Conservative amendment to the King's speech five Liberals, including Sir John Simon and the Chief Whip, Sir Robert Hutchison, voted with the Conservative Party. This was the start of the process of disintegration by which the Liberal Party was to tear itself apart over the next two years. However, in the short term, the Liberal and Labour leaders seemed to be moving into a closer and more formal relationship. In January 1931 the Liberals let the Trade Disputes Bill through; in February the Electoral Reform Bill began its slow passage in return. The Conservative opposition in the House of Commons seemed to be ploughing the sands, and the futility of their efforts inevitably reflected unfavourably upon their leader.

The decline in Baldwin's position during the winter and spring of 1931 was, however, largely of his own making. It provoked a crisis over his suitability as leader that had almost nothing to do with the Crusaders' activities. Indeed, the erosion of confidence in Baldwin was a far more serious danger than any challenge from Beaverbrook. The cause was Baldwin's failure in two respects: firstly in explaining and advocating the fiscal policy of the Party, and secondly in leading the opposition in the House of Commons. These were, of course, exactly the same problems that had undermined each previous re-imposition of control, although dissatisfaction with the official policy had then been an additional factor. Nevertheless, the continued existence of the other two problems was sufficient to cause the newly recovered morale of the parliamentary Party to dwindle away. Baldwin was no longer so vulnerable to the attacks of the Crusaders, having squared his policy, but his continued failure to provide an acceptable style of leadership in parliament was rendering him a dangerous liability to his immediate colleagues. It was this anxiety, rather than any plots or intrigues, which produced the leadership crisis of March 1931. For this reason Baldwin's cautious line in expounding his policy to the country was perhaps the less serious of the factors undermining his authority. However, it caused renewed criticism from the barely reconciled right wing, and certainly played into Beaverbrook's hands. Having at last refused to rule out food taxes, Baldwin still did not appear to want them. His speeches were apologetic in tone, and seemed to be full of qualifications. On top of this, Baldwin had once again relapsed into a mood of lethargy which Dawson likened to 'a sort of comfortable winter quarters', hardly the hallmark of vigorous or inspiring leadership.[11]

Two debacles of parliamentary mismanagement in November and December underlined the general dissatisfaction. The first was a dreadful speech by Baldwin on 27 November on a vote of censure against the Government's refusal to consider Bennett's imperial preference proposals.[12] This was all the more serious for the fact that the debate was on the very subject on which he needed to look like a new man. The vote of censure was a rushed and bungled job, in which Baldwin tripped over his own feet in his efforts to restore his position. Instead of raising his stock in the eyes of his colleagues and followers, it produced a 'profoundly depressing effect on our own people'.[13] A consequence of the decline in morale amongst Conservative MPs was absenteeism and apathy, a phenomenon similar to that of January 1930. This development led to a second humiliation, when on 10 December a Conservative motion critical of Government extravagance was counted out in the House due to lack of support. This amounted to a serious failure of organisation on the part of the whips and the front bench. As the issue of 'economy' was coming to be placed before all others by the Party at large, this fiasco produced howls of outrage and anger in the National Union.[14] At the same time, the leader's personal aloofness towards the younger backbenchers was becoming a serious bone of contention among the parliamentary party. Baldwin's alarming presentation of his views on the future of India in the debate of 26 January was only the final straw. Even the most staunchly loyal MPs were beginning to chafe.[15] Their loss of confidence was privately echoed to a greater degree than ever before amongst the inner circle of leaders. Cunliffe-Lister described the position as 'impossible', and Austen Chamberlain declared in February that another crisis was rapidly approaching.[16] The seriousness of the problem was admitted by such normally loyal figures as

Linlithgow, Hoare, and Neville Chamberlain, and had reached an acute stage by the second half of February. 'Only the absence of an obvious successor and the dislike of being coerced by the press has prevented things collapsing before now', considered Amery.[17] Baldwin's colleagues did not wish to see him go, but they were being inexorably pushed towards viewing that as the least damaging solution to the Party's difficulties. However, none of them was a clear candidate for the succession, none of them desired the leadership at a time when it was such a crown of thorns, and none wished to take the initiative in suggesting to Baldwin that he should, in the interests of his party, stand down.[18]

There were four possible contenders for the leadership if that should happen: Churchill, Horne, Hailsham and Neville Chamberlain. Of these, Churchill was the youngest at fifty-seven. However, he had seriously reduced his chances by resigning from the shadow cabinet, and he had almost no personal following amongst Conservative MPs. Although he reflected the views of the Diehards over India, he was not a favoured candidate with any section of the Party. Horne was a more serious contender, and was popular with the tariff reformers and the business element on the backbenches. However, though only sixty, he was not keen to return to the forefront of political life. Since June 1930 he had increasingly supported Baldwin as the best available leader, breaking with Beaverbrook in the process. In January 1931 his attitude remained one of loyalty to his leader, which was demonstrated when he publicly moved a vote of confidence in Baldwin at the Glasgow Unionist Association's annual meeting.[19] Horne might have accepted the leadership if it were thrust upon him, but there is no indication that he sought it. The strongest candidate was the fifty-nine year old Lord Hailsham, whose credentials with the right of the Party were solid, but who also had the trust of the moderates after his defence of Baldwin at the October party meeting. Moreover, he was currently the acting-leader in the House of Lords during Salisbury's lengthy illness. But Hailsham was a reluctant candidate. He too had taken Baldwin's part in the recent stages of the struggle with Beaverbrook, in spite of his belief that doing so damaged whatever prospects he may have had himself. Nevertheless, it was thought that if Baldwin were to go it was 'a strongish possibility that the two Houses would unite in choosing Hailsham as leader'.[20] Neville Chamberlain was the fourth possibility, and at the age of sixty-two the oldest. His spell as Chairman of the Party had firmly established his credentials as a figure in the very front rank. However, both Chamberlain and Hailsham were principally motivated by concern over party unity. This was being endangered not by them, but by Baldwin. Without unity, the overriding aims of getting Labour out and winning the subsequent election were unlikely to be attained. On the other hand, they appreciated that Baldwin's departure could cause rifts as damaging as those already in existence. When the anticipated crisis finally came, these concerns led the two men to agree on 5 March to stand together, each offering to serve under the other if he should be the chosen one. There is no doubt that this combination was widely favoured in the Party and would have swept the board in the event of a vacancy. The main reason for this was that it was thought likely to bring peace and security, with the minimum of fundamental change.

The concordat between Chamberlain and Hailsham was not the prelude of a plot to force Baldwin out, but the sensible precaution of pragmatic politicians who were simply preparing for a likely contingency. It was a reflection of the crisis of confidence in Baldwin's leadership in the spring of 1931, but not a contributory cause. In any case, there remained grave doubts as to whether Baldwin should withdraw. With all his defects, he still seemed to divide the Party least, for none of the other potential leaders had the complete confidence of the rank and file. Churchill was suspected of instability, intrigue, and coalitionist irredentism. Horne had also been a prominent figure in Lloyd George's ministry, and had not held office since its fall; in addition, he was much more involved in the City than the Commons. Hailsham was thought to be too impetuous, and though being in the Lords was not an insuperable barrier, his lack of contact with many MPs was a considerable practical reservation. Neville Chamberlain's occupancy of Central Office had not been an entirely unmixed blessing, for in carrying out his duties he had inevitably made some enemies. In addition, his personal manner was a serious defect. Headlam, describing him as 'a cold fishy creature who puts your back up in five minutes', was far from alone in his view.[21] To change horses in midstream therefore seemed to offer few advantages, especially as none of the jockeys were keen on the attempt. A further reason for avoiding change was the very spate of the flood. The renewed attacks from Beaverbrook and Rothermere in the by-elections of February and March augmented the sympathy for the leader, and at the same time raised the perennial problem of any appearance of bowing the knee to press dictation. Furthermore, no real differences of policy or approach divided Baldwin from his colleagues; they did not disagree with his strategy but merely despaired of his ability to carry it out. The crisis of spring 1931 was a matter of manner and style, of confidence and not of substance. The situation in February was also one of extreme uncertainty; 'I have never known such confusion in party politics', confessed Lord Robert Cecil.[22] The Conservative leaders were caught on the horns of a dilemma. Whilst increasingly regarding Baldwin's retirement as the lesser evil of the alternatives before them, they were so little attracted by the prospect that they continually shrank from taking any practical action to bring it about.

The Party's Principal Agent, Topping, felt that the situation was becoming so serious that he was duty-bound to put the facts before the Chairman in a formal memorandum. He pointed out in this document that although Beaverbrook's support had dwindled since October, at the same time there had grown a 'very definite feeling' that Baldwin was 'not strong enough to carry the Party to victory'.[23] Most of the memorandum was studiously vague, and its principal concern was not so much that Baldwin should go, but that if he did so the present confusion might result in the choice of Churchill for his diehard line on India. Topping's conclusion, however, was definite enough: the dissatisfaction with Baldwin was too widespread and dangerous to be ignored. Such an expression of opinion from the Party's senior official forced a decision on Chamberlain, which is doubtless what Topping intended. Chamberlain grasped at the memorandum as the solution to the conflict between his loyalty and his anxiety over the loss of confidence in Baldwin, writing to his sister that 'Topping has been the *deus ex machina*'.[24] The memorandum was not the spearhead of a plot, except in the possible sense that Topping may have deliberately painted an overly dismal picture, but was rather the final straw, convincing most of Baldwin's colleagues that he would have to withdraw from an untenable position. Far from rushing to exploit the opportunity, Chamberlain hesitated over the best course to take. Making no secret of the document's contents, he consulted a wide range of front-bench colleagues. All were unanimous that the memorandum should be shown to Baldwin. This consultation could not be taken for intrigue, for Chamberlain approached not only his brother Austen, Hoare, Cunliffe-Lister, and Hailsham; but also the Chief Whip, Eyres-Monsell, and Bridgeman, who was Baldwin's most trusted and loyal associate in the Shadow Cabinet. Hailsham, moreover, wanted Baldwin to be given a further opportunity to redeem himself with his forthcoming speech at Newton Abbot, and suggested holding the document back for another ten days. Neville Chamberlain was unhappy over this, thinking that greater damage might result from delay, but he agreed lest any haste be misconstrued as a cloak for his own personal ambition.

The incident which finally removed Chamberlain's doubts was, in many ways, the least significant of all. As a result of the sudden death of Worthington-Evans in mid-February, a by-election was about to be held in Westminster St. George's, one of the safest Conservative seats in the country. Moore-Brabazon, a junior minister in the last Conservative government who had been defeated in the 1929 election, was the front runner for selection by the local Association. However, when an independent Conservative challenger, Sir Ernest Petter, came forward with the backing of the press lords and declared that he would fight purely on the leadership issue, Moore-Brabazon announced on 28 February that he would withdraw as he felt unable to defend Baldwin. Embarrassingly, the local Executive Committee found themselves suddenly without a candidate willing to champion the leader of the Party. The crisis of confidence, not in the constituencies but amongst parliamentarians of the Moore-Brabazon type, was now clearly both acute and public. Faced with this, Neville Chamberlain concluded that he could withhold Topping's memorandum no longer. On the morning of Sunday, 1 March, he sent it by hand to Baldwin's London residence, together with a covering letter. After relating his actions since Topping had first given him the memorandum, he enclosed it without further comment beyond the conventional nicety of apologising for adding to Baldwin's anxieties at a difficult time. There was no suggestion that Baldwin should retire—a passage that might have given that impression was deliberately struck out of the draft—only the remark that Baldwin would no doubt wish to consult with his friends.[25]

The Topping memorandum was not sent to Baldwin to force his retirement, but rather in the hope that, one way or another, he would respond to the gravity of the position and thus resolve a confused and unhappy predicament. Thus, once the memorandum was delivered, the decision was left entirely to Baldwin, without any attempt to press him to resign. A close examination of the events of late February and early March provides no real evidence for any conspiracy theory of a plot to oust Baldwin, and loyalty played a greater part than ambition in the actions of his colleagues. In fact, Neville Chamberlain thought that the intervention of the press lords at St. George's would make it too difficult for Baldwin to go, and told his sister a few days later that he had not anticipated that this would be Baldwin's reaction on perusing the memorandum.[26] However, it was a feature of Baldwin's character that periods of complacency could swiftly alternate with despair over his prospects when he was confronted with a bleak picture by a trusted colleague. On this cold and snowy first weekend of March, Baldwin was already 'rather depressed', and his wife had been distressed by the receipt of 'an anonymous letter from the Carlton Club'.[27] He was in no mood to look critically at Topping's assessment. Instead, Baldwin's spirits sank to an apathetic low. Gloomily convinced that he had fatally lost the confidence of his party, he resolved to quit at once. In the grip of this mood, he summoned Neville Chamberlain by telephone, and at three o'clock on 1 March told him that he would announce his resignation from the leadership forthwith. That evening Baldwin discussed his future plans with his wife, and also considered retiring from the Commons before the next election. As they talked, *The Times*, unofficially informed of the day's events, was setting its first leader for the following day, ready to announce that 'Mr. Baldwin Withdraws'.[28]

As a consequence of Baldwin's decision to resign, it has been too readily assumed that his position was in real, rather than apparent, danger.[29] Paradoxically, despite the evidence of his resolve to retire, his position was not that weak. Baldwin could have ceased to struggle with the dissident elements in his party at any stage as a result of losing his personal confidence and becoming depressed; it does not mean that this coincided with the period of his greatest actual peril. He had already survived the most serious phase of the Party crisis in October 1930. The decision to withdraw taken on 1 March 1931 was the product firstly of his low spirits, and secondly of his misconceptions about the political realities. When these conditions ceased to apply, then naturally talk of resignation quickly became a thing of the past. In analysing Baldwin's decision to quit, the emphasis should be placed on the impact of events on his own morale, rather than on the intrinsic significance of the circumstances, for they were not of such gravity as to inexorably bring about the fall of a politician of major stature. Baldwin's determination to withdraw proved shortlived, for his mood was to change before the night was out.

Davidson had been at Baldwin's house on the morning of 1 March when Chamberlain's missive was delivered, and he recounted the subsequent events to Bridgeman, with whom he happened to be dining that evening. Bridgeman had never thought the position warranted resignation, although when consulted by Chamberlain he had agreed that Baldwin should see Topping's analysis. Bridgeman kept his finger on the pulse of the ordinary membership, and was astounded at the idea that, after the successes of October, Baldwin could possibly retire merely because Petter had come out as a candidate to challenge his leadership. After dinner he went with Davidson to Baldwin's house, arriving at ten o'clock to find their leader resolved on immediate resignation. Bridgeman rolled in like a breath of fresh air. Presenting the other side of the picture frankly and robustly, he dispelled Baldwin's gloom like the mists before the dawn. He argued that Baldwin should at least go out fighting on some great issue, either in favour of a conciliatory policy towards India, or in defence of the constitution against press dictatorship. To this end Bridgeman offered a practical suggestion. Baldwin should resign his Worcestershire seat in order to fight St. George's himself.[30] This was more in line with Baldwin's habitual instincts, and within the hour his attitude had been transformed. *The Times* went to press without any announcement about resignation. Instead Baldwin summoned Neville Chamberlain to call on him on 2 March, to discuss not the details of the succession problem, but a plan for contesting St. George's.

Baldwin's position was not without difficulties, but these could all be overcome. The danger lay within the Conservative ranks, in the collapse of confidence in his leadership within the parliamentary

Party. However, Bridgeman was correct in his analysis; the tide of opinion had begun to turn during the previous fortnight, though this had not yet filtered through to the shadow cabinet. The principal reason was the East Islington by-election, where polling took place on 19 February. The impact of the campaign and of the result superseded the sentiments that had forced Topping to write his memorandum. When the vacancy had occurred there in January, the Conservatives were already prepared with an able and popular young candidate, Thelma Cazalet, who looked poised to win the seat from Labour and thereby strike a blow at the tottering government. The intervention of the press lords, despite the fact that Cazalet's policy differed hardly at all from theirs on fiscal matters, interfered with this. Beaverbrook's first candidate was Springman, a respected and able young London barrister who had helped with Taylor's campaign in South Padding-ton. Sensing the hostility of local Conservatives to his nomination, he rejected Beaverbrook and after only a few days in the field withdrew in Cazalet's favour; later he spoke for her at meetings.

This was a serious blow for Beaverbrook, who seemed to have run into the sand. His response was swift but counter-productive; he found another and much less reputable candidate, and rushed him into the constituency. The new Crusade standard-bearer was Brigadier-General Alfred Critchley, who had fought the safe Labour seat of Manchester Gorton as a Conservative in 1929. However, his principal qualifications seemed to be that he had been divorced by the cousin of Beaverbrook's late wife, and that he had plenty of money.[31] The campaign was bitter, even violent. Passions over the by-election ran high in the Conservative Party, both nationally and locally. Meetings were disrupted, with fights breaking out between Crusade stewards and Conservative hecklers, and on several occasions disorder spread from the hired halls into scuffles and affrays outside. Events on the eve of the poll were described as 'sensational street scenes' by one national newspaper, with 'running fights'.[32] One cause of this violent reaction, reflected in verbal onslaughts from Party leaders such as Hailsham, was Beaverbrook's frank admission at one public meeting that if he could not force his policy on the Conservative Party, then he would set out to destroy it. Such sentiments naturally caused the Party to rally together against Beaverbrook's wrecking interventions.

The most serious consequence of East Islington was not the manner in which the conduct of the campaign placed Beaverbrook even further beyond the pale of respectable politics, but the result itself. Neville Chamberlain had thought before the poll that it might not be a bad thing if the seat were lost as a result of Beaverbrook's activities, for that would provoke a backlash which would be beneficial to the official leaders.[33] This was exactly what happened. With the Conservative vote split, Labour held the division at a time when Conservatives were increasingly desperate to chip away at the government's majority and morale.[34] East Islington destroyed the appeal of the Crusade, and gave a new lease of life to the traditional cry of unity, which in effect meant a rally round Baldwin. The conduct and consequence of the Crusaders' intervention in this by-election led directly to their final decline. Support for the Crusade from Conservative activists, always the real strength of Beaverbrook's movement, had ebbed away continuously since October 1930. The East Islington fiasco put the Crusade in its coffin and the result nailed down the lid. The significance of the St. George's by-election a few weeks later was not that it brought about the defeat of the press lords, but rather that it provided the opportunity for a public manifestation of the reaction against them which had been caused by East Islington the month before. In the wake of the latter, previously disaffected MPs, typical of whom was Sir Robert Gower, made clear their desire to see an end to faction.[35] The idea that the crisis of March 1931 was more serious than that of September 1930 is the erroneous product of viewing events too much from the parliamentary perspective. Even Topping acknowledged in his memorandum in mid-February that resolutions in support of Baldwin were being frequently received from local branches. This flow increased to a flood after the East Islington result, as the issue of press dictatorship came once again to the fore.[36] Even more telling than the large number of constituencies which went out of their way to pass resolutions proclaiming their loyalty, is the lack of any single instance where sentiments hostile to Baldwin were voiced, even by implication, in the private discussions of the constituency committees. This is in very marked contrast to the unrest and explicit antagonism that had been so visible in September and October 1930.

In the light of this, the validity of the picture painted in Topping's memorandum must be called into question. In February 1931 there was increasing dissatisfaction in the parliamentary Party with Baldwin's inability to lead, and this found an avenue of expression in the anxieties of the Diehards over Baldwin's support for the bipartisan approach to Indian affairs. In this area there is no doubt that the leader's position was shaky; but it was not hopeless, as he was shortly to demonstrate. However, in other areas Topping's opinions are open to serious reservations. The mood in the local associations was generally pro-Baldwin, and was far from the desperate straits that he had described. The Party had not slipped back to the nadir of September 1930, and even if they did not enthuse about Baldwin, they preferred him to any other alternative. A clear indication of the calmer atmosphere of 1931 can be found in the tone and resolutions of the meeting of the constituency delegates at the National Union Central Council on 24 February, held on the day before Topping passed his memorandum to the Party Chairman. The Principal Agent had also been influenced by an apparent decline in local subscriptions, which was being attributed to disgust with the leadership. In fact, this was the real cause in only a minority of cases. The Party continually faced the problem of apathy in the mid-term of parliaments, whether in or out of office; and these financial alarms paralleled those of 1927–1928 and 1933–1934. On this occasion the problem was exacerbated by the economic slump, rather than political disillusion. In one region where the question was directly confronted, the political explanation for the diminution of revenue was swiftly dismissed as being no more than a pretext, 'the real reason being that owing to the commercial depression, people were cutting down expenses, and made the first cut in their political subscriptions'.[37] Two other factors may have caused Topping to exaggerate the disaffection in the lower ranks. Firstly, he was naturally most familiar with opinion in Lancashire, where he had formerly been the Area Agent, and in London and the Home Counties, his immediate political environment. However, these were the two areas where anxiety about the Party policy on India was much more of a live issue than was the case elsewhere. In the other parts of the country unemployment, protection, and the related topic of government expenditure, were the vital issues of the day. Secondly, much of Topping's information was received at second-hand from the local agents. In the nature of their work, they tended to be more concerned about the vocal dissatisfaction of a minority, and as a result gave too much weight to that, whilst overlooking the loyal attitude of the silent majority of their local membership. In fact, evidence for the existence of a serious crisis within the Conservative Party in February 1931 is far from convincing.

A more accurate description of the problem facing Baldwin was a loss of confidence in his powers of leadership by almost all of his colleagues on the opposition front bench, by several officials in the central organisation, and by some sections of the parliamentary Party. The extent of the disquiet on the Conservative backbenches is by its nature difficult to quantify, but the dissatisfaction with the leader's recent performances, together with serious misconceptions over his intended line on India, clearly had affected a much wider spectrum than the predictably critical right wing. However, in the short term, this backbench sentiment was largely inarticulate. Furthermore, it could be swayed one way or the other by the nature and effectiveness of the lead from above that it was given. For this reason, the attitude of the front-benchers was the crucial factor. Once Baldwin decided to fight the supposed danger of Beaverbrook's threat from without, they had no option but to rally around the symbol of the leader. In this sense, the withdrawal of Moore-Brabazon presented Baldwin with the tactical key to the situation. Moore-Brabazon's action was not, of course, a press attack, but a further and public manifestation of the private disaffection of the parliamentarians. By switching the question at stake to that of the power of the press, Baldwin forced his colleagues to take sides on that basis instead. In a polarisation between Beaverbrook and Baldwin after the events of the previous six months there could be no sitting on the fence. The logic of the position meant that in defying the press lords the Conservative front bench had inevitably to support Baldwin.

This was the significance of his willingness to stand for St. George's; with Beaverbrook completely beyond the pale after East Islington, there was no surer device for rallying the Conservative Party around himself. With the sanctity of the constitution to be invoked, and the trumpet call of loyalty to be sounded, under a banner of 'pure' politics, the tactical balance had swung once more in Baldwin's favour. The suggestion that he should fight St. George's in person as well as in spirit did not need to be put into practice to produce the desired effect. Neville Chamberlain was very unenthusiastic about the proposal when Baldwin put it to him in their interview of 2 March, and the rest of his colleagues 'got a bad attack of second thoughts and cold feet'. They begged Baldwin not to take the risk, but admitted that 'it was impossible for him to go until after St. George's'.[38] The Conservative shadow cabinet still believed that Baldwin's departure had only been delayed, and was inevitable in the near future. In fact, the moment had passed, for the intervention of the St. George's campaign gave Baldwin a breathing space in which to resolve his difficulties. Suspending the leadership question over until after the by-election settled the issue in his favour, quite regardless of the outcome at St. George's. If Baldwin, or his candidate, should win, then after such a triumph the matter of his going would be a dead letter. But what his colleagues overlooked was that it would be equally impossible to drop Baldwin should the official candidate lose. This would seem to be a surrender to the press barons; and all were unanimous that that could not be considered for a moment.

Baldwin's mood had been transformed; by 2 March he was determined 'not to go unless he was kicked out'.[39] In a curious parallel with his sounding of Derby in October 1930, Baldwin asked Lord Lloyd on 4 March, in the course of an interview arranged to discuss the India question, whether he should resign. When Lloyd replied in the affirmative, this unwelcome advice once again seemed to make not the slightest impression.[40] The first step Baldwin took towards recovering the position was to find a suitable candidate willing to champion his leadership at St. George's. This problem was rapidly solved. Despite the complaints of some of the younger generation in the parliamentary Party, Baldwin still retained the support of many of the rising figures on the centre and left. Several of these had lost their seats in 1929, and were keen to return to the House at the first opportune by-election. One of this number was Duff Cooper, a man with little affection for the press lords on either political or personal grounds, and noted in January 1931 as being 'very pro-Baldwin'.[41] Surprised to learn of the difficulty being encountered at St. George's, he returned from a lecture tour abroad and, with the encouragement of Central Office, offered himself as candidate on 4 March.[42] Cooper was interviewed by the St. George's selection committee on the following day, and formally adopted on 6 March. It is sometimes said that Cooper abandoned the good prospect he was nursing at Winchester to take on a difficult struggle in St. George's, but in fact the reverse was the case. St. George's was an ideal constituency for a rising figure, and one of the safest seats in the country. Furthermore, given both the political issues that Cooper could bring into play and his personal appeal, victory was almost a foregone conclusion. Social deference remained an influence in this constituency, with its introspective regard for society figures. Man-about-town Duff, married to a Duke's daughter and leader of fashion such as Lady Diana, hopelessly outclassed Petter, an obscure manufacturer of diesel engines from the West Country. Given the view that the methods of the 'gutter' press were ungentlemanly, high society, which might simplistically have been expected to have favoured Rothermere's diehard policies, proved to be more concerned with image and personality, and came down overwhelmingly on Cooper's side. The great houses of the aristocracy displayed placards urging a 'Vote for Cooper'. The combination of Duff and Lady Diana was a formidable one; Cooper himself had a gallant war record, was a good speaker, and amongst the generation of junior ministers was frequently spoken of as a coming man. Dawson was certain that 'he and the Lady Diana between them will succeed in pulling it off'.[43]

With his back secured, Baldwin could address his energies to coping with the more serious problem facing him: the entangled questions of the confidence of the parliamentary Party and the future of India. Alarm over the latter emerged after the debate on the Round Table Conference on 26 January, when Churchill's dissent had become manifest. On that occasion Baldwin deviated from the agreed line, associating himself too closely with the Government, and his speech lamentably failed to reassure his followers. Genuine anxiety over India fed the flames fanned by those who were irreconcilably hostile to his leadership. Baldwin attempted to restore his position with moderate Conservatives in his next public speech. Without compromising the spirit of his views on India, his text at Newton Abbot on 6 March raised no further alarms. He dealt first with the topics of economy in government spending and tariffs in such a way as to align himself fully with rank and file opinion. Turning to India, he then went some way to appeasing anxiety by placing greater emphasis on the safeguards that must be put into any new constitutional legislation. Although rather a pedestrian performance, the Newton Abbot speech helped to shore up Baldwin's position.

For some time discontent had been channelled through the Party's Indian Affairs Committee. Despite the efforts of the loyalist chairman, Wardlaw-Milne, the right wing had been gaining ground within that forum since January. It was as a result of a meeting of this group on 9 March that Baldwin's prestige sank to a new low. Either through carelessness, or failure to realise the implications, he agreed that a resolution which had been passed at Churchill's instigation should be released to the press, despite the fact that it seemed to imply a humiliating retreat from his previous undertakings on India. Coming at such a time, it seemed to be the final demonstration of Baldwin's incompetence. Lane-Fox was 'afraid that it was really the end of him'.[44] However, Baldwin was able to recover even from this blunder. The conclusion of an agreement between Gandhi, leader of the Indian Congress, and Irwin appeared to be a vindication of the moderate policy with which Baldwin had associated himself and his party. News of the terms of the pact, received in London in the first week of March, caused 'a tremendous revulsion of feeling among our own rank and file' in Baldwin's favour; 'it has come as an absolute godsend to S.B.', noted Amery in his diary.[45] The pact strengthened Baldwin's personal standing at the same time as cutting most of the ground from under the diehard position. It was the foundation upon which the decisive step was based: Baldwin's triumph in the Commons debate on India of 12 March. His oration on this occasion was not only one of his most successful efforts, but was also delivered to the very audience whom he needed to recapture: not the electors of St. George's, but the moderate majority of backbenchers. More than simply an effective exposition of Conservative policy, or even an accomplished demolition of Churchill, the real value of the speech was that it showed fighting spirit, and demonstrated Baldwin's willingness to assert himself. This debate proved to be the turning point, rallying to Baldwin's standard all but the most extreme Diehards, and restoring the faith of the moderate centre.[46] It cleared the issue of India out of the way and in the process isolated Churchill and the irreconcilable minority from the bulk of the Conservative Party.

There remained no further barrier to prevent the Party from rallying round its leader on the issue of the power of the press. Baldwin was visualised by his followers in the role of a crusader, unafraid of doing his duty and attempting to clean the Augean stables of political life.[47] Attack from without usually had the effect of closing the Conservative ranks. Put simply, this meant a desire on the part of many ordinary Conservatives to make it clear now that they 'were

Baldwinites and not Rothermereites'.[48] The strength of grass-roots support for Baldwin in March 1931 is clearly evident in the chorus of resolutions, supportive both of himself as leader and of Duff Cooper as candidate for St. George's, that were pouring in from the local Associations.[49] A parallel indication of the changed mood in the parliamentary ranks was the demonstration of support from those Conservative MPs who happened to be voters in St. George's, the division being a fashionable and convenient location for residence during the parliamentary session. Forty-five out of the fifty-one, representative of a broad spectrum of opinion, responded to a request to sign an open letter of support for Cooper. Only the Diehard fringe remained hostile, but reduced to impotence. Gretton was the most prominent of the six who refused to sign, but only Sir William Wayland stepped so far out of line as to give public support to Petter. The new atmosphere was further emphasised by the fact that this gesture nearly led to his repudiation by his own constituency Association in Canterbury, in addition to the withdrawal of the Party whip.[50]

At the same time the attack on Baldwin at St. George's and in the columns of the hostile newspapers was being badly mismanaged. Beaverbrook was now paying the price of his dependence on Rothermere, firstly in the way in which hostility to the latter tarred him by virtue of the association, and secondly in the fact that Rothermere was diverting the campaign towards other issues. The balance of power in the alliance between the two press lords was swinging from Beaverbrook to Rothermere. Empire Free Trade was pushed into the background by India, on which both Petter and the *Daily Mail* concentrated throughout the campaign, culminating with the slogan 'Gandhi is watching St. George's'.[51] However, India was no longer such a good stick with which to beat Baldwin, and Beaverbrook later felt that he had made a fatal mistake. He admitted 'the defeat is due in part to my own stupidity: it was wrong of me to fight on India and the leadership of the Conservative Party'.[52] Another respect in which the tactics of the press lords were misconceived was the social composition of the constituency. Though a metropolitan division, it was not ideal Crusading territory; the influence of the *Daily Mail* and *Daily Express* was not as great here as in many middle class constituencies. In St. George's the leaders of opinion in the upper class residential areas tended to be readers of *The Times*, the *Morning Post*, or perhaps the *Daily Telegraph*, all of which were not only staunchly pro-Baldwin, but also accepted his contention that the issue of the day was the constitutional role of the press.[53] Apart from the wealthy quarters of Mayfair, the constituency also contained some working class housing in Pimlico. As none of the other parties were fielding a candidate, Petter may have picked up some votes here, although most Liberal or

Labour supporters would not have been attracted either by anti-Baldwinism or a hard line on India. However, one product of the hostility shown to Beaverbrook by the aristocratic element was his adoption of an even more demagogic, even populist, platform in his attempts to win over Pimlico, further alienating himself from the conventional and deferential Conservatism of respectable society. The greatest weakness of Petter's campaign was that the keynote was personal rather than political. This was not only counter-productive in itself, but it also gave Baldwin an excuse for making a direct intervention in the constituency. He spoke at the Queen's Hall on 17 March, two days before the poll, and inevitably the theme of his oration was a denunciation of the press lords' methods.

The significance of the Queen's Hall speech, and in particular the short extract from it in which Baldwin castigated the press barons for aiming at 'power without responsibility—the prerogative of the harlot throughout the ages', has been consistently overrated by historians, amateur and professional.[54] Baldwin did not crush the Empire Crusade by means of a phrase, or even a speech, however pungent and striking. Phrases from speeches do not normally have that kind of direct electoral impact, unless hammered home repeatedly in the media or by other forms of propaganda. Baldwin's almost vulgar summation received no such prominence at the time.[55] Contemporary observers considered it only a minor contribution to either Cooper's campaign or Baldwin's re-establishment, if they thought even that. The targets of the speech did not feel damaged by it: Hannon told Beaverbrook that he did not think Baldwin's speech would make a shadow of a difference to the battle in St. George's.[56] It played only a small part in Baldwin's strategy of raising the argument from the details of policy, whether it be tariffs or India, to the preservation of the constitution. Once he had succeeded in changing the nature of the controversy, in which he was considerably assisted by the misconceived tactics of his enemies, the latter were exposed in a politically untenable light.

The 'harlot' passage, and indeed the entire Queen's Hall speech, is significant as a supreme example of the defence that Baldwin adopted, by decision or by instinct. The impact of the 'harlot' image was not upon the electors of St. George's, but upon posterity. In retrospect it came to encapsulate, even for those intimately involved in these events, the keynote of the Party crisis. Due to its virtues of brevity and almost shocking pungency it was frequently taken out of context, and the writers of memoirs and later commentators used it to sum up the events of both 1930 and 1931.[57] This gave both the Queen's Hall speech and the St. George's by-election an irresistible impetus towards achieving historical significance. Yet its importance was far from clear at the time. The St. George's contest was largely won in other ways: not least by the personality of the candidate. It was probably won for Baldwin even before it began, in the sense that East Islington had exposed the Empire Crusade as a dangerously irrelevant political luxury, thereby producing the reaction exhibited at St. George's. On these terms East Islington, and not St. George's, was the turning point, and must be largely credited for both the existence and the scale of Cooper's victory on 19 March, when he defeated Petter by 5,710 votes. If any speech added to this majority, it was Baldwin's successful Commons performance on India. So far as the press was concerned, it seems clear that the personal attacks on Baldwin backfired. His true achievement at St. George's was that a majority of the electors, and almost all of his own party, accepted his analysis of the causes and solutions of the Party crisis, blaming the mischievous-ness of the press. This was a double victory, for as the precise details of the complicated sequence of events between 1929 and 1931 receded into memory, so the correctness of Baldwin's stand became an accepted fact.

The final reason why the importance of St. George's is so consisten-tly overrated is that in the week immediately following the poll Beaverbrook re-opened negotiations and made his peace with the Party. On this occasion, with both sides in a chastened mood after the result and reaction at East Islington, topped off and confirmed by St. George's, the prospects for concluding a deal were brighter than ever before. This was not so much the direct product of St. George's as of the whole trend of events since October 1930. Having eliminated the differences over policy, Neville Chamberlain had long wanted to end the rift, but felt no particular urgency in the matter until East Islington suggested that Beaverbrook might still have sufficient influence with the public in London and the home counties to undermine Conserva-tive prospects in a general election. After this, the December attitude of letting things drift became too risky. On Beaverbrook's side, two successive failures, with their accompanying bitterness, finally con-vinced him that his strength had passed its peak. The continuous strain of running what was effectively a one-man campaign was telling, and he was at least temporarily attracted to another truce. On 22 March, at Hoare's suggestion, Neville Chamberlain sent Beaverbrook a note suggesting a talk. This was quickly responded to, and the two men met on the 24th at Beaverbrook's residence, Stornoway House. During the following week most of the negotiations took place here, giving the agreement eventually concluded the name of the Storno-way Pact. The basic concord was drafted on 24 March, and hinged on Beaverbrook's concern over the position of British agriculture, which had now become his principal interest. The agreement contained nothing that was not already implicit in the Conservative agricultural programme and the free hand position on tariffs, but Beaverbrook half-heartedly attempted during the week after 24 March to amend the drafted letters so as to make it appear that he had scored a victory. To some extent he was encouraged in this by the newly formed Agricultural Party, based in Norfolk; but at this stage his desire for a truce was greater than his willingness, sometimes contemplated, to fight to the end by 'adopting Sinn Fein tactics'.[58] When Neville Chamberlain firmly resisted these modifications, Beaverbrook's opposition crumbled. The difficulties over Taylor's position at South Paddington which had proved the stumbling block on the last occasion were now swept aside, to be dealt with after a general settlement. Chamberlain secured the agreement of the shadow cabinet to the proposed exchange of letters between Beaverbrook and himself, and they were released to the press on 31 March. Chamberlain had moved swiftly, exploiting the mood he sensed in Beaverbrook, flattering and then bullying him into an agreement which was made public immediately, and from which Beaverbrook would have much more difficulty in disengaging than the previous truce of March 1930.[59] Neville Chamberlain himself had no doubt that the pact was a real victory, for which the Conservative leaders had had to make no concessions; it was Beaverbrook who now accepted their policy.

The tensions within the parliamentary leadership were resolved at the same time as the external battle with the press lords. There had been no plot against Baldwin, only anxiety and dissatisfaction; but in his fighting mood after 2 March Baldwin misinterpreted the actions of several colleagues, including Hailsham and Neville Chamberlain, as having been disloyal. One reason for this was an unexpected intervention from Austen Chamberlain at the shadow cabinet meeting on 11 March, at the height of the crisis, in which he demanded to know when Baldwin would release Neville from the confining position of Party Chairman. This additional complication was not a stab in the back at Baldwin, but a spontaneous initiative which Neville himself neither expected nor entirely welcomed.[60] It was the product of Austen's frustration over the general situation and his fear that Neville was damaging his own prospects by his tenure of the Chairmanship. Austen had always believed that taking that post was a mistake, but he could not see how to shield his younger half-brother from political damage.[61] At the heat of the crisis he was afraid that Neville might be dragged down with his leader, and took the first available chance, however maladroitly, to prevent this. Nevertheless, Baldwin felt threatened by the attitude of his colleagues, and allowed his resentment to become known. This in turn exacerbated their feelings, and in particular led to a period of personal coolness between Baldwin and Neville Chamberlain. Believing he had lost his leader's confidence, the latter indicated that, the matter having been raised, he would like to quit the Chairmanship. Paradoxically, this led to a clearing of the air. After the dust had settled at St. George's, Neville Chamberlain, piqued at the apparent mistrust which he considered his loyal conduct had not deserved, insisted on a private interview on 24 March. Baldwin was now keen to avoid any further rift, and when Chamberlain put his grievances before him, responded apologetically. Chamberlain stuck to his wish to stand down from the Chairmanship of the Party organisation, declaring that he had carried through the required reforms, but he retained control of the Conservative Research Department. The meeting between the two men was a considerable success, removing the clouds that had darkened their personal and political relationship.[62] A similar pattern was repeated at the shadow cabinet meeting the following day. Baldwin's colleagues were able to vent their frustrations to his face, a process which reduced the pressure of their discontent through a relatively harmless letting off of verbal steam.

In real terms it was Baldwin who had gained most politically from recent events. He had been forced to concede nothing of consequence, and his position and powers had remained intact. The price of hearing some critical comments was not a high one to pay for re-establishing his pre-eminence as leader and preserving the solidarity of the front bench. Bridgeman perceptively analysed the realities of the position at the end of March. 'I think it can be assumed that they have said all they mean to say, and will now come into line', he wrote to Baldwin; 'I noticed that they all spoke of you as their Leader'. His conclusion was definite: Baldwin's position was secure. The crisis had become a thing of the past, as had talk of Baldwin's retirement, and there was 'a general atmosphere of relief'.[63] In the face of the impending economic and political crises facing the nation, unity came above all else in Conservative politics in 1931. This was the lesson taught by East Islington, tested but accepted on the issue of India, and confirmed at St. George's. In such a period of national peril, internal dissension was a dangerous luxury. It was in this mood, against the background of economic recession and financial crisis, that in the summer of 1931 Baldwin and his colleagues set about the restoration of order in Conservative politics.

CHAPTER 8

The Impact of the Slump

In Victorian and Edwardian Britain the Conservative Party had traditionally been associated with the landed or agricultural interest, and this relationship was perpetuated in the inter-war period. Close links existed with the National Farmers Union, and the rural county divisions were a substantial and significant element of Conservative electoral support. However, the character of the Party was changing as the Liberal Party declined and was replaced on the left by the rise of a Socialist party. The influx of business and financial interests, though a trend evident before 1914, was altering the balance within the parliamentary Conservative Party by the late 1920s. The increasing prominence of the business mentality had been a particular source of comment during the post-war coalition parliament, but it had not then been so predominant over the agricultural interest. Indeed, these amorphous groups were not in conflict with each other, for a protectionist policy was attractive to them both. Fear of Socialism assured their active support for the Conservative Party during the early 1920s, and went a long way to explain the polarisation of anti-Socialists behind Baldwin, and the consequent decline of the Liberal centre. However, the period of tranquillity provided by Baldwin's 1924–1929 government significantly reduced these tensions, a process in which the defeat of the General Strike had played a large part. By the general election of 1929 both conservative interest groups had reason to feel dissatisfied with the Conservative ministry. This translated into the apathy amongst the rank and file which had contributed to defeat.

After the 1929 election, the running was initially made by the vocal dissatisfaction of the agricultural interest.[1] The effects of the slump hit British agriculture first, coming on top of nearly a decade of depression. The primary cause of the slump of 1929 was a collapse in world commodity prices, and this of course affected British farmers as well.

151

The wheat growers were especially vulnerable to overseas competition, and in late 1929 the price paid for grain fell by nearly 20%. This increased the clamour of the British producers for agricultural protection, and for government action to prevent the 'dumping' of subsidised imports from abroad upon the home market. As the Liberal and Labour parties were doctrinally committed to maintaining free trade, the agriculturalists could only look to the Conservatives for aid. However, at this time the Conservative leaders were far from offering the sort of protectionist policy that the stricken wheat farmers wanted. It was this political vacuum which Beaverbrook moved to fill in October 1929. His Empire Crusade campaign was as much about domestic agriculture as imperial trade, and began as an appeal to the farmers. Its greatest strength was always to be found in the south and in the arable counties of eastern England, above all in Lincolnshire and Norfolk. The National Farmers Union itself came close to breaking its informal but extensive links with the Conservative Party in frustration at the absence of a suitable agricultural policy. Its alienation did not result in serious damage in the county seats only because of the internal divisions within the Union itself, as it oscillated between affiliation to the Crusade and an ostensible 'above party' position. The suggestion of establishing a separate agricultural party, frequently voiced in the Union's councils, was a clear sign of loss of faith by a crucial pillar of Conservatism.[2]

Whilst keeping one eye on the electoral barometer of public opinion, Baldwin moved cautiously during 1930 to appease the agriculturalists. The truce with the Crusade in March 1930 removed much of the direct pressure. Before the truce collapsed, Baldwin finally presented his agricultural programme on 9 June at Glemham Park. This was designed to stop short of complete agricultural protection with its accompanying danger of food taxes. Further steps in that direction came as a result of the policy brought forward in October, which was based not on tariffs, but on the quota system. This provided the facade on the edifice of a popular Conservative agricultural policy. It was the product of negotiations with the National Farmers Union conducted by Lord Wolmer throughout the summer. The crucial point was that the quota system was favoured by the Union's leadership: it would give the wheat farmers the protection which they required.[3] The final stage in the conciliation of the farmers came in the winter of 1930, when their agitation against the dumping of ruinously cheap subsidised foodstuffs from abroad was met by the Party's adoption of the proposal for an 'emergency tariff', to be implemented the moment it returned to office.

However, this series of concessions could not hide the fact that by the end of 1930 the concerns of the agricultural interest were beginning to lose pride of place. Calls for further advances, under the code of seeking further 'definition' of policy, were seen as potentially divisive and no longer commanded the same degree of support at local level.[4] By the summer of 1931 the agricultural issue had been pushed into the background by the concerns of industry and finance with other aspects of economic affairs, and these received priority even where they cut across those of the farmers. Addison's useful Agricultural Bill was sacrificed at the altar of reducing government expenditure. The changed focus of attention was evident when on 20 July 1931 not one Conservative front bencher bothered to speak during a vote of censure debate on agricultural affairs. This subject had slipped to being always the last mentioned and least emphasised point in all the speeches and statements expounding the new Conservative programme.

This attitude reflected the maturing changes in the composition of the Party. By 1929 the landed group provided only 15% of the parliamentary Party, and the businessmen outnumbered them by 2 to 1. When taken together with the professional men, who were mainly lawyers linked more to finance and urban life than to the land or rural concerns, they accounted for more than two-thirds of Conservative MPs. Links with the atmosphere of the landed squirearchical party of the late-Victorian era were passing. Only forty Conservative MPs had sat before 1914, and many of these represented not the old style, but had themselves been harbingers of the new business ethos. This development was further matched by the increasing role of business in providing the Party's funds, both locally and nationally. That the business group did not dominate the Party in a more visible sense was due to the pre-eminence in the public eye of the career politicians, and to the corresponding inarticulateness of the business sector, as well as the poor reputation of that element known as the 'Forty Thieves'. In 1930 the impression that the views of the business bloc were being ignored resulted in the belief that collectively they were the motive force behind the right-wing revolt.[5] In reality this was far from the case. Certainly by the end of its term much of the enthusiasm for the Conservative government of 1924–1929 in business circles had evaporated. Baldwin had refused to act as the representative of any sectional interest, and Churchill's budgets did not deliver the desired reductions in expenditure and taxation. One result of this was the favourable reception given to Labour in 1929, when Macdonald was presented with the freedom of the City. The business world was mainly neutral during the Crusade campaign in early 1930. Cunliffe-Owen reported to Beaverbrook in May that the mood in the City was sulky and apathetic, and that there was little chance of raising money for political funds of any kind.[6] However, when this indifference began to evaporate during the last quarter of 1930, business in politics threw its weight on the side of the Conservative leadership, quashing dissent and rebellion, in order to restore the Party as an effective force enlisted under the banner of financial rectitude.

This return to political involvement was largely the product of factors external to Conservative politics. The first stage began with the hostility of the mineowners to the government's Coal Bill in 1929, although the Party was always reluctant to be tied to the chariot wheels of that particular interest group.[7] More significant were the actions of the Labour administration during 1930. Politically, it was proposed to remove the business franchise and plural voting. Economically, opposition was aroused by the addition of six pence to the income tax in the 1930 budget and the dismantling of the safeguarding duties, which had afforded certain industries a limited form of protection from overseas competition. Above all, the impact of the economic recession on the business world brought about a renewed and urgent concern with domestic politics by the winter of 1930. The decline in British exports gives some indication of the seriousness of the collapse; in 1929 these had been worth £839 million, in 1930 they fell to £666 million, and in 1931 they plunged to only £461 million. Domestic output was hit as badly. The results, of course, were not only a crash in the yield and value of stocks and shares, but a torrent of bankruptcies, and consequently sharp rises in unemployment. As a result of the slump, there was throughout 1930 a growing current of opinion in favour of protection of the home market, so that that policy was for the first time becoming a popular asset.[8] The Bankers' Manifesto of July and the Associated Chambers of Commerce in August advocated sweeping extensions of safeguarding, whilst in October the Federation of British Industries conducted an internal referendum which produced a 96% vote for protection, and even the Trades Union Congress began to make favourable noises by the winter.[9]

However, at the beginning of 1931 the dominant theme of the business sector was no longer simply the need for protection. It was their belief that the principal cause of the slump and the main barrier to any recovery was the burden of taxation imposed by central and local government. This had been the concern of finance and industry for many years, and had been the rationale behind the Conservative de-rating policy of 1928–1929. As the central tenet of financial orthodoxy, it inevitably returned to the forefront of the political stage when the onset of an economic trough was combined with the existence of a government committed on principle to a high level of expenditure on the social services. Even in the most prosperous of times these were considered in the Conservative frame of mind to be items carried on the luxury ledger, and were therefore the first target for reducing the load in times of difficulty. This attitude determined the decision in the spring of 1931 to wreck in the House of Lords the government's

Education Bill for being 'financially reckless'.[10] The Unemployment Fund was a much greater problem, for the escalating numbers in need of support were over-stretching its resources. In January 1930 the unemployment figure was 1,533,000; by March it had risen to 1,731,000; and by June it had reached 1,946,000. The increase in unemployment was even more rapid and severe during the last half of the year, and by December 1930 the total stood at 2,725,000. The rise in the first three months of the year, against the normal seasonal trends, upset the actuarial calculations upon which the finances of the Fund were based. To meet the difficulty, the Labour government chose not to increase contributions or decrease benefits, or to raise the state's statutory subvention, but to embark upon a career of borrowing. They did so from the belief that this was a freak crisis which would swiftly pass. However, this proved not to be the case, and as the figures continued sharply upwards, more and more borrowing was required. The Minister of Labour, Margaret Bondfield, had to return to the Commons on several occasions to ask for the necessary powers, but she could offer no prospects of improvement ahead. The government seemed simply to be living from hand to mouth.[11] During 1930 the financial community was becoming increasingly anxious about the repeated government borrowing for the Fund, which was clearly beyond its means. This gave rise to fears of an unbalanced budget, and the prospect of a large deficit by the end of 1931. In the economic orthodoxy of the day, that spelled national bankruptcy. Faced with such a peril, the business sector raised the twin standard of reduction of government expenditure and consequently of direct taxation. This was proclaimed to be the only sure path to the recovery of confidence and investment, and therefore to the reduction of unemployment and the return of prosperity. Protection, especially in the form of the emergency tariff on imports, could play its part in this. However, in the search for a remedy to the problem of massive unemployment, admitted by all parties in the inter-war period to be the most significant social problem facing the nation, the Conservatives were perceptibly turning away from their platform of 1923 that protection alone would suffice. The Party was not slow to respond to the mood of finance and industry, and by midsummer 1931 reduction of taxation was placed even above tariffs in the Conservative programme.[12]

The campaign for 'economy' had been an recurrent theme in Conservative politics for many years. It had been exploited by the Diehards as an issue with which to arouse wider support amongst Conservatives. They had been most successful in this with the Anti-Waste campaign of 1920–1922, precisely because the 'economy' cry had a more general appeal than any sectional complaint. In 1930, the Conservative leadership moved rapidly to take up the 'economy' campaign as its own. This was partly a result of their genuine community of interest and economic outlook with finance and industry, and partly because it was a cause too close to the hearts of the constituency activists to be safely ignored. But, above all, the 'economy' issue could unite all sections of the Party behind a potentially popular cry. Many Conservatives who had flirted with the Crusade in the early part of 1930 had done so not just because it offered a vigorous lead on protection, but also because they had hopes of turning Beaverbrook's movement into a campaign for other diehard causes in general, and the need for economies in particular. As anxiety about taxation and government expenditure came to the fore in late 1930, the Conservative leaders responded with a rapidity and commitment that was a revealing contrast with their attitude to the advocates of protection over the previous twelve months. In the press release which announced the policy advance at the time of the Imperial Conference it was noticeable that Neville Chamberlain, when drafting the leader's statement, put 'economy' first, the emergency tariff second, then repeated the pledges already given to agriculture, leaving empire trade to bring up the rear. By December 1930 Baldwin was emphasising the other face of 'economy' in his public speeches, declaring at Glasgow on the 12th that the most important thing was the reduction of taxation.[13]

It was clear that the main impact of the economies would be on the social services. They would involve cuts in the salaries of government employees and in capital expenditure on building projects. Most importantly, a reduction in the level of unemployment benefit and of the number of people entitled to receive it would be mandatory, for it was evident that the financing of this outlay threatened more than anything else to unbalance the budget.[14] The detailed planning of the Party's response on this issue had been one of the main tasks of the new Conservative Research Department during 1930 and 1931. A committee was set up under Sir Henry Betterton, who had been the parliamentary secretary to the Ministry of Labour during both Baldwin governments. Its report called for the reduction of the level of benefit, together with the adoption of a means test to regulate the recipients of the dole. The heart of their policy was a strict restoration of the insurance principle: that benefits could only be drawn where they had been covered by an individual's contributions. Expenditure would be kept in line with the Fund's receipts, and a properly balanced fund would no longer act as a drain on the national exchequer.[15] Conservative politicians continued to press the government on this issue throughout the last six months of 1930. However, without a policy of their own, and unwilling to humble themselves by adopting the favoured panaceas of either of the opposing parties, the Labour Government set up during 1930 and 1931 a series of committees and advisory councils on economic matters. All sounded impressive, but were essentially hollow. These delaying tactics were repeated in the case of the Unemployment Fund. Lacking any clear idea themselves of how to deal with the problem, the ministry fobbed off their critics by the expedient of appointing a Royal Commission. When this finally reported in early June 1931, the Conservatives accepted its findings in toto. This was partly because they were very close to the conclusions already arrived at by Betterton's committee, but it was mainly intended as a political move to increase the pressure on the Labour government. Not only did the Royal Commission lend prestige to the Conservatives' cause; it also served to blur the element of partisanship that was involved.

Inevitably, there were fears that the 'economy' policy would be unpopular with many urban working-class electors. This was a source of concern to some of the prospective candidates in the north, and to meet their anxieties Baldwin slightly watered down the presentation of the policy in his own public statements. Typically, he did so through remaining vague and avoiding any definite commitments, and this did not alter the Party's ultimate intentions. However, his caution on the issue was not shared by most of his colleagues, in contrast with previous similar fears about food taxes.[16] This was partly due to the fact that a reduction of the dole would only directly affect a minority of the working class, whereas a rise in the cost of living could alienate them all. There was also a case that after a decade in which prices had fallen, the unemployment benefit was now worth more in real terms. This was reinforced by the concurrent press campaign based on exposing abuses in the benefit system, which was producing an indignant response from grass-roots Conservatism. The abuses were held to be the direct result of the changes in the unemployment insurance regulations made by the Labour government since they had come into office. Some of the charges were more serious than others, and many of the more scandalous examples had little basis in reality, though this did not diminish their impact on the public mind. However, the increase in the number of married women claiming benefit, from only 86,000 in October 1929 to 240,000 twelve months later, was a particular target of Conservative criticism. The Party believed this to be the consequence of Labour's misguided relaxation of the stringency of the rules governing entitlement, and that furthermore women who had husbands to support them should not come within the purview of the act.[17] Another complaint was that the changed provisions were an encouragement to short-time working, with benefit being given for the idle days in each week. This was related to the most serious charge: that Labour's abandonment of the 'not genuinely seeking work' clause had given a licence to scroungers.[18] The difference between the two parties' outlook was fundamental. Conservatives and many Liberals were suspicious of centrally-administered state welfare, the system of doles. They did not accept Labour's belief that there was a right to maintenance that was unrelated to the amount of contributions paid. The Conservatives put great emphasis on thrift, and this was a view which found an echo not just with the middle class, but amongst many of the working class as well.

An even more significant element in the public reaction to the slump was the widely shared belief that no section of society could be immune from the wage reductions and other belt-tightening of recent years. This was a consequence of the economic orthodoxy of the day, accepted instinctively as common sense by all classes. People believed that their prosperity was bound up with that of the nation as a whole, and that anything which undermined that must be avoided. This attitude was revealed in the debate over the danger of a budget deficit; there was little argument that the country, like any individual family, could not live beyond its means. Economies were therefore not seen in class terms. One reason for this was the rhetoric with which an otherwise unpalatable package could be presented. The rallying cry used by the Conservative Party to avoid any potential class antagonisms that dole and wage cuts might produce was the widely accepted commitment to 'equality of sacrifice'. The economic crisis facing Britain was instead to be a cause for national solidarity. All parts of the nation, it was claimed, would face up to their duty. In such an atmosphere the Conservatives, with their self-image and public posture of being the patriotic party, were bound to be the beneficiaries of any evocation of national sentiment, and even to be in danger of being swept away by it.

The 'economy' issue came to the forefront of Conservative politics after the effective settlement of the tariff question in October 1930, and reaction to the Labour government's 'squandermania' became acute in the first quarter of 1931. Whilst protection had set north against south, industry against agriculture, the demand for budgetary sanity was one upon which all Conservatives could agree. On the same day that the local association in Halifax resolved 'economy is in the forefront of Conservative policy', Waldron Smithers, MP for Chislehurst and a prominent figure in the City, urged that the Party should 'put Economy first with a capital E'.[19] At the same time, in January 1931, Neville Chamberlain was publicly declaring that the first duty of a Conservative administration would be to cut national expenditure and call a halt to the extension of the social services. His theme was echoed by Baldwin a week later, and simultaneously taken up by other prominent figures.[20] Even in the dark days of the internal crisis in February, Chamberlain was carefully monitoring the effect of Labour's budgetary policies on the money market.[21] When making his crucial speech at Newton Abbot on 6 March, Baldwin significantly placed 'economy' firmly first of the four essential points of the Conservative programme. With the cessation of the Crusade campaign after the Stornoway Pact, the paramountcy of 'economy' became even more marked. At the Albert Hall on 15 May Baldwin outlined his priorities. 'Economy' was foremost, with the problem of foreign dumping and its solution in the shape of the emergency tariff second, followed by a vague promise to help agriculture. Noticeably, there was no discussion of the imperial dimension at all.

This hierarchy of issues was, however, completely in tune with the state of mind of the Party in the early summer of 1931. The clear message from all the policy discussions that took place within the local parties was that 'economy' took priority over everything else.[22] Constituency resolutions were couched in suitably apocalyptic terms; 'immense and immediate' reductions in public expenditure afforded 'the only means of economic salvation'.[23] The degree of concern was shown in February when Esher Conservative Association decided to circularise all the constituencies, calling for a chorus of resolutions on 'economy'.[24] The national peril became manifest when even the government acknowledged the seriousness of the position during the budget debates of April. Votes of censure on government overspending were moved on several occasions from the opposition front bench, and a national campaign was launched to provide an umbrella under which both Liberals and Conservatives could advocate large-scale reductions in expenditure. As the summer advanced the issue became an even more crucial concern, and the declarations of leading Conservatives adopted the language of alarmism. In January Hailsham had warned that if the burden placed on industry and property increased the whole economic structure of the nation might collapse. This danger became the dominant theme of the speeches of the spring and summer months; that 'unless we retrenched we were heading straight for bankruptcy and ruin'.[25]

Not unnaturally, such a serious situation produced considerable pressures for unity amongst Conservatives. This was exemplified by two manifestos issued in support of Duff Cooper at St. George's; the first by almost all the resident MPs, and the second by a circle of the most prominent businessmen and bankers. 'Economy' was pushing both protectionism and the India question into the background. It also served to smooth over another area of internal controversy. This was the revolt of the younger political generation against the predominance of a group of senior figures from the former Cabinet, many of whose careers had been rooted in the pre-war world. Stale, stuffy, and jointly responsible for the lacklustre image presented in the 1929 election, they were dismissively categorised as the 'Old Gang' by their impatient and energetic juniors. Sentiments of this nature are endemic to the younger backbenchers of all parties, but this was one of the facets which, cutting across conventional boundaries, symptomised the general political uncertainty of this particular period. Within the Conservative Party, the peaks of the agitation coincided with Baldwin's worst periods of parliamentary incompetence, policy vagueness, and personal aloofness; in brief, with the periods of lowest morale in the Party.[26] Baldwin's remoteness from the younger generation, and his apparent reluctance either to acknowledge their abilities or to dispense with any of his more senior colleagues, was at the root of the 'Old Gang' agitation. This obscured the fact that, with the exception of a minority of Diehard orientation, the younger men were mainly sympathetic to their leader's approach to public life.

Baldwin's lack of vigour was the problem which led the youthful rebels to flirt with alliances with politicians they would not normally be attracted to, such as Lloyd George and Sir Oswald Mosley, the bright new star in Labour's firmament. However, overriding frustration was not focused directly on Baldwin, but on the absence of drive and originality amongst the Conservative frontbenchers, whom they considered to be 'wooden' and uninspiring.[27] The 'Old Gang' syndrome was a symptom as well as a condemnation of the failures of leadership during the eighteen months since the defeat of 1929. The result was the willingness of the young men to applaud anyone who gave the appearance of energy. This instinct led firstly to sympathy with Beaverbrook's Crusade in its earlier stages, and secondly to a community of feeling with the 'economic radicals'. The common ground of impatience with orthodox remedies drew them together with Beaverbrook, Lloyd George, and Mosley.[28] The tension between the attraction of vigour and the instincts of party loyalty, the confusion over policy complicated by the frustrations of idle young men with abilities and ambitions, all combined to produce an atmosphere that was, paradoxically, both alarming for the Party leadership yet ultimately ineffective. Nonetheless, the mood of hostility to the old party shibboleths was very marked, and represented something more significant than merely the rhetorical cloak adopted by ambitious men. It synchronised with the feeling that party politics were in the melting pot, and could and should be recast in the image of the post-war generation.

In the guise of this general feeling, acknowledged even by the 'Old Gang' themselves, the young men's movement gave rise to considerable anxiety and discussion amongst the Shadow Cabinet. In November 1930, in the period of settlement after the peak of the Conservative crisis, the leadership tried to take the heat out of the agitation against the 'Old Gang' by the circulation of a self-denying ordinance amongst the front benchers. This enabled Baldwin to reassure his followers publicly that he had a 'free hand' in another sense; to appoint whom he pleased when the Party returned to office.[29] This token of appeasement was crucial in stemming the tide of dissatisfaction, so that when Mosley later formed his New Party the young turks' impotence was revealed. Much of their movement was simply hot air: the compiling of cabinets and cliques on the back of menu cards, the thrill of secret meetings with Lloyd George or with Mosley. Almost all of it evaporated in the cold world of political realities. If the new generation of Conservative MPs looked to any one individual as a leader amongst themselves, it was probably Walter Elliot.[30] However, when Elliot publicly indicated sympathy with Mosley's ideas, he was pulled back into line by a rebuke from Baldwin, and swiftly dropped any plans for cross-party groupings. When Mosley broke away from Labour to set up the New Party in February 1931 he was joined by only one Conservative MP, the Ulster Unionist W.E.D. Allen. The remainder were held back by a combination of personal mistrust of Mosley and pragmatic conformity to the established structure. There were fundamental reasons for the failure of the revolt of youth to materialise in any concrete form. Breaking away from the Conservative Party was not so attractive in reality as it had been to talk about.[31] Fusion with like-minded figures in other parties did not seem so practicable when the details came to be ironed out, and neither was switching to a different party an enticing prospect. Mosley's venture was admired only from afar.

The young men's clique was small in number, but included such rising talents as Walter Elliot, Oliver Stanley and Anthony Eden, who already had their feet set on the ladder of promotion and who had too much to risk by disloyalty. Apart from such expediency, many of the young men on the centre and left of the Party, of whom Duff Cooper was just one example, were determined to continue the struggle for the soul of the Conservative Party by supporting Baldwin against diehard reaction. The young men's circle lacked coherence. It included Diehards such as Edward Marjoribanks; moderates such as Victor Cazalet; maverick figures on the further fringes of the Party's left wing such as Harold Macmillan and Robert Boothby; and Churchill's fervent admirer and supporter over India, Brendan Bracken. There were ardent tariff reformers, and those like Walter Elliot and the Marquess of Hartington who were almost free traders. Nor was it more socially cohesive; there was a certain common privilege of background, without which entry into parliament at such a comparatively youthful age would have been impossible, but little else. Some of the young men were career lawyers like Terence O'Connor; others financiers or businessmen. Some came from academic or service families, others were aristocratic agriculturalists. There were also cliques within cliques, the best known of which were the remnants of the 'YMCA' of the previous parliament, and the

'Boys Brigade'. The latter had been set up as a more moderate counter to the ethos of the 'YMCA' group by four MPs first elected in 1929; R.A.Butler, Harold Balfour, Michael Beaumont, and Viscount Lymington. The flavour of the young mens' cabals was well caught by their titles. Equally typical was the way in which even these groups fragmented, the other three members of the 'Boys Brigade' parting company with Butler and turning against Baldwin's leadership in October 1930.

The only common link was the accident of youth and party circumstance. This produced a sense of frustration which was essentially caused by an absence of sympathy with the pragmatism and caution of the leadership, and which came to be symbolised by the generation gap. Once that breach was mended and the younger MPs reassured about their prospects, the bulk of them settled down. Whilst their leanings towards protection alienated them from the official policy in mid-1930, by and large India reunited them with their leader in 1931. In addition, the primacy of the 'economy' cry and the reality of the slump washed away the 'new' ideas. These had never been more than generalised concepts; aspirations rather than blueprints. The majority of the young men accepted the national peril, the need for unity, and the deflationary economic strategy. The youth movement existed through its very vagueness; definitions would only have divided its adherents, and their only common cause was hostility to the continued control of the pre-war generation. In the atmosphere of patriotism and national emergency, the young turks put these feelings on one side, and worked for a Conservative victory at the next election without having restructured either the Party or its policies.

The restoration of order and unity within the Party not only pushed the issues which had been causing divisions into the background, but also propelled the Conservatives towards alliance with other anti-Socialist forces. One immediate product of the 'economy' campaign was to foster a reconsideration of the thorny question of relations with the Liberal Party. The latter held the parliamentary balance, and the fate of the Labour government was in their hands. The new attitude contrasted sharply with the bitter hostility to the Liberals typical of the early months of opposition. Many Conservatives found these emotions hard to swallow even when, due to the overriding necessity of the national crisis, co-operation and coalition became necessary. Antagonism towards the Liberals was based more on the events of the past decade than on the pre-war divides. Conservative anti-coalitionist feeling still ran high, fed by rumour and gossip, and surfaced in constant suspicions. This was reinforced by antipathy to Lloyd George, for his coalition past, for his role in the 1929 election, for his subsequent support of the Labour government, and, above all, for his supposed unprincipled untrustworthiness. The Conservative rank and file blamed the Liberals for the loss of the 1929 election with a peculiar bitterness. Their intervention in such large numbers and their election promises were both condemned. The moral was clear: co-operation with Lloyd George and his followers was a political impossibility.[32] This feeling was only strengthened by Liberal support for the Labour government in the division lobbies on such crucial measures as the Coal Bill of December 1929. However, the principal issue which kept Conservatives and Liberals apart during 1930, and tied the Liberals to Labour, was that of protection versus free trade. The Labour Government's concession of establishing a conference on electoral reform was intended to make this division permanent. Whilst the Liberals looked for the salvation of proportional representation, the Conservatives stood only to lose their advantages of more ample financial resources, plural voting, and the University representation.

As identification of Labour as the greater danger became more pronounced, some Conservatives suggested attempting a deal with the Liberals through the electoral reform Conference.[33] However, the principal concern of the Conservative delegation, under Hoare's leadership, was to prevent any further consolidation of the Liberal-Labour front. By adroit exploitation of the divisions over detail between the other parties, Hoare was so successful in this endeavour that in the end the Conference had to be dissolved.[34] In 1930, dealing with Lloyd George was ruled out by the strength of party sentiment. Conservatives preferred to await the frequently anticipated collapse of the Labour government, or to work towards an accommodation with the Liberal right-wing. This had the advantage that it would not involve alliance with Lloyd George or require concessions on tariffs and electoral reform. Co-operation with other groups was made absolutely conditional upon the fact that it must not water down the protectionist policy arrived at in October 1930. That position was made public by Baldwin in December in the knowledge that it ruled out alliance with most Liberals.[35] This standpoint reflected the fact that by January 1931 the Liberals had entered into what amounted to an informal coalition with the Labour government, and were principally responsible for its continued existence. The government had passed through crises of their own in February and March 1931. Not only had Mosley and his small band of followers finally left the Labour Party, but not long afterwards Sir Charles Trevelyan, the education minister, resigned from the cabinet amidst mutual recriminations. However, these defections were resented by the mass of Labour MPs and, if anything, increased their stubborn cohesiveness and their support for their beleaguered cabinet. From February onwards Lloyd George drew most of the Liberal Party with him into closer links with the government, and by July there were indications that he might join in some senior cabinet capacity. The period of the Liberal–Labour pact saw new heights of Conservative hostility. The denunciation that the Liberals had allowed themselves to become so close to the Government that the Liberal Party 'was neither fish, flesh, fowl, nor good red herring' was only one example of the torrent of abuse rained down by Conservative speakers from the public platform.[36]

There was little likelihood of a Conservative arrangement with the official Liberal Party, unless a section of Liberals made themselves more amenable. As the economic depression intensified, the emphasis which the Liberals had hitherto placed on their manifesto of 1929, with its newly devised programme of expensive public works, receded into the background, shouldered aside by their more traditional cry for retrenchment. However, the main body of the Liberal Party, under the leadership of Lloyd George and his deputy, Sir Herbert Samuel, preferred to stick to the tactic of working to remedy the situation within the framework of a Liberal–Labour partnership, despite its declining popularity in the country. This became apparent on 16 April, when the Conservatives moved a vote of censure on unemployment. Instead of simply abstaining, Lloyd George led his followers into the same lobby as the government, giving it a comfortable majority. Other Liberals were unhappy about nailing their colours to the mast of Labour's drifting and ramshackle vessel, and five Liberal MPs repudiated Lloyd George and voted with the Conservatives. The impact of the slump in 1931 forced a convergence between the Conservative Party and this right wing of the Liberal Party, headed by Sir John Simon. The Simonite Liberals moved closer to the Conservative position not simply because of anxiety about their seats, but also because they shared similar fears of the economic consequences of the continued existence of the Labour government. At the same time, the overriding demand for 'economy' made the latter more desirous of a working partnership.

The crucial development was the Simonite Liberals' abandonment in slow stages of free trade in favour of the emergency tariff.[37] In consequence, they became politically acceptable allies for Conservatives, without provoking internal complaint. Simon himself was seen as 'rapidly coming our way'.[38] He was already a respected figure in Conservative circles as a result of his Report on India in 1930. His stock rose higher when he first distanced himself from requests for electoral reform and later repudiated not only the Liberal–Labour pact but also Lloyd George. On 26 June 1931 this culminated in his resignation of the Liberal Whip. Conservatives drew a distinguishing line between the followers of Lloyd George and Samuel, who moved closer to the government, and Simon's group, to whom they held out a hand in public. Hoare told his constituents at Chelsea in April that he was proud to fight side by side with Simon, for they were propounding the same programme.[39] This was, of course, the business and Conservative strategy of limited insular protection and rigorous economies, and Liberals who accepted this became the 'best type' of 'patriotic' Liberals. In light of this common ground a deal on seats for the next election became not a sordid intrigue but an honest alliance, and parallels were frequently drawn with the late-nineteenth century Liberal Unionist arrangement. These negotiations began after Simon's speech at Manchester on 3 March, where he came out strongly for 'economy' and hinted at a change of heart over free trade, and were dependent upon the fiscal acceptability of the Simonites' manifesto.[40] It was hoped that this realignment of the anti-Socialist forces behind the Conservative banner would be able to bring about the fall of the Labour government when the House of Commons reconvened after the summer recess. A pact would also limit splits in the anti-Socialist vote at the ensuing general election. The Conservative Party, as the predominant partner, stood to gain the most from a mutual withdrawal of candidates. Though not the only cause, these expectations reflected the optimism prevailing within the Conservative Party by midsummer 1931 about not only the imminence of a dissolution but also the prospects for a Conservative victory which this now offered.

The months after the crisis of March 1931 saw a restoration of order within the Conservative Party in which the established hierarchy were able to resume their former omnipotence. The most important cause of this was the accepted primacy and urgency of anti-Socialism. The message from the constituencies was clear: 'it would be a calamity if, at a time when we have the Labour Party on their knees, there should occur any serious rift which would divide the Conservative forces'.[41] Notwithstanding normal party antagonism, as a result of the economic situation this concern was even more pressing than it had been in 1929 and 1930. By the spring of 1931 the existence of the Labour government was regarded as a national calamity, and its continued existence was held by Conservatives to be a national peril. None would have dissented from the bleak view of the Chairman of the Bristol West association, that 'they had never been in greater danger of national disaster than they were today'.[42] As the pressure for Conservative unity was directly proportional to the degree of anxiety felt about the national situation, so these forces increased in effectiveness during the summer months of 1931. The catchword was 'closing the ranks', which inevitably meant drawing together around the position taken by the leader, with dissidents shifting their ground towards his and thereby reducing any need for any concessions to be made to their susceptibilities. The way in which the phrase was employed indicated the power of the leader's position and the unconscious desire for conformity. This was apparent even over India, on which Baldwin's views were farthest from those of many of his followers. At the meeting of the Party's India Committee on 22 June at which Irwin, who had recently returned to Britain at the end of his term as Viceroy, presented his apologia, the pressure for unity overcame the doubters. A strong appeal was made 'that every effort should now be made to close up the ranks in order that the Conservative Party might show a united front'.[43] Even Churchill was responsive to this mood. Although still concentrating his attention on the India question, he promised to 'take no factional attitude'.[44]

Closing the ranks was more than an exercise in papering over the cracks. By midsummer 1931 a new and stable consensus within the Party had been reached. This was especially true in the case of tariff reform, a policy that had consistently divided the Conservative forces since its first formulation in 1903. At that time Joseph Chamberlain had expected that a serious depression would turn the ordinary voter against free trade, and this finally occurred in the economic blizzard of 1930–1931. The evolution of opinion was exemplified by the protectionist resolution tabled in the Commons by Croft on 29 June 1931, to which all the Conservative backbench MPs save six attached their names. This represented a degree of unanimity within the Party in favour of tariff reform that had never previously been attained. Five days earlier a committee working through the Conservative Research Department, chaired by Cunliffe-Lister and including Amery, Lord Lloyd, and H.G. Williams amongst its members, presented a report on fiscal policy amounting to more than a hundred pages, in which the details were for the first time fully worked out.[45] Yet, though firmly established in the Party programme, protection was no longer the most urgent concern. In the interests of securing the floating voter, essential if the Conservatives were to regain power in the next election, Baldwin attempted to defuse the dangerous immediacy of the food tax. He brought forward the proposal, based on the Research Department's report, that the task of deciding which duties were required, and at what level, would be placed in the hands of a Royal Commission. In the interim, the emergency tariff was to hold the ring against dumping. This would protect domestic industry, but avoid the complications of the 'whole-hogger' position on agriculture. Once again Baldwin seemed to want to take the fiscal debate out of party politics; what was revealing was that on this occasion his initiative did not bring forth howls of outrage from his followers. In part this was because the emergency tariff gave most Conservatives what they urgently sought in the domestic dimension, whilst the commitment to call an imperial conference and set up the tariff commission appeared to be a firm promise for the future in the imperial dimension. In the political atmosphere of summer 1931 the issues which had dominated the Party's attention in the previous two years had been elbowed aside by other concerns. On the two key areas of protection and India, Baldwin's policy was acceptable to the broad majority of the Party, even if it did not satisfy the fanatical advocates of either cause. Just as the emergency tariff attained a consensus of approval in one area, so in the other Baldwin's public commitments to specific safeguards in Indian constitutional reform were sufficient to secure unity on his terms.

In the summer of 1931 other issues drew the Party together in opposition to the Labour government. The provisions in the budget for a tax on land values revived memories of the long-standing opposition to such policies of the late-Victorian and Edwardian eras.[46] Conservative ardour was also aroused by another partisan question from the more recent past: the attempt to reverse the industrial verdict of 1926 by repealing the Trades Disputes Act of 1927. In the eyes of the mass of the Party, that measure had been the most important product of the previous administration. They were determined that Conservatives in parliament should fight tooth and nail to prevent what they saw as a surrender to the sectional interests of the trade unions. The passion and bitterness of feeling that this matter aroused among the Conservative grass-roots can hardly be over-estimated. Coming as it did from all regions, it acted as a powerful spur to unite and invigorate the parliamentary opposition.[47] But 'economy' was the issue which by general agreement had come to hold pride of place in the Party manifesto. Naturally, while its effective consequences were relegated to the vague background, the advantages were not. The whole point about 'economy' was that it was much more than just a negative standpoint. The depression was thought to have been caused by the loss of business confidence and incentive, principally due to the high level of rates and taxes.[48] It was widely held that the result of a Conservative government coming into office, committed to cutting taxes and safeguarding industries, would be an instantaneous revival of confidence. Worthington-Evans had made this point the keynote of a vote of censure debate on 'economy' only days before his sudden death in February. 'Without confidence there can be no enterprise, and without enterprise there can be no revival of employment', he declared from the opposition front bench. If the government were turned out 'the psychological effect will be immediate'.[49] Instead, Labour continued to survive in office with Liberal support. As a result of this debate, and as a concession to pressure behind the scenes from their Liberal allies for economy, the government agreed to set up yet another committee to report on the size of the deficit and the amount of reductions required to balance the budget, under the chairmanship of a City businessman, Sir George May. Once again, the government had put off the evil hour, but the report of the May Committee was to

have explosive political effects when it finally appeared at the end of
July 1931.

The needs of agriculture still received frequent mention in the
Conservative programme, but its prominence had waned since 1929.
Not only was it usually relegated to a low position in the list of urgent
topics, but it was also usually referred to in the studiously vague terms
of 'help' for agriculture. This could be taken to mean almost anything,
or almost nothing. Contrasted with this, the concerns of industry and
finance received prominent and specific attention, a fact which reflected the changing nature of the Conservative Party since the turn of the
century. Reduction of expenditure was placed in the vanguard and a
pledge specifically given to impose an immediate emergency tariff,
which would at least mark the end of 'Cobdenism'. In the summer of
1931, Party policy was uniformly presented as a four-point programme. 'Economy' and protection for industry always came first.
Agriculture and imperial development, though still highly emotive
for many Conservatives, had been pushed to the bottom of the list by
the questions of domestic finance.

With unity established around that programme, and with the
pressures to maintain that unity effective throughout 1931, the internal condition of the Party showed a marked improvement over the
first three months of the year. There was 'a general feeling of renewed
courage and determination' which could be seen in the improved
morale and the better attendance of Conservative MPs.[50] The
improved performance of the opposition front bench in attack during
the suemer of 1931 also served to cloak what remained of Baldwin's
deficiencies as an opposition leader. Even in this department there was
some amelioration. This was partly a result of the plain talking in the
shadow cabinet at the end of March, but was mainly a consequence of
Baldwin's conclusion that public opinion had moved to a sufficient
extent that vigorous attacks were now a safe and sensible option.
Neville Chamberlain's conduct of the opposition to the 1931 budget
was a particular success, and marked the final stage of his emergence as
the second figure in the Party—an emergence which had a steadying
force of its own.

The improvement in the internal condition of the Party was also
demonstrated by the minimal concern shown over the occasional
rumblings of dissatisfaction from Beaverbrook after the Stornoway
Pact. These partly concerned the difficulties over the position of
Taylor, the Crusade MP for South Paddington, but were principally
the result of Beaverbrook's suspicion that Baldwin was welshing on
the agreed policy, especially over agriculture. One consequence of the
shelving of the landed interest during 1931 was Beaverbrook's progress towards basing his campaign on the disaffected agricultural
section. This was not because he had given up the concept of Empire

Free Trade, though by the time of the Stornoway Pact he had come to realise the difficulties posed by dominion reluctance. Initially at least, this was just a tactical move with which to maintain the pressure. Beaverbrook knew that his newspapers were not a powerful force on their own, and that they needed to vocalise and mobilise a real grievance felt by rank and file Conservatives. By April 1931 the only group available were the farmers. Single-issue pressure group campaigns were always Beaverbrook's metier, and it was hardly suprising or illogical that his Crusade evolved during 1931 into the Agricultural Party; food taxes were the common ground for both.[51] However, his new venture never had the appeal that the Crusade had possessed. Apart from an irreconcilable element in Norfolk, Lincolnshire, and some parts of rural East Scotland, his campaign failed to attract support. Most Conservatives accepted the validity of Baldwin's strictures on the press lords after the spectacles of the East Islington and St. George's by-elections. But more than anything else, Beaverbrook's complaints were over-trumped by the pressure for Party unity, so strongly felt during the growing national economic difficulties of 1931. It was not just the simple fact that the concerns of finance and industry had shouldered aside the economically weaker farmers, but also that the latter were themselves possessed of the same economic ideas, and were as receptive as any other group to the cry for 'economy'.[52] Indeed, in one sense this was a continuation of the counties' campaign during the previous eighty years to secure reductions in the burdens of local rates. Of all the available issues, 'economy' was the best rallying cry for the forces of anti-Socialism. As it was harnessed only to the less objectionable revenue or 'emergency' tariff, it posed a lesser barrier to drawing into the fold the 'patriotic' Liberals. The programme enunciated in July 1931 was therefore in tune with the electoral and tactical needs of the Conservative Party. It was designed to eject the Socialist government and establish a new national consensus. Along the way the unique sectional claims of agriculture, of the Indian trade, and of the imperial federationists, were relegated to the backwaters of politics.

There could be little doubt by the end of July that the course of British politics was moving in the direction of a return to power by the Conservative Party in the near future. All the indicators suggested that the Labour government had not long to live, and that the Conservatives and their Simonite allies would win the following general election. The shift of opinion in favour of the Conservative economic policy was gathering pace into a landslide. Neville Chamberlain was reliably informed by local sources in May that the Party would make a clean sweep of Lancashire and Yorkshire in an election.[53] The by-election results between April and July confirmed this impression. An early harbinger was the Conservative gain at Ashton-under-Lyne on

30 April. The trend became unmistakable in the three by-elections that took place in June. These proved in the event to be the last of the parliament: Gateshead on the 8th, Manchester Ardwick on the 22nd, and Liverpool Wavertree on the 23rd. Though none changed hands, at an average of 12% the scale of the swing to the Conservatives was enormous. The most significant aspect of these by-elections was their geographical location, for they indicated to Baldwin that his pragmatic strategy was bearing fruit in the industrial north.[54] The reason for this was undoubtedly the rise in unemployment. In 1929 unemployment had averaged 9.7%, in 1930 it had leaped to 16.2%, and in the first eight months of 1931 it reached 22%. Both 'economy' and protection for the home market were policies that were simple to put across, and obvious in their relevance to the worsening industrial climate.

The Conservatives could now look forward with optimism to regaining the ground in the urban areas that they had lost in 1929, and therefore to a majority in the House of Commons. Hannon noted that Gateshead had had a 'considerable stimulating effect' on the parliamentary Party, and that MPs had 'become quite bright and cheerful'.[55] Experienced electoral strategists were convinced that the Party was heading towards a victory on the scale of 1924, even if they would not have gone as far as Baldwin's claim at the end of June that there was not a seat in the country which the Conservatives could not win.[56] Outside parliament, the Stornoway Pact and the arrangements with the Simonite Liberals reduced the likelihood that splits would dissipate the maximum potential of the anti-Socialist vote. The apathy so remarked upon in 1929 and 1930 had vanished as the mist before the dawn of the national crisis. Because of the frequent scares over the possible fall of the government, the local associations were prepared for an election at any time. Inside parliament, secure in the knowledge of the swing of public opinion, the Party began for the first time to use its dominance in the House of Lords to wreck controversial government legislation, in a deliberate attempt to force a dissolution. In view of the government's own internal weaknesses, it was thought that even if it lasted to the recess it would fall on the re-opening of parliament in the autumn. The combination of all these factors made possible and effective the restoration of order in the Party, the cement for which was the prospect of imminent victory.[57]

Optimism over the electoral position went hand-in-hand with pessimism about the national situation. Since the winter of 1930 the dominating theme had been the increasingly evident fact that the troubles within the Party had become overshadowed by a national crisis. Given the self-image of Conservative politicians and their conception of the role of their party as the defender of the realm when in peril, such a realisation required the supercession of the debate over the future path of the Party. Thus the politics of Conservatism were fundamentally reordered from the posture of 1929–1930. Primacy was now placed upon party solidarity. One aspect of this was that further assaults intended to change Party policy, whether on empire trade or India, were counted out. The other aspect dictated that, in order to maintain and preserve that united front, the policy advances of 1929–1930 must be retained as the basis of any Conservative manifesto. The impact of the financial crisis was to fossilise the evolutionary process in Party policy for the foreseeable future. It arrested further development, and preserved in tablets of stone the attitudes and remedies which had been arrived at by July 1931. The commitment to the budgetary podicy summed up by 'economy', to the emergency tariff, and to the bi-partisan approach to India, provided the foundation for Conservative policy when the Party found themselves involved in the crisis of August 1931 and the formation of a National Government.

CHAPTER 9

The National Crisis

The economic and political crisis of August 1931 was the most important event of the inter-war period, and had profound consequences for subsequent British history. The events of August created a multi-party National Government, which went on to win a landslide majority in a general election and to govern for the rest of the decade. The crisis which created the National Government has proved to be of enduring historical fascination. However, attention has been focused hitherto upon the problems of the Labour Government, the vacillations of Ramsay Macdonald, and the interventions of King George V.[1] As a result the role of the Conservative Party, often portrayed as the sole benefactor from these events, has been either neglected or misunderstood.[2]

In the light of the events of August, one of the foremost themes has been the question of whether such a coalition was already in the making before the financial crisis broke. The concept of an all-party coalition, or 'national government', had been floated in the press at frequent intervals during the previous year, but most of these suggestions came from figures on the fringes of political life, such as John Seely, once a Liberal Cabinet minister before the first World War; the former Conservative MP Warden Chilcott; and the increasingly erratic editor of the *Observer*, J.L.Garvin. None of these initiatives bore fruit. However, taken together with the occasional rumours current about the position of Macdonald, they required some reaction from the Conservative Party. The hints concerning the Prime Minister were the result of his characteristic habit of painting a dire picture of his problems in an appeal for the sympathy of his listeners. In the social circle which Macdonald habituated, the audience often consisted of Conservatives or City figures who passed on his table-talk to the Conservative leaders in the belief that they had been selected as political go-betweens. Their presumptions cannot alone be taken as satisfactory evidence of Macdonald's true intentions. Too much weight can be given to those scattered occasions when the Prime Minister acknowledged the minority position of his government with references to Parliament acting less in partisan fashion and more in the capacity of a Council of State, and to those periodic unavoidable contacts between the leaders of the various parties over the official business of the day. The explanation of the formation of the National Government as a plot by Macdonald has been discredited and can be dismissed.[3] Certainly, there was nothing in the contacts between Macdonald and Baldwin to suggest anything more sinister than the fact that they did not dislike each other.

The reaction of the Conservative Party to the public and private talk of coalition was consistently to dismiss it. Throughout the year before the crisis broke Baldwin went out of his way in public speeches to discount the possibility. Co-operation with other parties was ruled out because of the fundamental division over economic policy on the issue of protection versus free trade. The only kind of alignment the Conservatives would consider would be upon the basis of accepting their cherished policy of tariff reform. Conservatives looked upon their own party as being the embodiment of national unity, and believed that such unity was attainable not by their fusion with other parties but by drawing into the Conservative ranks all those of patriotic outlook. They saw the Conservative Party as being 'the greatest unity of individuals in the country', comprising within itself a complete political spectrum from left to right. This, Baldwin insisted, was the only foundation upon which the country 'can form, and we hope to form, a national party'.[4]

The private response of the Conservative leadership was no different from the public one. In early June Lord Stonehaven, the new Chairman of the Party organisation, relayed some supposed feelers from Macdonald to Neville Chamberlain. The latter realistically dismissed them as no more than an expression of Macdonald's weariness. If meant seriously the Prime Minister 'must have got a long way off realities, for such a combination is clearly impossible'.[5] Chamberlain considered that it would produce a right-wing revolt, and that the component parts of this unnatural alliance would find themselves unable to work together. He mentioned the idea to Baldwin, and both concluded 'our party would not stand it for a moment'.[6] Despite this, by the end of July there was so much speculation in the press about a 'national government' that the Conservative leadership felt obliged to discuss and define their position once more. None of the shadow cabinet wanted a coalition and all sought to avoid it, although it was realised that under the pressure of a crisis or of a panic in the City it might become difficult to stand aside.

In such a case the Party would insist that any combination must be temporary, limited solely to the financial issue, and swiftly dissolved. It should be followed immediately by a general election, which would be fought upon the present party platforms. This was to be the basis of Conservative reactions during the crisis of the following month.[7]

It has been suggested that the formation of the National Government, though no conspiracy, was the result of a Conservative bid for power, in which Neville Chamberlain consciously pursued a strategy which ensured Labour's downfall and prepared the way for a coalition ministry under Conservative control.[8] In truth, the actions of the Conservative opposition during the August crisis were not so purposeful. The Conservative Party was blown off course at least as much as Labour. Far from seeking to lay the foundations for a coalition 'ramp', the Conservative leaders continued until the crisis broke upon them strenuously to encourage friendly elements in the press to damp down any discussions of all-party combinations. Although the holiday period was normally almost devoid of political speeches, those given by prominent Conservatives in early August continued this theme by specifically pronouncing a 'national government' impossible. The reasons for this were simple and pragmatic, and far outweighed any dubious gains that such an alliance might have brought. Electorally the Party had nothing to gain from such a strategy. Conservatives were anticipating a full term of office in which they would for the first time ever have a mandate to enact a 'free hand' protectionist tariff policy. Since 1922 the Party had developed an instinctive hostility to coalitions, due to the belief that they necessarily involved compromising the purity of political principles. It was this which led to the adamant rejection of any combination not based on the common ground of the Conservative economic approach. The strategy which the Conservative leadership followed in August did not concentrate upon the destruction of Labour either as a government or as a political force, but was based consistently upon the issue which, over the spring and summer of 1931, had evolved to the foremost position on the Conservative agenda: the reduction of government expenditure and the levels of direct taxation.

The financial crisis of August 1931 was the product of two distinct problems: a banking crisis which had its origins in central Europe and which had left the position of the City of London exposed, and the prospective British budget deficit of £120 million pounds in the financial year 1931–1932. The latter was underlined by the report of the May Committee, published on 31 July, the day after Parliament rose for the summer recess. Both these factors combined to produce a serious run on the gold reserves, and sterling's position could only be saved by propping up the parity through loans from financiers in the markets of Paris and New York. The experts of the Bank of England advised the Labour Cabinet that these could not be obtained unless they were able to restore overseas confidence by demonstrating their determination to balance the budget. This would require a substantial reduction of expenditure, in particular in the area of the unemployment benefit, which under the impact of the slump was a heavy charge on the Treasury. In other words, the crisis had become as much political as financial.

So far as it affected the Conservative Party, the crisis of August 1931 occurred in four distinct phases. The first of these began on 11 August when the Labour government agreed to a request by the Bank of England that they be allowed to inform the leaders of the opposition parties about the implications of the accelerating flight from the pound. As a result of the bankers' warnings, Baldwin was summoned back from his holiday in France and Neville Chamberlain came down from his Perthshire retreat. Both men arrived in London early in the morning of 13 August. At 10.30 a.m. they met with Horne, one of the Party's leading financial figures, who declared that the government must restore confidence by orthodox measures and 'put its house in order'.[9] Baldwin invited Chamberlain to accompany him to an impromptu interview at 10 Downing Street with Macdonald and Philip Snowden, the Chancellor of the Exchequer, at 2.00 the same afternoon. The government ministers sought to secure opposition approval for their measures to balance the budget, as they could not rely upon their own backbenchers in such a matter. They revealed that they would ask both the Conservative and Liberal leaders to assent to their proposals, which they hoped to have ready within the week. At this preliminary stage Chamberlain enquired whether the amount of the deficit to be met by economies in their plan would equal the May Committee's recommendation of £96.5 million. Snowden, though warning that the deficit was even larger than May had predicted, agreed that it would. Chamberlain declared these economies to be adequate, but went on to remark that it might be difficult for the Conservative Party to endorse any increase in direct taxation. No conclusions were arrived at in this exploratory stage, but Macdonald indicated that if assured of opposition support he would recall Parliament for early September, and place before it a linked emergency Budget and Economy Bill. On leaving Downing Street the two Conservative leaders met with the Bank officials, who shook them further by warning that the situation was extremely serious. Subsequently Baldwin, sensing that his party's position could become compromised if it became too entangled in the crisis, left again for France. He devolved responsibility for meeting the government the following week onto Neville Chamberlain, leaving him with a watching brief.

The mood of the Conservatives at this stage was clearly not in favour of any close involvement in the government's problems. Chamberlain assured Gwynne that there was no suggestion of a 'national government', and he evidently expected the ministry to survive the crisis.[10] Baldwin viewed the problem as being the result of mismanagement by Labour, and saw no reason to risk burning his hands by helping to get their chestnuts out of the fire. The Conservatives sited their defensive position around their distinctive policy of the emergency tariff. Horne urged this on Baldwin on 15 August, and the same day the Party leader instructed Chamberlain to bring it forward at his next meeting with the Prime Minister. This was a deliberate tactic to distance the Conservatives from both Labour and their Liberal allies, whom Baldwin held equally responsible for the deficit. The prevalent fear of entanglement was echoed by Bridgeman, who advised forcing acceptance of the tariff as the price of compliance, for the Party held 'the strongest hand' and 'must not be prevented from taking advantage of it'.[11] Similarly, Neville Chamberlain's projection of the probable result of the crisis was an eventual election 'in conditions offering us the utmost advantage', in which the Party would 'concentrate on tariffs and imperial preference as the restorers of prosperity'.[12]

The second stage opened with the conference between the leaders of the three parties on Thursday 20 August. With Baldwin abroad, Chamberlain asked Hoare to accompany him. Sir Herbert Samuel and Sir Donald MacLean represented the Liberals, and the Prime Minister and the Chancellor the government. Snowden put before them a plan for economies of £78.5 million. Chamberlain thought this was not unreasonable, until the Chancellor revealed that the estimated deficit was now £170 million, implying that the remaining 90 millions would have to be found by new taxation.[13] At once Chamberlain reverted to his original proposition that the economies must be the larger part, certainly not less than the £96 million recommended by May, and must include more than merely cosmetic cuts in the unemployment dole. Macdonald and Snowden indicated their personal agreement, and sought to use the opposition's stand as a lever with which to force the Cabinet into accepting a higher figure as the price of political survival. They arranged to see the other parties next day after the Cabinet had discussed the issue further. Later on 20 August Chamberlain and Hoare had three further meetings. The first was with the bankers, who were pleased with the line taken, but at the same time emphasised that 'the sands were rapidly running out'.[14] The second appointment was with the other Conservative front-benchers then available in London: Hailsham, Cunliffe-Lister, Kingsley Wood, and Eyres-Monsell. All were agreed that the vital point was retrenchment. The final incident in a crowded day was an impromptu rendezvous with the two Liberal leaders, who indicated their general accord with the Conservative position on the scale of economies required.

At 3.00 on the afternoon of 21 August the four opposition representatives were summoned back to Downing Street and told that the Cabinet would only accept economies of £56 million. Macdonald, in weary disillusion, seemed to wash his hands of the responsibility should this be insufficient to restore financial confidence. For the Conservatives, Hoare protested vigorously against both the smallness of the amount and the Prime Minister's conception of his duty. In reply Macdonald made a celebrated remark, delivered in a 'semi-jocular way', enquiring whether they were 'prepared to join the Board of Directors'. Hoare replied that 'if seriously made that was a proposition which would demand serious consideration'.[15] This exchange has been much misunderstood, for Macdonald's phrase was only the throwaway retort of a weary man at his wits' end. More importantly, Hoare's response was not one of approval, but a classic blocking manoeuvre to evade commitment on a question where it is difficult to refuse point-blank. His reply, far from opening up the topic, quite clearly ended all discussion of such an eventuality at that time. Instead of coalescing with Macdonald the two opposition groups withdrew to an upper room at No. 10 to consult each other. The conclusions they drew were that a crash must be avoided at all costs, that the government must face up to their responsibilities, and that the way to make them do so was by threatening to oust them—not by any offer of a helping hand.[16]

After leaving Downing Street, and informing their waiting colleagues of events, Chamberlain and Hoare returned at 9.30 in the evening for the second three-party meeting of that day. Here the strategy agreed earlier with the Liberals of threatening the government was put into effect. Nothing was said on the topic of a 'national government', although the position of the Conservative leadership had begun to shift under the pressure of the crisis atmosphere, and they no longer ruled out such an eventuality. After a lengthy digression on his own troubles, Macdonald promised to try to carry his cabinet once more the next day. As the four opposition politicians were about to leave No. 10, the two Liberals were summoned back for a private session with Macdonald. It was the Liberals, the unofficial allies of the government, and not the Conservatives, who were closest to the Labour leaders. Thus Chamberlain and Hoare departed alone for another meeting with their colleagues and with Sir Ernest Harvey, who was acting as Governor of the Bank of England during the convalescence abroad of Montagu Norman.

The three pairs of leaders gathered again at 12.30 p.m. next day, Saturday 22 August, for a meeting which appeared to achieve the outline of a solution to the crisis. This was not the suggestion of coalition, but a proposal from Macdonald to bring forward economies of £68.5 millions, which would include a 10% cut in the dole, and to save a further £50 million by suspending payments to the sinking fund for the national debt. The Conservatives agreed to this on the proviso that the bankers affirm that the economies were sufficient for their purposes. Neville Chamberlain believed after this that both the financial and political problems had been resolved, and he continued to think so until the afternoon of the following day. He interpreted the fact that Macdonald was to see the King when the latter returned as 'merely part of Ramsay's game to put pressure on his Cabinet'. Chamberlain wrote to his wife that he believed that the Cabinet would grudgingly accede to the settlement: 'the crisis is over and I should be able to go north tomorrow'.[17] However, the optimism voiced at the end of this second stage of the crisis collapsed due to Macdonald's inability to secure sufficient Cabinet support for economies which included any real cut in the dole.

The third phase began on Sunday 23 August with the return to London of the two principal actors in the drama which was to lead to the actual creation of the National Government: Baldwin, who had arrived late on the previous evening; and King George V, who returned from Balmoral at 8.00 a.m. that morning. At 10.30 the King saw Macdonald, who informed him that the Cabinet situation made it impossible for him to continue, and advised the monarch to see the Leaders of the other two parties. In the meantime Baldwin had walked out to consult Dawson, and lunched with him at the Travellers Club. Dawson urged that Labour should be supported in carrying through the economies. Baldwin assented without enthusiasm, although he made it clear he expected that the Labour government would fall and that he would be invited to form a Conservative administration. The remainder of the meal was passed in discussing the personnel of such a ministry.[18] The King's Private Secretary, unable to locate Baldwin, summoned Samuel to the Palace first. The acting-leader of the Liberals saw the King at noon, and strongly reinforced his already existing inclination towards the idea of a 'national government'. As a result, when Baldwin was admitted to the royal presence at 3.00 p.m., the King opened the audience by asking him outright whether he would serve under Macdonald in a crisis national ministry, an appeal from the monarch which a Conservative politician could hardly refuse. Baldwin considered such a promise unlikely to be taken up, and this view could only have been strengthened when the King told him that if Macdonald's last effort with his Cabinet that evening failed, then he would be summoned the following day to receive the royal commission to form a government.[19] After leaving Buckingham Palace Baldwin conveyed this news to Neville Chamberlain, and they debated their strategy. Chamberlain urged that, in view of the balance of forces in the Commons, Baldwin would have to invite the Liberal leaders to come in under him. As he could not hope to construct a purely Conservative ministry before the election, he should therefore also try to secure Macdonald and Snowden. Baldwin reluctantly acknowledged these constraints on his freedom of manoeuvre and agreed with Chamberlain's suggested course of action.[20]

On the evening of 23 August the Labour Cabinet broke up with the refusal of almost half the ministers to accept the economy package, and the Prime Minister left at 10.00 p.m. for the Palace, declaring that he was going to throw in his hand. However, the King persuaded him to sleep on it, assuring him that 'he was the only man to lead the country through this crisis' and that he could count on Conservative and Liberal support in restoring the financial stability of the country.[21] In response to this Macdonald asked the King to preside over a meeting of the three pairs of party leaders the next morning. Even so, Macdonald was still undecided about his own future. On his return to Downing Street at 11.00 p.m. he summoned the four opposition politicians, and informed them that he had told the King he could not go on, and that there would be no point in his joining the succeeding government. It was only at this literal eleventh hour, and in the context of his discussion with his Leader earlier that afternoon, that Chamberlain made his appeal to the Premier to reconsider the latter part of his decision, and give support from within rather than without the new administration. Though Samuel supported this plea, Chamberlain noted that Baldwin 'maintained silence and we did not pursue the matter further'.[22] Thus stood matters at midnight on 23 August, with everyone expecting Macdonald to withdraw, and that after the conference on the following morning Baldwin would be invited to kiss hands as Prime Minister of a government which Macdonald was unlikely to join.

The fourth and final stage, the events of Monday 24 August, produced an unexpected reversal of this position. When Macdonald, Samuel and Baldwin met with George V at Buckingham Palace at 10.00 a.m., it was the King who dominated events and set the tone in favour of an all-party solution. He specifically stated 'that he trusted that there was no question of the Prime Minister's resignation', and hoped that Macdonald would form a 'national government' which would be 'supported by the Conservatives and the Liberals'. The monarch also put the three politicians under further pressure by insisting that, in the national interest, a decision be hammered out there and then for immediate release to the press. After having put the case in favour of a 'national government' for over half an hour, and extracted from Samuel and Baldwin fresh promises to serve under Macdonald, George V then withdrew, leaving the three only 'to settle the details'.[23] Macdonald had been swayed into reversing his decision to quit, and as a result Baldwin was left without any respectable means of blocking the formation of a coalition; thus the crucial decision to form the National Government was taken.

The remainder of the discussion was occupied in drafting the new ministry's terms of reference. Many of the provisions of this six-point memorandum reflected Baldwin's reluctance, and were included to satisfy the demands of the Conservative Party rather than the needs of either of the other two leaders. In particular, three promises were intended to assuage Conservative anxieties. These were that the new government was not a coalition but only a short-term expedient; that economies would equal the amount of any taxation imposed; and that the ensuing general election would be fought after a return to present party positions.[24] The first undertaking aimed to lay the ghost of a return to the experiences of the Lloyd George Coalition, whilst the last offered reassurance that the tariff policy had not been abandoned. The new Cabinet of ten, with four Labour and two Liberal free-traders outweighing the four protectionist Conservatives, could hardly be considered a step forward for the party committed to the introduction of an emergency tariff. However, under the combined pressures of the royal personification of national unity, the bankers' clamour that national ruin was only hours away, and the restraint of having to work within the existing balance of forces in the Commons, the Conservative leadership reluctantly acquiesced in the inevitable.[25] Their aims had remained consistent, although by 24 August the means of achieving them had come to include the possibility, but not the desirability, of a temporary coalition.

One of the most important causes of this transformation was the sudden eruption of the crisis. This combined with the crucial consideration that there were apparently only hours in which to stave off national catastrophe. In July, the Conservatives had been slowly proceeding with the strategy of seeking an alliance with the Simonite Liberals, in order to eject the government when the House reassembled in the autumn. These plans were overtaken by the dramatic march of events; 'things suddenly boiled up in the City'.[26] As the crisis progressed, the pressure of time increased, for it was widely accepted that it was a matter of hours, a fact which in itself changed the attitude of many Conservatives to the expediency of co-operation. In view of the emergency the Conservative Party could, without sacrifice of principle, work with other parties for 'economy'. This new common ground could only be short-lived, for once the cuts were secured, the tariff question would come to the fore. To have reached the point where a 'national government' was no longer being ruled out was certainly a change in the Conservative position. However, it could only be indicative of the dawning realisation that time and circumstance might compel such a resolution. On the day that the National Government was established Austen Chamberlain acknowledged that 'it has been—perhaps still is—a question of hours between this country and the deluge'.[27]

In this belief, and in their consequent actions, the Conservative leaders were constricted by their unquestioned support for the position of the bankers. Horne spoke for the City when putting the facts before Baldwin, in particular by directing attention to the need for cuts in the unemployment benefit.[28] At the end of the parliamentary session in July Neville Chamberlain watered down his speech in the finance debate, and passed up the chance of party advantage, because of the anxiety in the City lest he paint too dark a picture. Indeed, it was as a result of the Bank's initiative that Baldwin and Chamberlain were requested to return to London and became involved in the first place. From that moment onwards the Party came close to being an echo of the City, and it was no surprise that the bankers approved of the politicians' conduct on 20 August, and were intimately involved in the counsels of the front-bench leadership. The role of the financial community was not the sinister one of seeking to destroy the Labour government; it was not that subtle. The bankers were desperately anxious over their own professional arena of finance, and were simply seeking to impress upon all parties the gravity of that position in order for some solution to be contrived.[29] However, the politicians of all three parties deferred to their expert knowledge of the arcane mysteries of finance, and took their cue from them as to what was and was not possible. Thus the Conservatives looked to the bankers for guidance on the scale of the economies required. Similarly, they accepted the bankers' declaration of 22 August that the line could only be held for another four days.

One consequence was that all other possible solutions to the crisis, several of them politically more attractive, were ruled out. Within the leadership only Amery questioned the urgency, and the wisdom of putting 'economy' before tariffs, declaring that 'in these matters I think we are all too inclined to take the bankers at their word'.[30] Against the policy of deflation he set the alternative of a high wages policy hand-in-hand with vigorous empire development, but this could be dismissed as the crotchet of a tariff 'faddist'. Another possibility was raised by Beaverbrook, who argued that the accession to office of a Conservative government would have been sufficient on its own to restore confidence and secure the loans. A final option was also ruled out by the bankers. This was Neville Chamberlain's brief flirtation with the idea of a capital levy to reduce the national debt, and thus remove the need for £100 millions of interest charges from a balanced budget. The financiers' disapproval of this concept, admittedly for fear that it would backfire and cause a flight from the pound, was so evident that Chamberlain swiftly dropped it.

The large-scale economies sought by both the financial interests and the Conservative Party were not without political complications. These were firstly the question of the amount of new taxation to be imposed, and secondly their possible electoral unpopularity. Economies on the scale desired were accepted as being unattainable unless they were matched by some increase of taxation, but it was the concern of both the City and the Party to keep the latter at a minimum and the former at a maximum. For this purpose the Conservatives insisted upon the doctrine of equality of sacrifice, and they established at their first interview with Macdonald and Snowden on 13 August that the budget must be balanced in accordance with this principle. This was the only method by which the Labour leaders could be committed to a decision that economies should provide at least half the amount required. The crucial point is that the Conservatives were mainly concerned with the avoidance of further burdens of taxation, and thus placed the emphasis throughout on the role of 'economy'.[31] The doctrine of equality of sacrifice was not a magnanimous gesture on the part of the better-off to share the consequences of the financial crisis, but on the contrary was designed for the reverse purpose. In part it was a product of fears that a Labour government would be tempted to soak the rich by going for a populist 'people's budget'. This was considered a danger for three reasons. The first was the simple instinct of self-preservation, in that it would hit hardest the Conservative sources of support. The second was the genuinely-held belief that the slump was due to over-burdening local and national taxation, sapping domestic confidence and investment. Finally, as the overseas bankers adhered to the same economic model, the vital loans would not be forthcoming if a high-taxation policy was adopted. As both Horne and Neville Chamberlain declared, it was not simply a question of finding any method to deal with the deficit: the budget had to be balanced in the right way.[32]

Equality of sacrifice was designed to ensure that the government could not meet their target without a real cut in the unemployment benefit, and that the unemployed could not be considered a special case immune from the financial debacle. Thus it was as much a political doctrine as a fiscal one. It was for this reason that Chamberlain sought to preserve freedom of action in the matter of approving proposals for new taxes in the agreement of 22 August, through which he believed the crisis had been resolved. He was willing to accept a plan which committed the Labour Cabinet to proposing real economies when parliament reconvened, but left the Conservative forces free to propose amendments. With Liberal support they would later be able to increase the economies and limit the taxation. This was not a subtle ploy to split the Labour Party, but a determined effort to minimise the impact of new imposts. Once Macdonald and Snowden had accepted equality of sacrifice their conceptions of a solution were converging with those of the other party leaders. Although it had involved accepting coalition and the retention of Macdonald as Premier along the way, the final position arrived at was, in economic terms, acceptable to Conservatism. Not only would the amount raised by taxes be kept to a minimum but, in the light of the rumoured changed attitude of Macdonald to the concept of the revenue tariff, there was also a good prospect that the major proportion of the money raised would be through indirect duties.

Having made the key Labour figures of Macdonald and Snowden face the need for economies, the logical consequence was to seek to involve them in the passage of the necessary measures.[33] Although the scale of the crisis had swept aside most of their reservations, Conservative politicians still felt a residue of anxiety about the possible unpopularity of economies passed by an 'upper class' government, as opposed to the approval that proposals which had the imprimatur of the leaders of Labour opinion might receive. The scenario Conservatives feared most was that, if they alone attempted to impose economies before the dissolution of parliament, they would make themselves vulnerable at the polls.[34] Having appeased the demands of supporters who had pressed for 'economy', they would find themselves left alone to face the backlash from the victims of the cuts. The advantage of being in opposition would then be reaped by Labour, who might thereby restore their unity and vigour. As a result, the Conservatives could end up losing the election they seemed poised to win. This was the particular fear of those who placed tariffs before economies, but it was also of serious concern to Conservative prospective candidates in the northern constituencies, where unemployment was at the highest levels.[35] Although the 1931 election later demonstrated that public opinion had not developed along these lines, this does negate the fact that this possibility preoccupied the minds of the Party leadership in late August. It was an incentive for retaining both Macdonald and Snowden at their present posts. The rationale behind the desire to involve some Labour figures in a Baldwin ministry, which until the very end had been thought the most logical product of the crisis, was not a stratagem to split the Labour movement, but a simple device to spread the load of unpopularity across as many shoulders as possible. It was only a short step from this to accepting that if the premiership was the only post Macdonald would take then it was not too high a price to pay for insurance in what would be, after all, only a temporary expedient.

The Conservative Party sacrificed much in tactical terms and risked much more in electoral terms by its actions during the crisis of August 1931. Where it gained, it gained in policy; though only in one of its two aims, economies but not tariffs. This was the prize for which the Conservative Party adhered to the National Government, so far as it had a choice at all. In view of their uncritical acceptance of the bankers' urgency and therefore of the limitations on their freedom of action whilst parliament remained adjourned, it can be argued it was the Conservatives, more than any other party, who were the victims of a bankers' 'ramp'. Neville Chamberlain's desire to have Labour involvement in the new administration reflected not his political sophistication, but his greater responsiveness to City opinion. To suggest that any Conservatives were principally concerned during the August crisis with cunning notions of wrecking the Labour Party is patently absurd. Conservative leaders knew that Macdonald and Snowden would not have more than a handful of supporters amongst the Labour backbenchers, though they might have some standing in the country. The Conservative leaders were worried men, concentrating on saving national solvency and prestige, and thus on the position of sterling and the relationship thereto of proposals for economies or direct taxation. They risked sacrificing the political interests of their own Party at that altar, although this was partly a consequence of their notions about patriotism and duty. Any damaging side effects on the Labour Party only came into the picture as an added bonus. Joining a 'national government' was not an end in itself for the Conservatives in August 1931, but rather became the means of achieving their ends— the reversal of recent trends in the growth of government bureaucracy and of national and local expenditure, and therefore of the levels of direct taxation. Thus, at the height of the crisis on 21 August, the Conservative leaders were agreed 'that retrenchment was the vital thing' and that they must 'concentrate entirely on that'.[36]

Neville Chamberlain has been described as the architect of the National Government, the man who foresaw every contingency and who dominated the situation.[37] The latter he certainly was not; Chamberlain acted only in an advisory capacity to Baldwin. He was not present at either of the two crucial audiences at Buckingham Palace on 23 and 24 August, where the political context was so completely transformed. Far from anticipating this, Chamberlain believed on the 22nd that the agreement outlined then had dealt with the crisis. During Baldwin's absence in the early stages of the crisis his position had been that of an observer, not an executive, and once matters became serious he sent for his leader and called his other frontbench colleagues into consultation. The decision to join the National Government was initially taken by Baldwin, and subsequently approved by the collective leadership and the Party as a whole. Casting Chamberlain as the creator of the National Government is also inherently unsatisfactory, for it is based on the premiss that, of all politicians, only Neville Chamberlain was unaffected by the alarms of the City, the atmosphere of panic, and the appeal of sacrificing party at the altar of the national interest. Chamberlain's eleventh-hour remarks did not seduce Macdonald into an all-party coalition. Although not entirely without effect, they were only a minor influence on the Labour leader. Macdonald regarded Chamberlain as the embodiment of partisan Conservatism, and was too experienced a parliamentarian to accept his advice as being disinterested. He was even less likely to be moved by an appeal that was so markedly unsupported by Chamberlain's leader, a man for whom Macdonald had a much higher regard. The King, impelled by his sense of duty to act in what he regarded as the national interest, persuaded both Macdonald to remain as Premier and Baldwin to serve under him. No other figure commanded the prestige or respect necessary to sway either man into such a course of action.

Chamberlain was more concerned with the financial position than the political one. On this, he followed the strategy which the Party in general adhered to. The suggestions sent on 17 August by the Conservative Research Department's principal salaried official, Joseph Ball, who was holidaying in Cornwall, were very close to the positions actually taken up by Chamberlain during the following week.[38] There can be no suggestion that Chamberlain was Ball's puppet: rather, it is a demonstration that his line was not of his own invention. On 20 August he told Hoare that the essential problem was the restoration of foreign confidence in British credit, and that this could only be achieved by a cut in the annual recurrent expenditure of a severity which would demonstrate that the British people were facing up to their perilous position.[39] Chamberlain now felt that to secure the reductions with the approval of a Labour Cabinet was 'so important in the national interest that we MUST give it our support'.[40] The only proviso was strict adherence to the doctrine of equality of sacrifice. Conservative leaders were fully aware that 'the danger from our point of view is the "sacrifice" by the Rentier'.[41] Chamberlain concluded that if all or some of the Labour leaders meant business on this matter, then 'our duty seems to me plain enough'. The Conservatives must give assurances of their support and 'hope that we shall not as a party suffer for it'.[42] He sought to associate Labour with the economies in order to increase the chances of their passage, and his early moves were designed to aid Macdonald in carrying his Cabinet towards accepting a larger sum.

The Conservative position evolved on a day-to-day basis throughout the crisis, but it was always consistently founded upon these assumptions. Neville Chamberlain's concerns became apparent on the one occasion when he did appear to consider the political consequences of his policy. He had toyed with a partisan strategy on 22 August. This would have meant remaining as unfettered as possible, not of joining a coalition. Looking back on the arrangement concluded that day, he noted that the Conservatives had committed

Labour to economies, yet had kept their own hands free on the issue of taxation.[43] The plan swiftly collapsed, not just because the Labour Cabinet would not accept the outline agreement, but also because the bankers made it clear that the constraints of time would not permit such a delayed resolution of the crisis. The incident nevertheless demonstrates that those partisan instincts which Chamberlain possessed urged the keeping in office of a weak Labour government, and the retention by the Conservatives of the safe harbour of opposition until the election should come. Thus, Chamberlain's urgings to Macdonald late at night on 23 August in reality represented the final fling of his hope that the Labour government could be made to shoulder the responsibility of its own overspending. It was an attempt to obtain some form of Labour involvement with the economy package, and should not be misread as part of some preconceived strategy aiming at a 'national government' for its own sake. Chamberlain came to favour a temporary coalition, not for its impact on domestic politics, but for the very reason he gave Macdonald—that the Prime Minister's name carried weight overseas and his presence would increase the chances of restoring confidence in foreign financial markets.[44]

Baldwin's views paralleled these; if anything he was even more hostile to the idea of becoming involved in another coalition. He thought the government was about to fall, and as late as the evening of 23 August was engaged in planning the composition of his new Cabinet. It was because he feared that involvement might prevent such an outcome that he distanced himself from the crisis in its early stages, but, despite this, co-operation became inescapable. Nevertheless, as he arrived at Buckingham Palace at 10.00 a.m. on 24 August, Baldwin expected to become the Prime Minister, even if the government was not to be exclusively Conservative.[45] One reason why he did not leave the Palace as Premier was Baldwin's acceptance of both the bankers' diagnosis and their prescribed cure. However, the crucial element was the *fait accompli* with which he was presented by the fact that Macdonald had not resigned, and was now prepared to lead a national ministry. Baldwin gave in, not without reluctance, to the appeals of the King. Given that both George V and Samuel, who controlled the balance of power in the Commons, were keen to support Macdonald; given the attitude of the City that hours were vital; and in view of the hypothetical undertaking Baldwin had made the previous day (and he was not a man to break a pledge to his liege), Baldwin had lost the freedom of manoeuvre which he had tried throughout to maintain. He found himself carried along by events, but unable to shape their course.

Despite all the talk of a 'national government' over the previous year, it was George V who turned the concept into reality. The King acted according to his own conception of the constitutional duty of the monarch as custodian of an impersonal 'national interest'. Most important was his repeated refusal to accept the Prime Minister's resignation, and his encouragement flattered and sustained Macdonald in these crucial hours. When Baldwin and Samuel arrived at Buckingham Palace on 24 August Macdonald 'told them acting under great pressure from the King he had decided to try and form a national government'.[46] George V always favoured this type of solution to grave national difficulties, and promoted it vigorously. When, on the morning of the 23rd, Macdonald had advised him to see the leaders of the other parties, the King's response had been that he would strongly advise them to support the Premier.[47] Thus the monarch pre-empted the issue when he talked with Baldwin later that day, and again set the tone in his opening address at Palace on the following morning. The role of the King was not necessarily unconstitutional, for he always had the right to advise and to encourage his Ministers. However, during the August crisis he pressed his viewpoint with unusual but effective emphasis. His pivotal position gave him a unique opportunity to influence the three party leaders. It was at his monarch's request that Baldwin, though a former Prime Minister, made the critical concession that he was prepared to serve under Macdonald if this was necessary 'for the sake of the country'.[48]

In the decision to form the National Government, Samuel played a part second only to that of the King. The policy of the Liberal leaders towards the crisis was rooted in assumptions almost identical to those of the Conservatives. They too were influenced by the City and the Bank of England, and considered the financial aspects of the crisis to be more serious than the political. The Liberals were equally determined to emphasise the need for greater economies, and indeed Samuel rejected the solution of the emergency tariff partly because he more strictly saw it as another form of increasing taxation. The Liberal leaders were concerned to avoid a socially divisive solution to the crisis, and deprecated a purely Conservative government as likely to have difficulty in ensuring popular support for the necessary measures.[49] They also sought to involve Labour figures in the economies as a means of carrying the working-classes with them.[50] If this could not be done through the medium of the existing Labour Cabinet, then the Liberal leaders thought the next best thing would be a 'national government' with Macdonald as Premier. Samuel's effective advocacy of this solution strengthened the King's inclinations towards it.[51] Nevertheless, of the three parties only the Liberals stood to gain from an all-party coalition. Naturally, they preferred to retain as Prime Minister and Chancellor figures with whom they had been in informal alliance during the previous two years, and who were known free traders. The formation of a coalition might postpone an election until a time when the Liberals might be better placed to withstand the anticipated Conservative landslide, for it would give them an opportunity to gain office and prestige. They could also forward their aims by playing each party off against the other; economies would be achieved by Liberal-Conservative pressure, but tariffs avoided by a Liberal-Labour block. An alliance in which the dogmatic Gladstonian Snowden was re-established at the Exchequer was hardly an advance on the road along which the Conservatives wanted to travel, but it suited the Liberals well enough.

The Conservative Party responded to the crisis in terms of its self-perceived patriotic duty, believing the country to be facing a peril as great as that of the First World War. The Party Chairman declared that 'the Industrial, Social, and Economic Order was at stake', and Conservatives accepted that the crisis was 'unparalleled in the history of the country'.[52] On 24 August, in a statement commended by *The Times* for its patriotic spirit, Baldwin explained that it was their bounden duty to put aside party differences for the time being in favour of national interests. Conservatives, even those at the apex of the Party, held comparatively unsophisticated conceptions of the proper role of government and opposition in periods of grave crisis: it was the Prime Minister's 'duty to avoid that catastrophe and ours to do all we could to help him'.[53] In accordance with this, if the government did its duty, Conservatives promised to refrain from exploiting the opportunity for party gain, and would act with equal responsibility. As the Party had been poised to win an election on the scale of 1924, this was no small gesture. The fact that it did not lead, as feared, to electoral unpopularity, should not obscure the rationale behind the Conservative response to the crisis of August 1931.

The reaction of the Conservative Party to the formation of the National Government revolved around the restrictions placed upon it. The measure of Baldwin's reluctant acquiescence can be found in the document hammered out at Buckingham Palace on 24 August, for of the three leaders he was the most concerned to avoid entanglement in a coalition. Baldwin placed much emphasis on the concept that the government was only the co-operation of certain individuals. The declaration that there was no question of any permanent alliance was all the more credible when it came from the lips of the man most closely associated with the repudiation of coalition in 1922.[54] Such promises were required to soothe the instinctive reactions of a party for whom during the previous nine years Disraeli's dictum that 'England does not love coalitions' had become an article of faith. The inclusion of Labour ministers was not the principal problem, for their presence was psychologically desirable. However, co-operation with the Liberals, who were led by Samuel and the widely detested Lloyd

George, was a more difficult pill to swallow.[55] For these reasons
Baldwin was also keen to limit the Cabinet to only ten. Austen
Chamberlain, one of the excluded Conservative leaders, acknowledged that this made clear the temporary and emergency character of
the arrangement.[56]

In selecting his colleagues to fill the other three Conservative places
in the new Cabinet, Baldwin sought to reassure his followers that the
gains of the past year had not been surrendered. Two of his choices
symbolised the tariff policy: Neville Chamberlain, a known protectionist and the architect of the advances of October 1930 and the
Stornoway Pact; and Cunliffe-Lister, President of the Board of Trade
in the last Conservative government, who had supervised the drafting
of detailed tariff provisions by the Party's Research Department. The
appointment of Hoare to the India Office was crucial, as he stood for
the determination to ensure that while the Round Table policy on
India would be continued, it would be tempered with caution and
hedged with safeguards.[57] Although Chamberlain was 61 years old, in
political terms all three personified the promotion of newer faces at the
expense of the 'Old Gang'. The omission of certain Conservatives
from the first National Government has been given undue significance, due to the ministry's later permanence. Austen Chamberlain,
Hailsham, Amery, and even Churchill might have been included in
the less restricted confines of a purely Conservative administration;
indeed the first two did receive high office outside the new cabinet a
few days later. The arrangements of August were only intended to be
temporary, and several of the omitted front-benchers were out of the
country during the critical week. The principal reason for their
omission was not so much their political unorthodoxy as the need to
maintain consensus within the Party by demonstrating that the 'Old
Gang' would not be allowed to dominate the next Conservative
cabinet. This priority eased aside some members of the last Conservative Cabinet, such as Peel, whilst in Hailsham's case Baldwin did not
press his claims over Macdonald's objections. That the exclusion of
these figures was only temporary was a theme Baldwin went out of his
way to stress when he first addressed the Party a few days later.

The temporary nature of the new government, and the fact that it
would swiftly lead to a general election, was repeatedly emphasised.
Its limitation to enacting only an Economies Bill and passing a
balanced Budget was crucial in respect of the Conservative Party's
tariff policy. The view that drastic economy must be the first target,
and that the tariff battle would be fought afterwards, was held by a
large majority of the Conservative Party. The minority, who had
been uneasy about this order of priorities, reluctantly acquiesced on
the understanding that protection would nonetheless swiftly follow.
An emergency session of the Empire Industries Association had been

summoned by Amery and Croft for 27 August. Before it met, they
were appeased by explicit assurances from Baldwin that the position
on tariffs had not been compromised, and unity was maintained.[58]
The new government would dissolve in a matter of weeks and
nothing would prevent the Party from appealing in the ensuing
election for a 'free hand' on tariffs.[59] This was important because of
the general view in the Conservative Party that, whilst economies
were the short-term solution to the crisis, only a protectionist policy
could bring prosperity in the longer term. Tariffs were more than
merely a party shibboleth: they were considered essential for any
national recovery. Indeed, the crisis of August 1931 increased the
urgency for fiscal reform; it was held that 'we cannot recover any
revenue or any industry now without a tariff', and so it was all the
more important that the opportunity should not be lost now that
public opinion had at last come round to the point where 'we can carry
protection in the country at an early general election'.[60]

In being swayed by the pressure of events the Conservative leadership reflected, rather than created, the mood of its followers. As a
result, entry into the National Government did not produce a rift
between leaders and led. The Conservative rank and file were swept
along as much as their leaders by the extraordinary atmosphere of the
crisis weeks. Ironically, Baldwin's stock rose dramatically in the eyes
of his supporters through being forced to sacrifice the Party's interests. Their approval of his statesmanship went far in obliterating
memories of his weakness as leader of the opposition since 1929, and
completed the process of rehabilitation which had begun in October
1930. In the August crisis Baldwin's reluctance or inability to act as a
partisan leader for once accorded with the conceptions of the Party
grass-roots, rather than as previously fanning the flames of internal
conflict. The Party's acceptance of the National Government was far
from automatic, but was directly dependent upon the restraining
conditions under which it had been established. However, within
days the momentum of approval gathered irresistible force. This was
demonstrated in the meetings of the Party's representative institutions
held on 28 August: firstly an emergency session of the Executive
Committee of the National Union, and secondly a party meeting of
peers, members of parliament, and prospective candidates, addressed
by Baldwin at the Kingsway Hall. At the Executive Committee, the
temporary nature of the government was stressed yet again, and
attention was directed away towards the forthcoming dissolution,
before which the tariff programme was to be strongly pressed home in
the constituencies by a propaganda offensive. Having been soothed by
these reassurances, Lord Derby's resolution approving the leader's
recent actions was passed unanimously.

At the party meeting later in the day, Baldwin candidly explained

the events of the previous weekend, and made it clear that the decision
to form a national ministry, though accepted by him, had been neither
his desire nor his suggestion. He closed with a typical appeal to the
instincts of loyalty and unity, and promised that the Party's position
on the tariff question remained intact. The resolution of support was
moved by a trio of figures associated with the right; Hailsham,
Gretton, and Croft. All three set their seal of approval on the new
government, though none welcomed it. Gretton warned that even
modest amounts of new taxation would be a grievous burden, and
must be only a temporary sacrifice in the interval before the revenue
tariff could come to the rescue of both the taxpayer and the unemployed. Croft pointed to the fact that the new Cabinet had a free trade
majority, but he accepted that, due to the pressure of time, there had
been no alternative. All those present at the meeting appeared to
approve of Baldwin's actions; at the end, after rounds of cheering,
'God Save The King' was struck up spontaneously.[61] What was being
hailed, however, was not a party success, but a patriotic sacrifice in the
national interest. As Croft had observed in his speech, many MPs
were disgruntled that the Conservatives might have been jockeyed
out of a certain electoral triumph. The mood at the Kingsway Hall was
consistent with the sentiments of the local Associations up and down
the country. There was no dissent, implicit or explicit, from the
decision to join the emergency government.[62] Apart from concern
that the tariff policy should not be shelved as the price of all-party
unity, approval was unanimous. However, it was invariably couched
in the language of patriotism, duty, and party sacrifice in the national
interest. The view that Baldwin had justified their trust in him by
putting country before party was typical of the reactions of the Party
activists.[63]

The National Government was from the outset a development unfavourable to the Conservative Party, and genuinely seems to have been
intended by Baldwin only to have been temporary. By nature an
optimist, he assumed that the future course of events was guaranteed
by the conditions written into the founding document on 24 August.
However, under the pressure of events it proved increasingly difficult
for the new alliance to break up, and the prospect of the parties being
able to return to their previous positions receded. The formation of
the National Government did not resolve the financial crisis. The
drain on the Bank of England's reserves was reduced and the temporary credits were secured from the overseas bankers, but pressure on
the currency continued at a dangerous level. Against this continued
background of crisis the lesser offices in the new ministry were filled
during the last week of August, and agreement was reached within the
Cabinet by 3 September on a programme of economies. Parliament

was recalled, and on 10 September Snowden's emergency budget passed through the Commons with the support of Conservative, Liberal, and a handful of Labour MPs. Although this put into effect most of the May Committee's recommendations, the tide of withdrawals from London could not be stemmed. It became a flood with the news on 15 September of a mutiny in warships of the Royal Navy at Invergordon, whose crews refused to muster in protest at the severity and the inequalities of the cuts in service pay. Maintenance of the gold standard became impossible. After the events of this 'terrible week' the Cabinet admitted defeat on 20 September.[64] Next day the Bill to suspend payments in gold was passed through all its stages. The new government had failed in its primary task, but its members remained prisoners of the situation. Preservation of the National Government, as a solid rock in a sea of political and economic chaos, became an end in itself. The Conservative leaders were still bound by the views of the bankers. The advice they received was unanimous: only the existing government, symbolic of national unity and resolve, could grapple with Britain's economic predicament. The National Government could not break up; the problem was on what basis it could remain intact. Whilst there had been a consensus amongst the politicians who had come together on 24 August on the measures necessary to balance the budget, there was no such consensus on the means to restore the balance of trade, for this brought the Cabinet face-to-face with the issue of tariffs. On that question, as Cunliffe-Lister admitted at the beginning of September, 'no-one can suggest any policy on which we could possibly agree', let alone go to the country.[65]

At the same time, pressure was building up within the Conservative Party for an early general election. The first cause of this was the continuing anxiety about the impact which the economy measures might have on public opinion before an election could take place. The cuts would have aroused a predictable short-term storm of protest, without there being time for the long-term economic picture to improve and justify the severity of the measures. On 16 September Central Office warned Baldwin of the dangers of delay. The Party's Area Agents were unanimous that if the election were postponed for several months, the prospects of success would slip away.[66] These fears were further increased by the declarations of the T.U.C. and the Labour opposition, who had broadened their attack from the manner of the National Government's formation to every aspect of its measures. Even worse was Labour's claim to have the support of the people, and the atmosphere of class warfare which they seemed to be promoting.[67] Without an election, this could not be put to the test, nor could the financial markets regain that precious but elusive confidence. 'The T.U.C. undo 90% of what we do', exclaimed Cunliffe-Lister.[68] The election which had seemed out of the question whilst the gold standard was being defended, seemed to most Conservatives by mid–September to be not just possible but essential. Equally, as the financial picture darkened, the need for tariff protection became ever more clear and urgent. Only by such means could the balance of trade be restored and foreign 'dumping' eliminated. Conservatives did not want to break up the National Government, and their advocacy of tariffs was not a partisan proposal; they simply could not envisage any other effective policy.[69] At the Kingsway Hall Baldwin had promised 'a straight fight on tariffs and against the Socialist party' once the budget was balanced. Since that meeting the Conservative Party, with only a handful of exceptions, had come to accept that a simple return to previous party positions was no longer possible. The banner of national unity had great appeal, so long as it was not transformed into a wet blanket smothering the tariff policy. These different strands were drawn together in the last week of September into an inexorable demand by Conservatives for a dissolution as soon as possible. In the ensuing election the National Goverment, untrammelled by limiting pledges, would appeal for a completely free hand in economic affairs. Hoare admitted that concern within the Party had reached such a level that if it was not satisfied, the leaders in the Cabinet would be left 'high and dry'.[70]

The first phase of the National Government's existence was the defence of the gold standard, between 24 August and 21 September. The second phase was the struggle within the Cabinet over the question of an election: when, in what combination, and under what manifesto. After the failure to defend the parity Macdonald had a nervous collapse, and withdrew to Sandwich to recuperate between 22 and 25 September. In his absence, the election issue came onto the open agenda. Samuel circulated a Cabinet memorandum on 24 September, putting the case for delay. On the same day the Conservative leadership met and resolved to press for 'an early election, a national appeal, no whittling down of our tariff policy', though they were also ready to continue serving under Macdonald.[71] The government had been poised on the brink of a crisis over its future path; now it was plunged into it. Macdonald had already come to the reluctant conclusion that an election, though undesirable, was inevitable. On his return he circulated a memorandum to his Cabinet colleagues accepting this, but also insisting that the government must go to the country united and intact. Characteristically, he dwelt on the public's perception of his own position, should the Liberals or some of his Labour supporters withdraw. Two days later, on 28 September, Macdonald was expelled from the Labour Party by its National Executive Committee. This not only wounded the Prime Minister, it also reduced his future options. The result was on the one hand to make him look more favourably on a showdown with his critics and an end to the present uncertainty; on the other it made him even more dependent on his Liberal and Labour allies.

The Conservative Party provided the mass of the National Government's parliamentary support, but this did not mean that they held the whip hand. Their freedom of action was severely circumscribed by three factors. The first of these was the pressure from the financial community, which was favourable to the National Government and to Macdonald's continued presence at its head. The second factor was the continuing impulse to put the interests of the country before those of party. Within a matter of days, the National Government had come to regarded by many Conservatives as a blessed deliverance; it was an absolute necessity for as long as the crisis lasted.[72] The third factor was the minority position of the Conservatives within the cabinet. The combination of the first two factors meant that they could not force a solution to the third by riding roughshod over the Liberal and Labour members of the government. The break up of the government, or even several resignations, might provoke an even worse collapse of the financial situation. A solution had therefore to be found within the existing framework.

In the event, the problem of the Conservatives' minority position in the cabinet proved to be more apparent than real. The Prime Minister was the crucial figure. He was indispensable to any cross-party appeal, quite apart from his constitutional prerogative of asking for a dissolution. However, Macdonald was increasingly open-minded on the merits of protection, although he was determined to maintain the all-party complexion of the government. He was fearful of becoming, or even of seeming to become, what his enemies on the opposition benches derided him as—the catspaw of the Tories. Repudiated by his former party, Macdonald sought to keep the new ship from foundering at once. This was not so much because he wanted to remain Prime Minister, but rather stemmed from a characteristic combination of a sense of duty and the vanity of feeling indispensable, in which the King had encouraged him. Of his three Labour colleagues, Thomas was almost belligerently in favour both of tariffs and of an election. Sankey, whose main interest and attention was being given to the second stage of the Indian Round Table Conference, would follow where Macdonald led on these matters. Snowden was no longer the insuperable obstacle, having announced his intention to retire to the Lords. His invective was beginning to turn against his former party, and he seemed unlikely to resist to the point of resignation. The defence of free trade therefore devolved on the party most closely identified with it: the Liberals. However, one of the two Liberals in the Cabinet, Lord Reading, was also closer to Macdonald's own position. Provided a formula could be found which would neither break up the government nor alienate the Liberal rank and file, he would remain and support it. Thus the apparent barrier of six free traders dwindled to only one: Sir Herbert Samuel. The stresses within the government were compounded by Conservative attitudes to Samuel personally. He was regarded with mistrust and contempt, tinged with anti-semitism. Some Conservatives, in particular Neville Chamberlain, actively sought to force his resignation. Samuel, although the key to the situation, was also isolated and under conflicting pressures from the various factions within the Liberal Party and from its leader, Lloyd George, recovering at his country home from a prostate operation. Samuel's aim remained consistent throughout the crisis: to avoid an election in circumstances so unfavourable to the Liberals. He had the crucial support of Macdonald who, though often as angry at his actions as at those of the Conservatives, wanted to keep the acting-leader of the Liberals in the National combination. On the other hand, Samuel was also influenced by his many contacts in the City, and saw little point in making a futile gesture of solo resignation.

The result was a struggle within the government between Samuel and the Conservatives, with Chamberlain rather than Baldwin forcing the pace, whilst Macdonald took the role of referee. A series of cabinet meetings was held almost daily between 28 September and 5 October, debating the election issue in an increasingly fraught and fractious atmosphere.[73] This process of going round in circles, whilst it drove Neville Chamberlain to despair, clarified the position for both Samuel and Macdonald. It became apparent that all other options, ranging from the dissolution of the government to continuing without an election, were impossible. At the same time, it was also made clear to the Conservatives that some concessions, even if only of a face-saving kind, would have to be made. They abandoned their aim of committing the government as a whole to protection, seeking instead to ensure that it was not hampered by any commitments against it. On 5 October, at the very moment when it seemed that the Cabinet were breaking up, and as Baldwin was delivering some typical valedictory remarks, Samuel interrupted him with a pre-viously prepared and typed statement.[74] In this he accepted that the government as a whole would make no statement on tariffs, and that each party woudd be free to advoaate whatever measures it felt were necessary to restrict imports and restore the balance of trade. Within a matter of minutes the crisis was over, and the policy of separate appeals under the national umbrella accepted. The next day Macdo-nald asked for and obtained a dissolution of parliament.

Macdonald's role in the decisions of late September was crucial, and it is clear that by agreeing in August to his retention of the premiership the Conservatives had made no small concession. Macdonald had used his position to avoid a joint manifesto which included a positive protectionist platform, and to prevent the Conservatives squeezing out of his cabinet any of its Liberal or Labour members. He did not do this for Samuel's sake, but for his own; the non-Conservative elements in the government were his allies and his alibi. Macdonald succeeded in his aims; the government remained intact and he remained in control. This was not necessarily in the Conservatives' interest. The appeal by the National Government for a 'doctor's mandate' and separate party manifestos was not the best they could do, but the least. The greatest irony of all was that Baldwin had fulfilled all the promises made to the Party on the formation of the government: limitation of legislation to the budget and economies, an early election, and no inhibition of Conservative freedom to seek a mandate for the free hand—and yet this represented a defeat for Conservative ambitions, not a victory. Once again, the Conservatives had been jockeyed out of the most advantageous position, and into a lesser one. As a result, Baldwin found himself leading his party into the general election of October 1931 as part of a National coalition, with Macdonald still Prime Minister and Samuel still a key figure in his Cabinet. The rank and file of the Party were only too well aware that they were accepting something less than their desired tariff policy, for the sake of the national interest.[75]

The continued atmosphere of crisis ensured the painless acceptance of this, without the corollary of apathy or disunity. Indeed there was a considerable measure of enthusiasm, for the enemy was clear. 'We try to beat as many Socialists as possible', wrote Cunliffe-Lister on 6 October. He spoke for most Conservatives both in his unhappiness with the Cabinet compromise on protection, and his acknowledgement that even so 'this is better than a simple dog-fight'.[76] The Conservatives did not expect a landslide victory; they were still fearful of the effects of the cuts. However, they were encouraged to a moderate optimism by the fact that the national appeal would spread the odium incurred by economies whilst at the same time hampering the opposition. Baldwin talked of winning perhaps 350 seats, a figure regarded by other Conservative leaders as probably twenty or thirty seats too high.[77] The election campaign was short and intense, with polling on 27 October. It was also frequently bitter and rancorous, not only between the divided sections of the former Labour government, but also between the constituent parties of the National Government. Although some Conservative candidates withdrew, mainly in favour of Macdonald's small band of National Labour followers or of Simonite Liberals, several local Associations refused to stand down for the free-trade followers of Samuel.[78] This included the Conservatives in Samuel's own constituency of Darwen, though he was able to fend off this challenge. When the results were declared the Conservatives found they scored a sweeping victory. 473 Conservative MPs were returned, by far the predominant element amongst the 554 supporters of the National Government. The Labour Party's vote had not collapsed, but their parliamentary strength was smashed. The official opposition were left with a mere 52 seats.

This result gave the Conservatives further advantages, but it did not transform their political situation. They had still to work within the National Government, and Macdonald was even more irremovably ensconced as Prime Minister. The introduction of tariffs was still restrained by their colleagues and partners. The free traders within the enlarged Cabinet, Snowden, no longer Chancellor but still a symbolic figure, and the Liberal contingent of Samuel, Maclean, Sinclair, and, to a lesser extent, Runciman, impeded or watered down one protectionist proposal after another. These difficulties continued throughout November and December, culminating in January 1932 over the key measure, the Import Duties Bill. Only another agreement to differ, devised by Hailsham, by which the free trade ministers would be permitted to suspend the doctrine of collective cabinet responsibility on this one occasion to speak and vote against the Bill, enabled the government to avoid a collapse. The Conservatives could not afford this; for it would have been blamed by the Liberals and National Labour on Conservative intransigence and the aggressive use of a majority obtained by exploiting the national appeal.

Between November 1931 and January 1932 the Conservatives won the battle for the revenue tariff, though not without difficulty. Achieving Joseph Chamberlain's goal of imperial preference took longer still. It was only after further rifts within the government, which finally brought about the resignations of Snowden and Samuel on 28 September 1932, that the agreements negotiated at the Imperial Conference held at Ottawa in July and August were put into effect. Neville Chamberlain, Chancellor of the Exchequer since Snowden's retirement in November 1931, introduced these with appropriate homage to his father's memory. However, this emotional occasion drew attention away from the real theme of his management of the Treasury. This was not the wide imperial vision, sought after by Beaverbrook or Amery, but the narrow application of rigid economy. Thus, by the end of 1932, the four point programme around which consensus within the Conservative Party had been eventually created in the spring and summer of 1931 was finally carried out, though by a strange and circuitous route and under a hesitant and sometimes hostile Prime Minister.

The pressures of political and economic circumstance between 1929 and 1931 had radically reshaped British politics. The three-party battle of the 1920s was replaced by a system of two groupings: the purged Labour Party on the one hand, and its opponents on the other. The latter, left in possession of the middle ground by the resigning Labour ministers in August 1931, dominated British politics for the following decade. The National Government, after 1935 led by Conservative premiers, was only cast down from these heights by the political and social cataclysm of another world war. Even so, the vitality of the Conservative Party and the depth of its roots in the country made possible a remarkably quick and complete recovery from the defeat of 1945. One reason for this was the operation of the two-party system which, re-established as a result of the events of 1929–1931, formed the undisputed framework for political activity in Britain for the next fifty years.

Conservative leaders are vulnerable in opposition, but have much greater resources to call to their aid when in office, and Baldwin was never again to face such a challenge in the remaining half of his career. The revolt over India rumbled on, reaching peaks of public in-fighting between the publication of a White Paper in 1933 and the passage of the Government of India Act of 1935. However, this rebellion, though consuming much of the leadership's attention, marked the refusal of the Diehards to accept the decisions about India which had been taken between 1929 and 1931. With the security of office, and with slow but visible improvement on the economic front after 1933, Baldwin was well able to fend off the assaults of Churchill and his allies on the backbenches. Although Macdonald remained Prime Minister until 1935, Baldwin, holding the prestigious but non-departmental post of Lord President of the Council, was clearly the second man in the ministry. As Macdonald's health and grasp declined sharply in his last two years, Baldwin regained the substance of power before he traded offices with Macdonald and became premier for the third time in June 1935. After re-shuffling his team, Baldwin won a final general election victory in November 1935, the last held before the end of the Second World War. In his final two years as Prime Minister and party leader Baldwin certainly had serious problems to cope with. In domestic politics the antics of the new monarch, Edward VIII, took up much time and energy, and the growing problems of foreign and defence policy surfaced in particularly acute form over the Hoare-Laval Pact in December 1935. These and other difficulties undermined Baldwin's health, and in 1936 he passed through a period of nervous debility and exhaustion, and political decline. Yet none of these issues ever seemed likely to bring about a change in the party leadership, and at the end of 1936 Baldwin emerged from these shadows to adroitly handle the Abdication crisis. He was able to go at a moment of his own choosing, at the height of public acclaim. Waiting until the coronation of King George VI, he retired from political life in May 1937, taking a peerage as the first Earl Baldwin of Bewdley, and passing an uncontested succession to his heir apparent, Neville Chamberlain.

The period of opposition during the second Labour Government was a vital phase in the career of Neville Chamberlain, for it transformed him from being merely one amongst several promising ministers to the position of second figure to Baldwin and thus, eventually, to both the leadership and the Premiership. Chamberlain had been one of the successes of the 1924–1929 Government, but in a minor department and on a politically dull programme. His spell at the Ministry of Health had demonstrated talent as an administrator and legislator, but it was by no means clear that he had qualities of leadership. He was 'more at home in the frozen regions of politics', and thought to be too bureaucratic.[79] His political sense was open to doubt after having been, together with Churchill, responsible for the disastrously unpopular de-rating programme. Neither this, nor other expensive social legislation, carried much credit with most ordinary Conservatives. By the time the end of the parliament was approaching in 1929, Chamberlain had become aware of the limitations of the Ministry of Health. He wanted to move to the Colonial Secretaryship, where his assumption of his father's mantle might mend some bridges. However, the anticipated re-shuffle did not occur before the dissolution, and defeat removed the opportunity from his grasp. Political reputations are far more variable than is often depicted, and in the closed circles of Westminster the index of political standing fluctuates as frequently as the prices on the Stock Exchange. After the general election of May 1929 Chamberlain was in decline, and for the remainder of the year he fruitlessly sought opportunities to restore his influence. In the immediate aftermath of the election he took a public stand in favour of reconsidering the fiscal policy, but first Amery's hints in favour of food taxes and then Beaverbrook's sudden eruption into an outright campaign for them caused him to pull in his horns. Unclear as to what line to take, he kept a low profile throughout the summer recess of 1929, and followed this with a lengthy absence in East Africa during the winter. This was only partly the result of exhaustion after five strenuous years in office; it was also a reaction to his altered political position.

On his return he resolved to use the newly created Conservative Research Department, of which he had been given control, to influence Party policy.[80] However, the Research Department was founded with the intention of filling the place of the civil service in providing briefs for the Party, and no more than that: it was never intended to direct policy. For Chamberlain, such a back-room position remained essentially unsatisfactory. It could only be a first small stage in rehabilitation. Nevertheless, the usefulness of the Research Department was a revelation to Chamberlain, and led his thoughts to the possibility of combining the Party Chairmanship with it. Baldwin was manoeuvred by Chamberlain, who exploited the growing hostility to Davidson, and created a position in which his own control of Central Office, either through an intermediary or directly, would be assured. In May 1930 Chamberlain's position in the Party hierarchy was still open to question, and he coveted the Chairmanship as a means of asserting his centrality on all matters.[81] In this sense his vision of the Central Office as being the directing force of the Party, literally the central organ, rather than another administrative workhorse like the Research Department, explains his desire for the position. Chamberlain was always happier in a defined institutional role in which he possessed executive power. At the Research Department he had been dependent upon Central Office without clear powers over it; but now he could emerge from the shadows.

The appointment to the Party Chairmanship in June 1930 was the first step in Neville Chamberlain's rise. This fell into three phases between June 1930 and November 1931, by which point his pre-eminence was completely assured. The Chairmanship filled a crucial role in this process, for it was a position of unique importance in the Party during periods of opposition. Indeed, apart from the leader himself there was no other position which ensured a voice in every significant decision; certainly membership of the former cabinet or the Business Committee did not do so.[82] Chamberlain exploited this during the first stage of his emergence, from June to October 1930. In this period he slowly built up his reputation, endeavouring to conci-liate Beaverbrook and secure the dropping of the referendum for the free hand. His political maturity emerged in the initiatives which he took in September and October 1930, firstly in the 'Unauthorised Programme', and secondly in masterminding the response to Bennett's declaration. Chamberlain avoided many of the pitfalls of his office by simply not doing the same job as his predecessor. Davidson had been a long-term working organiser. Before his own appoint-ment, Chamberlain was careful to have it made public that his own tenure was only to be temporary. This he did for two reasons. He wished to highlight his role as a new broom with a mandate to reform the Central Office from above; not cut out from the normal pattern of Chairmen, but attending to grand policy rather than the grind of detail. Essentially, Davidson had been an administrator, attending to the minutiae of organisation, management, and fund-raising. Cham-berlain's reforms of Central Office reflected his style of Chairmanship. They were designed to liberate the Chairman from such work in order that he might take on a more overtly political role. He also saw his relationship with the leader in a different light. Davidson had seemed too much the personal secretary. Chamberlain intended to be chief counsellor and to use his institutional access to the leader to mould his outlook to the shape which Chamberlain wanted the Party to adopt. In short, he intended to be an active, interventionist power in his own right—as no Chairman previously had been. Thus he maintained a high profile, distancing himself from mere management except where, as in the case of the crucial by-election contests or the control of the Party publicity machine, such powers brought solid advantages. The coup of restoring the leadership's position in October 1930 provided the kind of return that Chamberlain had been hoping for when he had invested his political capital in the Chairmanship. He told his sister with satisfaction: 'as we thought, the Chairmanship of the Party does enable one to direct the policy'.[83]

The remaining months spent as Chairman, between November 1930 and April 1931, comprised the second step in Neville Chamberlain's ascent to the position of unchallengeable heir apparent. He had been careful to make clear that his tenure of the Chairmanship did not rule him out from accepting cabinet office should the Labour government fall. Nevertheless, he was still vulnerable to the changing tides of fortune. The Central Office was inevitably embroiled in every internal dispute. Furthermore, Chamberlain was still in danger of being too closely identified with Baldwin, and of being dragged down with him when his position once again seemed on the verge of collapse in March 1931. Although increasingly spoken of as a candidate for the succession, Neville Chamberlain was still only one amongst several possible contenders. The third and most crucial phase of all was his capitalisation of his opportunity in the period after stepping down from the Chairmanship. Between April and November 1931, Chamberlain consolidated his position as the second man in the Conservative Party and gradually left his rivals behind. He returned to the front bench team in April with new prestige, and scored an immediate success in spearheading the attack during the budget debates.[84] He was an essential figure in the negotiations of August 1931, and in the Conservative group in the emergency cabinet of ten. With Horne effectively in retirement, Churchill in revolt, and Hailsham, though recently appointed leader in the Lords, eclipsed and marginalised by his omission from the cabinet, Neville Chamberlain had conclusively emerged as the future leader.

It was inevitable that this should be confirmed by his return to the Exchequer after the 1931 election. The circumstances of this second appointment as Chancellor, and its political significance, were quite different from his first brief tenure of the position during the Party's disunited condition in 1923. On that occasion he had been keeping the seat warm for the return of his half-brother Austen, himself twice formerly Chancellor of the Exchequer. In 1931, no such special circumstances applied; Neville Chamberlain had regained by right the position which had first come his way only by chance and circumstance. Chamberlain has acquired the historical reputation of having been a progressive figure. However, on tariffs and 'economy', two out of the three issues that really mattered within the Party in this period, he, more than any other figure in the leadership, was saying the kind of things that the right-wing and constituency activists wanted to hear. He was, perhaps, the only figure in the Party to gain in prestige from the tangled and unhappy events of the Party crisis. Yet the circumstances of 1931 also set an important limit upon Chamberlain's advance. Though crown prince, he would have to bide his time with as much patience as he could muster until his leader chose to retire, an event for which he had to wait another six years.

CONCLUSION

Power and Authority in Conservative Politics

The Conservative Party has always been as much a matter of men as of measures. More revealing than the mechanics of policy making were the fortunes and influence of the Party leadership, and, above all, of the leader. Individually he had the widest discretion in formulating policy, which only he could authoritatively pronounce.[1] It was his sole prerogative to select his front bench colleagues and to appoint the holders of the key posts in the Party organisation. The leader of the Conservative Party set its tone; to change the policy of the Party, it was necessary to force a change of leader. However, the leader was able to exploit for his personal advantage the Party's instinct for unity and solidarity. This manifested itself in the closing of ranks around the leader, which had the effect of making his critics appear as the divisive force. In turn this was reinforced by the fact that in times of crisis, internal debate was seen as a dangerous luxury. As a result, the leader of the Conservative Party possessed an immensely powerful position, whether used for creative initiation or defensive obstruction. Nevertheless, the leader was by no means immune from criticism or even direct attack from within the ranks of his followers, nor was he sheltered from the pressures of external forces. One of the best definitions of the leader's role was given by Baldwin in his speech to the party meeting of 30 October 1930:[2]

> Whenever a party chooses its leader it invests that leader by that action of selection with the right of putting forward the party policy. There has never been any other course pursued in this Party. But the leader in doing that, of course, has to be guided by his own common sense. He has to be guided by his own knowledge of the currents of opinion in the country, and he has to be guided by keeping in close touch with all that goes on and with the Resolutions

that are passed at the meetings of the National Union of Conservative and Unionist Associations.

The leader of the Conservative Party was expected to fulfil three requirements. Firstly, he had to give an adequate lead to the parliamentary Party in the House of Commons. His front bench colleagues could assist him in this role, but not substitute for him. Secondly, the leader had to satisfy the bulk of Conservative supporters in the country by accommodating the policies of the Party to a position that would at least ensure their continued active adherence to the cause. If the leader failed in this respect, he could himself be portrayed as the cause of division. Finally, the leader had to provide some prospect of leading his forces to victory at the polls, and therefore to power. This meant more than just pandering to the middle way in politics, for one significant practical brake upon the leader's authoritarian position was the fact that he must not split his forces, but by consultation and persuasion carry at least the bulk of his colleagues and his followers with him. To be secure, the leader of the Party needed to perform satisfactorily in at least two of these areas. His position would rapidly become untenable if he failed in all three, or even in two, for more than a short interval.

No politician is a paragon, and all the leaders of the Conservative Party in the first part of the twentieth century were stronger in some of these respects than others. The third Marquess of Salisbury, leader of the Party from 1885 to 1902, had been the most successful in all three roles, though as Prime Minister in the House of Lords he depended to some extent upon his chosen deputy in the lower chamber. From 1891 this was his nephew, Arthur Balfour, who succeeded him in 1902 and remained the leader until 1911. Though generally very capable as a parliamentarian and administrator, Balfour was unable to cope with the difficulties posed by the division over tariff reform after 1903, and did not effectively communicate his case to either the Party or the public. His difficulties in these second and third areas of leadership contributed to the renewed strife within the Party in the closing two years of his tenure, and led to his decision to stand down in 1911. His unexpected successor, Andrew Bonar Law, proved also to have unexpected strengths. Many of these came from his embodiment of the values and opinions of rank and file Conservatism, by whom he was trusted and valued. Bonar Law's principal difficulty during his first long term as leader, from 1911 to 1921, was his weakness as a parliamentarian, and the low opinion that was held of him by many of his immediate colleagues. Coming into the leadership whilst the Party was in opposition was not an advantage, for Bonar Law lacked the prestige and patronage of the premiership, which later cushioned Baldwin at his accession, and he had even less ministerial experience, never having sat at the cabinet table. When Bonar Law retired due to ill-health, he was replaced as leader of the Conservative Party by Austen Chamberlain, the man who had been forced to stand aside in his favour in 1911. Austen Chamberlain's tenure of the leadership was the briefest of all, and he was the only leader of the Party never to become Prime Minister. His position between 1921 and 1922 as leader of the largest element in the Lloyd George Coalition government was certainly a difficult one, but it is clear that Chamberlain's personal unsuitability for the position exacerbated the rift within the Party and contributed to his own destruction. He markedly failed in all three areas of leadership, and especially in the last two. By failing to make his own position clear, he appeared to disaffected followers among the junior ministers, on the backbenches, and in the constituency associations, to be at the same time both weak and stubborn. Worst of all was the fact that he seemed to be putty in the hands of Lloyd George. By allowing it to be thought that he was unwilling to lead the Conservatives into the impending general election as a separate force under their own leaders, he forced many of them to cast round for a leader whom they could trust to preserve their party. They found such a man in Bonar Law, who was waiting in the wings, having temporarily recovered his health.

The strain of leadership and office brought about the final collapse of Bonar Law's health in May 1923, only six months after he had replaced Chamberlain and led the Conservatives to victory in the 1922 election. His successor was Stanley Baldwin, who remained leader until he retired in 1937. Whilst Prime Minister, Baldwin was usually adequate in the House of Commons, and his occasional oratorical triumphs, together with the support of effective front-bench colleagues, masked the erratic quality of his parliamentary performance. He had been less satisfactory in the eyes of his followers in the formulation of Party policy. In 1923 he was able to survive the defeat into which he had led the Conservatives because the tariff reform platform on which he had gone to the country was endorsed by most of his followers. However, in his new departure between 1924 and 1929 Baldwin was taking calculated risks by deliberately moderating the Party's image and programme. At first these paid off in the sweeping electoral victory of 1924, but in the last two years of his second premiership, between 1927 and 1929, the Conservative activists began to feel thwarted and even betrayed. Baldwin took the biggest gamble of all in nonetheless sticking to the approach of 1924, symbolised by the slogan 'Safety First', in the general election of 1929. When this resulted not in victory but defeat, his position as leader became seriously exposed.

The second and longer spell in opposition between 1929 and 1931 clearly revealed his drawbacks as a parliamentarian. His performance made a dismal contrast with that of Lloyd George, who in these years was at the top of his debating form. These problems in the Commons were additional to the rift which had opened up between Baldwin and the rank and file. His definitions of Party policy were out of tune with a large element of his followers until October 1930. At the peak of the crisis within the Party, in September and early October 1930, it seemed as if the majority of Conservatives might desert in favour of false gods. If Baldwin was clearly failing in respect of the first two duties of a Conservative leader, the role of the third, the prospect of electoral victory, was more complicated. On the one hand his limited policy between May 1929 and October 1930 was an anathema to the protectionists, who believed that only a bold programme, vigorously marketed, could attract the voter. On the other hand, it was widely accepted that, despite all his faults, Baldwin was an electoral asset for whom there was no suitable replacement. Even so, if the Party crisis between May 1929 and March 1931 was caused by unrest over the parliamentary performance and political stance of the leadership, there can be no doubt that it was exacerbated by the frustrations of the electoral situation. In the first half of the parliament the Conservatives trailed dismally in the wake of a popular Labour administration; during the second half they seemed unable to gain any profit from the growing discredit of that government. Then, by the same process, disunity in the Conservative ranks was dampened down when public opinion seemed at last to move in their favour, culminating in the whiff of victory scented in the by-elections of June. Combined with this was the fact that the leader's policies now wore an acceptable face. This had been true of fiscal policy since October 1930. It was also true with regard to India, so long as sufficient emphasis was placed upon the safeguards to be built into any constitutional advance. The growing primacy of the 'economy' issue from late 1930 onwards was most important, for here the leadership had never been out of touch with their followers. By coming back to a position which his party found acceptable, Baldwin was able to isolate the press lords' campaign. The traditional hierarchies and the powers and position of the leader, which had come into question, were restored. Baldwin had come very close to losing that minimum of confidence without which no leader can function, but managed to pull back from every brink, when even his closest advisors thought his situation to be beyond all hope of recovery. Yet the end of this period found him in a position as strong as that which he had held between 1924 and 1926. Not only was he back in step with the desires of his partisan supporters; his approach was clearly also destined to lead to a historic victory at the ballot box.

There is no simple explanation of Baldwin's success in preserving his position during the Party crisis of 1929 to 1931, for it was the product of a variety of forces. Defensively, Baldwin made adroit tactical use of the tradition of loyalty. At the same time he endeavoured to accommodate party policy to the twin, and at first conflicting, demands of party and public opinion. So far as protection went, Baldwin was malleable. He sought the path of least resistance, trying always to find a median position in the Party. Where he embodied negativism, this was not rooted in principle, but was the expression of electoral pragmatism. It was directly related to the most obvious task before him: the recapturing of the key constituencies in the urban midlands and north of Britain, without which a return to power would be impossible.[3] Baldwin also exploited the weaknesses of his opponents. For most of the period, with the single but crucial exception of the months between July and October 1930, he was able to keep the grumbling support of the moderate majority in the centre of the Party. Baldwin's concentration on the matter of political methods was especially important, for he was able to alter the substantive issue from being a debate over ends to a debate over means, and in the process he split the protectionists against each other. As so often throughout his career, playing the constitutional card served Baldwin very well.

Many of the leader's problems were, consciously or otherwise, of his own making. The decision to resist Empire Free Trade was partly electoral caution, and partly the refusal of an experienced statesman to be tied to a policy which he did not believe could be put into practice. But the strains which resulted from denying the aspirations of many of his more vocal followers were multiplied by his personal limitations. Baldwin's mood during the Party crisis was a mixture of nervousness and complacency, irresolution and sudden attack. These are conflicting descriptions, but they represent a complex and often contradictory personality, whose moods and conduct were unpredictable and who was under considerable stress. He was most often criticised for his complacency, though its cause may have been as much an instinctive appreciation of the latent strengths of his position as of any inability to perceive its difficulties. Certainly, Baldwin was always sceptical of his power to change the political environment through creative acts of leadership and energy. The lethargy which resulted from this drove such colleagues as Amery and the Chamberlains almost to distraction, for they held the opposite view, and chafed at inactivity.

Baldwin's combination of complacency and indecision was the result of his reliance on being able to understand and respond to a political atmosphere, and of the conflicting signals which he detected at various stages of the crisis from the different regions. He tended always to come down on the side of caution in timing his advances of policy. This was without doubt a weakness in his character, and there were others which added to his difficulties in this period. Though Baldwin could often charm, he lacked tact. He was uncommunicative and maladroit in handling his principal colleagues, and distant from many of his backbenchers. He clung to certain individuals to whom he felt sympathetic in spite of their unpopularity, to the point of endangering himself. His personal preference for the 'Old Gang', and the consequent frustration of the rising younger men, was a sign both of his indolence and insecurity. He was always reluctant to change his advisers, for he had grown accustomed to their faces. Most important, however, was his failure to act as leader of the opposition in the normal partisan fashion. As a result, many of his followers came to believe that the Party had lost its sense of purpose.

Against this was balanced the strength of the position of the leader of the Conservative Party. Baldwin's shortcomings, which strained the internal cohesion of the Party, were not quite serious enough to destroy this. He survived by exploiting the powers of his office and the general loyalty of his followers, which hamstrung the efforts of his enemies within the Party on the few occasions when they felt bold enough to move openly against him. To these institutional advantages Baldwin added an often underestimated skill of timing. Above all, he was able to produce an oratorical triumph when it was most needed. Baldwin's choice of strategy was acute, for the lack of political respectability of his opponents was their gravest disadvantage. But there can be no doubt also that he benefited from that most elusive quality, luck: above all in the outcome of the Irwin-Gandhi talks in March 1931.[4]

One of the factors which made for a more secure tenure of leadership was the absence of an alternative leader, or even a clearly established succession.[5] One consequence of the Party crisis was the almost complete reshaping of the dominant group within the leadership, of which the agitation against the 'Old Gang' was a symptom and cause. Several of the older generation fell away into retirement or obscurity, whilst others such as Hailsham lost influence with their exclusion from important office in August 1931, never to regain it. Horne was never again thought of as a possible leader; Churchill and Amery were to remain in the wilderness for the rest of the decade. It is not in the nature of British party politics for men to rise from nowhere overnight, but it is true that only a handful of figures in any Cabinet set its tone, dominate its debates, and are familiar to the people. The new faces in the Conservative inner circle had all held office before, in or out of the Cabinet, but what was significant was their transition from minor appointments to the major posts. Although the Conservative Party was the dominant force in British government between 1918 and 1940, the leadership of the 1920s was a different group from that of the 1930s. Walter Elliot, Kingsley Wood, Anthony Eden, Duff Cooper, and William Ormsby-Gore represented a change of generation. However, the two most important developments in the Conservative leadership were the rise of Sir Samuel Hoare, and the emergence of Neville Chamberlain as Baldwin's clear and inevitable successor.

If Baldwin and Chamberlain can be described as the winners of the struggle within the Conservative Party between 1929 and 1931, the press barons are commonly held to be the losers. Their campaign has been accepted on Baldwin's terms, as an attempt at dictatorship by the press, in which the dragon was slain at St. George's. The role of the press in a parliamentary democracy, and the relationship between party politicians and the owners of newspapers was much more complex than this. The Conservative press acted as a forum for the development and presentation of issues of policy within the Party. This applied as much to the mass circulation popular titles as to the more prestigious metropolitan quality press and the varied range of major provincial newspapers. The press was not a creative element in its own right, but a medium of expression for opinion formed elsewhere. Formally in its columns or informally in discussion with journalists, editors, and owners, the press provided a sounding board for debating policy and strategy. Such figures as Dawson, Garvin, and Gwynne, no less than Beaverbrook, were as significant in their private role as confidants and mediators as in the public exhortations of their printed editorials. The Conservative press had no institutionally defined relationship with the structure of the Party or with its leader, for it was largely a matter of informal interaction. Nevertheless, it had a clearly understood function, all the more important for its possession of an independent power base and thus a certain freedom of action and opinion.

The Conservative press varied in political weight, that intangible but important quality, but most of its members were not dissimilar in the respect which their views could command from the parliamentary front bench. Editors and owners were scattered along a linear spectrum of lesser or greater affinity with the leadership and its policies. Dawson was always closest to Baldwin's position, with Garvin less so on protection as was Gwynne on India. Beaverbrook and Rothermere were simply removed further still, but should not be thought of as being on a different plane altogether. However, there was a distinction drawn between those newspapers whose political line was laid down by an editor who had been accorded the traditional independence, and those where the course was set by a 'dictatorial' proprietor. If there was a sense in which Beaverbrook and Rothermere were regarded as outsiders, this was not due to any feeling of snobbery for the market and readership at which their newspapers were aimed, but rather to the feeling that their managerial methods, journalistic tactics, and political pretensions were neither proper nor respectable. At several points in the history of the Party, Conservative newspapers had attempted to marshal resentment from below against the official line, or even, as in 1911, against the leader. Beaverbrook and Rothermere were only novel in the scale of their activities, not in their intention.

The strength of the Empire Crusade did not lie in the circulation figures of the newspapers that supported it, although there is no doubt that their initial advocacy enabled it to get started in a spectacular fashion, at least in the south. As Hailsham noted in his speech at the second Caxton Hall meeting: 'it is significant that those parts of the country where the agitation is strongest, those parts where even members of parliament have felt the pressure, are those parts, the south of England, where that press is read'.[6] Outside the southern counties, which were dominated by the metropolitan press, the daily morning and evening newspapers published in the major provincial centres were still powerful and effective voices in Britain between the wars. The average middle-class voter in the West Riding was as likely to have the *Leeds Mercury* or the *Yorkshire Post* on his breakfast table as the *Daily Express* or the *Daily Mail*; if he did read either of the latter, this would probably be as supplements rather than replacements.[7] In this sense it was *The Times*, rather than any of the press lords' titles, which could be said to have had a truly national influence. Furthermore, although the circulation of *The Times* was only one-tenth that of the *Daily Mail*, it was overwhelmingly the predominant newspaper read by the upper strata of British society, and therefore not only by Members of Parliament but also by the leading figures in the constituency associations (see Appendix 3).

Beaverbrook freely acknowledged that his campaign was based on the rank and file in the Conservative strongholds in the southern half of England.[8] So long as his movement embodied their otherwise inarticulate demands, he would represent a force to be reckoned with in Conservative politics. However, as Sir Basil Peto observed, 'it is not a question of Beaverbrook and Rothermere starting this feeling, but it is merely a question of their putting a match to the fire already laid'.[9] Disillusion with Baldwin's second government since 1927, rather than the charisma of the Crusade, was the motivating force. What mattered was that the Empire Crusade was able to mobilise a significant proportion of disaffected Conservatives at the lower levels of the Party organisation, and amongst the general public. These people gave substance to the press lords' shadow army. In addition, it was the backbench members of parliament who reflected these views, whether from sympathy or simple necessity, who gave the unrest a presence in the parliamentary Party.

Even when it engaged the fervent sympathy of so many Conservatives, any campaign like the Empire Crusade was still struggling against the pull of the Party's instincts of loyalty and unity. Beaverbrook's movement suffered from other fundamental weaknesses which prevented him from fully exploiting the vulnerability of the official clique of leaders between October 1929 and October 1930. Principal amongst these was the equation by which Beaverbrook was the Crusade, and the Crusade Beaverbrook. The fight for Empire Free Trade was a one man band and thus dependent upon the dynamism of its promoter. The loneliness of his position, and a mistaken belief that an increase in press circulation strength would augment the impact of the Crusade, led Beaverbrook to cling to his partnership with Rothermere, although the alliance was itself one of his weakest points.[10] In the spring of 1930 Beaverbrook's role as a herald moving before the advance guard of the Party, preparing the ground, was accepted as valid even by Baldwin himself. In the middle of 1930, after the collapse of the truce, many Conservatives still made a distinction between the political acceptability of the two press lords. There was a tendency to polarise all the odium on Rothermere, and all the tolerance on Beaverbrook.[11] The connection with Rothermere proved the barrier to successive attempts to come to terms in the summer months. South Paddington changed this picture radically, as also did the accommodation between the Party leaders and their followers in October 1930. Once the difference of policy largely disappeared, so also did the justification for continuing the pressure of the Crusade. This was recognised by Melchett and Elibank, who promptly withdrew their support. Beaverbrook's difficulty was that he had lost all faith in Baldwin, and now believed that his removal was an essential requirement before his programme could succeed. However, his motives could now be portrayed as based purely on personality, and he was indicted as the cause of faction within the Party.

The strategy of intervention in by-elections was at once the best card the Empire Crusade could play, and its greatest gamble. The problem was that Beaverbrook was not so much trying to appeal to new and unaffiliated voters, but that he was competing for the Conservative vote. In a similar manner to the experience of the Liberal Party during the Macmillan and Heath governments some decades later, the Crusade was able to attract a protest vote when Conservative voters were alienated from their leaders, but not to sustain it. In both periods, it was the safer seats, where the local organisation had never needed to be strong or effective, which proved the most volatile. The selection of a weak or unpopular candidate, as in South Paddington or over thirty years later in Orpington, only made matters worse. However, Beaverbrook's by-election strategy backfired at East Islington, and discredited him by seeming to give aid to the Socialists. Already isolated, Beaverbrook lost the last shreds of tolerance and support by his reckless and wrecking intervention. This was the situation which Baldwin did not create, but only confirmed, by emphasising the constitutional question at St. George's. The verdict at St. George's was a condemnation of the conduct and result of East Islington. It also reflected the fact that the issue of 'economy' was taking precedence in the concerns of Conservative supporters over the fine details of protection for agriculture; for most of them, the adoption of the free hand policy in October 1930 was sufficient. The press campaign blew hot and cold in direct relation to one factor only: the degree of rank and file Conservative disaffection which it could vocalise.[12] Its pressure manifested itself not by means of the newspapers that promoted it, but through the orthodox political activities of recruiting members, forming constituency branches, raising funds, and contesting elections. It is for this reason that the history of the Empire Crusade belongs with the history of pressure groups, and not with the history of journalism.

So far as it could express a genuine body of opinion, the press could play a role in the formulation of Conservative policy. This could be described as the search for a programme acceptable to the widest possible range of support in the Party and the nation. Considerations of electoral pragmatism had to be balanced against the need to keep the flame of party spirit burning brightly. There was not always a direct contradiction between party and public opinion, for both were affected by the same social and economic forces. The difference was one of degree, and dangerous only when an attitude or aim was central to the partisan supporters' *raison d'être*, yet in conflict with the public mood. This affected the political fortunes of the Party when the matter in question was one of the crucial issues of the day. On this criterion, the Conservative Party was out of touch with the electorate at the time of the 1929 election, and remained so for another year. During 1930, Party and nation moved independently onto converging courses, so that by mid-1931 they were broadly of the same mind on the foremost matter, the impact of the slump. Of course, public opinion was not a homogenous unit, and cannot historically be treated as such. Large numbers of people remained hostile to the Conservatives and the National Government even at the height of their popularity in 1931. What had shifted was the balance; but, in a first-past-the-post electoral system, where a handful of votes in a handful of constituencies decided the day, that was enough to remove one party from power and replace it with another. In the 1931 election the movement was larger than on most occasions, and over half the constituencies changed hands. Even so, the Labour vote fell by less than two million from their high point of May 1929. The Conservative Party improved its poll by more than three million votes, but it is clear that much of this is accounted for by the fact that the Liberals ran over three hundred and fifty fewer candidates than in 1929, and most Liberal voters followed their leaders in supporting the National government.

Even where a political party is successful in creating an affinity with a majority of voters, this does not mean that the public shares every tenet of the activists' faith. In the summer of 1931 the Conservative position on tariffs and 'economy' appeared to be attracting increasing support, but it should not be supposed that this was equally true of other attitudes. Many ordinary Conservatives were hostile towards further disarmament and dubious about the League of Nations, or made frequent and vocal pleas for the restoration of the powers of the House of Lords, but on these matters the 'man in the street' remained indifferent. Party policy was not created by public opinion; it welled up from the hearts of the Party activists, and was only then offered to the wider audience in the expectation that it would strike a chord with them as well.

In theory, policy was the sole province of the Party leader. In practice, it was moulded by the four elements of Party opinion. Firstly, the leader was constrained by the need to retain a consensus amongst the frontbench team. Secondly, the confidence and morale of the parliamentary forces was essential to success, and their views had also to be taken into account. Thirdly, the sections and classes from which the Conservative Party normally expected to draw its support exerted more general pressures. This was communicated upwards through the fourth and final element, the representative institutions of the National Union. Public opinion was a more amorphous concept, but attention was specifically directed to the state of opinion in key marginal regions, such as Lancashire, and to the results of by-elections. The evolution of Party policy was a process of attempting the most satisfactory compromise between these forces. However, different persons and groups within the Conservative political world started out from different standpoints, and as a result had varying perspectives on the order of priorities. Members of Parliament were often pre-occupied by unrest within their local constituency organisations, whilst both prospective candidates and the Party leader were more concerned about the non-Conservative voter.

Another factor was the growing complexity of political issues, and the need for detailed planning in policy formulation. Baldwin was notorious for not consulting his colleagues, and even for seeming to make up policy as he went along. This impulsiveness led to several difficulties, most obviously in the origins of the 1923 general election. Although a planning apparatus was set up in opposition in 1924, it fell into decay as soon as the Party returned to power. The poverty of ideas about long-term policy was revealed when the manifesto for the 1929 election came to be drawn up, and it was one reason for the choice of a strategy of pointing to what had been done, and criticising the plans of others. After this reliance on ad hoc methods had led to another defeat, the Conservative Research Department was established in November 1929. Baldwin took little interest in its work, but he was the last leader of the Party to be able to avoid the detailed formulation of policy. His successor, Neville Chamberlain, thrived on such work, and held on to the Chairmanship of the Research

Department from 1930 until his death ten years later. Although Winston Churchill shared Baldwin's reluctance, after the defeat of 1945 he was forced into endorsing the proposals of his more eager colleagues. Since the Second World War, the range and complexity of issues has become such that, inevitably, the leader's role has been encroached upon, and policy-making has become a more collective matter.[13] But as late as 1931 defining the Party's views on the vital issues of the day remained a reasonably simple matter, within the compass of even such a slow-moving individual as Baldwin. For that reason, the influence of the Party's newly-created civil service in the Research Department mattered very little, when compared to the more traditional contributions of other sections of Party opinion.

Within the Party, the transition from being based on a landed interest to industry and commerce brought with it important changes in attitude. At the same time the attention to imperial questions was giving way to an increasing insularity of approach. Specific Conservative policies were related to these changing emphases. The pressure for the readoption of tariff reform reflected the failure of 'Safety First' to capture sufficient public support in 1929. Added to this was the pressure from business that the policy of safeguarding should be extended in its application, to include iron and steel. However, the element of imperial preference in the protectionist programme was soon being set aside in the interests of the domestic market. Agriculture was a less successful interest group, partly because of its diminished importance both economically and politically, and partly because public opinion was thought likely to balk at duties on imports of cheap food.

The difficulty of balancing between Party opinion and public opinion was a central theme in the Conservative crisis of 1929–1931. In the immediate aftermath of the election defeat, the leadership was understandably determined to remain in step with what it thought was the public mood. Whilst constituency and backbench hostility to the Liberals prevented the former Coalitionists from having meaningful negotiations with Lloyd George, the leadership on the other hand was equally able to block the ardent desire of the protectionists to commit the Party to a bolder but electorally dangerous platform. The resultant stalemate led only to further apathy, and played into the hands of the Empire Crusade, which drew its strength from local Conservatism in rural and southern England. However, in 1929 not all Conservatives were favourable to protection, and in northern urban areas it was unpopular with both Party and public opinion. As a result, the leadership strove to concede as little as possible to the pressure from below for an advance towards full safeguarding for industry, even if not for agriculture. Baldwin's speeches at the 1929 Conference, at the Coliseum, and at the Hotel

Cecil were exercises in rhetoric rather than substance in an attempt to paper over this gap.

In this he was unsuccessful; and the widening rift between leader and followers produced the peak of the Party crisis in the summer of 1930. At this point Baldwin appeared to be failing in all three aspects of leadership. His Commons performances were visibly unsatisfactory, his policy was unpopular and creating division, and he could provide no prospect of electoral victory. In addition he was losing control over feeling in the Party. Unrest was rife amongst both his colleagues in the leadership and his backbench followers in parliament. In the country, for the only time in his fourteen years as leader, he was losing the loyalty of the chairmen of the local associations. Recovery was achieved in the nick of time. Business opinion, and public feeling more generally, appeared during 1930 to be shifting towards protection, even in the former strongholds of free trade. By the end of the year this drift had become such a landslide that even food taxes no longer provoked more trouble than they were worth. Adjustments of policy to appease the Party stalwarts thus became practical politics. Baldwin was able to exploit a suitable pretext to make concessions to his party when the Canadian Prime Minister made his offer of reciprocity at the Imperial Conference in October, without losing face by surrendering to the pressure of the Empire Crusade.

Over the next six months the Party continued to be racked by doubts over Baldwin's personal fitness as leader, and over his deliberately moderate stance on India. These were primarily concerns of the parliamentary Party, and Baldwin was able to meet the fears that he himself had raised in both areas by producing the speech of his life, just when he most needed it, in the debate on India of 12 March 1931. The agitation over India had little impact on the wider public, though critics of the bipartisan line could always attract an audience within the parliamentary ranks. The attitude of Conservatives towards the future political development of India was strongly influenced by parallels with the Irish question during the previous fifty years.[14] Baldwin drew the lesson that for the health of the empire such matters must not become the stuff of dispute between the parties. However, the imperialist wing of the Conservative Party arrived at different conclusions from the events in Ireland, especially since the end of the First World War. Its members placed more emphasis on the importance of strength and consistency, and the purity of a policy of refusing to negotiate with seditious native elements.[15] From such a perspective, Baldwin's self-confessed aim of 'trying to liberalise the Tory Party' on India appeared to be stark defeatism.[16] However, Baldwin expected that the other parties, which were equally aware of the need for unity, would moderate their course in the light of Conservative fears and requests for safeguards. Baldwin, Irwin, and many other Conservatives felt that the implications of British policy in India in the past had limited their freedom of manoeuvre, and that the pattern of Indian development had already been determined. The Montagu-Chelmsford reforms in 1921 'had set our feet upon the permanent road' of devolution, whilst the reaction to the Amritsar massacre had sounded the death knell of any simple reliance on repression of native opinion.[17] In the matter of India, as with tariff reform, the division in the Conservative Party lay between the pragmatists, surrounding and influencing the Party leader, and the purists or idealists, who were normally kept in the position of a vocal fringe group. In both these areas of imperial politics the leadership managed to retain the crucial confidence of the central mass of the Party, both in the Commons and in the constituencies.

From November 1930 onwards Conservatives found common ground in placing foremost on their agenda the dangers of national bankruptcy, for which the solution was 'economy'. This outstripped both tariffs and India in the Party rhetoric of 1931 precisely because it was the one area on which Party and public opinion were at their closest. The by-elections of 1931 denoted that Baldwin was now satisfactorily performing all three of the leader's functions, in terms of parliamentary performance, policy-making, and standing with the public at large. The adoption of the twin policies of 'economy' and protection restored unity of purpose to the Party in 1931. In all these respects, the solid mass of moderate backbenchers played a crucial role, acting as a thermometer measuring the twin effects of Party and public opinion blowing hot and cold. On most occasions in the first half of the parliament these forces pulled in opposite directions and produced only paralysis; but perhaps this mattered less in the politics of inter-war Britain than it would have done before 1914. Once these forces began to come together in the second half of the parliament, the Conservative Party responded vigorously.

Nonetheless, it remains true that they did so in the wake of the movement of public opinion, as an effect and not as a cause. The Conservatives' renewed popularity was more the result of the Labour government's failure to deal with unemployment than of any initiative on their own part. Certainly, the opposition in parliament played little part in reviving the fortunes of the Conservatives. Even in terms of the least ambitious aim of an opposition, that is, to obstruct government business, success was due more to the lack of clear ideas on Labour's part, or to the Liberals balking at some government proposal either out of a desire to demonstrate independence or genuine disagreement. The Conservative preponderance in the House of Lords was never used until the government was already in such difficulties that it shrank from accepting the challenge and calling an election. The Conservative leaders were to the end careful not to present their opponents with any popular issue upon which a cry of peers versus people could be raised—in that sense at least they had learned the lesson of 1910. Insofar as there were prospects of the fall of the ministry, these were not the product of effective opposition, but of the decay of the government from within and of the drift away from them of floating voters. The move towards alliance with the Conservatives by the Liberal wing under Sir John Simon might indeed produce the fall of Labour, but this move was the result of the pressure of public circumstances which ground the Liberal Party between the upper and lower millstones of the larger parties, forcing a choice of lesser evils upon them.

Between 1929 and 1931 the position of all of the political parties was transformed. So also was their relationship with each other, and with the public at large. However, the position of the Conservatives after the general election of 1929 had been far from assured, and the strengths of the Party were less apparent to contemporaries than they might be from a historical perspective. There existed the capacity for the Conservative Party at several points during this period to damage itself so seriously as to be excluded from power for years to come. That this danger was avoided might be considered an inverted form of success. The Party could have broken up as badly, if not more so, as it had in 1903, 1911, or 1922. As the experience of the Liberals during the 1920s had shown, prolonged public disunity could extract its own price and ultimately become a prime cause of a party's decline. The Conservatives narrowly avoided splitting their party in the efforts of the leadership to remain close to the middle ground of public opinion; by doing so they escaped being once again locked into the electoral trap of the Edwardian period. Instead, they were manoeuvred into the National Government. Although the Conservative Party took its place in the emergency Cabinet assembled on 24 August 1931, and although that decision was apparently received with general approval throughout the Party, this outcome was neither sought nor desired. The panic atmosphere of late August stampeded the Conservatives into decisions not of their own free choice. The National Government was accepted with misgivings, firstly as being the only possible solution to the crisis, and secondly as being a matter of patriotic duty.

As a result of developments during the spell in opposition between 1929 and 1931, the formation of the National Government found the Conservative Party united around particular policies and leaders, having evolved a political posture to face the issues of the foreseeable future both at home and abroad. On the one hand, the Conservatives refused to allow their own right-wing to drag them away from the middle ground for the sake of imperial or foreign policy. On the other, the preoccupation with the concerns of business limited the Party's options. Government intervention, regardless of the colour of the party in power, was condemned as expensive, profitless, and socialistic. Though important measures were passed in the 1930s, the Conservative Party never again presented itself as the engine of energetic social reform in the way that it had begun to do during the government of 1924–1929. Between 1929 and 1931 changes in the direction and outlook of the Party became crystallised into a pattern in which they remained set until the Second World War, if not longer. A different face was shown after 1931, with the emphasis upon welfare through means-tested official charity and the strictest economy in local and national expenditure.[18] This outlook also contributed to the difficulties of rearmament after 1934; in the refusal to organise or compel industry in any way; in the dilemma over the question of legitimate profits; and in the humiliating withdrawal of the National Defence Contribution proposals of 1937.[19] Similar attitudes were to hamstring the Conservatives when the Beveridge Report was published in 1942. Their legacy was the popular revulsion from the political image of the depression years which contributed so greatly to the catastrophic defeat of the Conservative Party in 1945. The policies associated with R. A. Butler and Harold Macmillan from 1948 to 1963 rejected these inter-war values, and were based instead upon the twin pillars of the welfare state and Keynesian economic management. When, by the 1970s, the continued relative decline of Britain caused that post-war optimism to tarnish and fade, the Conservatives swiftly and naturally reverted to holding the same basic ideas and assumptions about the role of government in the fields of welfare provision, intervention in the economy, taxation, and expenditure, as those mobilised in response to the impact of the slump in 1931.

There has been a tendency to categorise Mrs Thatcher as if she were some sort of new departure in terms of the history of British Conservatism. It is supposed that she and Baldwin symbolise entirely opposite traditions within the Conservative pantheon. Indeed, for sound reasons of political tactics, it has been part of that lady's strategy to present herself as a radical break with the past. But the changes are ones of rhetoric, not of substance. The mass of the Conservative Party, in the constituencies and on the backbenches, are not intellectuals. They have not been converted since 1975 to an economic ideology for which 'monetarism' or 'Thatcherism' are abbreviations, nor have they been captured by ideologues. On the contrary, the reason for the appeal of that policy is that it is, under the cover of much economic jargon, the traditional, indeed the instinctive, Conservative remedy in times of recession. Between 1929 and 1931 the Conservative Party under Baldwin's aegis revealed itself to be operating on the basis of 'housewife economics': the same thing as the constant demand for the approach of the 'practical men' of business. It was alarmed at the levels of local rates and national taxation, and it was determined to reduce the scale of government activity and expenditure. Apart from the substitution of Europe for the empire as the trading area to be sheltered behind preferential tariff walls, there has been no fundamental change in policy. In facing the problem of mass unemployment, then as now the major social and political issue of the day, the Party was profoundly sceptical of the claims of the proponents of programmes of great public works, and profoundly hostile to the financing of these by the increase of government borrowing. At its most basic levels, the Conservative Party was never really converted to ideas of Keynesian economics. If any period in the history of the Party does not represent the norm, it must be the period from the late 1940s to the early 1960s, which was itself so much a conscious reaction and rejection of the image and approach of the Conservative Party of 1931.

APPENDIX 1

Constituency Opinions on the Causes
of the 1929 Defeat

On 2 July 1929 the Central Council of the National Union resolved to send a letter to every constituency, asking for their views on the causes of the defeat in the general election. This enquiry only involved the English and Welsh seats: Scotland, which has a separate organisational structure, did not conduct any parallel exercise. Three hundred and fifteen replies were eventually received by Conservative Central Office, but they were not kept. All that survives is a general analysis of their collective content in the draft report of the enquiry sub-committee (see p. 32). As a result, local Party opinion can only be traced with any precision through the constituency minute books. Many Associations recorded the fact that they had sent a reply, without giving any indication of its content. However, the sample of surviving records was found to include fifteen constituencies where full details of the response were minuted: Bath, Bristol West, Camborne, Chelmsford, Chippenham, Ealing, Gravesend, Kennington, Knutsford, Lewisham West, Oxfordshire North, Shrewsbury, Sowerby, Torquay, and Winchester. There were also four examples of detailed reports which, though not specifically stated to be responses to the national enquiry, must nevertheless have formed the basis of a reply: Guildford, Keighley, Ipswich and Wolverhampton West. The table below is derived from the information in this total of nineteen reports. Allowance must be made for the fact that there is a bias in the sample towards the safer and southern seats. Seven of the seats were in the south east, with an average Conservative percentage of the poll in 1929 of 47.2%. Five were in the south west, with an average Conservative poll of 45.9%. Four were in the midland or eastern counties, with an average Conservative vote of 43.4%. The remaining three seats were in the north, with the much lower average Conservative poll of 37.1%. Of the total of nineteen seats, fourteen were held by the Conservatives, four were lost (Kennington, Sowerby, and Wolverhampton West to Labour; Camborne to the Liberals), and one (Keighley) was already held by Labour. In other respects, the selection of data has been by the random circumstance of survival, and there is no reason to assume that it does not represent an accurate microcosm of the state of feeling within the Conservative Party. The percentage figure in the table below refers to the proportion of these constituencies which mentioned the item in question. Only items listed by more than one Association have been included.

Proportion	Item Mentioned
78.9%	Criticism of the de-rating policy and the reassessment of rateable values
73.6%	Absence of any 'positive', i.e. protectionist, policy, and criticism of the 'Safety First' strategy
57.9%	Criticism of the granting of the 'flapper' vote
57.9%	Attacks on the Party by a hostile press
42.1%	Leadership out of touch with the rank and file, and the ignoring of policy resolutions sent up through the Party organisations
36.8%	Intervention of a Liberal candidate
26.3%	Safeguarding not sufficiently emphasised
26.3%	Failure to modify the Defence of the Realm Act, and criticism of the Home Secretary
26.3%	Effects of the 'swing of the pendulum'
21.0%	Misrepresentation by opposition parties
21.0%	Failure to economise & reduce local and national government expenditure
15.8%	Failure to reform the House of Lords
15.8%	Criticism of the petrol tax
15.8%	Criticism of reforms in local government
10.5%	Criticism of the betting tax

APPENDIX 2

The Membership of the Empire Crusade

The Beaverbrook papers include a number of documents which list the Empire Crusade membership for certain constituencies, and one memorandum which gives figures for all the divisions in the county of Lincolnshire. These are mainly undated, but cover the period from February to November 1930. Although they do not amount to a complete register of the Crusade membership, they demonstrate a number of significant factors. The following table compares the Crusade membership with the total of votes cast for the Conservative candidate in the same constituency in the general election of May 1929. It must be remembered that only a small proportion of Conservative voters would be active members of their local Association, a factor which makes the size of the Crusade membership even more impressive. Its strength was far from inconsiderable: in several constituencies it had enrolled close to, or more than, a thousand electors. However, this strength is concentrated in distinct areas. The highest totals are found in southern England (especially in the suburban environs of London) and in the agricultural parts of eastern England. The Empire Crusade was especially strong in the arable farming districts of Lincolnshire and Norfolk, and it was from this area that Beaverbrook's later venture of the Agricultural Party drew its firmest support. Equally significant is the almost total absence of any lists for northern constituencies. Excluding the Lincolnshire seats, only five of the twenty-six divisions for which a figure can be traced are located north of the river Trent. It is no coincidence that these, together with the Lincolnshire division of Brigg (which included Scunthorpe and other industrial areas), comprise the six weakest constituencies from the Crusade's point of view.

Constituency	Crusade Membership	Conservative Vote in 1929	Crusaders as % of Cons vote
Holland	1643	15877	10.3
Bromley	1411	14025	7.4
Brentford	1044	14025	7.4
Horncastle	926	12837	7.2
Grantham	1103	16121	6.8
Epsom	1603	24720	6.4
Hastings	956	15928	6.0
Lincoln	613	11978	5.1
Chislehurst	802	16909	4.7
St Albans	943	20436	4.6
Thanet	1009	22595	4.4

Table continued

Table continued

Constituency	Crusade Membership	Conservative Vote in 1929	Crusaders as % of Cons vote
Hythe	565	12982	4.3
Chelmsford	724	17094	4.2
Westbury	532	12907	4.1
Wycombe	946	23231	4.0
Stamford	460	12607	3.6
Bristol West	883	25416	3.4
Putney	625	19657	3.1
Evesham	464	14694	3.1
Louth	422	13999	3.0
Chippenham	395	13550	2.9
Gainsborough	283	10058	2.8
Grimsby	719	27001	2.6
Worcester	345	13182	2.6
Salisbury	382	15672	2.4
Fareham	399	19756	2.0
Dorset West	251	12247	2.0
Bristol Central	290	16524	1.7
Portsmouth Central	217	13628	1.5
Brigg	129	12506	1.0
East Renfrewshire	170	18487	0.9
Sunderland	191	29180	0.6
Cleveland	102	15255	0.6
East Toxteth	41	17678	0.2
Scarborough	40	20710	0.1

In addition, there is also a total for the Crusade membership in all four Nottingham seats. When compared to the total vote given for the four Conservative candidates in Nottingham in 1929, this produces the following figure:

City	Crusade Membership	Conservative Vote in 1929	Crusaders as % of Cons vote
Nottingham (4)	1360	46826	2.9

Source: Beaverbrook MSS B214–218, 224, 227, 233, 237–240.

APPENDIX 3

Social Class and the Readership of Newspapers

The table below gives a social profile of the readership of the main national newspapers, by means of a percentage estimate of the degree to which each newspaper was taken by a given group of the population. The five income bands are based upon the earnings of the chief bread-winner of the family, and the class descriptions attached to each of these are intended as approximate and not absolute distinctions. The figures are derived from data collected in 1935, and there seems no reason to suppose that the character of newspaper readership had varied significantly since 1930. However, it should be borne in mind that the *Daily Mail* suffered a decline in circulation from 1,845,000 to 1,719,000 between 1930 and 1935, and was surpassed by the *Daily Express*, whose circulation rose from 1,693,000 to 1,911,000. The *Daily Mirror* and the *Daily Sketch* had almost no political content, and have been omitted from the table.

Income of Chief earner p.a.	Families in group as % of population	% of group taking each newspaper						
		The Times	Morning Post	Daily Telegraph	Daily Express	Daily Mail	Daily Herald	News Chronicle
Upper Class more than £1000	0.9	54.1	19.5	29.3	12.3	31.6	1.2	4.0
Upper Middle Class £500–£1000	3.4	20.7	11.7	23.9	16.8	35.0	1.2	5.6
Lower Middle Class £250–£500	14.3	2.6	2.9	11.0	26.4	31.7	6.2	10.2
Upper Working Class £125–£250	57.5	0.1	0.1	1.9	20.0	12.3	21.4	13.4
Lower Working Class below £125	24.0	0.02	0.01	0.4	7.8	4.5	20.7	7.6

Source: Incorporated Society of British Advertisers, *The Readership of Newspapers and Periodicals in Great Britain 1936* (London, 1937), p. 1A.

NOTES

In addition to the standard abbreviations, the following have also been used:

AC	Austen Chamberlain MSS
AGM	Annual General Meeting
An	Annual
CA	Conservative Association
CRD	Conservative Research Department
EIA	Empire Industries Association MSS
Exec	Executive Committee
Div	Division
F&GP	Finance and General Purposes
GM	General Meeting
GP	General Purposes
HC Debs	House of Commons Debates
IES	Indian Empire Society (Stuart) MSS
JIL	Junior Imperial League
NC	Neville Chamberlain MSS
NFU	National Farmers Union MSS
NU	National Union of Conservative and Unionist Associations
Prov	Provincial
Res	Resolution
SUA	Scottish Unionist Association

Unless otherwise stated, all references to the Halifax MSS are to the papers at the India Office Library, all references to the Selborne MSS are to the papers at the Bodleian Library, and all references to the Dawson MSS are to the papers held in the *The Times* Archive (except references to the Dawson diary, which has been deposited at the Bodleian Library). In the nature of the constituency material, for most points a large number of references could be given. In order to economise on space, the policy which has been followed is to cite a selection of representative examples.

Introduction

1. K.O.Morgan, *Consensus and Disunity: The Lloyd George Coalition Government 1918–1922* (Oxford, 1979); M.Cowling, *The Impact of Labour 1920–1924* (Cambridge, 1971); M.Kinnear, *The Fall of Lloyd George* (London, 1973); C.Cook, *The Age of Alignment* (London, 1975).

2. T.Wilson, *The Downfall of the Liberal Party 1914–1935* (London, 1966); M.Bentley, *The Liberal Mind 1914–1929* (Cambridge, 1977); R.I. McKibbin, *The Evolution of the Labour Party 1910–1924* (Oxford, 1974); J.M. Winter, *Socialism and the Challenge of War* (London, 1974).

3. Wilson, op. cit.; J.Campbell, *Lloyd George: The 'Goat' in the Wilderness 1922–1931* (London, 1977).

4. R.Skidelsky, *Politicians and the Slump: The Second Labour Government 1929–1931* (London, 1967); R.I.McKibbin, 'The Economic Policy of the Second Labour Government 1929–1931', *Past and*

Present, No. 68, (1975); D.Marquand, *Ramsay Macdonald* (London, 1977).

5. R.Bassett, *1931: Political Crisis* (London, 1958); Skidelsky, op. cit.; Marquand, op. cit.; H.Berkeley, *The Myth That Will Not Die: The Formation of the National Government 1931* (London, 1978); H.Nicolson, *King George V* (London, 1952); K.Rose, *King George V* (London, 1983).

6. R.Blake, *The Conservative Party from Peel to Churchill* (London, 1970); J.D.Fair, 'The Conservative Basis for the Formation of the National Government of 1931', *Journal of British Studies*, Vol. 19, 1980.

7. R.Blake, op. cit.

8. J.Ramsden, *The Age of Balfour and Baldwin 1902–1940* (London, 1978).

9. R.Rempel, *Unionists Divided* (Newton Abbot, 1972); A.Sykes, *Tariff Reform in British Politics 1903–1913* (Oxford, 1979); P.Fraser, 'Unionism and Tariff Reform: the crisis of 1906', *Historical Journal*, Vol. 5, 1962; N.Blewett, 'Free Fooders, Balfourites, and Whole Hoggers: Factionalism within the Unionist Party 1906–1910', ibid., Vol. 11, 1968.

10. R.Blake, *The Unknown Prime Minister: The Life and Times of Andrew Bonar Law* (London, 1955); J.Campbell, *F.E.Smith* (London, 1983); K.Middlemas & J.Barnes, *Baldwin* (London, 1969); H.M.Hyde, *Baldwin* (London, 1973); M.Gilbert, *Winston S. Churchill: Vol. 5 1922–1939* (London, 1976). D.Dilks, *Neville Chamberlain: Vol. 1* (Cambridge, 1984).

11. A.B.Cooke & J.Vincent, *The Governing Passion: Cabinet Government and Party Politics in Britain 1885–1886* (Brighton, 1974); M.Cowling, *1867: Disraeli, Gladstone, and Revolution* (Cambridge, 1967): M.Cowling, *The Impact of Labour 1920–1924* (Cambridge, 1971).

12. McKibbin, *Evolution of the Labour Party;* B.Pimlott, *Labour and the Left in the 1930s* (Cambridge, 1977);

T.Stannage, *Baldwin Thwarts the Opposition: The British General Election of 1935* (London, 1980).

13. R.J.Olney, *Lincolnshire Politics 1832–1885* (Oxford, 1973); P.Thompson, *Socialists, Liberals, and Labour: The Struggle for London 1885–1914* (London, 1967); P.F.Clarke, *Lancashire and the New Liberalism* (Cambridge, 1971).

14. Memo by Pollock, 'The Fall of the Coalition Government', Hanworth MSS d.432/133–188.

15. A.J.P.Taylor, *Beaverbrook* (London, 1972), p. xiv.

16. G.Peele, 'Revolt Over India', G.Peele & C.Cook, eds., *The Politics of Reappraisal 1918–1939* (London, 1975).

17. D.Butler, ed., *Coalitions in British Politics* (London, 1978), pp.55–59.

18. Amery diary, 31 July 1931.

19. This aspect has been more fully discussed elsewhere; see S.Ball, 'Failure of an Opposition? The Conservative Party in Parliament 1929–1931', *Parliamentary History*, Vol. 5, 1986.

Chapter 1

1. Sykes, *Tariff Reform*, passim.

2. R.F.Mackay, *Balfour* (Oxford, 1985), pp.137–155, 195–203.

3. Morgan, op. cit., pp. 1–45.

4. Kinnear, op. cit., pp. 63–134.

5. Ramsden, *Balfour and Baldwin*, pp. 174–207.

6. Reeve to Smithers, 2 Mar. 1929, Artindale to Smithers, 22 Mar. 1929, copies to Baldwin, Baldwin MSS 55/35–48.

7. Joynson-Hicks to Baldwin, 23 Jan. 1928, Baldwin MSS 163/167–168.

8. Northwich CA, Exec., 20 Dec. 1928; Chippenham CA, Exec., 1 Feb. 1929.

9. Hoare to Baldwin, 26 Sept. 1927, Baldwin MSS 162/166–168; Chelmsford CA, Exec., 23 Jan. 1928.

10. P.Williamson, 'Safety First: Baldwin, the Conservative Party, and

and the 1929 General Election', *Historical Journal*, Vol. 25, 1982, pp.385–409.

11. Crawford to Irwin, 13 May 1930, Halifax MSS EUR.C. 152/19/1/57a.

12. Hyde, *Baldwin*, pp.32–91; Middlemas & Barnes, *Baldwin*, pp.39–94.

13. L.S.Amery, *My Political Life* (3 Vols., London, 1953–5), III, p.224.

14. *The Times*, 26 Oct. 1923; Hyde, *Baldwin*, pp.174–177.

15. Speech of 6 May 1924, S.Baldwin, *On England* (London, 1926), p.6; Ramsden, *Balfour and Baldwin*, pp.207–215.

16. D.Cannadine, 'Politics, Propaganda, and Art: The Case of Two Worcestershire Lads', *Midland History*, Vol. 4 (1977).

17. J.Campbell, 'Stanley Baldwin', in J.P.Mackintosh, ed., *British Prime Ministers in the Twentieth Century: Volume One* (London, 1977), p.210.

18. Baldwin to Mrs. Davidson, 16 Jan. 1922, in R.R.James, ed., *Memoirs of a Conservative: J.C.C.Davidson's Memoirs and Papers 1910–1937* (London, 1969), p.112.

19. For an unsolicited view from a 'man in the street', see Fleet to Hannon, 1 Jul. 1930, Hannon MSS 19/1; J.A.Ramsden, 'Baldwin and Film', N.Pronay & D.W.Spring, eds., *Propaganda, Politics, and Film 1918–1945* (London, 1982), pp.126–143; Cannadine, op. cit.

20. Williamson, 'Safety First', pp.387–390.

21. Jones diary, introduction, p. xxx.

22. Amery, *My Political Life*, II, p.505.

23. Irwin to Davidson, 25 Feb. 1930, James, *Memoirs*, p.306.

24. Bridgeman journal, II, p.183; Amery diary, 3 Mar. 1930.

25. Austen to Ida Chamberlain, 22 Jun. 1930, AC 5/1/506.

26. Neville to Ida Chamberlain, 11 Oct. 1930, NC 18/1/712.

27. Austen to Hilda Chamberlain, 21 Mar. 1931, AC 5/1/535; Bridgeman journal, II, p.183.

28. Austen to Hilda Chamberlain, 14 Jun. 1930, AC 5/1/504.

29. Austen to Hilda Chamberlain, 21 Mar. 1931, AC 5/1/535.

30. Neville Chamberlain diary, 8 Dec. 1929, NC 2/22.

31. H.Macmillan, *Memoirs: Vol. 1— Winds of Change 1914–1939* (London, 1966), p.313.

32. Bridgeman journal, II, pp. 221–223; H.Balfour, *Wings Over Westminster* (London, 1973), p.76; Hannon to Beaverbrook, 12 Sept. 1955, Hannon MSS 17/1.

33. Austen to Hilda Chamberlain, 21 Mar. 1931, to Ida Chamberlain, n.d. but c.Jun. 1931, AC 5/1/535, 541.

34. Bridgeman journal, II, p.183; Amery diary, 2 Aug. 1930.

35. Hope to Neville Chamberlain, 3 Jul. 1930, NC 7/11/23/6.

36. Austen to Ida Chamberlain, 2 Jul. 1931, AC 5/1/545; Amery diary, 24 Feb., 8 Oct. 1930.

37. Jones diary, introduction, p. xxx.

38. Hilton Young's draft autobiography, Kennet MSS 82/1/49–50.

39. Bayford diary, 18 Mar. 1925; R.R.James, ed., *Chips: The Diaries of Sir Henry Channon* (London, 1967), p. 39.

40. Ramsden, 'Baldwin and Film', pp.128–142; Cannadine, op. cit., pp.100–101.

41. Dawson to Irwin, 17 Jun. 1930, Dawson MSS.

42. Bridgeman journal, II, p.181.

43. Amery, *My Political Life*, II, p.398.

44. Smithers to Salisbury, 19 Aug. 1930, Hatfield MSS S(4)136/148.

45. Dawson to Irwin, 17 Jun. 1930, Dawson MSS.

46. Dorset West CA, Exec., 24 Aug. 1927; Hitchin CA, AGM, 22 May 1928; Horncastle CA, Exec., 22 Oct. 1928; Stafford CA, Exec., 15 Mar. 1929.

47. Memo on Selection of Candidates, Bowyer to Baldwin, 12 Dec. 1930, Baldwin MSS 48/187–192; Uxbridge CA, Exec., 17 Nov. 1923; Bradford South CA, Exec., 24 Jun. 1926; Reigate CA, Exec., 25 Feb. 1929.

48. J.M.McEwen, 'The Unionist and Conservative Members of Par-

liament 1914–1939', University of London Ph.D thesis, 1959, pp. 289–306.
49. ibid.
50. ibid.
51. Crawford diary, 5 Jun. 1929.
52. Butler to his father, 4 Mar. 1931, Butler MSS D48/792–795.
53. Crawford diary, 19 Nov. 1910.
54. [Lady] Peto diary, 23, 29 Jan. 1930.
55. For lists of Diehard MPs, see signatories of memorials from Gretton to Baldwin, 25 Jul. 1929, 27 Jan., 3 Apr. 1930, Baldwin MSS 164/66–67, 31/13,70–71.
56. Ramsden, *Balfour and Baldwin*, p.298; 'List of Progressive Unionists who lost their seats', Astor MSS 1416/1/1/120.
57. McEwen, loc. cit.

Chapter 2

1. Williamson, 'Safety First', p.409.
2. Dawson diary, 1 Jun. 1929; Whitehall diary, 20 Jun. 1929.
3. Memo by Stamfordham, 2 Jun. 1929, Royal Archives RA.K.2223/30.
4. Derby to Baldwin, 3 Jun. 1929, Baldwin MSS 36/225; Worthington-Evans to Hall, 4 Jun. 1929, Worthington-Evans MSS c.896/197.
5. Campbell, *Lloyd George,* pp. 244–245.
6. Headlam diary, 18 Jul. 1929.
7. Irwin to Davidson, 25 Feb. 1930, James, *Memoirs*, p. 306.
8. Churchill to Baldwin, 23, 26, 29 Jun. 1929, Baldwin MSS 51/85–86, 165/58–61, 164/36–37.
9. Bridgeman journal, II, p. 175; Worthington-Evans to Birdwood, 24 Jun. 1929, Worthington-Evans MSS c.896/203–204.
10. Neville Chamberlain diary, 8 Jun. 1929, NC 2/22; Austen to Ida Chamberlain, 7 Jun. 1929, AC 5/1/475.
11. Steel-Maitland to Collier, 3 Jun. 1929, Steel-Maitland MSS SRO GD193/251/4.
12. Amery diary, 3 Jun. 1929.

13. Peterborough CA, Exec., 8 Jun. 1929; Accrington CA, AGM, 11 Jun. 1929; Bradford CA, Central Ctte., 22 Jul. 1929; Cochrane to Gilmour, 1 Jun. 1929, Gilmour MSS GD383/29/16.
14. Stockton CA, 3 Dec. 1929; Yorkshire Prov. Area, An. Report, 1929; Moray & Nairn CA, Agent's Report, 31 Dec. 1929.
15. Uxbridge CA, Exec., 12 Oct 1929.
16. NU Exec., 16 Jul., 3 & 22 Oct. 1929, 14 Jan. 1930.
17. Draft Report of NU Exec. Sub-Ctte., 7 Jan. 1930, Bull MSS 5/24.
18. Wolverhampton West CA, Management Ctte., 26 Jun. 1929.
19. Bath CA, Exec., 13 Sept. 1927; Yorkshire Prov. Area, Council, 10 Dec. 1927; Chichester CA, GP Ctte., 23 Jan. 1928; Rotherham CA, AGM, 30 Apr. 1928; Ealing CA, Exec., 20 Aug., 30 Nov. 1928; Memo by Blair, 'Impressions of the General Election', for SUA, copy in Gilmour MSS GD383/29/32–35.
20. Oxfordshire North CA, Exec., 24 Sept. 1929; Shrewsbury CA, 5 Jul., 16 Oct. 1929; Kennington CA, Exec., 27 Sept. 1929; Lewisham West CA, Council, 11 Oct. 1929.
21. Ealing CA, Exec., 13 Sept., 11 Oct., 9 Dec. 1929.
22. NU Exec., 22 Oct. 1929; NU Conference Res., 1929.
23. Moore-Brabazon to Baldwin, 28 Nov. 1929, Moore-Brabazon MSS.
24. 'Memorandum Upon Mr. Baldwin's Changes of Policy', Nov. 1930, Croft MSS 2/2.
25. Beaverbrook to Rothermere, 3 Jul. 1929, Beaverbrook MSS C284; Neville Chamberlain diary, 26 Jul. 1929, NC 2/22.
26. Amery to Croft, 6 Jun. 1929, Croft MSS 1/2/Am8; Amery diary, 4, 11 Jul. 1929.
27. Bridgeman journal, II, p. 199; Amery diary, 9 Jul. 1929; Crawford diary, 19 Oct. 1927.
28. Salisbury to Baldwin, 13 Jul. 1929, Baldwin MSS 36/261–262; Hartington to Salisbury, 11 Jul. 1929, Hatfield MSS S(4)130/124–126.

29. Derby to Baldwin, 17 Jul. 1929, Derby MSS 920DER(17)/33.
30. Hoare to Baldwin, 12 Jul. 1929, Baldwin MSS 36/260.
31. Neville to Ida Chamberlain, 13 Jul. 1929, NC 18/1/661; Amery diary, 11 Jul. 1929.
32. Baldwin to Derby, 18 Jul. 1929, Derby MSS 920DER(17)/33; Amery diary, 17 Jul. 1929.
33. Neville to Ida Chamberlain, 13 Jul. 1929, NC 18/1/661.
34. Taylor, *Beaverbrook*, pp.24–210.
35. Lockhart diary, 30 May 1929; Beaverbrook to Birkenhead, 7 Jun. 1929, Beaverbrook MSS C41.
36. Lockhart diary, 22 May 1929.
37. Beaverbrook to Caillard, 22 Jul. 1929, Beaverbrook MSS B94.
38. Beaverbrook to Melchett, 9 Oct. 1929, ibid. C243.
39. Beaverbrook's circular to NFU branches, 15 Oct. 1929, ibid. B99.
40. Beaverbrook to Elibank, 23 Nov. 1929, ibid. C126.
41. Beaverbrook to Ruggles-Brise, 27 Jan. 1930, ibid. B133.
42. Beaverbrook to Bossom, 4 Jun. 1930, ibid. B132.
43. Beaverbrook to Turton, 27 Oct. 1929, ibid. B119.
44. Beaverbrook to Elibank, 23 Nov. 1929, ibid. C126.
45. Beaverbrook to Melchett, 15 Oct. 1929, ibid. C243; Amery diary, 13 Jul. 1929.
46. Beaverbrook to Garvin, 12 Jul. 1929, Beaverbrook MSS C140.
47. Derby to Beaverbrook, 20 Nov. 1929, Derby MSS 920DER (17)/33.
48. Neville Chamberlain diary, 26 Jul. 1929, NC 2/22.
49. Austen to Hilda Chamberlain, 13 Jul. 1929, AC 5/1/478.
50. Ferguson to Beaverbrook, 2 Jul., Beaverbrook to Ferguson, 3 Jul. 1929, Beaverbrook MSS B100.
51. C.Cook & J.A.Ramsden, eds., *By-Elections in British Politics* (London, 1973), pp.75–76.
52. Baldwin to Ferguson, 23 Jul. 1929, Baldwin MSS 36/268–269.
53. Amery diary, 17, 22, 23 Jul. 1929.
54. Gretton to Baldwin, 25 Jul. 1929, Baldwin MSS 164/66–67; Gretton to Heneage, 19 Jul. 1929, Heneage MSS HNC 1/G.
55. Birmingham CA, Agent's Report, 11 Oct. 1929; Chippenham CA, Exec., 14 Jun. 1929; Sowerby CA, Exec., 27 Sept. 1929.

Chapter 3

1. Beaverbrook to Bailey, 19 Jul. 1929, Beaverbrook MSS B90; Amery diary, 13 Jul. 1929.
2. Beaverbrook to Rothermere, 24 Oct., to Moody, 23 Oct. 1929, Beaverbrook MSS C284, B110; Amery diary, 22, 24 Oct., 24 Nov. 1929.
3. Copies in Beaverbrook MSS B99; Beaverbrook to Deeley, 20 Oct. 1929, ibid. B97.
4. *Observer*, 27 Oct. 1929.
5. Cecil to Salisbury, 24 Feb. 1930, Cecil MSS Add.51086/82; Ramsbotham to Beaverbrook, 28 Oct. 1929, Beaverbrook MSS B113.
6. Wessex Area, AGM, 12 Oct. 1929.
7. Kent Prov. Div., AGM, 15 Oct. 1929, copy in Hatfield MSS S(4)131/107; Metropolitan Area Res., NU Exec., 20 Nov. 1929.
8. Hemel Hempstead CA, Council, 26 Oct. 1929.
9. N. to Ida Chamberlain, 23 Oct. 1929, NC 19/1/673.
10. Speaker's Report on Cornish and Devon Constituencies to EIA Headquarters, 22 Oct. 1929, copy in Beaverbrook MSS C153; Winchester CA, Council, 18 Nov. 1929.
11. Skidelsky, op. cit, pp.185–186,224; Butler, *Coalitions*, p.56.
12. N. to Hilda Chamberlain, 26 Oct. 1929, NC 18/1/674.
13. N. Chamberlain diary, 4 Nov. 1929, NC 2/22.
14. ibid., 5 Nov. 1929.
15. ibid., 12 Nov. 1929.
16. A. to Ida Chamberlain, 18 Nov. 1929, AC 5/1/487; Lockhart diary, 23–24 Nov. 1929; Amery diary, 11, 22 Nov. 1929.

17. Walsall CA, Emergency Ctte., 19 Nov. 1929.
18. Derby to Baldwin, 22 Nov. 1929, Derby MSS 920DER(17)/33; Moore-Brabazon to Beaverbrook, 22 Nov. 1929, Moore-Brabazon MSS; Headlam diary, 22 Nov. 1929; Yorkshire Area, Council, 7 Dec. 1929; Islington East CA, Exec., 12 Dec. 1929.
19. Lewisham West CA, Council, 13 Dec. 1929; NU Exec., 14 Jan. 1930.
20. '1922' Ctte., 27 Jan. 1930; North West Area, Council, 18 Jan. 1930; Hemel Hempstead CA, Council, 25 Jan. 1930.
21. Beaverbrook to Cole, 2 Dec. 1929, Beaverbrook MSS B138; Elibank ['Empire Free Trade'] diary, [November 1929-May 1930], [Elibank MSS SRO/GD/32/25/74] f.4; Draft Constitution of the Empire Crusade, copy in Hannon MSS 18/1.
22. Beaverbrook to Lynn, 21 Jan. 1930, Beaverbrook MSS B164.
23. Stigant to Salisbury, 26 Feb. 1930, Hatfield MSS S(4)133/183–4; Gravesend CA, Exec., 13 Dec. 1929; Uxbridge CA, Council, 7 Dec. 1929; Lewisham West CA, Exec., 27 Feb. 1930.
24. Bristol West CA, Exec., 15 Jan. 1930; Accrington CA, Exec., 21 Jan 1930; Cornwall North CA, Exec., 25 Jan. 1930; Lincoln CA, Exec., 27 Feb. 1930.
25. Salisbury to Baldwin, 29 Jan. 1930, Baldwin MSS 31/29–33; List of free-trade MPs in Beaverbrook to Rothermere, 19 Feb. 1930, Beaverbrook MSS C284.
26. Bayford to Baldwin, 28 Jan. 1930, Baldwin MSS 165/18; Horne to Hughes, 3 Mar. 1930, Beaverbrook MSS B236.
27. Gwynne to Northumberland, 18 Dec. 1929, Gwynne MSS 21.
28. N. Chamberlain diary, 8 Dec. 1929, NC 2/22; Bridgeman journal, II, pp.181–183; Lady Lloyd of Dolobran diary, 25 & 28 Jan. 1930.
29. Beaverbrook to Derby, 7 Mar. 1930, Derby MSS 920DER(17)/33.
30. Peto diary, 23 Jan. 1930.
31. Derby to Blumenfeld, 17 Feb. 1930, Blumenfeld MSS D/Der.45; Skidelsky, op. cit, pp. 255–257.
32. Davidson to Baldwin, 1 Jan. 1930, Davidson MSS.
33. JIL, Council, 8 Feb. 1930, Conference Agenda, 31 May 1930.
34. Gwynne to Baldwin, 21 Feb. 1930, Gwynne MSS 15; Amery diary, 28 Jan. 1930.
35. Peto diary, 23, 29 Jan. 1930.
36. Gwynne to Beaverbrook, 3 Feb. 1930, Gwynne MSS 14; Birkenhead to Beaverbrook, 28 Jan. 1930, Beaverbrook MSS C41.
37. Ramsden to Baldwin, 24 Jan. 1930, Baldwin MSS 31/39; Bayford diary, 7 Feb. 1930; EIA, Exec., 18 Feb. 1930.
38. Campbell, Lloyd George, pp. 248–249, 258.
39. Memo of conversation with Baldwin, 28 Jan. 1930, Hatfield MSS S(4)133/67–71; Amery diary, 30 Jan. 1930.
40. Baldwin to Beaverbrook, 29 Jan. 1930, Beaverbrook MSS C19.
41. Peto diary, 5 Feb. 1930.
42. Gretton to Baldwin, 6 Feb. 1930, Baldwin MSS 31/25; EIA, Parl. Council, 6 Feb. 1930; Clitheroe CA, AGM, 15 Feb. 1930; Headlam diary, 5 Feb. 1930.
43. Amery diary, 5 Feb. 1930.
44. Kent Agents' Union, 19 Feb. 1930; Eastern Area, AGM, 5 Feb. 1930; Aberdeen South CA, Political Ctte., 20 Feb. 1930.
45. Newcastle West CA, Women's Council, 13 Feb. 1930.
46. Elibank diary, f.6; Beaverbrook to Baldwin, 5 Feb. 1930, Beaverbrook MSS C19.
47. Elibank diary, f.5; Hilton Young to his wife, 1 Mar. 1930, Kennet MSS 107/3.
48. Beaverbrook to Gwynne, 19 Feb. 1930, Beaverbrook MSS C5; Amery diary, 12 Feb. 1930.
49. Elibank diary, f.7–8; Gwynne to Baldwin, 21 Feb. 1930, Gwynne MSS 15.
50. Beaverbrook to Chivers, 25 Feb. 1930, Beaverbrook MSS B136;

Beaverbrook to Amery, 22 Feb. 1930, ibid. C5.

51. Beaverbrook to Grey, 18 Feb. 1930, ibid. B152.

52. Derby CA, GP Ctte., 28 Feb. 1930.

53. Thirsk & Malton CA, Exec., 28 Feb. 1930; Ipswich CA, AGM, 21 Feb. 1930; Ashley to Mills, Mar. 1930, Ashley MSS BR/78.

54. Elibank diary f.8; Erskine to Beaverbrook, 24 Feb. 1930, Beaverbrook MSS B145; Sutton CA, Exec., 27 Feb. 1930, Astor MSS 1416/1/1/122.

55. Gwynne to Beaverbrook, 18 Feb. 1930, Gwynne MSS 14; Amery diary, 18, 19 Feb. 1930; Amery to Beaverbrook, 19 Feb. 1930, Beaverbrook MSS C5.

56. Beaverbrook's memorandum, 7 Mar. 1930, Beaverbrook to Londonderry, 9 Mar. 1930, to Marjoribanks, 6 Mar. 1930, ibid. C284, C224, B167.

57. Memorandum given by Beaverbrook to Gwynne, 19 Feb. 1930, Beaverbrook to Gwynne, 25 Feb. 1930, ibid. C149.

58. Elibank's Memorandum of conversation with Baldwin, 28 Feb. 1930, Elibank MSS SRO/GD/32/25/74 f.57–59.

59. Horne to Beaverbrook, 25 Feb. 1930, Beaverbrook MSS C178.

60. Elibank diary, f.15.

61. ibid. f.20–21; Amery diary, 3 Mar. 1930.

62. Beaverbrook to Baldwin (via Horne), 3–4 Mar. 1930, Baldwin MSS 57/25–26.

63. Amery diary, 24 Feb. 1930.

Chapter 4

1. EIA, Exec., 11 Mar. 1930; Cayzer to Baldwin, 5 Mar. 1930, Baldwin MSS 31/58; *Observer*, 9 Mar. 1930.

2. Basingstoke CA, Exec., City of London CA, Exec., 6 Mar. 1930; Ipswich CA, Exec., 7 Mar. 1930; Bath CA, Exec., 11 Mar. 1930; Warwick CA, Exec., 13 Mar. 1930; Dorset West CA, AGM, 21 Mar. 1930; Amery diary, 6 Mar. 1930.

3. Bradford CA, Central Ctte., 26 Mar. 1930; Yorkshire Area, AGM, 22 Mar. 1930; Birmingham CA, Council, 21 Mar. 1930; SUA, Western Div. Council, 5 Mar. 1930.

4. Beaverbrook to Abbott, 8 Mar. 1930, to Clyne, 5 Mar. 1930, Beaverbrook MSS B123, B137.

5. *The Times*, 8 Mar. 1930; Amery diary, 7 Mar. 1930.

6. Beaverbrook to Amery, 7 Mar. 1930, Beaverbrook MSS C5.

7. Beaverbrook to Edwards, 8 Mar. 1930, ibid. B144.

8. Beaverbrook to Croft, 9 Mar. 1930, ibid. C101.

9. Davidson to Beaverbrook, 7 Mar. 1930, ibid. C111.

10. Memo of conversation with Beaverbrook, 12 Mar. 1930, Davidson MSS.

11. Memo of conversation with Beaverbrook, 14 Mar. 1930, ibid.

12. Elibank diary, f.35–37.

13. Outhwaite to Beaverbrook, 3 Apr. 1930, Beaverbrook MSS C284.

14. Elibank diary, f.43.

15. Amery diary, 1, 2 Apr. 1930; JIL, Conference Agenda, 31 May 1930.

16. Croft to Salisbury, 3 Apr. 1930, Hatfield MSS S(4)134/122–3; EIA, Exec., 2 Apr. 1930.

17. Elibank diary, f.49.

18. *The Times*, 26 Mar. 1930; Davidson to Neville Chamberlain, 26 Mar. 1930, Davidson MSS.

19. Beaverbrook to Elliott, 9 Apr. 1930, Beaverbrook MSS C129.

20. Neville Chamberlain to Beaverbrook, 15 Apr. 1930, ibid. C80.

21. Croft to Beaverbrook, 24 Mar. 1930, ibid. C101.

22. Beaverbrook to Rothermere, 24 Apr. 1930, ibid. C284.

23. Beaverbrook to Gwynne, 9 May 1930, Gwynne MSS 14.

24. Baldwin to Beaverbrook, 7 May 1930, Beaverbrook MSS C19.

25. *The Times*, 12 Apr. 1930.

26. Beaverbrook to Neville Chamberlain, 8 Apr. 1930, Beaverbrook MSS C80.

27. Beaverbrook to Davidson, 7 Apr. 1930, Beaverbrook MSS C111.

28. NU Exec., 16 Jul., 22 Oct., 10 Dec. 1929; Guildford CA, Exec., 2 May 1930; *Weekend Review*, 17 May 1930.

29. Remer to Baldwin, 7 Apr. 1930, copy, Beaverbrook MSS B172; Courthope to Beaverbrook, 17 May 1930, ibid. B139; Ramsden, *Balfour and Baldwin*, p.301.
30. Derby to Beaverbrook, 6 Mar. 1930, ibid. C113; Elibank diary, f.28, 47; Amery diary, 20, 22 May 1930.
31. North West Area, Council, 18 Jan. 1930; Accrington CA, Exec., 21 Jan. 1930.
32. *Home and Empire*, Vol. 1, No. 3, May 1930; Central Office circular, copy in Beaverbrook MSS C111; JIL, Conference Agenda, 31 May 1930.
33. Birmingham CA, Agent's Report to Council, 5 Jun. 1930; Walsall CA, Exec., 30 May 1930; Knutsford CA, AGM, 3 May 1930; Stockton CA, Agent's Report, Exec., 2 Jun. 1930.
34. Ashford CA, Standing Ctte., 3 May 1930; Oxfordshire South CA, Exec., 7 May 1930; Dorset East CA, Exec., 7 Apr. 1930.
35. Chichester CA, F&GP Ctte., 28 Apr. 1930; Brighton CA, Res., 17 Apr. 1930, copy in Beaverbrook MSS C111.
36. Beaverbrook to Amery, 14, 20, & 25 Apr. 1930, Beaverbrook MSS C5.
37. *The Times*, 16 Apr. 1930.
38. Austen to Hilda Chamberlain, 14 Jun. 1930, AC 5/1/505.
39. Croft to Beaverbrook, 6 Jun. 1930, Beaverbrook MSS C101.
40. Derby CA, AGM, 15 Apr. 1930; Skipton CA, Exec., 29 Mar. 1930; Kennington CA, Exec., 21 May 1930; Thirsk & Malton CA, AGM, 24 May 1930.
41. Wakefield CA, Council, 18 Jun. 1930; Oxfordshire South CA, AGM, 31 May 1930; North West Area, Council, 12 Apr. 1930.
42. Chelmsford CA, Exec., 13 Jun. 1930; Finchley CA, Council, 20 Jun. 1930; Wessex Area, AGM, 2 May 1930; JIL, Conference Agenda, 31 May 1930.
43. Marquand, op. cit., pp.530–531.
44. ibid., pp.546–547; Campbell, *Lloyd George*, pp.260–262.
45. Skidelsky, op. cit., pp.207–214.
46. Headlam diary, 19 May 1930; Brent-

ford to Salisbury, 17 Apr. 1930, S(4)134/ 159.
47. Bridgeman journal, II, pp.221–3; Baldwin to Smithers, 28 Jul. 1930, Smithers MSS.
48. Churchill to Baldwin, 17 May 1930, Baldwin MSS 117/53–54; NU Exec., 17 Jun. 1930.
49. '1922' Ctte., 5, 12 May 1930; Peto diary, 15 May 1930.
50. Neville to Ida Chamberlain, 17 May 1930, NC 18/1/695; Amery diary, 12 May, 2 Jun. 1930.
51. Neville to Ida Chamberlain, 20 Apr. 1930, NC 18/1/692.
52. Dawson to Beaverbrook, 24 Apr. 1930, Beaverbrook MSS B141.
53. Beaverbrook to Hall, 25 Apr. 1930, ibid. B153.
54. Memo, Topping to Davidson, 2 May 1930, James, *Memoirs of a Conservative*, pp.335–336.
55. *The Times*, 2 Jun. 1930.
56. Amery diary, 26 May 1930.
57. Beaverbrook to Hoare, 15 May 1930, Templewood MSS VI/I.
58. Beaverbrook to Croft, 19 May 1930, Beaverbrook MSS C101; Neville to Hilda Chamberlain, 25 May 1930, NC 18/1/696; Lockhart diary, 11 May 1930.
59. Elibank diary, f.55.
60. *The Times*, 22 May 1930.
61. [Lady] Smithers diary, 20 Oct. 1930.
62. Beaverbrook to Bridgeman, 15 May 1930, Beaverbrook MSS C133.
63. Beaverbrook to Horne, 28 May 1930, ibid. C178.
64. Neville to Ida Chamberlain, 4 Apr. 1930, NC 18/1/689.
65. J.A.Ramsden, *The Making of Conservative Party Policy: The Conservative Research Department since 1929* (London, 1980), pp.37–41.
66. Neville to Ida Chamberlain, 25 May 1930, NC 18/1/696.

Chapter 5

1. NU Exec., 17 Jun. 1930.
2. Neville to Hilda Chamberlain, 25 May 1930, postscript, NC 18/1/697.
3. Neville to Hilda Chamberlain, 21 Jun. 1930, NC 18/1/701.

4. Neville to Hilda Chamberlain, 26 Oct. 1929, NC 18/1/674.
5. Smithers to Salisbury, 19 Aug. 1930, Hatfield MSS S(4)136/148; Derby CA, GP Ctte, 23 Jun. 1930; Peto diary, 24 Jun. 1930.
6. Neville to Hilda Chamberlain, 21 Jun. 1930, NC 18/1/701.
7. Bridgeman to Baldwin, 22 Jun. 1930, Baldwin MSS 165/28–29.
8. Baldwin to Salisbury, 23 Jun. 1930, Hatfield MSS S(4)135/184.
9. The Times, 25 Jun. 1930.
10. Hannon to Beaverbrook, 12 Sept. 1955, Hannon 'Secret Memo', 21 Jun. 1930, Hannon MSS 17/1.
11. Lane-Fox to Irwin, 25 Jun. 1930, Halifax MSS EUR.C.152/19/1/87.
12. The Times, 25 Jun. 1930.
13. Wakefield CA, Council, 18 Jun. 1930: York CA, Special Exec., 1 Jul. 1930; Neville Chamberlain to Scott, 17 Jul. 1930, Scott MSS 119/3/P/Ch/5.
14. Kennington CA, GP Ctte., 21 Jun. 1930.
15. Amery to Baldwin, 4 Jul. 1930, Baldwin MSS 31/133–134.
16. Austen to Hilda Chamberlain, 30 Jun. 1930, AC 5/1/508.
17. Lane-Fox to Irwin, 25 Jun. 1930, Halifax MSS EUR.C.152/19/1/87; Amery diary, 5 Jun. 1930.
18. Austen to Hilda Chamberlain, 28 Jul. 1930, AC 5/1/509; Hope to Neville Chamberlain, 3 Jul. 1930, NC 7/11/23/6; Amery diary, 7, 14, 16, 20, 21 Jul. 1930.
19. Butler to his father, 11–14 Jul. 1930, Butler MSS D48/744–754.
20. ibid.; Beaverbrook to Astor, 6 Jul. 1930, Beaverbrook MSS C14.
21. Beaverbrook to Amery, 12 Jul. 1930, to Macmillan, 12 Jul. 1930, ibid. C5, C236.
22. Beaverbrook to Bowker, 8 Aug. 1930, ibid. B132.
23. Neville Chamberlain diary, 25–30 Jul. 1930, NC 2/22.
24. Neville to Anne Chamberlain, 30 Jul. 1930, NC 1/26/433.
25. Report on Bromley By-Election, Campbell to Bowyer, 15 Sept. 1930, Baldwin MSS 51/13–15.
26. Ormsby-Gore to Irwin, 3 Jul. 1930, Halifax MSS EUR.C. 152/19/1/19a; Imperial Economic Unity Group, Res., 20 Jul. 1930, Hannon MSS 18/3.
27. Marquand, op. cit., pp.554–564; Campbell, Lloyd George, p.280.
28. Don Valley CA, Res., NU Exec., 16 Jul. 1930; Bolton CA, Women's Exec., 29 Jul. 1930; SUA, Central Council Exec., 10 Sept. 1930; Yorkshire Prov. Area, Council, 4 Oct. 1930.
29. Wells CA, Exec., 11 Sept. 1930; Renfrewshire West CA, Council, 6 Oct. 1930.
30. Chippenham CA, Exec., 27 Jun. 1930; City of London CA, AGM, 12 Jul. 1930; Horncastle CA, Finance Ctte., 1 Aug. 1930; Norwich CA, Advisory Ctte., 29 Sept. 1930; Cambridgeshire CA, Res., NU Exec., 14 Oct. 1930.
31. Beaverbrook to Williams, 24 Sept. 1930, Beaverbrook MSS C324; Sevenoaks CA, An. Report, 1930; Bristol West CA, Agent's Report, Exec., 9 Sept. 1930.
32. Dixon to Heneage, 30 Sept. 1930, Heneage MSS HNC/4/40.
33. Neville Chamberlain to Bridgeman, 5 Oct. 1930, Bridgeman MSS SRO 3389/98.
34. Austen Chamberlain to Carnegie, 9 Oct. 1930, AC 4/1/1302; President, Wrekin CA, letter to The Times, 8 Sept. 1930.
35. St. Albans CA, Exec., 30 Jun. & 25 Jul. 1930; Wells CA, Exec., 11 Sept. 1930; Chelmsford CA, Exec., 26 Sept. 1930; Aberdeen South CA, Political Ctte., 25 Sept., 3 Oct. 1930; Lewisham West CA, Council, 6 Oct. 1930; Uxbridge CA, Council, 11 Oct. 1930.
36. Chairman, Whitstable CA, to Beaverbrook, 15 Oct. 1930, Beaverbrook MSS B171; Northern Daily Telegraph, 23 Aug. 1930; Liverpool Daily Post, 24 Sept. 1930.
37. Torquay CA, Ctte., 7 Jul. 1930; Altrincham CA, Res., NU Exec., 16 Jul. 1930; North Norfolk CA, Res.,

NU Exec., 14 Oct. 1930; Lewisham West CA, Council, 6 Oct. 1930.

38. Derby to Neville Chamberlain, 10 Oct. 1930, Derby MSS 920DER (17)/33; North West Area, Council, 4 Oct. 1930.

39. Ormsby-Gore to Salisbury, 5 Oct. 1930, Hatfield MSS S(4)137/44–45; Headlam diary, 24 Sept. 1930.

40. Croft to Neville Chamberlain, 4 Oct. 1930, Croft MSS 1/7/Ch34; Dawson diary, 6 Oct. 1930.

41. Hoare to Neville Chamberlain, 8 Oct. 1930, Templewood MSS VI/1.

42. Austen to Ida Chamberlain, 4 Oct. 1930, AC 5/1/516.

43. *The Times*, 30 Sept. 1930.

44. CRD/1/9/5; Ramsden, *Party Policy*, pp.45–46, 51–53.

45. Neville to Hilda Chamberlain, 21 Sept. 1930, NC 18/1/742.

46. Austen to Neville Chamberlain, 9 Oct. 1930, AC 39/2/40; Neville Chamberlain to Bridgeman, 5 Oct. 1930, Bridgeman MSS SRO 3389/98.

47. Neville Chamberlain to Bridgeman, 8 Oct. 1930, NC 8/10/13d.

48. Neville Chamberlain to Salisbury, 11 Oct. 1930, Hatfield MSS S(4)137/60–62.

49. Hilton Young to Baldwin, 9 Oct. 1930, Kennet MSS 4/11.

50. Neville Chamberlain diary, 11 Oct. 1930, NC 2/22; Amery diary, 9 Oct. 1930.

51. Neville Chamberlain to Bridgeman, 15 Oct. 1930, Bridgeman MSS SRO 3389/102.

52. Chelmsford CA, Exec., 17 Oct. 1930; Lewisham West CA, Council, 27 Oct. 1930; Knutsford CA, Exec., 31 Oct. 1930; Uxbridge CA, Council, 15 Nov. 1930.

53. Lewes CA, Exec., 27 Oct. 1930; Ipswich CA, Exec., 16 Oct. 1930; Sowerby CA, Exec., 31 Oct. 1930; North West Area, Council, 15 Nov. 1930.

54. Birmingham CA, Council, 10 Oct. 1930; Inverness CA, AGM, 16 Oct. 1930; Lancaster CA, Exec., 18 Oct. 1930; SUA, Eastern Div. Council, 22 Oct. 1930; Torquay CA, Exec.,

29 Oct. 1930; Harborough CA, Council, 1 Nov. 1930; Kensington South CA, Chairman's Agenda, 4 Nov. 1930; NU Exec., 14 Oct. & 12. Nov. 1930.

55. Neville to Hilda Chamberlain, 18 Oct. 1930, NC 18/1/713.

56. Derby to Beaverbrook, 21 Oct. 1930, Derby MSS 920DER(17)/33; Salisbury to Baldwin, 14 Oct. 1930, Baldwin MSS 31/168–170.

57. Bridgeman to Neville Chamberlain, 16 Oct. 1930, Bridgeman MSS SRO 3389/103; Bridgeman to Baldwin, 17 Oct. 1930, Baldwin MSS 165/33–34.

58. Neville Chamberlain to Bridgeman, 18 Oct. 1930, Bridgeman MSS SRO 3389/104.

59. Peto diary, 28, 30 Oct. 1930.

60. *Morning Post*, 30 Oct. 1930; Lane-Fox to Irwin, 29 Oct. 1930, Halifax MSS EUR.C.152/19/1/154a; Winchester CA, Council, 5 Nov. 1930; Renfrewshire West CA, AGM, 29 Oct. 1930; Tynemouth CA, Exec., 24 Oct. 1930.

62. Austen to Ida Chamberlain, 2 Nov. 1930, AC 5/1/519.

63. Headlam diary, 30 Oct. 1930; Amery diary, 30 Oct. 1930.

64. Wraxall to Bull, 31 Oct. 1930, Bull MSS 5/25; Butler to his father, 4 Nov. 1930, Butler MSS D48/756a–762.

65. Wraxall to Bull, 31 Oct. 1930, Bull MSS 5/25.

66. Austen to Ida Chamberlain, 2 Nov. 1930, AC 5/1/519.

67. R.R.James, *The British Revolution* (London, 1977), II, p.220.

68. Bridgeman to Baldwin, 22 & 25 Jun. 1930, Baldwin MSS 165/28–30.

69. Bridgeman to Davidson, 22 Oct. 1930, James, *Memoirs of a Conservative*, pp.350–351; Neville Chamberlain diary, 26 Oct. 1930, NC 2/22.

70. Amery diary, 24 Jun. 1930; Peto diary, 25 Jun. 1930; Butler to his father, 4 Nov. 1930, Butler MSS D48/756a–762; Lane-Fox to Irwin, 29 Oct. 1930, Halifax MSS EUR.C.152/19/1/154a.

71. Lockhart diary, 7 Oct. 1930; Amery diary, 30 Oct 1930.
72. Derby to Beaverbrook, 21 Oct. 1930, Beaverbrook MSS C113.
73. Baldwin to Mrs. Davidson, 2 Nov. 1930, James, *Memoirs of a Conservative*, p.354; Halsbury to Salisbury, 30 Oct. 1930, Hatfield MSS S(4)137/94.
74. Headlam diary, 25–29 Oct. 1930.
75. Bridgeman journal, II, p.225.
76. *Daily Telegraph*, 30 Oct. 1930; Peto diary, 31 Oct. 1930.
77. Beaverbrook to James, 26 Oct. 1930, Beaverbrook MSS B158.
78. Neville Chamberlain to Bridgeman, 1 Nov. 1930, NC 8/10/16c.

Chapter 6

1. Baldwin to Irwin, 26 Jun. 1927, 10 May 1931, Halifax MSS Borthwick Institute, A4/410/14/2, A2/278/24; Memo of Conversation with Irwin, 28 Jul. 1929, Hatfield MSS S(4)197/103.
2. Amery diary, 30 Oct. 1929.
3. A. Chamberlain to Peel, 30 Oct. 1929, AC 38/3/115.
4. Hoare to Irwin, 13 Nov. 1929, Halifax MSS EUR.C.152/18/1/298; Amery diary, 23 Oct. 1929.
5. Crawford to Irwin, 8 Nov. 1929, ibid. 152/19/1/162a.
6. Dawson to Irwin, 3 Nov. 1929, ibid. 152/18/1/290.
7. A. to Ida Chamberlain, 11 Nov. 1929, AC 5/1/486.
8. Dawson to Irwin, 31 Oct. 1929, Dawson MSS; Davidson to Irwin, 9 Nov. 1929, Davidson MSS.
9. Hoare to Irwin, 13 Nov. 1929, Halifax MSS EUR.C. 152/18/1/298.
10. Davidson to Irwin, 9 Nov. 1929, Davidson MSS.
11. Memo of Conversation between Davidson and Stopford, 4 Nov. 1929, ibid.
12. Hailsham to Salisbury, 2 Apr. 1931, Hatfield MSS S(4)140/58–61.
13. Chelsea CA, Newsletter, March 1931, copy in Templewood MSS VI/1; Hoare to Irwin, 24 Dec. 1929, Halifax MSS EUR.C.152/18/1/339.
14. Hailey to Irwin, 6 Jan. 1931, ibid. 152/19/1/201; Butler to his father, 14 Jul. 1930, Butler MSS D48/744–754.
15. Peele, 'Revolt over India', pp. 126–127.
16. Cecil to Irwin, 31 Jul. 1930, Halifax MSS EUR.C.152/19/1/104a.
17. Memo on Bromley By-election, Campbell to Bowyer, 15 Sept. 1930, Baldwin MSS 51/13–15.
18. Dixey to Baldwin, 8 Sept. 1930, ibid. 165/104–106; Croft to Beaverbrook, 5 Nov. 1930, Beaverbrook MSS C101; Bayford diary, 22 Mar. 1931.
19. Lane-Fox to Irwin, 11 Dec. 1929, Halifax MSS EUR.C. 152/18/1/328; Amery diary, 27 Jun., 11 Jul. 1929; Beaverbrook to Guest, 22 Nov. 1929, Beaverbrook MSS C27.
20. Elibank to Beaverbrook, 18 Jun. 1930, ibid. C126; Amery diary, 26 May 1930; R.R.James, *Churchill: A Study in Failure 1900–1939* (London, 1970), pp.176–240.
21. Lane-Fox to Irwin, 21 Jan. 1931, Halifax MSS EUR.C. 152/19/1/211; Lockhart diary, 23 Jan. 1930.
22. Churchill to Beaverbrook, 23 Sept. 1930, Beaverbrook MSS C86.
23. Churchill to Baldwin, 14 [not sent] & 16 Oct. 1930, Churchill MSS pp. 191–194; Tom Jones to E. Jones, 9 Feb. 1930, Whitehall Diary; Amery diary, 30 Jan., 25 Feb. 1930; N. Chamberlain diary, 19 Oct. 1930, NC 2/22.
24. Peele, 'Revolt over India', pp. 121–125.
25. Beaverbrook to Churchill, 19 Jan. 1931, Beaverbrook MSS C86.
26. Churchill to Irwin, 1 Jan. 1930, Halifax MSS EUR.C.152/19/1/1; *The Times*, 21 Aug. 1930.
27. Peele, 'Revolt over India', pp. 124–125.
28. A. to Hilda Chamberlain, 28 Jul. 1930, AC 5/1/509.
29. Draft resignation letter, June 1931, Hatfield MSS S(4)140/98–102.
30. Notes on a Meeting between Gandhi and a delegation of MPs, 23 Sept. 1931, Beamish MSS 3/3.
31. Ramsden, *Balfour and Baldwin*, p.304.

32. Lloyd to Irwin, 31 Jul. 1929, Halifax MSS EUR.C.152/28/8; Lloyd to Baldwin, 2 Mar. 1931, Lloyd of Dolobran MSS 19/5.
33. Dawson to Irwin, 13 Mar. 1931, Dawson MSS.
34. Hailey to Irwin, 6 Mar. 1931, Halifax MSS EUR.C.152/19/1/253; Manchester CA, Res., NU Exec., 12 May 1931; Peele, 'Revolt over India', pp. 131–132.
35. Stuart to Cotton Spinners and Manufacturers Association, 7 May 1931, IES MSS c.609/20; Conway diary, 20 May 1931.
36. Ormsby-Gore to Irwin, 3 Jul. 1930, Lane-Fox to Irwin, 25 Jun. 1930, Halifax MSS EUR.C.152/19/1/91a & 87; Unionist India Ctte. Res., The Times, 15 Jul. 1930.
37. Hoare to Irwin, 15 Jul. 1930, Halifax MSS EUR.C. 152/19/1/100; Butler to his father, 14 Jul. 1930, Butler MSS D48/744–754.
38. Lane-Fox to Irwin, 28 Jan. 1931, Halifax MSS EUR.C.152/19/1/221; HC Debs., 5th series, vol. 247, cols. 689–703, 744–748; Amery diary, 26 Jan. 1931.
39. A. to Ivy Chamberlain, 2 Feb. 1931, AC 6/1/785.
40. Baldwin to MacDonald, 2 Mar. 1931, Baldwin MSS 104/216; Unionist India Ctte., The Times, 17 Feb. 1931; Peto diary, 24 Feb., 6 Mar. 1931; Lloyd to Baldwin, 5 Mar. 1931, Lloyd of Dolobran MSS 19/5.
41. NU Council, 24 Feb. 1931; The Times, 25 Feb. 1931.
42. Gwynne to Baldwin, 1 Feb. 1931, Gwynne MSS. This was not, however, Lord Lloyd's analysis: Memo of conversation with Baldwin, 4 Mar. 1931, Lloyd of Dolobran MSS 19/5.
43. IES Exec., Greenway to Baldwin, 9 Mar. 1931, Baldwin MSS 104/230–232.
44. N. to Hilda Chamberlain, 31 Jan. 1931, NC 18/1/724.
45. Lane-Fox to Irwin, 12 Mar. 1931, Halifax MSS EUR.C. 152/19/1/266; Dawson to Irwin, 13 Mar. 1931, Dawson MSS; Amery diary, 12

Mar. 1931; The Times, 13 Mar. 1931.
46. Churchill's press release, The Times, 21 Jan. 1931.
47. Beaverbrook to Borden, 7 Jan. 1931, Beaverbrook MSS C52.
48. Churchill to Rothermere, 3 Feb. 1931, Churchill MSS p.259; Lady Astor to Subbarayan, 9 Apr. 1931, Astor MSS 1416/1/1/1011.
49. Mid-Bedfordshire CA, Res., NU Exec., 12 May 1931.
50. NU Council, 30 Jun. 1931; JIL, Exec., 21 Apr. 1931, Conference Agenda, 9 May 1931.
51. Clitheroe CA, Exec., 15 Apr. 1931; Chichester CA, Exec., 13 Apr. 1931; Aldershot CA, Council, 11 Apr. 1931; Wells CA, Exec., 17 Mar. 1931; Winchester CA, Exec., 10 Feb. 1931.
52. Cirencester & Tewkesbury CA, Exec., 18 Feb. 1933; Cornwall North CA, AGM, 11 Apr. 1933; Wells, AGM, 5 May 1933; Camborne CA, Exec., 26 May 1933, 15 Dec. 1934; Oswestry CA, Exec., 1 Dec. 1934.
53. Sheffield Ecclesall CA, 19 Jun. 1933; Uxbridge CA, Council, 3 Dec. 1934; Wells CA, Exec., 1 Feb. 1935; East Grinstead CA, AGM, 16 Mar. 1935.
54. Bayford diary, 22 Mar. 1931.
55. Stonehaven to Irwin, 17 Mar. 1931, Halifax MSS EUR.C. 152/19/1/271; Headlam diary, 10 May 1930.
56. Baldwin on 12 Mar. 1931, HC Debs., 5th series, vol. 249, col. 1418.
57. The Times, 13 Mar. 1931.
58. Knox to Sydenham, 24 Jun. 1931, IES MSS c.620/59.
59. James, British Revolution, II, pp.225–226; Peele, 'Revolt over India', pp.132–142; Ramsden, Balfour and Baldwin, pp.332–336.
60. Irwin to Davidson, 31 Mar. 1931, Halifax MSS EUR.C.152/19/2/306.

Chapter 7

1. '1922' Ctte., 24 Nov. 1930; Metropolitan Area, Res., NU Exec., 12 Nov. 1930; Northern Area, Res.,

NU Exec., 9 Dec. 1930; Somerset Prov. Div., Council, 3 Nov. 1930; Inverness CA, Exec., 9 Dec. 1930; JIL, Council, 8 Nov. 1930.

2. Bridgeman journal, II, p.227.
3. *Daily Telegraph, Morning Post*, 1 Nov. 1930.
4. Neville Chamberlain diary, 6 Nov. & 5 Dec. 1930, NC 2/22.
5. Lockhart diary, 15 Dec. 1930.
6. Beaverbrook to Horne, 23 Jan. 1931, Beaverbrook MSS C178.
7. Beaverbrook to Lush, 24 Jan. 1931, to Gray, 19 Mar. 1931, to Fitzalan, 24 Mar. 1931, ibid. B200, B197, C134.
8. Beaverbrook to Amery, 14 Jan. 1931, ibid. C5.
9. Edinburgh West CA, Agent's Report to AGM, 27 Nov. 1930.
10. Campbell, *Lloyd George*, p.274.
11. Dawson to Willingdon, 16 Dec. 1930, Dawson MSS.
12. Austen to Ida Chamberlain, 30 Nov. 1930, AC 5/1/522.
13. Amery diary, 27 Nov. 1930; Lane-Fox to Irwin, 3 Dec. 1930, Halifax MSS EUR.C. 152/19/1/180.
14. NU Exec., 13 Jan. 1931; Kensington South CA, Exec., 13 Dec. 1930; Amery diary, 22 Jan. 1931.
15. Smithers to Fry, 1 Jan. 1931, Baldwin MSS 166/275–278; Amery diary, 26, 27 Feb. 1931; Lane-Fox to Irwin, 28 Jan. 1931, Halifax MSS EUR.C.152/19/1/221.
16. Austen to Ida Chamberlain, 28 Feb. 1931, AC 5/1/532; Baldwin to Gilmour, 18 Feb. 1931, Gilmour MSS GD383/34/1; Bayford diary, 22 Mar. 1931.
17. Amery diary, 2 Mar. 1931; ibid., 22, 24 Feb., 6 Mar. 1931.
18. Dawson to Irwin, 5 Mar. 1931, Dawson MSS.
19. Amery diary, 20 Jul., 16, 27 Nov. 1930; Glasgow CA, AGM, 26 Jan. 1931.
20. Neville to Hilda Chamberlain, 1 Mar. 1931, NC 18/1/728.
21. Headlam diary, 3 Dec. 1930, 10 Mar. 1931; Dawson to Irwin, 28 Sept. 1930, Dawson MSS; Amery diary, 16 Nov. 1930.

22. Cecil to Irwin, 9 Mar. 1931, Halifax MSS EUR.C.152/19/1/262.
23. Memo, Topping to Chamberlain, 25 Feb. 1931, Baldwin MSS 166/50–53.
24. Neville to Ida Chamberlain, 1 Mar. 1931, NC 18/1/728.
25. Chamberlain to Baldwin, 1 Mar. 1931, NC 8/10/24.
26. Neville to Ida Chamberlain, 7 Mar. 1931, NC 18/1/729.
27. Cazalet diary, 1 Mar. 1931, R.R.James, *Victor Cazalet* (London, 1976), p.134.
28. Jones diary, 11 Mar. 1931; Neville Chamberlain diary, 1 Mar. 1931, NC 2/22; Dawson diary, 1 Mar. 1931.
29. Ramsden, *Balfour and Baldwin*, pp.310–314; Blake, *Conservative Party*, p.234; G.Peele, 'St. George's and the Empire Crusade', Cook & Ramsden, eds., *By-Elections*, p.79, 107; M.Beloff, *Wars and Welfare; Britain 1914–1945* (London, 1984), p.175; Macmillan, *Memoirs*, I, p.252.
30. Bridgeman journal, II, pp.229–233.
31. Beaverbrook to Rothermere, 3 Feb. 1931, Beaverbrook MSS C285.
32. *News Chronicle*, 19 Feb. 1931; Lockhart diary, 5–10 Feb. 1931; Amery diary, 8 Feb. 1931.
33. Neville to Ida Chamberlain, 8 Feb. 1931, NC 18/1/725.
34. *Daily Telegraph*, 19 Feb. 1931.
35. Press report, 21 Feb. 1931, Gower MSS.
36. East Midlands Area, Council, 15 Jan. 1931; City of London CA, AGM, 14 Feb. 1931; York CA, Exec., 9 Mar. 1931; Bradford Central CA, AGM, 12 Mar. 1931; Ipswich CA, AGM, 13 Mar. 1931.
37. SUA, Eastern Div. Council, Treasurer's Ctte., 12 Feb. 1931.
38. Davidson to Irwin, 6 Mar. 1931, Halifax MSS EUR.C. 152/19/1/254; Amery diary, 2, 6 Mar. 1931; Dawson diary, 3 Mar. 1931.
39. Neville Chamberlain diary, 11 Mar. 1931, NC 2/22.
40. Memo of conversation with Baldwin, 4 Mar. 1931, Lloyd of Dolobran MSS 19/5.
41. Lockhart diary, 25 Jan. 1931.

42. Winchester CA, Exec., 9 Mar. 1931; St. George's CA, Exec., 2, 5 Mar. 1931; D.Cooper, *Old Men Forget* (London, 1953), p.173.
43. Dawson to Irwin, 5 Mar. 1931, Dawson MSS.
44. Lane-Fox to Irwin, 12 Mar. 1931, Halifax MSS EUR.C.152/19/1/266.
45. Amery diary, 5 Mar. 1931.
46. Freemantle to Salisbury, 14 Mar. 1931, Hatfield MSS S(4)140/20–21; Dawson diary, 12 Mar. 1931.
47. Sevenoaks CA, AGM, 28 Mar. 1931; Bristol West CA, AGM, 20 Mar. 1931; Winchester CA, AGM, 14 Mar. 1931; Skegness CA, AGM, 25 Mar. 1931, copy in Haslam MSS 276/2.
48. Denbighshire CA, Southern Area AGM, 21 Mar. 1931; South East Area, Women's Advisory Ctte., 18 Mar. 1931.
49. More than 120 constituency Associations from all parts of the country sent messages of support: List of telegrams and letters of support received by Baldwin and Cooper during the St. George's by-election, Cooper MSS 2/8.
50. Canterbury CA, Emergency Meeting, 28 Mar. 1931.
51. *Daily Mail*, 18 Mar. 1931.
52. Beaverbrook to Pinckard, n.d. but c.25 Mar. 1931, to Parker, 23 Mar. 1931, Beaverbrook MSS B203, C267.
53. Lawson to Cooper, 9 Mar. 1931, Dawson to Cooper, 10 Mar. 1931, Baldwin to Cooper, 12 Mar. 1931, Cooper MSS 2/8.
54. F.Williams, 'Challenge to the Press Lords', in J.Raymond, ed., *The Baldwin Age* (London, 1960), pp.160–175; H.Cudlipp, *The Prerogative of the Harlot: Press Barons and Power* (London, 1980), p.274; Hyde, *Baldwin*, pp.326–327; Blake, *Conservative Party*, p.234; Peele, 'St. George's', p.100.
55. *Daily Telegraph, Morning Post*, 18 Mar. 1931.
56. Hannon to Beaverbrook, 17 Mar. 1931, Beaverbrook MSS C155.
57. James, *Memoirs of a Conservative*, p.361; Macmillan, *Memoirs*, I, p.254; Earl Winterton, *Orders of the Day* (London, 1953), p.170.
58. Lockhart diary, 24 Mar. 1931.
59. Neville Chamberlain diary, 25–31 Mar. 1931, NC 2/22.
60. Neville Chamberlain to Baldwin, 13 Mar. 1931, Baldwin MSS 166/58–61; Amery diary, 11 Mar. 1931.
61. Austen to Hilda Chamberlain, 7 Mar. 1931, AC 5/1/533.
62. Neville Chamberlain diary, 25 Mar. 1931, NC 2/22; Amery diary, 25, 26 Mar. 1931.
63. Bridgeman to Baldwin, 25 Mar. 1931, Baldwin MSS 166/36.

Chapter 8

1. Eastern Area, Exec., 10 Oct. 1929.
2. NFU, Parliamentary Ctte., 17 Dec. 1929, 17 Jun., 14 Oct. 1930, 17 Feb. 1931.
3. Wolmer to Ball, 2 Jan. 1931, Selborne MSS c.998/3–5; negotiations with NFU, Jun. 1930-Feb. 1931, Baldwin MSS 31/236–346; Memo by Philpotts, 13 Dec. 1930, Beaverbrook MSS B218.
4. NU Council, 25 Nov. 1930.
5. Remer to Taylor, 31 Oct. 1930, Baldwin MSS 31/185–187.
6. Cunliffe-Owen to Beaverbrook, 30 May 1930, Beaverbrook MSS C107.
7. Correspondence with Coal Owners Association, Nov.-Dec. 1929, Steel-Maitland MSS SRO/GD/193/437/ 7–12,92–98.
8. Newcastle West CA, Finance & Emergency Ctte., 19 Aug. 1930.
9. Skidelsky, op. cit., pp.257–259.
10. Memo on Education Bill, Hatfield MSS S(4)139/1; Neville Chamberlain to Hilton Young, 8 Nov. 1930, Kennet MSS 16/4.
11. Skidelsky, op. cit., 100–101, 143–148, 168–170.
12. Memo, 'Causes of the Slump', prepared for the Party by Hilton Young, 1931, Kennet MSS 81/1.
13. *The Times*, 13 Dec. 1930.
14. Conservative Research Dept. Memos on Unemployment Insur-

ance, CRD/6, CRD/9, copies in AC 49/1/6.

15. CRD/1/14/2–4,6; Ramsden, *Party Policy*, pp.46–47.

16. Neville to Hilda Chamberlain, 20 Jun. 1931, NC 18/1/744.

17. Newcastle West CA, Women's Council, 5 Feb. 1931; Skidelsky, op. cit., pp.142–152, 344–345.

18. Edinburgh North CA, Council, 29 Apr. 1931.

19. Halifax CA, Exec., 12 Jan. 1931; Smithers to Fry, 12 Jan. 1931, Baldwin MSS 47/233–235.

20. *The Times*, 9 Jan., 30 Jan., 4 Feb., 27 Feb., 5 Mar. 1931.

21. Neville to Hilda Chamberlain, 14 Feb. 1931, NC 18/1/726.

22. SUA, Conference Res. No. 1, 12 Dec. 1930; Dorset West CA, Exec., 30 Jan. 1931; City of London CA, AGM, 13 Feb. 1931; NU Exec., 19 Feb., 12 May, 16 Jun. 1931.

23. Somerset Prov. Div., Council AGM, 13 Feb. 1931; Yorkshire Area, Council, An. Report, 24 Jan. 1931; Wessex Area, AGM, 29 May 1931.

24. Esher CA circular, copy and Res. endorsing same, York CA, Exec., 9 Mar. 1931.

25. *The Times*, 7 Mar. 1931.

26. Memo by Macmillan, 5 Nov. 1929, Beaverbrook MSS C235; '1922' Ctte., 26 May 1930; Whitehall diary, 26 Oct. 1930; Nicolson diary, 2 Jul., 6, 30 Nov. 1930, 15 Feb. 1931.

27. Neville Chamberlain to Bridgeman, 18 Nov. 1930, Bridgeman MSS SRO 3389/106.

28. Hall Caine to Beaverbrook, 20 Nov. 1929, Beaverbrook MSS B94; Beaverbrook to Mosley, 17 Jul. 1930, ibid. C254; Conway diary, 29 Oct. 1930, 21 Aug. 1931.

29. Bridgeman to Baldwin, 15 & 26 Nov. 1930, Baldwin MSS 165/35–39; NU Council, 25 Nov. 1930.

30. Jones to Moorhead, 20 Jan. 1931, Jones diary.

31. Nicolson diary, 30 May 1931.

32. Corres. on election results, Baldwin MSS 36/218–269, 37/60–155; Amery diary, 17 Jul. 1929.

33. Hugh Cecil to Baldwin, 28 Jul. 1930, copy, Hatfield MSS S(4)136/85.

34. Memos on Electoral Reform, Templewood MSS VI/2, Hatfield MSS S(4)136/62–63, Baldwin MSS 52 267–273.

35. *The Times*, 18 Dec. 1930.

36. *The Times*, 31 Jan. 1931; Butler, *Coalitions*, pp.57–59; Campbell, *Lloyd George*, pp.286–293.

37. *The Times*, 30 Jan., 14 Feb., 4 Mar., 15 May 1931; Amery diary, 26 Mar. 1931.

38. Hannon to Beaverbrook, 10 Jun. 1931, Hannon MSS 18/3; Neville to Ida Chamberlain, 5 Dec. 1930, NC 18/1/719.

39. *The Times*, 21 Apr., 29 Jun. 1931; Finchley CA, Council, 30 Jun. 1931.

40. Neville to Ida Chamberlain, 7 Mar., 18 Apr. 1931, NC 18/1/729, 734.

41. White to Derby, 6 Feb. 1931, Derby MSS 920DER(17)6/33; Ipswich CA, AGM, 13 Mar. 1931; Reigate CA, AGM, 18 Mar. 1931; SUA, Eastern Div. Council, 25 Mar. 1931; Thirsk & Malton CA, AGM, 9 May 1931.

42. Bristol West CA, AGM, 20 Mar. 1931; Gillingham CA, AGM, 25 Mar. 1931, Gower MSS.

43. Unionist India Ctte., *The Times*, 23 Jun. 1931.

44. *The Times*, 13 Jul. 1931.

45. CRD/1/2/6–12; Ramsden, *Party Policy*, pp.52–53.

46. Garvin to Simon, 16 Jun. 1931, Simon MSS 68/90.

47. Res. from East Midlands, North West, and Northern Areas, NU Exec., 19 Feb. 1931; from Somerset Prov. Div. and Metropolitan Area, NU Exec., 10 Mar. 1931.

48. Horne to Neville Chamberlain, 15 Aug. 1931, Baldwin MSS 44/25–34.

49. HC Debs., 5th series, 248/427, 11 Feb. 1931.

50. Moore to Neville Chamberlain, 31 Mar. 1931, NC 7/11/24/24.

51. Beaverbrook to Rothermere, 12 Jan., to Dykes, 4 Jul., to Pinckard, 20 Jul., to J.H.Macdonald, Jan.-Dec. 1931, Beaverbrook MSS C285, B194, B203, B201.

52. NFU, Parl. Ctte., 17 Mar. 1931; Eastern Area, AGM, 5 Feb. 1931.
53. Neville to Hilda Chamberlain, 2 May 1931, NC 18/1/736.
54. *The Times*, 19 Jun. 1931.
55. Hannon to Beaverbrook, 10 Jun. 1931, Hannon MSS 18/3; Amery diary, 30 Apr. 1931.
56. *The Times*, 29 Jun. 1931; Bridgeman journal, II, note following p. 243.
57. Hannon to Beaverbrook, 1 Apr. 1931, Hannon MSS 17/1.

Chapter 9

1. Bassett, *1931*; Berkeley, op. cit; Marquand, *Ramsay MacDonald,* pp.604–653; R.Dare, 'British Labour, the National Government, and the "national interest"', *Historical Studies*, Vol. 18, 1978–79; Nicolson, George V; Rose, George V.
2. Fair, 'Conservative Basis'.
3. Marquand, *Ramsay Macdonald*, pp.604–653; Berkeley, op. cit.
4. *The Times*, 18 Dec. 1930 17 Jul. 1931; Amery diary, 31 Jul., 11 Aug. 1931.
5. Neville to Ida Chamberlain, 11 July 1931, NC 18/1/747.
6. Neville Chamberlain diary, 6 July 1931, NC 2/22.
7. Neville Chamberlain diary, 24 July 1931, NC 2/22; Steel-Maitland to Baldwin, 28 July 1931, Steel-Maitland MSS SRO GD193/94/2/179–181.
8. Fair, 'Conservative Basis', p. 143.
9. Memo by Neville Chamberlain, 'The Financial Crisis', to Austen Chamberlain, 14 Aug. 1931, AC 39/3/26 [hereafter cited as 'Financial Crisis']; Lloyd to Cunliffe-Lister, 14 Aug. 1931, Swinton MSS I(174)/2/1/26.
10. Neville Chamberlain to Gwynne, 13 Aug. 1931, Gwynne MSS 17; to Cunliffe-Lister, 15 Aug. 1931, Swinton MSS I(174)/ 2/1/11–12.
11. Bridgeman to Baldwin, 16 Aug. 1931, Baldwin MSS 44/35–38; Baldwin to Neville Chamberlain, 15 Aug. 1931, NC 7/11/24/1.

12. Neville to Hilda Chamberlain, 16 Aug. 1931, NC 18/1/752.
13. Neville Chamberlain diary, 22 Aug. 1931, NC 2/22.
14. ibid.; Neville to Anne Chamberlain, 21 Aug. 1931, NC 1/26/446; MacDonald diary, 20 Aug. 1931, MacDonald MSS 30/69/1753/1.
15. Neville Chamberlain diary, 22 Aug. 1931, NC 2/22.
16. Memo by Samuel, 'Course of Events 20–23 August', 23 Aug. 1931, Samuel MSS A/78/7/5.
17. Neville to Anne Chamberlain, 3.00 p.m. 23 Aug. 1931, NC 1/26/447.
18. Memo by Dawson, 'Events of Sunday 23 August', 24 Aug. 1931, Dawson MSS [hereafter cited as Dawson's Memo].
19. Baldwin to his wife, 24 Aug. 1931, Hyde, *Baldwin*, p. 336; Neville Chamberlain to his wife, 23 Aug. 1931, NC 1/26/447.
20. Neville Chamberlain diary, 23 Aug. 1931, NC 2/22.
21. Memo by King George V's Private Secretary, Sir Clive Wigram, 'Memorandum of Events surrounding the formation of the National Government 22–24 August 1931', 27 Aug. 1931, Royal Archives RA.GV.K.2330(2)/1 [hereafter cited as Wigram's Memo].
22. Neville Chamberlain diary, 23 Aug. 1931, NC 2/22.
23. Wigram's Memo.
24. Memorandum written at the Conference at Buckingham Palace after the King had withdrawn, 24 Aug. 1931, Samuel MSS A/78/11.
25. Neville Chamberlain diary, 24 Aug. 1931, NC 2/22; Austen to Ivy Chamberlain, 24 Aug. 1931, AC 6/1/800; Cunliffe-Lister to his wife, 24 Aug. 1931, Swinton MSS III(313)/1/5.
26. Neville to Hilda Chamberlain, 16 Aug. 1931, NC 18/1/752.
27. Austen to Ivy Chamberlain, 3.00 p.m. 24 Aug. 1931, AC 6/1/800.
28. Horne to Baldwin, 15 Aug. 1931, Baldwin MSS 44/22–24.

29. Peacock to Wigram, 23 Aug. 1931, Royal Archives, RA.GV.K. 233O(1)/6; P.Williamson, 'A Bankers Ramp? Financiers and the British Political Crisis of August 1931', *English Historical Review*, Vol. 99, 1984.

30. Amery to Gwynne, 8 Sept. 1931, Gwynne MSS 14; Amery diary, 21, 25, 29, & 30 Aug. 1931, Amery MSS.

31. Horne to Neville Chamberlain, 15 Aug. 1931, (copy), Baldwin MSS 44/25–34.

32. Neville Chamberlain diary, 22 Aug. 1931, NC 2/22; *Evening Standard*, 17 Aug. 1931.

33. Cunliffe-Lister to his wife, 24 Aug. 1931, Swinton MSS III(313)/1/5; Dawson's Memo.

34. Austen to Ivy Chamberlain, 24 Aug. 1931, AC 6/1/800; Bridgeman to Baldwin, 16 Aug. 1931, Baldwin MSS 44/35–38.

35. Amery to Beaverbrook, 26 Aug. 1931, Beaverbrook MSS C6; Beaverbrook to Elliott, ibid., C129; Headlam diary, 24 Aug. 1931.

36. Neville to Anne Chamberlain, 21 Aug. 1931, NC 1/26/446.

37. Fair, 'Conservative Basis', p.154.

38. CRD/1/13/3; Ramsden, *Party Policy*, p.57.

39. Neville Chamberlain diary, 22 Aug. 1931, NC 2/22; *The Times,* 14 Aug. 1931; Amery diary, 25 & 29 Aug. 1931.

40. Neville to Hilda Chamberlain, 16 Aug. 1931, NC 18/1/752; Amery diary, 25 Aug. 1931.

41. Lloyd to Cunliffe-Lister, 14 Aug. 1931, Swinton MSS I(174)/2/1/26–28.

42. 'Financial Crisis'.

43. Neville to Anne Chamberlain, 23 Aug. 1931, NC 1/26/447.

44. Neville Chamberlain diary, 23 Aug. 1931, NC 2/22.

45. For Baldwin's views during the crisis see: Baldwin to his wife, 23 Aug. and 24 Aug. 1931, Hyde, *Baldwin,* pp.334, 336; Butler to his father, 28 Aug. 1931, Butler MSS D48/873; Hankey diary, 6 Sept. 1931; Lockhart diary, 21 Sept. 1931.

46. Maclean to his wife, 24 Aug. 1931, Maclean MSS c.468/127–128.

47. MacDonald diary, 23 Aug. 1931, MacDonald MSS 30/69/1753/1.

48. Wigram's Memo.

49. Samuel's Memo, 'Course of Events 20–23 August 1931', Samuel MSS A/78/7/8; Shaw to Samuel, 21 Aug. 1931, ibid., A/78–9; Samuel to MacDonald, 21 Aug. 1931, ibid., A/78/10; Maclean to his wife, 18, 21, 24 Aug. 1931, Maclean MSS c.468/116–128.

50. Wigram's Memo.

51. Note of 25 Sept. 1931, attached to Wigram's Memo.

52. West Midlands Area, Executive Ctte., 18 Sept. 1931; Astor to Munday, 5 Sept. 1931, Astor MSS 1416/1/1/1040; SUA, Western Division Council, 9 Sept. 1931.

53. Neville to Anne Chamberlain, 23 Aug. 1931, NC 1/26/447.

54. Baldwin's press statement, *The Times*, 25 Aug. 1931; Finchley CA, Council, 25 Sept. 1931.

55. Ormsby-Gore to Baldwin, 24 Aug. 1931, Baldwin MSS 44/50; Horne to Neville Chamberlain, 15 Aug. 1931, (copy), ibid., 44/25–34; *The Times*, 21 Aug. 1931.

56. Austen to Ivy Chamberlain, 24 Aug. 1931, AC 6/1/801.

57. ibid.; Hilton Young to his wife, 26 Aug. 1931, Kennet MSS 107/3; Stopford to Peel, 26 Aug., 7 Sept. 1931, Stopford MSS EUR.E.346/7.

58. Amery diary, 27 Aug. 1931; Steel-Maitland's 'Diary of Events during Crisis 1931', Steel-Maitland MSS SRO GD/193/120/3/443–448; EIA Council Minutes, 27 Aug. 1931.

59. Croft to Baldwin, 25 Aug. 1931, Croft MSS 1/2/Ba9; Baldwin to Croft, 26 Aug. 1931, ibid., 1/2/Ba10.

60. Ormsby-Gore to Baldwin, 24 Aug. 1931, Baldwin MSS 44/50; Gretton to Baldwin, 27 Aug. 1931, ibid., 44/60–61.

61. Headlam diary, 28 Aug. 1931; Conway diary, 28 Aug. 1931, Conway MSS 7676/463.

62. In one constituency a month later, one lone dissenting vote was cast

against a resolution of confidence in the National government, but there is no other case in any of the other associations examined of even such minority opposition: Lewes CA, Exec., 21 Sept. 1931.

63. Ealing CA, Exec., 31 Aug. 1931; Waterloo CA, Council, 4 Sept. 1931; Bath CA, Exec., 8 Sept. 1931; SUA, Western Div. Council, 9 Sept. 1931; Uxbridge CA, Council, 12 Sept. 1931; Sowerby CA, Exec., 25 Sept. 1931; Abingdon CA, Council, 26 Sept. 1931.

64. Neville to Ida Chamberlain, 19 Sept. 1931, NC 18/1/755.

65. Cunliffe-Lister to his wife, 1 Sept. 1931, Swinton MSS III(313)/1/5.

66. Gower to Baldwin, 16 Sept. 1931, Baldwin MSS 44/141–142; Glasgow CA, General Ctte., 7 Sept. 1931.

67. Butler to his parents, 10 Sept. 1931, Butler MSS D48/877–880.

68. Cunliffe-Lister to his wife, 8 Sept. 1931, Swinton MSS III(313)/1/5.

69. Wessex Area, Council, 10 Sept. 1931; Uxbridge CA, Council, 12 Sept. 1931; Peterborough CA, Exec., 3 Oct. 1931; Derby CA, Exec., 28 Aug. 1931.

70. Hankey diary, 25 Sept. 1931.

71. Austen to Ida Chamberlain, 26 Sept. 1931, AC 5/1/555.

72. Flintshire CA, Management Ctte., 9 Sept. 1931; Clapham CA, Council, 14 Sept. 1931; Bristol West CA, Exec., 15 Sept. 1931.

73. Memo by Hankey, 'Note of Events during the week ended Saturday October 3rd', Hankey MSS 1/8/46–66; Hankey diary, 25 Sept.-5 Oct. 1931.

74. Sankey diary, 5 Oct. 1931; Hankey Diary, 5 & 6 Oct. 1931.

75. SUA, Western Div. Council, 7 Oct. 1931.

72. Cunliffe-Lister to his wife, 6 Oct. 1931, Swinton MSS III(313)/1/5.

77. Austen to Ivy Chamberlain, 7 & 8 Oct. 1931, AC 6/1/825–826.

78. For candidates withdrawn, see: Flintshire CA, Special GM, 12 Oct. 1931; Dumfriesshire CA, Emergency GM, 15 Oct. 1931. For refusals to stand down, see: Kincar-dine & West Aberdeenshire CA, Exec., 6 Oct. 1931; Cornwall North CA, Exec., 29 Sept., 12 Oct. 1931; Dorset East, Exec. & GM, 12 Oct. 1931.

79. Hannon to Beaverbrook, 15 Aug. 1930, Beaverbrook MSS C154; Bridgeman journal, II, p. 207.

80. Neville to Ida Chamberlain, 22 Mar. 1930, NC 18/1/686.

81. Amery diary, 20 Jul. 1930.

82. Bridgeman to Salisbury, 5 Nov. 1930, Hatfield MSS S(4)138/14–15.

83. Neville to Hilda Chamberlain, 18 Oct. 1930, NC 18/1/713; Neville Chamberlain to Bridgeman, 15 Oct. 1930, NC 8/10/15.

84. Amery diary, 15 Apr. 1931.

Conclusion

1. M. Wolff, 'Policy Making in the Conservative Party', J. Mackintosh, ed., *People and Parliament* (London, 1978); Ramsden, *Party Policy,* pp. 1–10.

2. *The Times,* 31 Oct. 1930.

3. Amery diary, 26 May 1930.

4. ibid., 5 Mar. 1931.

5. ibid., 2 Mar. 1931; Gilmour to Provand, 19 Mar. 1931, Gilmour MSS GD383/34/6.

6. *The Times,* 31 Oct. 1930.

7. Political and Economic Planning, *Report on the British Press* (London, 1938), Figure 10, p.237, p.29, pp. 242–247.

8. Beaverbrook to Horne, 28 May 1930, Beaverbrook MSS C178.

9. Peto diary, 22 Feb. 1930.

10. Amery diary, 18 Feb., 7 Mar. 1930.

11. Lewisham West CA, Council, 6 Oct. 1930.

12. Amery Diary, 19 Jul. 1930.

13. Ramsden, *Party Policy,* pp.2–5, 22–60.

14. Stopford's diary notes, 5 Oct. 1930, Stopford MSS EUR.E.346/6.

15. Lloyd to Baldwin, 5 Mar. 1931, Lloyd of Dolobran MSS 19/5.

16. Lytton to Irwin, 20 Nov. 1929, Halifax MSS EUR.C.152/18/1/309.

17. Irwin to Churchill, 26 Dec. 1929, ibid. EUR.C.152/18/2/419; to

Hugh Cecil, 29 Aug. 1930, ibid.
EUR.C.152/19/2/136e.

18. F.M.Miller, 'The Unemployment
Policy of the National Government
1931–1936', *Historical Journal*, Vol.
19 (1976), pp.453–459.

19. R.P.Shay, *British Rearmament in the
Thirties: Politics and Profits* (Princeton, 1977), pp. 92–93, 246–263.

BIBLIOGRAPHY

In addition to the standard abbreviations, the following have also been used:

BLPES	British Library of Political and Economic Science
CA	Conservative Association
Ctte	Committee
NU	National Union of Conservative and Unionist Associations
RO	Record Office
SUA	Scottish Unionist Association

Where no other location is given, primary sources remain with their original owners. Unless otherwise stated, secondary works were published in London.

I PRIMARY SOURCES

1. **Private Papers**

(a) *The Conservative Leadership*

Amery MSS	(Courtesy of Rt. Hon. J. Amery, London)
Ashley MSS	(Southampton University Library)
Baldwin MSS	(Cambridge University Library)
Balfour MSS	(British Library)
Bridgeman MSS	(Shropshire RO)
Bridgeman Journal	(Courtesy of the late Lord Bridgeman)
Cecil of Chelwood MSS	(British Library)
Austen Chamberlain MSS	(Birmingham University Library)
Neville Chamberlain MSS	(Birmingham University Library)
Churchill MSS	(M.Gilbert, ed., *Winston S. Churchill, Companion Vol. 5, Part 2* (1981).)
Davidson MSS	(House of Lords RO)
Derby MSS	(Liverpool RO)
Gilmour MSS	(Scottish RO)
Halifax MSS	(Borthwick Institute, York University)
Halifax MSS	(India Office Library)
Hatfield (Salisbury) MSS	(Hatfield House)
Londonderry MSS	(Durham RO)
Steel-Maitland MSS	(Scottish RO)
Stonehaven MSS	(National Library of Australia)

Swinton MSS	(Churchill College, Cambridge)
Templewood MSS	(Cambridge University Library)
Worthington-Evans MSS	(Bodleian Library)

(b) *Conservative MPs, Candidates, and Peers*

Atholl MSS	(Blair Castle, Blair Atholl)
Astor MSS	(Reading University Library)
Bayford MSS	(Bodleian Library)
Beamish MSS	(Churchill College, Cambridge)
Bull MSS	(Churchill College, Cambridge)
Butler MSS	(Trinity College, Cambridge)
Conway MSS	(Cambridge University Library)
Cooper MSS	(Churchill College, Cambridge)
Crawford MSS	(J. Vincent, ed., *The Crawford Papers* (Manchester, 1985).)
Croft MSS	(Churchill College, Cambridge)
Crookshank MSS	(Bodleian Library)
Elliot MSS	(National Library of Scotland)
Gower MSS	(Tunbridge Wells Library)
Hammersley MSS	(Manchester Central Library)
Hannon MSS	(House of Lords RO)
Hanworth MSS	(Bodleian Library)
Haslam MSS	(Lincolnshire RO)
Headlam MSS	(Durham RO)
Heneage MSS	(Lincolnshire RO)
Kennet MSS	(Cambridge University Library)
Lloyd of Dolobran MSS	(Churchill College, Cambridge)
Marriott MSS	(York RO)
Moore-Brabazon MSS	(Royal Air Force Museum)
Morrison-Bell MSS	(House of Lords RO)
Peto MSS	(courtesy of Mr. J. Peto, Woodbridge, Suffolk)
Scott MSS	(Warwick University Library)
Selborne MSS	(Bodleian Library)
Selborne MSS	(Hampshire RO)
Smithers MSS	(courtesy of Sir D. Smithers, Knockholt, Kent)

(c) *The Empire Crusaders*

Beaverbrook MSS	(House of Lords RO)
Blumenfeld MSS	(House of Lords RO)
Elibank MSS	(Scottish RO)
Lockhart MSS	(House of Lords RO)

(d) *Other Collections*

Cabinet Papers	(Public Records Office)
Dawson MSS	(Bodleian Library)

Dawson MSS	(Times Newspapers Archives)
Empire Industries Association MSS	(Warwick University Library)
Indian Empire Society (Stuart) MSS	(Bodleian Library)
Gwynne MSS	(Bodleian Library)
Hankey MSS	(Churchill College, Cambridge)
Jones Diary	(T.Jones, ed., *A Diary With Letters* (1954).)
Lloyd George MSS	(House of Lords RO)
Macdonald MSS	(Public Records Office)
Maclean MSS	(Bodleian Library)
National Farmers Union MSS	(Institute of Agricultural History, Reading University)
Nicolson Diary	(H.Nicolson, ed., *Diaries and Letters, Vol.1: 1930–39* (1966).)
Royal Archives	(Windsor Castle)
Samuel MSS	(House of Lords RO)
Sankey MSS	(Bodleian Library)
Simon MSS	(Bodleian Library)
Stansgate MSS	(House of Lords RO)
Stopford MSS	(India Office Library)
Whitehall Diary	(K.Middlemas, ed., *Thomas Jones: Whitehall Diary, Vol. 2: 1926–1930* (1969).)
Wrench MSS	(British Library)

2. Conservative Party Records

(a) *National Records*

NU, Executive Ctte.
NU, Reports of Executive Ctte.
NU, Central Council
NU, Annual Reports of Council
NU, Conference Agendas and Minutes
NU, Labour Advisory Sub-Ctte.
Junior Imperial League
Conservative Central Office
Conservative Research Department
Conservative Private Members '1922' Ctte.
    All at Conservative Party Archive, Bodleian Library)
National Society of Conservative Agents   (Westminster Library)

(b) *Regional Records*

SUA, Executive and Central Council
SUA, Annual Conference   (all at Scottish Conservative
SUA, Eastern Divisional Council   Central Office)
SUA, Western Divisional Council

East Midlands Area
Eastern Area   (Bodleian Library)
North West Area   (Bodleian Library)
South East Area   (Bodleian Library)
Wessex Area   (Bodleian Library)
Western Area   (Bodleian Library)
West Midlands Area
Yorkshire Area
Cornwall Provincial Division   (Bodleian Library)
Somerset Provincial Division   (Bodleian Library)
Kent Conservative Agents
   Union   (Canterbury CA)
Birmingham CA   (Birmingham Central Library)
Bradford CA   (Bradford Central Library)
Glasgow CA   (Scottish Cons. Central Office)
Leeds CA   (Leeds RO)
Sheffield CA   (Sheffield Central Library)

(c) *Constituency Records*

Aberdeen South CA
Abingdon CA
Accrington CA   (Manchester University Library)
Aldershot CA   (Hampshire RO)
Ashford CA
Ayr Burghs CA
Barkston Ash CA   (Leeds RO)
Basingstoke CA
Bath CA   (Bath RO)
Bewdley CA   (Worcestershire RO)
Blackpool CA   (Lancashire RO)
Bolton CA
Bradford Central CA   (Bradford Central Library)
Bradford East CA   (Bradford Central Library)
Bradford South CA   (Bradford Central Library)
Bridgeton CA   (Scottish Cons. Central Office)
Bristol East CA   (Bristol RO)
Bristol West CA   (Bristol RO)
Camborne CA   (Cornwall RO)
Cannock CA
Canterbury CA
Chelmsford CA   (Essex RO)
Chichester CA   (West Sussex RO)
Chippenham CA
Cirencester & Tewkesbury CA
City of London CA   (Westminster City Library)
Clapham CA   (BLPES)
Clitheroe CA   (Lancashire RO)
Cornwall North CA   (Cornwall RO)

Cornwall South East CA	(Cornwall RO)
Darlington CA	
Darwen CA	(Lancashire RO)
Denbighshire CA	(Clwyd RO, Ruthin Branch)
Derby CA	(Derbyshire RO)
Derbyshire West CA	(Derbyshire RO)
Dorset East CA	(Poole CA)
Dorset West CA	(Dorset RO)
Dumfriesshire CA	
Ealing CA	(Greater London RO)
East Grinstead CA	
Edinburgh North CA	(Edinburgh Central CA)
Edinburgh West CA	
Epsom CA	
Finchley CA	
Flintshire CA	(Clwyd RO, Hawarden Branch)
Fylde CA	(Lancashire RO)
Gravesend CA	(Kent RO)
Guildford CA	(Surrey RO, Guildford Branch)
Hackney North CA	(North East London Cons. Group)
Halifax CA	
Harborough CA	(Leicestershire RO)
Harwich CA	
Hemel Hempstead CA	
Herefordshire North CA	(Herefordshire RO)
Hitchin CA	
Horncastle CA	(Lincolnshire RO)
Inverness CA	
Ipswich CA	(Suffolk RO, Ipswich Branch)
Islington East CA	(North East London Cons. Group)
Keighley CA	(Leeds RO)
Kennington CA	(BLPES)
Kensington South CA	
Kincardine & West Aberdeenshire CA	(Kincardine & Deeside CA)
Kinross & West Perthshire CA	(Tayside North CA)
Knutsford CA	
Ladywood CA	(Birmingham Central Library)
Lancaster CA	
Leeds West CA	(Leeds RO)
Lewes CA	
Lewisham West CA	
Lincoln CA	
Loughborough CA	(Leicestershire RO)
Maidstone CA	(Kent RO)
Maryhill CA	(Scottish Cons. Central Office)
Melton CA	
Middleton & Prestwich CA	(Lancashire RO)
Moray & Nairn CA	

Newark CA
Newcastle West CA   (Tyne & Wear RO)
Northampton CA   (Northamptonshire RO)
Northwich CA   (Cheshire RO)
Norwich CA
Oswestry CA
Oxford CA
Oxfordshire North CA   (Oxfordshire RO)
Oxfordshire South CA   (Oxfordshire RO)
Penistone CA
Peterborough CA
Petersfield CA
Reigate CA   (Surrey RO, Kingston Branch)
Renfrewshire West CA
Ripon CA   (Harrogate CA)
Rochester & Chatham CA
Rother Valley CA   (South Yorkshire Cons. Federation)
Rotherham CA   (South Yorkshire Cons. Federation)
Rothwell CA   (Wakefield CA)
Rushcliffe CA   (Nottinghamshire RO)
Rye CA
St. Albans CA
St. George's CA   (Westminster City Library)
Sevenoaks CA
Sheffield Central CA   (Sheffield Central Library)
Sheffield Ecclesall CA   (Sheffield Central Library)
Sheffield Park CA   (Sheffield Central Library)
Shrewsbury CA
Skipton CA
Southport CA
Sowerby CA
Stafford CA   (Staffordshire RO)
Stirling & Falkirk Burghs CA   (Falkirk CA)
Stirlingshire West CA   (Stirling CA)
Stockton CA   (Durham RO)
Stone CA   (Staffordshire RO)
Thirsk & Malton CA
Torquay CA
Tynemouth CA   (Local Studies Centre, North Shields)
Uxbridge CA
Wakefield CA
Walsall CA
Warwick & Leamington CA   (Warwickshire RO)
Waterloo CA   (Lancashire RO)
Wells CA
Winchester CA   (Hampshire RO)
Wirral CA
Wolverhampton West CA   (courtesy of Prof. G. Jones, London
                                        School of Economics)

Wood Green CA	(Greater London RO)
Woolwich West CA	(Greenwich Local History Library)
Worcester CA	
York CA	(York City Archives)

(d) *Party Publications*

Ashridge Journal
Conservative Agents Journal
Gleanings & Memoranda
Home & Politics (from March 1931 *Home & Empire*)

3. Newspapers

(a) National

Daily Express
Daily Herald
Daily Mail
Daily Telegraph
Evening News
Evening Standard
Morning Post
News Chronicle
Observer
Times
Sunday Dispatch
Sunday Express
Sunday Times

(b) Provincial

Aberdeen Press and Journal
Birmingham Post
Courier and Advertiser (Dundee)
Eastern Daily Press
Glasgow Herald
Leeds Mercury
Liverpool Daily Post
Manchester Guardian
North Mail
Northern Daily Telegraph
Northern Echo
Nottingham Guardian
Scotsman
Western Mail
Yorkshire Post

4. Memoirs and Contemporary Publications

Amery, L.S., *My Political Life*, Vols. 2 and 3 (1953 and 1955).
Avon, Earl of, *The Eden Memoirs: Vol. 1: Facing the Dictators* (1922).
Balfour, H., *Wings Over Westminster* (1973).
Banks, R.M., *The Conservative Outlook* (1929).
Beaverbrook, Lord, *My Case for Empire Free Trade* (1930).
Boothby, R., *I Fight to Live* (1947).
Bryant, A., *The Spirit of Conservatism* (1929).
Butler, Lord, *The Art of the Possible* (1971).
Camrose, Lord, *British Newspapers and their Controllers* (1947).
Cecil of Chelwood, Lord, *All The Way* (1949).
Chamberlain, Sir A., *Down The Years* (1935).
Chilcott, W., *Political Salvation 1930–32* (1932).
Christiansen, A., *Headlines All My Life* (1961).

Cooper, D., *Old Men Forget* (1953).
Cooper, Lady D., *The Light of Common Day* (1959).
Croft, Lord, *My Life of Strife* (1949).
Elibank, Lord, *A Man's Life* (1934).
Feiling, K., *What Is Conservatism?* (1930).
Gerhardi, W., *Memoirs of a Polyglot* (1931).
Halifax, Earl of, *Fulness of Days* (1957).
Herbert, D.H., *Backbencher and Chairman* (1946).
Londonderry, Lady, *Retrospect* (1938).
Londonderry, Lord, *Wings of Destiny* (1943).
Macmillan, H., *Memoirs, Vol. 1: Winds of Change 1914–39* (1966).
Midleton, Earl of, *Records and Reactions* (1939).
Moore-Brabazon, J.T.C., *The Brabazon Story* (1956).
Oman, Sir C., *Things I Have Seen* (1933).
Percy, Lord E., *Some Memories* (1958).
Percy, Lord E., *Democracy on Trial* (1931).
Portsmouth, Earl of, *A Knot of Roots* (1965).
Rentoul, Sir G., *This Is My Case* (1944).
Samuel, Viscount, *Memoirs* (1945).
Simon, Viscount, *Retrospect* (1952).
Stuart of Findhorn, Lord, *Within The Fringe* (1967).
Swinton, Lord, *Sixty Years of Power* (1966).
Templewood, Viscount, *Nine Troubled Years* (1954).
Winterton, Earl, *Orders of The Day* (1953).
Zetland, Lord, *Essayez* (1957).

II SECONDARY SOURCES

1. Biographies

Adam, C.F., *Life of Lord Lloyd* (1948).
Baldwin, A.W., *My Father—The True Story* (1955).
Birkenhead, Earl of, *FE: Life of FE Smith, First Earl of Birkenhead* (1959).
Birkenhead, Earl of, *Halifax* (1965).
Blake, R., *The Unknown Prime Minister: The Life and Times of Andrew Bonar Law* (1955).
Bolitho, H., *Alfred Mond, First Lord Melchett* (1932).
Brodrick, A.H., *Near to Greatness: Life of the 6th Earl Winterton* (1965).
Bowle, J., *Viscount Samuel* (1957).
Boyle, A., *Poor, Dear Brendan* (1974).
Bryant, A., *Stanley Baldwin* (1937).
Campbell, J., *Lloyd George: The Goat in the Wilderness 1922–1931* (1977).
Campbell, J., *F.E. Smith: First Earl of Birkenhead* (1983).
Carlton, D., *Anthony Eden* (1981).
Charmley, J., *Duff Cooper* (1986).
Charmley, J., *Lord Lloyd and the Decline of the British Empire* (1987).

Churchill, R., *Lord Derby: King of Lancashire* (1959).
Coote, C.A., *Companion of Honour: the story of Walter Elliot* (1965).
Cross, J.A., *Sir Samuel Hoare* (1977).
Cross, J.A., *Lord Swinton* (1982).
Dilks, D., *Neville Chamberlain: Vol. 1, Pioneering and Reform 1869–1929* (Cambridge, 1984).
Driberg, T., *Beaverbrook: A Study in Power and Frustration* (1956).
Dutton, D., *Austen Chamberlain* (Bolton, 1985).
Eade, C., ed., *Churchill By His Contemporaries* (1953).
Egremont, M., *Balfour* (1980).
Elletson, D.H., *The Chamberlains* (1966).
Feiling, K., *Life of Neville Chamberlain* (1946).
Gilbert, M., *Winston S. Churchill, Vol. 5: 1922–39* (1976).
Green, J., *Mr. Baldwin: A Study in Post-War Conservatism* (1933).
Heuston, R.F.V., *Lives of the Lord Chancellors 1885–1940* (1964).
Howard, A., *Rab: The Life of R.A.Butler* (1987).
Hyde, H.M., *Baldwin* (1973).
Hyde, H.M., *Neville Chamberlain* (1976).
Hyde, H.M., *Lord Reading* (1967).
James, R.R., ed., *Memoirs of a Conservative: JCC Davidson's Memoirs and Papers 1910–37* (1969).
James, R.R., *Victor Cazalet* (1976).
James, R.R., *Anthony Eden* (1986).
James, R.R., *Churchill: A Study in Failure 1900–39* (1970).
Jenkins, R., *Baldwin* (1987).
Judd, D., *Lord Reading* (1982).
Lysaght, C.E., *Brendan Bracken: A Biography* (1979).
Mackay, R.F., *Balfour: Intellectual Statesman* (Oxford, 1985).
Mackenzie, F.A., *Lord Beaverbrook* (1931).
Macleod, I., *Neville Chamberlain* (1961).
Marquand, D., *Ramsay MacDonald* (1977).
Middlemas, K. & Barnes, J., *Baldwin* (1969).
Nicolson, H., *King George V* (1952).
Pelling, H., *Winston Churchill* (1974).
Petrie, Sir C., *Life and Letters of Sir Austen Chamberlain: Vol. 2* (1939).
Roberts, B., *Stanley Baldwin* (1936).
Rose, K., *The Later Cecils* (1975).
Rose, K., *King George V* (1983).
Rowland, P., *Lloyd George* (1975).
Sampson, A., *Harold MacMillan* (1967).
Skidelsky, R., *Oswald Mosley* (1975).
Smith, J.A., *John Buchan* (1965).
Somervell, D.C., *Stanley Baldwin* (1953).
Steed, W., *The Real Stanley Baldwin* (1930).
Sykes, C., *Nancy: The Life of Lady Astor* (1972).
Taylor, A.J.P., *Beaverbrook* (1972).
Taylor, H.A., *Jix, Viscount Brentford* (1933).
Wrench, J.E., *Geoffrey Dawson and Our Times* (1955).
Young, G.M., *Baldwin* (1976).

Young, K., *Arthur James Balfour* (1963).
Young, K., *Baldwin* (1976).
Young, K., *Churchill and Beaverbrook* (1966).
Young, K., ed., *The Diaries of Sir Robert Bruce Lockhart, Vol. 1: 1915–38* (1973).
Zebel, S.H., *Balfour* (1973).

2. **Books**

Bassett, R., *1931: Political Crisis* (1958).
Beloff, M., *Wars and Welfare: Britain 1914–1945* (1984).
Bentley, M., *The Liberal Mind 1914–29* (Cambridge, 1977).
Berkeley, H., *The Myth That Will Not Die: The Formation of The National Government 1931* (1978).
Blake, R., *The Conservative Party from Peel to Churchill* (1970).
Blake, R., *The National Union 1867–1967* (1967).
Boyce, G. & Curran P., eds., *Newspaper History: From the 17th Century to the Present Day* (1978).
Bromhead, P.A., *The House of Lords and Contemporary Politics 1911–1957* (1958).
Brookes, P., *Women at Westminster: an account of Women in the British Parliament 1918–1966* (1967).
Butler, D., ed., *Coalitions in British Politics* (1978).
Butler, D., *The Electoral System in Britain Since 1918* (second edition, Oxford, 1963).
Butler, Lord, ed., *The Conservatives* (1977).
Cambray, P.G., *The Game of Politics* (1932).
Carlton, D., *MacDonald versus Henderson: The Foreign Policy of the Second Labour Government* (1970).
Clarke, P.F., *Lancashire and the New Liberalism* (Cambridge, 1971).
Comfort, G.O., *Professional Politicians: A Study of the British Party Agents* (Washington, 1958).
Cook, C., *The Age of Alignment* (1975).
Cook, C. & Ramsden, J., eds., *By-Elections in British Politics* (1973).
Cooke, A.B., & Vincent, J., *The Governing Passion: Cabinet Government and Party Politics in Britain 1885–1886* (Brighton, 1974).
Cowling, M., *1867: Disraeli, Gladstone, and Revolution* (Cambridge, 1967).
Cowling, M., *The Impact of Hitler: British Politics and British Policies 1933–40* (Cambridge, 1975).
Cowling, M., *The Impact of Labour 1920–24* (Cambridge, 1971).
Cudlipp, H., *The Prerogative of the Harlot: Press Barons and Power* (1980).
Dean, K.J., *Town and Westminster: A Political History of Walsall* (Walsall, 1972).
Douglas, R., *History of the Liberal Party 1885–1970* (1971).
Drummond, I.M., *British Economic Policy and the Empire* (1972).
Fawcett, A., *Conservative Agent* (1967).
Goodhart, P. & Branston, U., *The 1922: The Story of the Conservative Backbenchers Parliamentary Committee* (1973).

Granzow, B.A., *Mirror of Nazism: British Opinion and the Emergence of Hitler 1929–1933* (1964).

Guttsman, W.L., *The British Political Elite* (1963).

Gwyn, W.B., *Democracy and the Cost of Politics in Britain* (1962).

Howell, D., *British Social Democracy* (1976).

Incorporated Society of British Advertisers, *The Readership of Newspapers and Periodicals in Great Britain 1936* (1937).

James, R.R., *The British Revolution: Vol. 2: British Politics 1914–1939* (1977).

Jones, G.W., *Borough Politics: A Study of the Wolverhampton Town Council 1888–1964* (1969).

Kinnear, M., *The Fall of Lloyd George* (1973).

Koss, S., *The Rise and Fall of the Political Press in Britain, Vol. 2: The Twentieth Century* (1984).

Layton-Henry, Z., ed., *Conservative Party Politics* (1980).

Lindsay, T.F. & Harrington, M., *The Conservative Party 1918–1979* (1979).

McKenzie, R.T., *British Political Parties* (1955).

McKenzie, R.T. & Silver, A., *Angels in Marble* (1967).

McKibbin, R.I., *The Evolution of the Labour Party 1910–1924* (Oxford, 1974).

Middlemas, K., *Politics in Industrial Society* (1979).

Morgan, K.O., *Consensus and Disunity: The Lloyd George Coalition Government 1918–22* (Oxford, 1979).

Nordlinger, E., *The Working-Class Tories* (1967).

Norton, P. & Aughey, A., *Conservatives and Conservatism* (1981).

Olney, R.J., *Lincolnshire Politics 1832–1885* (Oxford, 1973).

Pelling, H., *A Short History of the Labour Party* (1961).

Petrie, Sir C., *The Carlton Club* (1955).

Petrie, Sir C., *The Powers Behind the Prime Ministers* (1958).

Pimlott, B., *Labour and the Left in the 1930s* (Cambridge, 1977).

Political and Economic Planning, *Report on the British Press* (1938).

Pugh, M., *The Tories and the People 1880–1935* (Oxford, 1985).

Ramsden, J., *The Age of Balfour and Baldwin 1902–40: History of the Conservative Party, Vol. 3* (1978).

Ramsden, J., *The Making of Conservative Party Policy: The Conservative Research Department Since 1929* (1980).

Raymond, J., ed., *The Baldwin Age* (1960).

Rempel, R., *Unionists Divided* (Newton Abbot, 1972).

Robb, J., *The Primrose League* (New York, 1942).

Seymour-Ure, C., *Press, Politics, and Public* (1968).

Shay, R.P., *British Rearmament in the 1930's: Politics or Profits* (Princeton, 1977).

Skidelsky, R., *Politicians and the Slump: The Labour Government of 1929–31* (1967).

Stannage, T., *Baldwin Thwarts the Opposition: The British General Election of 1935* (1980).

Stevenson, J. & Cook, C., *The Slump: Society and Politics during the Depression* (1977).

Southgate, D., ed., *The Conservative Leadership 1832–1932* (1974).

Sykes, A., *Tariff Reform in British Politics 1903–13* (Oxford, 1979).

Thompson, N., *The Anti-Appeasers: Conservative Opposition to Appeasement in the 1930s* (Oxford, 1971).

Thompson, P., *Socialists, Liberals, and Labour: The Struggle for London 1885–1914* (1967).

Waller, P.J., *Democracy and Sectarianism: A Political and Social History of Liverpool 1868–1939* (Liverpool, 1981).

Webber, G.C., *The Ideology of the British Right 1918–1939* (1986).

Wiener, M.J., *English Culture and the Decline of the Industrial Spirit 1850–1980* (Cambridge, 1981).

Wilson, T., *The Downfall of the Liberal Party 1914–35* (1966).

Winter, J.M., *Socialism and the Challenge of War* (1974).

Young, K., *Local Politics and the Rise of Party: The London Municipal Society and the Conservative Intervention in Local Elections 1894–1963* (Leicester, 1975).

3. **Articles**

Ball, S.R., 'Failure of an Opposition?: The Conservative Party in Parliament 1929–1931', *Parliamentary History*, Vol. 5 (1986).

Ball, S.R., 'The Conservative Party and the Formation of the National Government: August 1931', *Historical Journal*, Vol. 29 (1986).

Beattie, A., 'Neville Chamberlain', Mackintosh, J.P., ed., *British Prime Ministers in the Twentieth Century, Vol. 1* (1977).

Beichman, A., 'Hugger-Mugger in Old Queen Street: The Origins of the Conservative Research Department', *Journal of Contemporary History*, Vol. 13 (1978).

Blewett, N., 'Free Fooders, Balfourites, and Whole Hoggers: Factionalism within the Unionist Party 1906–10', *Historical Journal*, Vol. 11 (1968).

Bridge, C., 'Conservatism and Indian Reform 1929–1939', *Journal of Imperial and Commonwealth History*, Vol. 4 (1975–76).

Campbell, J., 'Stanley Baldwin', Mackintosh, J.P., ed., *British Prime Ministers in the Twentieth Century, Vol. 1* (1977).

Cannadine, D., 'Politics, Propaganda, and Art: The Case of Two Worcestershire Lads', *Midland History*, Vol. 4 (1977).

Close, D.H., 'Conservatives and Coalition after the First World War', *Journal of Modern History*, Vol. 45 (1973).

Close, D.H., 'The Collapse of Resistance to Democracy: Conservatives, Adult Suffrage, and Second Chamber Reform 1911–28', *Historical Journal*, Vol. 20 (1977).

Close, D.H., 'The Re-Alignment of the British Electorate in 1931', *History*, Vol. 67 (1982).

Dare, R., 'British Labour, the National Government, and the "National Interest" 1931', *Historical Studies*, Vol. 18 (1978–79).

Fair, J.D., 'The Conservative Basis for the Formation of the National Government of 1931', *Journal of British Studies*, Vol. 19 (1980).

Fair, J.D., 'The Second Labour Government and the Politics of Electoral Reform 1929–31', *Albion*, Vol. 13 (1981).

Fraser, P., 'Unionism and Tariff Reform: The Crisis of 1906', *Historical Journal*, Vol. 5 (1962).

Ghosh, S.C., 'Decision-Making and Power in the British Conservative Party: A Case Study of the Indian Problem 1929–34', *Political Studies*, Vol. 13 (1965).

Glickman, H., 'The Toryness of English Conservatism', *Journal of British Studies*, Vol. 1 (1961).

Hearder, H., 'King George V, the General Strike, and the 1931 crisis', Hearder, H., & Loyn, H.R., eds., *British Government and Administration* (Cardiff, 1974).

Layton-Henry, Z., 'Democracy and Reform in the Conservative Party', *Journal of Contemporary History*, Vol. 13 (1978).

McKibbin, R.I., 'The Economic Policy of the Second Labour Government 1929–31', *Past and Present,* No. 68 (1975).

Miller, F.M., 'The Unemployment Policy of the National Government 1931–1936', *Historical Journal*, Vol. 19 (1976).

Moodie, G.C., 'The Monarch and the selection of a Prime Minister: A Re-examination of the crisis of 1931', *Political Studies,* Vol. 5 (1957).

Peele, G., 'Revolt Over India', Peele, G., & Cook, C., eds., *The Politics of Reappraisal 1918–39* (1975).

Ramsden, J., 'Baldwin and Film', Pronay, N., & Spring, D.W., eds., *Propaganda, Politics, and Film 1918–45* (1982).

Rasmussen, J.G., 'Government and Intra-Party Opposition: Dissent within the Conservative Parliamentary Party in the 1930's', *Political Studies*, Vol. 19 (1971).

Seymour-Ure, C., 'The Press and the Party System Between the Wars', Peele, G., & Cook, C., eds., *The Politics of Reappraisal 1918–39* (1975).

Sykes, A., 'The Radical Right and the Crisis of Conservatism before the First World War', *Historical Journal*, Vol. 26 (1983).

Williamson, P., 'Safety First: Baldwin, The Conservative Party, and the 1929 General Election', *Historical Journal*, Vol. 25 (1982).

Williamson, P., 'A Bankers Ramp? Financiers and the British Political Crisis of August 1931', *English Historical Review*, Vol. 99 (1984).

Wolff, M., 'Policy making in the Conservative Party', Mackintosh, J., ed., *People and Parliament* (1978).

Wrench, D.J., ' "Cashing In": The Parties and the National Government, August 1931—September 1932', *Journal of British Studies*, Vol. 23 (1984).

4. Theses

Dean, D.W., 'The Contrasting Attitudes of the Conservative and Labour Parties to Problems of Empire 1922–36', University of London, Ph.D. (1974).

Herzog, R.D., 'The Conservative Party and Protectionist Politics 1918–1932', University of Sheffield, Ph.D. (1984).

McEwen, J.M., 'The Unionist and Conservative Members of Parliament 1914–39', University of London, Ph.D. (1959).

Ramsden, J.A., 'The Organisation of the Conservative and Unionist Party in Britain 1910–30', University of Oxford, D.Phil. (1975).

Rolf, K.W.D., 'Tories, Tariffs and Elections: The West Midlands in English Politics 1918–35', University of Cambridge, Ph.D. (1975).

Self, R.C., 'The Conservative Party and the Politics of Tariff Reform', University of London, Ph.D. (1982).

Shorter, P.R., 'Electoral Politics and Political Change in the East Midlands of England 1918–35', University of Cambridge, Ph.D. (1975).

INDEX

Dissolving the Family Company

Dissolving the Family Company

Second Edition

Paul Seal FCA CTA(Fellow) TEP

Tottel Publishing, Maxwelton House, 41–43 Boltro Road, Haywards Heath, West Sussex, RH16 1BJ

© Tottel Publishing Ltd 2008

A CIP Catalogue record for this book is available from the British Library.

ISBN: 978 1 84766 157 9

Typeset by Phoenix Typesetting, Chatham, Kent
Printed and bound in Great Britain by Athenæum Press, Gateshead, Tyne & Wear

Preface

These are changing times. At the time of publication of the first edition of this book the economy was buoyant and the underlying assumption of much of the publication was that we were dealing with the distribution of assets from a successful family company at a time when the proprietors wished to retire to enjoy the fruits of their labour. How times have changed. In the current climate there will, of course, still be successful family companies and funds available to distribute to the shareholders. However, equally, there will be many who are currently operating what appear to be successful businesses but with an eye to preserving the assets that they have already built up and no wish to see the business decline as a result of the current credit crunch. They may take the decision to close the business down earlier than might otherwise have been the case to preserve the assets presently accrued.

If the intention is to preserve what we already have then the ideas, techniques and advice contained within this publication will be of assistance. I have always taken the view that the amount of tax that an individual or company pays is of less importance than the value on which that tax charge bites. After all if a business paid no tax whatsoever then the likelihood is, in the great majority of cases, that there are no profits and, ultimately, without profits there would be no business. Maximising the after tax retention should be the most important objective.

Some years ago a client was proposing to sell building land and the best advice was that a tax charge of approximately £700,000 would apply. Following the sale the revised calculations showed an increased tax charge of approximately £1.5 million. Of course the reason for the increase was that the proceeds of sale were so much greater than had been anticipated so that the net of tax figure was also very much greater than the client was expecting, but that was a good result it seems to me.

Since the first edition there have been changes, principally the abolition of capital gains tax taper relief and its replacement by CGT simplification and entrepreneurs' relief, clarification of the bona vacantia provisions and the circumstances in which the issued share capital of a dissolved company can be claimed by HM Treasury as well as clarification and extension of HMRC's undertakings in relation to ESC C16; the relevant sections reflect these changes.

The original inspiration for this publication was the dissolution of a substantial family company where the shares were widely held and where assets used by the company were personally owned. As I could find no single source as to how to approach the required task, or more importantly, how to identify the potential pitfalls, I began to gather together much of the information that appears in this publication. In advance of my meetings with that particular client I had rather assumed that they would have all the information that was needed to proceed and it was only when I began the task that it became clear that there were many factors to be considered and that a quick and cheerful dissolution would not have resulted in the most tax-efficient distribution of assets to the shareholders.

This publication is intended as a practical guide to the factors and processes that need to be considered when dissolving a family company. Its purpose is to help others avoid the dilemma that I faced. Apart from a few specific references to dissolution or liquidation there are few techniques or planning ideas that cannot be applied in other circumstances, but the purpose of this publication is to review those ideas and established practices and to apply them to a solvent dissolution in order that the dissolution process can be carried out in an appropriate manner and that events are organised at the appropriate time.

It is also intended to cover those areas, perhaps rarely encountered in practice, which when met may require research and consideration before an appropriate conclusion is drawn. If this publication prevents some users from reinventing the wheel then it will, I believe, have served its purpose.

The appendices include an extended case study originally based upon the case that triggered my interest in this area but, naturally, suitably modified to protect the innocent (and guilty) and updated for the current CGT regime. Its purpose is to demonstrate how factors that are often met in practice may be resolved. In addition copies of appropriate HMRC practice and concessions are included.

In particular Appendix 9 includes a detailed checklist which is a much expanded version of my original checklist and although, in many cases, a significant number of the answers will be 'not applicable' it will act as an *aide-mémoire* to provide reassurance that no matters have been overlooked.

I would like to thank my professional colleagues who have offered advice, criticism and suggestions as to the ways in which matters might be presented. However, as always, responsibility for any sins of omission or commission rest solely with the writer.

I would also like to thank my wife, Nola, for her assistance in working on the book, being able to read most of my scribble and for her support in dealing with the manuscript.

Finally I would like to dedicate this book to my father, Leslie Seal, who died just as this publication went to print. Without his belief, kind words and guidance, my career would have been very different and his support over the years is something that I will greatly miss.

Paul Seal
Norwich
December 2008

Contents

Contents

Table of Statutes

[All references are to paragraph number and appendices]

Table of Statutory Instruments

[All references are to paragraph number]

Table of Other Materials

[All references are to paragraph number and appendices]

Table of Cases

[All references are to paragraph number and appendices]

Chapter 1

Setting the background

1.1   Over a number of years my work required me to become involved in advising an increasing number of businesses that had become limited companies where, as a result of changed circumstance, the company was no longer required. The circumstances have varied from the death of the main shareholder in a situation where the family no longer required the business to be carried on, to individuals who wished to retire and, at the extreme, to individuals who had literally come to blows over the future policy of the company.

Much of the research I carried out was spread amongst a wide range of publications, legislation and other resources, but no single resource drew together all the desired information; hence the incentive to produce this publication.

For some, the additional administration and red tape of operating as a company are just too much. They look back to the days when they operated as a sole trader or partnership, when truly the bank balance was their money and nothing HMRC could do or say could stop them drawing a cheque for personal expenditure.

One memorable case involved an individual whose company made profits of about £180,000 per annum, with personal expenditure, funded by dividends, of only £30,000 per year; so, apparently, an ideal candidate for continued trading as a limited liability company. However, a single PAYE audit, where there were no adjustments except for an overdrawn director's loan account of only £150, was sufficient to decide the company's fate!

Despite the thrust of this publication, and despite much of the effort that we put into our professional work, not all clients are driven by tax. Some just want a quiet life, and if extra tax is the price to pay, then so be it. However, when it came to the crunch, even the client tipped over the edge by a PAYE audit required the dissolution to be tax efficient so, perhaps in truth, no single client can ever claim to be totally uninterested in the tax consequences of their actions.

1.2   There is much in the public domain as to the mechanisms for transferring a business to a company, see (for example) Roger Jones, *Incorporating a Business,* 3rd edn (Tottel Publishing), and the best approaches to achieve taxation advantage from that process. However, there is little available for advisers seeking to reverse the procedure. This process is just as important, certainly no less so, because the proceeds of a successful business, about to be dissolved, may be required to fund a new business, provide for retirement, or simply allow individuals to pursue their own interests. In all cases the maximisation of after-tax cash will be a primary requirement.

If a business can be sold, and a purchaser can be persuaded to acquire the company through a share sale, then much of this publication is redundant. From a client's perspective the sale of shares will be the best option. Equally, from a purchaser's perspective, they may not want the company because they cannot be certain that they will not be taking on responsibility for the sins of omission and commission of your client. The value of any warranty is only as strong as the financial capacity of the person who has given the warranty. Certainly within the writer's experience, when looking to enforce warranties, there has often been an obstacle to any claim being settled in full.

The legal costs of selling shares, warranties and due diligence, all of which are outside the scope of this publication, will in many cases more than outweigh the theoretical extra proceeds obtained by selling shares, as well as causing the death of a few trees. In these circumstances, it is usually the purchaser who has the whip hand; there are few well advised purchasers who will take the company on. Accordingly, the perspective of this publication is that, even assuming that a client can sell the trade, they will usually be left with dissolving the company in order to realise shareholder value.

Equally (unfortunately), there will be circumstances where the family company is no longer solvent and therefore may be forced into insolvent liquidation. Alternatively, the family may want to preserve the business by creating a new vehicle because they have the funds available to do so and want to achieve whatever taxation advantages are available.

We are used, as part of our professional lives, to simply considering the taxation values when undertaking tax planning, even if the tax value is supposed to be a commercial value. That is not wholly the case here. The taxation consequences within the company of asset sales will be based upon tax values that may or may not reflect the true commercial value. However, when considering the extent of any capital gains tax liability on shareholders, it is only the true commercial value that has an impact. It may be the taxation value that determines the corporation tax liability, but it will be the true market value of the assets (whether that value is determined by arm's length sale or negotiation) that is important. Here we are not dealing with a deemed value or even a value, as in share valuation, that is often so artificial that no one recognises the value as having any impact upon the real world. What we are looking at is the value that the company will realise. It is for this reason that emphasis is placed upon the impact of the actual balance sheet of the company, adjusting for the impact of any notional values that may have been used to achieve a tax credit or charge. One of my children's teachers was fond of saying 'you have to go out into the big wide world sometime'. Here the tax planning taken has real and particular consequences; it is not a case of holding over tax to a later date and putting the problems onto our successor. This is the big wide world and our advice will affect the tax and, therefore, the net proceeds ultimately received.

1.3   Inevitably, with the increased popularity of trading through the incorporated medium, there will be a corresponding increase in the number of companies that become surplus to requirements for a whole range of reasons. Just as we spend considerable professional time ensuring any new company trading structure is appropriate and tax efficient, so we should make sure that the escape route is equally properly structured. The shareholders may continue as clients so we should not simply assume they are a lost client with proceeds taxable as capital gains.

There are, in the writer's view, two main areas that need to be addressed in the dissolution process:

(i)   managing the financial position of the soon-to-be-dissolved company and ensuring that all relevant claims are made, both so far as corporation tax relief is concerned and in relation to other direct or indirect taxes, that may arise as a result of the dissolution process; and

(ii)   what impact does the decision to dissolve have upon the shareholders and the employees? For the most part, assuming (as this publication does) that the dissolution is a solvent arrangement, payments to shareholders can usually be treated as a capital payment subject to capital gains tax, and here we need to explore the interaction of the post-5 April 2008 CGT regime, entrepreneurs' relief, and the optimum time for a distribution to be made.

Equally, the cessation of a trading company may have an impact upon the inheritance tax position of the shareholders – 100% business property relief on a trading company whilst it continues, but perhaps no relief once trading has ceased or when the proceeds are distributed as a bundle of assets.

1.4   Other areas that should be reviewed include the process by which the company is dissolved and the arrangements for removing the company from the Registrar of Companies database. The timing of these arrangements can have an impact upon the taxation position, as well as costs, so we need to ensure that our timing is appropriate.

This publication sets out a number of appendices, including relevant statutory matters, a number of precedents (including a checklist of matters to be addressed) as well as an extended case study that draws together a number of the main issues discussed. The case study, although based upon a number of cases the writer has dealt with, has been modified both to protect the innocent (or the guilty) but also to hopefully draw out the principles involved, and is designed to cover a typical example encountered in practice without the marginal complications.

1.5   Therefore, the underlying premise of this publication is that we are dealing with a company that is solvent, or at the very least solvent enough to allow the shareholders the possibility that they will receive a return on their share investment. Where, as is occasionally the case, an apparently solvent company turns out to be insolvent then the relevant issues are touched upon (see para **2.29** and **2.33**). However, a detailed review of the custom and practice of insolvency, the steps undertaken by insolvency practitioners and the taxation of insolvent companies is outside the scope of this publication.

Inevitably with any publication, a number of conventions have to be adopted in order to avoid an excess of either/or computations. As a general rule, unless the stated circumstances indicate otherwise, the following are basic assumptions:

- all capital gains realised are in respect of post-5 April 2008 gains that, unless otherwise indicated, are subject to tax at 18%;

- any income receipts are taxed at higher rates;

- the annual CGT exempt amount is £9,600 (2008/2009);

- fees to the Registrar of Companies are as at 1 July 2008;

- the law is as stated at 1 July 2008 but includes relevant matters published in Finance Act 2008.

1.6   There will have been a range of reasons why individuals established a company and, until now, were content to allow trading to continue through such a structure. Such arrangements may have been instigated for the following reasons:

- the business is long established, and when grandfather set it up there were advantages to the company structure;

- the enterprise was high-risk, so some limited liability protection was required, ignoring personal guarantees; where the business sector is very competitive or subject to technological change or fashion, this could be the structure of choice;

- everyone in my industry trades as a company, so people will not give me work unless I trade as a company – for some, this is the only incentive to have a company;

- a limited company sounds like a more impressive structure than a sole trader; customers may believe your business is more important than the reality indicates; in some industries, appearance is everything;

- I want to be a company director (even though whenever the writer sees the description applied in the local press, the description sometimes has the appearance of being slightly less than reputable);

- the structure provides a better method to assist the company obtaining credit because financial institutions are able to take security in a stronger form, perhaps by way of a debenture over the whole of a company's assets; this may be particularly important where the promoter has few personal assets to provide security;

- there are some taxation advantages; in recent times a dominant objective for many small businesses, although it must be acknowledged that, equally, there can be taxation disadvantages;

- a company may be able to put more funds into a director's pension fund than can the equivalent sole trader/partner; assuming pension provision is considered worthwhile.

- assets can in part be passed down to a younger generation without the present owners losing control by, for example, retaining at least 51% of voting shares or transferring some shares to a trust where the donor is a trustee. Giving someone a share in a partnership gives them more theoretical power as well as responsibility – although if the partnership is substantial, the scope for independent action may be restricted by the partnership deed.

Other publications deal with the move from sole trader (or partnership) to company. In this publication it is assumed that, for whatever reason, the company is no longer required and the assets are to be distributed; that may be on cessation of trade, or to restart as a sole trader or partnership. Accordingly, unless referred to specifically within the text, it is assumed that maximising the value distributed to shareholders is the primary concern. On this occasion, taxation is the primary driver.

1.7   The usual underlying approach within this publication is that the dissolving family company is solvent and, accordingly, that the shareholders are seeking methods by which the assets available to them can be maximised through:

- minimising the administration costs;

- minimising the tax costs in the company before distribution;

- maximising the expenditure eligible for corporation tax relief;

- reducing the shareholder's personal tax on any proceeds distributed; and

- achieving what the client wants.

1.8   Each situation will require specific analysis, but the three typical scenarios that are examined here are:

- the termination of the trade and the sale of the residual assets;

- the sale of the trade to an unconnected third party; or

- the disincorporation of the trade into a sole trader/partnership but essentially under the same ownership.

Where relevant, the application of company law and tax law to the different circumstances envisaged will be made, as well as comment on commercial best practice and other factors that may be considered relevant. The process of disincorporation is not exclusively a tax driven exercise, although that is important. Of equal or perhaps greater value is the management of the transaction, ensuring that matters are dealt with promptly and that administrative delay or inertia (an assumption that once the business ceases matters of timing are of no importance) must be avoided.

There are many circumstances where 'professional experience' is often of more assistance than a detailed review of tax or company law. Those elements are important, but the techniques indicated here are not exclusive to the disincorporation of the family company. They are likely to apply to a range of circumstances, but this publication seeks to use those techniques in a particular direction. Equally, there is no single tax element that overrides other considerations. The process of dissolving the family company begins from consideration of the latest published accounts and seeks to review the progress of the business from those accounts through to the distribution of cash or assets to the shareholders. In the majority of cases, we attempt to undertake this in a controlled manner so that events take place at our bidding rather than allowing events to dictate the pace. It is for this reason that establishing a timetable at the very outset is regarded as an essential tool. Not only does a timetable set expectations, but it also gives the appearance of control and, importantly, the timetable can be adjusted as events conspire to affect the smooth progress of the dissolution. As Harold Macmillan once said in relation to politics, the most dangerous force was 'events, dear boy, events', and so it is here that a timetable should allow control to be introduced at each stage of the process.

1.9   Equally, there will be circumstances where the dissolving of the family company does not take place in a controlled environment, where once there were funds or assets available to distribute to the company shareholders, but instead the company has sustained such losses that it is forced to cease trading and the company is dissolved either under a creditor's voluntary winding-up or under a compulsory winding-up. This publication does not address taxation issues relating to the consequences of insolvent liquidation except to the extent that consideration of the circumstances is relevant to the taxation position of shareholders.

However, if a company is dissolved with the result that shareholders and directors do not, or cannot, recover monies originally invested, there is included in Chapter 4 an overview of the areas where relief can be obtained for any losses made and the circumstance in which some tax relief (for which much thanks) can be obtained to ease the loss of asset value.

Dissolving the family company requires an interaction of income tax, capital gains tax and corporation tax as well as VAT. All these can, and do, reduce the funds available to the shareholders. Equally, proper appreciation of the issues can ensure that tax costs are managed to the benefit of the company and its shareholders, with the consequence that the available funds are not diminished but improved. However, tax is not the only answer. There are company law issues to be properly addressed to ensure that costs do not reappear many years later, perhaps because creditors come to light that had been conveniently forgotten in the hope that they would go away (see para **2.20**).

Within the writer's experience, many creditors cannot tell the difference between a solvent and an insolvent liquidation – the description liquidation is enough to trigger the assumption that all is lost. Clients should not use the confusion to ignore genuine claims. Equally, if we are assisting the directors, our procedures should ensure that we identify all the areas. Included in Appendix 8 is an extensive checklist of matters that require attention (drawing on their own experiences, many may wish to include other matters in this list). Using a checklist will assist dialogue with the client and identify areas of concern. Inevitably any sins of omission or commission undertaken by the client will be placed at our door because we will have access to funds; the shareholders relied upon our expertise and have spent the distribution. We should treat the dissolution process in exactly the same way as we approach any other professional project. To assume that all we are doing is acting as undertakers and that our omissions will also be quietly buried invites problems arising to haunt both us and the directors/shareholders.

Equally, there is the need to be aware of accounting issues and the impact of accounting adjustments upon value distributed. Just because an item of income or expenditure is either not taxable or not tax deductible does not mean that the particular item has no impact upon the value distributed. Part of this publication concentrates upon minimising the tax and administration costs within the company, but once that process has been completed we then proceed to tax the proceeds distributed to shareholders, which may or may not have featured in the taxation process.

Our training and skills are often directed at the taxation values of a transaction whether that is a transfer between connected parties or when considering capital gains tax computations. After all, the 31 March 1982 CGT value has no commercial significance to our clients unless, coincidentally, that was the day the company started. The date is merely one of a number of artificial elements that we build into our calculations. Whilst minimising the tax payable is one important element of the work that we undertake, it is only *one element*. What is of equal importance is maximising the proceeds of sale and telling the clients how much they can expect to receive. If we know how, but cannot tell the clients how much, then we have achieved only part of the transaction. Whilst we may derive satisfaction from the elegance of a technical tax point, what drives our clients is how much is left and what they can spend.

Accordingly, the matters dealt with here are more than simply a review of the technical issues involved, important though they may be. What is also important is to grasp the commercial realities of the process and to adjust the company accounts both for tax charges and real changes in value, so that the calculations we prepare accurately show the true amount of cash that the shareholders can expect to receive. Not just how, but how much.

1.10   In the case of a company that has ceased to be required (either because the trade has been sold or because the trade has ceased and the assets sold off), the shareholder proceeds should simply be the cash available in the company bank account. However, in circumstances where the trade is to be disincorporated and perhaps resumed under common ownership, we need to be aware of the connected party rules of ITA 2007, ss 993–994 (formerly ICTA 1988, s 839). The value that is distributed to the shareholders is never likely to be the balance sheet value of the assets, which almost certainly will not reflect current value, either because assets have not been revalued or depreciated under conventional accounting procedures, or are simply not shown in the balance sheet. Typical examples will include:

- freehold or leasehold property;

- plant and machinery;

- intangible assets, including goodwill, know how or patent rights, where these have been developed in house;

- stock and work-in-progress;

The issue of whether a phoenix sole trader/partnership will trigger a charge under ITA 2007, s 682 onwards (formerly ICTA 1988, s 703) on assets distributed from a predecessor company is discussed at para **5.17**.

PROVISIONS AND DEFERRED INCOME

1.11   When assessing the value that is likely to be distributed to the shareholders, care needs to be taken to consider in detail the balance sheet of the company and the impact of cessation of trade. Often included within the accounts of a limited company will be the following:

- deferred taxation;

- provisions for liabilities, guarantees and similar where the expense has not yet been incurred;

- deferred income where monies have been received from customers but the payment represents a service to be given over perhaps a 12 -month period.

When assessing the value of the balance sheet, and hence the potential distribution to any individual shareholder, any items that do not represent true and immediate liabilities, such as deferred taxation, will not be a deduction in calculating the value of the company distributed to the shareholders. But, equally, just because an asset is not immediately disclosed on the published balance sheet does not mean that there is no addition to the value of the company. Goodwill is just as much an asset to be reflected in the company value as the vans or stock. As indicated elsewhere, cash and assets are king.

Also, any amounts of income deferred, for whatever reason, if they do not have to be repaid to customers or paid over to any trade successor, will be taxable as income. The amounts will be taxable on the last day of trading so, again, an unexpected credit – net of any tax charge – may impact upon the amount of funds available for distribution. A typical company with deferred income might well be a refrigeration engineer or perhaps a security alarm maintenance provider, who collects annual service charges but where the company's year-end is not coincidental with the year-end of the service charge.

Example

Docking Ltd services security alarms and ceased to trade on 31 October 2008 when the alarms business was sold to a competitor. At the last balance sheet date of 30 June 2008 there was deferred income of £25,000 representing the unexpired portion of service contracts and, at 31 October 2008, the company paid £10,000 to the successor business to take over the contracts. The difference of £15,000 will represent income earned in the final accounting period.

1.12   As a general proposition, the valuation of assets, when distributed to shareholders, has to be at current market value. Therefore, in any shareholder CGT computation, this is the value that has to be used. To simply assume that the balance sheet values represent the appropriate tax value is to invite enquiry. Accordingly, when contemplating a shareholder distribution, we need to review the entire balance sheet, not only to ensure that full provision has been made for known liabilities and provisions (see para **3.9**) but also that all assets are stated at their current value. This may well result in costs being incurred with valuers, estate agents and others, but represent costs that have to be incurred if unacceptable and unexpected tax charges are to be avoided. When preparing accounts for clients, we have to ensure that they show a true and fair view, but that is a concept that can represent a very flexible approach to both value and creditor provisions. Where a company is ongoing, we are often prepared to accept that a variation of up to perhaps 20% in asset value (simply because too much or too little depreciation has no impact upon tax) as well as an understating or overstating of profit by a range that professional experience says is not material in the particular facts of the case (the extent of the range depending upon the size and financial strength of the company) but which still allows us to say that the accounts show a true and fair view. Such a view may not be accepted by HMRC, where, in the writer's experience, amounts as small as £1,000 in a company with profits of £500,000 were disputed, but the alignment of tax law and practice with generally accepted accounting principles should produce a narrowing to areas of dispute. The valuation of many items in a set of accounts are matters of judgement and the writer's assessment of the strength or weakness of any particular factor influencing the valuation will be different to everyone else's but since the effect of alternative views is merely to accelerate or defer a tax liability from one year to another, the practical effect is (in most cases) incidental. Some tax inspectors might take a different view, but now that taxation computations are supposed to reflect normal accounting conventions, this should be less of a problem. However, there is still a widespread belief that 'true and fair' means 'correct' and this can and does cause conflict with the regulators.

However, when contemplating a distribution to shareholders when a company is to be dissolved, we need to assess the balance sheet in a proper manner so that there is evidence of the values chosen that ultimately lead towards the shareholder CGT computation. Some values can be agreed by the company under the CG34 procedure because they will trigger a capital gain in the company's computation, but other values need to be supported by sensible computations and may also need to be agreed by shareholders. If the same values impact upon several shareholders then it may save time and professional fees if the values can be agreed by a single agent. Even if the values are challenged, so long as there is evidence of care being taken to

9

calculate the value used, the scope for HMRC being able to impose significant penalties may be reduced.

The CG34 procedure, post-transaction valuation checks for capital gains allows a taxpayer or their adviser to submit to HMRC a draft capital gains tax computation and to agree, where the computation includes estimated or unknown values, those values in advance of any taxation liability becoming payable. It is the intention that the valuations should be agreed after the transaction has been completed but before any tax becomes payable.

Values that might be disputed will include 31 March 1982 value, an acquisition value where the assets were acquired by way of gift and at acquisition both donor and donee elected for the SP8/92 procedure to avoid negotiating values at that time, or the disposal value depends upon agreeing the market value of assets transferred to connected parties that may in part comprise the disposal proceeds.

The process begins by completing form CG34, which is available from the HMRC website, which requires disclosure of the identity of the taxpayer, the date of disposal, the purpose for the valuation and an indication as to the assets that have to be valued. In addition, there is a checklist that requires submission of a number of supporting documents, including a capital gains tax computation, copies of any valuation reports and any land valuations that are available. Once the documents have been submitted, HMRC will then consider the values proposed and either agree the suggested values or begin the process of negotiation through either the District Valuer or Shares Valuation.

Statement of Practice 8/92 allows donor and donee to avoid having to negotiate a disposal value where, because a claim for holdover relief has been made, there will be no tax at stake. It saves the taxpayers costs of agreeing a value that has no immediate impact and it also assists HMRC in not having to allocate resources to agree a value that is not going to immediately produce revenue.

If you have not acted for the company for the whole of its history then, again, care will need to be taken in regard to values. Clients will have no record, or will conveniently forget that the 31 March 1982 value was actually negotiated in 1989 and that this affects current tax planning. The local tax district may have had a record but this will now be in archive and take considerable research to find. Equally, the previous agents will have shredded their old files. In practice the only reliable source of historical data is likely to be the District Valuer or Shares Valuation. Time and professional costs can be saved by a timely telephone call to the relevant office to obtain details of any previously agreed values.

Therefore, we need to prepare a notional balance sheet when dissolution is in prospect that shows the expected out-turn to shareholders with all assets and liabilities shown at current values, wherever possible supporting those values by either external professional valuations or by internally generated values that are within our competence. This needs to be prepared soon after the decision to dissolve the company is taken and copies provided to the directors. If there are shareholders who are not involved in the day-to-day management of the business then consideration should be given as to whether that information, or at least an executive summary, is issued. Care must be taken not to be over optimistic and, where matters are in dispute, it is prudent to take the pessimistic view. We all spend what we anticipate we will receive and this situation is no different. Accordingly, any significant variables should be disclosed unless to do so may impact upon any litigation or informal negotiations or values that might be realised. The decision to disclose will remain that of the directors. They retain responsibility for the company and have to satisfy their responsibilities. However much we think we know how our clients operate, we cannot know the true commercial practices. Therefore, the decision to keep minority shareholders informed rests with the directors. The writer's view is that, wherever possible, disclosure should be made, but if it is not then both we and the directors need to document the decision.

1.13   As matters progress, the notional balance sheet at the anticipated distribution date needs to be updated regularly to reflect additional tax payable and fluctuations in realised value, whether from higher or lower proceeds or from additional costs. Care should be taken to preserve each intermediate step, particularly if interim distributions are based upon intermediate accounts. Equally, any impact of any sale to connected parties at less than market value needs to be known so that adjustment can be made back to open market value. Occasionally, shareholders will agree a value between themselves for distribution purposes, but adjustment still needs to be made for the true value in all tax computations.

Consider the following circumstances where the trade ceases but a connected party resumes the trade.

Example

Walsingham Ltd is to be disincorporated and managed by its shareholders as a partnership and, at the date of disincorporation, the published balance sheet shows the following position.

Fixed assets	30,000
Current assets	
Stock	14,000
Debtors	10,000
Cash at bank	30,000
	54,000
Current liabilities	
Trade creditors	20,000
Net current assets	34,000
Shareholders funds	64,000

The application of ITA 2007, ss 993–994 (formerly ICTA 1988, s 839) means that £64,000 is unlikely to be the value that falls to be used in any appropriate CGT computation so far as the shareholders are concerned, equally the published values will not affect the company's corporation tax position. We need to look beyond the accounting values to assess the open market value of the business. A review of the balance sheet shows the following.

Within fixed assets, the book values and market values are:

	Book value	Market value
Plant and machinery	£10,000	£16,000
Freehold	£20,000	£50,000

For all other currently disclosed assets, the accounting and current values are identical.

However, the directors of Walsingham Ltd recently received an offer for the business, which valued it at £150,000 ie £64,000 being balance sheet value plus the increased fixed asset values of £36,000 plus goodwill of £50,000. The offer was turned down by the directors because they believed the offer to be too low. They arranged for the family lawyer to dismiss the offer in precisely those terms and a copy of that letter resides in your files. Therefore, the value to be distributed to shareholders, reflecting current market values could, as a minimum, be restated as follows:

Fixed assets	66,000
Goodwill	50,000
	116,000
Current assets	
Stock	14,000
Debtors	10,000
Cash at bank	30,000
	54,000
Current liabilities	
Trade creditors	20,000
Net current assets	34,000
Shareholders funds	150,000

As already indicated elsewhere, it is not sufficient to simply look at the balance sheet values and assume that those same values will apply on any subsequent disincorporation. The provisions of ITA 2007, ss 993–994 apply equally here as they would in any transaction between related parties. Given the existence of the lawyer's letter, the directors must consider if the restated balance sheet is reliable or whether a further uplift is required. It may be that the directors have an inflated view of the company's value, but whatever value is to be used it must be documented and include an assessment of all known factors.

It is not enough just to look at the values of assets, although they are likely to be the main items on the balance sheet where the published value is unlikely to be the market value. Most accounts for companies that have been trading for some years will include within the balance sheet a number of provisions against anticipated liabilities or falls in value or, more conveniently, because a provision was required to reduce the taxable profit. Surely not, but the writer has seen examples even in the case of subsidiaries of quoted companies where the only purpose of a provision was to suppress profit because the preliminary consolidation showed that the profits expected by the Stock Exchange had been exceeded. Provisions for bad debts, fall in value of stock to the director's assessment of net realisable value and for liabilities that may or may not be contingent, all need to be reviewed and a fresh assessment made of the required provision. Some will be increased, others may no longer be relevant so need to be written back. Such adjustments may affect the value available to the shareholders, either positively or negatively, but will also affect the tax position of the company.

As a first step, the effect of provision adjustments must be reflected in the revised balance sheet at cessation of trade and, in line with other realisations, the revised provisions adjusted as more information becomes available as the assets are realised.

1.14   However, it would not end there. Any revaluation of assets to open market value has an impact upon both the tax position of the company (considered in Chapter 3) and on those of the shareholders (where the impact is discussed in Chapter 6). It is no use ignoring increases in value that will increase the tax cost of disincorporation simply to satisfy the client. The balance sheet provided needs to be critically reviewed, certainly where the trade is transferred, that market value must be assessed.

Although much of this publication will concentrate upon matters relating to trading companies because for most practitioners such companies represent the average company dealt with, nevertheless, some investment companies may wish to disincorporate and again, where relevant, separate issues are considered.

1.15   Disincorporation of a solvent company can be dealt with in one of two methods.

(i)   The company passing a resolution to be wound-up under the terms of a member's voluntary winding-up, which results in the appointment of a liquidator who has to be a licensed insolvency practitioner.

Not every firm will have such a practitioner in house so there may be a reluctance to use this route, the costs of which are discussed at para **2.30**, but within the writer's experience if the formal procedures are required, many licensed insolvency practitioners are happy to allow the instructing accountant to undertake much of the routine administration, to reduce costs, with only the formalities being dealt with by the duly appointed liquidator.

(ii)   Dissolving the company under Companies Act 2006, ss 1000–1002 (formerly Companies Act 1985, ss 652), and Companies Act 2006, ss 1003–1011 (formerly CA 1985, ss 652A–652F), by application to the Registrar of Companies and payment of the modest (currently £10) fee coupled with an application to HMRC for confirmation that ESC C16 will apply to allow distributions to shareholders to be treated as capital payments.

1.16   As will be seen later at paras **6.10** and **6.12** onwards, there may be circumstances in which full capital status is not appropriate. In some circumstances allowing for higher rate tax on income distributions a combination of partial capital elements (to use up annual CGT exemptions) – is a more favourable option.

1.17   This publication continues to refer to 'the ss 652, 652A procedure', notwithstanding we are now governed by Companies Act 2006, on the basis that most practitioners will still refer to the scheme in that way. The ss 652, 652A procedure has the advantage that professional costs are much reduced, as compared with formal liquidation, but the procedure has some disadvantages under company law (see para **5.27**). However, for many small companies this route will be the procedure of choice simply because there is no desire to spend funds on the payment of a liquidator where the perception of risk is reduced because the directors should know what has happened within the company.

The position may be different for larger companies where, in any event, the liquidator's fees should be a smaller proportion of any distribution. Perhaps where the business has been organised on semi-autonomous division lines, where the directors have historically trusted the local managers, there will be greater risk because matters can be hidden away and only occasionally surface in auditing scandals. In such cases the main board may be unaware of the detail and cannot say that they are aware of all known creditors; it may then be more appropriate to use the liquidation route to gain the added protection that is available. The liquidation route may also be more appropriate in a group situation for the same reasons, where the subsidiaries have been managed by local managers.

If the ss 652, 652A procedure is to be adopted within groups where the holding company directors also control the subsidiaries, it may be possible to close down the subsidiaries and to distribute the reserves up to the holding company by way of inter-group dividend to avoid any CGT on any excess above holding company CGT base cost and then have the now dormant subsidiaries struck off. In this circumstance, care will be required particularly where the holding company does not trade and is merely the holding company of a trading group because once the last trading subsidiary has gone, the group is no longer trading which may impact upon the availability of entrepreneurs' relief.

1.18   The choice of procedure needs to be carefully considered (see discussion at para **2.22** onwards). The decision taken must be made by the client, who may be guided by us, but must not be taken by us, simply because as advisers we know that our preferred option is the one the client would choose. Most accountants and tax advisers believe that they know how their client's business works but, in practice, rarely do. We see the snapshots our clients allow us to see when the annual records are produced. They will not reflect the commercial reality of operating the business. Sometimes we are told more information than we really want and certainly, following the changes to the money laundering rules, the flow of information is likely to significantly reduce. However, in most cases it seems, within the writer's experience, that we are told less than we need to understand how the business works. The extra knowledge the directors have must be used to determine the correct dissolution process.

1.19 As always in any review, taxation is not the only answer. There are a range of tax and commercial requirements to be considered and reviewed before the disincorporation process decision is taken. If the situation is that the business is to be sold to an independent third party or simply discontinued, the review of the available options may simply concentrate on maximising the distribution to the shareholders.

1.20 If, however, the company aiming to disincorporate is doing so just to achieve a perceived future tax saving, perhaps in much the same way as they rushed to incorporate a few years ago, then separate review and assessment criteria are required.

To a considerable extent, the tax cost of incorporation can be controlled either by capital gains tax holdover or planning the date of cessation and claiming appropriate reliefs. But the reverse process has no such parachute to ease the tax cost. Perhaps that is the correct statutory approach, implying that the choice of business structure should not be determined simply by any short-term advantage.

In much the same way as we undertake risk assessment for clients entering a corporate structure (because we know from their sole trader/partnership days that the basis upon which they use the business is as a personal piggy bank, but in that situation the tax consequences are not too onerous) so risk assessment is required for the reverse process. However, that attitude applied to a corporate vehicle is a recipe for uncontrollable and unpredictable tax charges. Wherever possible, we try to instil in our clients a sense of responsibility and provide guidelines to be adopted. Therefore, if a client is proposing to disincorporate then our assessment of the procedures should be equally formal and any assessment of tax costs should not be on the basis of an optimistic valuation but on a reasonable and reliable basis.

DISTRIBUTING THE CASH

1.21 Elsewhere in this publication, detailed consideration has been given to the taxation consequences and the tax planning opportunities of distributions to shareholders. No company's accounting records are immediately accurate, perhaps because suppliers are slow in sending invoices or because returns from branches are late. As part of the normal accounts process, we are used to examining after-date transactions to establish assets and liabilities that arise after the year end. This process can impact here and therefore (as part of the dissolution management process) when distributing cash to shareholders, it is generally desirable to retain some cash against the possibility of additional or unknown

15

creditors coming forward. Certainly, sensible management would say that too early a distribution of funds may well result in having to ask shareholders to refund cash to meet outstanding liabilities.

1.22 It is not possible to suggest a standard percentage of the funds to be held back, rather it will be a matter for judgement based upon the size of the company, the evidence that is available of known creditors and an assessment of the accounting skills of the directors. If a company deals with a few major suppliers then, perhaps, the reserved cash can be relatively low in relation to the overall assets of the company, whereas if the directors are always chasing discounts and use a high number of suppliers then a more conservative approach to cash balances may be appropriate. It would be appropriate for the directors to assess the amount of cash required and to ensure that the cash reserve is placed on deposit for the appropriate length of time. Just as there is no simple formula for calculating the cash balance so there is no simple formula for determining the length of time that it might be appropriate to hold the cash balance before it is distributed to the shareholders.

FINANCE ACT 2004

1.23 Many small businesses were incorporated in the pre-Finance Act 2004 frenzy, so it may help to review the position that existed prior to 17 March 2004. No one should have changed their business structure simply because they might save a small amount of tax, but many traders, encouraged by the 0% corporation tax rate and no further tax on dividends (provided you were a basic rate taxpayer) transformed their window-cleaning round, their mobile hairdressers or even their tax advisory business into 'Basic Rate Avoidance Limited'.

Example

By way of illustration and comparison, let us consider the case of Joanna who operated a ladies hairdresser's business and made profits of £14,615 (ie £10,000 + 2003/2004 personal allowance). As a sole trader, her 2003/2004 tax position was:

Profits	14,615
Less Personal allowance	4,615
	10,000
1,960 @ 10%	196.00
8,040 @ 22%	1,768.80
	1,964.80
Class 4 (14,615 – 4,615 @ 8%)	800.00
Total due	2,764.80

Assuming the same position for 'Basic Rate Avoidance Limited', the position might have been, for 2003/2004:

Profits	14,615
Less Salary	4,615
Profit distributed as dividend	10,000

Corporation tax of £0 (£10,000 × 0%) to achieve a tax saving of £2,764.80 from which were deducted the additional costs of operating a company – which might be between £500 and £1,000 – to produce a cash saving of (say) £1,750.

As a result of the Finance Act 2004 changes, the personal position for 2004/05 would remain broadly unchanged as follows:

Profits	14,615
Less Personal allowance	4,745
	9,870
2,020 @ 10%	202.00
7,850 @ 22%	1,727.00
	1,929.00
Class 4 (14,615 – 4,745 @ 8%)	789.60
Total due	2,718.60

But the company position might have been as follows, with the profits available for distribution reduced to £8,404 using up all the available profit:

Profits	14,615
Less Salary	4,745
Profit	9,870
Dividend	8,294
Minimum tax charge 19%	1,576
	9,870

As a sole trader, the after-tax cash in 2004/05 might have been £11,897 (£14,615 – £2,718), but as a company the after-tax cash is £13,039 (£8,294 + £4,745); even at this level there is still a margin to be made – not as much as there was before 17 March 2004, but certainly enough to persuade Joanna to remain a company.

1.24 At a more typical level in 2008/09, say profits of £26,035, the position would now be:

Profits	26,035
Less Personal allowance	6,035
	20,000
20,000 @ 20%	4,000.00
Class 4 (26,035 - 5,435 @ 8%)	1,648.00
Total due	5,648.00

Assuming the same profit level for 'Basic Rate Avoidance Limited', the corporation tax position might now be:

Profits	26,035
Less Salary	5,460
Profit	20,575
Dividend	16,254
Tax charge at 21%	4,321
	20,575

As a sole trader, the after-tax cash was £20,387 (£26,035 – £5,648), but as a company the after-tax cash is £21,754 (£16,254 + £5,460), therefore there is still a margin of £1,367 to be made. This is not as much as the saving was in 2003/04, but probably still enough to cover the costs of a company. Certainly there is not enough to justify the costs of disincorporation.

1.25   It would seem that at very low profit levels current less favourable corporation tax regime has not provoked a rush to disincorporation; rather a slowing down in the numbers of incorporations, although for most businesses a limited company still seems the medium of choice even without any tax advantages but, as indicated above, there still remains some advantage in operating as a limited company. Therefore, in the great majority of cases, the factors that influence disincorporation are likely to be the same factors that have always influenced clients:

● the business is to be sold;

● the trade has come to an end; or

● there is no longer a commercial justification for the company.

1.26   Whatever combination of arrangements is undertaken to distribute cash or assets, or a combination thereof, reliable calculations need to be prepared so that the full tax cost of any action can be assessed and the shareholders are aware of the amount they might expect to receive. Equally, timing of the cessation of trade and distributions needs to be explored – a lower CGT cost will arise from two separate capital distributions either side of 5 April, rather than a full distribution in one year, because extra annual CGT-exempt amounts will be available, and wherever possible the higher distribution should be made after 5 April rather than before because there will be a greater period of credit before the majority of any CGT is paid (a gain from interest on investment of that part of the distribution to be paid over).

1.27   Within these parameters this publication seeks to address the available tax mitigation techniques, as well as administrative matters, to ensure that any proposed disincorporation is dealt with in an appropriate manner. However, it is also clear that, as always, direct tax should not be the only factor that has to be taken into account. Subsequent chapters review not only direct tax consequences but also indirect (VAT and some stamp duty and stamp duty land tax matters) as well as accountancy and

Companies Act issues. Agreeing the tax values are only the first steps in a process that requires a detailed review and assessment of the impact of those first steps, as well as future actions, on the cash that shareholders may receive from the dissolution of their company.

Throughout this publication the term 'dissolution' is used as convenient shorthand for the process of dissolving a company under either a formal liquidation or under the informal ss 652, 652A procedure, unless otherwise stated.

OPENING THE FILE

1.28   Dissolving the family company is a microcosm of all the factors that we generally need to take into account when dealing with any matters with our client. There are time limits for actions, taxation opportunities change with either delay or progress, and the client wants matters dealt with now. Whilst the company plods on from year to year the value of its assets, other than as a base from which income is generated, is often of academic interest but once the prospect of available personal cash is in sight then a different set of concerns applies.

This process has few hard and fast rules that do not apply elsewhere but (and it is a big 'but') there is no opportunity to put right next year what went wrong in last year's accounts. Here we are dealing with the last year. We need to be aware of the process, make sure matters are dealt with in the correct way, or if a decision is made to short cut, that all parties are aware of the impact. However, it is more than a simple application of a few taxation rules. There are a range of skills and processes that require mastering. Within some firms, accounting, taxation, Companies Act compliance and VAT will be dealt with by separate individuals. In other firms, it's just you. The aim of this publication is to indicate that the process is an organic whole where nothing can be considered in isolation. Every action produces a reaction – sometimes helpful, sometimes not – but solutions to most areas that will be encountered are set out here.

PLANNING POINTS

1.29

- Make sure the balance sheet at the planning stage reflects true values, not values that are accounting-convenient.

- Consider all aspects of the business to ensure the correct result for the shareholders.

- Prepare a detailed timetable of expected events: who is to deal with them and the reporting obligations.

- Assess the nature of the trade, potential liabilities and value of available assets to decide if formal liquidation or the concession route is to be preferred.

- Consider if there is sufficient margin in the available assets to be confident that the company will remain solvent throughout the process.

- Make sure that all shareholders support the required actions.

- Do not dissolve the company as a knee-jerk reaction to any apparently adverse tax changes. Tax should not have been the answer when incorporating; it should not be the answer now.

Chapter 2

Companies Act and Registrar of Companies formalities

2.1   When a company is to disappear, and it is proposed to distribute the assets to the shareholders, the proprietors of a private company have two options available to them. They can either make use of HMRC ESC C16 in conjunction with Companies Act 2006, ss 1000–1002 (formerly CA 1985, s 652) and Companies Act 2006, ss 1003–1011 (formerly CA 1985, ss 652A–652F), which operate as an informal basis, or a formal liquidation involving the appointment of an insolvency practitioner to act as liquidator.

HMRC procedures for the informal route are quite straightforward and are set out at para **5.3** below. Any company that has ceased trading can make the application on Form 652a to the Registrar of Companies by paying the appropriate fee. The circumstances in which this might be appropriate include:

- the trade has been sold to a third party and the shareholders require funds;

- funds were subscribed in anticipation of developing a trade, but upon enquiry the trade never developed and the shareholders want the residue of their monies back; or

- the owners of the business no longer wish to trade as a limited company and wish the assets to be transferred to them personally.

2.2   The application to the Registrar of Companies cannot be made until the company has stopped trading for at least three months (as indicated at para 5.3 the requirement of ESC C16 are different), but the Registrar of Companies does give some guidance as to circumstances in which trading no longer applies. The sale of trading stock would be regarded as continuing to trade, whereas the sale of assets used in the trade would not extend the trading period. Therefore, a Companies Act application cannot be made until all trading stock is sold, but assets do not have to be sold before the application is made. Care would be required in this circumstance to avoid the possibility that the company is struck off before all the assets are sold and distributed, with the result that ownership passes *bona vacantia* to the Treasury. Extremely detailed advice as to the application of the *bona vacantia* rules are set out in the Treasury Bona Vacantia website at www.bonavacantia.gov.uk.

Prudence would suggest that no Companies Act application is made until the major assets of plant and machinery and land and buildings have been sold. If restoration then becomes a requirement this is an expensive process (see para **2.24**); certainly the six-month period between receipt of the paperwork by the Registrar of Companies and dissolution can quickly pass if the company is waiting to sell land. If urgency is truly required then perhaps the earliest that Form 652a is submitted should be when property contracts are exchanged where completion is within the six-month window. However, since this is an administrative process, it is difficult to imagine how or why dissolution would be required early.

Certainly we should make sure that all assets are sold, and all cash distributed, before the formal dissolution takes place. A review would also be appropriate no more than one month before the dissolution date.

Historically there always was a suggestion that there was a conflict between company law and tax law in relation to issued share capital (and other undistributable reserves) that may pass *bona vacantia* to the Treasury. A discussion of the issues is included at para **5.27** onwards. If the share capital is nominal, the concerns may not be of any practical importance, but where the issued share capital exceeds £4,000 then further advance planning will be required.

REGISTRAR OF COMPANIES FORMALITIES

2.3   Once all the assets are distributed to shareholders, the company is then dissolved under Companies Act 2006, ss 1000–1002 (formerly CA 1985, s 652) and Companies Act 2006, ss 1003–1011 (formerly CA 1985, ss 652A–652F) (or any comparable provisions) after application to the Registrar of Companies using Form 652a and after paying the required fee (currently £10). The company is treated as dissolved six months after the Registrar of Companies application; the company receiving notice about 14 days before the date of dissolution; at this time the process is irreversible.

2.4   The Form 652a application preferably needs to be signed by all directors, although a majority signing is acceptable and also requires them to give broadly similar assurances as those that have to be given to HMRC. These are that the company has not in the three months prior to the application:

- traded or changed its name;

- sold assets that would normally be sold as part of the trading activities of the company;

- engaged in activities other than settling its affairs in preparation for dissolution; or

- been subjected to insolvency action.

2.5   In effect therefore, because of the requirement not to have traded for the previous three months, no action can be taken to dissolve the company until at least three months have elapsed from the date upon which trading ceased. This is generally not so important because this action has no impact upon the taxation consequences of any distribution to shareholders.

2.6   The Form 652a notice contains a warning that to complete the application knowing that it is false, perhaps with the intention of arranging for an insolvent company to be struck off in an attempt to avoid settling liabilities, is a criminal offence.

The Form 652a procedure is not a seamless process. If there are creditors who are unpaid or there are organisations who believe that there are outstanding matters that require to be dealt with then they can, and will, raise objection to the dissolution process. Once an objection is raised then the process is suspended until the objection is removed. Within the writer's experience HMRC are the usual objectors where, for example, statutory returns are outstanding or tax is currently unpaid.

When application is made to the Registrar of Companies to have the company struck off under the informal arrangements, the company gives the various undertakings as set out in para **2.4**.

WHEN THE FORM WILL BE REJECTED?

2.7   It would however seem apparent, judging by the standard letter of rejection that is issued by the dissolution section at Companies House, that there are at least four common circumstances in which the form is rejected.

- *Insufficient signatures* – A majority of the directors must sign. Therefore, if there are four directors then at least three must sign otherwise the form will be rejected.

    Provided the directors are all in agreement that the company is to be dissolved but, for whatever reason, a particular director is unavailable over an extended period to sign, then it may be appropriate for one or more directors to resign so that a majority of the remaining directors can sign and any delay waiting to obtain a majority is reduced. Curiously, although a director has to sign to indicate their consent that they are willing to act as a director, there is no corresponding requirement to confirm a wish to retire. If this option is chosen then Form 287b recording the necessary resignations must be filed before Form 652a so that the Companies House record shows the reduced number of directors.

    Therefore, you need to allow time for Form 287b to be placed in the public file. As a minimum, this is likely to be between six to seven working days. This is because the dissolution section that receives Form 652a then review the Companies House public record to ensure the form is signed by a majority of directors.

- *The form is incomplete* – It is difficult to imagine the circumstances where this may apply. Where the forms are submitted by professionals then there should be no excuse but, presumably, degrees of incompleteness include omitting the company number or indeed the company name.

- *No fee* – The form clearly states the required fee.

- *Faulty cheque* – By presumably sending an unsigned cheque.

Failing to deal with the preliminaries merely holds up the date of dissolution and therefore we should make sure that the routine administrative matters are dealt with without delay.

Example

Trimingham Ltd traded as furniture manufacturers and stopped taking orders on 30 June 2008 but continued to supply furniture to existing customers until 30 September 2008 when the company's freehold premises were offered for sale.

On 1 December 2008, the remaining stock and work-in-progress was sold and on 28 March 2009 the company's premises and vehicles were sold.

The three-month non-trading period could begin 1 December 2008, so application could be made on 1 February 2009. The subsequent sale of assets does not extend the trading period.

But if application were made on 1 February 2009 this would mean that the company is dissolved on or about 1 August 2009. At 1 February 2009, could the directors be certain the premises would be sold on 28 March?

2.8   It would be good practice for the directors, assuming that they are not shareholders, to advise a number of interested parties of the process. Certainly the company will not want interested parties objecting to the process simply because this would delay dissolving the company and, ultimately, may impact upon the capital gains position of the shareholders. Interested parties could include the following:

- *fellow directors* – if they form a minority of those who have not signed the form.

- *employees of the company* – in particular, if all the employees are to be made redundant sufficient notice must be given to avoid any claim for unfair dismissal (see para **3.16**).

2.9   General creditors (see para **2.12**), must be informed, but if this is a solvent dissolution it would also be prudent to send all known suppliers a letter with payment for any current balances setting out a cut-off date for supplies to be made to the company. The letter should be sent not only to current suppliers but also to suppliers used with the last 12 to 24 months so that the prospect for fraudulent orders from aggrieved employees is minimised.

2.10   The shareholders must be informed, although in close family arrangements there is unlikely to be any significant disparity between directors and shareholders. Occasionally, there will be a minority who play no part in the management of the company, perhaps because of family disputes. It is essential they are informed as otherwise there may be a risk that action could be taken for unfair prejudice – what before 1980 was known as 'oppression'. Such action, if taken by a minority, will result in costs to all parties, usually those causing the unfair prejudice. At the very least, such action will delay the dissolution process with the result that the consequences may spread further than merely resolving the company law issues. If the trade has already been sold, by the time any unfair prejudice action reaches the courts, the effect of any delay may result in all shareholders ending up paying more tax. The dissolution process is initiated by the directors because they sign the application to the Registrar of Companies, but any action should not be taken unless informed agreement has been obtained from the shareholders. Some shareholders may not want the company dissolved, even if its existing trade has ceased. They may have an alternative use for the company and may be prepared to pay the shareholders, who want to realise value for their shares, a higher price than can be achieved by dissolution.

2.11 All the relevant statutory authorities should be advised, including the relevant divisions of HMRC, Inland Revenue, Customs & Excise, and other parties, including trustees of the company pension scheme.

2.12 A copy of Form 652a must be provided to all interested parties (see above) within seven days of the form being submitted to the Registrar of Companies and, equally, a copy of the form must be submitted to anyone who becomes a creditor after the date of filing.

The photocopy of Form 652a is to be either posted to the creditor's address, if a partnership or sole trader, or to the registered office if the creditor is either a company or a partnership (including an LLP).The Registrar of Companies guidance says that you must also deliver a copy of the notice to every separate branch of suppliers that the dissolving company has had dealings with.

Example

Yaxham Ltd operated as builders, and purchased goods from Builders Merchants Ltd at their branches in Norwich, King's Lynn, Fakenham and Great Yarmouth.

The Form 652a was submitted to the Registrar of Companies on 7 October 2008, so a copy of the form will need to be sent to all the four branches mentioned before 14 October 2008.

ACKNOWLEDGEMENT FROM REGISTRAR

2.13 Provided the form is completed properly, the Registrar of Companies will send an acknowledgement to the address shown on the form. As a protection against fraudulent applications for dissolution, an acknowledgement will also be sent to the registered office if that is a different address.

It would be good practice to send a copy of that acknowledgement to the directors and the shareholders where different if the registered office is at the accountant's or solicitor's office. Simply keep all parties informed of the process.

CREDITOR OBJECTION

2.14   Any of the interested parties referred to in para **2.12** can object to the dissolution process by writing to the Registrar of Companies and, in doing so, are expected to provide evidence of their claim. If the objection is successful then the dissolution process will be suspended. In the writer's experience, the commonest objectors are HMRC, either Inland Revenue or Customs & Excise, either because there are outstanding returns or they believe that there is outstanding tax payable.

Other typical circumstances might include:

* a dissident director who does not want the company to be dissolved;

* a creditor who has not been paid, if the company is in dispute with any creditor where, typically, the creditor will be claiming more than the company wants to pay – then these disputes must be resolved otherwise there is a risk of objection to the dissolution process;

* the company has become subject to formal insolvency proceedings.

CHANGING YOUR MIND

2.15   If the company decides that, partway through the dissolution process, it does not wish to proceed to dissolution then Form 652c must be submitted. Again, curiously, whereas Form 652a has to be signed by a majority of the directors, Form 652c has to be signed by only one director. In the event of a dispute between the parties, is there a scope for mischief here? Perhaps it is much better to arrange matters irrespective of the statutory position so that they are agreed formally between all the parties.

2.16   Again the Registrar of Companies guidance sets out a number of circumstances that might provoke a withdrawal of the process, but the commonest would seem to be:

* changing the company's name – if the current owners of the business wish to preserve the name, for commercial purposes, and they want to achieve this by forming a new company with the existing name, by a name swap, then this needs to be effected before the application for dissolution is made; or

* the company continues to trade or engages in some other activity, perhaps not its original trade, but some other activity during the dissolution period so that, in effect, it never ceased to trade and the three-month gap is never achieved.

ADVERTISING THE DISSOLUTION

2.17   Notice will be published in the London Gazette, with the cost being settled by the Registrar of Companies, whereby the Registrar invites those who have knowledge of the notice to make objection to the dissolution process. Provided there are no objections, or the application is not withdrawn, then three months after the notice has appeared in the London Gazette the company will be dissolved. In practice, the only parties who are likely to scrutinise the London Gazette will be the statutory authorities, HMRC, the company's bankers and most insolvency practitioners. Normal trade creditors are unlikely to have had notice which is the purpose of requiring a copy of Form 652a to be sent to all known creditors.

There is also no need for the company or its shareholders to continually search the Registrar of Companies database. A letter will be sent to the contact name shown on Form 652a to confirm that dissolution has been completed and to confirm the date.

FALSE CLAIMS

2.18   The application process under s 652A is a relatively informal process. It might therefore be thought open to some abuse, perhaps because the company is in dispute with a creditor and wants to get the company struck off before a legal claim can be formulated, or simply because there are disputes between the directors and shareholders, and the dissolution process is seen as a way of imposing commercial pressure to reach a compromise. There are a number of offences that the directors who sign the form can commit and these are:

- failing to withdraw the application if the company becomes ineligible for the process;

- failure to provide a copy of a Form 652a notice to all relevant parties within seven days of filing;

- providing false or misleading information in respect of the application; and

- applying when the company is not eligible for striking off.

2.19   Clearly, if a company is in a dispute with a creditor, or is tempted not to send a copy of a s 652A notice to them, with the consequences that the process becomes flawed, this is almost certainly not only inviting an objection but also encouraging the creditor to make a complaint to the Registrar, which may result in criminal proceedings.

The majority of the offences can result in a fine upon conviction of up to £5,000, where matters are dealt with before the magistrates' court or, if dealt with before a jury, an unlimited fine.

2.20   If the directors know that the company is insolvent and hope to avoid liabilities by having the company struck off, or fail to notify any interested party, then upon conviction they might also be subject to up to seven years' imprisonment and be disqualified from acting as a director for up to 15 years.

DEALING WITH THE ASSETS

2.21   It is implicit within the context of this publication that the assets are to be distributed to the shareholders, however, the directors only have power to deal with the assets so long as the company is active and on the company register. If assets arise after the date of dissolution then those remaining assets no longer belong to the company but instead are *bona vacantia* as property of the Crown. They can be reclaimed by the company but only by satisfying a formal legal process (see para **2.24**) to restore the company to the Companies House register, which includes application to the Crown. Applications should be made, except in the case of companies whose registered office is either in Lancashire or in Cornwall and the Isles of Scilly to:

> The Treasure Solicitor (BV)
> Queen Anne's Chambers
> 28 Broadway
> London SW1H 9JS

For companies whose registered office was in Lancashire, applications should be made to:

> The Solicitor to Duchy of Lancaster
> Farrer & Co
> 66 Lincolns Inn Fields
> London WC2A 3LH

If the companies registered office was either in Cornwall or the Isles of Scilly then the application should be made to:

> The Solicitor to Duchy of Cornwall
> 10 Buckingham Gate
> London SW1E 6LE

WHO ELSE CAN DISSOLVE THE COMPANY?

2.22   There are many companies on the company register that have never traded and the Registrar would be concerned to weed such companies out of the public record. Accordingly, if the Registrar of Companies takes the view that a company is no longer in business, then he can take steps to have the company removed from the Register. The Registrar might form such a view if, for example, post that has been sent to the registered office is returned undelivered or the company has failed to submit accounts or annual returns.

2.23   The Registrar is not allowed to simply strike the company off but must write to the company It may simply be that the directors are inefficient, but if no positive response is received then again a notice is placed in the London Gazette to the effect that the company will be struck off three months after the date of the notice. To assist anyone in searching the Companies House index, a copy of the notice will be placed on the public file.

Typical examples of the Registrar becoming interested in a company and considering whether the company should be struck off will include late returns, late accounts and no directors listed. This seems to be a common occurrence within the first few months of a company's life whereby the formation agents will have resigned as first directors and the promoters of the company have failed to appoint themselves.

REVIVING THE COMPANY

2.24   In some cases a company, which has been removed from the register under the s 652A procedure, could be restored within 20 years under Companies Act 1985 if particular circumstances exist, but Companies Act 2006 generally sets a six-year limit for restoration. The Registrar cannot simply revive the company but can do so if in receipt of a copy of a formal court order.

Application must be made to the courts that can either be the Registrar of Companies Court in London or district registries or any county court that would have the authority to order the winding-up of the company.

Restoration may be allowed if the courts are satisfied that the applicant was not properly informed of the procedures or the company's application was (in some cases) in error or (a catch all) it is just and reasonable to restore the company.

A shareholder or creditor can apply, as can the DTI if there are matters of public interest.

Example

Mistley Ltd was dissolved on 28 February 2005 and all the known assets have been distributed to the shareholders. Unfortunately, the directors forgot that they were members of a class action in the United States of America, which was successfully concluded on 5 April 2008 when the courts awarded £15,000 to Mistley Ltd.

These monies belong *bona vacantia* to the Crown and so can only be obtained for the benefit of the shareholders if an application is made to restore the company.

TIME LIMIT

2.25   In general, an application for restoration under Companies Act 2006 must be made within six years of the date of dissolution, but in some unusual circumstances (rarely met in practice) there is no time limit at all. A company can be restored at any time if restoration if required in order to bring legal proceedings for compensation for damages for personal injuries, including any sum under the Law Reform (Miscellaneous Provisions) Act 1934, s 1(2)(c) (funeral expenses) or damages under the Fatal Accident Act 1976 or under the Damages (Scotland) Act 1976.

For companies that anticipate claims, perhaps for product liability, then they should make sure that any insurance policies that they have at the date of dissolution would cover any subsequent claims in respect of events that must have taken place whilst the company was trading, either by obtaining from their insurers formal comfort or by making an additional payment to cover the post-dissolution period.

APPLYING TO RESTORE THE COMPANY

2.26   When an application to restore the company is to be made, the necessary notices must be served on the solicitor dealing with the *bona vacantia* assets at the addresses indicated at para **2.21** and to the Registrar of Companies restoration section. If there is any documentation in support of the application to restore, then copies of this must be sent to all interested parties and reasonable notice, which is not less than ten days, must be given.

There are a number of formal matters that need to be included in such an application, for example, formal information about the company, its date of incorporation, and objects and copies of Certificate of Incorporation of Memorandum and Articles. Such matters are best dealt with by lawyers who specialise in this area. Other examples are as follows:

• details of shareholders and directors;

• background information and indication of the date when trading stopped;

• explanation of failure to submit information to the registrar of Companies;

• other information to assist the application.

2.27   Normally, in the run up to dissolution, the company will not file final accounts or annual returns simply because it knows that the company will be dissolved. However, in support of any application to restore, it will be necessary to bring the file at the Registrar of Companies up-to-date by, for example, filing annual returns and filing any accounts that are now late.

Example

Mistley Ltd filed its last accounts up to 31 August 2004, but as the application to dissolve would result in the company being removed from the Register within the ten-month filing period, the company did not file those accounts with the Registrar.

By the time it discovers the additional funds from the California class action, the ten-month period for the accounts to 31 August 2004 has elapsed and a number of further sets of accounts are also now outstanding. Accordingly, in support of any application to restore, it must file all the outstanding accounts and suffer any penalties for late filing (see **2.28** below) that arise.

COSTS

2.28 The party making the application to restore the company will incur their own legal costs, but, in addition, they will generally be required to meet the costs of the Treasury Solicitor who acts for both the Treasury and the Registrar of Companies. If there are any outstanding late filing penalties, these must also be paid, but once the order for restoration has been made it is effective from the date that the order is delivered to the Registrar.

Example

Mistley Ltd's application for restoration was dealt with by the courts on 21 July 2008 and the order dealt with. The order was filed with the Registrar on 1 August 2008, so that is the date from which restoration is regarded as being made.

VOLUNTARY LIQUIDATION

2.29 In some circumstances, perhaps where there are a large number of shareholders or matters that are likely to be disputed, it may be more appropriate to deal with the dissolution to shareholders under the terms of a voluntary liquidation. There are two types of voluntary liquidation:

- a member's voluntary liquidation, where the directors are able to swear a statutory declaration that the company is solvent; or

- a creditor's voluntary liquidation, where the directors believe that the company is insolvent where the only element that is voluntary is the description of the process. The basis is only voluntary because it is not compulsory.

2.30 Both forms of liquidation have to be dealt with by a licensed insolvency practitioner and the formalities that the insolvency practitioner will deal with are outside the scope of this publication. However, brief outlines of matters relevant to this publication are set out. Where the matter is to be dealt with by a licensed insolvency practitioner then the minimum cost is likely to be in the range of £5,000 to £10,000, partly because of the advertising costs, but also because of the need for a fidelity bond, the cost of which varies with the value of the assets. Certainly, for very small companies the formal liquidation costs will fall disproportionately on the value of the assets distributed.

2.31   As has been indicated elsewhere, the underlying premise of this publication is that the company is solvent. Therefore, a member's voluntary liquidation would be the appropriate method to adopt. This is achieved by a majority of the directors of the company making a statutory declaration to the effect that the company is solvent, with such declaration being made within five weeks of any resolution to wind-up the company being passed. The statutory declaration states that the directors, having made full enquiry into the company's position, are satisfied that the company is solvent and can pay its debts within 12 months of the start of the winding-up process. There will also be the need to include a statement of the company's assets and liabilities as at a recent date. Having made the statutory declaration, this may often be arranged with the assistance of an insolvency practitioner, the liquidation process then proceeds.

If circumstances change and it appears that the company is no longer solvent then a member's voluntary liquidation is no longer appropriate. In such circumstances, the voluntary liquidation must be converted into creditor's voluntary liquidation by the calling of a meeting of creditors within 28 days of the liquidator becoming aware that the company is no longer solvent.

MEMBER'S VOLUNTARY LIQUIDATION COMPLETE

2.32   When a liquidator is satisfied that the company's affairs are fully wound-up, they call final meetings of creditors and members – although in practice these are rarely well attended – and, within one week of those meetings having taken place, final accounts of the liquidator's transactions must be filed with the Registrar of Companies. Except in circumstances where the courts order a deferral, any company subject to members' voluntary liquidation is dissolved three months after the forms are placed on the public record at Companies House. The advantage of a formal liquidation is that creditors who did not come forward cannot subsequently affect the distribution of the assets.

COMPULSORY LIQUIDATION

2.33   There is a third form of liquidation known as compulsory liquidation, which is generally initiated by a creditor of a company who is owed more than £750 who issues a formal demand for payment to the company and, as a result of that formal demand, the company has failed to pay. Once the courts are satisfied that the company has failed to pay then the company is deemed to be insolvent and it is then appropriately wound-up.

Other circumstances for compulsory liquidation to apply can include application from the Secretary of State for Trade and Industry or the Financial Services Authority or the Official Receiver or where it is considered to be in the public interest for the company to be wound-up. This might be, for example, where the company was involved in some form of fraudulent or illegal activity and a liquidator is appointed to protect what assets remain.

Example

New Bolingbroke Ltd invited applications from investors to acquire ostriches as an investment activity, but was never registered with the Financial Services Authority and, following much public discussion in the Sunday papers, the Secretary of State for Trade and Industry made a formal application for the company to be wound-up to protect any available assets. Such applications are often made where there is evidence of fraud.

2.34 However, for our purposes, it is likely that in both a creditor's voluntary liquidation and a compulsory liquidation there will be no monies available for the shareholders. All that the shareholders can consider is how they can get tax relief for any losses that they may have incurred, whether in respect of shares or in respect of loans to the liquidated company. Indeed, the term 'creditor's voluntary liquidation' is something of a misnomer as in most cases there is very little that's 'voluntary' about it – the directors taking steps to put the company into liquidation, at a time when they hope there might be some assets, as opposed to waiting for a compulsory liquidation where all the assets may well be dissipated. In either instance, the conduct of the directors may be reported to the Department of Trade and Industry and steps taken to have the directors banned from acting as directors for a period. In most circumstances, the courts will be more lenient where a creditor's voluntary liquidation has been arranged and there were assets, as compared with a situation where there are no assets and the directors are forced by creditors to recognise the position.

PLANNING POINTS

2.35

- Ensure sufficient directors will be available on the designated date to sign any required forms.

- If there are contingent assets, perhaps those that depend upon an outstanding court case, consider delaying matters until the outcome is known. Maintaining the company in a period of suspense will be cheaper than having to apply to reinstate the company to the register.

- Resolve disputes with creditors so that the scope for creditor objection is minimised.

- Prepare lists of creditors the branches the company deals with, and related information, so that any required paperwork can be sent promptly in one single mailshot.

- Establish the date on that trading ceases, so that it will be known in advance when the three-month interregnum ends.

- Ensure any name change, perhaps to preserve an historically important name, is dealt with before the three-month interregnum begins.

- If the dissolution turns out to involve an insolvent company, deal with changing the process promptly; the directors must appoint a liquidator as otherwise they may face action from the DTI who may seek to have them barred from acting as a director of any company for an extended period.

- Agree with a liquidator in advance, if the formal route is chosen, the division of duties between the company adviser and the liquidator.

Chapter 3

Taxation position of the company before and after cessation of trade

3.1 In the run up to dissolution, whether by formal liquidation or by the C16 concession, the timing of expenditure and income needs to be carefully monitored to ensure that, wherever possible, tax relief is obtained. Although taxation is never the primary objective for undertaking any transaction, we know there will be many who formed companies in recent years solely on that premise. We need to make sure that, wherever possible, expenditure is eligible for tax relief. We must take into consideration the dates on which expenditure is incurred and, if losses are occurring in the final trading period, make sure that those losses are properly relieved.

DATE OF CESSATION OF TRADE

3.2 For a number of purposes referred to in this publication, it is important to be able to ascertain when a trade has ceased. It, generally, will be a question of fact and in most cases the position will be straightforward. In the case of *Speck v Morton* (1972) 48 TC 476, a speculative builder completed a development and prepared accounts on the basis that the trade ceased when construction ceased, but properties remained unsold. However, the stock of houses was subsequently sold over an extended period. Initially, the Revenue accepted that stopping construction was a cessation but, subsequently, it was agreed on a determination by the Special Commissioner that trading continued whilst the properties were sold. In some cases a business will have more than one trade and in these circumstances the cessation tests have to be applied to each separate trade to determine a date of cessation. In *Highland Rail Co v IT Special Commissioners* (1885) 2 TC 151, the company operated both steamships and a railway. It was held that the continuance of the railway had not caused a cessation of all the trading activities. In other cases, the courts, have decided equally that what appears to be two separate trades are merely one business, even though they may be operated in two departments. For example, in *Howden Boiler and Armaments Co Ltd v Stewart* (1925) 9 TC 205 the company originally made boilers but in the 1st World War obtained contracts for making armaments; even though the activities were carried out in two separate premises there was only one profit and loss account and costs were not apportioned between the two activities – result: a single trade. By contrast in *Scales v George Thompson & Co Ltd* (1927) 13 TC 83, the company apparently had two businesses of ship-owning and insurance underwriting. In that case it was held that there were two separate trades. Perhaps the distinction between the *Howden Boiler* and *George Thompson* cases is that in the first the company seems to have regarded the whole activity as one, a form of metal transformation in both cases, because that is what the

35

accounting records showed, whereas it was easier to be able to demonstrate that ship-owning and insurance underwriting were clearly two separate trades.

3.3   Perhaps a clearer view can be obtained by considering a number of the cases relating to the commencement of trading and then, in effect, reversing the test to determine whether any activities that are still carried out amount to trading. In *Birmingham District Cattle By Products Co Ltd v IRC* (1919) 12 TC 92, the company was incorporated on June 1913 and, until October 1913, was constructing its factory and entering into contracts for supply of raw material and sale of products. Trading was held to have commenced on 6 October 1913, being the first date that raw material was received. Similarly, in *Cannop Coal Co Ltd v IRC* (1918) 12 TC 31, the company was established to operate coalmines and, although the company was incorporated in 1906, the pits were not complete for full production until 1911. However, from 1908 onwards coal began to be extracted, which was primarily used in the construction process, but surplus coal was sold. Accordingly, it was held that trading had commenced in 1908. Finally, in *O'Loan v Noon & Co* (1948) (Irish tax case 71), the original business had been as fruit merchants, both wholesale and retail but, as a result of wartime restrictions, the trade declined and in early 1943 the company diversified by acquiring land containing coal and production began on 1 April 1943. It was held that trading commenced when the production of coal began, the acquisition of the coal mine merely being a preparatory act.

3.4   Therefore, by reversing the tests in relation to commencement of trading, the cases suggest that cessation of trading is likely to take place either when manufacturing ceases or when sales are no longer made. Accordingly, if it is important to keep the trade going for a period for any of the particular taxation advantages discussed in this publication then the proprietors of a dissolving company must make sure that any activity that is carried out is clearly recognisable as trading. Most of the cases referred to are no longer relevant to the particular legislation that required the case to be brought, but what they tell us is a more important issue that where we need to know when trading began, or ceased, that these are the principles to be applied.

ALLOWABLE EXPENDITURE

3.5   For most practitioners, the application of the 'wholly and exclusively' rule which allows or denies relief for a particular item of expenditure will be well known, but for businesses that are currently operational, we tend to overlook the fundamental requirement of ICTA 1988, s 74(1)(a), which is that an item of expenditure has, firstly, to be for trade purposes to be deductible. On most occasions when we consider the rule, assuming there is detailed consideration of the underlying requirements, our client's business is ongoing so the business is trading. Once that hurdle has been overcome, in the majority of circumstances it is then possible to demonstrate that an advantage endures to the trade as a result of the expense being incurred, so tax relief is available for the relevant expense. However, in this publication we are considering the position of a business on the cusp of ceasing to trade, so that in the absence of a particular statutory relief, once trading has ceased, the business falls outside of ICTA 1988, s74(1)(a), with the result that expenditure may no longer be tax deductible. This does not mean that the expense does not have to be incurred by the company; it simply means that tax relief cannot be obtained. Accordingly, the date on which particular items of expenditure are incurred and, being able to demonstrate that there is a trade advantage is important so that (if the cost does not come within a particular statutory relief) wherever possible, relief is obtained.

3.6   Advantage accrues to the dissolving company because corporation tax may be regarded as a subsidy for any tax deductible item of expenditure. Since the usual purpose of dissolving the family business is to maximise the value of assets in the hands of the shareholders, this is a relief that should not easily be discarded.

Tax rate	Effective cost
21%	79%
28%	72%

For those companies who are in the marginal transition between £300,000 and £1,500,000, where the marginal rate is 29.75%, the net cost is 70.25%.

Tax relief for the expense, in these circumstances, as with a number of other concepts is a matter of considering the expenditure, the timing, and making sure, if there is likely to be any doubt that the 'wholly and exclusively' rule may not apply, that there is contemporary evidence of:

● the purpose for the expenditure;

● the basis of calculation;

● when the liability to pay was determined; and

● did a trade advantage accrue?

3.7   There are many tax cases on the 'wholly and exclusively' test of ICTA 1988, s 74 (1)(a), which set out guidance as to the areas of expenditure that might be deductible, and the details of three are set out below. The statutory test, ICTA 1988, s74, indicates that deductions not allowable are:

'(1) Subject to the provisions of the Corporation Tax Acts, in computing the amount of the profits to be charged to corporation tax under Case I or Case II of Schedule D, no sum shall be deducted in respect of—
(a)   any disbursements or expenses, not being money wholly and exclusively laid out or expended for the purposes of the trade or profession ...'

Therefore, the fundamental point to be established is whether expenditure incurred has been incurred for the purposes of the current existing trade or whether the expenditure has been incurred merely because the currently existing trade is about to cease or, more plainly, the expense was only incurred because of an anticipated cessation of trade.

It is not sufficient to concentrate upon the taxation consequences of the assets being distributed to the shareholders. In much the same way as we spend time planning for corporation tax reduction whilst a business is ongoing, so equally we need to spend time reviewing taxation issues surrounding the cessation of trade. Therefore, we need to consider areas where expenditure may or may not be tax deductible or, indeed, areas where income may or may not be taxable. When a business is about to terminate there is often expenditure incurred that is particular to the closing down of a business. As a general proposition, such expenditure is unlikely to satisfy the provisions of ICTA, 1988 s 74(1)(a) as being neither wholly or exclusively for trade purposes. Such expenditure, being concerned with the structure of the business, is more likely to be regarded as capital expenditure in the widest meaning of the term because it has been incurred to allow the assets of the business to be realised. The consequence being that unless there is a specific statutory relief or supporting judicial decision, no corporation tax relief will be obtained for the expense.

ALLOWABLE COSTS

3.8   In exactly the same way as we should seek to minimise tax liabilities arising on the shareholders of a family business because this maximises the after tax proceeds, so equally we should seek to minimise the corporation tax liability in periods running up to cessation of trade. In particular, we need to make certain that items of expenditure are, so far as possible, tax deductible. Typical items of expenditure will be:

- general trading expenses;

- pension contributions;

- redundancy and other costs relating to severance of employment; and

- costs of dissolving the company and costs incurred in respect of managing the dissolution.

GENERAL TRADING EXPENSES

3.9   These should all be allowed, provided they satisfy the general 'wholly and exclusively' test and so long as full provision is made for them in any final accounts up to the date of cessation of trade. Such expenditure does not have to be paid before the cessation date because, as always, some suppliers will send invoices in late, but full provision must be made.

If provision has not been made and further expenses come to light at a later date, there is no general basis upon which such items of expenditure can be subsequently allowed. There are rules for Schedule D trades where such expenses can be allowed against post-cessation receipts, with a result that the net post-cessation receipts are taxed, but if there are no post-cessation receipts there is no basis upon which post-cessation expenses can be relieved. ITA 2007, s 96 provides the general authority for tax relief on post-cessation expenses, and in general when dealing with the final accounts of a company, it makes sense to delay submitting to HMRC the corporation tax return covering the final period of trading to make sure that adequate provision for all known and anticipated expenses has been made to avoid the possibility of expenses being incurred that can not ultimately be relieved.

3.10   Within the writer's experience, it is more unusual for post-cessation receipts to arise simply because income sources in a company are generally known and recorded. Where post-cessation expenses arise, it is generally because the owner or manager of the business has closed their eyes to a supplier dispute and has not wanted to make provision in the accounts whilst the business was ongoing. They may argue that such a provision is merely a contingent liability, that the legal advice is that they will have no liability and to provide one would merely encourage the supplier. However, the date of cessation of trade sets a line in the sand and expenses confirmed after that date will not be allowable unless provision is made in the final accounts. To the extent that provisions turn out to be excessive then any surplus provision will be taxed under Case VI in the particular post-cessation accounting period that any excess provision becomes confirmed. That is not to say that the provision may not be disputed by HMRC, but provided it is included within the cessation accounts, the principle is established and subsequent events may allow the correct liability to be allowed in those accounts.

Example

Corpusty Ltd normally made its accounts up to 31 December 2008, but ceased to trade 30 May 2008. In the final accounts, provision was made for a legal claim for breach of patent rights in the sum of £100,000 against a claim from the creditor of £200,000.

The £100,000 would be allowed as an expense against profits to 30 May 2008.

The claim was settled 16 February 2009 by a payment of £85,000 with both parties covering their own costs. Corpusty Ltd's costs were £10,000. The excess provision of £5,000 would be taxed in the year to 30 May 2009.

3.11   The same approach needs to be made in respect of bad and doubtful debts. Again, there is no advantage to the dissolving family company to pay corporation tax on debts that may never be paid, so again full provision needs to be made. If the provision proves to be excessive then the excess provision will be taxed as Case VI in the accounting period that the debt is recovered. The general charging provisions are contained within ICTA 1988, s 103(1) as follows:

'(1)   Where any trade, profession or vocation the profits of which are chargeable to tax under Case I or II of Schedule D has been permanently discontinued, tax shall be charged under Case VI of that Schedule in respect of any sums to which this section applies which are received after the discontinuance.'

3.12 Therefore, accounts and tax computations in the final pre-dissolution trading period will follow generally accepted accountancy practice where provision for creditors will achieve relief even though a particular creditor has not been paid. Apart from the provisions relating to tax relief on remuneration set out in FA 1989, s 43 (where any provision must be paid within nine months of the end of the accounting period where the provision has been made to obtain tax relief in the accounting period, or interest payable to related parties where the interest must be paid within 12 months of the year end to which it relates), there are no other time limits for relief; so long as the provision is a true liability and satisfies the 'wholly and exclusively' test and is ultimately paid, the expense should be relievable.

PENSION PREMIUM RELIEF

3.13 There is one area, particularly when a trading company is coming to the end of its useful life, where timing and the payment date can be crucial. The general proposition is that pension premiums are only allowed in the chargeable period when paid. However, Finance Act 2004, s 199 allows some payments made after the date of cessation of trade to be deemed to have been incurred in the final trading period, so that there is no restriction on relief. The statutory position is:

'(1) This section applies where a sum is paid to the trustees or managers of a registered pension scheme by an employer in or towards the discharge of any liability of the employer under—

(a) section 75 of the Pensions Act 1995 (c 26) (deficiencies in the assets of a pension scheme), or

(b) Article 75 of the Pensions (Northern Ireland) Order 1995 (SI 1995/3213 (NI 22)) (corresponding provision for Northern Ireland).

(2) The making of the payment is to be treated for the purposes of—

(a) Part 2 of ITTOIA 2005 (trading income) or Case I and II of Schedule D,

(b) section 75 of ICTA (expenses of management: companies with investment business), and

(c) section 76 of ICTA (expenses of insurance companies),

as if it were the payment of a contribution by the employer under the pension scheme.

(3) Subsections (4) and (5) apply if the employer's trade, profession, vocation or business is discontinued before the making of the payment.

(4) The payment is to be relieved—

(a) to the same extent as it would have been but for the discontinuance, and

40

> (b)   as if it had been made on the last day on which the trade, profession, vocation or business was carried on.

(5)   And for the purposes of section 76 of ICTA it is to be treated (to the extent that it would not otherwise be) as part of expenses payable falling to be brought into account at Step 1 in subsection (7) of that section.'

This removes the practical difficulty that many companies will not have the cash to allow the arrears of already agreed contractual pension provision to be made until all the assets have been sold. But for the above provision, the trade would have ceased and relief could otherwise be precluded.

However, in general the extent of relief for directors/employees will be limited to the annual allowance on the basis that any excess will be the subject of a tax charge on the employee even though there may not be any restriction on the amount the company can deduct. The annual allowances in future years are as follows.

2008–09: £235,000
2009–10: £245,000
2010–11: £255,000

Example

Little Snoring Ltd operated a pub and restaurant and the proprietor wished to pay £250,000 into his pension fund to provide for arrears of funding to improve the available pension and to save corporation tax on the sale of the freehold. The freehold sale is completed on 31 July 2008, which is the accepted date that the trade ceases and three days later £250,000 is paid to the insurance company.

Although this is after the trade has ceased, relief is allowed under FA 2004 as the purpose of the payment is to make good any deficit in the scheme funding.

If any part of the pension contribution was simply to provide for a pension and also achieve a reduction in corporation tax, where no contractual arrangements were in place, then that part would only be deductible if the relevant contributions were paid before trading ceased.

3.14   Whilst a company continues to trade, there are regulations governing the allowability of contributions to a pension fund. Contributions, which are described as 'ordinary' contributions, are allowed when paid irrespective of their size. If, however, special contributions are paid and the purpose of such special contributions is to make good any shortfall in either the fund or the benefits for the employees (and this includes director employees), relief is only available in full provided the amount paid is less than £500,000.

Where the amount exceeds £500,000 the potentially spreading of contributions can apply but in order for spreading to apply then the following conditions must be present.

41

- The company must have paid contributions in successive accounting periods.

- Contributions paid in the second year must be more than 210% of the contributions paid in the first year.

- The contributions paid in the second year are more than the aggregate of 110% of the first year's contributions and £500,000, so the spreading rules then apply to the excess of the contributions above 110% of the contributions in year one.

Example

Outwell Basin Ltd paid pension contributions of £300,000 in the accounting period ended 31 August 2008 and in the year ended 31 August 2009 paid £900,000.

This is more than 210% of the year one contribution so the premium potentially subject to spreading is;

Premium – year to 31 August 2009	900,000
Less: £300,000 × 110%	330,000
Excess contributions	570,000

If the amount is more than £500,000 then tax relief is spread forward on the following basis:

Special contribution	Years of spread
More than £500,000 but less than £1,000,000	2
More than £1,000,000 but less than £2,000,000	3
More than £2,000,000	4

Thus in the Outwell Basin Ltd example, £285,000 would be allowed in each of the two years ended 31 August 2009 and 31 August 2010.

For most companies the preferred strategy would be to either ensure that the excess of additional pension contributions is below £500,000, or to regularly step up normal contributions so that whenever the possibility of restriction applies, the 110% multiplier applies to an enhanced figure.

However, it is not simply the amount of contribution that causes the above spreading rules to apply. If the pension scheme actuary can certify that the only reason for making additional contributions is to cover cost of living increases for existing pensioners then this amount is excluded from the spreading provisions and allowed in the year in which the contribution is made.

In some circumstances it may be possible that a company is making a number of special contributions in the run up to cessation of trade and the spreading provisions applied, in the years before the cessation of trade, to restrict the current relief. If the contributions would otherwise have been spread forward beyond the date on which trading ceases, relief will not be lost but instead FA

2004, s 199 deems such contributions to have been incurred on the last day of trading. However, the premiums deemed to have been paid after cessation of trade can be allowed over an extended period by FA 2004, s 198(4) on the basis of the following example set out in HMRC Manual RPSM05102130.

Example

JMG Ltd ceased business on 15 November 2008. In the period ending 30 September 2008 JMG Ltd paid pension contributions that result in the tax relief being spread as follows:

£493,200	Period ending 30 September 2008
£493,200	Period ending 30 September 2009
£493,200	Period ending 30 September 2010

As the company ceased business in the period ending 30 September 2009, it will not get full tax relief on the pension contribution unless it uses the cessation of business spreading rules. JMG Ltd can choose to:

- have the last £493,200 put into what would have been the period ending 30 September 2009, ie the company's last chargeable period; or

- have the last £493,200 treated as paid daily from 1 October 2007 to 15 November 2008. The daily amount will be £1200 (£493,200/411 days). This gives £55,200 in the final chargeable period (period ending 30 September 2009) and £438,000 in the period ending 30 September 2008.

See also the following example.

Example

Laxfield Ltd made its accounts up to 31 December 2006 and in the year to 31 December 2006 paid excess contributions, after the 110% deduction, to its pension fund of £1,200,000. Under the normal spreading rules the expenditure would have been relieved in the three years to 31 December 2006, 2007, and 2008 as to one third in each year and therefore £400,000 was allowed in each of the two years to 31 December 2006 and 2007 with the final £400,000 to be allowed in the year to 31 December 2008.

However, Laxfield Ltd ceased to trade on 30 June 2007 and the first spread amount would be allowed in the period to 30 June 2007.The balance of £400,000 would also fall to be allowed in the period to 30 June 2008 under the provisions of FA 2004, s 198 or spread backwards under the JMG example. Therefore, contributions required to make good any shortfall in benefits (within the writer's experience, many small private companies have under-funded pension benefits for directors for many years) will be allowed.

There is no need for the contributions to be paid before trading ceases but, instead, a tax efficient amount can be paid after the computations are prepared, perhaps to take the profit levels below £300,000. However, for those generally exceptional companies where matters are more up-to-date, if the contributions that are to be paid are no more than 'ordinary' contributions funding current benefits, without any need to make good a shortfall or deficiencies in the assets of a scheme, then it will be important to ensure that such premiums are paid before commercial activity ceases.

REDUNDANCY PAYMENTS

3.15 One major cost in any cessation of trade will be the costs of redundancy, where the trade cannot be sold as a going concern. Set out below is a discussion of the various cases in relation to such payments. Under current regulations, statutory redundancy pay is limited to £330 per week, which applies to redundancies after 1 February 2008; for redundancies in earlier periods, lower rates applied. The payments that are required to be made will vary depending upon the age and service of the employee but, for example, an employee aged 40 with 20 years' service would be entitled to redundancy of £6,270 under the statutory scheme, whereas an employee aged 60 would be entitled to £9,735. Additionally, there are special rules that abate the entitlement by $\frac{1}{12}$ once an employee is aged 64 for every complete month up to age 65. For any employee aged 65 or over, no statutory redundancy is due.

Further information including a guide for employees is available at the Department for Business Enterprise and Regulatory Reform which includes an online calculator, at www.businesslink.gov/redundancy calculator.

Many companies will decide, where the trade has ceased and, particularly, where longstanding and loyal employees have to be made redundant, to make payments to their employees in excess of the statutory redundancy amounts. ICTA 1988, s 90 allows such additional payments to redundant employees of up to three times the statutory amount and the position is set out in various Revenue Interpretations, in particular RI 103 and RI 200, which need to be read in conjunction with the discussions set out below. It does, however, follow that if a company decides to make a redundancy payment in excess of three times the statutory amount, that only the excess falls to be disallowed.

Example

The new owners of the Little Snoring Inn do not wish to take on the existing manager and deputy manager who, under statutory redundancy, are entitled to £6,500 and £4,200 respectively.

The directors of Little Snoring Ltd make payments of £10,000 to both employees. As this is less than three times the statutory entitlement, full relief is available.

In the above example, if £20,000 were paid to the manager this would be more than three times his statutory entitlement of £6,500 so the limiter would apply at £19,500 with the excess, in this case £500, being disallowed.

CONSULTATION WITH EMPLOYEES

3.16 As part of the process of closing the business down, where there are significant numbers of employees it will be necessary to give all employees the appropriate statutory notice period. The extent will depend upon the individual employee contacts and advice should be obtained from a specialist employment lawyer to ensure that the correct procedures are followed.

For any organisation that has more than 20 employees, there is a statutory obligation for employers to consult with employee representatives in advance of the intended dismissal date. Consultation should normally be with union representatives, but if there are no union representatives then consultation needs to take place with duly appointed representatives of the workforce and in addition the employer needs to notify the Department for Business, Enterprise and Regulatory Reform by letter or using form HR1 which can be downloaded from the Insolvency Service website. There is a wider range of information available on the government Business Link and Department for Business Enterprise and Regulatory Reform websites but the consultation process must begin well before the dismissal date and, in any event, at least 30 days before the anticipated redundancy date.

The consequences of failing to comply with any required consultation process is that the affected employees may then have further claims for compensation which within the parameters of this publication implies a reduced amount to be received by the shareholders. So getting the consultation right preserves shareholder funds.

IS THERE ANY MINIMUM PERIOD FOR CONSULTATION?

3.17 Unless prevented by special circumstances, the employer must begin the process of consultation in good time and, in any event, at least:

- 30 days before the first of the dismissals takes effect in a case where between 20 and 99 redundancy dismissals are proposed at one establishment within a 90-day period;

- 90 days before the first of the dismissals takes effect, in a case where 100 or more redundancy dismissals are proposed at one establishment within a 90-day period.

An employer who has already begun consultations about one group of proposed redundancy dismissals and later finds it necessary to make a further group redundant does not have to add the numbers of employees together to calculate the minimum period for either group.

In a case where employee representatives are to be specially elected because there is no union representation, the employer will need to ensure that the election is completed and the representatives are in place (having had an opportunity for appropriate training if necessary) in time to allow for the minimum period for consultation to be met.

WHAT INFORMATION MUST BE DISCLOSED?

3.18   The employee representatives will need enough information about the employer's proposals to be able to take a useful and constructive part in the process of consultation. An employer must therefore disclose certain specified information *in writing*. This must be:

- handed to each of the appropriate representatives; or

- sent by post to:

  – an address notified to the employer; or

  – in the case of a trade union, to the address of the union's head or main office.

The information the employer must disclose is:

- the reasons for the proposals;

- the numbers and descriptions of employees it is proposed to dismiss as redundant;

- the total number of employees of any such description employed by the employer at the establishment in question;

- the proposed method of selecting the employees who may be dismissed;

- the proposed method of carrying out the dismissals, taking account of any agreed procedure, including the period over which the dismissals are to take effect; and

- the proposed method of calculating any redundancy payments, other than those required by statute, that the employer proposes to make.

3.19   Giving the correct notice to employees complying with any required consultation procedure and other matters are important issues that need to be dealt with. Failure to deal with matters properly may result in the dissolving company being taken to an employment tribunal for issues of unfair dismissal with the result that significant compensation may have to be paid to employees who were consulted improperly.

Although the statutory obligations begin where 20 employees are involved, the Department for Business Enterprise and Regulatory Reform publications suggest that best practice would involve consultation with all affected employees, even if the numbers were smaller. Since our purpose in dissolving the family company is to maximise the proceeds for the shareholders, there will certainly be no desire to have those proceeds reduced by any employment tribunal awards.

EXPENSES OF DISSOLVING THE COMPANY

3.20   Apart from the various statutory allowances and prohibitions that are discussed above, any item of expenditure has to satisfy the provisions of ICTA 1988, s 74 as being wholly and exclusively for business purposes. Where expenditure has a dual purpose then unless the expense can be apportioned in such a way as can be demonstrated that the apportioned expenditure was wholly and exclusively for trade purposes then the whole of the expenditure falls to be disallowed. The difference can be illustrated by comparing petrol usage and the cost of a haircut. A tank of petrol could, in part, be consumed wholly and exclusively for trade purposes because it is possible to demonstrate as a question of fact that some of the petrol is used for trade purposes with the remainder for non-business use, whereas it is not possible to allocate a proportion of the expense of a haircut to business to leave a remainder for other purposes. Therefore, the haircut is not wholly and exclusively business, but some of the petrol could be.

A further consequence is that if expenditure can be established as being capital expenditure or expenditure incurred for a capital purpose, it cannot be tax deductible. The effect of this rule is that any expenditure incurred to achieve the dissolution of the family company or to transfer assets to the shareholders is expenditure incurred in dealing with the capital of the company. Accordingly, no relief is due against the corporation tax profits.

Example

Blakeney Ltd ceased trading 30 September 2008 and on 10 December 2008 received a bill from its accountants comprising the following elements:

- drafting the accounts to 31 August 2008 – £3,500;

- application for ESC C16 – £500;

- cost of PAYE inspection with HMRC – £750;

- dealing with advances to shareholders – £750.

The costs of application for ESC C16 and distributing capital to shareholders are both costs of dealing with capital and therefore are not deductible against any company profits.

3.21   There is often no doubt that a business has had to incur a particular expense but that in itself does not result in a tax deduction. The leading case on this issue is *CIR v Anglo Brewing Co Ltd* (1925) 12 TC 203, where it was held that payments made by the company to facilitate the winding-up of the company were not tax deductible. Care must be applied when reviewing the leading cases in this area because much of the specific subject matter of the cases (for example, redundancy payments) are now allowed by statute, but the continuing purpose of the cases is to illustrate the allowability, or non-allowability principle.

In *Anglo Brewing*, a decision to close down the business had been made. Whilst the company continued to trade, generous provision had been made to pay pensions to former employees and, at closure, the company made comparable payments to the existing workforce for both pensions and redundancy. In the High Court it was held that the payments were not tax deductible because they had not been made to allow the trade to continue, but were only made as a consequence of the cessation of trade. This conclusion was different to the position of any earlier payments that the company had made because in those earlier circumstances the company was continuing and there was an enduring benefit to the company in that, apart from other considerations, satisfactory treatment of former employees provided an assurance to existing employees that they would receive similar treatment and their ongoing cooperation was secured.

There are now statutory provisions that allow the items of expenditure that were the subject of the *Anglo Brewing* case; in respect of the redundancy (see para **3.15**), and in respect of pensions costs (see para **3.13**), the case confirms that the payments to facilitate going out on business are not tax deductible.

3.22   In the case of *O'Keefe v Southwell Printers Limited* (1984) 58 TC 88, payments made to employees in order to secure their cooperation whilst the company was still trading, albeit in anticipation of closing down, were held to be allowable.

This case distinguishes the *Anglo Brewing* rule to allow expenditure, which is stated to be for the benefit of the current trade, even if there has been a decision to close the business down. In this particular case, the business was to close at a known date, but the company's management were concerned that the workforce would prove to be uncooperative in the period before closure. Any such actions would have further damaged the trading position of the company even though the company was already loss making. Accordingly, it was agreed that payments would be made to the employees where the stated purpose was to ensure their cooperation whilst the company continued to trade. The company succeeded in its claim, partly on the strength of evidence before the Special Commissioners by the company's management, in that the only purpose for the payment was to ensure efficient and satisfactory current trading in the run up to closure.

3.23   This may seem a fine line between the two cases simply because the payments, in both cases, were only made because the trade was about to cease. Had *Southwell Printers* (see para **3.22**) continued to trade, the payments would not have been required, but if any business intending to disincorporate is proposing to make such payments it will be important to ensure that satisfactory evidence of the trading purposes of the payments is available. This may take the form of, for example:

- minutes of meetings with staff taking care to record any reaction from employees;

- letters to all employees setting out the terms and purpose of the payment;

- Board minutes agreeing to the payment;

- correspondence with professional advisers.

Accordingly, the test, required to decide whether the expense incurred is corporation tax deductible, is concerned with the impact of the expense on the activities of the company before or after the trade ceases and the purpose for which the expense was incurred. Expenditure that either increases trading profit or activity or, conversely, reduces or minimises trading losses (provided it is incurred before trading ceases) should be tax deductible. By contrast, expenditure that merely achieves an efficient close-down of the trade will not be deductible.

Example

North Wootton Ltd makes payments of £10,000 to employees to assist in removing plant and machinery from the company's premises to auction after trade has ceased. The expenditure is not deductible.

However, overtime payments to employees in a closing down period, to complete existing orders or to realise stock, would be deductible because the company was then still trading even where, by comparison with previous payment levels, the amounts might seem excessive.

CONTRACTUAL OBLIGATION

3.24   One further circumstance where expenditure can be deducted is if there is a pre-existing contractual arrangement between company and recipient that requires the payment to be made.

Often this type of expenditure will be in relation to payments to employees under the terms of, for example, pay in lieu of notice, bonuses relating to the trading or payments agreed to be made if the trading were to cease. This includes redundancy payments (see para **3.15**), but only up to the extent of the contractual or statutory provision.

Example

Spooner Row Ltd employ a manager under the terms of a contract that requires them to make a payment of £100,000 should his employment be terminated as a result of the business closing down.

Closure of the business on 30 September 2008 triggers the payment, which is tax deductible, since it is a contractual arrangement.

It would follow that if the trade were simply disincorporated and subsequently carried on as a sole trader/partnership, the payment would not be triggered because the manager's employment should be protected under the transfer of undertaking (protection of employment rights (TUPE) arrangements.

3.25   There is a clear distinction between contractual arrangements, which are tax deductible, and non-contractual arrangements, which are not. This issue was addressed in the case of *Cosmotron Manufacturing Co Ltd v CIR*

(1997) 70 TC 292. This case was an appeal against a Hong Kong decision where the House of Lords sat as the Privy Council, but the case is important to UK law because their Lordships decided, as a question of fact, that there was no significant difference between the provisions of ICTA 1988, s 74(1)(a) and the comparable Hong Kong legislation that was the subject of the appeal.

Cosmotron Manufacturing had an obligation imposed by Hong Kong employment law to make redundancy payments to employees of two or more years' standing. The business closed down and the appropriate compensation payments were made. The Hong Kong authorities refused a deduction on the basis that they had only been made as a result of a cessation of trade and not to generate future profits. The local Board of Review accepted that the company's contention was valid that the payments were made as an integral part of the costs that were incurred when the employees had originally been employed. Therefore, they related to the trading position of the company.

The case was appealed by the Hong Kong authorities, but at both the Court of Appeal and Privy Council levels the taxpayer succeeded. The possibility of having to pay redundancy is simply part of the ongoing cost of employing any staff. The fact that a particular payment arises because of cessation of trade does not make any difference. The potential for payment arose when the staff were employed, so the redundancy payments were incurred for the purpose of trade.

3.26   Accordingly, it follows that if there was a contractual obligation to make the payment had the company continued to trade, that any corresponding payments made at cessation of trade are also tax deductible. However, does the matter end there? Are there circumstances in which non-contractual payments can be deducted?

The custom and practice of making particular payments to employees, even if they are not part of the contractual employment package, may establish a precedent that allows payments to be made. Certainly, the writer has knowledge of cases where 'ex gratia' payments to former employees have been challenged by HMRC as taxable because the majority of former employees received ex gratia payments, so that there was an expectation that whenever employment ceased that a payment would be made, so they were similar to a contractual obligation. On that basis, HMRC's purpose was to make the payments taxable, but our purpose would suggest that there is an argument for saying that such quasi contractual payments could be tax deductible because they are, by custom and practice, an expected part of the employment package.

Example

Berney Arms Halt Ltd enrolled all its employees as members of a local sports and leisure club. Over the years, a practice had arisen of making a payment to cover one year's subscription for any employee who either retired or was made redundant. At cessation of trade, such payments should be tax deductible on the basis that there was a quasi-contractual expectation that such payments were to be paid.

3.27   In a further case, *Godden v A Wilson's Stores (Holdings) Ltd* (1962) 40 TC 161, HMRC succeeded at Court of Appeal level, but not at Privy Council. *Godden v A Wilson's Stores (Holdings) Ltd* (1962) (40 TC 161) is a case that follows on from the *Anglo Brewing* decision (see para **3.21**). In this case, the company's trade was discontinued and a manager was paid six months' salary in lieu of notice, as well as the anticipated commission that he would have earned in the six-month period after cessation of trade. The case went to appeal and the courts identified two categories of expenditure:

- payments made to allow a trader to go out of business where they were not made to improve the existing trade arrangements; and

- expenditure to escape from onerous service contracts.

It is clear from the decision in the Court of Appeal that because the expense was made for the purposes of discontinuance (indeed the commercial reality was that it was made to prevent the employee suing the company once the trade ceased) that the payment was not allowable.

3.28   As in so many cases, if the taxpayer had ordered matters differently, the expenditure may have been allowed. In the *A Wilson's Stores* case the judges stated that if the employee had proved awkward then the tax consequence might have been different. In effect, the conclusion may well have been, as in *O'Keefe v Southwell Printers Ltd*, that the expense would have been allowed. In other circumstances, the courts can only consider the facts that actually happened, not the facts that might have been more desirable to happen.

The Master of the Rolls, Lord Evershed, expressly commented, in the *Wilson's Stores* case, on the issue that had the company arranged their affairs differently, the payment may well have been deductible (40 TC at p 175 of the report):

> 'As I have said, it might have been put so that Mr Paton could have been invited to say: "I accept six weeks' notice instead of six months' provided that my salary for the six months now pending is doubled"; and that would have been reinforced, perhaps, because, as (the taxpayer's barrister) Mr Borneman pointed out, it was essential that the rubber plantation should be continued and handed over as a going concern. Indeed, the argument for its sale required its continuance as a going concern afterwards. But we can decide this case only upon the material as it took shape.'

3.29   This case has, however, now been superseded by the decision in *Cosmotron Manufacturing Co Ltd* and from guidance in HMRC Business Income Manual (see for example, paragraph BIM38390) that the *Godden* case will not be used by the Revenue to challenge such payments.

Therefore, in the Spooner Row example (see para **3.24**), if the company decided to pay £200,000 instead of paying the £100,000 contractual payment, perhaps because the managing director's future employment prospects were poor, the extra £100,000 would not be deductible. There could be a view that any payment in excess of a contractual payment taints the whole payment, resulting in a failure to satisfy the 'wholly and exclusively' test, but HMRC BIM42955 confirms that, in this circumstance, in effect only the excess over the contractual entitlement is disallowed.

If payments are to be made to employees in excess of any existing contractual amounts then there will be a need to ensure that the payments are for a trade purpose if a corporation deduction is required. The contractual payments and other payments should ideally be made by separate cheques and such additional payments need to be clearly identified as relating to a trade purpose if that can be demonstrated, perhaps based upon the family company's trading results or indeed employee cooperation (see para **3.22**). Such payments need to be carefully minuted and evidenced, but perhaps a tax inspector may prove sceptical if the stated purpose is a bonus based upon trading results if the company has never previously made such payments or, indeed, in the period in which the payments are made profitability and turnover are falling.

EX GRATIA PAYMENTS

3.30   These are unlikely to satisfy the provisions of ICTA 1998, s 74(1)(a), if paid at the same time as the trading ceases. It has always seemed to the writer that the only justification for ex gratia payments is to avoid management time being involved in costly disputes, to allow it to be directed towards the business of earning profits. That purpose cannot be achieved if there is no future trade because the trade is being shut down.

The same situation is likely to apply if the business is being disincorporated into a sole trader/partnership. The payment is certainly not for the benefit of the trade as owned by the limited company, but perhaps may be for the benefit of the trade owned by the sole trader/partnership. In either event, it is not likely to be tax deductible since it will not have been made by the person who will obtain the benefit.

3.31   The expenditure areas discussed above represent typical expenditure incurred by companies ceasing to trade, or about to cease to trade, in anticipation of a solvent disincorporation with distribution of assets or cash to shareholders. It is the role of management and their advisers to ensure that the costs are managed in an efficient manner, and that includes not only keeping the costs within acceptable levels but also ensuring that, so far as possible, tax relief is obtained for the payments that are to be made. This is because there is often no choice but to make the payments and because the shareholders will want to generate the maximum funds available to them. Tax relief, at either 21% or 28%, reduces the costs of closing down the business so will increase the funds available to shareholders.

Just as in other areas considered in this publication, advance planning can improve the administrative efficiency of disincorporation, so advance planning for costs can also improve the tax efficiency of closing down. Clients often accept that particular items of expenditure have to be incurred whilst trading continues and, although the attendant tax relief is welcome, there is a general expectation that most items of expenditure incurred whilst trading continues to make a contribution to future profits, whether it is advertising, purchase of machinery or even redundancy costs, will improve future prospects. There is no such expectation at cessation of trade and costs incurred at this point are simply regarded as unwelcome overheads. Therefore, the more efficiently they can be managed, the greater will be the benefit for the shareholders.

CORPORATION TAX RELIEF FOR LOSSES

3.32 What happens if, as a result of any of the above allowable expenses, a loss is incurred in the final trading period? As a result of ICTA 1988, s 393A(2), losses incurred by trades that are continuing can only be carried back twelve months. However, when the trade has discontinued, a terminal loss relief claim under ICTA 1988, s 393A(2A) can be made.

Terminal loss relief claims can be made under ICTA 1988, s 393A to carry back losses made in the final 12 months of trading against profits made in the previous 36 months. In respect of losses that occur in the final period when the trade is discontinued, they can be carried back in full, assuming there are profits to cover the losses, for the three years prior to the accounting period in which cessation takes place.

Terminal loss may also arise in respect of losses for the final period of trading of 12 months so, where this straddles two CTAPs, an apportionment must be made in respect of the 12-month period of accounts that ends within 12 months of cessation to arrive at the net loss that can be carried back for three years.

Example

Raynham Park Ltd's normal accounting date is 30 April 2008 and ceases to trade on 30 September 2008. The results for the last two periods are:

Year to 30 April 2008	Loss	£24,000
Period to 30 September 2008	Loss	£5,000

The terminal loss is:

$$£5,000 + \frac{7}{12} \times £24,000 = £19,000$$

which is the loss for the final 12 months of trading.

The loss is to be set first against profits for most recent periods before being set against profits for earlier periods.

Equally, the terminal loss claim can be set against any other taxable source such as Schedule A income and capital gains and is a more flexible relief than the simply ongoing loss relief, which can only be set back 12 months.

Example

Salhouse Ltd ceased to trade 31 August 2008 and normally made its accounts up to 31 December. In the period 1 January 2008 to 31 August 2008, a loss of £40,000 was made.

In the year to 1 January 2007 to 31 December 2007, the company made a profit of £24,000.

Therefore, the terminal loss will be £40,000, which can be carried back to any earlier years.

As indicated, terminal loss is used first against more recent profits and only then against earlier profits.

Example

If the profits of Salhouse Ltd in earlier periods were as follows then the terminal loss relief claim set-off would be, as below, against the most recent period first.

Profits year to 31 December 2007	£24,000 (set-off of £24,000)
Profits year to 31 December 2006	£16,000 (loss set-off of £16,000)
Profits year to 31 December 2005	£8,000 (no relief)
Profits year to 31 December 2004	£6,000 (no relief)
Total profits	£54,000

If there were sufficient losses to carry back to the year to 31 December 2004, perhaps because the terminal loss could have been augmented by a share of any time apportioned loss in the year to 31 December 2007, the maximum loss that can be offset for that period would be £2,000. If the terminal loss were to be enhanced by a pro rata share of loss for, in this case, the year to 31 December 2007 then, for the element from the year to 31 December 2007, a strict 36-month limit on carry-back applies, so loss relievable profits at 1 September 2004 to 31 December 2004 are 4/12 × £6,000, ie £2,000.

3.33   Repayment supplement is unlikely to be an issue because entitlement only depends and accrues from the period in which the terminal loss claim is made.

At the current time, if the effect is to carry losses back to a period prior to 31 March 2007, then the overall value in terms of cash recovery of terminal loss relief may be significantly restricted. It is not possible to restrict the loss relief claim to a figure in any particular year that will restrict the taxable profits to £10,000 on which the tax might be for so some loss relief may fail to produce any refund of tax.

TOO MUCH LOSS RELIEF

3.34 What happens if the terminal loss, or indeed any of the losses, that the company has incurred exceed the profits previously made by the disincorporated company with the result that loss relief cannot be carried forward? Is there any mechanism for ensuring that the shareholders can benefit from those losses in the future either because they succeed to the trade or, more generally, against other income sources?

The short answer is no. Although there are provisions under ITA 2007, s 86 to allow trading losses made prior to incorporation to be carried forward by the (new) shareholders, provided particular requirements are satisfied, to be set by them against income received from the successor company, there are no corresponding provisions to allow the reverse position to apply.

Example

John transferred his sole trade business to Gunton Ltd in exchange for shares on 1 January 2008. At that date he had unused losses of £10,000, which he set against his salary from Gunton Ltd in the year to 31 December 2009.

If, in the Salhouse Ltd example (see para **3.32**), the terminal loss claim had exceeded £54,000, ie the profits in the period 1 September 2004 to 31 August 2007, then the excess would not be available to set against any other income source.

This is another of those examples, that appear throughout this publication, of a concessionary or statutory path to assist a company and its shareholders to transfer a trade from sole trader/partnership to a company but retain taxation benefits, whether by way of retained losses to reduce future taxable profits or deferment by CGT holdover where the reverse procedures are not protected by a tax shield.

3.35 If the trade is simply ceasing then any inability to carry losses forward may not cause any ongoing financial hardship other than perhaps a dissatisfaction that the losses have disappeared.

However, if the company is being dissolved because the trade is to be transferred to a revived sole trader/partnership under the same ownership then any loss relief trapped in the disincorporated company may cause financial hardship.

Accordingly, the shareholders and their advisers will need to manage, if this is possible, the extent of loss relief claimed. Therefore, we were aware of the need, in company accounting periods before 31 March 2006, of restricting capital allowances claims to ensure that the taxable profits fell below the £10,000 0 per cent band because below that figure there is no cash value in the capital allowances that, for example, reduced the taxable profits from £10,000 to £8,000. A similar view may need to be taken in the run up to disincorporation.

CESSATION OF TRADE

3.36   All companies have a corporation tax accounting period (CTAP) to which, generally, accounts will be made up, tax computations prepared and a return submitted to HMRC. In accordance with normal provisions, corporation tax will be payable nine months and one day after the end of the accounting period.

Example

Gorleston North Ltd makes its accounts up to 30 September 2008, so the tax for profits earned in the year to 30 September 2008 is payable on 1 July 2009.

However, the cessation of trade of a company brings to an end a CTAP. Unless this is at a normal accounting reference date, the effect will be to accelerate the date upon which tax becomes payable.

Example

Suppose Gorleston North Ltd ceased to trade on 31 December 2008. It would have a CTAP for the trading period 1 October 2008 to 31 December 2008 and tax on any profit earned in that period would be payable on 1 October 2009.

If the dissolution of Gorleston North Ltd was over an extended period then there would be a second CTAP for the period post-cessation from 1 January 2009 to 31 December 2009 and for this period tax would be payable at the normal payment date of 1 October 2010.

Bringing forward the tax payment dates should not cause any difficulty provided the issue is recognised early; increasingly, purchasers of a business are unwilling to pay the full price when the transfer takes place but, rather, want to pay by instalments. If you act for the vendor of a business, the proceeds will be taxable in the accounting period to cessation of trade whether they have been received or remain unpaid. Accordingly, we need to make sure that the client receives sufficient cash from the initial payment to meet any taxation liabilities that arise.

The previous paragraph referred to the normal basis for 'small' companies where tax is paid nine months and one day after the end of the accounting period. Larger companies have to make quarterly payments on account with the first payment being due six months and 13 days after the beginning of the accounting period. The remaining three instalments are due at three monthly intervals thereafter so that the final payment for any particular year will be due three months and 14 days after the end of the accounting period.

Example

Magdalen Road Ltd has an accounting period ended on 31 December 2008 so the quarterly instalments would have been due on 14 July 2008, 14 October 2008, 14 January 2009 and 14 April 2009.

For this purpose a company is regarded as large and therefore has an obligation to make quarterly payments if the chargeable payments are more than £1,500,000. If there are active companies in a group then this limit is spread proportionately between the active companies in the group.

Where, as a result of a change in circumstances, a company discovers it has paid too much under the quarterly payment regime, and such a circumstance might be the decision to dissolve the family company, it may apply to HMRC to have tax refunded if the anticipated profits are below the large company thresholds.

3.37   The clear objective of tax planning in relation to expenditure incurred in the run up to dissolution or on the sale of the trade and its assets should be to either maximise the tax relief that is available on expenditure that has to be incurred or to maximise the proceeds of sale. In either instance, the economic cost of tax relievable expenditure of £1,000 will vary between £790 and £720 (see para **3.6**) depending on the corporation tax rate, whereas an increase in sale proceeds of £1,000 will increase the cash available to shareholders by between £790 and £720, again depending on the corporation tax rates. If the proceeds can be in tax-free form, £1,000 proceeds equates to £1,000 for the shareholders.

It might be implicit in the foregoing paragraphs that the company has sufficient taxable profits in its final trading period to ensure that full relief is obtained for expenditure that has been incurred. That may not always be the case. In anticipation of dissolving the company, the enthusiasm of the shareholders and management may decline, the marginal cost of operating the business increase and the effect may well be a loss arising in the final corporation tax trading period that cannot otherwise be relieved. If the trade is to be transferred to a partnership controlled by the current shareholders, what can be done?

One way of achieving this will be for assets eligible for capital allowances to be sold at a value that incorporates unrelieved losses to be carried forward. Surprisingly, there is no requirement for capital allowance transactions to be at market value as between connected persons for assets within the general pool, although market value rules do apply to expensive motor cars and short life assets (see paras **3.40** and **3.41**) where arranged by a sale, so it would be possible to transfer tax relief from Family Limited to Family Partnership by arranging for plant and machinery to be sold at an appropriate value. Where plant or machinery is disposed of by a company, or any other business, then the disposal is valued in accordance with the table set out in CAA 2002, s 61. In effect, this means that the parties to a transaction, where they are connected and want to achieve a particular tax advantage are free to do so.

Certainly taxpayers and their advisers should avoid the idea, perhaps for a tidy file that the transaction has to be at market value. Unless there is an election under CAA 2001, s 266 to transfer at tax written down value, it is open to the parties to achieve a sale at whatever value they consider appropriate.

Example

Dersingham Ltd is about to cease trading and transfer the trade to its shareholders. At 31 August 2008, the tax written down value of the general capital allowances pool is £30,000, market value is £25,000, and in the final accounting period the company incurred £3,000 of additional expenditure.

Dersingham Ltd will have at cessation losses that cannot be relieved by terminal loss claims amounting to £14,000.

If an election were made under CAA 2001, s 266, the tax written down value would be inherited by the successor partnership as follows:

Tax written down value	30,000
Additions	3,000
Tax value	33,000

If there were to be a sale at less than market value, in this case less than £25,000, then disposal event 2 of CAA 2001, s 61(2)(Table) would require Dersingham Ltd to achieve the following result:

Tax written down value	30,000
Additions	3,000
Tax value	33,000
Less market value	25,000
Balancing allowance	8,000

3.38   However, here we are looking at a company who already has losses that will be lost on a disincorporation because they remain ring fenced in the company so an extra £8,000 of losses is of no use to the company or its shareholders, shortly to be partners, who would like to use as many of the losses as possible in the new trade, particularly if they can obtain relief at either 28% (basic rate plus Class 4) or even 41% or 48%. What the company can do is use the definition in disposal event 1 of CAA 2001, s 61(2)(Table), which states that the disposal value is the actual sale proceeds, except in a case where the plant and machinery is sold at less than market value. This view is confirmed by HMRC Capital Allowances Manual 23250, where the relevant extracts state:

'**Disposal values [September 2007]**
Section 61(2)–(5), Section 62 & Section 63 CAA 2001; Paragraph 9(3)(c) Schedule 18 FA 2002. These are the disposal values for the various disposal events in CA23240.'

Disposal event	Disposal value
Sale of the asset	*Net proceeds of sale (see CA11540) plus any insurance money received as a result of an event affecting the sale price and any other capital compensation received*
Sale of the asset at less than market value	*Market value unless there is a charge under ITEPA on the buyer or the buyer can claim PMAs or RDAs on the asset and the buyer is not a dual resident investing company connected with the seller*

Therefore, Dersingham Ltd could achieve the following result, but since the company has losses of £14,000 this result is tax neutral so far as the company is concerned, but the new partnership has allowances of £47,000 available.

Tax written down value	30,000
Additions	3,000
Tax value	33,000
Sale proceeds	47,000
Balancing charge	14,000

The balancing charge of £14,000 is covered by losses that might otherwise be unrelieved. Finally, the sale proceeds cannot exceed original cost because any balancing charge is limited by this value. Therefore, if the original cost of Dersingham Ltd's capital allowance eligible assets was, for example, £44,000, this would be the maximum sale proceeds that could enter the above calculation so the balancing charge would be restricted to £11,000, and so (in this instance) £3,000 of losses (losses £14,000 − balancing charge £11,000) would be lost.

3.39   There is however one important factor that needs to be taken into account in order to achieve this arrangement, which is that there must be a sale from the company to the new sole trader/partnership. If there is no sale then the market value rule of disposal event 2 of CAA 2001, s 61 requires the disposal to generate the balancing allowance we are trying to avoid (for example, see para **3.37**). Therefore, in the circumstances envisaged by this publication, the mere distribution of the plant and machinery to the shareholders at dissolution would be a disposal at market value because it would not be regarded as a sale for this particular purpose, even though market value would be taken into account for capital gains tax purposes. If a particular planning result needs to be achieved then a sale is required. That sale may be subject to VAT (unless the TOGC rules set out in para **9.10** can be met), but at worst that would merely be a timing difference.

3.40 This technique does not, however, work for all assets eligible for capital allowances. In the case of expensive motor cars, the effect of CAA 2001, ss 79 and 213 is to impose market value on any transaction. Because of the restriction of capital allowances to £3,000 until written down value reduces below £12,000, the likely effect is that expensive motor vehicles will be carried at a tax value in excess of market value so the impact will be a balancing allowance in the computations of the vendor, in this case the Family Company. Accordingly, it is probable that an election to transfer at tax value will be relevant here to ensure the successor business gets full value for capital allowance eligible assets.

Example

Buckenham Ltd owns a BMW with a tax written down value of £44,000 but has a market value of £26,000; on transfer to shareholders, the position without an election is:

Tax written down value	44,000
Market value	26,000
Balancing allowance	18,000

3.41 A similar position exists with short life assets still within the first four years of ownership. Where there is a transfer between connected parties and the usual ICTA 1988, s 839 rules apply, the purchaser and vendor have the choice of continuing the short life regime by election under CAA 2001, s 89(6) with the result that the transfer will be at tax written down value. If the parties do not elect, the effect of CAA 2001, s 89(4) – because this is a transaction between connected parties – is that the transfer is at the lower of either market value or cost so, unless market value is lower than tax written down value, no balancing allowance will arise, although it is possible that there will be a balancing charge because in most cases market value will be lower than cost.

3.42 So far as Industrial Buildings Allowance and Agricultural Buildings Allowance are concerned where the sale, or disposal took place before 21 March 2007 it was possible to achieve some modest tax planning gains by triggering a balancing charge to allow the original cost of the asset to be transferred to a successor where the balancing charge event was within the first 25 years following construction. That ability has now passed and the successor merely gains the normal annual writing down allowance because there was no balancing charge on the vendor. Indeed after 31 March 2011 there will be no allowances for either industrial buildings or agricultural buildings. It would have been unusual to elect to achieve a balancing allowance or charge in respect of agricultural buildings, but it was possible under CAA 2001, s 380, otherwise transfer was at capital allowance value but no longer for disposal on or after 21 March 2007.

LOANS TO PARTICIPATORS

3.43 It will often be the case that companies approaching dissolution or liquidation have made loans to directors or shareholders in circumstances that forced a loan of tax to HMRC under ICTA 1988, s 419 to be made. Some authorities suggest that the Companies Act 1985 restrictions on loans to directors have had the direct consequence that such loans are less common than they may previously have been. Others may realise that within companies that are director-/shareholder-controlled, the tendency to treat the company bank account as a private bank account is still prevalent with the consequence that loans are frequently made. Accounting gymnastics are frequently undertaken in order to make sure that the loans are repaid before any charge under ICTA 1988, s 419 becomes payable, but that is not always possible.

Where a company is being dissolved, recovery of any ICTA 1988, s 419 tax may be an important element in the funds available for shareholders. Where, as part of the dissolution process, monies due to a particular shareholder are withheld and used to settle sums due to the company, it is possible to make a recovery of the tax previously paid. In normal circumstances, there would be an expectation that cash should be repaid to the company, but HMRC Company Taxation Manual, para 61605 confirms that book entries are an acceptable basis to prove repayment. Therefore, there will be a book entry to record repayment of the loan and a book entry recording payment of the gross balance due to a shareholder with the cheque showing the net position. This mechanism allows the company to recover any advance corporation tax paid on the loan.

> **'BOOK ENTRIES**
> You need not object to repayment via book entries if those entries reflect the underlying reality of a transaction and they are properly recorded in the company's books (see the comments of Vinelott J in *Minsham Properties Ltd v Price* (63 TC 570 at p.585) beginning "There can be no doubt that a book entry can constitute payment". But a repayment by this means should only be treated as taking place at the date the book entries are made and it is only at that date that the Section 419(4) relief is due.'

Example

Arthur Peacock, a shareholder in Aldeby Ltd received a loan from the company of £25,000 in circumstances where the company made a payment to HMRC under ICTA 1988, s 419 of £6,250.

The company is due to be dissolved and as the first distribution, Arthur was due to receive £30,000. In fact the company holds back the loan and only makes a payment to Arthur of £5,000. Therefore, it will be possible to recover the £6,250 ICTA 1988, s 419 payment.

CORPORATION TAX RATE APPLYING IN DISSOLUTION

3.44 Under the terms of ICTA 1988, s 13A, any close company in the process of being wound-up, either through a formal liquidation or by the concession route, is a close investment-holding company, with the consequence that the benefit of the lower rates of corporation tax are not available. Accordingly, any profits subject to corporation tax should be subject to a current rate of 28%. However, a degree of relief is available through Revenue Interpretation 21 (see Appendix 7), which states that if a company was a trading company in the accounting period prior to liquidation then it will not be regarded as a close investment-holding company in the accounting period immediately following liquidation. In effect, for small companies the higher rate of tax will not apply provided the liquidators can sell the assets within 12 months of either the date of liquidation or cessation of trade (see the 'Beccles Ltd' example below). This also applies if the company is being wound-up under the s 652 and s 652A procedures.

3.45 The close investment-holding company rules apply because when a company is in liquidation it no longer exists for trading purposes but instead exists solely for the purposes of realising its assets and making distributions to its shareholders and creditors.

Example

Beccles Ltd's normal accounting period is up to 31 December 2008, but in the accounting period ended 31 December 2008 it is placed in liquidation on 30 September 2008.

Under Revenue Interpretation 21 the trading accounting period comes to an end on 30 September 2008 and thereafter, whilst the company is in liquidation, accounting periods then end on the 12-month anniversary of the appointment of the liquidator. Accordingly, if the company can dispose of all of its assets by 30 September 2009 it will have the benefit of Revenue Interpretation 21, if the lower tax rates applied before cessation of trade.

3.46 So far as companies in formal liquidation are concerned, the date upon which the trading accounting period ends is, as in other cases discussed in this publication, fixed at the date on which the liquidator is appointed. For companies applying ESC C16, the date may be less clear-cut and will be a question of fact. The factors discussed in paras **3.2–3.4** need to be taken into account in determining the end of an accounting period. The relevant date is likely to be the date trading ceases, so Revenue Interpretation 21 should apply for the 12 months beyond the date of cessation of trade.

3.47 HMRC Company Taxation Manual 60780 contains a further relaxation of the strict rules. This covers the situation where a company ceases to trade but the liquidator is not appointed until some time later. This is because if there is a gap between trading ceasing on the appointment of the liquidator, on a strict interpretation the company would be a close investment-holding company in that final trading period because it would not satisfy ICTA 1988, s 13A(4). The relevant manual paragraph is set out below.

'Where a close company commences liquidation, Section 13A(4) ICTA 1988 provides that it is not to be treated as a close investment-holding company (CIC) in the accounting period immediately following the commencement of winding-up if it was not a CIC in the accounting period immediately before liquidation commenced. In any subsequent accounting period a close company in liquidation will be excluded from being a CIC only if it then meets the usual conditions of Section 13A(2) – see CTM60710.

It may happen that there is a very short gap between the end of a period in which the company was not a CIC and the commencement of winding-up, so that strictly the company will not have the benefit of Section 13A(4). This may cause difficulties in some cases and an undertaking has been given to review the position where a company has not been able to avoid a short gap and would suffer significantly if not given the protection of Section 13A(4).'

Example

Brampton Ltd's accounting period usually ran to 31 January 2009, but on 31 August 2008 it ceased to trade. A liquidator was formally appointed on 1 November 2008, but by virtue of Company Taxation Manual 60780 the period from 1 August 2008 would be eligible for the small companies' rates.

3.48   There is much that can be achieved in managing the corporation tax position of the company during a period approaching dissolution. The aim must be to ensure that, wherever possible, full relief is obtained for items of expenditure that have to be incurred in dissolving the company, such as redundancy payments, but equally to ensure that loss relief does not become locked in the company that is to be dissolved. As indicated in para **3.38,** where the limited company is to be dissolved but the current shareholders are to carry on the same trade in succession then there is some scope for transferring losses through the medium of enhanced capital expenditure.

There is no substitute for sitting down and looking at the facts, making sure that matters are discussed properly with the client, equally making sure that the client discusses matters properly with you to ensure that timing of expenditure and/or transactions are appropriate.

PLANNING POINTS

3.49

- Ensure that evidence is available to support the tax deductibility of particular items of expenditure.

- Ensure that if professional advisers incur costs, which are either allowable or disallowable, that their invoices reflect the different areas of concern.

- Consider carefully the timing for when expenditure has to be incurred and/or paid to obtain tax relief.

- Review carefully the balance sheet at the date of cessation of trade to make sure that assets are stated at their lowest realisable value, ie full provision has been made for bad doubtful debts and any other fall in value.

- Equally make sure that full provision has been made for all known liabilities. The normal rules apply for provisions and make sure that any item included in the cessation of accounts is for a specific purpose and can be supported by data.

- If pension planning is a key element either of the post-cessation personal position of the shareholders or the company's corporation tax planning, make sure that payments are made at the appropriate time.

- Consider what evidence is required, and actually available, to define extra costs incurred in the run up to trading ceasing as assisting current trading conditions rather than assisting the close down of the business.

- Wherever possible ensure asset sales are made whilst the company is not treated as a Close Investment Company to ensure a lower corporation tax rate.

Chapter 4

Shareholder issues

4.1   When considering the tax position of shareholders in a company that is about to be dissolved, it is not just the CGT issues that require to be addressed. The shareholders may have organised their personal affairs tax efficiently in relation to funds currently used by the family company in order to maximise income tax relief whilst the company was trading, but cessation of trade and proposals to distribute funds to them may cause the previous planning to unravel. Accordingly, there are issues that need to be addressed so that although the loss of some income tax relief during the dissolution period is inevitable, we need to ensure that this loss is managed and that monies received are used against loans or other arrangements in the correct order to ensure interest is not paid that is not tax relievable. If the shareholder simply reinvests the company proceeds on deposit, the interest received will be taxable but there will be no relief for the interest on any loan balances.

LOSS OF INTEREST RELIEF

4.2   In the circumstances envisaged by this publication, loan interest relief is likely to have been available to shareholders, and in some cases employees, in the following circumstances.

- Under the terms of ITA 2007, s 390 (formerly ICTA 1988, s 359) – in respect of a loan to buy plant and machinery in circumstances that allow the holder of an office or employment to claim capital allowances, where the relevant asset is used in the office or employment. For this relief there is a time limit where interest relief is restricted to the year in which the loan is taken out and the next three tax years.

- Under ITA 2007, s 392 (formerly ICTA 1988, s 360) – where the money is used to purchase either ordinary share capital in a close company or in making a loan to that close company where the loan is ultimately used for trading purposes.

- Under ITA 2007, s 396 (formerly ICTA 1988, s 361)– being a loan to purchase an interest in an employee-controlled company.

4.3   There are a number of requirements to be satisfied in relation to the payment of interest so that it can be allowed for tax purposes. When considering the dissolution of a family company, as will be seen below, at some point during the dissolution process the company is likely to fail the necessary qualifying conditions with the consequent result that interest relief, for the shareholder or employee paying the interest, is lost.

Where relief is claimed under ITA 2007, s 390 (formerly ICTA 1988, s 359), it is sufficient that the equipment purchased with the loan is used in the office or employment. There is no requirement for the office or employment to be related to a trade; it follows that if the employee works in a company, that interest relief continues to be available even if trading has ceased, so long as the relevant individual remains an employee. This appears to be confirmed by Revenue Manual RE402 and EIM 36500, that the only requirement is the equipment is used for the employment or duties.

Under ITA 2007, s 392 the tests are that the company must be a close company and exist wholly or mainly to carry on a trade or trades on a commercial basis. There are additional qualifications where the monies are used for an acquisition in relation to a group, but again the fundamental purpose for which the group exists must be to conduct or coordinate trading arrangements. The proceeds of any loan must be used to acquire either ordinary share capital or to make a loan to the company; again a requirement is the money should be applied for trade purposes within a reasonable time from being advanced.

An individual will be able to claim interest relief either from controlling at least 5% of the company, in some form whether on their own or with associates or, if the individual owns less than 5% of the shares, is employed for the greater part of his time in the management of the company. For this purpose, the greater part of a person's time is considered to be more than 50% of a working week (see Relief Instructions Manual 423.)

4.4 The most common position that causes a reduction in loan interest relief is when an individual recovers capital from the business. That situation is certainly going to exist on the dissolution of a family company because the value of the company, and loans and related assets are to be distributed back to the shareholder borrower.

4.5 Again, once trading has ceased (in whatever circumstances), whether or not the assets have already been distributed to the shareholders, it cannot be said that the company any longer exists wholly or mainly for the appropriate qualifying purposes. Accordingly, loan interest relief will stop from the date trading ceases and if any interest is paid after the date of cessation, no relief will be available. There are no provisions whereby the loan interest can be time apportioned between periods that are eligible and periods that are ineligible. Accordingly, in order to maximise any available relief, a borrower should approach his lender and make sure that they pay interest before the trading has ceased up to the date trading is expected to cease.

The shareholder's bankers will continue to charge interest even though it may no longer qualify for tax relief. Accordingly, in order to minimise the interest payable, it may make sense to apply the first amounts received to repay any loans. Some taxpayers will have taken out loans that carry penalties if redeemed early and if penalties apply to any early redemption, the possible penalty needs to be compared to the interest payable if the loan is allowed to continue.

Example

Joan Smith has a loan from her bank of £20,000, which she advanced to Hemsby Ltd, a trading company, where the trade is to cease on 30 September 2009 and the value of the company is to be distributed to the shareholders. Joan's bank charges interest monthly, in arrears, on the first day of each month, so to maximise relief she contacts the bank manager and arranges for interest up to 30 September 2009 to be paid in September 2009.

She subsequently recovers £15,000 as the first payment of her entitlement on 20 December 2009. No income tax relief is due on any interest charged between 1 October 2009 and 20 December 2009, but she applies £10,000 to repay the loan. Interest will continue to be charged on the balance of £10,000, but no interest relief is available.

4.6   Matters in relation to the recovery of capital from a close company are set out in ITA, ss 406–407 (formerly ICTA 1988, s 363), and the rules there make no distinction between amounts advanced to the close company by way of loan or in respect of monies that have been used to acquire shares in the close company. Recovery of capital is simply deemed to go against all the loans. It is not possible to ring fence separate advances in respect of monies used to make a loan to a close company and monies used to acquire shares in order to continue relief.

Example

Peter owned 20% of Stowe Bedon Ltd and at various times had taken out loans totalling £40,000, being £15,000 to acquire shares in the company and £25,000 to advance monies to the company.

As part of a reorganisation, he sold half of his shareholding to bring his holding down to 10% for £35,000. The whole of this sum counts as a capital recovery and therefore the interest relief, for the future, will be restricted to a loan of £5,000.

INCOME TAX RELIEF FOR CAPITAL LOSSES

4.7   Income tax relief can be available on a capital loss arising on shares against other taxable income. The loss is only available when the individual concerned has subscribed for the shares, ITA 2007, s 131 (formerly ICTA 1988, s 574), and the disposal must be either by way of a bargain at arm's length or arising from a distribution in the course of the dissolving or winding-up of the company; or a negligible value claim has been made under TCGA 1982, s 24(2). Accordingly, when considering the dissolution of the company, there may be circumstances where the company is solvent and therefore shareholders will receive some money, but the amounts received are less than the amount subscribed by them. Accordingly, an income tax claim can be made.

For transactions that took place before 5 April 2000, there were some restrictions on claiming this relief on a dissolution of the company where matters were governed by ESC D46, although this is now obsolete and relief is now governed by ITA 2007, s 131 (formerly ICTA 1988, ss 574, 575).

Example

Elizabeth subscribed for 25% of the shares of Wolferton Ltd at a cost of £25,000, which represented 250 ordinary shares of £1 each at a premium of £99 per share. The trading was moderately successful, but the shareholders all agreed that the company should be dissolved and funds returned to them. On dissolution, Elizabeth received £30 per share, ie £7,500, so will be entitled to make an income tax claim for the balance of the amount subscribed of £17,500.

CREATING A TAX CHARGE

4.8   When considering the capital gains tax position on part disposals (see para **6.13**), reference is made to Inland Revenue Capital Gains Manual CG 40432 where, on a part disposal, HMRC will accept almost any value for the remaining shares provided the valuation seems reasonable and the liquidation is expected to be completed within two years of the date of the first distribution.

4.9   HMRC are aware (see Venture Capital Schemes Manual 45800) that it might be possible to exploit the valuation flexibility referred to above in order to increase the amount of relief obtainable under ITA 2007, s 131. Where a number of distributions take place in a winding-up, the effect of understating the residual value in the part disposal formula could be to inflate the amount of loss relief available under ITA 2007, s 131 on the early distributions, with the result that, perhaps on the final distribution, there might be a capital gain that may be covered by the annual exemption.

HMRC Venture Capital Schemes Manual 45800 also confirms the contrary position that if the residual value is overstated then this has the effect of restricting the relief under ITA 2007, s 131, although it is difficult to envisage the circumstances in which a taxpayer would want to understate the relief. Perhaps the only circumstances in which an apparent advantage might be obtained is if a taxpayer was only a basic rate taxpayer in the year in which a first distribution is made, but it is likely to be a higher rate taxpayer in a year in which a subsequent second distribution is to be made and, therefore, manipulation of residual values could increase the loss eligible for ITA 2007, s 131 relief in a particular year. Inspectors who are aware of the advantages are instructed to refer valuations to Shares Valuation to determine the residual value where, following a distribution, either:

- a chargeable gain arises on an interim distribution and relief is claimed under ITA 2007, s 131 in respect of a later distribution; or

- relief is claimed under ITA 2007, s 131 in respect of an interim distribution, and the residual value shown in the computation is known not to be in accordance with the aggregate amount of all later distributions.

4.10 As indicated above, the essential requirement in order to claim the relief is that the company where a loss is claimed must have been a trading company. In addition, the shares must be shares that the claimant has subscribed for; they cannot be shares that have been acquired from a previous shareholder. Accordingly, identification rules apply where a shareholder wants to make a claim but has a holding that comprises both subscribed shares and purchased shares. In effect shares are, from 6 April 2007, matched on a last-in first-out basis which may have the effect of denying or allowing relief depending upon the order of acquisition. In most cases it might be thought that the effect of the matching will be to deny relief on the basis that within most companies there is usually only an initial subscription and any subsequent reorganisation of shareholdings occurs when shareholders acquire shares from each other.

Example

Joan has a holding of 50,000 shares in Dunham Ltd, comprising 30,000 subscribed for in April 2002 and 20,000 acquired in July 2008. If she sells 10,000 shares in January 2009, they will be matched against the July 2008 acquisition, so no relief under ITA 2007, s 131 would be available.

A sale of 25,000 shares equally would only allow a loss relief claim on 5,000 shares on the basis that the matching exhausts the July 2008 acquisition and then applies to the first acquisition.

RELIEF FOR LOSSES ON LOANS MADE TO A FAMILY COMPANY

4.11 In the circumstances envisaged by this publication, the distribution of assets from a solvent company (relief for losses on loans made to traders under TCGA 1992, s 253) is unlikely to be applicable. However, where a loan becomes irrecoverable from a company where a shareholder has made a loan – perhaps where loan interest relief was previously obtained under ITA 2007, s 392 (see para **4.2**) – then the lender can obtain a capital gains loss in respect of any loss on the loan provided they satisfy particular requirements:

- the borrower company used the money wholly for the purposes of a trade carried on by them;

- the company was resident in the United Kingdom;

- the borrower's debt is not a debt on security as defined in TCGA 1992, s 132;

- the loan must have become irrecoverable and the loss must belong to the person who had the original loan; and

- the right to loss relief is lost if the original lender assigns their debt to another person.

4.12 If a claim is made, and accepted, under TCGA 1992, s 253 for the full amount of the loan but, at a later date, a recovery has been made then that recovery is treated as a separate capital gain that arises in the tax year in which the recovery is made.

Example

George advanced a loan to Overstrand Ltd of £50,000. On 10 September 2008, the company goes into insolvent liquidation and George only recovers £5,000 of his original loan. He may therefore make a claim under TCGA 1992, s 253 for the amount not recovered of £45,000.

Sometime later, the liquidators of Overstrand Ltd succeed in a legal claim against the company's bankers with the result that they recover sufficient funds to make a further payment to George of £20,000 on 14 September 2010. The £20,000 is treated as a capital gain arising in 2010/11.

CONVERTING LOANS INTO SHARES

4.13 It will occasionally be suggested that shareholders/loan creditors in trading companies, which are going through a difficult time and where it might be anticipated that the company will go into insolvent liquidation at some point in the future, would be advised to convert loan capital in the company into share capital. This is so that they might take advantage, at a future date, of a claim for income tax relief under ITA 2007, s 131, on the general presumption that most taxpayers will, at some time, have income rather than seeking to rely upon the TCGA 1992, s 253 relief because, in most cases taxpayers do not generally produce taxable capital gains on a regular basis. This particularly might be the case if an individual has previously been the shareholder in a failed company. If this situation arises then it is generally disadvantageous to convert a loan into shares because the consequence is likely to be a loss of relief. A shareholder who converts a loan into share capital in circumstances where the company subsequently becomes insolvent can not then make a claim for relief under TCGA 1992, s 253 because at the date of liquidation the loan no longer exists. It has been converted into share capital.

Equally, relief under ITA 2007, s 131is unlikely to be available because the subscription for the shares is deemed to take place under the provisions of TCGA 1992, s 17 at market value. It therefore follows that if the shareholder/loan creditor is involved in a company, which was insolvent at the date of conversion, then the acquisition value for the shares may well be £nil, or so close to £nil that the effect of restricting the available relief is that no relief is available.

Example

Penny is a shareholder in Old Leake Ltd and, at 31 August 2008, the balance sheet showed a deficit on reserves of £50,000 after taking account of a loan from Penny of £25,000.

She agrees, under pressure from the bank, to convert her loan capital into shares, but even after the conversion the company remains insolvent because the net deficit still remains at £25,000, so under TCGA 1992, s 17 the acquisition value for Penny's 25,000 shares is likely to be £nil.

4.14   It is insufficient to simply look at the face value of the debt in relation to the overall assets of the company and to say that, as a result of converting loan capital into shares, the company has become solvent and that the value of the new shares (for any purpose, including ITA 2007, s 131) must be the extent of the disclosed balance sheet surplus. What requires assessment is market value, which must include consideration of the amount that anyone would pay to acquire the debt, or even what the loan owner would accept to sell the debt. These types of arrangements are often only considered in respect of companies close to insolvency. The market value of the debt will be a significant discount to face value. Agreeing the value will be a share valuation exercise outside the scope of this publication, but (as discussed elsewhere) the face value of any asset or liability is only the starting point.

Example

Suppose that instead of a deficit of £50,000, Old Leake Ltd only had a deficit of £10,000 and that Penny's loan was £40,000.

As a result of converting her entire loan into shares, the company now becomes solvent to the extent of £30,000. However, the acquisition value of Penny's additional shares is unlikely to be £30,000 because that will not represent the market value of her loan. In this circumstance the acquisition value would have to be negotiated, but it is likely that the value will show a significant discount to the £30,000 anticipated value.

4.15   As mentioned above, the income tax relief under ITA 2007, s 131 is likely to be more valuable than the relief under TCGA 1992, s 253, simply because most taxpayers are more likely to have income rather than capital gains. Few promoters of a business consider the tax advantages that might arise if the business fails. Equally, advisers are likely to suggest, in most cases, that a company be formed with minimal share capital and a maximum of director loan. This is perceived to have a number of advantages:

- the director/shareholder can charge the company interest, which is tax deductible;

- the director's loan account can be repaid as the business develops and therefore money can be extracted tax-free; and

- share capital can only be realised on a liquidation or sale.

If, however, it is recognised that the newly promoted company may be subject to higher risk factors where there is a possibility that the company will fail then the shareholders/promoters of the business would be better advised to subscribe all their funds as shares for cash so that in the event of failure there is unlikely to be any dispute as to the market value of the shares because, at the date of subscription, the company would have been solvent and no restriction would apply under TCGA 1992, s 17.

PAYMENTS UNDER GUARANTEE

4.16   One final area where shareholders or directors may find themselves having to make payments on behalf of an insolvent company will be where they have agreed to guarantee the company's overdraft or other borrowings. Where an individual has guaranteed a loan then a capital gains tax loss can be claimed for payments made under TCGA 1992, s 253 of the amount paid by the claimant guarantor, less any amounts he is able to recover from his co-guarantors.

There are ranges of conditions that have to be satisfied in order for the payment to generate an allowable capital cost, of which the most important are the following.

- The loan must have been of money.

- The loan was used wholly for the purposes of the borrower's trade, profession or vocation, but the trade does not consist of lending money.

- The loan was used for the purpose of setting up a trade provided a trade is actually set up.

- The loan was made to a borrower resident in the United Kingdom.

As in the case of claims under ICTA 1988, s 363, if there are subsequent recoveries (see HMRC Capital Gains Manual 66071 and 66072) then these are deemed to be capital gains arising in the year of recovery (see para **4.12**).

CREDITOR VOLUNTARY ARRANGEMENTS

4.17   Creditor voluntary arrangements ('CVA') sit uneasily within this publication because they are neither a solvent situation nor are they a circumstance where an immediate liquidation will take place. In effect, they are often the last throw of the dice by both the company and its suppliers. There is a recognition that the company cannot pay its dues and demands in full, probably cannot pay at all, but equally the creditors know that if they all step off the edge and force insolvency, that the best they can achieve is tax relief for the bad debt and, perhaps, some VAT refunds. If the company continues to trade, the creditors may gain because they will make a profit out of future sales to the company and the company may also benefit because it survives. Within the assumptions of this text, a CVA may offer planning opportunities that are not available at any other time. If the company fails then the shareholders will have lost any value subscribed for the shares (and relief will be available as discussed above), but if the company comes through the CVA then significant future value may have been extracted from the current shareholder's estates at a modest cost.

Under CVA, a company that can not pay its creditors enters into a binding agreement with those creditors that – over a period of time (conventionally three to five years) and provided that a relatively nominal payment is made towards the monies due – at the expiry of the CVA period, any balance due to the creditors will be written off. For most creditors, this is simply accepting the best of a bad job because, if the company were forced into liquidation, nothing would be received. Such arrangements are becoming more common because the philosophy of insolvency practice is to try to save businesses wherever possible.

WRITE BACK OF CVA DEBTS THAT WERE FORGIVEN

4.18 In normal circumstances, the writing back of a trade creditor that has not been paid is simply a taxable credit to the profit and loss account in accordance with established principles. Under the provisions of ICTA 1988, s 94, such an amount is taxable. That seems correct, both in terms of the legislation and also under the terms of current accounting treatment that would treat a creditor write back as an addition to the published profit. Current practice is now to seek to align tax computations and treatment with the relevant accounting treatment, unless a specific statutory provision determines otherwise, and these would treat the write back of a creditor as a credit to the profit and loss account. Therefore any creditor write back would be taxable.

However, if the credit to the profit and loss account is by way of a release of the balance creditor under the terms of a CVA then this amount is not taxable because the release under a CVA is as part of a relevant arrangement or compromise:

Under ICTA 1988, s 94:

'(1) Where, in computing for corporation tax purposes the profits of a trade or profession, a deduction has been allowed for any debt incurred for the purposes of the trade or profession], then, if the whole or any part of the debt is thereafter released otherwise than as part of a statutory insolvency agreement, the amount released shall be treated as a receipt of the trade or profession arising in the period in which the release is effected.

(2) In subsection (1) above 'relevant arrangement or compromise' has the same meaning as in section 74.'Company Taxation Manual 6260 includes the following comment:

'Under Section 144 FA 1994, from 30 November 1993, where trade debts have been foregone as part of a voluntary arrangement under the Insolvency Act 1986 the release will not however result in a charge under Section 94. If evidence comes to light that this provision is being used to counteract the relevant liabilities restriction a report should be made to CT&VAT (Technical).'

Therefore, where creditors are forgiven as a result of a CVA then there can be no doubt that the release does not generate a tax charge. This may be important because the shareholders may decide, once they are through the CVA and the company has returned to a form of solvency, that they will then decide to dissolve the company. Any tax charge at that stage would be unwelcome.

INHERITANCE TAX POSITION

4.19 Ownership of shares in a CVA company that carries on a trade entitles the owner to BPR (see para **11.1**) because the company is still trading. If the shareholders are confident that the business can be revived then this may be an appropriate time to make gifts to other family members because the transfer value will be low.

Current value	Low?
Less BPR (100%)	Low?
Taxable value	Low?

Even if claw back applies – if the company is sold on within the seven-year post gift period – or the donor dies, the amount subject to taxation as a failed PET will also be low because it is the original transfer value, ie £Nil in the above illustration, not the proceeds achieved on sale that become taxable.

OTHER TAXATION ISSUES

4.20 Whilst the CVA is underway, the CVA supervisor will be holding funds on deposit whilst creditors make claims and those claims are agreed. Any interest that arises is income belonging to the company and will need to be returned on the appropriate corporation tax return. Accordingly, details of interest and tax deducted will need to be obtained each year.

Any expenses incurred by the company in connection with the CVA are unlikely to be eligible for tax relief because they may not satisfy wholly or mainly the requirements of ICTA 1988, s 74, as not being related to trading activities.

ACCOUNTING TREATMENT

4.21 The payments to the CVA supervisor, in part settlement of the balances due to the company's creditors, are not tax deductible in the years in which they are paid. This is because they are simply a reduction of the amounts that are due to the relevant creditors, where the liability is already reflected in the value of any corporation tax losses carried forward. The amounts paid to the CVA supervisor should simply be deducted from the creditor balance.

Example

Fakenham West Ltd owed its creditors a total of £400,000 at 31 July 2005 when it entered into a CVA.

Under the terms of the CVA, the agreement was that £10,000 would be paid to the CVA supervisor for each of the next five years.

Therefore, in the accounts to 31 July 2006, the creditor balance would be shown as £400,000, less one year's contribution to the CVA supervisor. This process would continue for the full five years of the arrangement.

4.22   The balances due to the creditors cease to be claimable only when the conditions of the CVA had been satisfied, as in the above case by the expiry of five years. If the company were to go into insolvent liquidation prior to the five-year period, the whole of the balance of the creditor theoretically becomes due, although in practice it would simply become a claim in the liquidation.

At the expiry of five years, the creditor balance – which is no longer payable – should be credited back to the profit and loss account, with no adjustment through the corporation tax computation (see para **4.18**).

The adjustment should be made in the accounting period that the creditor voluntary arrangement is satisfied. This is because, under accounting standards, this is a non-adjusting post balance sheet event; it is only at the date the voluntary arrangement is satisfied that an adjustment can be made.

Example

Walsingham Ltd makes its accounts up to 30 September 2008, but the CVA was agreed on 31 July 2008.

The five-year period expires on 31 July 2013 so the adjustment will be made in the accounting period 1 October 2012 to 30 September 2013.

This would be the case even if the accounts to 31 July 2012 had not been drafted at the time the CVA was satisfied. This is because it is a non-adjusting post balance sheet event.

PLANNING POINTS

4.23

- Consider carefully the capital structure at commencement, or at any other stage, to ensure optimum tax relief is available.

- Use any advances from the company to repay borrowings to avoid interest charges that are not deductible.

- Assess the value of recoveries to see if any income tax relief claim can be made under either ITA 2007, s 131 or TCGA 1992, s 253.

- Consider if converting loans into share capital whilst the company is apparently insolvent is an appropriate action and what tax benefit accrues.

- Prepare detailed calculations to demonstrate that the B factor in any partial disposal calculation is based upon future distributions.

Chapter 5

Extra Statutory Concession C16

5.1   Extra Statutory Concession C16 is often considered appropriate for small-scale dissolutions where the costs of a liquidator are substantial in relation to the assets available. Paragraph **2.30** set out an indication of the minimum level of a liquidator's fees and the factors that result in costs at that level being required. The concessionary treatment will be cheaper, simply because the tax adviser writes a short letter to HMRC and submits the company and shareholder undertakings set out in Appendix 3 and 4 and, in most cases, the consent is obtained. Until a few years ago, it was enough for the adviser to give the undertakings on behalf of the company, but even with the current requirement for shareholders to sign the additional administration costs should be modest. Additionally, the client can undertake most of the tidying up of assets and settlement of liabilities.

The reasons for the additional administration and the need for shareholder undertakings are set out in para **5.5**

ESC C16 REQUIREMENTS – HMRC

5.2   An alternative to the appointment of a liquidator for clients who wish to save costs or where the company is solvent but the value of the assets does not justify the cost of a liquidator, is to apply to HMRC to use Extra Statutory Concession C16. The effect of HMRC consent is that payments to shareholders are treated as capital sums and therefore subject to the CGT regime.

In all other circumstances, a distribution to shareholders by a company is always treated as an income distribution and therefore subject to the income tax regime on dividends.

In most circumstances, providing certain assurances are given to HMRC and generally best practice is to apply before the event, the Revenue is prepared – for tax purposes – to regard the distribution as though it was made under a formal winding-up so that the proviso to ICTA 1988, s 209(1) applies. The value of the distribution is then treated as a capital receipt of the shareholders for the purpose of calculating any chargeable gains arising to them on the disposal of their shares in the company.

It must however be remembered that the distribution is still legally a dividend, albeit subject to the legal fiction that it is now taxed as capital. Accordingly there will be a need for minutes to declare the relevant dividends and a need to ensure that excessive dividends are not declared where any excess paid out to shareholders over distributable reserves might be treated as a loan to a participator, with all the ICTA 1988, s 419 consequences that may then ensue.

5.3   The assurances, as indicated in HMRC guidance, to be given include that:

- the company:

    (i)   does not intend to trade or carry on business in future;

    (ii)   intends to collect its debts, pay off its creditors and distribute any balance of its assets to its shareholders (or has already done so); and

    (iii)   intends to seek or accept striking off and dissolution.

- the company and its shareholders agree that:

    (i)   they will supply such information as is necessary to determine, and will pay any corporation tax liability on income or capital gains; and

    (ii)   the shareholders will pay any capital gains tax liability (or corporation tax in the case of a corporate shareholder) in respect of any amount distributed to them in cash or otherwise, as if the distributions had been made during a winding-up.

In addition, recent HMRC practice now seems to require two additional undertakings which are designed to draw the attention of the applicant to the possibility of assessment under ITA 2007, s 698 (formerly ICTA 1988, s 703) where the distributed proceeds are then used to fund a parallel company undertaking many of the same activities of the dissolved company, known in some circumstances as 'phoenix' companies:

- the company will not transfer or sell its assets or business to another company having some or all of the same shareholders; and

- the arrangement is not a reconstruction in which some or all of the shareholders in the original company retain an interest in the second company.

It might be considered best practice to now include these additional assurances as standard, assuming they represent the true intentions of the shareholders.

DEALING WITH THE ELEMENTS OF THE UNDERTAKINGS

5.4   There are a number of practical elements that need to be considered in relation to the undertakings, as follows.

- The company will cease trading at some point in the future. The trade does not have to have ceased when the application is made, but it is implicit that the application will only be made when the end is in sight. Perhaps application should be made no more than three to six months before trading ceases. If cessation is delayed beyond that, it would be sensible to write to HMRC to obtain confirmation that the concession previously given still applies.

- The company intends to distribute any balance of its assets to its shareholders (or has already done so). Accordingly, the concession only applies to companies that are solvent. The clearance for the concession to apply does not have to be obtained before assets are distributed but best practice would be to apply in advance so that, in the unlikely event the application of the concession is refused, alternative planning can be undertaken.

- The company will apply to the Registrar of Companies and will be struck off. This is not a procedure that will allow profits to be extracted as capital and also allow the company to then recommence its trade.

- The company – or failing the company, its shareholders – agree they will supply enough information to allow HMRC to agree any corporation tax liability of the company and that the shareholders will pay any tax due if, for any reason, the company fails to pay.

- Where tax is due on the distribution(s), the shareholders will ensure that they pay tax on the amounts received either through a self-assessment return or, in the case of company shareholders, through the CTSA return.

5.5 HMRC require the company secretary and all shareholders to give the ESC C16 assurances whereas, historically, it was the adviser who made the application on behalf of the company and gave the appropriate assurances. It is understood that the procedure was changed because in a number of cases advisers gave the required assurances on behalf of the company, but the shareholders then refused to pay any arrears of tax because they had not given the assurances. ESC C16 is unclear as to who is required to give the assurances; although for most cases the adviser's assurances were sufficient. To avoid possible loss to the public purse, the procedure has now been changed so that those who receive the distribution also provide the assurance that there is no possibility of a shareholder escaping their obligations. Appendices 3 and 4 set out suggested precedents for the required assurances, which include the additional items referred to in **5.3** above.

WHEN TO APPLY

5.6 Often the application to use ESC C16 is made after the trade has ceased and the company has effectively become dormant, although this may not always be the case. A company can continue to be active even though it does not carry on a trade. The directors expend energy selling the trade for the best price and generally tidying up matters, but lose interest once the trade has ceased; there is a belief that, once the assets have been realised, matters can proceed at a leisurely pace. Generally once the business has ceased, the separate shareholders will want to go their separate ways, so dealing with matters as quickly as possible is usually the better option.

Accordingly, the application should be made at the earliest opportunity. There is no reason why the application can not be made before the trade has ceased so as to ensure that the period of delay between cessation of trade and distribution to shareholders is at a minimum.

Certainly, adviser and client need to cooperate to ensure that periods of delay are at a minimum, otherwise the client may seek compensation for any extra tax that arises. There is a temptation for some advisers to ignore completing the accounts and tax returns for a soon-to-be dissolved client on the basis they are about to cease as a client of the firm, so it is better to spend time with developing clients.

5.7   Action that may need to be taken on the part of the company to minimise delay includes:

- sale of the company premises, either freehold or leasehold, to include (where relevant) agreeing with the landlord responsibility for dilapidations;

- sell the trade as a going concern;

- if there are assets that a purchaser will not want then make sure they are sold as soon as possible – do not wait until after trade ceases, a closing down sale may allow you to realise all that stock that might one day be worth keeping;

- make sure the accounts are up-to-date and can be delivered to the accountant as soon as possible after the trade is sold – do not think that they can wait (delay may increase your tax bill);

- plan ahead – most businessmen plan to make a profit whilst trading, so why not make a profit out of dissolving the business?

5.8   Action that may need to be taken on the part of the adviser, to minimise delay, includes:

- talk to the client so that the ESC C16 application is made promptly;

- plan when the books can be received to allow accounts to be prepared promptly and tax liabilities to be established;

- do not let the accounts fester in the 'in jobs' cupboard just because this is the last set of accounts;

- tell the client how the tax may increase if there is delay – this will encourage him to get matters done on time, but will also provide you with a reason to get on with the job.

IS THERE A COST FROM DELAY?

5.9   Under the pre-6 April 2008 CGT taper relief regime, there was a need to distribute as quickly as possible because delay could cause dilution of the business asset taper entitlement. Under Finance Act 2008 CGT simplification, all gains are subject to a flat 18% charge unless covered by the entrepreneurs' relief regime. In respect of the entrepreneurs' relief regime, under the convention generally assumed for this publication, that the assets of a solvent trading business are distributed to its shareholders, there is only a cost of delay if distributions are delayed more than 36 months after the date on which trading ceases. In the writer's view, such cases are likely to be the exception rather than the rule.

WHAT INFORMATION WILL HMRC REQUIRE?

5.10   Once agreement to use the concession has been given, returns continue to have to be made to HMRC, but this should not involve full accounts as would normally be prepared for the Registrar of Companies and to HMRC. It will be enough to provide sufficient information to show that all taxes due from the company have been agreed and paid. A set of management accounts and computations should (in most cases) be sufficient, together with a CT600, and any appropriate supporting schedules.

In some cases, a computation together with Form CT600 may suffice if, since the previous return, all that has happened is realisation of assets and receipt of investment income. Therefore, there would be a need to provide an explanation of the transactions and why no accounts are provided, but that should satisfy most inspectors. Remember to tick the box on Form CT600 and explain why no accounts have been prepared.

Corporation tax is dealt with under a form of self-assessment known as CTSA, which requires a company to complete a Form CT600, calculating their tax liability for a particular accounting period and to submit this to HMRC within 12 months of the end of the taxable period together with a detailed computation as well as a set of accounts for the same period. Where a business is in the process of disincorporation, accounts may not be prepared so, when submitting Form CT600 for any final period, it is important to tell HMRC that no accounts are submitted, otherwise the return may be rejected and will need to be re-submitted with enough information to allow an Inspector of Taxes to agree the return.

Where directors and others have been in receipt of salary through the PAYE system then complete a P35 early and supply all former staff with a P45. If the trade has been sold as a going concern, the new employer will require a P45 from his new employees, so complete the P35 and close the PAYE scheme down. At the same time, complete any necessary P11Ds and pay over the appropriate National Insurance charge.

CAN YOU ALWAYS USE THE CONCESSION?

5.11   The writer saw it suggested, during the taper relief regime for CGT, that advantage could be taken of the lower tax rates that apply to capital gains, and simply accumulate profits within a series of companies, applying to dissolve them in succession every two or three years. Such an arrangement, if it worked, would have been more attractive in the taper relief era because the effective CGT rate on business gains was only 10%. Presumably if the gain could be made to come within entrepreneurs' relief, then again an effective CGT rate of 10%that might result in a tax charge of 10% provided CGT status is agreed but, in practice, the effective charge may be something less if the annual CGT exemption (£9,600 for 2008/09) is available. The following examples suggest the processes involved.

Example

Hilary is a part-time author and, in addition to her main employment, writes regularly for the press. The fees amount to about £7,500 per year and she arranges for them to be paid to Hilary's Writing Ltd. In two years the company received £15,000, there were a few costs, but Hilary's intention was to build up a nest egg. After 26 months she applies to use ESC C16, consent is given and the funds are distributed.

Suppose the available funds are £10,000, after tax and costs, just above the annual CGT exemption, so perhaps only £70 in tax. At the same time, Hilary's Writing 2 Ltd begins to trade and the cycle continues.

Example

Quentin is a successful interior designer and appears regularly on house transformation shows on television; on the strength of his appearances, his biography 'It's only MDF but I like it', was an unexpected success. Quentin earns £300,000 per year but has a modest lifestyle, as the television companies for whom he works pay most of his living expenses.

His accountant organises Quentin's Interiors Ltd and after 26 months the company has accumulated £300,000, which is available for distribution. After 26 months, consent to use ESC C16 is given and the funds are distributed.

Entrepreneurs' relief means an effective tax rate of 10%, so only tax of approximately £28,300 is payable. At the same time, Quentin's Interiors 2 Ltd begins to trade and the cycle continues.

Does this work?

5.12   There might be a number of objections or pitfalls to the suggested scheme. Firstly, if the company simply consists of a money box with only cash assets at the date of application and throughout its operation it may not strictly satisfy the trading company definition.

Secondly, we need to look at the preamble to booklet IR1, which reads as follows.

'An extra statutory concession is a relaxation which gives tax payers a reduction in tax liability or which they would not be entitled under the strict letter of the Law. Most concessions are made to deal with what are, on the whole minor or transitory anomalies under the legislation and to meet cases of hardship that the margins of the code were a statutory remedy would be difficult to advise or would run to a length out of proportion to the importance of the matter.

The concessions described within are of general application, but it must be borne in mind that in a particular case there may be special circumstances which will need to be taken into account in considering the application of the concession. A concession will not be given in any case where an attempt is made to use it for tax avoidance.'

What weight should we place on the warning? Well, we should be aware that HMRC do refuse to apply concessions. The concessionary exemption is not given where the taxpayer attempts to use it for tax avoidance purposes. There have been few cases where taxpayers have resorted to the courts to seek to require HMRC to apply the concessions; perhaps because in most cases the warning contained in IR1 persuades them or their advisers of the weakness of their case. In a number of cases it is clear that concessions are concessions – they cannot be relied upon to achieve a tax favourable result. In *R v IRC ex p Fulford-Dobson* 60 TC 16811, a case concerning ESC D2 and an attempt to achieve split year status for capital gains tax on leaving the UK, the taxpayer sought to rely upon ESC D2 for their tax avoidance scheme to work. This indicates that, normally HMRC will treat the periods in a tax year before and after departure as separate periods with the result that a capital sale after departure would be United Kingdom CGT-free. The court upheld the Revenue's refusal to grant the taxpayer concessionary exemption from capital gains tax on the grounds that the whole transaction amounted to a scheme devised to gain a tax advantage. Therefore, relying upon a concession to obtain a tax advantage will not work.

5.13   If HMRC refuses to adopt a concession, what steps are open to a taxpayer, or their advisers, to try to force the issue in their favour? In *R v HM Inspector of Taxes ex p Brumfield* [1989] STC 151, counsel for the Inland Revenue (Mr Moses) accepted, according to the following judgment:

'That notwithstanding that the application relates to an extra statutory concession, the Court has jurisdiction to hear the application. He does not challenge, in my view rightly, the ability of a taxpayer to seek judicial review of a decision made by an Inspector not to allow the taxpayer the benefit of a Revenue concession, provided that the taxpayer can satisfy the Court that the taxpayer's circumstances fall within the scope of the concession. Nor has Mr Moses sought to draw any distinction between a published extra statutory concession and a concession such as that relied on in the present case (*R v HM Inspector of Taxes ex p Brumfield* [1989] STC 151), being one where the practice has been allowed by the Revenue even though it did not appear as an extra statutory concession published by the Revenue before the facts alleged to fall within the circumstances covered by the concession occurred.'

5.14   However, a review of cases where taxpayers have sought reliance upon either a concession or a Statement of Practice does not, generally, suggest that taxpayers can expect much sympathy from the judges. There is a view, that seems widely expressed in judgments, that judges are generally unsympathetic to concessions; their view is that the law is the law and that HMRC cannot, by concession, alter what Parliament has decided; they see their role as upholding the law.

USE OF THE CONCESSION IS REFUSED

5.15   In many cases, ESC C16 is used because there are insufficient assets in the company to justify the costs of employing a liquidator; even in straightforward cases the costs are unlikely to be less than £5,000 and could extend up to £10,000, which clients simply see as an extra cost in much the same way as tax. Many cases are likely to involve very small distributions where such costs cannot be justified. If the concession is refused, shareholders will not be prepared to incur the costs of a liquidator. One alternative may be to distribute all the proceeds as dividends. In the example below, a distribution of £14,000 is assumed to be the net proceeds on liquidation or dividend. In this case there are proceeds of £14,000, but if the costs are £5,000 to a liquidator, that is equivalent to a tax charge of virtually 35%. At that level of costs, distribution by way of dividend becomes an attractive option.

Example

A distribution of £14,000 as a dividend is equivalent to a gross sum of £15,555, so higher rate tax would be £5,055 less basic rate credit of £1,555 to leave £3,500 payable and net proceeds of £14,000 less £3,500, or £10,500.

Treating the same transaction as capital could result in liquidator's fees of £5,000, to produce a net sum of £9,000, which may or may not be subject to CGT in the hands of the recipients. In 2008/09 once an annual exemption are deducted, no tax is likely. Therefore, the comparison is £10,500 as income or £9,000 as capital.

5.16   For many taxpayers, the distinction between income and capital is largely academic. If you are a basic rate taxpayer, and always likely to remain one, then it is possible that refusal to allow the concession does not cause hardship (defined here as extra tax) so the profits can be distributed to the shareholders by way of dividend, perhaps over two or three tax years, and the same effective nil tax result is achieved. However, this section considers the situation of individuals with a paying hobby who want to receive the results of their labours tax-free. Accordingly, it might be considered that such individuals are more likely to be higher rate taxpayers because they can afford to leave the cash unspent. Certainly for illustration purposes, the tax differentials are most highly illuminated on that basis, but that may be a particular conceit that only applies in some parts of the country. Many traders operating through a company only earn an average wage so are always basic rate taxpayers.

Example

Joanna operates Joanna's Services Ltd and draws £2,000 per month from the company. She proposes to retire on 28 February 2009 and distribute the reserves of £30,000, all of which have already suffered corporation tax, to herself as sole shareholder.

If the whole amount were paid out as a dividend before 5 April 2009 then Joanna's gross income in 2008/09 would be:

Salary	22,000
Dividend	33,333
Total	55,333

This is comfortably within the higher rate band, which in 2008/09 begins at approximately £40,800 (including personal allowances) so a higher rate liability on the excess above say £40,800 will apply at the dividend rate of 32.5% to result in tax of approximately £3,050 (£13,533 @ 32.5%) less tax credit.

Suppose, instead, a dividend of £13,500 (net) was paid in 2008/09 and the balance in 2009/10: there exists the possibility that some or all of the reserves are only subject to basic rate tax. The assessment for 2008/09 becomes:

Salary	22,000
Dividend	15,000
Total	37,000

The balance of £15,000 (gross £16,666) will fall in 2009/10. Taxability will depend upon other income in 2009/10, but if Joanna has retired, her total income may be below the higher rate threshold for that year.

TRANSACTIONS IN SECURITIES

5.17 The major possible objection from HMRC to the use of ESC C16 to a number of successor companies each of whom trade for two years, build up reserves and then distribute those reserves as a capital transaction has already been explored. Remember, a concession is only a concession if the Revenue agrees to apply it. However, equally, a taxpayer may have established a pattern of such companies and the Revenue previously given consent. But once a pattern emerges, they will refuse all future applications, and yet, equally, may instead seek to cancel any tax advantage previously obtained by an assessment under ITA 2007, s 682 (formerly ICTA 1988, s 703). The effect is likely to be that amounts previously distributed would be reclassified as dividends with a consequent exposure to a higher tax charge. ITA 2007, ss 682–685 state as follows:

's 682 Overview of Chapter

(1) This Chapter makes provision for counteracting income tax advantages obtained or obtainable by persons to whom section 684 applies in respect of a transaction or transactions in securities.

(2) See section 698 (counteraction notices) for the way in which the income tax advantages may be counteracted.

s 683 Meaning of "income tax advantage"

(1) In this Chapter "income tax advantage" means–

    (a) a relief from income tax or increased relief from income tax,

    (b) a repayment of income tax or increased repayment of income tax,

    (c) the avoidance or reduction of a charge to income tax or an assessment to income tax, or

    (d) the avoidance of a possible assessment to income tax.

(2) For the purposes of subsection (1)(c) and (d) it does not matter whether the avoidance or reduction is effected–

    (a) by receipts accruing in such a way that the recipient does not pay or bear income tax on them, or

    (b) by a deduction in calculating profits or gains.

(3) In this section "relief from income tax" includes a tax credit.

s 684 Person liable to counteraction of income tax advantage

(1) This section applies to a person in respect of a transaction in securities or two or more such transactions if the person is in a position to obtain or has obtained an income tax advantage–

    (a) in circumstances where any of the provisions specified in subsection (2) applies in relation to the person, and

    (b) in consequence of–

        (i) the transaction, or

        (ii) the combined effect of the transactions.

(2) The provisions are–

    section 686 (abnormal dividends used for exemptions or reliefs (circumstance A)),

    section 687 (deductions from profits obtained following distribution or dealings (circumstance B)),

    section 688 (receipt of consideration representing company's assets, future receipts or trading stock (circumstance C)),

    section 689 (receipt of consideration in connection with relevant company distribution (circumstance D)), and

    section 690 (receipt of assets of relevant company (circumstance E)).

(3)   For the purposes of this Chapter an income tax advantage is treated as obtained or obtainable by a person in consequence of–

(a)   a transaction in securities, or

(b)   the combined effect of two or more such transactions,

if it is obtained or obtainable by the person in consequence of the combined effect of the transaction or transactions and the liquidation of a company.

(4)   This section is subject to–

section 685 (exception where no tax avoidance object shown),

section 696(3) (disapplication of this section where person receiving preliminary notification that this section may apply makes a statutory declaration and the relevant officer of Revenue and Customs sees no reason to take further action), and

section 697(5) (determination by tribunal that there is no prima facie case that this section applies).

s 685 Exception where no tax avoidance object shown

(1)   Section 684 does not apply to a person in respect of a transaction in securities or two or more such transactions if the person shows that the transaction or transactions meet conditions A and B.

(2)   Condition A is that the transaction or transactions are effected–

(a)   for genuine commercial reasons, or

(b)   in the ordinary course of making or managing investments.

(3)   Condition B is that enabling income tax advantages to be obtained is not the main object or one of the main objects of the transaction or, as the case may be, any of the transactions.'

In the circumstances envisaged here, the tax advantage obtained is having funds taxed as capital rather than income with the consequent exposure to higher rates of tax. In *IRC v Cleary* (1968) 44 TC 399, two sisters owned all the share capital of both Company G and Company M, and their holdings in Company M were sold to Company G for cash. The view taken was that the funds of Company G could equally have been used to pay dividends and that the method chosen was merely an attempt to convert what might otherwise have been income to capital. Indeed, the position is made clear that capital distributions are not excluded from action under ITA 2007, s 682.

5.18   What other weapons does HMRC have to attack the use of liquidation (or the concession) to achieve capital gains tax status where the commercial reality is that the procedure is being misused or might be interpreted as being misused? Taxation advantages that accrue from capital treatment with tax at a maximum of 18%, or an effective 10% if entrepreneurs' relief can apply as compared with perhaps 32.5% for income status, are well understood.

One possible attack would result from the Revenue serving notice under ITA 2007, s 698 on the basis that the liquidation, or at least the proceeds, amount to a transaction in securities. The key elements of s 698 are:

's 698 Counteraction notices

(1) If–

(a) a person on whom a notification is served under section 695 does not send a statutory declaration to an officer of Revenue and Customs under section 696 within 30 days of the issue of the notification, or

(b) the tribunal to which such a declaration is sent under section 697 determines that there is a prima facie case for serving a notice on a person under this section,

the income tax advantage in question is to be counteracted by adjustments.

(2) The adjustments required to be made to counteract the income tax advantage and the basis on which they are to be made are to be specified in a notice served on the person by an officer of Revenue and Customs.'

The current provisions in ITA 2007, s 683 are set out above, and within ICTA 1988, s 703(2), the predecessor legislation, the following was the statutory position:

'(2) For the purposes of this Chapter a tax advantage obtained or obtainable by a person shall be deemed to be obtained or obtainable by him in consequence of a transaction in securities or of the combined effect of two or more such transactions, if it is obtained or obtainable in consequence of the combined effect of the transaction or transactions and the liquidation of a company…'

which suggests that the draftsman at that time did not consider liquidation alone might represent a transaction in securities. However ITA 2007, s 689 in subparagraph (2)(a) makes the position clear:

's 689 Receipt of consideration in connection with relevant company distribution (circumstance D)

(1) This section applies in relation to a person if subsections (2) to (4) apply.

(2) The person receives consideration in connection with–

(a) the distribution, transfer or realisation of assets of a relevant company (see section 691), or

(b) the application of such assets in discharge of liabilities.

(3) The consideration–

(a) is or represents the value of–

(i) assets which are available for distribution by way of dividend by the company, or

88

(ii)   assets which would have been so available apart from anything done by the company,

(b)   is received in respect of future receipts of the company, or

(c)   is or represents the value of trading stock of the company.

(4)   The person so receives the consideration that the person does not pay or bear income tax on it (apart from this Chapter).

(5)   The assets mentioned in subsection (3) do not include assets which are shown to represent a return of sums paid by subscribers on the issue of securities, despite the   fact that under the law of the country in which the company is incorporated assets of that description are available for distribution by way of dividend.

(6)   In this section references to the receipt of consideration include references to the receipt of any money or money's worth.'

However, the intentions of the draftsman are of little account in deciding the interpretation or application of statute. In *IRC v Joiner* (1975) STC 657, it was argued by HMRC that the distribution of assets where arrangements were put in place to allow the assets of one company to be transferred to a second company, both controlled by the same taxpayer, arising from a winding-up was a transaction in securities. Again, the notice under what was then TCGA 1988, s 704 was upheld. In effect, the transaction was intended to allow the taxpayers to receive accumulated profit in a capital form. In this case, in respect of transactions that took place before 1965, the consequence would have been that anything received as capital would have been tax-free, but even under current rules the availability of taper relief will provide a tax advantage.

However, the courts did not express any opinion as to the merits of the argument, but a Parliamentary reply in relation to this case produced the following answer:

'In 1960 the then Attorney-General gave an assurance that [what is now TA 1988, s 703 (ITA 2007, s 682)] would not be applied to an ordinary liquidation. In Joiner's case the court did not express any opinion on the argument for the Crown that a distribution of assets to a shareholder in a winding up is itself a transaction in securities.

Until such time as there is a decision of the court giving further guidance on this issue, the Revenue is advised on the basis of recent decisions that for the purposes of [TA 1988, s 703 (ITA 2007, s 682)] a distribution to a shareholder in a liquidation is a transaction in securities. It does not propose any change of practice in relation to an ordinary liquidation, that is to say the bona fide winding up of a business as a discrete entity, whether the business with its concomitant goodwill then comes to an end or is taken over by some other concern which is under substantially different control. On the other hand, the Revenue would not regard as 'ordinary' a liquidation which is part of a scheme of reconstruction which enables the old business to be carried on as before with substantially the same shareholders, directly or indirectly, in control. [TA 1988, s 703 (ITA 2007, s 682)] does not of course apply where a taxpayer can show that the transaction or transactions were carried out for bona fide commercial reasons or in the ordinary course of making or managing investments and that the main object or one of the main objects was not the obtaining of a tax advantage.'

The Parliamentary reply is clear so far as sales to third parties are concerned, with the happy consequence that ITA 2007, s 682should not apply. It does not give the same assurance if there are sales to associated businesses where, to quote the Parliamentary answer, 'as part of a scheme of reconstruction which enables the old business to be carried on as before with substantially the same shareholders deriving or obtaining control'. Therefore, it may be considered that where a company is being liquidated to allow the trade to be carried on by the same shareholders, albeit in a different guise, the proper conclusion is that a liability under ITA 2007, s 682 is a real possibility.

5.19   The wide nature of ITA 2007, s 682can be demonstrated by some of the many cases on this particular statute. In *IRC v Cleary* (1968) 44 TC 399 (see para **5.17**), two companies under common control became a group by one acquiring the other for cash. The House of Lords decided that income tax status was appropriate to the monies paid for the acquisition of shares. In particular, consequence ITA 2007, s 689 (circumstance D) which envisaged the assets available by way of dividend, see above.

5.20   Accordingly, it is clear that considerable care is required to achieve a situation where assets can be transferred to shareholders if a trade is to continue in a new form. There are exemptions for bona fide commercial transactions, but it may be considered that, particularly where a business was incorporated to obtain a taxation advantage, any subsequent disincorporation is not carried out for bona fide commercial purposes.

If a company is to be placed into formal liquidation then clearance under ITA 2007, s 682 can be requested, provided a full statement of the facts and circumstances – including details of any assets to be sold to existing shareholders – as well as a full explanation of the bona fide commercial purposes for which the clearance are required. The same information should be supplied, as would be supplied in respect of any other application for clearance, ITA 2007, s 682. Similarly, where the application for clearance is under the C16 concession then again full disclosure must be made to the local inspector in order that a proper assurance under the concession can be obtained.

The Inspectors Manual at para 4519, which is no longer in the public domain, indicated that there was a real conflict in these circumstances:

'4519. Security transactions: Liquidation
An ordinary liquidation (in which a company is wound up following the complete cessation of its business or the transfer of that business to a person unconnected with its original shareholders) is not within the scope of ICTA 1988, s 703. ICTA 1988, s 703 can, however, apply to counteract a tax advantage obtained in consequence of a liquidation combined with a transaction in securities.

EXAMPLE

A, B and C are shareholders in X, a trading company with substantial amounts of cash representing undistributed profits. They subscribe for shares in a newly incorporated company Y in the same proportions as their shareholding in X. Company Y now acquires the trade and assets of X in exchange for an issue of its own Ordinary shares and begins carrying on the trade previously undertaken by Y.

Company X is now put into liquidation and its assets (including the shares in Y) are received by A, B and C in the form of a capital distribution.

ICTA 1988, s 704D applies to the cash etc received by A, B and C in the liquidation (except to the extent that it represents the return of the amounts subscribed for the share capital in X). ICTA 1988, s 704E may also apply to any subsequent repayments of the share capital in Y.'

Company Tax Manual at 36875, to which reference has already been made, indicates that where HMRC identify tax advantages that are capable of counteraction, specialist advice be obtained in a range of circumstances that include the transfer or sale by a company of its assets or business to another company having some or all of the same shareholders followed by the liquidation of the company whose assets etc have been acquired, or the sale of shares in either company, or receipt of capital consideration by shareholders of a company or group following a demerger or scheme of reconstruction from the sale or liquidation of one demerged company where the same shareholders retain an interest via another company involved in the transactions.

5.21   Although the points raised here are specific, they do raise the more general point that in any correspondence with HMRC where clearance is sort, full disclosure must be made. This is equally important when an application to apply a concession is made since the concessions are a less strict application of tax law. The preamble to the Extra Statutory Concessions makes it quite clear that they are only concessions. Failure to supply a key fact, particularly if it runs counter to the circumstances in which a counteraction notice can be given, will render valueless any confirmation that has been given by HMRC and allow HMRC to take an alternative and generally less favourable view to our client's cause. Transactions where HMRC acknowledged that, had application for the concession been made (notwithstanding unusual facts), they would have been prepared to allow the concession because the circumstances envisaged were within the spirit of the concession, even if they did not wholly satisfy the standard circumstances, have been encountered by the writer. However, since no application had been made they would insist upon the strict statutory position applying.

It should not be considered that the threat of action under (formerly) ICTA 1988, s 703 is an empty gesture. Two recent Special Commissioner decisions in 2008 reflect the continuing HMRC attention in this area. In *Snell v Revenue and Customs Commissioners* [2008] SpC 699 the conclusions make it clear that a tax advantage that is more than *de minimis* can be a 'main object' of the transaction and thus capable of a counter notice.

Even where there are bona fide commercial considerations if elements are inserted that produce a tax advantage, usually ensuring what could be taxed as a dividend being taxed as capital, then that is sufficient. In *Snell* the issue was highlighted to HMRC by the client's accountants who in a series of (refused) s 703 clearance applications, gradually refined, attempted to establish what figure would be regarded as *de minimis* to prevent a counter notice under s 703 but unsurprisingly no confirmation was offered. In the event a tax saving of £12,500 was not *de minimis* even though the overriding bona fide commercial pressure to undertake the transaction was the preservation of the family business albeit under a different corporate structure.

Lloyd v Revenue and Customs Commissioners [2008](SpC 672) was a more classic tax advantage arrangement where shares in a company were purchased by a holding company, specially formed for the purpose, using cash provided by an inter-group dividend from the (now) subsidiary company so again the tax advantage obtained was the creation of a sum intended to be taxed as capital rather than one taxed as income which would have been the consequence if the holding company had not been created and the dividend simply paid direct to the shareholders of the target company.

WHAT IS THE DOWNSIDE OF USING ESC C16?

5.22   As demonstrated in para **5.2,** the advantage to a company using ESC C16, and a subsequent application to have the company struck off under Companies Act 1985, s 652A, is a saving in the costs of a liquidator that can be substantial. However, where dissolution under Companies Act 2006, ss 1000–1002 (formerly CA 1985, ss 652) and Companies Act 2006, ss 1003–1011 (formerly CA 1985, ss 652A–652F) differs from a formal liquidation is the degree of protection that is available against a claim from (usually) an aggrieved creditor who believes that the company should never have been struck off and, accordingly, makes an application to have the company restored to the register. Companies Act 2006 provisions in general set a six-year time limit for action, whereas under the provisions of Companies Act 1985 s 653 it is possible for a company to be reinstated for up to 20 years after the date of striking off. The time limit under Companies Act 2006 runs from the date of dissolution, which is taken to be the date of receipt of the notice by the Registrar, while under Companies Act 1985 time runs from the date advertising the proposed dissolution in the London Gazette.

Clients who are planning to adopt the s 652A procedures need to review the history of the company and its financial obligations and make a judgement as to whether there are skeletons in the finances and, if so, the likely maximum extent of any claims. If the amounts are less than the costs of employing a liquidator, then the administratively simpler route can be adopted.

Example

Postwick Ltd adopts the s 652A procedure, having been quoted fees of £5,000 for formal liquidation. The directors are aware of a contingent claim, strenuously disputed, of £1,500 so conclude that even if the sum has to be paid, they gain advantage of the administratively simpler route.

5.23 By contrast if the contingent claims are substantial, then formal liquidation is likely to be the favoured route, particularly where there are several shareholders obtaining cash. Once distributions have been made, satisfying a claim can be difficult. In many family situations, the family may hold together whilst the company subsists, but once the bond is broken, the family disputes arise again.

Example

Limpenhoe Ltd is considering adopting the ESC C16/s 652A procedure, having been quoted fees of £6,000 for formal liquidation. The directors are aware of a contingent claim, strenuously disputed, of £55,000 for breach of patent rights relating to their major product, which will go to court. The directors conclude that formal liquidation is appropriate.

DISTRIBUTING THE CASH

5.24 Elsewhere in this publication, it is implied that funds are simply distributed on a single occasion, but that is not always appropriate or possible. Often the purchaser of the business, assuming one can be found, will want to pay by instalments to ensure that what is being sold is of value or, more typically, does not have the funds to meet the agreed sale price and wants to pay for the business out of future profits.

5.25 Equally, does it make any difference as to the nature of the payments that are made? In most family businesses, some shareholders on dissolution may expect payments to be made to them from a number of sources, but typical payments will be:

- payment for ordinary shares;
- repayment of debentures;
- repayment of director's loan;
- repayment of preference shares.

The immediate temptation will be to repay the director's loan as the first tranche, perhaps because the company know what that figure is, perhaps because the payment will be received tax-free and to then make other payments as assets are realised. The directors will have to comply with any regulations set out in, for example, debenture deeds or preference share rights, but if there is any flexibility in the basis of repayment then it will generally be more tax efficient to repay ordinary shares as the first tranche and to repay the other categories at a later date. A particular order of preference only has to be adopted in insolvent liquidations where loan creditors must be repaid first and any shortfall is suffered by the ordinary and preference shareholders. Generally, debentures, directors' loans or preference shares do not give rise to any taxable capital gains so within a dissolution situation this is unlikely to be an issue, provided the time limit to obtain entrepreneurs' relief is not exceeded.

EMPLOYEE SHAREHOLDERS

5.26 The majority of the illustrations contained in this publication are based on the assumption that recipient shareholders generally have a material interest in the company and, therefore, the effect of trade ceasing is generally to allow gains to be covered by entrepreneurs' relief. However, for shareholders who do not have a material interest and whose shareholdings fail the tests set out below, even if they are also employees of the company, the fact that the company was a trading company at a particular date will have no impact upon their failure to gain entrepreneurs' relief. For entrepreneurs' relief to apply, the relevant shareholder must:

● have been an officer or employee of the company, or of a company in the same group of companies, and

● own at least 5% of the ordinary share capital of the company, which holding enables the individual to exercise at least 5% of the voting rights in that company.

Therefore, for employee shareholders holding modest numbers of shares, the date of cessation of trade will have no impact upon their entitlement to entrepreneurs' relief, because they have none. Such employees will pay tax at the normal 18% rate, with a consequence that they will have a higher liability to tax than they would have had under the taper relief regime. The particular basis on which this applied was discussed in the first edition of this publication.

Example

Betty was an employee shareholder in Barway Drove Ltd and owned 100 out of 10,000 shares. When she realises her investment, because she owned less than 5% of the shares, any gain suffers tax at 18%.

CONFLICT WITH COMPANY LAW

5.27 One issue that will now cause difficulty was initially explored in the ICAEW Tax Faculty Newsletter 'Taxline', where it was suggested that if the issued share capital, together with any share premium account or other undistributable reserves, is more than nominal, the consent under ESC C16 only applies to the distributable reserves of the company and that HMRC consent only extends to allowing the fiction that the distributions of accumulated profits and other distributable reserves are treated as capital. They do not extend to the issued share capital or to any other undistributable reserves and, in consequence, any amounts represented by those sums belong *bona vacantia* to the Crown. Inevitably, if the amount at stake is a nominal issued share capital, typically £100 for many small companies, then there is little concern, but if the amount involved is more substantial then there was concern that funds may be at risk of payment to the Crown. However, as in many areas within the public domain, this was not a matter about which there was universal agreement. It was said by some that HMRC act as agents for the Crown and as such give consent to the distribution of all funds in the company to the shareholder. Therefore, distribution of any monies comprised within the share premium account or share capital can safely be distributed to the shareholders because the Crown, through the agency of HMRC, has given their direct agreement to these matters. It is equally suggested that HMRC do not and cannot act as agent for the Crown, even though they have encouraged a strike-off under the ESC C16 procedures and that another Crown agency could claim the assets *bona vacantia*.

5.28 It was accepted by most correspondents that this was a technical breach and equally most seemed relaxed where the amounts involved were modest. Certainly, it might have seemed inequitable if the Crown, having encouraged companies to be dissolved by a combination of the s 652 procedure and ESC C16, were then to make a claim for the share capital (and any other non-distributable reserves) under the *bona vacantia* provisions. Within the experience of the writer dealing with matters, this issue had been raised on a number of occasions and, on one occasion, advice was obtained from counsel. This concerned a case where a demerger was being effected and the client was unwilling to pay a liquidator the very substantial fee they required. Instead, ESC C16 was used to transfer the assets of Oldco to each of two Newcos, once consent from the company's HMRC office had been obtained for the use of ESC C16. The issue was further clarified with HMRC Specialist Divisions who had given the initial required clearances and they confirmed that they had no objection to the procedure, provided the local inspector whose responsibility it was to guard the ESC C16 consent had no objection. In that case the position of the issued share capital, which amounted to £10,000, was raised by Counsel on the basis that, strictly, those monies might belong to the Crown under the *bona vacantia* rule, but the advice given was that this was not an issue that was likely to cause concern. The further clarification provided was, however, that it was permissible if a *bona vacantia* claim was made to deduct the costs of winding-up and dealing with the company's assets from the share capital – certainly, for companies with very small authorised share capitals on this netting down basis, little value would remain for a *bona vacantia* claim.

5.29 The vast majority of companies have a low issued share capital, notwithstanding the advantage that might arise under para **4.15** of a higher issued share capital and, therefore, if netting down can apply, the value potentially at risk is going to be modest. Conversely, companies that have more complex share capitals or higher issued share capital, perhaps with share premium account or other forms of capital reserve, are likely to be (in any event) more substantial organisations where perhaps, on balance, the company and its advisers will generally take the view that formal liquidation may be the preferred option. If, however, ESC C16 is to be adopted in such cases then it may be appropriate to seek Counsel's opinion as to the extent of the risk.

Certainly care will be required because, ultimately, all HMRC are agreeing to is that the distributions are to be treated as capital rather than income. The writer takes the view that although the Registrar of Companies guidance indicates that this procedure is not an alternative to formal liquidation, because in that instance there would be the rights and payment to creditors to be considered, nevertheless, the distributions to the shareholders are of monies due to them in exactly as they would be in a formal liquidation.

The concern in respect of issued share capital and the bona vacantia provisions has now been clarified through notice BVC 17 on the Treasury Bona Vacantia website, and it is now confirmed that where the share capital, and other non-distributable reserves, distributed amount to less that £4,000, even though, under the s 652 procedures, the distributed share capital belongs to the Crown, no claim will be made. The level has been fixed at £4,000 on the basis that the figure represents a typical cost of liquidation, so that if a company had gone through the liquidation process those funds would, in any event not be available.

Accordingly it follows that where the issued share capital distributed to shareholders is in excess of £4,000, there is a risk that the Crown, through the Treasury Solicitor, will ask for the unlawfully distributed funds to be paid back to them. BVC 17 indicates that the Treasury Solicitor will not seek out cases and will only enforce the rules where the matter is brought to their attention and where there is a reasonable possibility of those recovery proceedings being successful. The writer's view is that if the aggregate of issued share capital and non-distributable reserves is marginally above £4,000, no action would be pursued. Indeed BVC 17 indicates that if there are circumstances where the company can be restored to the register, recovery proceedings would not be commenced, equally that if recovery proceedings could be made, that they might not be considered if the action was unlikely to be financially successful.

So what type of case might be pursued? Perhaps where former shareholders fall out after the event and attempt point-scoring, or where there are creditors whose contingent claims ultimately prove unenforceable but who want some satisfaction? The message is clear. If the aggregate of issued share capital and non-distributable reserves is greater than £4,000, then those funds must legally be reduced below the £4,000 threshold before an ESC C16 distribution is made.

The most straightforward method is by a purchase of own shares, passing the appropriate resolutions and settling the stamp duty cost of 5% (rounded up to the nearest £5). In a dissolution situation there is unlikely to be any value shift as between the shareholders because all will be expecting their proportionate share of the company's funds, so there will not be any need to apply for HMRC consent, but notification to the company's tax district should be made after the event.

Example

Hethersett Ltd is about to be dissolved but has an issued share capital of £200,000, held by four shareholders who each own 25%. A purchase of own shares is effected to reduce the issued share capital to £2,000 and once that has been achieved the s 652 procedure can proceed because there is then no risk that the *bona vacantia* claim will be made.

Extra cost is incurred because there will be a stamp duty cost in this case of £990 and the cost of effecting the purchase of own shares, but the aggregate is considerably less than the loss that might result from a payment to the Crown under the *bona vacantia* procedure.

In the above example, the whole of the company's value, including share capital, can be paid out. However, if the amounts are substantial, then perhaps the formal liquidation route should be applied. Certainly, if the issued share capital and the value of other non-distributable reserves are substantial, there is likely to be more commercial justification for formal liquidation and the additional protection that that procedure offers from unexpected restoration to the register, simply because there may be unknown liabilities or concerns. Within the writer's experience, if the capital reserves to be distributed are substantial, perhaps in excess of £100,000 to £150,000, then the assets to cover the costs of a liquidator are available even if the issued share capital is modest. At lower levels, the ability to deduct capital accountancy and legal costs (see para **5.28**) will reduce the potential *bona vacantia* claim to a negligible amount.

PLANNING POINTS

5.30

- Apply to use the concession at the earliest possible date.

- If the issued share capital is substantial, consider whether the conflict between company law and tax law will cause a problem.

- Consider a purchase of own shares if the issued share capital is above £4,000.

- Make sure all shareholders are available to sign the undertakings.

- Prepare estimated CGT computations to prove to shareholders the effect of delay on any CGT payable.

- Prepare a timetable, agreed between the adviser and the directors, of actions required to achieve speedy dissolution.

Chapter 6

Capital gains tax – shareholder issues

6.1   The first edition of this publication dealt with capital gains tax issues as impacted by the different financial results that could have been achieved on dissolution depending upon whether the assets realised qualified for either business taper relief or non-business taper relief where timing was a crucial element in minimising the capital gains tax liabilities that would arise on shareholders following the cessation of the trade. Following the capital gains tax simplification announced, initially, in the pre-Budget report of 9 October 2007, now confirmed in Finance Act 2008, there are a range of different issues that apply to the computation of capital gains under the new post-5 April 2008 regime which this chapter seeks to address.

Unless gains qualify for entrepreneurs' relief on only the first £1 million of lifetime business gains per individual, the basic rate of capital gains tax is 18%, whether those gains are realised by individuals, trusts or settlements or an estate.

6.2   For some gains arising from the disposal either of an interest in a business, for the purposes of this publication usually shares, or assets used in the same business, usually freehold or leasehold property, then provided the person making the disposal meets the appropriate qualifications, they suffer an effective rate, under entrepreneurs' relief, of 10% on the first £1 million of gain, but as will be clear, the reduced gain is still subject to tax at 18%.

In general, in relation to personal assets used in the business it will be more certain that entrepreneurs' relief can apply if the disposal of those assets broadly takes place at the same time as the disposal of the interest in the business. As is discussed in para **6.6**, the disposal of assets used in the business has to be associated with the withdrawal from the business, and it might be considered more difficult to establish a link between the two transactions if there is a large time gap between the two events.

Many advisers still talk about an effective rate of 10% in exactly the same way as we used to talk about an effective rate of 10% under business taper relief for capital gains. Accordingly, in advising clients in relation to the dissolution of a family company, it is the availability of entrepreneurs' relief that is going to be the key element in establishing the full extent of any tax liability that will arise from the dissolution of the family company.

ENTREPRENEURS' RELIEF

6.3   Entrepreneurs' relief is targeted at individuals who have a minimum interest in a business, provided that interest has been owned for at least 12 months prior to the disposal. It applies to the first £1 million of gain realised by an individual over their lifetime on both interests in businesses and assets used in those same businesses.

Entrepreneurs' relief is available on the disposal of shares in a trading company, provided it can be defined as the shareholder's 'personal company'. The requirements to make a company a 'personal company' are as follows:

- The shareholder must be either an officer or employee of the company.

- The individual must own at least 5% of the ordinary share capital of that company and be capable of exercising at least 5% of the voting rights in that company.

- The qualifying interest in the business must have been owned for at least 12 months.

In most cases it will be quite clear whether an individual has 5% or more of the shares, but difficulty can arise where there is a joint holding of less that 10%.

Example

Lucy and Rob are both full-time employees of Gorleston North Limited, a trading company, and jointly own 9.5% of the share capital.

Accordingly, unless there is any evidence to the contrary, they will each be regarded as owning 4.75%, so both would fail the entrepreneurs' relief tests.

On the basis that they are husband and wife it would be possible to make an inter-spouse transfer of shares to result in two separate holdings, such that one spouse would qualify for entrepreneurs' relief, or more sensibly transfer the whole holding to one spouse.

The acquisition of shares to take a shareholder through the 5% qualifying threshold does not result in an immediate entitlement to entrepreneurs' relief. Twelve months from the share transfer between spouses must elapse, in circumstances where, as in the indicated example, the initial aggregate holding is less than 10%, before the spouse whose shareholding has increased can satisfy the 'personal company' requirement.

The relief has to be claimed – it is not given automatically, as was retirement relief, which this relief partially resembles – within 22 months of the end of the tax year in which the transaction to which the relief is to apply took place, thus the normal self assessment time limit. Where the relief is to apply to an individual, then they must make the claim and in a case where the relief is transferred to trustees, both the individual and the trustees have to make a joint claim, see para **6.8**.

6.4   By contrast, if one spouse already has an interest in at least 5%, and satisfies the other requirements for the company to be their 'personal company', an advantage might be obtained if the other partner does not satisfy the 'personal company' test on the basis that they are, perhaps, neither an employee nor an officer of that company, or they own less than 5%. If there is a transfer at that point, there would be no need to wait 12 months before entrepreneurs' relief is available on the transferred shares.

Example

Paul and John, members of a registered civil partnership, own respectively 15% and 10% of the issued share capital in Lenwade Limited. John is a full-time employee of the company but Paul has other business interests and is neither a director nor an employee. The business is about to be dissolved and the value of the company distributed.

If Paul transfers his shares to John, immediately, then subject to the £1 million overall limit, John should be able to claim entrepreneurs' relief on the entire 25% holding.

REALISATION AFTER CESSATION OF THE TRADE

6.5   In cases where a shareholding is immediately sold and the proceeds received in full, the availability of entrepreneurs' relief should not be in doubt, provided the relevant requirements are satisfied. However for the purpose of this publication the general scenario is that the trade has ceased either because it had been shut down or sold, and that the proceeds are then distributed to the shareholders either by way of a formal liquidation or under the terms of ESC C16.

Inevitably, in those circumstances, there is likely to be a delay between the date on which trading ceased and the date on which the proceeds are ultimately distributed to the shareholders. Entrepreneurs' relief will be available on any distributions made within three years of the date on which the trading ceased. In the great majority of cases the full proceeds will be distributed well within the appropriate time limits, but it might be appropriate, in exceptional cases, to make sure that as much as possible is distributed before the three-year anniversary, if that makes a difference to the effective tax rate that would apply to the disposal.

Example

Julian is a shareholder in Ely Limited, which sold its trade on 10 September 2007, but as a result of an ongoing legal dispute, distribution of the funds is delayed. Only distributions made before 10 September 2010 will qualify for entrepreneurs' relief.

ASSETS HELD OUTSIDE A BUSINESS USED IN THE BUSINESS

6.6   It is extremely common for individuals who have trading companies to separately own assets which are used in the trade of that company, where usually the decision to retain personal ownership was influenced by the need to protect the assets from creditors and to avoid any double taxation that can arise where an asset is owned by a company and the proceeds then distributed. Typically this will be the premises from which the company conducts its trade, and again subject to satisfying the appropriate requirements, entrepreneurs' relief can be available subject, as always, to the overall £1 million limit per individual.

Essentially the asset on which it is wished to claim entrepreneurs' relief on an associated disposal must have been used in a company that qualifies as the individual's 'personal company', as indicated above, and the disposal must be taking place as part of the withdrawal of the shareholder from participation in the 'personal company'.

Example

Suppose Lucy and Rob (see para **6.3**) own Guestwick Works, the premises from which the trade of Gorleston North Limited is conducted.

Unless there is a share reorganisation along the lines indicated in para **6.3** above, neither will qualify for entrepreneurs' relief on an associated disposal of that property because the shares that they own do not qualify for entrepreneurs' relief and it is essential that where relief for an associated disposal is sought, the primary asset, in this case the shares in Gorleston North Limited, qualify for entrepreneurs' relief.

Where assets are held outside of the business they can only qualify for entrepreneurs' relief as an associated disposal. That is, the disposal of the personal asset must be associated with the sale or realisation of the shares in the personal company. Thus assuming that Rob and Lucy qualified for entrepreneurs' relief but that they simply sold Guestwick Works without disposing of their shares, they would be unable to obtain entrepreneurs' relief on the gain, and accordingly any gain would suffer tax at 18%.

Effectively the entrepreneurs' relief regime mirrors the old retirement relief requirement, that the disposal must be of an interest in a business, in the example a disposal of the shares in the family trading company, to then allow the extension of entrepreneurs' relief to an associated disposal. However the relief does not extend to the sale of an asset of the business if the trade continues. Accordingly it seems to the writer that problems may be encountered if the assets potentially eligible for associated disposal relief are sold at a date significantly before the share value is realised. It will be a matter of fact but if this is a risk, then there will be a need to ensure that the client preserves information that supports the tax advantageous consequence that the associated sale is a consequence of a withdrawal from a business.

Curiously, although there is a time limit of three years from cessation of the trade for gains deriving from realisation of the shares to qualify for entrepreneurs' relief, there is no indicated time limit for the realisation of gains on associated disposals. The disposal merely has to be 'as part of the withdrawal from participation in the business', see TCGA 1992, s 169K. Whether in time the courts or HMRC practice will determine that a time limit should apply to any interval between the sale of the business interest and the associated disposal, we shall have to wait and see.

Some comfort may be obtained in this regard in respect of statements by the government during the Finance Bill debates, where the then Economic Secretary to the Treasury, Kitty Ussher MP, stated during the report stage: 'There must be a link – an association between the withdrawal from the business and the associated disposal of the asset'.

Similarly the then Financial Secretary to the Treasury, Jane Kennedy MP, in the committee debate stated: 'It is possible for someone to withdraw from a business and make an associated disposal at a later date. If the disposal is linked to the withdrawal from participation, the individual may receive relief. We need to take a fair view of the case based on the facts.'

Where difficulty may arise is in relation to the quality of evidence that any associated disposal is a consequence of the withdrawal from participation in the business, if there is a long period of delay between the sale of shares and the sale of the associated asset. What may also cause difficulty is if the sale of the associated asset takes place well before the sale of the shares.

Certainly where there is going to be a long gap between events, taxpayers and their agents need to preserve evidence of intention that both the shares and the associated assets are intended to be sold within a corresponding time frame and as transactions that are linked in terms of purpose.

Even if some evidence is available that the reason for the sale of the 'associated assets' is part of a withdrawal and realisation of the business, if the ultimate consequence is that the 'associated assets' are sold but the value of the company is not realised, then the events that transpire may govern the taxation consequences, and thus the gain on the 'associated assets' would then be subject to tax at 18% rather than the favoured effective 10% rate. This problem may be less of an issue where the company is dissolved under ESC C16 because, presumably, the shareholders have control over the date of dissolution, but there could easily be circumstances where there is an offer for the 'associated assets' but the company cannot realise its own assets to allow the dissolution to proceed.

Example

The shareholders in Ryston Ltd own two separate properties which are occupied by branches of the business in King's Lynn and Stoke Ferry, and it is proposed that ultimately the company will be dissolved under the concession. Ryston Ltd owns the head office property and factory.

In October 2008 the decision to cease trading is made and all the property assets are put up for sale. Those that are personally owned are sold in April 2009 but although there are a number of offers for the head office property, they successively fail to complete. In the meantime the directors continue to operate the trade until November 2011, and in December 2011 the head office property is sold and funds can then be distributed.

Can it be said that the sale of the 'associated assets' in April 2009 is part of the withdrawal and realisation of the business? It will depend on the facts. If there is evidence that all the assets are to be sold and are offered for sale at the same time, evidence of negotiation and correspondence with prospective purchasers is available, and continual efforts to sell the assets have been undertaken, then realisation of both shares and associated assets may all be part of the withdrawal from participation in the business.

6.7   However there seem to be two separate circumstances, both of which are likely to be encountered when considering the tax position of shareholders in a soon to be dissolved company which might restrict the availability of entrepreneurs' relief on a property which might otherwise appear to qualify for the associated disposals relief.

If a property has not been occupied exclusively by the personal company but, perhaps part has been let out, or the property was only occupied by the relevant business for part of the period of ownership, then only the proportion of the gain attributable to the part of the property occupied by the personal company will be eligible for entrepreneurs' relief.

TCGA 1992, s 169P(4) and (5) which apply the market rent restrictions to entrepreneurs' relief do not contain any time limits, so in the absence of any transitional relief, payment of rent in the taper relief regime would have restricted the amount of relief available on a current sale. Fortunately TCGA 1992, s 169S(6) provides transitional relief to counter the effect of TCGA 1992, s 169P(4) and (5) which would otherwise restrict the relief not simply to the period post-5 April 2008, but for the entire period that the property has been owned. Accordingly it follows that if rent is stopped from 6 April 2008, the effect of TCGA 1992, s 169S(6) is that it is only the rent paid in the period after that date which has an impact.

Under the entrepreneurs' relief regime, payment of market rent, even to the owner of the business that is paying the rent, means that entrepreneurs' relief cannot be available on the associated disposal, but the effect of TCGA 1992, s 169S(6) is that we only need to consider the post-5 April 2008 period in relation to any rental payments and whether there is a restriction because market rent is charged, but in determining the period that has to be taken into account for entrepreneurs' relief, the full period of ownership, apparently without limit, is relevant.

This is good news because under the CGT taper relief regime before 6 April 2008, the payment of rent from the personal company to the property owner did not jeopardise entitlement to taper relief. It did not matter whether the rent paid was a market rent or less than market rent, and even in circumstances where the property owner was not a shareholder in the company, for periods between 6 April 2000 and 5 April 2008, business taper still applied.

Example

Paul owned premises from 6 April 1996 which were used by his family company, and which are to be sold in April 2010 in circumstances where 'associated disposal' relief would apply to the gain. No rent was charged to the trading company, but from 6 April 2008 until sale the building was only 50% used for the trade, with the other 50% let out and full market rent received from the tenant.

The property was owned for 14 years of which only two are restricted in relation to entrepreneurs' relief, so we have 12 years at 100% entitlement and two years at 50% entitlement, so overall approximately 92.8% of the gain may potentially be eligible for entrepreneurs' relief (12 × 100% + 2 × 50%/1,400).

Example

Wilbur has owned Parker House which is occupied by Overstrand Limited, his family company, since 5 April 2000 and took a market rent until 5 April 2008 but because he was well advised he stopped taking a rent from 6 April 2008. If the property was sold on 6 April 2010, 100% of the gain would be eligible for entrepreneurs' relief because the rental period pre-6 April 2008 is ignored.

Accordingly it follows that if the rent charged is less than market rent, a proportion of the gain would only be eligible for entrepreneurs' relief to the extent that the actual rent charged was less than market rent.

Example

Ashley acquired Enterprise House on 6 April 2004, the office block from which his trading company, Raynham Park Limited conducts its trade, and a rent of £30,000 per annum is charged, because Ashley needs income in order to ensure tax relief is obtained for interest on the loan he took out to buy the property. A full market rent would be £50,000.

Accordingly it follows that on any associated disposal of the property, only 40% of the gain would be eligible for entrepreneurs' relief, but again the restriction only applies from 6 April 2008.

Thus if rent paid in any period after 5 April 2008 is less than market rent, being paid by your own family company, the proportion of the gain eligible for entrepreneurs' relief will be calculated as to the percentage rent unpaid as a proportion of market rent along the lines of the Ashley example above.

What the transitional regime does mean is that where the owner of property occupied by their family company needs to charge a rent in order that the interest may be tax relieved, there is no immediate need to stop payment of rent, because it is only the period post-5 April 2008 that causes a dilution of entrepreneurs' relief entitlement so, for example, to apply the Paul example, every year that the rent paid post-5 April 2008 is 50% of market rent means that, approximately, only an extra 2.5% of the overall associated gain fails to qualify for entrepreneurs' relief, so even by 6 April 2016, 66.6% of the gain still remains eligible for entrepreneurs' relief.

Gains on associated assets only arise when there is a disposal of main assets (for the purposes of this publication, generally shares in the family company) and it might not be unreasonable to assume that the disposal of those shares will also generate gains that might in turn also be eligible for entrepreneurs' relief, so the amount of tax at stake where some dilution of entitlement occurs as a result of rental payments being less than market rent may be modest.

Therefore, depending upon how long the premises have been owned, there may not need to be any immediate rush to discontinue rental payments where the alternative to rental income, conveniently NIC-free, might be salary where the ongoing costs of employer's and employees' NIC will inevitably exceed the tax difference between an effective 10% and the main 18% rate.

TRUSTS INTERESTS

6.8   It will not be unusual for individuals, who might otherwise qualify for entrepreneurs' relief, to have shares or associated assets held in a trust in which they have an appropriate interest in possession as a 'qualifying beneficiary' in either the settled property in its entirety or in that part of the settled property used in the personal company of the qualifying beneficiary.

The way in which the rules apply is that entrepreneurs' relief is only available to trustees if the qualifying beneficiary qualifies for relief to make the relevant company their personal company. Thus the qualifying beneficiary must satisfy the requirements set out in para **6.3** before any surplus entrepreneurs' relief can be transferred to the interest in possession trustees.

Assets held by trustees can qualify for relief under the 'associated disposals' rules, again provided the relevant interest in possession beneficiary satisfies the requirements for the company in which the assets are held to be their personal company.

The trust has to satisfy the timing requirements in exactly the same way as any other associated disposal except that it also has to satisfy the 'qualifying beneficiary' test.

It is important to realise that extending the relief to a trust does not increase the amount of entrepreneurs' relief that an individual has. The trust merely shares the £1 million allowance of the relevant qualifying beneficiary, so any proportion that is agreed to be transferred to the interest in possession trustees reduces the allowance available to the individual.

Example

Rebecca owns 50% of the share capital in Dunham Limited, the remaining 50% being owned by interest in possession trustees for her benefit. On the dissolution of Dunham Limited in 2010, each of the two shareholders will make a gain of £400,000 and in addition Rebecca will make a gain of £400,000 selling the premises from which Dunham Limited conducted its trade.

Rebecca has entrepreneurs' relief as of right, on the basis she satisfies the qualifying conditions, but she can only transfer part of her relief to the interest in possession trustees by making an appropriate election.

In order to transfer the relief an election must be made to surrender a specified part of the individual's entrepreneurs' relief by the 31 January following the 31 January after the end of the year in which the gain arose. Thus if the gain arose in the year ended 5 April 2010, the election would have to be made by 31 January 2012. This is of course the usual time limit requirement in relation to self-assessment.

SHOULD A TRANSFER OF RELIEF BE CONSIDERED?

6.9   There are two issues that require consideration here.

Firstly the £1 million entrepreneurs' relief is an individual lifetime limit. Accordingly it would seem sensible that if the individual concerned is a serial entrepreneur and the current disposal is simply one of a number of disposals that the individual expects to make during their lifetime to retain the relief for their own benefit. Will they be best advised to allow part of their lifetime limit to be transferred to interest in possession trustees, even if those interest in possession trustees hold the funds for their benefit?

Secondly, what is the basis of compensation for the individual who has to agree to surrender their entrepreneurs' relief, for giving up relief that they might use on another occasion?

In the Rebecca example above, there is a surplus of £200,000 of entrepreneurs' relief, which if transferred to the interest in possession trustees would reduce their liability by £16,000. It might generally be considered appropriate for the interest in possession trustees to make a payment to Rebecca for her agreeing to surrender entrepreneurs' relief. This may be more important in relation to an interest in possession settlement where, for example, the trust assets do not ultimately pass to the same family as the existing life tenant.

Any payment that the individual receives will be a capital gains tax disposal taxable in the year in which the payment was made, but perhaps there exists some scope for a payment, which commercial reality suggests might be less than an annual CGT exemption, for surrender of the relief, particularly where the remainderman is not a member of the same family as the existing life tenant.

INVESTMENT COMPANIES – CAPITAL GAINS TAX TREATMENT IS NOT ALWAYS THE ANSWER

6.10   However, when the company being dissolved is an investment company, or other company where entrepreneurs' relief does not apply, then we need to consider whether capital distribution is the most appropriate course of action. Such disposals suffer tax at 18%, whereas perhaps if matters can be appropriately organised, the 10% tax credit on distributions may be the extent of the liability. However it is only likely to be the case where most or a significant proportion of the funds are subject to tax at basic rate.

The following example shows that distribution basis will not result in greater funds being available.

Example

Brandon Ltd is an investment company that was incorporated on 10 July 1990 with an issued share capital of £10,000 owned equally by Mr & Mrs Brandon. The current value of the company, net of all liabilities is £200,000 and it is proposed to distribute the funds on 20 September 2008 to the shareholders.

For illustration purposes, it is assumed that both Mr & Mrs Brandon are 40% taxpayers. The position on a capital distribution of £100,000 each would be as follows:

Sale proceeds	100,000
Less cost	5,000
Gain	95.000
Less: Annual Exemption (say)	9,600
Taxable gain	85,400
Tax payable	£15,372
Net proceeds (£100,000 – £15,372)	£84,628

Alternatively, if the funds are distributed by way of an income distribution, then the maximum payable will be 25% of the funds distributed.

Example

Income distribution	£100,000
Tax credit	£11,111
Taxable income	£111,111
Higher rate tax at 32.5%	£36,111
Less Tax credit	£11,111
Higher rate tax payable	£25,000
Net proceeds (£100,000 – £25,000) =	£75,000

Thus where the income distribution is taxed at higher rates, each shareholder ends up with £75,000 on the income distribution but £84,628 on the capital route, so here capital distribution is appropriate.

6.11   As indicated elsewhere, if capital distributions could take place in two tax years, then a further saving can be made but, overall, those further savings are likely to be modest . It is not considered that HMRC would attack payment in a number of tax years as an artificial arrangement. Certainly, in instances where application for a clearance has been made on a sale of a business, within the writer's experience any indication that the planning envisages the use of the annual exemptions amongst a number of family members causes no difficulty.

The examples here indicate the potential tax savings that can be achieved when dissolving an investment company by arranging for the majority of the proceeds to be distributed as an income distribution. If the approach taken is to achieve part as capital and part as income then there will be a need to make sure that the income distributions are made before any application is made to HMRC for the application of ESC C16 or before the appointment of a liquidator. Income distributions need to be properly minuted, Companies Act requirements satisfied, and separate cheques issued to the shareholders. This is to avoid tainting either the income or capital distributions.

BASIC RATE TAXPAYERS

6.12   The previous example, and most of the examples in this publication, assume that on dissolution the shareholder recipients are higher rate taxpayers. However, as we know from practice, the great majority of our clients only suffer tax at basic rate. Accordingly, if the shareholders, or a majority of the shareholders, remain basic rate taxpayers after the company has been dissolved then a significant advantage may be achieved by income status for the distribution of reserves. This may require the company to continue for a year or two in order to achieve maximum advantage. Remember that we can get payments into three separate tax years over only 13 months, provided the timing is right by making distribution in, for example, March 2009, April 2009 and April 2010.

Example

Nora, a basic rate taxpayer, is due to receive £20,000 being her share of reserves in Catfield Ltd, an investment company, and after the annual exemption of £9,600 (2008/09) she would have a taxable gain of £10,400 on which capital gains tax of £1,872 would be payable.

Nora's income once trading ceases will be low, consisting only of the retirement pension and a small amount of investment income. Accordingly, the £20,000 could be distributed to her without giving rise to a higher rate liability. In this circumstance there would be no additional tax payable so Nora saves

£1,872. As indicated, if the amounts are distributed in a single year and would give rise to a higher rate liability, consideration should be given to a number of interim income distributions in separate tax years to minimise the impact of higher rate tax. There may be some additional costs involved in administration, filing fees and the like but these are likely to be less than the income tax saving.

The same planning technique, to distribute all the reserves as income may also apply to trading companies where all, or a majority, of shareholders are basic rate taxpayers. The availability of entrepreneurs' relief and any annual exemptions are likely to result in rather more being distributed as capital and lower income distribution levels, to achieve a similar taxation result to the Nora example where the aggregate of income distribution and capital gain keeps the majority of the shareholders within the basic rate band.

Example

Albert, a basic rate taxpayer with a gross annual income of £20,000, is due to receive £40,000, being his share of reserves in Skegness Ltd, a trading company where the funds are available to be distributed in March 2009. Albert is entitled to entrepreneurs' relief. Therefore perhaps £18,000 could be distributed as income and £17,280 as capital before 6 April 2009. £17,280 after reduction of 5/9 gives a gain equivalent to the annual exemption, so in 2008/09 a total of £35,280 has been distributed; Albert's income, even with the above, remains within the basic rate band.

The balance can be distributed shortly after 6 April 2009 as capital and will be covered by the 2009/10 annual exemption.

CAPITAL GAINS TAX PARTIAL DISPOSAL

6.13   Most solvent distributions, by whatever method, where proceeds are paid out in a number of instalments over a number of tax years, will be partial disposals under TCGA 1992, s 42 requiring use of the formula:

$$\frac{A}{A + B}$$

with an appropriate reference to the Inland Revenue, using the CG34 post-transaction procedure, to agree the value of 'B'. Where there is likely to be a succession of part disposals, neither the taxpayer nor the Revenue will want to be involved in a series of negotiations that will not materially alter the tax payable. Particularly, if the liquidation distributions take place over a relatively short period of time, there is a relaxation, by concession, to avoid the costs of negotiation. Extra Statutory Concession D3 allows the 'B' element in the part disposal fraction to be agreed informally provided certain matters are satisfied.

The concession is set out in Appendix 6 and predates self-assessment since it refers to the making of an assessment, but does indicate that no enquiry into the 'B' value will be made unless more than two years elapse after the dissolution begins or the proceeds have exceeded allowable cost. This seems a case for relevant entries to be made on the white space of a tax return, both to advise that the concession is being used and to provide enough information to confirm that matters are dealt with in accordance with the concession. Certainly, when preparing CGT computations for clients where there are a series of interim distributions, we need to be sure that our assessment of the 'B' value does satisfy the spirit of the concession.

6.14   An alternative approach, if the capital distributions are small in value, allows them to be deducted from cost so that gains only become chargeable once cost has been used up (TCGA 1992, s 122). Revenue Interpretation 164 (see Appendix 6) regards a capital receipt as small whenever the amount is £3,000 or less, irrespective of whether the amount received is more than 5% of the overall value of the shares. However, it is probable that the number of occasions where a taxpayer will want to take advantage of TCGA 1992, s 122 are likely to be few and far between. This is because, ultimately, any decision to reduce cost without having a gain to assess has the effect of increasing the gain assessed on any final distribution from the company. Therefore, if the dissolution is delayed beyond three years, there is the possibility that gain that might have qualified for entrepreneurs' relief and an effective tax rate of 10% would then suffer tax at 18%. Additionally, there is the possibility that CGT annual exemptions will be wasted that might otherwise be used against interim distributions, either in part or in full, because in the great majority of solvent dissolutions there will be a surplus over allowable cost.

Example

Rose owns shares in Acle Ltd with a current value of £40,000 and a base cost of £5,000, being the share subscription on 31 January 1998. The company is a trading company and therefore, when it ceased to trade on 30 September 2008, Rose was entitled to entrepreneurs' relief, if the funds could be distributed to her at that date.

She receives an interim distribution of £3,000 on 30 September but has already used up her annual capital gains tax exemption. If use were made of ESC D3, her base cost would become £2,000 (£5,000 – £3,000), but if the £3,000 were accepted as taxable in 2008/09, Rose would have a taxable gain of perhaps £2,625 at, say 10%, withtax payable of ££262.50.

Suppose interim distributions proceed in 2009/10 and 2010/11 each September, they will qualify for entrepreneurs' relief

If the balance of £37,000 were distributed to Rose on 30 September 2009 then at that date she would have an extra £3,000 subject to tax, ie the taxable gain is £37,000 less residue of cost £2,000. The result is likely to be marginal and affected by Rose's tax position in the two years.

6.15   Accordingly, it would seem that advantage of ESC D3 should not be taken if the company is a trading company if the effect of reducing cost is to increase the gains at a later date when some of the gain will be subject to tax at the 18% normal rate. By contrast, if the proceeds being distributed are in respect of an investment company where the proceeds are not eligible for entrepreneurs' relief, it is possible in extreme or unusual circumstances that there may be an advantage in deducting proceeds from cost so that, ultimately, any tax liability is delayed. However, given that the concession can only apply to small distributions, it is probable that in most cases it will be better to simply accept the capital gain in the year of distribution and rely upon it being covered by the annual exemption. The evidence available to the writer from tax returns clearly shows that it is the exceptional client who uses up their annual CGT exemption every year.

CAPITAL GAINS TAX PLANNING FOR THE FAMILY

6.16   One area that clients often want to explore, particularly where cash is available for the first time on a proposed disincorporation, is to make gifts to their children and grandchildren. Previously, such gifts were simply not a possibility either because they did not have cash to fund gifts or the owner-generation were reluctant to transfer shares in the family company whilst it was active.

One advantage of transferring shares to family members is the possibility of multiplying the available capital gains tax exemptions, which for 2008/09 are £9,600. Even if the gifts of shares are to minor children, the settlement provisions of ITTOIA 2005, ss 625, 626 (formerly ICTA 1988, s 660B) only apply to income and not to capital, provided the capital remains the child's. Therefore, it is only income generated from any subsequent investment of the proceeds of disincorporation that may be taxable as a parental settlement, but the settlement provisions do not deny entitlement to capital gains tax annual exemption.

It will be important to ensure that once the cash has been distributed to the minor shareholders that the money is not recycled back to the donor. Such action risks the whole transaction being attacked as a sham or, indeed, a series of pre-ordained events whereby it was always intended to pass the cash back (perhaps the minor children did not even know the funds were expected) with the result that the intermediate additional annual exemptions are denied. This is, in any event, a settlement under TCGA 1992, s 77 and would result in the gain being assessed upon the parent, whether the apparent beneficiary was a minor or child.

TIMING OF THE GIFT

6.17   If shares producing gain in excess of the annual exemption are to be given then such gifts need to be made whilst the company is still trading to (potentially) take advantage of holdover relief under TCGA 1992, s 165.

One consequence of the gift of shares is that unless the gifted holding allows the recipients to qualify for entrepreneurs' relief, a shareholding of 5% and full-time working the gain will be taxed at 18%, so perhaps the gift should be of only sufficient shares to ensure that gains equal to the annual exempt amount are realised by the recipient.

However, it may be possible to make a partial claim for holdover to ensure that the gift by the donor simply realises his or her annual exemption. This might be achieved by two separate gifts on separate dates, one the subject of a holdover claim and the other left taxable where the gain is equivalent to the annual exemption.

Example

Julia owns 500 shares of £1 each in Yaxham Ltd, a trading company, which have been owned for many years and were acquired at par. The company plans to disincorporate in November 2008 and Julia anticipates that on each share she will make a gain of approximately £1,500, to make proceeds of £750,000.

She wants to give shares to her son and daughter to allow them to realise sufficient gains to use their own annual exemptions. If no gifts were made then, on disincorporation, Julia's position would be:

500 × £1,500	£750,000
Less: entrepreneurs' relief	£333,333
Annual exemption (say)	£9,600
Taxable gain	£407,067

Therefore, the residual taxable gain attributable to Julia will be subject to tax at 18%.

Her son and daughter are both university students so, ideally, they would want to realise gains in the region of £30,000. In any event, although Julia is intending to be generous she is also nervous about giving too much money to her children who may fritter the cash away. This could be achieved in one of two ways:

Gifts of shares (25) – gain	£37,500
Less Gain held over	£37,500
Julia's liability	Nil

Each child would receive value of £37,500 on dissolution from which they would deduct an annual exemption and have taxable gains of approximately £27,900, a tax charge of £5,022 at 18% and net proceeds of £32,478.

6.18   It will be for the client to consider the appropriate sum that they are happy to give away. Using the facts in the above examples, it is unlikely that most clients will want to give each child as much as £37,500 simply because they would be concerned that children could dissipate the money. In the above example, we have assumed a gain of £37,500 to each child but, at best, this results in CGT of £5,022. If Julia took all the gain herself and then made a cash gift, the tax payable on those same 25 shares might be only £3,750 (£37,500 – at the effective entrepreneurs' 10% tax rate), whereas each child would pay tax of £5,022.

Therefore, in practice, there seems little advantage in making gifts to family members where the recipient will generate a CGT liability on the dissolution proceeds that cannot, in turn, be reduced by entrepreneurs' relief. Accordingly, it would seem that the optimum value to give away is no more than the annual exemption that each recipient will have.

If the recipient has CGT losses that might otherwise not be used then an advantage may be obtained by creating a transfer that allows those losses to be used, but otherwise it seems limiting the gift to any recipient so the annual exemption is the favoured arrangement. This may only save £960 per recipient where the donor could otherwise claim entrepreneurs' relief, but in some circumstances it might well be the trigger for inheritance tax lifetime giving, which may produce other advantages.

TRANSFER INTO TRUST

6.19   Prior to the Finance Act 2008 changes to capital gains tax regime there were, in some circumstances, advantages to be obtained in transferring assets to an interest in possession settlement in order to avoid any dilution of entitlement to business asset taper that would result from holding shares until the dissolution proceeds were received. The detail was set out in paragraph **6.17** onwards of the first edition of this publication, but it seems probable that as a result of the new legislation giving shareholders up to three years to realise the assets after trading has ceased, in most cases transfers into trust will not be appropriate. However there may well be some unusual circumstances where, for example, it is not possible to achieve distributions within the three-year window, and the consequence would be that entitlement to entrepreneurs' relief would be lost. Some examples where this might occur are as follows.

- The trade has been sold but the premises remain owned by the trading company and there is a long delay in achieving a sale of the property. The 'credit crunch' of 2007/2008 inhibiting the ability of purchasers to acquire appropriate loan finance.

- There are ongoing legal disputes following the sale of the trade in relation to, perhaps breach of copyright, infringing patent rights and the life and it would be imprudent to make distributions until those disputes are completed.

- There might be a view that the shareholders want the company to continue and that the funds from the sale of one business are then used to purchase a replacement business but ultimately no replacement business is found within the three-year window. In the event that the three-year window approached there may then be an advantage in transferring the shares into an interest in possession settlement.

6.20   By way of illustration as to the way in which costs of transfer can easily eat into the apparent tax saving, consider the following example.

Example

Louise owns the freehold of property used in her family company, Stanhoe Limited, in circumstances where the company has ceased to trade and the proceeds are to be distributed to Louise, resulting in a gain of £250,000. The freehold property is also to be sold for £700,000, which will result in a gain of £250,000.

CGT at the effective entrepreneur rate would produce a liability of £25,000, whereas at the normal 18% a liability of £45,000. Thus there is a £20,000 difference in the two liabilities.

Similarly entrepreneurs' relief could be made to apply to the freehold property, as an associated disposal, and then a further £20,000 in CGT might also be saved. However there would be associated legal costs payable immediately, which might reduce the tax saving that would otherwise be available, making the transfer into a trust not cost effective.

It always has to be born in mind that the tax saving is always a percentage of the realised gain, whereas costs of transferring assets very often are based upon the gross value of the assets.

In the December 2003 pre-Budget report it was announced that holdover relief under either TCGA 1992, s 165 or s 260, would no longer apply where there was a transfer to a settlor interested trust. Historically, a settlor interested trust was used either to bank an entitlement to capital gains tax retirement relief or, more recently, before 12 December 2003 in order to restart the taper relief clock. However, in the circumstances envisaged here, a claim for holdover relief would not be anticipated because the purpose of the transfer to a settlor interested trust would be to bank any entitlement to entrepreneurs' relief to allow any resultant gain to suffer an effective rate of tax on the first £1 million.

6.21   Care may be required to ensure that the shareholders ultimately receive sufficient cash in time to pay any capital gains tax due on the transfer into trust, but otherwise the use of a settlor interested trust may result in the banking of entrepreneurs' relief and achieve a maximum tax saving of £80,000.

Example

Henry Brown owns 50% of Brixham Ltd, a trading company of more than ten years standing. The business of Brixham Ltd is to be sold on 1 September 2008 but on terms whereby 25% of the proceeds will be received in October 2009 and the balance in October 2011.

A review of Henry's shareholding indicates that he can expect to realise a gain of £250,000 on his shares and, if no amounts are paid out until, say, 6 April 2012, the effect is entrepreneurs' relief will be lost.

Distribution 1 September 2008

Gain	250,000
Less: Entrepreneurs' reduction	111,111
Taxable gain	138,888
Tax payable	25,000

Distribution 6 April 2012

Gain	250,000
Taxable gain	250,000
Tax payable	45,000

The tax payable reduces to £25,000 rather than £45,000.

So long as Henry transfers his shares to a settlor interested trust before 1 October 2011, his entitlement to entrepreneurs' relief would be preserved and, since the capital gains tax on that transfer will not be due until (say) 31 January 2013, this allows sufficient time for the company to receive all its proceeds and make an appropriate distribution to Henry to put him into funds to meet his liability.

6.22   However, it is not as simple as assessing the value based upon an uncompleted sale, transferring the shares, or other assets, to a settlor interested trust and then banking the entrepreneurs' relief. The transfer into trust will generate a real CGT liability and the need to agree a real disposal value. This is a share valuation issue, which is outside the scope of this publication but, in general terms, the transfer value will need to represent the price someone would pay for the shares on the day of transfer. Therefore, if the ultimate dissolution proceeds depend upon monies being received in instalments from a purchaser of the trade or the trade has not yet been sold then a discount would be expected from the theoretical received value for a number of reasons.

This might be because each individual shareholder only owns a minority interest, so the transfer value reflects the minority status on normal share valuation principles.

6.23   Alternatively, there will be a risk that the trade purchaser may themselves become insolvent and be unable to pay the agreed price, there may be guarantees and warranties but they may be of little comfort if the purchaser defaults.

Alternatively again, full dissolution proceeds may depend upon achieving a sale of company assets at a future date, perhaps once planning permission has been obtained, either under a conditional contract or option agreement.

In all these circumstances it is possible to calculate the amount we might expect to receive if everything goes according to plan, but any third party purchaser will discount the price now to allow for risk. The same principle applies in determining the transfer value into trust.

6.24 Where the values are known and there is little possibility of downward discount on the transfer value then a transfer into trust to bank entrepreneurs' relief may produce tax savings. This issue is explored in some detail in the Brundall Gardens Halt example in Appendix 5, but perhaps the appropriate conclusion is that a transfer into trust that goes counter to the anti-avoidance rules of Finance Act 2004, Sch 21 may only be advantageous either where the discount from dissolution proceeds is slight or in circumstances where the value is known but third party sales may take some time. Certainly it may be better in the post-5 April 2008 regime to wait and use the three-year window that is available to allow distribution of dissolution proceeds without having to incur the cost of establishing a trust and negotiating appropriate values.

This may also involve the transfer of property owned by shareholders outside the company. The property cannot be sold until after the trade has ceased, but the value will be the value with little discount. As is illustrated in the Brundall Gardens Halt example (see Appendix 5), there may be little advantage in transferring shares if the discount from anticipated proceeds is significant because within the recipient trust. The consequences will be that the discount, when redeemed on dissolution, will be subject to 18% tax.

6.25 If property used in the trade of the soon-to-be-dissolved company is personally held and entrepreneurs' relief appears to be available, then again there might be an advantage in transferring the relevant property into an interest in possession trust to preserve entrepreneurs' relief. The position with regard to property was much clearer-cut in the taper relief regime, because there was no limit to the amount of business taper relief that could be obtained. Accordingly, in the post-5 April 2008 regime where there will be an overall limit of £1,000,000 to the amount of gain eligible for entrepreneurs' relief, there may be less of an incentive to transfer freehold property to an interest in possession settlement.

The purpose of transfer into trust is to save the extra 8% between the normal capital gains tax rate and the effective entrepreneurs' relief capital gains tax rate, but the following factors would need to be taken into account.

- What are the legal costs of transferring the property into trust? SDLT should not be an issue, but for a property worth more than £500,000 legal fees might be 5% of the asset value. Not a significant difference from the amount of CGT that might be saved.

- Transferring into settlement will accelerate the tax charge and there might be funding issues if cash has to be borrowed.

- There may be cost implications in terms of value in the property, negotiations and again there might be a discount from open market value where that discount might ultimately be taxed at 18% rather than the effective 10% rate.

PLANNING POINTS

6.26

- Will advantage be obtained by a transfer into a settlor interested trust to preserve entrepreneur relief?

- Make any gifts of share before trade ceases, so that TCGA 1992, s 165 holdover relief is available.

- Review the shareholdings to ensure that 5% minimums are held by spouses or registered civil partners.

- Make sure that any assets that might be eligible for associated disposal entrepreneurs' relief are held by the correct spouse or registered civil partner.

- Assess part disposal 'B' value on the basis of known information.

- Assess whether there is any advantage in allowing surplus entrepreneurs' relief to be transferred to interest in possession settlements.

- Make sure the maximum distributions are made before the three-year window expires where entrepreneurs' relief remains available.

- Review the income tax status of the shareholders to see if capital treatment is always the correct approach.

- Assess the tax cost of income status.

- Consider if, as adviser, you can act for all shareholders or, if there is likely to be conflict, between the interests of the shareholders.

Chapter 7

Continuing the trade under a new structure

7.1 Previous chapters considered the probability that the family company is to be dissolved simply because the trade has either ceased or because the trade has been sold to a non-family member – in effect, a new family take-over. However, just as there was a rush to incorporate following the Finance Act 2001 corporation tax nil-rate band introduction, some commentators (before the detailed provisions were known) suggested an equal rush to reverse as a result of Finance Act 2004 which resulted in the withdrawal of the £10,000 nil rate band. Since then there has been little evidence of any reluctance either to carry on with the companies formed in the Finance Act 2001 rush, or of a cessation of new company formation. The effect of the current circumstances is to reduce, but not eliminate, the tax reductions achieved by incorporation.

The reduction in tax advantage may discourage some at the margin from incorporating; there will not be many who will want to accept the additional administration costs, in terms of cash and time, for a tax reduction of less than £1,000. For many companies, and their shareholders, the primary motive for incorporation is often a reduction in tax – in effect, an increase in take-home pay. They are prepared to put up with the additional administration and supervision the company enjoys, but if the advantages of operating through a company become marginal then is there any advantage in retaining your trade within a limited company? That is a decision only the proprietors can take, but if they do decide the company has had its day, what are the disadvantages of attempting to extract the trade from the family company? It is assumed that, in most cases, the advantages of incorporation are implicit and were accepted when the trade was incorporated.

7.2 The current corporation tax rate for small companies, and these are likely to be the companies most practitioners will deal with, is 21% (from 1 April 2008) and with the parallel reduction in mainstream corporation tax rates it might be surmised that ultimately the two rates will meet somewhere in the middle. The consequence would then be that if there were a universal rate of perhaps 25%, that that would not be significantly different from the effective rate paid by a basic rate unincorporated business of 28% (20% tax and 8% Class 4 NIC).

Except for very small companies (which probably should never have incorporated), the impact of increased corporation tax rates will be marginal. Companies are used to including in their cash flow a tax payment nine months after the end of the accounting period; companies paying quarterly instalments are unaffected because their profit levels are too high.

7.3 Although there are procedures available to allow a business to transfer from sole trade/partnership to company in a relatively painless way, the same cannot be said for the reverse process. In particular, it cannot be assumed that CGT treatment will apply to any reserves distributed to existing shareholders to allow them to carry on the same trade under a new structure – see para **5.17**, which discuss the very real risk that ITA 2007, s 682 onwards (formerly ICTA 1988, s 703) may apply to any value received in these circumstances.

NO HOLDOVER RELIEF

7.4 On incorporation holdover relief is available on the transfer of assets to the family company under TCGA 1992, s 162 or s 165, depending upon the precise mechanism that has been chosen for incorporation.

7.5 Equally, the balance on capital account within a partnership or sole trader business, when transferred to a family company, is not then subject to a further tax charge. The value is generally either credited to a director's or shareholder's loan account under TCGA 1992, s 165 or subsumed into the value of shares that the family company issues under TCGA 1992, s 165. Some will withdraw capital immediately before incorporation so that the new company takes over an overdraft, then the cash is reintroduced as a loan and not subsumed into the value of shares.

7.6 By contrast, chargeable assets owned by the family company, if they have appreciated in value during the family company ownership, will be subject to corporation tax on the profit, subject only to the deduction of indexation allowance. There is no mechanism to allow holdover relief on exit from the family company.

7.7 Equally, if a family company has generated profit and loss account reserves on which corporation tax has already been paid, then the distribution of those reserves to shareholders will be subject to capital gains tax. Indeed, there are strong arguments for saying that the distribution of reserves to the shareholders in circumstances where the trade is to be carried on by those same shareholders, in a new venture, would result in an assessment under ITA 2007, s 682 because a tax advantage is obtained by having the reserves assessed to CGT rather than income tax. This issue is explored in greater detail in paras **5.11–5.21**. Certainly, extracting a trade from a company will not be a seamless exercise.

7.8 In effect, both tax charges would not have arisen but for disincorporation and the desire to extract the trade from the family company. The tax charges apply equally to all assets, but perhaps bite hardest on freehold property. Property may have been introduced into the family company by minority shareholders in order to achieve 100% BPR because the assets are within the corporate window rather than the 50% business property relief ('BPR') that would be available in private ownership, but only to a controlling shareholder. The owners may have taken the view that the trade was unlikely to be sold so that the better advantage was to have the property owned by the corporate vehicle, despite any concerns as to double tax charges if the property were ever desired to be extracted. Ownership of freehold or leasehold property through a family company is generally considered undesirable because of the double charge to tax that will arise when the property is sold and the profits distributed to shareholders. But, if the freehold property would be owned by a minority shareholder, the advantage of obtaining 100% BPR, if the property is within the corporate envelope, may more than outweigh any extra tax charge that may arise if the property is subsequently sold and the proceeds then distributed to the shareholders.

Example

Dogdyke Ltd, a trading company, owns the freehold from which the trade is conducted having acquired the property in April 1998 for £50,000. The property is sold in May 2008 for £100,000.

The impact upon the shareholders, assuming Jones Ltd is then immediately dissolved, is as follows:

Sale proceeds	£100,000
Less cost	£50,000
Indexation allowance (say)	£12,500
	£62,500
Profit	£37,500
Corporation tax at 21%	£7,875

Increase in value of reserves	
Profit on sale	£50,000
Less corporation tax	£7,875
Increase	£42,125

If that £42,125 is distributed to shareholders entitled to entrepreneurs' relief and thus taxable at an effective 10%, then, ignoring the annual exemption, the cash to shareholders would be £37,912 (£42,125 – £4,213).

7.9 By contrast, if freehold property had been owned personally either because the trade was conducted as a sole trader/partnership or indeed the trade was carried on through the family company but the property retained privately, then the cash to shareholders would be as follows:

Sale proceeds	100,000
Less cost	£50,000
Taxable gain	£50,000

At the effective entrepreneur rate of 10% this would produce a tax charge of £5,000 so the net profit to the shareholders, ignoring return of capital of £50,000, would be £45,000, ie £100,000 – £50,000 – £5,000. Therefore, on personal ownership the shareholder would save approximately £7,088 in income taxes, being the difference between the aggregate of corporation tax and personal CGT.

7.10   As indicated in para **7.8**, income taxes are not the only factor to be considered. Capital taxes also need to be considered if there is a choice between corporate or personal ownership. Where assets are personally owned, BPR is only available if the owner is a controlling shareholder and then only at the reduced 50% rate. Therefore, £7,088 in income taxes would be saved if the asset were held personally, but if the same shareholder were to die as a minority shareholder owning the asset, there would be an inheritance tax charge on the owner of a £100,000 property of £40,000.

7.11   It is entirely possible that, in seeking to extract the trade from the family company, the tax charges that arise on disincorporation may exceed the tax saved by any previous incorporation because of the double tax charge of both tax in the family company on realisations and tax in the hands of the shareholders on distributions. The availability of entrepreneurs' relief may reduce the impact of the double charge, but the charge still exists. However, in the post-5 April 2008 era if a profit is made there will be double tax because there will always have been a charge within the company (assuming a profit in excess of indexation relief) and a minimum effective 10% charge on the shareholders or potentially 18% if the company is not a trading company or the individual shareholders have used up all their £1,000,000 entrepreneurs' entitlement.

7.12   There have been a number of proposals and suggestions over the years to achieve a situation where disincorporation does not produce an immediate tax charge, but these have never produced legislation. It is difficult to envisage, in the current climate, that HMRC would be sympathetic to shareholders who incorporated to save tax and now want relieving legislation to allow them to disincorporate to save tax. A case of biter bit? It is difficult to consider that any concessions would be offered to disincorporation.

7.13   Chapter 5 above discusses in detail the application of ESC C16, but it must be remembered that the concession is precisely that. The introduction to the concessions includes the warning set out at para **5.12**, which also includes a discussion of cases where the courts had decided that the concession should not be applied and also speculation as to other circumstances.

If you are to disincorporate a trade that has successively been a sole trader and family company in order that the trade can revert to sole trader status, and it is clear that the only or main reason for change is a reduction in income tax, is this a circumstance where capital status should be allowed?

Certainly, Company Taxation Manual 36875 still refers to the possibility of assessment under ICTA 1988, s 703 (ITA 2007, s 682) for either a company reconstruction, in which some or all of the shareholders in the original company retain an interest in the second company, or where there is a sale of shares under any agreement whereby the shares themselves or the underlying assets are capable of being subsequently reacquired by the vendor. Certainly, it will be a live issue because Company Taxation Manual 36220 which is the main area where ESC C16 is discussed, is cross-referenced back to Company Taxation Manual 36875.

DISTRIBUTION AS INCOME

7.14 Where the value of a company is distributed on disincorporation as income, because ESC C16 has been refused, or the advisers decide that an assessment under ITA 2007, s 682 is the logical consequence of the proposed transactions, and the shareholders decide that the costs of a formal liquidation are too great, then any value distributed will be taxed at the recipient taxpayer's marginal tax rate. In the year of disincorporation, this may well be 32.5% being the rate applicable to dividends but because the profits of the disincorporated and now resurrected sole trader/partnership will also be taxed in the same year some income may suffer 40% tax.

Unlike incorporation where it is often possible to ensure that no income arises from the company post-incorporation until 5 April following incorporation (either by drawing cash from a director's loan account or by simply living off savings, but replenishing these after the 5 April after incorporation by dividend or salary), under disincorporation, no such mechanism is available to the born again sole trader. The Schedule D profits are immediately subject to tax and have direct tax consequences.

Example

John owns 50% of John's Plumbers Ltd, which at disincorporation has a value, net of director's loan account balance, of £54,000. Therefore, on disincorporation as an income event, John receives £27,000 net of 10% tax credit. The disincorporation takes place on 30 September 2008 and, from 1 October 2008, John's Plumbers commences to trade.

John's Plumbers makes an annual profit of £60,000, so John's 2008/09 tax charge is as follows:

	Gross	Tax
John's Plumbers – Sch D	30,000	
John's Plumbers Ltd – dividend distribution	30,000	3,000
	60,000	3,000
Less Personal allowance	6,035	
	53,965	
23,965 @ 20%	4,793.00	
10,835 @ 10%	1,083.50	
19,165 @ 32.5%	6,228.62	12,105.12
53,965		
Class 4 NIC (30,000 – 5,435 at 8%)		1,965.20
		14,070.32
Less suffered at source		3,000.00
Tax due 31 January 2010		£11,070.32

Of course he is now also on the self-assessment treadmill, so on 31 January 2010, in addition to the balancing payment, he will also have to make a 2009/10 payment on account of perhaps £5,535.16; therefore, a total liability of £16,625.48. As always with self-assessment, if the taxpayer can show that the 2009/10 liability will be less than £11,070.32, a postponement claim can be made.

CHARGEABLE ASSETS IN THE COMPANY

7.15 Paragraph **7.8** discussed the taxation position of freehold property being owned by the family company, but there will be other chargeable assets that will be subject to capital gains tax on a disposal.

Goodwill

7.16 This is likely to be one of the major assets of any business. Many may not have thought so prior to incorporation of the business, but on new incorporations in 2001 and 2002 many advisers created a director's loan account balance by selling goodwill to the new family company, often at a figure that, conveniently, did not give rise to a CGT tax charge. In many cases this seems to have been achieved by the convenient exploitation of a sale for £30,000, 75% taper relief and the available annual exemption multiplied up if a partnership.

Example

John the plumber, or at least his accountant, thought it was a great wheeze to sell John's goodwill to John's Plumbers Ltd on incorporation on 1 August 2001 for £30,000 so that the CGT position net of 75% business asset taper relief was a taxable gain of £7,500, which was covered by the annual CGT exemption.

The value was reviewed by HMRC, but the inspector accepted that the calculation basis stated of one year's net profit was reasonable.

At disincorporation the company's profits are now £60,000 per annum so should the goodwill now be valued at £60,000? The valuation basis of goodwill is outside the scope of this publication but perhaps a harder line on valuations offered where, on exit from the family company, a low valuation is required in order to avoid a tax charge may be expected.

Example

If we assume on disincorporation that the goodwill on John's Plumbers Ltd is £60,000 then the position is as follows:

Proceeds	£60,000
Less cost	£30,000
Indexation allowance (say)	£6,600
	£36,600
Taxable gain	£36,600
Corporation tax at 21%	£7,686

However, the increase in value of the goodwill, because this is a transaction between connected parties, will also have an impact upon the value of the company that is distributed to John and his other shareholders. So whereas the illustration in para **7.14** assumed no change in value of goodwill, if goodwill is now truly worth £60,000, assuming it always did have a value, the consequence is that the value of the company increases by £22,314, so John's income distribution would then amount to £38,157, so there is a further liability to higher rate tax, but this time on an asset that John never knew he had before the accountant's wheeze in August 2001.

Although the John example produces significant tax charges because much of the reserves of the company will suffer tax at higher rates there might be examples where taxing the dissolution distribution as income does not cause so great a tax charge.

Example

Suppose the shareholders in Jeff's Plasterers Ltd consisted of three plasterers, and their partners in circumstances where the settlement provisions are not an issue. They generally produce profits of approximately £25,000 per year per plasterer, their partners typically earn similar amounts, and in consequence when they decide to revert to a partnership the accumulated reserves of £50,000 when distributed between the six shareholders produce just over £8,000 each, so there is no exposure to higher rates.

In effect this is an extension of the Nora example at para **6.12**.

Purchased goodwill

7.17   Goodwill, if purchased after 1 April 2002 by a company from unconnected parties, is eligible for tax relief on the depreciation that is claimed within a company environment. Accordingly, in circumstances where it is anticipated that the business is to close and, equally, it is anticipated that it will not be possible to sell the goodwill to a successor company, it will be important for the directors of the company to carry out impairment reviews on a regular basis. This is something that should always be undertaken in any trading company on a regular basis but is drawn into sharper focus where the trade is about to cease. It may, for example, be that the company ceasing trading is operating in an industry where technological advance has passed the ceasing company by, but there is customer loyalty but only to the current proprietor. The client base may ultimately be passed on to a competitor, but the competitor will not make any payment. The purpose of any impairment review is to ensure that the company obtains corporation tax relief for any reduction in purchased goodwill value whilst it is still trading. If there are a series of impairment reviews then these will cause an immediate reduction in corporation tax liabilities, and therefore a cash flow advantage to the company, but, equally, if an impairment review is only carried out at the date on which the trade ceased then any diminution in value can only form part of the terminal loss relief claim and that may result in relief being denied if the effect is to make the quantum of the terminal loss relief claim greater than the profits made in the final three years of trading.

Example

Hunstanton Ltd makes its annual accounts up to 30 June each year and on 1 July 2004 purchased goodwill with a cost of £100,000. Within six months of purchase, a technological advance means that Hunstanton Ltd would have to incur substantial capital expenditure if it wishes to continue to trade and exploit its purchased goodwill. However, the proprietor of Hunstanton Ltd believes that he can continue to trade for a further five years, but he would then no longer be able to trade because further technical advances would mean his remaining equipment is totally obsolete.

On 30 June 2005, the company carry out an impairment review and write off one-fifth of the purchased goodwill of £20,000.

In the year to 30 June 2006, Hunstanton Ltd decides that their previous estimate of five years trading was optimistic and that four years is more likely. Accordingly, for the year to 30 June 2006, they undertake a further impairment review and write off £30,000. This process continues on an annual basis so that by the time Hunstanton Ltd ceases to trade on 30 September 2008, all the purchased goodwill has been written off and tax relief obtained.

7.18   If the accounts up to cessation of trading are submitted to HMRC and no impairment review has been taken of purchased goodwill in the completion of the cessation accounts then, under the provisions allowing relief for post-cessation expenses, if the purchased goodwill is ultimately sold at a loss there are no provisions whereby that loss can be carried back into the trading period. Accordingly, it is essential for any company that has purchased goodwill to, as a minimum, undertake an impairment review at the date of cessation of trade and to reflect the effect of that review in the corporation tax computation for the final accounting period. If that review results in a corporation tax loss then, equally, a terminal loss relief claim would be appropriate.

7.19   If the reason the company is being dissolved is to allow the trade to be carried on by a sole trade or partnership it must be remembered that for successor self trader or partnership, no relief is due on the value of the goodwill or other intangible asset acquired by successor business. Therefore it is equally important that an impairment review is undertaken at the date of transfer. Even if it is not, Finance Act 2002, Sch 29, para 92 requires the transfer to be at market value. Since Finance Act 2002, Sch 29, para 92(5) defines market value as the price the asset might reasonably be expected to fetch on a sale on the open market, it is likely to correspond with the value achieved by the impairment review. Therefore, this provision would prevent the directors of the dissolving company from saying that the value of the goodwill and other intangibles is nil simply to obtain corporation tax relief for the loss in value when the reality was that the asset still has a value.

Finance Act 2002, Sch 29, paras 95, 118 in effect prohibit a deduction where the intangible asset has been acquired from a related party. Finance Act 2002, Sch 29, para 84 allows a continuation of the relief on a company reconstruction where the trade transfers from one company to another, provided the transferor company received no part of the consideration of the transfer other than the recipient company taking over all or part of the liabilities of the business. However, this does not extend the relief to a transfer from a company to a sole trader or partnership. Therefore, even though the company would have been eligible for tax relief on purchased goodwill, assuming it was purchased from an unconnected party (so not a purchase of goodwill of the John's Plumber variety), and the successor partnership will not, simply because provisions of Finance Act 2002, s 85 do not allow any relief where purchased goodwill is acquired by a non-company business.

7.20 The provisions of Financial Reporting Standard 10, coupled with Finance Act 2002, s 84, allow a company a measure of relief for goodwill and other intangibles (where these are purchased) after 2002 for the amount written off as depreciation under an impairment review, provided the writing off basis is reasonable. As always, it is open to HMRC to challenge the basis upon which the impairment review has been undertaken but it is insufficient, particularly when a company is in the process of being dissolved or such action is being contemplated, to simply accept that a single impairment review undertaken when the goodwill was purchased should remain the position for all time. It is open to the directors to undertake an impairment review on an annual basis and this is certainly something that should be done. Within the writer's experience, those businesses that may pay for goodwill are, equally, those where technological advantages or fashion can render the value of that goodwill worthless within a matter of months or years so the earlier the relief for any reduction in value is obtained, the better.

Example

Using the Salhouse terminal loss example (see para **3.32**) but assuming the company had purchased goodwill of £150,000, as a result of the original impairment review by the date of cessation of trade, goodwill was written down to £100,000. On 31 August 2008 the goodwill is actually sold for £10,000, which would have the effect of increasing the terminal loss by

£90,000. On the facts shown in the Salhouse example, this would mean that some of the losses are unrelieved.

7.21 It is possible that if impairment reviews were more honestly undertaken, some of that locked-in loss relief would have been relieved. Historically, when accounts were prepared, because no relief was available for purchased goodwill, directors were reluctant to write the expenditure off. Equally today, because tax relief is now available, they are more likely to want to write goodwill off but, equally, they do not want to dilute the balance sheet. FRS 10 imposes an obligation to undertake an impairment review on a regular basis so that review should be undertaken.

Excessive impairment reviews may ultimately have an impact upon the ability of a company to buy back its shares, particularly if the share buy-back is required to reduce the issued share capital below £4,000 before tangible assets have been realised at a gain which will achieve realisable profits, so the initial purchase of shares may be out of capital. Companies Act 2006 has eased the requirements for purchase of shares out of capital for private companies, but except in the case of a company with a very high level of issued share capital and a low balance on profit and loss account, this is unlikely to cause any practical problems.

Capital allowances

7.22 On the transfer of assets eligible for capital allowances from sole trader to family company it was possible to elect, under CAA 2001, s 266, to transfer the assets at tax written down value. Equally, on disincorporation the same election will be available.

However, it is also possible to transfer plant and machinery eligible for capital allowances at market value. There are, in effect, three options open to the disincorporating business:

- make an election under CAA 2001, s 266;

- substitute market value so that there might arise either a balancing allowance or balancing charge depending upon the market value of the assets; or

- control the extent of the balancing allowance or balancing charge by having actual consideration and arranging for the new sole trader to pay cash to the former family company for the plant and machinery.

7.23 The advantages and disadvantages of all three options are discussed at para **3.37**, but the main criteria is likely to be the amount of tax relief that can be obtained either through the family company or through the sole trader/partnership business. If the sale route produces a balancing charge then it will be subject to corporation tax at either 21% or 28% (ignoring the interim marginal banding), whereas the writing down allowance in the sole trader business would be eligible for tax relief at either 28%, (being basic rate of 20%

plus class 4 NIC of 8%) or 41% (being higher rate tax of 40% plus 1% class 4 NIC) or indeed 48% if the sole trader income is subject to higher rate tax but also the first band of class 4 NIC.

Cash flow considerations may impact here but, generally, it will be the potential relief that is available on writing down allowances that should be the determining issue.

7.24   If a sale is made then for VAT purposes, this is likely to be a transfer of a business as a going concern (TOGC) so long as both the family company and the proposed sole trader satisfy the TOGC rules (see para **9.10**).

7.25   Within this section we have considered the impact on corporation tax or income tax of a disposal of plant and machinery and the circumstances in which an election of the CAA 2001, s 266 might be made. However, this election only applies for either income tax or corporation tax purposes. It does not apply for capital gains tax purposes when considering the value of the company distributed to a shareholder.

Therefore, in the example set out in para **3.37**, if an election were made to transfer plant and machinery in the capital allowance pool at the tax written down value of £25,000, you would still need to include in your valuation of the company, for distribution purposes, the current market value of the plant and machinery. Therefore, the difference between book value and market value, if any, will increase or reduce the value of the company potentially subject to either capital gains tax or income tax on dissolution.

PLANNING POINTS

7.26

- Think, and think again, before disincorporating simply to counteract any Finance Act changes from a single year, even those for 2004 that commentators feared would slay the golden goose but, upon mature reflection, do not.

- Consider the cash flow implications of a sole trader/partnership resuming Schedule D payments on account.

- Assess the true value of the assets to be distributed.

- Calculate the cost of an ITA 2007, s 682 assessment if this were raised on the shareholders. Of course if there were a number of shareholder/partners who were to start again it is possible, depending upon the number of shareholders, the amount of income-assessable reserves, and their personal tax positions, that income basis may produce a lower tax charge, on the basis any deemed basic rate liability is covered by the dividend tax credit.

Chapter 8

Stamp Duty and Stamp Duty Land Tax

8.1   During the course of dissolution, whether through the formal or through the informal liquidation route, it is possible that assets will be transferred to shareholders in full or in part settlement of any entitlement to the company's assets as represented by their shareholding. Such distributions could consist of either:

- cash; or

- assets of the company, including freehold and leasehold property.

So far as cash is concerned, there would be no liability to either Stamp Duty or Stamp Duty Land Tax.

8.2   In respect of any liability to Stamp Duty Land Tax (SDLT), the position is governed by Finance Act 2003, Sch 3, para 1, which states:

'A land transaction is exempt from charge if there is no chargeable consideration for the transaction.'

This position exists whether the asset is distributed by the liquidator or through the more informal ss 652, 652A procedure.

ASSUMPTION OF LIABILITIES

8.3   The only occasion on which a charge to SDLT might apply is if any land and property, which is transferred to a shareholder in full or partial settlement of their entitlement under the dissolution, is transferred subject to the assumption of a debt or subject to a requirement to make a payment to the company. In this instance, the FA 2003, Sch 3, para 1 exemption would not apply to the value of the consideration paid, ie the value of the debt attached to the property or the cash payment made to the company.

Example

Alice, a shareholder in Fransham Ltd, had passed to her, as part of her entitlement in the dissolution, a freehold property with a value of £350,000. The property is subject to a mortgage of £200,000, which is assumed by Alice, so there will be a liability to SDLT at 1% of the value of the debt; in this case £2,000.

If, however, the company could arrange to repay some of the mortgage from realisation proceeds so that the debt assumed is less than the 1% thresholds, from 23 March 2006, of £150,000 for commercial property or £125,000 for residential property, assuming the temporary uplift in the threshold for residential property to £175,000 from 3 September 2008 for 12 months is reviewed in 2009 there would be no exposure to SDLT.

8.4 The same potential exposure to SDLT would apply even if the debt was not directly secured on the property. Suppose, in the above example, that Alice's entitlement in the liquidation was £280,000 but she decided that she wanted to have the property in circumstances where the original mortgage had been repaid from asset realisations. In order to allow the company to make distributions to other shareholders, she agreed to make a cash payment to the company. This would be treated as consideration for the property and therefore is potentially subject to SDLT, depending upon the type of property being transferred and whether the payment was above the relevant SDLT threshold. The same situation would also subsist if a shareholder was not required to make a physical payment or assume responsibility for debt, but instead agreed not to receive the full balance on a director's loan account in order to allow other shareholders to receive their appropriate share in cash, so a contra book entry also potentially triggers a SDLT liability. However, the amount of SDLT payable will depend upon the nature of the property any particular shareholder acquires.

8.5 It will be seen from the tables below that there are two different scales of SDLT, which apply from 23 March 2006 as follows.

- In the case of commercial property, a higher 1% threshold applies so that SDLT only applies where the consideration exceeds £150,000.

- By contrast, if the property concerned is residential property then SDLT becomes payable once the consideration exceeds £125,000 but see below for details of the temporary raising of the residential limit to £175,000 for transactions between 3 September 2008 and 3 September 2009.

Example

Alfie is due to receive property from Wrabness Ltd, which has a value of £140,000. SDLT would be due at 1% if this were residential property, but at 0% if it were commercial property.

Accordingly, if any property that is transferred to a shareholder, in partial satisfaction of their dissolution entitlement, is commercial property, and if the market value is below the £150,000 threshold, no SDLT would be due. SDLT would, however, become payable if the property transferred were residential property where the market value exceeds £125,000.

WHAT RATES OF STAMP DUTY LAND TAX MAY APPLY

8.6   Two different scales of SDLT apply to freehold property. The scale for residential property is as follows:

Consideration does not exceed £125,000	0%
Exceeds £125,000 but less than £250,000	1%
Exceeds £250,000 but less than £500,000	3%
Exceeds £500,000	4%

On 2 September 2008 the government announced a temporary raising of the 0% band to £175,000 for transactions that take place between 3 September 2008 and 3 September 2009. Whether this temporary arrangement, which has been designed to provide some measure of support for the housing market in the 2007–2009 credit crunch, will ultimately become permanent, time will tell. However, for the moment, for non-residential property, conventional commercial property or property that has a mixture of residential and non-residential (for example, a shop with a flat above), the rates are:

Consideration less than £150,000	0%
Exceeds £150,000 but less than £250,000	1%
Exceeds £250,000 but less than £500,000	3%
Exceeds £500,000	4%

Separate rates of SDLT apply to leases and, again, there are different rates depending upon whether the lease is of residential property or non-residential (or indeed non-residential and residential as a mixed property):

The rates are

Residential consideration does not exceed £125,000	0%
Consideration exceeds £125,000	1%

For non-residential (or mixed leases) the rates are

Consideration does not exceed £150,000	0%
Consideration exceeds £150,000	1%

Within the above table for the period 3 September 2008 to 3 September 2009 the initial threshold of £125,000 is replaced by £175,000, so the 1% band only covers residential properties that sell for between £175,001 and £250,000.

The amount of tax payable is a straight percentage of the chargeable consideration; therefore the Stamp Duty scheme of rounding up to the nearest £5 is abandoned.

In most property transactions, consideration whether a premium on a lease or the sale of a freehold, will be the price paid by an unconnected third party for the property or, if the transaction is between connected parties, the open market value. In the circumstances envisaged by this publication, consideration subject to SDLT is only likely to apply to the value of liabilities assumed by a recipient of property.

8.7   One helpful modification following from the introduction of SDLT is the abolition of any charge to SDLT on notional VAT on leasehold transactions where there was no VAT payable because the option to tax had not been made (see Chapter 9). In respect of transactions that took place before 1 December 2003, Stamp Duty was payable on the value of a leasehold transaction (plus notional VAT) unless the contract contained provisions that prevented VAT being charged, as a contractual matter, so long as the vendor had a choice.

Example

Snape Ltd granted a lease on 10 July 2003 at a premium of £450,000 but had not elected to charge VAT on the property. Nevertheless, notional VAT would be added, and Stamp Duty, because this was a pre-1 December 2003 transaction, is due on £528,750 (£450,000 + 17.5%). Therefore, Stamp Duty of 4% is due on £528,750 rather than 3% on £450,000.

The introduction of SDLT now means that a leasehold transaction will now only result in an SDLT liability on VAT where it is charged on the property, usually where the option to tax has been made. If no VAT is charged then SDLT is only payable on the consideration that passes between the parties. Therefore, for transactions that take place after 1 December 2003, there is no difference between leasehold and freehold transactions, so far as exposure to SDLT on VAT is concerned. It is only payable on VAT charged by a vendor.

Example

Assume the same facts as above but Snape Ltd now grant a lease on 10 January 2005 at a premium of £450,000 and have not elected to charge VAT on the property. SDLT will only be due on £450,000 at 3%.

WHEN IS THE TAX PAYABLE?

8.8   The tax is payable 30 days after the earlier date of completion of the contract or the date when commercial reality indicates the transaction is complete – this is to prevent SDLT avoidance by arranging for cash to pass, but avoiding completing the contract.

An indication of commercial completion would be if most of the consideration monies had passed; payment of 90% of consideration monies is considered effective commercial completion.

If the purchaser does not bother to pay the SDLT on time then it will be possible for the Inland Revenue to raise an assessment to recover any lost tax.

OTHER MATTERS

8.9   The position under SDLT for land transactions that take place after 1 December 2003, where property is distributed to shareholders, is clearer than the position that potentially existed with regard to Stamp Duty charges prior to 1 December 2003.

Under the Stamp Duty (Exempt Instruments) Regulations 1997, category 1 exempted from Stamp Duty any conveyance or transfer by a liquidator of property that formed part of the assets of a company in liquidation to a shareholder of that company (or his nominee) in or towards satisfaction of the shareholder's rights of the winding-up.

If the dissolution of the company and the asset distribution to the shareholder were effected under the ESC C16 mantle, then there was some doubt as to whether exemption from Stamp Duty under category 1, as it was then, applied. It was, however, accepted by the Stamp Office that the transfer of property, subject to the debt point (see para **8.3**) was on conveyance other than on sale and therefore would only have attracted a fixed duty of £5 under FA 1999, Sch 13, para 16.

Prior to 1 December 2003, there was of course only one nil rate band of £60,000 whether the property was commercial or residential but, in the great majority of cases, this may not have been the issue.

SALE OF ASSETS

8.10   If the company sells freehold land or leasehold property as part of the realisation of the company's assets then any purchaser of those assets will be subject to SDLT in the usual way.

PURCHASE OF OWN SHARES

8.11   Where the company has an issued share capital in excess of £4,000, then in general it will be advisable to undertake a purchase of own shares before any distributions to shareholders, to reduce the value of the issued share capital below £4,000 to avoid the risk that the bona vacantia provisions will result in a claim from the Treasury. The transaction is returned to the Registrar of Companies on form G169 but the price paid is subject to Stamp Duty at ½%, rounded up to the nearest £5, which must be paid to HMRC before the form is filed with the Registrar of Companies.

PLANNING POINTS

8.12

- Review the arrangements to see if SDLT will arise on any distribution to a particular shareholder that involves either directly or indirectly the assumption of liabilities.

- Ensure any SDLT due is paid within the normal 30-day period.

- If property is to be transferred to a shareholder, where there are assumption of liabilities, can the liabilities be reduced so that one of the higher rates of SDLT thresholds are not exceeded?

8.12 *Stamp Duty and Stamp Duty Land Tax*

- For commercial property, keep the debt assumed below £150,000, £250,000 or £500,000 if possible.

- For residential property, keep the debt assumed below £125,000 (£175,000 if within the period of temporary uplift), £250,000 or £500,000.

Chapter 9

Value Added Tax

9.1   Although this publication is primarily concerned with the direct taxes – income tax, capital gains tax and corporation tax – it would be inappropriate to ignore the major indirect tax of Value Added Tax (VAT) because, in seeking to transfer or sell the assets of a dissolving company, it is probable that VAT liabilities will arise that will reduce the funds available to be distributed. VAT is much more than a sales tax and, for some businesses, represents a significant cost that needs to be managed. Some practitioners will have in-house VAT specialists who can advise on the areas that need to be reviewed but others need to understand the areas of concern so that, at the very least, the appropriate questions are asked. The problem with VAT for most direct tax practitioners is that it is generally viewed as an 'in-and-an-out' without any significant impact upon the tax computations. In dealing with the sale of assets, we are primarily concerned with the net cash that is realised. Simply treating matters as an 'in-and-out' could not be further from the truth, particularly in the circumstances envisaged by this publication where often the main concern will be the capital assets of the business where specific and unexpected VAT charges can arise if the correct preventative action is not taken in advance.

In exactly the same way as direct taxes need to be managed to ensure that the appropriate minimum is paid, so VAT needs to be managed to achieve the same objective.

9.2   Most companies of any significant size will be VAT registered or will have been registered at some time in their period of existence and, therefore, when the company is no longer required because the company is to be dissolved, as a minimum there will be administrative matters to be dealt with to allow the company to cease to be a VAT registered business. For many, VAT is regarded as a sales tax but it has moved on since 1973 when the then Chancellor described VAT as a 'simple tax'.

There are a number of additional circumstances that may apply, some only occasionally, but nevertheless do require and repay attention. Equally, just because a company is not currently registered does not mean that circumstances may not arise during dissolution that will require re-registration and payment of VAT to HMRC.

9.3   Within this chapter there will be an initial overview of VAT and then a detailed look at the different circumstances that may apply whether the business is fully taxable so far as VAT is concerned. In most cases, full recovery of VAT charged on costs can be made. Otherwise, the business is partially exempt whereby some restriction on the recovery of VAT charged on costs will be made, or the business is only engaged in the making of exempt supplies where, conventionally, no recovery of VAT charged on costs can be made.

The contrast between direct and indirect taxation is stark. When we are reviewing the accounts in order to prepare a tax computation, all we are interested in is the profit or loss on a particular transaction or whether a cost already incurred is tax deductible. In such circumstances, the company – at worst – will pay an extra 21% or 28% on any additional profit that results from an expense being disallowed. In the case of VAT, the tax cost may only be 17.5%, but it will be on the whole transaction – the profit made has no interest here unless the client is operating one of the special second-hand margin schemes. In general (for the purposes of this publication), we are considering capital assets where such schemes do not apply.

Example

Massingham Ltd, in the run up to dissolution, sold a commercial building that was less than three years old for £500,000, but forgot to charge VAT. Within the costs incurred to make the sale were legal fees of £10,000, which the local Inspector of Taxes insisted were not allowable.

So far as direct taxes are concerned, the tax bill of Massingham Ltd will increase, at most, by £2,800. Failure to deal with VAT properly results in a VAT charge of:

$$£500,000 \times \frac{7}{47}$$

amounting to £74,468.

Although Massingham Ltd's profit on the transaction will be reduced by tax relief on the additional VAT charge, they will still be out of pocket by 72% of the charge if a large company, or £53,617.

9.4   VAT charges if identified incorrectly can creep up and significantly reduce the available cash. All transactions undertaken in the run up to dissolution need to be monitored closely to ensure the correct result is obtained and the minimum of cash goes out in respect of VAT output tax.

THE BASICS OF VAT

9.5   There are three basic concepts that may apply to any particular company. The importance of each concept is that the application of the detailed rules to the particular circumstances of a transaction determines the ability or inability of the business to recover VAT charged to it by its suppliers, or may generate a liability on asset transactions that might otherwise be avoided. These concepts are:

- fully taxable transactions;
- fully exempt transactions; and
- partially exempt businesses.

Fully taxable transactions

9.6   The great majority of businesses are involved in taxable transactions where VAT is charged on most transactions, but this may include charging tax at either 17.5% for standard-rated transactions, 0%, for zero-rated transactions or 5% for lower rate transactions. Typically, accountants' and solicitors' fees are standard-rated, most food is zero rated and new houses are also zero-rated. In all cases the business should be able to recover any VAT charged to it by its suppliers provided the business has full evidence of the payment. This will include obtaining and retaining proper VAT invoices that show the goods supplied and that have a proper VAT registration number appropriate to the supplier. It is, unfortunately, all too common for false invoices to be supplied where the VAT number appears to be authentic but that is merely part of an elaborate fraud.

This is an important area to be reviewed because, particularly following the money laundering obligations, recovering VAT that a business is not entitled to recover will be a reporting offence. In the great majority of cases, businesses do not carry out VAT number verification but, if we are involved, this may be an area that we should review, particularly for the final return. If a business has claimed back VAT for genuine transactions but has not verified the VAT number, then it would seem that there is no reporting obligation, particularly if there has been an HMRC inspection. Paragraph **9.38** includes a discussion of money laundering and reporting obligations. However, fraud is not always perpetrated on the directors, occasionally it is the directors who perpetrate the fraud. In such circumstances, the discovery by an adviser would result in a need to report matters to the Serious Organised Crime Agency (SOCA).

Some years ago, one client was carefully extracting money from his own company with fictitious invoices that were correct in every detail, including VAT number and goods of a type used in the trade as well as being printed at an external supplier. Unfortunately, the address chosen (granny's) was in the street where one of the audit team lived, and the fraud was discovered. The fraud was quietly put right, but today we would need to consider not just the tax consequences but also any money laundering reporting obligations.

Fully exempt transactions

9.7   These are where no VAT is charged by the business making the sale; typical examples will include insurance premiums or funerals as well as the redevelopment of second-hand houses. In these cases none of the VAT on costs should be recovered, subject to the situation where a business, which is partially exempt, may be treated as able to recover all its VAT on costs attributable to fully exempt transactions.

In dissolving the family company there will often be transactions involving land. Such transactions can be either exempt or fully taxable at the taxpayer's option and here is one pitfall that may affect businesses that previously never had to consider the impact of VAT on a property transaction where the impact of the Capital Goods Scheme (para **9.23**) may result in unexpected VAT charges. Failure to identify the risks and opportunities can give rise to additional VAT charges that may reduce the available cash for shareholders. As with tax transactions, once the event triggering the tax charge has passed, it is not possible to go back to revise the VAT effect of the transaction to a more favourable regime. The Capital Goods Scheme is considered in detail at para **9.23**.

Partially exempt businesses

9.8   These are businesses that only charge VAT on some parts of their sales. A typical example would be a building company who will charge VAT on repair work at 17.5% and on new houses (albeit at 0%), but who will also renovate second-hand houses where the sale of these are exempt sales.

Some transactions will be a mixture of taxable and exempt transactions; one example is the purchase or sale of a Public House. The cost attributable to living accommodation, typically 10% of the sale price, will be exempt, whereas the commercial parts will be standard-rated provided the vendor has elected to charge VAT on the sale.

Businesses that are partially exempt can recover all VAT on costs attributable to taxable transactions and may also be able to recover VAT attributable to exempt transactions provided the VAT attributable to exempt sales is both less than £7,500 and less than 50% of all VAT incurred by the business within a particular VAT year (having carried out the partial exemption calculation with regard to 'non-attributable' VAT costs where the proportion relating to exempt transactions is included in the VAT attributable to the £7,500 exempt limit). Therefore, when dealing with such a business that is in the process of disincorporation, it will be important to ensure that the partial exemption recovery rules are satisfied.

A business makes its VAT year up to either 31 March, 30 April or 31 May depending upon when the normal VAT quarterly or monthly return within that period is due. The concept of VAT year is important because, particularly, it needs to be used for any annual adjustments that are relevant in respect of either the Capital Goods Scheme or the Partial Exemption *de minimis* limits.

Example

County School Ltd makes its VAT returns to coincide with its accounting reference date of 31 December. Therefore, its VAT year will be 31 March.

This is an important area to monitor because, in the run up to disincorporation, a business that was always regarded as fully taxable may incur VAT attributable to activity that is exempt or is outside the scope of VAT, so a possible inability to recover VAT will increase the cost of disincorporation.

Outside the scope of VAT

9.9 These will be transactions that result in no VAT being charged to the customer but where, provided the statutory rules are satisfied, any VAT incurred to make those sales can be recovered. The commonest examples, outside the scope, are sales outside the European Union or the transfer of a business as a going concern.

Example

If an auctioneer sells goods that are located outside the European Union (EU) then the auctioneer's services will be outside the scope of UK VAT and any other EU VAT authority. Therefore, no VAT will be charged but input VAT on related costs will be recoverable in full.

TRANSFER OF A BUSINESS AS A GOING CONCERN (TOGC)

9.10 This category is the one most likely to be encountered on disincorporation because the business, or parts of the business, may be sold to someone who wishes to continue the trade and the sale of business assets may be regarded as the transfer of a business as a going concern (TOGC). Provided the detailed rules, which are set out in HMRC (Customs & Excise) Notice 700/9, are complied with, such transactions are outside the scope of VAT and no tax is charged by the vendor on such a transaction.

There are advantages to a purchaser of a business having the acquisition treated as a TOGC. However, there are a number of requirements to be complied with to achieve this:

- a business must be carried on both before and after the sale;
- both purchaser and vendor must be VAT registered; and
- where part of a business is sold, that part must be capable of independent operation.

In most cases it will be clear that a business was carried on before the sale, but sometimes the 'part of a business' test may cause difficulty: in one case where the facts were unusual, it was held that the sale of a single machine used to embroider sweaters was a TOGC. If there is doubt then HMRC will give clearance if all the facts are disclosed.

9.11 The main advantage of a TOGC for a purchaser is that they do not have to pay VAT on the assets purchased and finance it until a refund is claimed via the next VAT return. Normally, VAT is not charged on a TOGC – the only exception to this is in respect of new commercial buildings (under three years old). Here VAT must be charged by the vendor unless the purchaser also opts to tax and the property is being used in the same capacity by both the vendor and purchaser. The purchaser must also confirm to the vendor that their option to tax is not disapplied by the statutory block, VATA 1994, Sch 10, para 2(3AA). Therefore, if company A sells a property, which it previously owned as an investment, to company B who will also own the property as an investor then the transaction can be a TOGC. If company B proposes to use the property in its trade then this cannot be a TOGC; both vendor and purchaser must own and operate the premises in the same capacity, ie both must either be trader or both must be landlord.

If a purchaser is charged VAT and the matter is subsequently treated as a TOGC then a refund of the tax cannot be obtained from HMRC because a TOGC is regarded as being outside the scope of VAT; if VAT appears to be charged then, although it will be 17.5% of the price, it is not VAT. If there is dispute between the parties then the disputed VAT needs to be held by both the solicitors dealing with the transaction whilst the matter is resolved.

Examples of TOGC

Burnt House Ltd owns an opted building, which they own as landlord. A sale to West Fen Drove Ltd to own as landlord could be treated as a TOGC.

A sale to West Fen Drove Ltd to allow them to run a business from there would not be a TOGC even if West Fen Drove Ltd were VAT registered because the nature of ownership before and after the sale is different, ie one is a landlord and one a business owner.

Whitlingham Ltd owns a newspaper round that covers the villages of Brundall, Blofield and Great Plumstead. The part of the round covering Great Plumstead is sold to Brundall Ltd; this is treated as a TOGC because it is capable of independent operation.

Normally, a TOGC will apply provided the economic activity is carried on in the same manner by the vendor and the purchaser.

9.12   Any company about to be disincorporated should be a vendor of assets so they will need to make certain that any purchaser of assets intended to be treated as a TOGC is VAT registered for the TOGC arrangements to apply. The purchaser must either be registered for VAT already or be required to be registered as a result of the transfer – if the part of the business being transferred has generated a taxable turnover in excess of the registration limits in the past 12 months, then the purchaser is required to be registered. In this case, the transaction would be the transfer of a going concern whether or not the purchaser realises their responsibilities and registers for VAT. In all instances of a TOGC, apart from a transaction regarding property, no VAT is to be charged. Even when the transaction involves property in a situation whereby VAT is not charged, further rules need to be observed if this desirable position is to be achieved. Where the TOGC includes property then VAT may have to be charged on the sale of property if the vendor has previously elected to charge VAT, or even if the vendor elects just before the sale. If this is the case then, unless the purchaser opts to tax the property, a vendor will have to charge VAT but only on the property, not on any other assets. This matter is dealt with in detail at para **9.23** onwards.

APPROACHING CESSATION OF TRADE

9.13   In a simple case, the trade will cease and the assets, stock, goodwill and plant will be sold off piecemeal and, at the appropriate date, VAT deregistration will be effected.

Compulsory deregistration is required in a number of circumstances, but for our purposes the relevant situations are:

• taxable supplies are no long made;

• the business is sold;

• the legal status changes, perhaps because the trade previously carried on through a limited company is now to be carried on by a sole trader (in some circumstances the previous VAT registration number can be retained by completing form VAT 68);

• the business never actually commenced and therefore taxable supplies are no longer to be made.

9.14   Voluntary deregistration can also apply although perhaps, in the circumstances envisaged by this publication, a voluntary deregistration will be unlikely. Circumstances in which voluntary deregistration apply are as follows.

• HMRC are satisfied that the taxable turnover from the date of application will be less than the deregistration limit (from April 2008 £65,000).

• Part of the business is closed down and again HMRC are satisfied that the taxable turnover for the residue of the business will be below the deregistration threshold (from April 2008 £65,000).

• The tax exclusive turnover in the past 12 months has been below the current registration threshold.

• The turnover of the business currently exceeds the registration limit but consists mainly of zero-rated supplies in circumstances where the input tax claimed normally exceeds the output tax due on standard-rated sales. In effect, HMRC will deregister a business that normally receives repayments of VAT.

9.15   In terms of dissolving the family company, voluntary deregistration is only likely to be appropriate where, perhaps, the activity undertaken by the business is being reduced, either because most of the trade has been sold or the client is simply downsizing in anticipation of retirement. In such circumstances, the costs of maintaining a limited company may outweigh any perceived taxation advantages and there is, therefore, a wish to trade, in the future, as a partnership or sole trader.

ACHIEVING DEREGISTRATION

9.16   The first stage is to send to HMRC Form VAT 7 (available from HMRC website), which is the application to cancel registration. It requires the company to show the usual registration details and to explain to HMRC the reasons why deregistration is required. There are ten options that reflect the summary circumstances set out in para **9.13** above.

The VAT registered trader is also required to confirm to HMRC the value of stocks and other assets on hand for which output VAT may be due, whether the cash accounting scheme has been used and whether there is any property subject to an option to tax. Each of these circumstances may result in the registered trader having to pay VAT to HMRC and, as part of their risk management processes, HMRC will want to establish traders where the relevant rules apply. The VAT consequences of the questions are set out in paras **9.18**, **9.19** and **9.20**.

9.17   Once Form VAT 7 has been completed, and it must be completed within 30 days of the deregistration event occurring, it should be submitted to HMRC. Once the form has been processed, HMRC will issue the trader with a final VAT return to the agreed deregistration date. This return is subject to the same 30-day filing deadline as other VAT returns.

ASSETS ON HAND AT DEREGISTRATION

9.18   Where a VAT registered trader ceases to be VAT registered, there is a presumptive requirement to pay over to HMRC VAT on the value of any assets held at the date of deregistration. This is entirely logical because the trader will have reclaimed VAT paid on purchases and the expectation of HMRC would have been that they in turn would receive output VAT on any subsequent sale. However, where the amount of tax payable on assets on hand at deregistration would only be a nominal amount, a *de minimis* limit means that VAT does not always have to be paid over.

If the amount of VAT due on the market value of all assets held at the date of deregistration is below the *de minimis* limit of £1,000 then no VAT has to be paid to HMRC on those assets. In effect, if the market value is below £5,714, no VAT is due.

However, within the *de minimis* limit there are two important tests that have to be satisfied before the limit itself can be reviewed. The first is 'all assets'. This would include plant and machinery, trading stock and any assets to which the cash basis applies (see paras **9.19** and **9.20**), but not goodwill as this is a service for VAT purposes not goods. There are, however, some important exceptions in respect of some assets that can be ignored when determining whether the *de minimis* limit applies.

Secondly, 'market value', which applies to all assets except land and buildings covered by the Capital Goods Scheme (see para **9.23**) where any output VAT is calculated by reference to original cost.

9.19   There are also a number of exceptions and exclusions that allow a trader to treat, at the deregistration date, some business assets as excluded from inclusion in any calculation of whether the VAT payable on assets on hand at deregistration exceeds £1,000 and these are as follows:

- goods purchased from unregistered businesses;

- motorcars where a claim for input VAT has not been made;

- goods bought under the VAT second-hand margin scheme;

- goods used in an exempt activity unless input VAT was recovered (wholly or partly) under the partial exemption rules;

- land or buildings that were obtained VAT-free even though the company may subsequently have exercised the option to tax the property, or the property was used for a standard-rated purpose such as furnished holiday lets.

Example

Attleborough Ltd at deregistration has the following assets on hand:

Stock	£3,250
Plant and machinery	£5,000
Motor vehicles	£7,250
Freehold premises (VAT free)	£65,000

It is only the stock and the plant and machinery on which output VAT would have to be paid. Since VAT at 17.5% on the aggregate value of £8,250 exceeds £1,000, VAT has to be paid to HMRC.

Many businesses will not have maintained the records to allow them to calculate with any accuracy the extent of any assets that fall within any of the exemption classes detailed above. However, where the value of assets is close to the £5,714 value limit then time should be spent to see if there can be identified sufficient exempt assets to bring the value below the limit where payment would not be required. Some of the assets could also be sold prior to deregistration to leave the residue with a value of under £5,714 so that the *de minimis* limit can be taken advantage of.

Any business that operates on the cash basis so that output VAT is only paid on debtors when funds are received from customers will have to include, within the calculation of goods on hand at deregistration, the recoverable value of debtors and pay the output tax over. The advantage of cash basis whilst the trade continued was that automatic VAT bad debt relief applied. As in the case of other assets, it is the value expected to be received that is important, not the book value as the sales ledger printout. A full bad debt evaluation must be carried out prior to completing the final return. If debts turn bad later, there are no provisions to allow recovery of excessive tax declared on the final return.

INPUT VAT AFTER DEREGISTRATION

9.20   Most VAT registered businesses will, after deregistration, continue to incur small amounts of VAT typically in respect of accountancy, legal and other professional costs in dissolving the family company. Once the business has been deregistered for VAT, there are no ongoing quarterly returns to allow input tax recovery. Instead, a claim must be made on Form VAT 427 to the company's local VAT office. When submitting a claim under the VAT 427 procedure, the originals of all invoices have to be submitted in support of the claim.

In respect of this procedure, it is important to recognise that once deregistration has been effected it is not possible to recover input VAT paid on goods supplied to the business. Accordingly, in order to recover input VAT on goods supplied to the business, the last competent input tax claim must be made, at the latest, on the final VAT return. Therefore, where a business has operated its VAT accounting on the cash basis, a claim for input VAT in respect of unpaid creditors – where they relate to goods supplied to the company – must be made through the final VAT return. This is an anti-avoidance rule because once deregistration is complete, the dissolving company will be unable to charge VAT on any sales so it would be illogical if VAT could be recovered through VAT 427 because HMRC cannot receive output VAT but the business would otherwise have claimed it back.

PARTIALLY EXEMPT AT DEREGISTRATION

9.21   Where a business is partially exempt or uses a VAT scheme at deregistration, the company must continue to follow the rules for those schemes. Detailed consideration of these is outside the scope of this publication, but companies affected should refer to HMRC's (Customs & Excise) Notice 706 on partial exemption and Notice 727 on retail schemes. It should not be forgotten that the term 'company' can and does include unincorporated associations such as members' clubs. As such, they are subject to the same statutory requirements as incorporated companies. Accordingly, if the purpose for which the unincorporated association was formed has come to an end, the members, naturally, will want to realise the value of the funds, the direct tax consequences of which are dealt with in Chapter 10, but, so far as VAT is concerned, they must deal with matters in the manner set out here.

If a partially exempt company has deregistered before a sale of property that is to be an exempt supply, then there is no facility to recover input tax on the legal and agent's costs because the *de minimis* limits for partial exemption do not apply after the date of deregistration. Therefore, the VAT here cannot be recovered under the VAT 427 procedure indicated above. Accordingly, if an exempt sale is to be made, and it is desired to recover the VAT on costs under the partial exemption rules (see para **9.8**), the sale needs to be made before deregistration. It is not permissible to simply retain the registration and claim input VAT through a return in order to circumvent the VAT 427 procedure if the circumstances in para **9.13** are satisfied. To do so would result in input tax recovery that was not permitted and may result in money laundering implications (see para **9.40**).

RETAINING THE REGISTRATION

9.22   In some cases, if the trade is to be transferred to a new business under common ownership, it is possible, sometimes desirable, for the VAT number of the old business to be transferred to the new trader. This may be desirable if the owners wish to demonstrate continuity and maintain goodwill; retaining the registration number is one way of demonstrating business as usual. However, this does mean that the successor business takes on full responsibility for any tax arrears of the old business. Form VAT 68 sets out the undertakings and consequences and is available from the HMRC website. If there are disputes likely to result in any objection to striking off under the s 652, s 652A procedure then this option may be appropriate. If there are sins of omission or commission that the business proprietors want to leave behind then retaining the registration transfers the liabilities. Equally, a new registration in this circumstance may result in the professional adviser having to make a report to SOCA if they know or discover the arrears that are apparently unknown to HMRC (see para **9.40**).

CAPITAL GOODS SCHEME

9.23   The Capital Goods Scheme applies to any commercial property sold within ten years of construction or acquisition, but only where the cost was more than £250,000. It makes no difference the use that the property has been put to, provided the vendor was VAT registered either when the property was purchased or when more than £250,000 was spent on an extension or refurbishment. This can cause difficulty if the company being dissolved has had no experience of dealing with property and VAT complications, because up until now they have been a fully taxable business. If they purchased a new building and VAT was charged then that tax was recovered through the quarterly returns. Because the business sold only either standard-rated or zero-rated sales, any annual Capital Goods Scheme adjustment had no cost impact. Similarly, if an extension was constructed, it was always for trade purposes and the VAT incurred remained fully recoverable because the taxable business activity was continuing. Commercial property sold within three years of construction is a compulsory standard-rated taxable sale without the need for an option to tax.

Commercial property companies are likely to have opted to tax all or most of their properties because, if an actively trading property, they would otherwise be affected by the partial exemption limits. In respect of exempt property transactions, it does not take long to incur £7,500 in VAT attributable to exempt activity when only about £40,000 of services are reached. Accordingly, such companies will be aware of the need to opt to tax; others may not.

If the dissolving company is selling significant property assets and the company has not opted to tax then even if the option to tax only enables them to recover VAT on solicitors fees and agents fees, it may be worthwhile.

9.24   The scheme only applies to commercial property (it does not apply to residential property) where the property is either less than ten years old and has cost more than £250,000 or the main property is more than ten years old but an extension has been constructed within the last ten years before sale costing more than £250,000.

In either case, the vendor has to provide the purchaser with details of the VAT claimed on original construction, the percentage of the VAT recovered in the first year and how many years have elapsed since the expenditure was incurred.

9.25   The purpose of the scheme is to ensure that a VAT registered trader does not recover more VAT than they are entitled to under the input tax recovery rules. The scheme requires a business to adjust the input tax recovery to take account of any exempt use that the property has had.

Example

Holme Hale Ltd constructs a warehouse to be used for their trade at a cost of £400,000 plus VAT of £70,000. They are a fully taxable trade, ie they charge VAT on everything they sell, and can recover all the VAT on the construction costs. Therefore, the recovery rate in year one is 100%.

In year three, as a result in a downturn in trade, they let 20% of the building out and do not exercise the option to tax. They therefore have to pay back to HMRC a proportion of the VAT previously claimed, in this case £1,400 as follows:

$$£70,000 \, \frac{1}{10} \times \frac{20}{100} = £1,400$$

This adjustment continues on an annual basis for ten years from construction so if the percentage rented out increases, the annual adjustment will increase up to 10% of the input tax in any one year and therefore the maximum adjustment in a single year will be £7,000.

9.26   Most landlords will be aware of the scheme and will have opted to tax relevant properties. It is owners of buildings used in a trade who are unlikely to be aware of the scheme. The exempt sale of a building previously used for a taxable trade can cause a vendor to pay VAT back to HMRC, which had not been budgeted for.

Example

Holme Hale Ltd sells the warehouse after five years as business has now recovered and they need extra space but do not opt to tax the sale. As there are five years still to run on the Capital Goods Scheme adjustment periods, they are treated as being 100% exempt for the balance of five years and therefore have to pay back tax previously recovered of £35,000 as follows:

$$\frac{£7,000 \times 5}{10} \, 100\% = £35,000$$

Opting to tax the property would have meant that the final adjustment would be treated as 100% recoverable and so no VAT would be paid back to Customs, avoiding the above £35,000 pitfall.

SALE OF PROPERTY AT A LOSS AND ANTI-AVOIDANCE PROVISIONS

9.27   In circumstances where the trade is to continue under the same effective ownership, but the ownership structure is to change, then the dissolution may come within anti-avoidance provisions. HMRC are concerned that taxable businesses may sell property on which VAT had been claimed at a loss to an associated business, which is an exempt trader, with the result that, in effect, associated businesses can recover more VAT than is appropriate. If a business sells a property at a loss to an associated business then input tax recovery is restricted to the amount of tax charged on the sale.

Example

Instead of selling the warehouse to an unconnected business, Holme Hale Ltd sell the property as an exempt sale, after five years, to an associated Insurance Broker business (who are exempt traders) to use as storage for £200,000. They would have to pay back all the tax originally recovered of £70,000 even though they may have been a fully taxable business in the five years prior to the sale.

If Holme Hale Ltd opted to tax the sale then they would charge the Insurance Broker £250,000 plus VAT of £43,750. Therefore, they would retain £35,000 of the tax originally recovered but have to pay over to HMRC the balance of £26,250, as well as the £43,750 charged to the Insurance Broker.

CLEARANCE PROCEDURE

9.28   If the sale is at a genuine price because the market has moved then application can be made to HMRC for confirmation that the anti-avoidance rules do not apply, which in the above example would result in Holme Hale

Ltd not having to pay over the £26,250, but if the option to tax were not exercised then the normal adjustment discussed in para **9.26** would apply.

STEPS WE SHOULD TAKE

9.29   Assuming that our permanent files do not carry enough information to resolve matters, we need to ask any vendor client sufficient questions to ensure that the sale is correctly treated for VAT purposes. It will not be enough to ask if they have opted to tax.

INFORMATION THAT HAS TO BE PROVIDED TO THE PURCHASER

9.30

- The date of acquisition and how much more of the ten-year period is left.

- The input tax claimed on construction.

- The percentage of input tax recovered in year one.

It is important we obtain enough information to ensure that we can advise the client correctly. Many clients will not be aware of the position but will blame us when it goes wrong. Once the sale has been made, it is too late.

AUTOMATIC STANDARD-RATED SALES

9.31   Land and buildings sold within three years of construction are automatically standard-rated sales, even where the vendor has not elected to charge VAT.

Some other property transactions are also automatically standard-rated, even where the property is more than three years old. Examples include: sporting rights, holiday accommodation (such as time-share or a chalet on a chalet park, caravans and houseboats), holiday accommodation in tents, letting of caravan pitches, and letting of sports stadiums.

Charging VAT on any of the above depends upon the vendor being VAT registered. Therefore, the chalet park owner may charge VAT on the sale to a private individual, but the same private individual would not charge VAT when he comes to sell the chalet, unless he was VAT registered and operated a business of letting out holiday accommodation.

BUSINESS NO LONGER VAT REGISTERED

9.32   Once an owner has elected to waive the option to tax on property then the consequences of that option to tax continue even if the owner is subsequently deregistered. This circumstance is often overlooked where a business in anticipation of dissolution has continued to trade, but deregistered because the turnover has fallen below the registration threshold (from 1 April

2008 £67,000). If a company owned property where the option to tax has previously been made, there would be a need to account for output VAT on the sale of the opted property at deregistration where:

- input VAT was claimed when the property was purchased;

- the property was opted property when acquired as a TOGC, or as part of the assets acquired on a TOGC;

- the property is new commercial property less than three years old that is always a compulsory standard-rated supply.

It therefore follows that if a company elected to waive exemption on a property in order to recover VAT on refurbishment costs where the property was previously acquired as an exempt purchase then on deregistration, no VAT would have been payable.

Example

North Wootton Ltd acquired Carr Stone Industrial Estate in April 2002 for use in its own trade. In July 2005 they opted to tax because some of the properties were to be let, and input VAT of £37,000 was incurred on refurbishment.

In July 2007 the company deregistered as total income was below £58,000 and no VAT was payable.

WHAT HAPPENS AFTER DEREGISTRATION

9.33 In the above example, Carr Stone Industrial Estate remains opted property so long as it is owned by North Wootton Ltd, so on any subsequent sale there remains an obligation to reregister if the proceeds of sale exceed £67,000. It will be the exception rather than the rule for any property transaction to be for less than £67,000.

Example

North Wootton Ltd is about to be dissolved and on 31 October 2008 agrees to sell the remaining units at Carr Stone Industrial Estate for £400,000 – the draft contract makes no mention of VAT.

The proceeds exceed the current registration limit so the company would have to register for VAT and consider charging VAT on the sale price as the business is now reregistered.

Following re-registration, the only circumstance in which VAT need not be charged is if the sale can be classified a TOGC (see para **9.10**), but even in this circumstance there remains the requirement to register and deregister all on the same day simply to allow the transfer to achieve TOGC status.

9.34 The consequence of failing to recognise this circumstance is that the vendor company is likely to face a charge to VAT from HMRC, which it will then be unable to recover from the purchaser because one of the following may apply:

- the contract for sale does not cover the charging of VAT;

- the purchaser will claim that the price is VAT inclusive;

- the vendor forces possible penalties and surcharges because, in the above example, £70,000 of VAT will have been paid late.

Property sales can be a minefield and the opportunity to achieve substantial unexpected liabilities exists. When dealing with the dissolution of a company, we need to review all the property owned by the company to ensure that on a subsequent sale the correct tax treatment is applied.

LATE RETURNS

9.35 One possible consequence of commencing the procedure to disincorporate is that attention to routine administration may be overlooked and, in particular, VAT returns submitted late. This is a significant possibility if the business has closed down, the administration staff are no longer employed and the proprietor is relying upon himself to organise matters properly. All VAT returns must be submitted within one month of the VAT period ending; if they are not, there is a default.

The submission of one late return does not result in any penalty payment, it merely results in the issue of a notice from HMRC, which states that if a second return is filed late within 12 months of the first return then a default surcharge will apply.

9.36 When a second or subsequent return is late, a default surcharge of the higher of £30 or a specified percentage of the VAT due will apply. The specified percentages of the VAT due are as follows:

- first late return 2%;

- second late return 5%;

- third late return 10%;

- any subsequent return 15%.

9.37 In much the same way as HMRC are not interested in small amounts of tax, so there are some concessions that, for small businesses, will reduce the practical impact of the surcharges to negligible amounts.

- For the second and third defaults, ie the 2% and 5% occasions, no surcharge is payable if the surcharge will be less than £400.

- The surcharges do not automatically apply to any business with a turnover of less than £150,000.

Once the warning letter has been received, the submission of the next four returns on time causes the warning notice to lapse so that a subsequent late return, once four returns have been submitted on time, merely triggers the issue of a further initial warning, not a demand for surcharge. The four-return rule applies equally to traders who are on either monthly or quarterly returns.

Example

Felixstowe Beach Ltd submits the return to 30 November 2008 on 10 January 2009, so they receive a warning letter.

The return to 28 February 2009 was submitted on 10 April 2009 with net VAT payable of £6,000 so that the surcharge would be £120 but, as it is less than £400, it is not payable.

The return to 31 May 2009 is submitted on 28 July 2009 but shows tax due of £9,000. The surcharge at 5% amounting to £450 is payable as it exceeds the *de minimis* limit.

AVOIDING THE SURCHARGE

9.38   Apart from the obvious requirement to get the VAT return in on time, there are two further methods whereby the imposition of surcharges may be avoided simply by a claim by the trader to have a default notice withdrawn, but remember, HMRC can and will challenge the assertions made.

- *The return was lost or delayed in the post* – On the first occasion, this is likely to result merely in a warning letter, but any subsequent claim that delay was caused by the post again is likely to provoke the suggestion that it is not the post but some other underlying cause that has resulted in the return being late.

- *Reasonable excuse* – again HMRC take a hard line, for example, the illness of the accounts clerk responsible for preparing the return is likely to carry more weight in a small organisation than a large organisation where it might reasonably be expected that work-sharing procedures would cover such an eventuality. Again, this excuse cannot be used for a series of late returns because the expectation is that an organised businessman would take steps to obtain cover for a sick employee once they have been absent for a short period.

ACTION OF LAST RESORT

9.39   If all else fails, the submission of an estimated return based upon available evidence, perhaps using the figures from the corresponding return for the previous year, adjusted in line with current activity, may avoid a warning or late payment surcharge. In order to submit an estimated return, permission must be obtained from HMRC and, of course, the estimated VAT due must be paid on time. The extent that there is an adjustment required, as compared with the estimated return, should be adjusted on the subsequent return.

MONEY LAUNDERING OBLIGATIONS

9.40   There has been much information issued concerning the scope of the Proceeds of Crime Act 2002 and the Money Laundering Regulation 2003 whereby any suspicion relating to the process of any criminal offence must be reported to the Serious Organised Crime Agency (SOCA), even where the amounts might be regarded as trivial. This new regime impacts upon every area of practice and dissolving the family company is no exception.

VAT is one area where we are likely to have an obligation to make a report to SOCA simply because many clients will have claimed back more VAT than they are entitled to claim. The writer has seen many sets of company accounts where there are provisions representing VAT that was over-claimed in past accounting periods but where the company has failed to repay the amounts back to HMRC. As a client approaches the dissolution of his business, there will be a temptation to simply write the money off, perhaps because HMRC rarely revisit a trader who has deregistered in an attempt to increase the funds to be distributed. Such an action is likely to be regarded as 'theft by finding' because, in effect, the client has previously gained either by achieving a larger than justified refund or has paid less than was their true liability.

Most professional organisations have provided guidance to their members to indicate the extent of our obligations. Certainly, the initial reaction must be that if there is activity that is doubtful then a report must be made to SOCA (even if the client refuses to allow the matter to be reported to HMRC to allow matters to be put right). However, even notifying HMRC may result in delay in making shareholder distributions and may impact upon the after tax proceeds received by shareholders whilst HMRC investigate the reported omission (as well as investigating any other possible omissions). This would seem to be another area, assuming the client is prepared to be cooperative, for putting matters right in advance of cessation of trade so that the dissolution is dealt with efficiently and with minimum time delay.

9.41   Clearly, we may only avoid a report to SOCA if the client company is prepared to make an immediate voluntary disclosure to HMRC, but care needs to be taken as to how the matter is discussed to avoid any possible claim that the discussions amount to tipping-off. In the scenario envisaged, underpaid VAT has generally accrued over a number of years and, despite our urging the client to do the right thing, nothing has been done. Therefore, it would seem that, inevitably, we must make a return to SOCA and await developments even though the omissions may have arisen before 1 March 2004. It is not the historical acts of omission that trigger the reporting obligation but the client's decision to dissolve the company with the intention of retaining monies that have been obtained improperly.

Other areas where a reporting obligation may arise will include customers who have overpaid and where no attempt has been made to refund the balances. This also amounts to theft by finding, so sales ledgers need to be reviewed as part of the pre-dissolution administration.

9.42 However, not every provision or apparent unpaid liability will be a reporting event, some will arise simply because of unidentified bookkeeping errors where the matter was not investigated properly at the time and the accounts clerk or bookkeeper was too lazy to come to a proper conclusion. If upon investigation we can be satisfied those such matters are simply errors then no SOCA report is required, but we should make detailed file notes as to the work undertaken and the reasons for our conclusions. Writing back such provisions will result in a corporation tax charge, but again, any refusal to allow that to occur is also a reporting event! However, in the great majority of cases the client is unlikely to intervene to overrule our computations so the matter is appropriately resolved.

9.43 There is much in dealing with VAT, regarding points of administrative detail and matters of principle, that needs to be addressed. Provided the issues are identified early enough in the dissolution process then dealing with matters properly, so far as our vendor client is concerned, should achieve appropriate results. Particularly where property is concerned if VAT is to be charged then this needs to be advised to a purchaser as soon as possible to ensure that the purchaser's funding arrangements allow for the payment. In this circumstance, the VAT may only be 'an-in-and-an-out' exercise, but finance needs to be in place to cover the cost whilst the next VAT return is completed, and there will also be an impact upon the Stamp Duty/Stamp Duty Land Tax payable (see Chapter 8). If such matters are disclosed part way through the transaction, the risk is that a purchaser withdraws or, at best, delays matters whilst funding arrangements are adjusted. If this delay takes place once trading has ceased then the main impact may be that the proportion of any gain on dissolution proceeds, subject to capital gains tax non-business taper relief, may increase. Therefore, an apparent failure to deal adequately with one tax impacts elsewhere in the dissolution process. Our aim of dealing with matters promptly is affected.

PLANNING POINTS

9.44

- Identify all transactions involving land and make sure the correct treatment is applied.

- If no election to waive exemption on property owned has been made then consider making the election.

- Set up a system that ensures all VAT returns, post-cessation of trade, are submitted on time.

- Review critically the value of all assets held at deregistration if the tax will exceed £1,000.

- Make sure deregistration is effected at the appropriate date but include in the final return all input VAT in respect of goods on hand.

- If the company is currently not registered, establish if it ever was registered and whether this impacts upon opted property.

- Make sure the purchaser and vendor satisfy the TOGC rules.

- If the business is a partially exempt trader, identify any leeway in the £7,500 or 50% of all input tax parameters.

- Do not take on the old VAT number of the disincorporating business unless you can be certain there are no sins of omission likely to appear.

- Make all appropriate returns to SOCA, but avoid discussing the issues in such a way as amounts to tipping off.

Chapter 10

Unincorporated associations

10.1 Throughout this publication we generally consider the position in relation to companies formed under the Companies Acts, whether they are limited liability, limited by guarantee or unlimited, but there are certain unincorporated associations that also fall within the charge to corporation tax. Such organisations may, generally, be involved in some form of mutual trading so that no corporation tax liabilities may arise on a year-by-year basis, apart from perhaps minimal liability on investment income.

Indeed, such organisations are generally not required to make a return to HMRC on the basis that all profit arises from mutual trading and, even if there is investment income, such income has generally suffered tax at source.

Accordingly the absence of a relationship with HMRC may result in unfortunate consequences whenever the decision to bring the association to an end. However, here just as in other circumstances, the full extent of any tax consequences needs to be assessed.

One practical point that may arise following the introduction and subsequent abolition of the £10,000 nil rate corporation tax band is that whilst the nil rate band was in place, most unincorporated associations may have been excluded from making HMRC returns on the basis that any taxable income either from investment income or minimal non-mutual trading was below the £10,000 threshold. Following the withdrawal of the corporation tax nil rate band, there may be some unincorporated associations that will need to bring up to date their compliance obligations, and pay any arrears of tax and penalties, before any application to distribute funds to the members is made. Certainly any unexpected tax liabilities either in respect of tax or compliance penalties must be factored into any calculation of payment to members.

10.2 At a practical level, it is entirely possible that HMRC has no knowledge of many unincorporated associations because the secretary and treasurer are not aware that they fall within the charge to corporation tax and have no income that is normally taxable. In so far as tax advisers deal with such organisations, they are generally dealt with as semi-honorary jobs, perhaps with no involvement other than drafting the accounts when the books come in two days before the AGM! They are prepared by the cheapest member of staff and simply sent to the treasurer. You might even photocopy all the accounts for a modest fee, but we need to deal with matters properly and if such an unincorporated association is to cease, make sure that if we are acting in any capacity that matters are dealt with appropriately. In practice, the first we may know of any dissolution will be when the secretary writes to tell you that your services are no longer required and they have paid the monies out to members.

Strictly, such distributions to members are income distributions, but there is a concession available – ESC C15 (see Appendix 1) – which allows modest payments to be treated as capital with the consequence that, for most members of an unincorporated association, no tax would be payable because the distribution will be less than the CGT annual exemption (for 2008/09, £9,600). The concession operates in exactly the same way as ESC C16 to convert what would otherwise have been an income distribution to a capital distribution.

Conventionally, we are used to applying in advance for clearances. Application after the event is not fatal, but it is in the nature of unincorporated associations that tax is not generally the first item on the agenda. The treasurer may simply distribute, because the association has come to an end, and only contact you to thank you for your hard work in the past once the association has ceased. The concession does envisage circumstances where the claim to apply the concession is retrospective so we have the opportunity to put matters right. The concession (see Appendix 1) includes the following phrase, *'having the whole of the amounts distributed treated as capital receipts'*. If an advance clearance were required then it might state 'to be distributed' or a similar form of words but, just as with ESC C16, some limited retrospection can be appropriate.

10.3   Unincorporated associations will generally be small scale and local but some can and do build up substantial funds, which may be returned to members once the purpose for which the organisation was established has ceased. In many cases, the funds will simply be transferred on to a successor organisation but there is a procedure – ESC C15 – which achieves the same practical effect as ESC C16 to allow the funds of the association to be distributed to its members in a capital form. If the concession did not apply then any monies paid out would fall to be assessed as distributions under the terms of ICTA 1988, s 209.

In practical terms, this may not make much difference because the general body of taxpayers are basic rate taxpayers and as such the 10% notional tax credit that applies to dividends will cover most members' liabilities.

EXTRA STATUTORY CONCESSION C15 REQUIREMENTS

10.4   The association has the option of disapplying ICTA 1988, s 209 from any distribution to its members provided the following appropriate matters are satisfied:

- substantially, the whole of an association's activities are of a social or recreational nature;

- it has not carried on an investment business or trade, other than a mutual trade; and

- the amount distributed to each member is not large (that is, not more than £2,000 per member).

10.5   HMRC Company Taxation Manual 15540 indicates that the Revenue would agree to the application of the concession provided the amounts to be distributed to the members are not materially in excess of £2,000 per member.

APPLICATION PROCEDURE

10.6   The organisation would need to submit the pro forma applications (see Appendices 3 and 4) suitably modified. The shareholder undertaking (in Appendix 4) may be impractical in the case of a large association and it is possible that, if the amounts involved are very small where in the great majority of cases the amounts distributed will be covered by the CGT annual exemption, that the inspector will be prepared to accept simply an undertaking by the secretary and chairman of the organisation along the lines of Appendix 3. However, recent practice in relation to ESC C16 has suggested that in a case where there were many shareholders with less than 1% of the issued share capital, HMRC still required the undertakings to be signed by all eligible members, so perhaps this is something to be negotiated with the local tax office.

10.7   The association would also need to submit to HMRC a pro forma capital statement, if only to be able to indicate to the inspector that the amounts to be distributed are not materially in excess of £2,000 per member. There is no guidance within the Taxes Acts, or the Revenue Manuals as to what materially in excess might amount to. Such applications are very rare but, within the writer's experience (admittedly limited to only two cases), distributions of up to £3,000 per member might well come within the concession. The spirit of the concession can be used to assist a favourable agreement.

Example

The Limpenhoe Allotments Association operated for many years as a buying cooperative for seeds, fertilizers and other garden sundries, which were sold to members who have allotments at Limpenhoe. On 30 June 2008 there were 50 members with accumulated funds of £40,000 and, at that date, the association's purpose ceased as the allotments were acquired for housing.

The members resolve to distribute the funds and as the amount per member is £800 then ESC C15 should apply.

DO AMOUNTS HAVE TO BE EQUAL?

10.8   What is the position if the amounts distributed are not equal, with the result that some members receive more than the HMRC suggested maximum of £2,000 or thereabouts? The writer's copy of the Oxford English dictionary defines 'materially' as either substantially or considerably and takes the view that, perhaps, this might allow a leeway of up to 50% or 60% above the indicated level. However, in some cases HMRC regard 'materially' as being something other than negligible, but otherwise, a range within 20% of a particular item might not be material. The writer's experience suggests that if a case can be made that the payments are within the spirit of the concession, then a clearance will be given. Certainly, discussing the case with the Inspector of Taxes who is handling the request can often produce an acceptable response.

Example

Assuming the facts as the example above, suppose that the members of Limpenhoe Allotments Association agree that the surplus is to be distributed to members on the basis of the number of years of membership subject to a maximum payment of £3,000.

10.9   This would seem to fall within the spirit of the concession, even if it does not fall within HMRC Manual limits (see para **10.5**). In such cases, which are rare, it is suggested that since the majority of recipients are unlikely to pay tax on the distribution, even if treated as an income distribution because they are basic rate taxpayers and the dividend tax credit covers any liability, then HMRC consent would be forthcoming on the basis, perhaps, that the average distribution is less than (or at least not materially greater than) £2,000 – certainly there is no tax avoidance motive and the payments are within the spirit of the concession.

Equally because it may make no practical difference whether the payment is assessed as either capital or income and inspectors are often anxious to keep as many taxpayers out of the self-assessment net as possible – so, again, this may be persuasive to ensure the concession is applied.

10.10   Unincorporated associations are rarely encountered in practice and, equally, are rarely broken up because the funds are usually transferred to another organisation with similar aims and objectives; in the example chosen, the allotment owners are going to want to continue to purchase supplies at a discount so the funds are likely to be passed over to the equivalent organisation in the next village. However, where such organisations are broken up, it is more usual for the funds to be divided on the basis of years of membership as the second example, simply because that is seen as a fairer basis of distribution. Longstanding members, who are usually on the committee, feel that they have contributed to the funds to a greater extent than newcomers and, therefore, a differential subject to a meaningful minimum is often a more acceptable formula, in much the same way as some Building Society demergers gave a minimum as well as some extra for larger investors.

Consider if any distribution is to be made purely on the basis of membership at the proposed dissolution date or whether individuals who were members at any time within, say, the last five years should receive a share. It is the nature of unincorporated associations that membership is a loose concept where individuals may only pay once every few years, perhaps because the annual subscription is low, and it is not worth a treasurer's effort to chase. If a member contributes on any form of basis, it is undoubtedly equitable that they should receive a share of the pot. To bring the shutters down on a fixed day, perhaps without members being given a chance to confirm their membership, would be seen as inequitable.

10.11 Finally, in many unincorporated associations there will be life members, usually those who have contributed most to the association in years gone by but who are now forgiven payment of an annual subscription. They must be included on any list of recipients. The writer knows from his own experience that lists of honorary members are not well maintained and successive treasurers have to be pointed to the minutes to confirm the member's status.

PLANNING POINTS

10.12

- Make sure that dissolution of an unincorporated association is approved by all members; consider sending a pro forma letter with stamped addressed envelope requesting written agreement.

- Obtain possession of the assets from existing officers; there is a tendency for the officers of unincorporated associations to confuse what assets are their own and what assets are their association's.

- Ensure that there is an agreed list of members – again, within unincorporated associations, the concept of membership can be a loose arrangement. Ask to see the membership ledgers for, say, the last five years. It is not unknown for the treasurer to fail to remind members to pay their subscriptions in the run up to dissolution to increase their own share of the pot.

- Review the minute books of the association to establish if any rules have been established for honorary members.

- If, historically, members have never been excluded for non-payment of subscriptions, ask the committee to establish a list of members known to be alive and indeed seek confirmation that all those named on the list are still alive, particularly if a reduction in numbers may take the distribution materially above £2,000.

- Make sure the tax affairs of the association and payment of any outstanding tax liabilities are up to date, and that compliance has not fallen through the £10,000 nil rate band compliance relaxation regime.

Chapter 11

Inheritance tax relief

11.1 Prior to any decision being made to dissolve the family trading company, business property relief (BPR) would have been available on the value of the shares owned by any particular shareholder. That is provided the underlying business satisfied IHTA 1984, s 105 but did not fall foul of IHTA 1984, s 105(3), so that the business did not consist of wholly or mainly dealing in shares, stocks or shares, land or buildings or making or holding investments.

If the business did not fail IHTA 1984, s 105(3) then BPR would be available on the value of the shares. There has been in recent years considerable clarification through a range of cases where BPR was claimed where the courts, and in particular the Special Commissioners, have been required to consider the circumstances of whether the relevant company was involved in wholly or mainly the holding of investments. A detailed consideration of the facts in the particular cases is beyond the scope of this publication but useful cases to be considered, if the matter is an issue, include *Farmer and another (executors of Farmer deceased* (1999) STC 392, *Weston (executor of Weston, deceased) v IRC* (2000) STC 1064 and *IRC v George and another (executors of Stedman, decd)* (2004) STC 147, *Clark (executors of Clark deceased) v HMRC* [2005] and the recent case of *Exors of D W C Piercy* SpC 687.

11.2 Non-trading companies might, as an appropriate shorthand description, broadly be termed investment companies. Here, the previous unavailability of BPR may have been of less importance but, even here, there may be factors that need to be considered before the company is formally dissolved and before economic activity ceases. One of the possible advantages of holding family assets through an investment company is that an owner of 25% of the company would not be taxed for IHT on the full value, but on a discounted value to reflect tax charges and the fact that ownership is only of part of the assets. Even quoted investment trusts such as Foreign & Colonial trade at a discount to gross asset value. However, once the business is distributed to the shareholders they simply hold cash that will not be discounted. Therefore, even for owners of investment companies the dissolution affects their IHT position, simply because any value discount is reclaimed. Even a company that is a cash shell and about to be dissolved would still attract a discount if there were an IHT event before any distribution because any purchaser would require a margin. The case of *Re Courthorpe* (1928) 7 ATC 538 is statutory support for this principle because it was held that anyone acquiring a company in anticipation of liquidation would expect a reasonable profit from their activities, so an anticipated discount from asset value might be between 25% and 30%.

Certainly, *IRC v George and another (executors of Stedman, decd)* [2004] STC 147 does indicate that in some circumstances (provided the circumstances of the case we are dealing with can, broadly, be linked to the particular facts of that case) BPR may now be available in some companies that may previously have been considered only to undertake investment activities.

So far as trading companies are concerned, BPR is excluded under IHTA 1984, s 105 once a liquidator has been appointed. Therefore, even where a company in liquidation remains trading, it is the appointment of a liquidator that is the trigger for the loss of BPR, not the termination of the trade. From the date of appointment of the liquidator, any relevant shareholding no longer qualifies for BPR. Where a company is dissolved under ESC C16, BPR may continue to be available for a slightly longer period because the relief should be available until trading actually ceases, which might be after the application for the concession to apply, but the date of cessation of trade will be a question of fact.

11.3 The appointment of a liquidator removes BPR from the value of the shares in a soon to be disincorporated company that may ultimately be subject to inheritance tax. Therefore, when considering inheritance tax relief in a soon-to-be dissolved company, one of the main concerns of shareholders will be to preserve the availability of BPR for as long as possible, so that the impact upon any IHT ultimately payable is reduced to a minimum and to ensure that either existing reliefs are not lost by precipitate action or to recognise that the BPR can be preserved by investing the proceeds of liquidation into a future replacement activity.

11.4 The majority of this chapter concentrates on the availability of BPR because, for most practitioners, that is the relief that will more often be encountered. Consideration of the availability of BPR, beyond a broad distinction between trading companies and investment companies, is beyond the scope of this publication but practitioners do need to carry out an evaluation exercise on every company that is proposed to be dissolved. Once the company appoints a liquidator, or ceases to trade whilst using the concession option, BPR will be lost, unless a decision is made to reinvest the proceeds in a new business venture where the replacement property rules may apply.

Where clients have made gifts some time before the dissolution process begins then there may be an advantage in delaying the date on which BPR is permanently lost if the delay of a few months can ensure a major gift drops out because the seven-year potentially exempt transfer (PET) period has elapsed. Commercially, this only makes sense if the dissolution process can be controlled, does not result in the loss of a potential purchaser; or does not result in trading losses, in a period where it is known trading will cease and as a consequence trading is not pursued as vigorously as it was previously, exceeding the IHT at stake. If this is an issue then, if the formal route is chosen, no liquidator should be appointed until the full ramifications of that appointment are established.

WHEN IS BPR LOST?

11.5   Significantly, different criteria have to be considered to determine the date from which BPR is lost depending upon whether the company is being dissolved by the formal liquidation route or by the more informal concession route.

Therefore, IHTA 1984, s 105 indicates the date that BPR will be lost in respect of the shares in the trading company. With equal importance is the availability of BPR on assets, which are personally owned outside the trading company, where the availability of BPR on associated assets depends upon ownership of shares in the company that is having the benefit or use of the asset qualifying for BPR.

11.6   When a company goes into formal liquidation, the date on which BPR would be lost will be clear – it is the date that the liquidator is appointed, or the resolution to appoint has been passed. It is usual for the same date to apply to both, even if the trade continues beyond that date. The Inheritance Tax Act 1984, s 105(5) confirms that:

> 'Shares in or securities of a company are not relevant business property in relation to a transfer of value if at the time of the transfer a winding-up order has been made in respect of the company or the company has passed a resolution for voluntary winding-up or is otherwise in process of liquidation, unless the business of the company is to continue to be carried on after a reconstruction or amalgamation and the reconstruction or amalgamation either is the purpose of the winding-up or liquidation or takes place not later than one year after the transfer of value.'

11.7   Within IHTA 1984, s 105(5), BPR can be preserved where the purpose of appointing a liquidator is to achieve a reconstruction or amalgamation where BPR would continue to be available both before and after the reconstruction provided the activities both before and after do not then amount to wholly or mainly the holding of investments. The relevant extract of IHTA 1984, s 105(6) is set out below:

> 'Land, a building, machinery or plant owned by the transferor and used wholly or mainly for the purposes of a business carried on as mentioned in subsection (1)(d) or (e) above is not relevant business property in relation to a transfer of value, unless the business or the transferor's interest in it is, or shares or securities of the company carrying on the business immediately before the transfer are, relevant business property in relation to the transfer.'

11.8   Certainly, if there is a requirement to preserve BPR at least until a seven-year gift period had elapsed, it will be the responsibility of the directors to be aware of what gifts have been made and to set the date for the passing of the special resolution to appoint a liquidator accordingly. The same must be true of professional advisers, upon whom the directors will often rely, to make sure that the date of appointment of the liquidator is IHT efficient if this is an issue.

11.9 If ESC C16 is used, is there a date –which sets out an absolute date – in the same way as formal liquidation that provides certainty as to the date from which BPR is lost? It would seem that there is not; the trigger date will depend upon what actions are taken in the run up to dissolution by the directors and their advisers. Certainly, it might be any of the following dates:

- when the trade has ceased;

- when the application to HMRC to use the concession is made;

- when the first distribution is made to shareholders;

- when the directors resolve to close the company down;

- when the application is made to the Registrar of Companies;

- when binding contractual arrangements are complete to sell the trade.

In practice, it could be any of these dates subject to the overriding rule that if there are no contractual arrangements in place, the trade needs to have ceased. As indicated in para **5.6**, application for ESC C16 to apply is often made in advance of trade ceasing, so in those circumstances the request for the concession to apply should not be the trigger date for the loss of BPR. Therefore, perhaps, the concession offers rather more flexibility than formal liquidation in this area because BPR is lost once a liquidator is appointed under IHTA 1984, s 105, even though the trade, as a question of fact, may be continuing. Accordingly, under the concession the effective date that causes BPR to be lost is likely to be when trade has ceased or when there are binding contractual arrangements to sell the trade. The relevant extract of IHTA 1984, s 113, is set out below:

'Where any property would be relevant business property in relation to a transfer of value but a binding contract for its sale has been entered into at the time of the transfer, it is not relevant business property in relation to the transfer unless –

(a)   the property is a business or interest in a business and the sale is to a company which is to carry on the business and is made in consideration wholly or mainly of shares in or securities of that company, or

(b)   the property is shares in or securities of a company and the sale is made for the purpose of reconstruction or amalgamation.'

11.10 In terms of dissolution, it will be rare for the relieving elements of IHTA 1984, s 113(a)–(b) to apply because in most cases the owner of the trade assets is to be dissolved and the proceeds of selling the business distributed amongst all the shareholders, therefore there would be no successor company.

11.11 Because application for the concession to apply can be made in advance of trade ceasing, or indeed the trade may continue whilst a closing down sale takes place, it will often be a question of fact when trade ceases. Therefore, if there is the need to keep trading status whilst a PET passes through the seven-year barrier then the concession route may be preferred because it may enable the company to have a greater control over the trigger date for the loss of BPR. The issues relating to the factors that determine if trading has ceased are discussed in para **11.9**. Certainly, if evidence of continuing to trade is required then not only will the accounting records need to reflect trading actually taking place but the directors should also prepare minutes confirming an intention to dissolve, but also indicating that trading is to continue (perhaps by way of a closing down sale) until all stock is sold. If the date is crucial then there is a need to have contemporary evidence available to defend any challenge that BPR is no longer available.

11.12   Elsewhere in this publication, reference has been made to director's minutes and their importance so far as providing evidence that a particular event occurred on a particular date is concerned. In practice, save in the largest companies, the existence of board minutes is likely to be in the same category as the Loch Ness Monster or Big Foot. Everyone believes in them but in some companies there have been no definitive sightings in living memory. If minutes are important to establish a date then they must be prepared, even if historically the company never bothered.

Similarly, we need to make sure that we have detailed file notes. In extremis these can be used to prepare confirmatory notes, or minutes, of events that took place in the past. Such confirmatory documents should always have the current date of preparation and confirm that decisions were actually made on particular earlier historical dates. To prepare backdated minutes or other documents is a fraud, possibly false accounting, and certainly should never be adopted on the basis that no one will find out. Inevitably, errors arise that prove the lie. Paper used for minutes is date watermarked, the word processor references give the game away or, typically, the date chosen for the missing minuted meeting was a date when at least one of the alleged attendees was on holiday. If no contemporary minute was prepared a minute confirming that a transaction took place on an earlier particular date is not a backdated minute, with all the fraudulent consequences that that status implies, but is as strong as the event it confirms. Many advisers seem to prefer the backdated minute – somehow it seems more certain – but, if discovered, does draw into doubt not only the event apparently confirmed but also any other information associated with events that took place at the same time.

11.13   Essentially, when dissolving the family company we should be aware of the date on which BPR will be lost and whether that date has any impact upon planning that we undertook in the past. As part of the planning process, and the timetable envisaged in Appendix 9, we need to establish IHT relevant dates and review the planning process with these in mind; if they can be accommodated, so much the better. If they cannot then the directors and shareholders need to be aware of the consequences and the effect of clawback on gifts already made. In respect of any gift, the availability of BPR at the date of gift is usually only a reassurance that all will be well. The important date is the date that IHT becomes chargeable, so even if BPR was available at the date of the gift if it was not available at the date tax becomes payable then it is not available to reduce the tax then payable.

PERSONAL ASSETS

11.14   As indicated below, the availability of BPR on land and buildings and other assets used in the trade of a family trading company, but owned personally, is a much less certain relief but only at the lower rate of 50%. It depends upon the occupier of the premises (the family trading company) continuing to be trading and for ownership of the family trading company to be under the same ownership as the land, buildings and other assets. Additionally, the owner of the land and buildings or other assets used by the family trading company must own in excess of 50% of the shares, ie they must have control, even to get 50% BPR relief. Accordingly, there is a wide range of circumstances where BPR can be lost even before the business is closed down, typically where the controlling shareholder makes a gift of shares to a younger generation, to encourage their participation in the business, but omits to seek advice where the existence of a 50%+ shareholding is essential to preserve 50% BPR on collateral assets. There is no comparable BPR concept of 'occupied for the purpose of business' as applies for APR in IHTA 1984, s 115.

Example

George owns 55% in Downham Market Ltd, a trading company, and the premises Economy Works, from which the trade is conducted.

On 19 September 2008 he makes a gift of 15% of the shares to his son, so the consequence is that from that date because he no longer controls the company BPR is no longer available on Economy Works.

CLAWBACK

11.15   One, usually unforeseen, circumstance of dissolving the family company is the impact upon potentially exempt transfers previously made. At the time the gift was made, there was usually no doubt that the relevant company satisfied the 'wholly or mainly' tests for BPR and the anticipated position was as follows:

Value of 20% of Martham Limited	£100,000
BPR (100%)	£100,000
Taxable value	nil

The effect of appointing a liquidator or dissolving the company would cause BPR to be lost so that if a donor died within seven years of the gift but after trading ceased then clawback of anticipated BPR would occur so the position could be:

Value 20% of Martham Limited	£100,000
Less BPR (0%)	Nil
Taxable value	£100,000

Clearly, this puts at risk any IHT planning that was put in place some years ago. It should be good practice to review the share register of the company to be disincorporated, as well as other records, to establish if gifts previously made are going to be put at risk. As a general proposition, the timing of cessation of trade and either liquidation or the use of ESC C16 is a flexible arrangement and, therefore, it may be possible to arrange matters to avoid clawback on a previous PET. Alternatively, the client, in full position of the facts, may decide that you are being unduly cautious and go ahead with the procedures; as always, it is fatal to our credibility to fail to advise the clients simply because 'we know' what decision they would make.

11.16   This is one area that will benefit from forward planning, particularly where, for example, notice has to be given to employees of termination of employment or to a landlord to vacate leasehold premises. Again, knowing the client is going to disincorporate at some point in the future can allow a timetable to be put in place that attempts to cover most eventualities. If the decision to disincorporate is made, notice given to employees and the company premises vacated in circumstances where an ongoing PET would drop out of inheritance tax accumulation – say, six weeks after the effective date of cessation of trade – then that potentially unfortunate mismatch could be avoided if the required order of events were reviewed. Appendix 9 sets out a detailed checklist, which includes consideration of the inheritance tax position of the shareholders of the dissolving company.

Example

Aunt Jemima had made a gift of her shares in Dunham Ltd (a trading company) to her nephew Jim on 10 December 2002. She was, and is, in poor health. Jim wants to retire and says that he has informally agreed to sell the company to his cousin Penny on 30 September 2009.

Delaying the sale until after 10 December 2009 will ensure that Aunt Jemima's gift remains eligible for BPR if she were to die before 10 December 2009.

11.17   Certainly, it should be good practice to delay dissolving the company for a few weeks or months if such a delay can preserve a relief currently available. It is a matter of commercial judgement and agreement as between vendor and purchaser whether any delay is acceptable. However, tax pressures should not drive this or any other transaction. There is no advantage in risking the only sale in prospect where the price to be realised for the assets represents a premium above forced sale values. If the business has been up for sale for many years and the current offer is the only offer on the table then IHT clawback may be a risk that has to be taken, particularly if the donor whose gift might be affected appears to be in good health (a further example of commercial reality being more important than taxation advantage).

It has been held in a Special Commissioners' decision in *Brown's Executors v IRC* [1996] STC (SCD) 277 that a company that had sold its business and put the proceeds of sale in a short-term deposit account some 20 months before the deceased's death had not become an investment holding company, with the result that the deceased's shares in it still qualified for business relief on his death. The relevant factors were that the deceased (who was the principal shareholder and director) had been actively looking for another business to purchase throughout the period from the sale to his sudden death – the money was on short-term deposit in order to be readily available to make a speedy purchase, and the company's office dealing with administration and marketing continued to operate throughout the period. The problem with any judicial decision is that the facts are critical, so relying upon a decision in a published case carries risks; far better to organise matters so that the law, rather than a judicial interpretation, supports the claim.

11.18 The existence of a binding contract for the sale of a business does not automatically have the effect of a company's shares ceasing to be eligible for BPR if the decision in *Brown's Executors v IRC* [1996] STC (SCD) 277 can be made to apply. In the case of a company about to be dissolved, that case is unlikely to prolong the BPR eligible period because there will be evidence that the business is to be closed down and that the available cash is not to be used for new business purposes. Whether that is consideration of the appointment of a liquidator or application for ESC C16 to apply, the necessary ongoing commitment to continue a trade is unlikely to be present. Accordingly, if the trade is to be sold, at what point does BPR cease to be available? Perhaps the exclusion extends to a period of commercial delay where, to all practical intents and purposes, the contractual terms are already agreed but contracts have not been exchanged? The short answer is no because until contracts have been exchanged there is no binding contract.

Where there will be a risk of BPR being lost because of binding buy and sell arrangements is where one of the shareholders dies in the run up to liquidation (ie before the appointment of a liquidator or even before applying ESC C16), and the terms of the arrangements between the shareholders, whether in the memorandum and articles of association or in the shareholder agreement, create a binding buy and sell arrangement. This matter is covered in Statement of Practice 12/80 as well as in a Law Society Statement of 6 May 1981 and further comments in the Law Society's Gazette of 4 November 1992, Vol 89 No 40 p 30 and 4 September 1996. The Law Society statement sets out five possible circumstances that derive from SP12/80 and that are accepted by HMRC as being a true representation of their views. A similar clarification is also available in a guidance note published by the Institute of Chartered Accountants in England and Wales, TR 557, which was published in September 1984. The matter is also covered in HMRC Inheritance Tax Manual at 25292. The manual reassuringly indicates that it is only in exceptional circumstances that most agreements as between shareholders would cause a binding buy and sell arrangement to come into effect. For the agreement to come within IHTA 1984, s 113, the agreement would have to provide for the shares of the deceased shareholder to pass to their personal representatives and require the personal representatives to sell the shares to the surviving shareholders who were, in turn, obliged then to buy them. The more common arrangements are those where the shares pass into the estate of the deceased but where the surviving shareholders have an option to purchase them. It is also confirmed by HMRC Inheritance Tax Manual at 25292that these arrangements do not constitute a binding buy and sell arrangement.

11.19 Sometimes the vendor of a business and the purchaser of the business will both want a degree of certainty so that, in effect, the vendor is obliged to sell or, equally, the purchaser is obliged to buy. The existence of cross-options does not, themselves, amount to a binding arrangement, but if the dates of the arrangements are precisely coincidental this may cause difficulties.

What steps can a vendor and perhaps a potential purchaser take to secure a transaction will take place without achieving a binding contract that causes a premature loss of BPR? The vendor will want certainty because the value represented by the company is a key element of the family's wealth. The purchaser will want to be certain that any delay is not a scheme to flush out an alternative purchaser.

One solution would be for both purchaser and vendor to have 'put' and 'call' options allowing each party to call for the sale to be completed. It is important that the expiry dates are not precisely coincidental because if they are, HMRC's view is that the effect is to create a binding contract. The call option must expire before the put option can be exercised.

Example

Adopting the facts in the example set out in para **11.16**, Jim arranges for a call option to be in place expiring after 10 December 2009 on, say, 20 December 2009 because after 10 December 2009 Aunt Jemima's BPR is preserved.

Penny who wants to purchase the trade has a call option that covers the periods 28 December 2009 to 10 January 2010 and the trade is sold on 4 January 2010.

The option periods are not coincidental but both parties achieve the certainty that they desire.

11.20 The above observations, in connection with the need to ensure that a PET made perhaps more than six years ago will fall out of account whilst the company remains trading (involving a scrutiny of the share register) will equally apply to personal assets (although perhaps the professional adviser to the company who is advising on the dissolution of the family company may have less knowledge of assets that are personally owned, but used in the trade of the family company) where these may have been recently given away to other members of the family. Accordingly, the company records must be reviewed to see whether rent is payable to family members but, equally, there will need to be discussions with the directors to establish if there are any assets, usually land, which are used by the family company but where no rent is paid. Where rent is not paid then there is the distinct possibility that the asset may have changed hands, but there is no record in the data available to the professional advisers to confirm this. Accordingly, it will be good practice to establish from all shareholders whether any gifts of business-related assets have been made within the seven-year period prior to the proposed date of dissolution. However, since BPR for a personal asset is only available to majority shareholders, ie those who own more than 50% of a company, this is not an unduly onerous obligation because there can only ever be one majority shareholder in a company.

HOW CAN BPR BE PRESERVED? REPLACEMENT PROPERTY RULES

11.21 In the great majority of cases, the company will be dissolved, the assets sold and all business activity ceases. However, there may be circumstances in which one or more shareholders in a company will use the funds available to them to start a new business. The position is covered by IHTA 1984, s 107 to allow the proceeds of shares in one company (provided it previously qualified for BPR) to be invested into a new business (again providing it can be seen to be satisfying the BPR rules) to ensure there would be no loss of BPR in any period of interruption provided the interests in the two businesses had been owned for at least two years within the last five years prior to any event that requires the availability of BPR to be considered. Therefore, care must be taken to ensure that any gap period between the cessation of one BPR eligible asset and the creation of a new BPR eligible asset is not too great and does not cause the successor shareholding to fall outside the two years out of five years test.

However, be aware that using the assets distributed from one company to fund a second company does run the risk of assessments to income tax on the proceeds under ITA 2007, s 682 onwards (formerly ICTA 1988, s 703) on assets distributed from a predecessor company, as discussed at para **5.17**.

11.22 Alternatively, the taxpayer may choose to rely upon IHTA 1984, s 106. Provided the successor business qualifies as a trading business then once two years have elapsed from the original investment there would be no need to consider the replacement asset provisions of IHTA 1984, s 107 simply because the more straightforward circumstance is that the business now satisfies IHTA 1984, s106:

> 'Property is not relevant business property in relation to a transfer of value unless it was owned by the transferor throughout the two years immediately preceding the transfer.'

In effect, the replacement asset rules only cover any period between the cessation, or sale, of one BPR eligible asset and the acquisition of a second BPR eligible asset if any event requiring consideration of the availability of BPR occurs within the first two years of ownership of the replacement asset.

Care is required to make sure that the replacement asset is acquired within three years of the sale of the original asset. Certainly, where an individual intends to claim replacement asset relief, time is of the essence because if they die before acquisition no BPR will be available. In *Brown's Executors v IRC*

[1996] STC (SCD) 277, there was an enterprise in place at the date of death and the only issue was whether relief was due. Whereas if an enterprise has ceased to exist and the replacement asset has not been purchased, how can it be proved that there is an intention to acquire a new asset? The advantage of IHTA 1984, s 107 over IHTA 1984, s 106 is that once the business has been purchased and qualifies as a BPR eligible asset then there is no need to satisfy the two-year ownership test.

Example

Jim receives the proceeds from his shares in Dunham Ltd on 31 October 2007 and looks for a new business. He decides to invest the proceeds in a new venture. Following the sale of the trade of Dunham Ltd on 4 January 2007, the advisers assumed that BPR was lost from that date because after that date Dunham Ltd was only involved in dissolving the company and consequent administration towards that end.

Therefore, to take advantage of IHTA 1984, s 107, Jim needs to acquire a new BPR eligible business before 4 January 2010.

If he delays beyond that date then he will have to rely upon IHTA 1984, s 106 and then own the new assets for two years before BPR is available.

PERSONAL ASSETS

11.23   We have, therefore, considered the impact upon BPR available of shares in the family company but families will also have assets that are owned personally but used in the family company trade. Such assets are eligible for relief under IHTA 1984, s 105(1)(a) at the 50% rate, but only where the owner of the asset also has control of the company – therefore, for only the very closely owned family company is this likely to be an issue. Conventionally, it is usually the founder shareholder who will also own personal assets used in the trade of the company.

There is no statutory definition of 'business' for this purpose but rather it has its normal, dictionary definition. Indeed, the term 'business' has a wider definition than trade. However, there is still a requirement that activity is carried on and IHTA 1984, s 105 specifically disallows BPR if the business being carried on is wholly or mainly managing investments.

11.24   The Special Commissioners case of *Farmer* SpC 216 (1999), was the first of a number of cases concerning this area. The case is important because it sets out five points that have to be considered in determining whether an activity is wholly or mainly the managing of investments. It seems clear that the tests find favour with HMRC because they are used in modified circumstances elsewhere in HMRC guidance. The following factors were relevant to the *Farmer* decision of what the deceased's business mainly consisted:

- the overall context of the business;

- the capital employed;

- the time spent by employees;

- the turnover; and

- the profit.

11.25 There will, occasionally, be circumstances where a company and its shareholders know that the business is to be dissolved and there is an effective change in activity in the years running up to dissolution. The company may, for example, concentrate on converting trading stock into fixed assets, which are then held as investments, or begin to realise cash so that the dissolution process is more easily carried on. Revenue Interpretation 228 initially gave HMRC's view as to a trading company status for capital gains tax purposes, but Tax Bulletin 62 (reproduced in Appendix 6) has now superseded this. However, the article should provide assistance when reviewing the IHT position of shareholders.

11.26 In most cases, a company about to be disincorporated and having either sold its trade or its business assets, and that is currently continuing predominantly as a cash shell, is not carrying on a business. Therefore, so far as personal assets are concerned, they will also no longer qualify for BPR because they are no longer used by a company carrying on a business. If it is intended that a company will reinvent itself by carrying on a new trade, perhaps along the lines of *Brown's Executors v IRC* [1996] STC (SCD) 277, then the personal assets may continue to attract BPR because the user company remains trading, but that is unlikely to be the case where, for the purposes of this publication, the company is ultimately to be dissolved once the primary trade has been sold.

If, commercially, the company is to be disincorporated, the shareholders and asset owners need to recognise that their inheritance tax positions will alter once trading ceases. Whilst trading continues, prior to the existence of binding contracts for sale, the value of any shares qualifies for 100% BPR, and associated assets used in the trade may qualify for 50% BPR, but post-disincorporation (once the funds have been distributed) they merely hold cash and investment assets on which no relief is due. The inheritance tax planning techniques that need to be adopted in these changed circumstances are outside the scope of this publication, but recognising the alternative circumstances in the run up to liquidation or disincorporation will allow informed decisions to be made as to the appropriate commercial actions.

AGRICULTURAL PROPERTY RELIEF

11.27 So far as agricultural property relief (APR) is concerned, many of the same considerations as are indicated in relation to BPR for family trading companies will apply to the family farming company where the assets are ultimately distributed amongst the family members. In many cases, farmland being exploited by the family farming company will be personally owned and in these circumstances it is much easier to ensure that the farmland continues to remain eligible for APR even after the family farming company has been dissolved. The provision of IHTA 1984, s 115 is clear, for our purposes, although other publications, including *Business and Agricultural Property Relief* by Toby Harris (published by Tottel Publishing), contain greater detail. The relevant extract of IHTA 1984, s 115(2) is set out below:

> ' "agricultural property" means agricultural land or pasture and includes woodland and any building used in connection with the intensive rearing of livestock or fish if the woodland or building is occupied with agricultural land or pasture and the occupation is ancillary to that of the agricultural land or pasture; and also includes such cottages, farm buildings and farmhouses, together with the land occupied with them, as are of a character appropriate to the property.'

If the farm and farmhouse are owned outside the family company then, if the property is sold, the same inheritance tax consequence applies as in respect of business trading assets. Cash replaces the inheritance tax favourable assets. However, if the family farming company is being dissolved simply because the farming generation wish to retire and there is no one in the family to take the trade over then it is possible to preserve APR in a way which, for trading BPR assets, is not possible.

11.28 Agricultural property relief, see IHTA 1984, s 115, is available where property is occupied for the purposes of agriculture; this means that provided the land remains occupied for agricultural purposes, even if the family farming company (or even a member of the landowner's family) does not occupy it, the assets can remain eligible for APR provided the successor occupier uses the land for agricultural purposes.

Example

James owns the farmland and farm buildings that are currently exploited by Grimston Road Ltd, including the farmhouse, where it is proposed that Grimston Road Ltd will be dissolved following James's retirement in May 2009.

James will need income from the property and has no desire to sell the farm. Accordingly, he has discussions with a neighbouring farmer who wishes to expand and two separate proposals are made:

- the farmland will be rented to his neighbour at an appropriate agricultural rent but James will retain ownership and occupation of the farmhouse; or

- James will enter into a partnership arrangement with the neighbour and the profit share arrangements will give James an income equivalent to the agricultural rent and any contracting profit belongs to the neighbour.

In the first arrangement, APR will continue to be available on the farmland but will no longer be available on the farmhouse because the farmland has been let away from the house – the farmhouse is no longer occupied for the purpose of agriculture.

11.29   By contrast, provided the partnership/contracting arrangement with the neighbour is appropriately documented, this arrangement should preserve APR on both the farmland and on the agricultural value of the farmhouse because the farmhouse still remains occupied with the farmland within the same business, so APR remains available on the agricultural value of the farmhouse. There may be circumstances where this is no longer available, particularly where the amount of farmland is small in relation to the size and value of the farmhouse or the true farming decisions are made by the neighbour in his farmhouse.

CREDITOR VOLUNTARY ARRANGEMENTS

11.30   Creditor Voluntary Arrangements (CVAs) are not strictly a dissolution of the family company, although if they fail they may lead to the dissolution of the family company, generally in circumstances where a creditor voluntary liquidation is then appropriate. Nevertheless, there can be circumstances in which advantage can be achieved by making gifts whilst the company is in a CVA provided the shareholders are satisfied that, ultimately, the business will survive. This is because at the moment the CVA begins, the value of the company is likely to be low and therefore, potentially, value can be moved across at minimal IHT cost.

Such arrangements are entered into by the company and its creditors where the creditors are persuaded that they will gain more by allowing the company to continue to trade than they would by forcing the company into insolvent liquidation. By their very nature, such arrangements are generally only undertaken where the company is teetering on the brink of insolvency but has entered into formal arrangements with its creditors to allow it to pay a modest amount over a future period, typically five years, in settlement of existing claims. Such arrangements are often an arrangement of convenience but, particularly, offer unsecured creditors the prospect of something where the commercial reality is that any sensible review of the company's position is that nothing would otherwise be expected.

11.31   However, the act of entering into a CVA does not change the status of the company so far as BPR is concerned. The company is still trading because it needs to trade to generate profits to satisfy the CVA contributions and, accordingly, provided the company satisfies the trading requirements, BPR remains available under IHTA 1984, s 105.

The same consequence will apply to assets owned personally but used in the business – currently eligible for 50% relief. Perhaps the scope for current discount, whilst the company is in CVA, is less – this might be because any lease that the company has is more likely to be ultimately forfeit whilst a CVA is in place, because there might be a view that possession may be obtained as a result of a collapse into insolvency. In most cases, the value of property will remain unchanged irrespective of who is the tenant. Indeed, were the company to become insolvent, any lease may be forfeit, resulting in the property regaining any current value attributable to the leasehold interest. Whilst the company continues to trade, 50% BPR remains intact. Of course, if the company fails to satisfy its CVA obligations, the consequences are likely to be that the company's shares become valueless because all the creditors previously deferred by the CVA now become payable. Any assets outside the company, previously eligible for 50% relief, will now no longer satisfy the use in the business test required by IHTA 1984, s 113, so BPR will be lost.

11.32 One area of concern will be the status of a PET that fails, so IHT may become due because of the death of the donor whilst the CVA is in progress. Providing the trading requirements are satisfied, BPR will continue to be available on the basis described in para **11.31,** because whilst the CVA continues, in most cases the trading activity also continues, and thus no liquidator will have been appointed.

Example

Gavin made a gift of his 30% holding in Magdalen Road Ltd in July 2005 to his daughter Helen when the shares were valued at £200,000.

Helen proves incompetent and, on 10 August 2008, the company enters a CVA that continues. Gavin dies 31 January 2009, but because at that date the company is still trading, there is no claw back of BPR.

However, is the position different if, at the date of death, the CVA has failed, with the result that the company is then in liquidation and there is currently no value attributable to the previously gifted shares? Do the executors of Gavin's estate simply include a failed PET at £200,000 less BPR £nil to give a taxable value of £200,000? The answer would seem to be yes; all transactions are taxable on the basis of reliefs available at the date of death (or other event that results in an IHT charge) but at the value when the gift was made so that the executors have to make a return of a failed PET of £200,000, but there is no BPR available to reduce the taxable value. Therefore, the effect is that the clawback provisions apply, with the result that because the company is then in liquidation, there is no BPR available to reduce the taxable value. The gross value of the shares transferred will be liable to inheritance tax. This undoubtedly causes difficulty for the family because the donee may face a tax charge if the gross value of the PET exceeds the nil rate band at death, but there is no asset available to produce income or cash to satisfy the liability.

Even if the failed PET is below the nil rate band, with the result that there is no liability on the donee, the effect may still be that there is less nil rate band available to be set against the remainder of a donor's estate. If this situation subsists then it is not possible to take advantage of IHTA 1984, s 179 to arrange for a sale of the relevant shares to a third party so that the executors could make a claim to suffer IHT on the proceeds, which in the circumstances envisaged here might be £nil. This is because the ownership of the asset is in the wrong estate. In the example, it is Gavin's estate that is taxable but the asset is owned by Helen. Accordingly, the executors cannot organise a sale to take advantage of IHTA 1984, s 179.

11.33 What may cause even greater difficulty is if the shares that were given away were subject to a reservation. Here the rules require the 'PET' to be valued, at death, at the higher of the value when the original gift (albeit subject to the reservation) was made or the value when the reservation was lifted. Adapting the Magdalen Road facts, if the shares were given away in July 2005 but subject to a reservation not removed until August 2007 when the value of the shares was £150,000, reflecting Helen's abilities, what value applies on Gavin's death if the company had by then ceased trading? Again, it would be the original value when the 'gift' was made of £200,000 with no claim relevant under IHTA 1984, s 179.

11.34 Where a company goes into liquidation, after a gift of shares has been made within the following timetable, considerable hardship may ensue:

- gift made at a time when company is BPR eligible; subsequently

- the company is placed into liquidation; and finally

- the donor dies within seven years of the date of gift so that BPR is clawed back.

The donor's estate will face a charge on the gross value of the gift without the benefit of BPR. In this circumstance, there seems no action that can be taken to mitigate the charge.

If the shares in the company that has been placed into liquidation are sold to a third party, and the proceeds reinvested into new BPR eligible assets, then advantage may be taken of the replacement property rules in IHTA 1984, s 107.

Example

Adapting the facts in para 11.32 so that Magdalen Road Ltd finally collapses and is placed into liquidation on 31 October 2009

Helen sells her shares for £10 on 31 January 2010 and reinvests the money into an AIM listed company.

In this example suppose Gavin dies on 6 April 2010, but by then the shares in the AIM company are replacement property so BPR is preserved on the original gift.

If Gavin died before the company was placed into liquidation, and before Helen could arrange a sale of the shares and acquisition of new shares to acquire replacement property then the estate of Gavin would be subject to IHT on the full value of the failed PET at the value appropriate when the gift was made on the previously indicated basis. The IHT event has arisen so there is no scope for rearranging the wreckage.

In practice, the future availability of BPR on a gift made when the company was successful at a time when the shareholders are contemplating the wreckage is unlikely to be a prime concern. However, both donor and donee should always be made aware of the possibility of clawback on any gift and the position monitored. It will be bad enough that the value of the company has been lost, but to then face an IHT charge on a failed PET would be a crushing blow. Unfortunately, the writer's experience is that when a gift is made the concerns of the donor are always addressed, but it is often assumed that the donee's position requires little attention on the basis they now have the company and it is up to them to secure their own position. If the gift – once BPR is no longer available – is substantial then urgent consideration of the replacement property rules will be essential. Inheritance Tax Act 1984, s 107 is intended to restrict BPR to the amount that would have been available had the original asset been retained; it does not seem to apply to restrict the relief to the value of the replacement asset. The Inheritance Tax Manual does not contradict this view, the purpose of the legislation is to preserve the BPR that would have been available had the original asset been retained. Therefore, in the above example, if the subject matter of the original gift is replaced by a new BPR eligible asset then that is sufficient. There is no requirement for the old and current values to be identical. Therefore, even though the original value was £200,000 and the current value £10, that will not prevent retention of BPR on the original gift because a replacement asset has been acquired.

11.35   In the vast majority of dissolution cases, the impact of inheritance tax reliefs and charges may only have a marginal impact. For most cases, the particular relevant circumstances will be the time immediately before and immediately after the liquidation, or dissolution, which needs to be taken into account. Timing needs to be considered and, where possible, commercial arrangements tailored to make sure that relief is available.

PLANNING POINTS

11.36

- Review the share register to establish if any potentially exempt transfers are about to drop out of the count and, where possible, delay dissolving the family company until after that event.

- If any gifts are to be made in the run up to dissolution then make sure these are made as PETs, simply to avoid any potential immediate charge to inheritance tax, and made whilst the company remains trading so that holdover relief is available under TCGA 1992, s 165.

- Establish whether any gifts of assets used in the business have been made within seven years prior to death and again consider delaying dissolution if this will allow a gift to drop out.

- Arrange a full review of the client's inheritance tax position once the company has been dissolved. Business property relief may have removed any potential liability to inheritance tax whilst the trading company continued, but now the client will have cash or investments so their entire personal financial scenario has changed.

- Delay, so far as commercially possible, the cessation of trade so that if a proprietor dies whilst the dissolution is planned but not yet in effect, that BPR is not lost.

- If assets owned by the family include agricultural property on which APR is currently due, consider what replacement arrangements will preserve the relief.

- If a new business is to be started, consider how the replacement asset rules may assist the owners to preserve BPR, but take notice of ITA 2007, s 682 onwards (formerly ICTA 1988, s 703), particularly if the immediate income tax charge is significant in relation to the potential IHT relief sought to be preserved.

Chapter 12

Limited Liability Partnerships

12.1   The Limited Liability Partnerships Act 2000 (LLPA 2000) introduced a new form of corporate entity that, in effect, provides a degree of protection for partners to allow them to limit their liability although they are taxed, whilst the LLP is ongoing and active, as a partnership. Once the LLP ceases to be active, unless for a temporary purpose (see para **12.6**), then transparency is lost with the consequences set out below. The general purpose of the legislation is to create transparency between the business venture and the partners. In effect, each individual partner is taxed on their own share of income or profits so long as the business continues. LLPs are mainly used in high-risk professions, for example solicitors, surveyors and accountants, where the impact of uninsured professional negligence may apply.

12.2   There is a formal formation procedure that requires the LLP to be registered with the Registrar of Companies.

DISSOLUTION PROCEDURE

12.3   Equally, there is a formal procedure by which the business can be dissolved through the use of the ss 652/652A procedure, Companies Act 2006, ss 1000–1002 (formerly CA 1985, s 652) and Companies Act 2006, ss 1003–1011 (formerly CA 1985, ss 652A–652F), but using specially designated Form LLP652a (to apply to the Registrar to have the partnership struck-off) or Form LLP652c (to withdraw the dissolution process). The formal procedures are similar to those for companies with notice being advertised in the London Gazette.

CAPITAL GAINS TRANSPARENCY

12.4   Capital gains tax matters in relation to LLPs are governed by TCGA 1992, s 59A and cover fiscal transparency as between the business structure and the partners so long as the entity carries on trading.

12.5   However, when an LLP ceases to trade, or carry on any business with a view to profit, the capital gains tax transparency is lost and the LLP is then treated as a body corporate subject to tax in its own right (compare the position of an unincorporated association). Therefore, there may be a deemed disposal of chargeable assets potentially affecting the partners in the

LLP that triggers personal taxability of a gain previously rolled over into a replacement asset or where a gain might have been held-over under either TCGA 1992, s 165 or s 260. This will happen when a liquidator is appointed because the assets then vest in his ownership and he acquires those assets at the cost to the partnership, not the tax cost that, of necessity, would reflect any claim for rollover that the partnership, or the partners, has made. Therefore, in this circumstance the rolled-over or held-over gain crystallises and is assessed on the partner who made claim. This procedure is required because otherwise there exists the possibility that some gains would otherwise escape taxation. See HMRC Capital Gains Manual 28025 – Limited Liability Gifts holdover relief.

Example

Tim was a partner in Black Bank LLP. The partnership sold goodwill, and Tim's share of the profit, £50,000, was rolled-over into partnership property, of which Tim's share of the cost was £200,000. Therefore, his tax cost was £150,000.

The partnership went into liquidation on 14 August 2008 and the assets vest in the liquidator. Therefore, Tim's share of the property is acquired by the liquidator at £200,000. Tim faces a tax charge on the rolled-over gain of £50,000 in 2008/09.

TEMPORARY CESSATION IS NOT A TAXABLE EVENT

12.6   However, it is acknowledged that a temporary cessation of trading will not trigger a capital gains tax liability. See HMRC Capital Gains Manual 28007, which confirms that any gains realised during a temporary cessation of trading simply flow through to the partners.

INFORMAL WINDING-UP PROCEDURE

12.7   Where an LLP is wound-up in an informal way without the appointment of a liquidator, a process that might be considered comparable to the ESC C16 procedure but without any need to apply to HMRC for confirmation of its application, HMRC accept that fiscal transparency continues during the period required for settling outstanding liabilities and realising business assets provided the conditions set out in Capital Gains Manual 28009 are met. Those conditions are:

- that the LLP is not being wound-up for reasons connected in whole or in part in the avoidance of tax; and

- that, following the termination of the LLP's business, the period of winding-up is not unduly protracted taking account of the LLP's assets and liabilities.

If the winding-up is unduly protracted, and there is no definition of this, the fiscal transparency and the informal winding-up process can be lost. It would seem unreasonable for the period to be allowed to be less than the period that a prudent liquidator might take, if appointed. Therefore, a reasonable period of time might be considered (perhaps up to 24 months) to realise the assets and deal with the liabilities.

FORMAL LIQUIDATION

12.8 Where a liquidator is appointed then, as in the case of a trading company, fiscal transparency ceases at the date the liquidator is appointed. The liquidator must prepare his capital gains tax computations using the cost to the partnership when any asset was first acquired by the LLP.

Example

The Reepham LLP acquired freehold property on 10 April 2002 at a cost of £150,000. If the LLP goes into liquidation, it is this figure used as the base cost for any future capital gains tax computations.

Any gain realised by the liquidator is then assessed on each individual member of the partnership in the normal way.

12.9 What may cause difficulty is if any gains have been deferred, held-over or rolled-over against the purchase of the partnership asset. Because the assets of the LLP vest in the liquidator, and their capital gains tax computations are then based upon the cost to the partnership, there exists the possibility that gains previously held-over or rolled-over could otherwise fall out of account. Here the position is covered by TCGA 1992, s 156A, which brings back into charge the gain previously held-over.

Example

John is one of three partners in The Reepham LLP and contributed £50,000 towards the purchase of the property in the previous example. He rolled-over a gain of £35,000 on a previous asset so his capital gains tax base cost is £15,000.

On 10 February 2008, a liquidator is appointed to the LLP and the consequence is that the £35,000 rolled-over gain is immediately assessable on John in tax year 2007/08. A similar provision under TCGA 1992, s169A applies to reimpose any gain that was previously held-over by application of the gifts relief under either TCGA 1992, s 165(4)(b) or s 260(3)(b).

12.10 In respect of a trading LLP, provided the trade has been carried on for at least 12 months, then any consequent gain should qualify for entrepreneurs' relief up to the £1 million limit, so there will be an effective tax rate of 10%, failing which the gain will suffer tax at 18%.

However the gain imposed by TCGA 1992, s 169A arises as a consequence of a legislative imposition, not as a consequence of a sale of a business or interest in a business, and so any gain, as in the Reepham LLP example, should be taxed at 18% rather than the effective reduced 10% rate that applies with entrepreneurs' relief.

UNDULY PROTRACTED

12.11   In practice, the period of dissolution of an LLP is likely to be rather longer than the conventional trading company, simply because the nature of the professions involved. There will be a need to obtain insurance runoff – many of the projects will require completion in order to realise the fees owed – and therefore it is suggested that the phrase 'unduly protracted' used by HMRC should be a flexible time limit. If there are genuine commercial reasons for delay preventing realisation of the assets then the partner and/or the professional adviser dealing with the administrative matters must ensure that these are documented.

Where an LLP goes into liquidation or is informally wound-up then it may be possible to use the same planning techniques as applied when a limited company is to be dissolved, ie delay realisations until just after the end of the tax year or arrange for distributions to be in a number of tax years in order to multiply the available capital gains tax exemptions.

STATEMENT OF PRACTICE D12

12.12   In the unusual circumstances that the assets of an LLP are not realised but are instead distributed to the partners then there will be a capital gains tax liability, certainly when the assets are distributed by the liquidator for the reasons indicated above. Transactions between partners are governed by statement of practice D12; the same is true for the partners in an LLP.

Where there are rearrangements as between partners, perhaps on an informal dissolution of the partnership, then there is the possibility that separate partners will end up owning separate assets. Whilst the partnership continues, each partner is treated as owning an appropriate fractional share in each partnership asset and, correspondingly, on a disposal each partner disposes of a share of each partnership asset. This can lead to very complex computations, hopefully where a full cost history is available or, more likely, a need to review many years of transactions to obtain the cost history. The table below illustrates the simple history of ownership of what is now a five-partner LLP but which commenced as two partners to parity of ownership of all chargeable assets on the assumption that on each occasion when ownership proportions changed, equality of ownership was achieved, the items in brackets reflecting the elements sold by those partners reducing their share of the partnership assets.

A	B	C	D	E
1/2	1/2			
(1/6)	(1/6)	1/3		
(1/12)	(1/12)	(1/12)	1/4	
(1/20)	(1/20)	(1/20)	(1/20)	1/5

12.13   However, in practice, such a convenient history will not exist. A partner leaves, is not replaced immediately and has his assets bought by the remaining partners who then sell a proportionate share to a new partner when admitted. Conversely, a new partner may not acquire a full share of the capital assets reflecting their income profit-share immediately, nor will a retiring partner sell on retirement. In all cases, full capital histories need to be maintained so that proper computations can be prepared on each sale or transfer.

Equally, where there is a revaluation of fixed assets on each partnership change or, on a change of profit-sharing ratios, each partner will make either a gain or a loss. In the case of large LLPs, the gains are likely to be small because changes take place on a regular basis and will represent only a small portion of the LLP's property. The gain may be covered by the annual capital gains tax exemption (£9,600 for 2008/09), but proper records and allocation of costs will ensure a prompt and proper calculation of any gain.

12.14   The partners are connected persons within the meaning of TCGA 1992, s 18(3). However, this does not generally cause a problem either with off-set losses or with questions of value. There is an exception in relation to acquisitions and disposals of partnership assets pursuant to bona fide commercial arrangements. The bona fides of transactions are unlikely to be in question. No partner will sell for less than the proper price or pay more than the proper price. Where the transactions concern persons connected other than by membership of the partnership, if any valuation also impacts upon the other non-connected partners then there should be no difficulty with values.

Example

Suppose an LLP consists of mother, daughter and two unconnected persons. If mother were to sell an asset to all of the other partners, there should be no difficulty because mother is unlikely to want to convey bounty upon her unconnected partners.

However, HMRC Capital Gains Manual at paragraphs 27296–27298 indicates that market value rules may apply where partners are connected other than by partnership. For example, if they are mother and daughter, or even if not strictly connected (ie aunt and niece), they may not be acting at arm's length. There is an expectation that any transaction is on approximately the same basis as would have applied had the parties to the transaction been unconnected except by partnership.

Therefore, in the above example, a sale of an asset between mother and daughter at, say, 70% of market value would cause the market value rule to be invoked because there would be a presumption that the transaction was other than at arm's length. However, the same sale to one of the unconnected partners would not be reviewed.

When proposing to advise the members of an LLP as to their potential CGT liabilities on an informal or formal dissolution, there will be a need to establish a full CGT history adopting the principles outlined. In doing so, it is probable that unreported gains will be discovered but they will simply have to be reported as appropriately if the current evaluation is to be based upon a correct basis.

INHERITANCE TAX AND LLP

12.15   So far as inheritance tax is concerned in relation to an LLP, the position is straightforward. 100% BPR/APR will be available for assets held within the LLP. This will of course extend to land. Where land is held outside the LLP, as in a partnership, then the usual 50% relief will be available. In practice, it is more likely to be the latter relief, which will be the more common because generally the purpose of LLPs is to protect assets from the creditors and this would only be available if land is left outside the LLP. In effect, the potential extra inheritance tax charge is the insurance premium for protection.

PLANNING POINTS

12.16

- Review assets if an insolvent dissolution is anticipated so partners are aware of any exposure to claimed back roll-over relief.

- Ensure that the dissolution does not fall foul of the unduly protracted rule and fiscal transparency is lost.

- Prepare detailed CGT histories as the business develops on each occasion there is a change in ownership or profit-sharing ratios to ensure accurate computations are prepared.

- Ensure that you remain in contact with the partners once the business has ceased so that they can be advised of any personal gains.

- Ensure any required professional indemnity insurance for run-off periods is in place before dissolution commences.

Chapter 13

Other forms of dissolving the family business – insolvency

13.1   The primary purpose of this publication is to provide guidance as to the processes involved in a solvent distribution of assets to shareholders, whether in circumstances where shareholders receive a return or in such circumstances perhaps where the shareholders may receive some of their money back but not a full return on the amounts originally subscribed for share capital.

This latter instance may apply where, for example, a group of individuals agree to float a company to develop a particular project and subscribe for share capital – perhaps by issuing shares at a premium – where it quickly becomes apparent that the project is doomed or, at the very least, will not produce the anticipated return. The shareholders agree to go their separate ways and want their capital back. In such cases, the company is often funded by a mixture of loan capital and share capital and the funds of the company are sufficient to make a partial repayment of loan capital.

The reliefs that are available to shareholders in these circumstances are discussed in Chapter 4 and, in particular, paragraphs **4.7** and **4.11**. All third party creditors are repaid so that the only losers are the business promoters. In other cases, the company will have ploughed on, often in the face of factors that indicate almost certain disaster where all the promoters' funds are used up and there are balances due to third party creditors – so the only way of getting rid of the company is by a form of insolvency procedure.

For such arrangements, it will be necessary to use a licensed insolvency practitioner. The extent of their responsibilities is beyond the scope of this publication, but a general overview will assist general practitioners when faced with an apparently solvent family company that either turns out not to be as solvent as was hoped, or not solvent at all so insolvency is the only option.

13.2   Company insolvency procedure may consist of four distinct categories:

- creditor voluntary arrangements (see para **4.17**);

- administration;

- receivership; and

- liquidation, whether as a members or creditor's voluntary arrangement, where the company law aspects are discussed in Chapter 2.

ADMINISTRATION

13.3 An administrator is usually appointed by the courts to manage the affairs of the company to achieve certain specific objectives where the courts are satisfied that the company is insolvent or is likely to become insolvent and, as such, the company will be unable to settle its creditors. These include:

- the possibility that the company, or a significant part of its trade, will survive;

- that the creditors will approve a creditor's voluntary arrangement;

- that there will be a compromise under Companies Act 2006, s 895 (formerly Companies Act 1985, s 425); or

- that the appointment of an administrator will allow the company's assets to be realised for a greater sum than would be the case if the company were simply placed into liquidation.

The appointment of an administrator does not affect the corporation tax position of the company and so does not cause an accounting period to come to an end.

13.4 Whilst the administrator is in place, the directors usually have control of the company and are responsible for the company's actions. This will be the case even when the administrator is appointed to realise a particular asset subject to a particular charge and so is known as a 'fixed charge receiver'. Such an administrator will have no power to deal with the general trading of the company.

Therefore, responsibility for any corporation tax liability that arises either before the appointment of an administrator, or during any period that they are in office, remains the liability of the company.

RECEIVER

13.5 A receiver is often appointed under the terms of a floating charge, in which case they will have responsibility for dealing with all the assets of the company when they generally will trade, in which case the role of the directors will be correspondingly reduced.

Equally, a creditor holding a specific charge on specific assets of the company can appoint a receiver with the intention that the receiver should realise the asset or assets that provide the security in order that the creditor can be repaid. In the case of a specific charge receiver, they have no right to interfere in the administration of the company so, in this instance, the directors remain in nominal control of the company.

In practice, an administration or receivership will often lead to the appointment of a liquidator, but only once the administrator or receiver has realised as much as they can for the creditor who arranged their appointment.

LOSS OF CORPORATION TAX GROUP RELIEF

13.6   In a group situation where an administrator or receiver is in charge of only one or two companies in a group then it is understood that HMRC will argue that the companies subject to administration/receivership have ceased to be members of the group, using (as justification) ICTA 1988, s 410(1)(b)(ii). This subsection states 'any person has or could obtain, or any person together have or could obtain, control of the first company but not the second'. Therefore, HMRC argue that the administrator or receiver has control of the companies over which he has been appointed but that the existing shareholders have control of the remainder of the group and, therefore, group relief will no longer be available – and the ability to transfer assets around the group between the companies in administration or receivership and the rest of the group, without any taxation consequences, will be lost.

13.7   Any corporation tax liability that arises during the period of a receivership or administration is not the liability of the administrator or receiver but remains a liability of the company because, at this stage, the company continues trading – albeit that the effect of the appointment of a receiver or administrator is likely to significantly handicap the ability of the company to continue trading. For example, if a receiver sells assets of the company in order to repay a fixed charge, that may produce a profit subject to corporation tax. The liability for that tax is the company's liability, not the receiver's, nor is it the liability of the holder of the fixed charge. Accordingly, it will fall to be dealt with either as a payment by the company if it continues to trade or as a liability in any subsequent liquidation.

13.8   Where a receivership is dealt with under the terms of a floating charge in circumstances in which a liquidator is appointed either whilst the receivership is in progress or, indeed, was appointed prior to the appointment of a receiver, then the liquidator can be entitled to recover any tax liability that might arise when a receiver, under the terms of a floating charge, realises assets.

13.9   Otherwise, the appointment of an administrator or receiver has no direct impact upon corporation tax procedures or on the timing of any corporation tax liabilities. Equally, the inheritance tax position of the shareholders remains unchanged so that if a particular company, in receivership or administration, was a trading company before the appointment of a receiver (whilst the receiver is in place and after the receiver has been discharged) then BPR for inheritance tax purposes would continue to remain available throughout the period.

13.10   The rules in connection with companies in administration have been amended by Finance Act 2003, s 196 and Finance Act 2003, Sch 41. This introduced a number of changes following the passing into law of the Enterprise Act 2002 and, in particular, the following points may be relevant.

● If a company that is in administration is to be dissolved without passing into liquidation then corporation tax rates used to calculate any final liability will be those from the previous financial year of the company. Although we are now becoming used to the idea of corporation tax rates being announced in advance, the purpose is to assist the company in achieving an early settlement of its liabilities (ICTA 1988, s 342A(2)).

- If the only taxable income receivable by a company in administration in its final period is bank interest then, provided the amount does not exceed £2,000, the interest shall not be liable to corporation tax. This applies to companies that were in insolvent liquidation or insolvent administration immediately before 9 April 2003, or will go into insolvent liquidation or insolvent administration on or after that date (ICTA 1988, s 342A(4)).

- If a company has been in administration and passes out of administration then that will cause an accounting period to end (see ICTA 1988, s 12(3)(da)). Equally, applying for the company to be dissolved without first appointing a liquidator will cause an accounting period to end.

13.11 For a company that is in administration, the administrator may make an assumption in advance of the event of the date on which the company may be dissolved in order to agree the taxation liabilities of the company in advance. If, however, the estimated date proves to be incorrect then a further accounting period will commence on the original assumed date.

Example

The administrator of Union Mills Ltd estimates that the company will be dissolved on 15 December 2008. In the event the company is not dissolved at that time, on 15 December 2008 the administrator has to make a further assumption to indicate a likely new date of dissolution and that will be a further corporation tax accounting period for the period after 15 December 2008.

LIQUIDATION

13.12 When a company goes into insolvent liquidation, the current agent is unlikely to have any ongoing responsibility, save they may assist the company in agreeing taxation liabilities. As has been indicated elsewhere, the appointment of a liquidator has immediate corporation tax consequences and these include the following:

- an accounting period will cease on the date of an appointment of a liquidator;

- if there are group structures in place then the appointment of a liquidator to a particular company is likely to cause that group relationship to be broken;

- the liquidator becomes responsible for any corporation tax liability that arises during the liquidation period;

- the rate of corporation tax will be the rate for the previous year unless there has been a Budget Resolution to confirm the current rate (ICTA 1988, s 342(2)).

The effect of the appointment of a liquidator in a company that had been making profits immediately prior to the appointment of a liquidator (perhaps an unlikely concept in most cases but one the writer has met in practice) is to accelerate the date upon which tax might become payable.

Example

Spalding Ltd normally made its accounts up to 31 December, so the normal date for tax payment as a small company would be 1 October.

On 30 September 2008, the company was placed into liquidation, even though the period 1 January 2008 to 30 September 2008 was profitable. The appointment of a liquidator causes an accounting period to end so the tax for the final period, before a liquidator was appointed, is now due for payment on 1 July 2009. If the company continued to its normal accounting date, the tax would have been due on 1 October 2009.

13.13   Other matters in relation to companies in liquidation, whether they be a solvent liquidation or an insolvent liquidation, are discussed elsewhere in the text and, in particular, the ability of a close company that is in liquidation to retain the benefit of the lower rate band for the accounting period following liquidation is discussed at para **3.44**.

The detailed rules in relation to companies in insolvent liquidation are beyond the scope of this publication, which is intended to provide a general outline to advisers in practice dealing with matters up to the point at which responsibility is handed over to the liquidator. For those for whom insolvent liquidation represents a higher proportion of their work load, reference should be made to *Taxation of Corporate Insolvency* by Anthony Davis.

BANKRUPTCY

13.14   Generally, this publication deals with corporate matters and their impact upon the shareholders of companies that are to be dissolved. However, many of us will have acted for individuals who, perhaps through no fault of their own, have been made bankrupt but who wish to continue to trade.

So far as income tax is concerned, bankruptcy does not automatically result in a cessation, for income tax purposes of the business. The trustee in bankruptcy will be responsible (to be paid from the assets of the bankrupt available to them) for any liability up to the date of bankruptcy and for the tax year of bankruptcy irrespective of whether the trade ceases at the date of bankruptcy order or continues beyond that date but ceases before the following 5 April or indeed simply continues.

Once an individual becomes bankrupt, the entitlement to personal reliefs ceases on the basis that all assets and income vest in the trustee and, accordingly, any income that the bankrupt continues to receive is only a right of reversion to any balance after payments made to pay creditors (see *IRC v Fleming* (1928) SC 759).If the bankrupt receives income on his own account post-bankruptcy, then responsibility for the tax rests with the bankrupt.

Capital gains tax in bankruptcy

13.15   On the appointment of a trustee in bankruptcy, ownership of the assets vests in the trustee but this is not a disposal for capital gains tax purposes. Equally, any assets transferred back from the trustee to the bankrupt after the bankruptcy has ceased does not give rise to a taxable disposal. However, any gain that arises on the sale of assets by the trustee during the bankruptcy period is taxed on the bankrupt under TCGA 1992, s 66(1).

If a bankrupt dies during the bankruptcy period then the usual tax-free uplift on death applies under the provision of TCGA 1992, s 66(2), (3) and treats the assets as though they were held by the personal representatives of the deceased.

Income tax in bankruptcy

13.16   For the trustee, so far as income tax is concerned, there is a clear distinction between income retained by the bankrupt and income received by the bankrupt. In the case of *Hibbert v Fysh* (1961) 40 TC 305, an undischarged bankrupt claimed that personal earnings that he received and retained were not taxable by virtue of his bankruptcy. In that case, none of the earnings were paid over to the trustee in bankruptcy, but that would not seem to have made any difference. The earnings were taxable.

Income received and retained by a trustee in bankruptcy is taxable on the trustee and no personal allowances are available. This is because, in that instance, the income vests in the trustee with the bankrupt only having a right in reversion against the trustee; in effect, the bankrupt is in a similar position to a trust beneficiary. The trust is not entitled to personal allowances but once income is distributed or reverts to a beneficiary, that beneficiary then becomes entitled to a personal allowance.

INDIVIDUAL VOLUNTARY ARRANGEMENT

13.17   This is the personal equivalent of a creditor's voluntary arrangement for companies and operates in much the same way. The creditors of an individual are persuaded that it will be in their best interests to allow that individual to avoid bankruptcy by making an agreed payment in the pound for liabilities existing at the date the arrangement is agreed. Within the writer's experience, an individual voluntary arrangement is often used where a high earning individual has entered into a business arrangement outside of their core professional skills, which has turned out to be unsuccessful with the consequence that perhaps under joint and several liability they are the only individuals with assets that can support a guarantee.

Example

Henry is a successful tax consultant earning in excess of £100,000 per annum but agrees to go into partnership with his cousin redeveloping residential property from derelict commercial buildings.

Henry's cousin has no assets and, accordingly, Henry agrees to underwrite the partnership overdraft. All goes well for three years but in the fourth year there is a collapse in property prices as a result of the 'credit crunch', and they are forced to sell the current development at a large loss. The partnership is left with an overdraft of £500,000, which cannot immediately be met.

This is the only liability that Henry has of any consequence and his creditors agree to accept 40p in the £ under the terms of an individual voluntary arrangement payable over four years.

13.18   An individual voluntary arrangement has no direct impact upon personal taxation because it is probable that the core trade of the individual concerned will continue. It is, after all, required in order to provide the contribution to the creditors.

Similarly, there will be no inheritance tax issues except that, whilst the monies remain outstanding to the creditors, this will be a liability of the estate.

Finally, there will be no capital gains tax issues because ownership of any assets, which the individual involved in the individual voluntary arrangement has, will be retained in personal ownership.

CONCLUSION

13.19   Clearly, insolvent liquidation, bankruptcy or even an individual voluntary arrangement is likely to be commercially disadvantageous as far as the individual is concerned, whether as a shareholder in an insolvent company or having to settle the liabilities of (or at least make a contribution towards) a failed business. Any assets that the individual has will be sold in order to meet their liabilities, often with the consequence that what was once very high flying and valuable business now becomes an empty shell with no surplus available to return to the business proprietors. There are, generally, few tax advantages that can be achieved from an insolvent situation.

13.20   The assumption of this publication is to try to maximise the proceeds from a solvent dissolution of a business on the basis that the shareholders will receive £1, but will want to minimise the tax deductions that will apply to that £1. Whenever the writer has planning meetings with clients, he always takes the positive view that if a client has received £1 on which tax of 40p has to be paid, this means that 60p will be available for the client. Of course not all clients are in the happy situation of paying 40% tax, which must mean that their taxable earnings exceed, for 2008/09, approximately £40,000 and are therefore above national average earnings. For clients whose profits are below the 40% threshold, the most that may be deducted from £1 of profit is likely to be 28p (20p tax + 8p class 4 NIC) so 72p remains. With insolvent cases nothing is likely to be returned to shareholders so no matter how inventive any possible tax planning, the best that can be achieved is tax relief on a payment that has to be made. A poorly performing but consistent solvent business will always provide more for its owners than a high flying but ultimately failing business. Hopefully insolvency will only be faced by client businesses on an occasional basis, but when it does arise we need to be aware of the procedures so that they are pointed towards a licensed insolvency practitioner at the earliest opportunity.

13.21   Advisers should resist the temptation to believe that they can assist the proprietors to trade a failing company into solvency on the basis they 'know how to run their own businesses so how difficult can it be to run the business of a client?'. After all, the reasoning goes, they already know how the business currently operates. Nothing could be further from the truth. Just as Henry (see para **13.17**) knew how to run his own core business, so we know how to run our own businesses but can never understand the full knowledge required to run a client's business. Within the writer's experience, it is a sure sign of the property market overheating that a wider selection of clients begin a little property speculation. This has varied in recent times from a publican (persuaded by a bar room regular) to a solicitor (in this case persuaded by a golfing partner to join in the redevelopment of a nightclub because there was no risk). As a minimum, we all need to understand an outline of the insolvency procedures and tax consequences that may apply when matters go wrong. Particularly adopting the voluntary arrangement structures may ensure that bankruptcy or insolvency may be avoided. The consequence may be that the core business will survive to allow a solvent dissolution at some future date, at which juncture the techniques envisaged elsewhere in this publication may then apply.

PLANNING POINTS

13.22

- If there is the possibility of avoiding bankruptcy, explore the possibility of an individual voluntary arrangement with an insolvency practitioner at the earliest possible opportunity.

- If insolvency is a possibility, seek advice from an insolvency practitioner immediately.

- Try to discourage clients from entering into transactions beyond their core experience.

- If clients are determined to undertake speculative ventures then arrange as much protection against liabilities as is possible.

Chapter 14

Tying up the loose ends

14.1   As indicated in the preface, the purpose of this publication is to draw together those items that a general practitioner may need to consider when dissolving a typical family company. It is not concerned with the taxation of companies in insolvent liquidation, which is a more specialist area beyond the scope of this publication, but is aimed at assisting practitioners in dealing with the following questions.

- Assuming the client has a choice as to when the family business closes down, what is the optimum date?

- Do we dissolve the company by a formal liquidation or by use of the s 652A procedure?

- What are the advantages and disadvantages of either approach?

- If the s 652A procedure is adopted, do we wish to distribute the funds to shareholders as either income or capital?

- If the capital route is chosen, and in most cases this will be the appropriate route, how do we apply for ESC C16 to apply and what undertakings are required?

- In making distributions to shareholders from trading companies, how important is the timing of interim distributions to ensure entrepreneurs' relief (if available) is not lost as time passes from cessation of trade? Remember that any distribution to shareholders under the s 652A procedure is legally a dividend, and there is a requirement to prepare minutes and other statutory documentation so that the distributions cannot exceed the realised profits of the company. ESC C16 allows a legal fiction that the dividend is then taxed as a capital amount.

14.2   As with all taxation issues, there is no short cut but to prepare the tax calculations based upon any alternative choices. Instinctively, most advisers will believe that capital gains tax treatment on dissolution of the company will produce the most favourable result. However, as indicated at para **6.10**, there may be circumstances where income distribution is more favourable.

14.3   The examples at para **6.10** are a simplified version from a case involving an investment company where the shares were widely held amongst members of a family. In preparing the calculations, all the shareholders except one benefited from the income treatment. It was therefore agreed that income distribution should be on the basis of dissolution with the basic rate shareholders giving the shareholder who was liable to higher rates on part of his distribution an indemnity that they would settle his higher rate liability.

14.4   As should be clear, dissolving the family company is not simply a matter of agreeing the corporation tax liabilities up to dissolution and then considering what the capital gains tax position will be when the monies are distributed to the shareholders. No accountancy/taxation exercise, in the writer's experience, ever simply involved one tax. This interaction has been indicated elsewhere in this publication. Dissolution of the family company may potentially involve consideration of VAT, IHT (where we need to consider gifts that have been made in the past whether these are about to drop out because of the seven year limit), and SDLT.

All the taxes need to be carefully considered if the appropriate result for clients is to be achieved.

14.5   Dealing successfully with the dissolution of a family company does not simply require knowledge of taxation. It also involves accountancy skills and project management skills to ensure that:

- assets are realised at the appropriate time;

- timing of dissolution is considered;

- payments to shareholders are made as promptly as possible; and

- the company records and papers are dealt with promptly and retained for the appropriate period.

14.6   It cannot be stressed too often that when dealing with CGT issues it will be the market value of the assets, when they are distributed to a shareholder, that has to be taken into account in preparing the capital gains tax computations. The tax value of those assets may affect the way in which those assets are taxed in the company but that has little impact upon the capital gains tax computation.

14.7   When preparing the CGT computation for a client, in circumstances where you did not deal with the company either before or during dissolution, it is always important to obtain copies of the schedules prepared by the company or its accountants. Clients rightly regard the cash that they receive as being the most important element but the cash may have been reduced by entirely appropriate transactions but in circumstances where simply to insert the cash received into the capital gains tax computation will give an incorrect result.

In two cases that the writer was indirectly concerned with, the following instances both conspired to reduce the cash payment to the shareholder:

- The individual concerned had had a loan from the company and this was repaid to the company by deduction from an interim distribution in order that the company could recover any ICTA 1988, s 419 tax previously paid (see para **3.43**). The discrepancy was only picked up because husband and wife should have received the same amount for one of the interim distributions but, because of the loan repayment, the amounts were different.

- In a second case, a client wanted to purchase some plant and machinery for use in his own trade and agreed a price with his fellow shareholders. Again, no cash changed hands and the cost of the assets purchased was deducted from an interim distribution. In this instance, the matter only came to light when the annual accounts were prepared and the client had a VAT invoice for the purchase of equipment where payment could not be traced; the tax return had already been submitted to HMRC and it was therefore necessary to make a correction to the return.

WHAT IF IT ALL GOES WRONG?

14.8   The available funds will be distributed pro rata so this should not cause a problem. What may cause difficulty is if unknown liabilities arise. Occasionally, the company to be dissolved will pass cash over to the adviser so that he can deal with any necessary payments to suppliers and calculate the distributions to the shareholders, whether that is a single distribution or a series of interim distributions. Alternatively, the company will expect the adviser to assist them to calculate the amounts payable to each shareholder. In calculating interim distributions, full provision needs to be made for all future costs – including our own – so that cash is available to meet these as and when required. Unknown creditors do crawl out of the woodwork and therefore, if the adviser is dealing with both calculation and payment of monies to shareholders, they will need to obtain from all the shareholders a warranty that monies will be repaid in the event that additional costs come to light. As always, it would be better to retain cash until the position is clear because the value of any warranty depends solely upon the ability of the donor of the warranty having sufficient funds to make an appropriate repayment. In practice, if a payment under a warranty is required, some of the shareholders will not have the money, will blame their fellow shareholders, will blame the adviser and yet will be reluctant to produce their share of the cash; for shareholders who are able to produce the cash, this can cause family tensions.

14.9   Of equal importance – particularly for manufacturing companies being dissolved – is to ensure that all product liability insurance covers claims that may be made after the business has ceased to trade. It is understood in most cases that insurance will cover claims made after cessation of trade, simply because the event that gave rise to the claim occurred whilst the company was trading, but it is best to confirm the position with the company's insurance provider.

PHOENIX BUSINESSES

14.10   In recent years many clients happily converted what was previously a partnership or sole trader into a limited company and, for practical purposes, carried on in much the same way as before. Certainly, we are all aware that a sole trade/partnership can be converted into a limited company with a minimum of exposure to additional taxation, although some other publications indicate there are a range of complications. For individuals who wish to reverse the process and cease to trade as a limited company by extracting the assets from the previous limited company, there is the very real possibility that this action will give rise to an assessment under ITA 2007, s 682 onwards (formerly ICTA 1998, s 703). This matter is discussed in some detail at para **7.14** and in particular at para **5.17**. This is a real issue. HMRC Manuals (see, for example, Company Taxation Manual 36850) cover the point in some detail, so clearly it is a live issue for them just as it should be for advisers. Certainly, clients and their advisers who are considering a phoenix revival of a family trading company as a partnership/sole trader should carefully consider the downside of any assessment under ITA 2007, s 682.

CHECKLIST

14.11   Included in Appendix 9 is a checklist of issues that may, or may not, need to be considered in any particular dissolution. In many cases the response will simply be 'not applicable' but even in what appear to be straightforward cases, the writer used to use a version of the checklist, albeit a rather shorter version before this publication was in contemplation. It does make the adviser, and the company, consider matters that otherwise might be forgotten.

PUTTING IT RIGHT

14.12   It is fortunate that provisions of both ESC C15 and ESC C16 allow an application to be made for capital status after funds have been distributed. Those taxpayers who simply choose to shut the company down and empty the bank account can still gain the protection of capital status many months after the transactions have been effected. However ESC C16 needs to be made before the company is struck off. To apply after striking off risks the payments being categorised as dividends or relying upon an HMRC agreement within the spirit of the concession. Neither very satisfactory results.

14.13   An ability to deal with matters retrospectively may assist some who simply decide that the business is shut down and assume that what is left is theirs. This may particularly be the case where unincorporated associations are concerned because, the writer is certain, there may be many such organisations that should be recorded with HMRC but are not.

BURYING THE COMPANY

14.14   Just because all the assets have been paid out to the shareholders, and the corporation tax liability agreed and no visit from HMRC is anticipated, it does not mean that this is the end of the matter. The company's accounting records need to be retained for possible inspection. As indicated in HMRC

Guide for CTSA, the basic requirement is that records must be preserved for six years from the end of any period from which the company is required to deliver a return. In certain circumstances, the period of retention has to be extended where the notice to file a CTSA return is issued before the end of the six-year period and the relevant records must be kept until the later of:

- six years from the period for which the company may be required to make a return;

- the date on which an enquiry into the return is completed; or

- the date beyond which HMRC no longer has power to enquire into the return because the time limit for opening an enquiry has passed.

14.15 With some small companies, storage of accounting records may not be a problem. One archive box per year would cover the storage requirements. However, for very large companies storage of the records can be a problem. Accordingly, it would be appropriate to ensure that procedures are in place and storage capacity available to keep the records for the required period. Occasionally, a shareholder will be prepared to store the records on their premises, but more typically a storage provider will be required. The cost of this facility has to be factored into the distributions to shareholders and funds retained to make sure that the cost can be covered. Certainly, the last thing that the adviser wants is to have the books on his shelves for six years.

14.16 Dealing with storage of the accounting records should be the last event undertaken by the company and its advisers. Once all payments to shareholders have been made and cleared through the bank, the papers should be parcelled up and delivered to the archive facility. If storage is required for six years then a significant discount may be obtained on the storage costs if a prepayment is made for the full six years. Instructions should be given to the archive facility that the records are to be confidentially shredded once the six-year limit has expired and for the adviser to make a diary note to check that this has been done. Of course, prepaying the archive provider runs the risk that they themselves will become insolvent and what happens to the records after that date, but since the shareholders are likely to want to minimise the cost of archive storage there are some things in life that cannot be risk-free.

C15 Dissolution of unincorporated associations – distributions to members

Where a company which is an unincorporated association is dissolved, the distribution of its assets to its members is an income distribution within Section 209, ICTA 1988, limited where Section 490(1) or (4) of that act applies to the amount distributed out of profits brought into charge to corporation tax or out of franked investment income. If substantially the whole of the association's activities have been of a social or recreational nature, it has not carried on an investment business or a trade other than a mutual trade, and the amount distributed to each member is not large, it is given the option of not having Section 209 applied and of having the whole of the amounts distributed treated as capital receipts of the members for the purpose of calculating any chargeable gains arising to them on the disposal of their individual interests in the association.

Appendix 2

C16 Dissolution of companies under the Companies Act 1985, ss 652, 652A – distributions to shareholders

A distribution of assets to its shareholders by a company which is then dissolved under Section 652 or Section 652A Companies Act 1985 (or any comparable provisions) is strictly an income distribution within Section 209, ICTA 1988. In most circumstances, and providing that certain assurances are given to the Inspector before the event, the Revenue is prepared for tax purposes to regard the distribution as having been made under a formal winding up so that the proviso to Section 209(1) applies. The value of the distribution is then treated as capital receipts of the shareholders for the purpose of calculating any chargeable gains arising to them on the disposal of their shares in the company. The assurances include:

The company

● does not intend to trade or carry on business in future; and

● intends to collect its debts, pay off its creditors and distribute any balance of its assets to its shareholders (or has already done so); and

● intends to seek or accept striking off and dissolution.

The company and its shareholders agree that

● they will supply such information as is necessary to determine, and will pay, any Corporation Tax liability on income or capital gains; and

● the shareholders will pay any Capital Gains Tax liability (or Corporation Tax in the case of a corporate shareholder) in respect of any amount distributed to them in cash or otherwise as if the distributions had been made during a winding-up.

Appendix 3

Precedent for company application under ESC C16

Company Application under ESC C16

Company Name   An Example Limited
Inland Revenue Reference   529/

I, A N Other as Company Secretary of the above company, hereby apply to have the provisions of ESC C16 applied in the winding-up of the company.

The Company is in the process of selling its trading assets and once that process is complete does not intend to trade or carry on business in the future.

It intends to collect its debts, pay off its creditors in full and distribute any balance of its assets to its shareholders.

It intends to seek or accept striking-off and dissolution under the Companies Act.

The Company will supply such information as is necessary to determine, and will pay, any corporation tax liability on income or capital gains.

The company will not transfer or sell its assets or business to another company having some or all of the same shareholders.

The arrangement is not a reconstruction in which some or all of the shareholders in the original company retain an interest in the second company.

A N Other
Company Secretary   Date

Note: HMRC Company Taxation Manual at 36220 still includes a requirement that the undertakings include an agreement to settle any ACT liability under ICTA 1988, Sch 13, due on distributions made prior to 6 April 1999 but the latest edition of the Concession booklet excludes this requirement from ESC C16.

The supplementary undertakings referred to in chapter 5 are now included as part of the normal precedent.

Appendix 4

Precedent for application under ESC C16 — shareholder undertakings

Company Application under ESC C16

Company Name   An Example Ltd
HMRC Reference   529/

We, being all the shareholders in the above company, understand the company has applied to have the provisions of ESC C16 applied in the winding-up of the company.

We agree that we shall supply such information as is necessary to determine, and will pay, any corporation tax liability on income or capital gains liability.

We will pay any capital gains tax liability (or corporation tax in the case of a corporate shareholder) in respect of any amount distributed to us in cash or otherwise as if the distribution had been made during the winding-up.

A Shareholder
Date

Another Shareholder
Date

Note: This shareholder undertaking needs to be signed by all shareholders. Although it is understood that in some circumstances small minority shareholders may be excused from this warranty it is considered best practice to arrange for all shareholders to sign.

Case study – Brundall Gardens Halt Ltd

The purpose of the case study is to draw together the majority of the issues discussed in this publication to demonstrate how the issues impact upon one another and ultimately impact upon the cash distributed to shareholders.

BACKGROUND

Brundall Gardens Halt Ltd is a typical small/medium family-operated company formed on 1 March 1982 (when trading began) where the issued share capital of £100 is currently held as follows:

John Brundall	55
Helena Brundall	35
Peter Brundall (son)	5
Karen Brundall (daughter)	5

The business was very successful for many years and, over the period of time from commencement, considerable value has been built up within the company. The founder generation are currently running the business and now wish to retire but Peter, although he works in the business full time, has no wish to take over the business and Karen has developed a career away from home.

The company always made its accounts up to 30 April but the balance sheet at a recent date, 31 July 2008, showed the following position using book values:

Fixed Assets	
Plant and Machinery	185,000
Freehold Property	225,000
	410,000
Current Assets	
Stock	350,000
Debtors	600,000
Cash at Bank	240,000
	1,190,000
Current Liabilities	
Trade Creditors	102,000
Director's Loan Account	650,000
Taxation due for year to 30 April 2008	103,000
	855,000
Net Current Assets	335,000
	745,000

Shareholders Funds

Share Capital	100
Accumulated Profits	744,900
	745,000

Based upon management accounts and recent experience, the profit since 30 April has been earned at the rate of £10,000 per month after charging £2,000 depreciation.

The controlling shareholders draw a modest salary each month and draw any other cash from their loan account, which always remains in credit. At the end of the company's financial year in April they usually vote a dividend to top up the loan account. In April 2008 they voted and credited dividends amounting to £80,000, of which mother and father's share was £72,000, so any other taxable sources in 2008/09 will be subject to higher rate tax.

John Brundall personally owns the freeholds of two branches, which cost £25,000 each in July 1983 and have a current value of £250,000 each. John hopes to sell these within six months of trade ceasing.

In the run up to retirement, several attempts to sell the business were made, but no one has been prepared to pay the value John believes the company to be worth. Unfortunately, his view of the value of the business is tainted both by his long-term association with the company and a belief that although trading in this business sector is steady but slowly declining due to innovation elsewhere, his company (which, of course, is better operated than his competitors) should attract a premium.

Included within creditors is the sum of £10,000 due to HMRC in respect of an input tax over claim on the purchase of a fixed asset several years ago, before the present accountants acted, in a period that was never subject to a HMRC audit.

Within the balance sheet, the following assets are valued at values different to those of their balance sheet.

- The freehold property has a current use value of £600,000, the plant and machinery has a tax written down value of £190,000 and local specialist auctioneers estimate that no more than £185,000 would be achieved on a sale. Stock will realise £325,000 and the debtors are all considered recoverable except for £25,000 owed by a competitor.

- The company's freehold property was acquired on 5 April 1984 and any expenditure on this property, no matter how large the extent, has always been written off to profit and loss because John refused to believe that such expenditure results in any improvement to the property. However, a review of the corporation tax computations since incorporation shows that the following items of expenditure were disallowed as relating to improvements.

Year to 30 April 2001	£40,000
Year to 30 April 1993	£10,000
Year to 30 April 1986	£50,000

The company currently has 12 employees all of whom are entitled to statutory redundancy pay and their aggregate entitlement is £45,000. However, John agrees that he will double this so that the cost to the company is £90,000.

The corporation tax computations for the recent years show the following adjusted profits:

Year to 30 April 2008	£120,000
Year to 30 April 2007	£140,000
Year to 30 April 2006	£180,000
Year to 30 April 2005	£140,000

John, under pressure from his wife, agreed that the business be closed down on 30 September 2008 and took steps to begin the process of realisation. He contacted various business associates and managed to sell the stock and other assets immediately after 30 September 2008 for the values previously stated.

However, the only offer for the company's property is from a property developer who offers £800,000 for the site, but with a further payment in four years' time based on any increase in the average price of houses in the area between the date the initial payment was made and when the development was completed, or the average price of houses in four years' time, whichever event comes first. There is an active amenity group in the area and they immediately object to the planning application. However, the advice from the planning consultants is that, ultimately, planning permission will be obtained, although it may take perhaps two to three years to achieve this and a further two years to complete the development. John, on behalf of the company, signs an agreement to sell the property for £800,000 subject to a further payment once the development was complete.

John has also been talking to his pension adviser who explains that John had not made full provision over the years into his executive fund and, on 1 August 2008, the company needs to make a payment of £300,000 to top up John's pension. Under current rules it needs to be paid before trading has ceased, so in this case the required payment was made before 30 September 2008.

As a result of the various transactions, the corporation tax position of the company for the final period to 30 September 2008 is as follows:

Profit		60,000
Add Depreciation		12,000
		72,000
Less:	Redundancy	90,000
	Pension	300,000
	Balancing allowance	5,000
		395,000
Adjusted loss		323,000

The adjusted loss is set against the results for the earlier periods and gives rise to a corporation tax refund of approximately £65,000.

Accordingly, the balance sheet at 30 September 2008 can be recast as follows:

Fixed assets

Plant and machinery	185,000
Freehold property	225,000
	410,000

Current assets

Stock	325,000
Debtors	600,000
Taxation refund (estimated)	
Cash at bank	65,000
	240,000
	1,230,000

Current liabilities

Trade creditors	102,000
Director's loan account	650,000
Taxation due for year to 30 April 2008	103,000
	855,000
Net current assets	310,000
	785,000

Shareholders funds

Share capital	100
Accumulated profits	784,900
Reserves before sale of property	785,000

So far as John and Helena are concerned, their capital gains tax position is as follows, but only if the company were able to distribute the whole of the assets to them within three years of 30 September 2008.

The company also faces a capital gains tax charge on the freehold property that will need to reflect the possibility of extra consideration from the upward adjustment in house prices, under the *Marren v Ingles* [1980] STC 500 principle, but also to take account of the possibility of reduction in proceeds particular in the 'credit crunch' environment, as follows:

Market value		800,000
Possible uplift (say)		300,000
		1,100,000
Less:	Cost	225,000
	Disallowed improvements	
	Year to 30 April 2001	40,000
	Year to 30 April 1993	10,000
	Year to 30 April 1986	50,000
	Indexation on the above (say)	70,000
		395,000
Taxable profit		705,000
Corporation Tax due (say 28%)		198,500

This result feeds through into the balance sheet of the company, and therefore the CGT payable by the shareholders as follows:

Reserves before sale of property		785,000
Hope value		300,000
Uplift in property value	575,000	
Less tax charge	198,500	376,500
Sale proceeds		1,461,500
Less cost	100	
		100
		1,461,400
Taxable gain		1,461,400

Happily, the tax payable on proceeds of approximately £1.450 million is only £130,500 on the shares of John and Helena, provided the assets are distributed before 30 September 2011. However, this result may not be achieved because the company's freehold property cannot be sold until planning permission is obtained and, in September 2008, the best estimate is that this may not take place until September 2011. If the whole of the funds are held back until that date then John and Helena's liability would increase to approximately £235,000, because entrepreneurs' relief is not the available.

There remains the possibility that the planning will fail and, because the option agreement tied John to the purchaser for the full three-year period, there would then be further delay once the option has lapsed before John could realise value from the company by a sale of the property to someone else.

Finance Act 2004, Sch 21 introduced restrictions to the availability of capital gains tax holdover relief where trading assets, including shares in family trading companies, are transferred to interest in possession settlements where conventionally, before the December 2003 pre-budget announcement, the purpose of such transfers was to restart the capital gains tax taper relief clock to improve the rate of taper relief available or in earlier times to crystallise an entitlement to CGT retirement relief.

In the case of John and Helena, the loss of holdover relief is now of no interest. John and Helena want to preserve their right to entrepreneurs' relief at the reduced effective 10% rate. Accordingly, they could each transfer their shareholdings into separate interest in possession settlements before September 2011.

Because holdover is not available, nor desired, this would be a disposal for capital gains tax with the result that this is a disposal in 2011/2012 where the tax will be payable on 31 January 2013. John and Helena would need to make sure that they are paid sufficiently from the company by that date to ensure they are in funds to meet the immediate tax charge. It would seem that the financial position of the company is such that partial distributions could be made of sufficient magnitude to ensure that John and Helena are in funds before any tax becomes payable.

However, the issue that would need to be assessed is the value that would apply at the suggested disposal date of August 2011. At this date the proposed sale to a developer may not be certain and a share valuation exercise will need to be carried out to assess the value that would have to be included in the 2011/12 CGT computation.

There may be circumstances where the use of a trust can turn the anti-avoidance provisions of Finance Act 2004, Sch 21 to advantage. But one circumstance will not be where there will be a significant discount between the proceeds ultimately realised and any interim CGT valuation that determines the tax on transfer into trust. In the case of Brundall Gardens Halt Ltd, realisation of the full proceeds depends to a great measure upon hope value, but where the delay between cessation of trade and distribution has more to do with administrative matters – where the consequence is that any discount to value is likely to be minimised – then triggering a gain before trade ceases may produce an advantage for the client. However, as always, there is no alternative but to prepare detailed calculations.

In particular, John needs to consider what he will do with the two properties that he personally owns and which will be sold by approximately June 2005. At present, these qualify for entrepreneurs' relief, but assuming, as seems likely, the sale of these properties takes place before the realisation of the shares, the entrepreneurs' relief will dilute the claim that can be set against the realisation of the shares.

Sale proceeds	500,000
Less: cost	50,000
Taxable gain	450,000

In relation to the small number of shares held by the two children, Peter and Karen, the position in relation to entrepreneurs' relief is reasonably straightforward. So far as Peter is concerned, because he is a full-time working employee and has 5% of the shares, he will be entitled to entrepreneurs' relief on his gain, provided it is realised within three years of the date on which the company ceases trading, so again he will be subject to the same constraints and restrictions as his parents because of the potential delay in the sale of the property.

Karen, because she is not an employee, will not be entitled to entrepreneurs' relief. Whether she would be minded to, for example, transfer her shares to her brother to allow a claim for entrepreneurs' relief to be made, depends upon family circumstances. There might be an advantage to be obtained here, but she would need to transfer the shares whilst the company was still trading in order to ensure that holdover relief could be obtained. Of course this would mean that Peter would use up part of his lifetime £1 million entitlement, but if the consensus is that it is unlikely he will use that limit up, then there appears to be no reason why he cannot acquire a 10% holding and all would be covered by entrepreneurs' relief. Even if Peter then gives the after-tax proceeds back to his sister, there do not appear to be any anti-avoidance rules that might bite here.

This type of case, where there will be a delay in realising the full value, either because in the current climate the sale of commercial property is blighted by the 'credit crunch' or simply because the assets are complex and will take time to realise that the CGT simplification, originally announced on 9 October 2007 and included in Finance Act 2008 does in many respects make life easier for the Brundall family; the only immediate time-critical issue being any potential transfer of shares between Peter and Karen.

The relief which allows a three-year period for assets to be realised, in circumstance where trade ceases, does make the decision-making by the shareholders in a trading company somewhat easier. It might not be thought unreasonable that, in the great majority of cases, three years would be more than enough to realise the assets and distribute the proceeds to the shareholders. Accordingly, there is no urgent need for action on the part of most shareholders in the run-up to trading arrangements ceasing. It will only be if any proceeds cannot be realised within the three-year window that action then needs to be taken.

Where difficulty may arise is in relation to relief for associated disposals where, as was indicated previously, the gains in respect of associated disposals are not the subject of a time limit. It is merely necessary to be able to demonstrate that the gains on the associated disposals are associated with a withdrawal or realisation of the primary business asset. In the case of the Brundall family, it may well be self-evident that this is the case, because trading is ceasing and both associated and primary assets are in the process of being realised. It is simply that the processes by which the separate assets are realised may give rise to entirely different timescales.

Potentially the only circumstances in which urgent action might be required is in respect of any decision by Karen to transfer her shares to her brother where, presumably, she would want to make a claim for holdover relief and that means that the shares would need to be transferred before the company ceases trading.

As indicated elsewhere, the CGT simplification does at least give time for post-cessation planning to be organised in an appropriate timeframe.

Paragraph **5.29** discusses whether it matters if the director's loan accounts are repaid in advance of any interim share capital distributions. In the case of Brundall Gardens Halt Ltd, repayment of the loan need not be delayed because, unlike the position that existed under the CGT taper regime before 6 April 2008, unless the distributions are delayed beyond September 2011, CGT entrepreneurs' relief will be available and delay of that length of time does not seem to be an adequate reason to delay distribution of the director's loan accounts.

The accountants, in conjunction with John and Helena, review the balances in the company accounts on a monthly basis for the first year because within that period funds are being realised on a regular basis and make several interim distributions, but once all the debtors and other assets have been realised, the review need only take place quarterly until just before the property option is exercised when planning is made to distribute speedily thereafter.

So far as annual accounts are concerned, the company must make up and file with the Registrar of Companies the following accounts:

Year to 30 April 2008	File by 28 February 2009
Year to 30 April 2009	File by 31 January 2010
Year to 30 April 2010	File by 31 January 2011

It is possible that the accounts for the final period to 30 April 2008 may not need to be filed if an appropriate application is made to the Registrar to have the company struck off before the indicated filing date. This will depend upon whether the option to sell the property is exercised and outstanding matters resolved before 28 February 2009. However, the possibility that they will have to be filed needs to be recognised.

In addition, the company will have to comply with all other ongoing requirements including VAT returns and annual returns to the Registrar of Companies.

The PAYE scheme could be discontinued once the employees have been made redundant and all residual entitlements have been satisfied. Therefore, the return to 5 April 2009 is likely to be the final return. Brundall Gardens Halt Ltd remembers to submit final forms P11D for 2008/2009. If, however, John and Helena continue to receive remuneration or benefits, the scheme may need to be in place longer. In practice, it will make sense for John and Helena to cease employment at the earliest opportunity because the tax cost of salary and benefits will outweigh the tax cost on a dissolution distribution. If they remain directors simply to satisfy their formal Companies Act obligations then the PAYE scheme may be discontinued at an early date.

John and Helena both had company cars so once trading had ceased in September 2008, these were purchased from the company.

Chapter 9 considered the circumstances in which VAT deregistration is required but if the company anticipates incurring significant costs in terms of planning consultants and wants to recover the VAT it would have to opt to tax the freehold property, so in these circumstances VAT returns would continue to have to be made until the property is sold.

Throughout the dissolution process there was one matter that had not been resolved, and this was the over-claim from HMRC of £10,000. The accountant makes a number of representations to John that this amount must be declared to HMRC, being careful to ensure the conversation does not amount to tipping-off, but John is adamant that he will not do so. In part this is due to some perceived action that HMRC took many years ago, and John feels that two wrongs make a right. Nevertheless, retaining the money is an offence under the money laundering regulations and the accountant is obliged to make a return to SOCA of the circumstances. Whether anything will transpire of the report only time will tell.

Matters proceed to a satisfactory conclusion and the balance of the funds is distributed to John and Helena in January 2011 and the company is then struck off. However, some months later a visit from HMRC to review the records discovers a number of minor errors that need to be settled – but curiously not the £10,000 reported to SOCA!

D3 Company liquidations – tax on shareholders' capital gains

1. During the liquidation of a company the shareholders often receive more than one distribution. For capital gains tax each distribution, other than the final one, is a part disposal of his shares by the shareholder, and the residual value of the shares has to be ascertained in order to attribute a proportion of the cost of the shares to the distribution (unless the Inspector of Taxes accepts that the distribution is 'small' and can therefore be deducted from cost). It has been represented to the Commissioners for Her Majesty's Revenue and Customs that the making and formal agreement of these valuations is holding up the agreement of liabilities and that little if any change in the total tax is involved in the majority of cases.

2. Where the shares of a company are unquoted at the date of the first or later interim distribution, therefore, the Commissioners for Her Majesty's Revenue and Customs are prepared to authorise Inspectors of Taxes to accept any valuation by the taxpayer or his agent of the residual value of the shares at the date of the distribution, if the valuation appears reasonable and if the liquidation is expected to be completed within two years of the first distribution (and does not in fact extend much beyond that period). The valuation need not include a discount for deferment; and if the distributions are complete before the capital gains tax assessment is made, the Revenue will accept that the residual value of shares in relation to a particular distribution is equal to the actual amount of the subsequent distributions. In the normal way the Revenue will not raise the question of capital gains tax on an interim distribution until after two years from the commencement of the liquidation unless the distribution, together with any previous distributions, exceeds the total cost of the shares.

3. Where time apportionment (shares acquired before 6 April 1965) applies to a case within the scope of this practice, the Commissioners for Her Majesty's Revenue and Customs are prepared to calculate the gain on each distribution by applying the time apportionment fraction as at the date of the first distribution without further adjustment under paragraph 16(8) Schedule 2 TCGA 1992.

Appendix 7

Inland Revenue Interpretations

RI 21 Close investment-holding companies

A close company is a close investment-holding company (CIC) for any accounting period unless, throughout the period, it exists – as a question of fact – wholly or mainly for any of the purposes specified in TA 1988, s 13A(2). A principal effect of CIC status is that the company is not entitled to claim the small companies' rate of corporation tax for that accounting period.

A company in liquidation is normally a CIC. This is because a company in liquidation exists for the purpose of winding-up its affairs and distributing its assets to shareholders. Although during the winding-up the company might carry on a trade or business that it had carried on previously, it is unlikely that this will be other than incidental to its main purpose of winding-up its affairs.

There is, however, some uncertainty as to the application of s 13A(4). This provides that where a company in liquidation was not a CIC for the accounting period immediately before the commencement of winding-up, that status automatically continues for the first accounting period after the commencement of winding-up. A company that had previously carried on a trade but which ceased to carry it on some time before the commencement of winding-up, will normally be a CIC for the accounting period immediately before the commencement of winding-up. It is unlikely, therefore, to come within s 13A(4).

It is most unlikely, in any event, that a company in liquidation would be found not to be a CIC for any accounting period following the first accounting period after the commencement of winding-up.

RI 34 Small capital distributions

The receipt of a capital distribution from a company in respect of shares in that company is treated as a part disposal of those shares (TCGA 1992, s 122). The inspector may make a direction under TCGA 1992, s 122(2) if he or she is satisfied that the distribution is small compared with the value of the shares. In this context the Revenue consider the word 'small' to mean 5% or less. The effect of the direction is that the distribution is not treated as a disposal but the amount received is deducted from the recipient's allowable expenditure on the shares.

It is possible that a recipient may want to have a small distribution treated as a disposal and would prefer the inspector not to make a direction under s 122(2). This could be advantageous if, for example, any gain would be covered by the annual exempt amount. The Revenue will not insist on the application of s 122(2) if the recipient would prefer to have the distribution treated as a disposal. In practice this is most likely to apply to the sale of rights nil paid which TCGA 1992, s 123 treats as a capital distribution.

First publication Inland Revenue Tax Bulletin Issue 5, November 1992.

RI 93 Transfers of assets at undervalue to employees or directors – disposal consideration

Where an asset is transferred by an employer to an employee or a director in connection with the employment or services, TCGA 1992, s 17(1)(b) deems the consideration for the transfer to be at market value. For capital gains tax, therefore, the employer is treated as disposing of the asset at market value and the employee as acquiring it at that value.

But where the consideration actually paid by the employee is less than market value, the difference will usually be chargeable to income tax on him as a Schedule E emolument. In such circumstances it has been the Revenue's practice, in computing any capital gains tax payable by the employer on the disposal, and subject to certain conditions, to take the actual consideration paid, and not the market value of the asset, as the consideration for the transfer. The effect is to reduce the amount of the employer's chargeable gain. The employee continues to be regarded as having given market value consideration in calculating any gain on a subsequent disposal of the asset.

The Schedule E and the capital gains charges that can arise on such transfers at undervalue are quite distinct, arising on different taxpayers and separately calculated. The Revenue have concluded that there are no grounds for the continuance of this concessionary practice and it is therefore being withdrawn. The correct statutory treatment will apply to transfers of assets on or after 6 April 1995.

First publication Inland Revenue Tax Bulletin Issue 14, December 1994.

RI 95 Inheritance tax – business and agricultural relief

The inheritance tax legislation provides relief for transfers of agricultural property and for business property. The Revenue have been asked for their views on the availability of relief:

- where agricultural property is replaced by business property (or vice versa) shortly before the owner's death; and

- on the donor's death, where the donee of a potentially exempt transfer of agricultural property has sold it and reinvested the proceeds in a non-agricultural business (or vice versa).

A 'potentially exempt transfer' (PET) is a lifetime transfer, which only becomes chargeable to inheritance tax if the donor dies within seven years of the transfer.

Inheritance tax business and agricultural relief reduces the value of relevant business property, or the agricultural value of agricultural property, by either 50 or 100%. The rate of relief depends on the nature of the property and interest held.

The qualifying conditions for the relief include requirements of a minimum period of ownership and, in the case of agricultural property, of occupation of the property for agricultural purposes immediately before the transfer. If, and to the extent that, the same property may qualify for relief as both agricultural property and business property, IHTA 1984, s 114 prevents double relief.

There are also rules that allow for the sale and replacement of qualifying property. The replacement is qualifying property only if it, and the original qualifying property, have together been owned (and, in the case of agricultural property, occupied) for a combined minimum period.

In the Revenue's view, where agricultural property that is a farming business is replaced by non-agricultural business property, the period of ownership of the original property will be relevant for applying the minimum ownership condition to the replacement property. Business property relief will be available on the replacement if all the conditions for that relief are satisfied. Where non-agricultural business property is replaced by a farming business, and the latter is not eligible for agricultural property relief, s 114(1) does not exclude business property relief if the conditions for that relief are satisfied.

There could be cases where, for example, agricultural land is not part of a farming business, so any replacement could only qualify for business property relief if it satisfied the minimum ownership conditions in its own right. However, the Revenue's experience suggests such cases are likely to be exceptional.

Where the donee of a PET of a farming business sells the business, and replaces it with a non-agricultural business, the effect of IHTA 1984 s 124A(1) is to deny agricultural property relief on the value transferred by the PET. Consequently, s 114(1) does not exclude business property relief if the conditions for that relief are satisfied; and, in the reverse situation, the farming business acquired by the donee can be 'relevant business property' for the purposes of IHTA 1984, s 113B(3)(c).

RI 103 Redundancy payments and provisions

This article summarises the Revenue's current thinking on the treatment of redundancy costs in the computation of the taxable profits from a trade, profession or vocation – whether relief is available at all.

Under general Schedule D Case I and II rules, redundancy payments will normally be an allowable Case I and II deduction provided that:

- they are laid out wholly and exclusively for business purposes; and

- the payments are not of a capital nature.

In particular, redundancy payments made as an incident in the discontinuance of a trade are inadmissible on first principles. See *IRC v Anglo Brewing Co Ltd.*

Where a sum is not deductible under the general rules TA 1988, ss 90, 579, nevertheless, a deduction is given for:

- statutory redundancy payments; and

- additional payments, inadmissible on the Anglo-Brewing principle, up to three times the statutory payment made.

TIMING OF DEDUCTION

If the right to a tax deduction is dependent on TA 1988, s 90 or s 579 then relief is due for the period of account in which the payment is made. Where the payment is made after the discontinuance, it is regarded for this purpose as made on the last day on which the business is carried on.

Where instead a deduction is due under the general rules, the Revenue's view is that a provision for future payments may be allowed as a deduction so long as:

- the provision appears in the commercial accounts of the business in accordance with generally accepted accounting principles, including those in Financial Reporting Standard 3 para 18 where that is applicable; and

- a definite decision was taken during the period of account to proceed with the redundancy programme; and

- the provision was accurately calculated using the degree of hindsight permitted by Statement of Standard Accounting Practice 17 (an accurate calculation will normally require the individual employees affected to be identified); and

- payment was made within nine months of the end of the period of account, as required by FA 1989, s 43.

First publication Inland Revenue Tax Bulletin Issue 15, February 1995.

RI 130 Post-cessation business expenses – new relief

BACKGROUND

FA 1995, s 90 introduced, with effect from Budget Day (29 November 1994), a new relief for certain post-cessation expenses of persons who formerly carried on a business either alone or in partnership. The relief does not extend to companies, but individuals may claim relief against income and gains generally, of the year in which the expense is regarded as arising.

Before the new legislation took effect, there was no relief for expenses incurred after a business ceased, unless it was possible to deduct a provision for them in the final accounts or there were post-cessation receipts, charged under Schedule D Case VI, against which the expenses could be set.

Expenses qualifying for relief

The relief is for specific qualifying expenses paid in the year for which the relief is claimed and for trade debts that unexpectedly go bad after the business is discontinued. The qualifying expenses are payments made wholly and exclusively:

(a)   in remedying defective work done, goods supplied or services rendered while the business was continuing, or damages in respect of such work, goods or services;

(b)   legal and other professional expenses connected with such costs;

(c)   in insuring against such costs;

(d)   for collecting trade debts of the discontinued business.

To qualify for relief, the payment must have been made on or after 29 November 1994 and within seven years from the discontinuance. A claim to relief must also be made within two years of the end of the year of assessment in which the payment was made.

Professional indemnity insurance premiums for work undertaken in the course of the business will now, in principle, almost always be allowable. If incurred while the business is continuing they will be allowed as a deduction in computing profits within the ordinary rules of Schedule D Cases I/II. If paid after the business has ceased they will be within the terms of the new relief, subject to the seven-year rule. The Revenue would not seek to disallow such an insurance premium paid while the business continues on the grounds that the cover extends to claims lodged after it has ceased. This view supersedes that in Tax Bulletin Issue 4 (August 1992 p32: Revenue Interpretation RI 25).

Bad debts

The new relief also extends to bad debts. Trade debts that have been included in business incomings before discontinuance and that have not been the subject of an admissible bad debt provision sometimes turn out to be bad. Alternatively, debts may be sometimes wholly or partly released under a post-cessation formal 'voluntary arrangement'. The new rules deem a payment equal to the amount of the bad debt to qualify for relief, as described above, at the time the debt is 'proved' to be bad. That will normally be the date when the inspector is notified that the debt is irrecoverable.

The inspector must be notified that a debt has gone bad within seven years of the time the business is discontinued. He or she will need to be satisfied that the debt is irrecoverable, and may require further information for this purpose. In these circumstances the debt is proved to be bad when the inspector is first notified, provided that the debt is eventually shown to have been bad at that date.

The relief is not restricted to debts that have become bad on or after 29 November 1994. Relief is available for debts that otherwise qualify even if they were already bad at that date, so long as they are irrecoverable when they are subsequently notified to the inspector.

Insurance recoveries

Expenses that qualify for relief under the new provision may be reimbursed or refunded as, for example, insurance proceeds or premium refunds. This means that the cost will not be ultimately borne by the former trader. To take account of this, any sums received as reimbursements or refunds of a qualifying expense will be brought into charge as post-cessation receipts.

Unpaid expenses

In arriving at the taxable trading profits of the discontinued business, some expenses might have been deducted on normal accountancy principles, even though they had not been paid. If there are any expenses that remain unpaid at the end of a year of assessment for which the new relief is claimed, the amount of the relief is reduced by the amount of the unpaid expense. But if an unpaid expense that triggered such a restriction is later paid, relief will be given as if it were a qualifying post-cessation expense of the year in which it is paid.

Link with existing post-cessation expenses provision

The new relief exists alongside the rules already on the statute book for post-cessation receipts and expenses. Those rules provide that any loss or expense that would have qualified as a trading deduction had the business not ceased is relieved against post-cessation receipts. But where the deductions exceed the post-cessation receipts for a year of assessment, the excess can only be carried forward and relieved against any post-cessation receipts arising in later years. Where an expense qualifies for sideways relief under the new rules as well as for carry forward under the provision described above, the new rules thus take priority.

First publication Inland Revenue Tax Bulletin Issue 19, October 1995.

RI 164 Meaning of 'small' in TCGA 1992, ss 23, 116, 122, 133, 243

The above sections all contain provisions that apply where certain receipts are 'small' as compared to some other specified amount. The Revenue's long standing approach has been that 'small' means 5% or less. This view has been published in the Capital Gains Manual and (in relation to TCGA 1992, s 122) in Inland Revenue Tax Bulletin Issue 5, November 1992 Revenue Interpretation RI 34.

The Revenue have reconsidered their approach in these cases. The judgments in the case of *O'Rourke v Binks* indicate that what is 'small' is a question of fact and degree and has to be considered in the light of the circumstances in any particular case. The purpose of the legislation is to avoid the delay and expense of a full computation where this would be disproportionate, and to avoid the need for assessments in trivial cases.

The '5% test' continues to offer practical advantages and the Revenue will continue to accept that any case that meets that test can be regarded as small. To further reduce the likelihood of assessments in trivial cases, the Revenue will also now accept that these provisions can apply wherever the amount or value of the receipt is £3,000 or less – whether or not this would fall within the 5% test. This revised approach may be applied to existing cases where the point remains open at the date of publication of this article – 24 February 1997 – and to all future cases.

Exceptionally, taxpayers may wish to suggest that receipts above these limits should nevertheless be regarded as small, in the context of their particular circumstances, or, conversely, that receipts below these limits should not be so regarded. Any such cases will remain to be resolved on their merits, having regard to the dicta in *O'Rourke v Binks*.

First Publication Inland Revenue Tax Bulletin, Issue 27, February 1997.

RI 200 Schedule D Cases I and II – redundancy payments

The Revenue have been asked how the decision of the Judicial Committee of the Privy Council in *IRC v Cosmotron Manufacturing Co Ltd* affects the views the Revenue expressed in Revenue Interpretation RI 103.

The *Cosmotron* case concerned 'severance payments' which the company was obliged under Hong Kong law to make to its employees when making them redundant. Cosmotron closed its factory and ceased business, so making all its employees redundant. The company claimed a deduction for the 'severance payments' in computing its trading profits for tax purposes in the final period of trading. The Privy Council held that this deduction was allowable.

Although the relevant Hong Kong tax provisions were not identical to those in the UK, the Privy Council had UK case law cited to it, and expressly stated in its judgment that in applying the law to this case there was no difference between the test under Hong Kong law and the test in TA 1988, s 74(1)(a) that expenditure must be incurred wholly and exclusively for the purposes of the trade. The 'severance payments' passed this test because they were a liability assumed when employees were taken on for the purposes of the trade. The obligation to make them was contingent, but was nonetheless incurred as a necessary condition of retaining the services of the employees concerned. It was immaterial that in this case it was the cessation of the trade that crystallised the liability.

Although decisions of the Privy Council are only of 'persuasive' authority in UK tax law, we have decided to be guided by the decision. Accordingly, the Revenue will not argue that payments made:

• to an employee taken on for the purposes of the trade; or

• under a pre-existing contractual or statutory obligation, which was a consequence of their being employed for the purposes of the trade;

are disallowed by s 74(1)(a) just because it is the cessation of the trade that crystallises the liability to pay.

This does not apply to payments such as ex gratia payments that exceed an employee's pre-existing contractual or statutory entitlement and that are made for the purpose of closing down a business. Such payments continue to be inadmissible on general principles (*IRC v Anglo Brewing Co Ltd*), although they may be partly or wholly deductible by virtue of TA 1988, s 90.

First publication Inland Revenue Tax Bulletin Issue 39, February 1999.

RI 238 Change of interpretation – taxability of trade debt written-back

Accounting periods starting after 31 December 2001

We have been considering the tax treatment of trade debts written-back to the profit and loss account. This article sets out our revised view. We no longer consider that the decision in the 1932 tax case *British Mexican Petroleum Company Ltd v Jackson*, is applicable in determining the tax treatment of trade debt written-back. That case concerned a release of trade debt which was credited to balance sheet reserves in rather unusual circumstances. Modern accountancy practice is that a write-back of trade debt must always be credited to the profit and loss account to produce accounts which show a true and fair view. It is now our view that the correct computation of profits chargeable to tax under Schedule D Cases I and II should include the credit to profit and loss account of a trade debt write-back.

We propose to apply this change of interpretation for accounting periods starting after 31 December 2001. The current *(prior to 31 December 2001)* guidance *(was originally)* in the Inspector's Manual *(but now held in Business Income Manual 40265)* will be replaced by the following text. If you are reading this article some time after publication please check the relevant manual for the latest version of the guidance.

Business Income Manual (BIM) 40265

Trade debts written back to profit and loss account [*guidance adjusted* August 2006]

To produce a true and fair view, modern accountancy practice requires that the write-back of trade debt must always be credited to the profit & loss account. Our view is that the profits chargeable to tax under Schedule D Cases I and II include the credit to profit and loss account of a trade debt write back. This interpretation was explained in an article in TB56/01 (December 2001). This guidance supersedes that article and explains our previous practice, which applied to accounting periods starting before 1 January 2002.

Accounting periods starting after 31 December 2001

You should not make a computational adjustment to the accounts of a trade, profession or vocation which show a credit to the profit and loss account for trade debt written-back unless the debt is released as part of a voluntary arrangement (see BIM42740).

A trade debt is a debt that has been allowed as a deduction for tax purposes. The trader (including those carrying on businesses or professions) has received goods or services and has a legal debt to pay for them. It does not include debts incurred for capital or non-allowable expenditure. Loan relationships of companies have separate legislation, which is explained in the Corporate Finance Manual.

Accountants may refer to trade liabilities or trade creditors and to the crediting of the profit and loss account rather than trade debt write-back.

Section 94 ICTA 1988 and release

Section 94 ICTA 1988 deals with the special situation where a debt is formally released. It does not apply:

- if there is no release, for example because creditor merely writes off the debt, fails to invoice or demand payment, or fails to present a cheque for payment; or

- if the release is part of a relevant arrangement or compromise (see BIM42740).

Section 94 provides that where a deduction has been allowed for a debt that is later released, the amount released is treated as a receipt of the trade, arising in the period in which the release is effected.

The 'release' of a debt must involve a contractual agreement. A debt is not deemed to be released because the debtor is bankrupt or in liquidation. Where the release is under seal no consideration is necessary. All other releases must involve the debtor giving consideration for the release. The consideration may be in non-monetary form, for example shares. A formal waiver of remuneration is also a release of a debt.

Intra-group debt may be released as part of a sale agreement involving a change of control of a company. These transactions usually have to be examined in detail to ascertain what amounts are trade debt and whether there has been a release.

Intra-group debt may also be released as part of a 'hive-across' within a group, where all the assets and liabilities of a company are transferred to another company within the same group of companies, and as a result:

- the transferee assumes the obligation to repay the creditor, and

- the creditor consents to release the transferor from its obligations in return for the transferee accepting them.

In this situation there is a release of a debt so Section 94 applies, but Case I principles also require the consideration given by the transferor to the transferee for accepting the liabilities to be deducted in computing profits which include any Section 94 receipt. The net result is that if full consideration is given (by transfer of assets), the Section 94 receipt is matched in full by the related deduction.

Particular circumstances of a release

Where the release occurs after the business has been discontinued (or treated for tax purposes as discontinued), the amount released is to be treated as a post-cessation receipt under Section 103 ICTA 1988 (see BIM80500 onwards).

A charge to tax should not be imposed when a debt is formally released if:

- a charge has already been made because the debtor's accounts showed a write-back in the profit & loss account for the debt, and

- there have not been any intervening accounting entries reinstating the debt in the debtor's accounts.

Accounting periods which started on or before 31 December 2001

We no longer consider that the decision in the 1932 tax case *British Mexican Petroleum Company Ltd v Jackson* (1932) 16 TC 570, is applicable in determining the tax treatment of trade debt written back. But our previous practice, based on that case, may be applied for periods before our change of view was announced:

- Where a trade debt is wholly or partly released by the creditor then Section 94 ICTA 1988 applies (see above).

- Where a trade debt is written back to the profit and loss account but is not released a tax computation adjustment should be made to deduct the amount.

British Mexican Petroleum Company Ltd v Jackson

Two trade debts were formally released in this case. Under the terms of an agreement with an oil producing company, British Mexican Petroleum Company Ltd was released from part of its trade debt for oil supplied to it. The amount released was carried direct to the balance sheet and shown as a separate item under the head 'reserve'. The company was also released from a trade debt owing for ship charter hire and this sum was taken to its profit & loss account. It was only the taxability of the sum taken to reserve that was in dispute. The House of Lords decision was that the sum was not taxable.

Prior to December 2001, the Inland Revenue interpreted comments made in the House of Lords in this case to mean that write-backs of trade debt, apart from those brought into tax by Section 74 ICTA 1988, were not taxable. HMRC no longer consider this interpretation to be correct.

First publication Inland Revenue Tax Bulletin Issue 56, December 2001.

Appendix 8

Statements of Practice

D12 Partnerships

Note only those elements of D12 regarded as relevant are reproduced

This statement of practice was originally issued by the Board of Inland Revenue on 17 January 1975 following discussions with the Law Society and the Allied Accountancy Bodies on the capital gains tax treatment of partnerships. This statement sets out a number of points of general practice which have been agreed in respect of partnerships to which TCGA 1992 s 59 applies.

The enactment of the Limited Liability Partnership Act 2000 has created, from April 2001, the concept of limited liability partnerships (as bodies corporate) in UK law. In conjunction with this, new capital gains tax provisions dealing with such partnerships have been introduced through TCGA 1992 s 59A.

1 Nature of the asset liable to tax

TCGA 1992 s 59A treats any partnership dealings in chargeable assets for capital gains tax purposes as dealings by the individual partners rather than by the firm as such. Each partner has therefore to be regarded as owning a fractional share of each of the partnership assets and not for this purpose an interest in the partnership.

Where it is necessary to ascertain the market value of a partner's share in a partnership asset for capital gains tax purposes, it will be taken as a fraction of the value of the total partnership interest in the asset without any discount for the size of his share. If, for example, a partnership owned all the issued shares in a company, the value of the interest in that holding of a partner with a one-tenth share would be one-tenth of the value of the partnership's 100% holding.

2 Disposals of assets by a partnership

Where an asset is disposed of by a partnership to an outside party, each of the partners will be treated as disposing of his fractional share of the asset. Similarly, if a partnership makes a part disposal of an asset, each partner will be treated as making a part disposal of his fractional share. In computing gains or losses, the proceeds of disposal will be allocated between the partners in the ratio of their share in asset surpluses at the time of disposal. Where this is not specifically laid down the allocation will follow the actual destination of the surplus as shown in the partnership accounts; regard will of course have to be paid to any agreement outside the accounts. If the surplus is not allocated among the partners but, for example, put to a common reserve, regard will be had to the ordinary profit-sharing ratio in the absence of a specified asset-surplus-sharing ratio. Expenditure on the acquisition of assets by a partnership will be allocated between the partners in the same way at the time of the acquisition. This allocation may require adjustment, however, if there is a subsequent change in the partnership sharing ratios (see para 4 below).

3   Partnership assets divided in kind among the partners

Where a partnership distributes an asset in kind to one or more of the partners, for example on dissolution, a partner who receives the asset will not be regarded as disposing of his fractional share in it. A computation will first be necessary of the gains that would be chargeable on the individual partners if the asset has been disposed of at its current market value. Where this results in a gain being attributed to a partner not receiving the asset, the gain will be charged at the time of the distribution of the asset. Where, however, the gain is allocated to a partner receiving the asset concerned, there will be no charge on distribution. Instead, his capital gains tax cost to be carried forward will be the market value of the asset at the date of distribution as reduced by the amount of his gain. The same principles will be applied where the computation results in a loss.

10 SHARES ACQUIRED IN STAGES

Where a share in a partnership is acquired in stages wholly after 5 April 1965, the acquisition costs of the various chargeable assets will be calculated by pooling the expenditure relating to each asset. Where a share built up in stages was acquired wholly or partly before 6 April 1965, the rules in TCGA 1992, Sch 2 para 18 will normally be followed to identify the acquisition cost of the share in each asset which is disposed of on the occasion of a reduction in the partnership's share; ie the disposal will normally be identified with shares acquired on a 'first-in, first-out' basis. Special consideration will be given, however, to any case in which this rule appears to produce an unreasonable result when applied to temporary changes in the shares in a partnership, for example those occurring when a partner's departure and a new partner's arrival are out of step by a few months.

First publication Revenue Press Release dated 17 January 1975 but revised in October 2002.

SP 12/80 Business property relief – 'buy and sell' agreements

The Board understand that it is sometimes the practice for partners or shareholder directors of companies to enter into an agreement (known as a 'buy and sell' agreement) whereby, in the event of the death before retirement of one of them, the deceased's personal representatives are obliged to sell and the survivors are obliged to purchase the deceased's business interest or shares, funds for the purchase being frequently provided by means of appropriate life assurance policies.

In the Board's view such an agreement, requiring as it does a sale and purchase and not merely conferring an option to sell or buy, is a binding contract for sale within IHTA 1984, s 113. As a result the inheritance tax business property relief will not be due on the business property interest or shares. (IHTA 1984, s 113 provides that where any property would be relevant business property for the purpose of business property relief in relation to a transfer of value but a binding contract for its sale has been entered into at the time of the transfer, it is not relevant business property in relation to that transfer.)

SP 8/92 Valuation of assets in respect of which capital gains tax gifts holdover relief is claimed

Introduction

1   This statement sets out the Revenue's revised practice for dealing with the valuation of assets in respect of which a claim to capital gains tax gifts holdover relief has been made. It applies to both new claims to holdover relief and existing claims in relation to which valuation negotiations with the Revenue may already have started.

Circumstances in which capital gains tax gifts holdover relief is available

2   Subject to an appropriate claim, gifts holdover relief is available where –

– an individual makes a disposal not at arm's length of –

  (a)   an asset used for the purposes of a trade, profession or vocation carried on by the transferor, his personal company or a member of a trading group of which the holding company is the transferor's "personal" company – TCGA 1992 s 165(2)(a);

  (b)   shares in a trading company or holding company of a trading group which are either unlisted or are in the transferor's "personal" company – TCGA 1992 s 165(2)(b); or

  (c)   agricultural property as defined by IHTA 1984 – TCGA 1992 Sch 7 para 1;

– the trustees of a settlement make a disposal of certain settled property – TCGA 1992 Sch 7 paras 2, 3;

– an individual or the trustees of a settlement make a disposal of an asset not at arm's length which is either a chargeable transfer under IHTA 1984; or is one of a specified range of exempt transfers – TCGA 1992 s 260(2).

What is the held over gain?

3   In the absence of a claim to holdover relief, TCGA 1992 s 17 would treat both the acquisition and disposal of the assets transferred to be for a consideration equal to their market value. Where a valid claim is made the effect is that the transferor's chargeable gain is reduced to nil and the transferee's acquisition cost is reduced by the amount of the held over gain.

4   The held over gain is the amount of the chargeable gain which would have accrued to the transferor, but for the claim to holdover relief. To compute the chargeable gain, and hence the held over gain, it is necessary to establish the market value of the asset at the date of the transfer.

5   Where no other reliefs are involved, holdover relief will be available where the market value of the asset transferred exceeds the transferor's allowable expenditure and the amount of indexation allowance due up to the date of disposal. If holdover relief is claimed and no consideration is paid then the transferee's acquisition cost will be equal to the sum of the transferor's allowable expenditure plus indexation to the date of transfer. In holdover relief cases, assuming none of the restrictions described in paras 6 and 13 below apply, agreement of the market value of the asset at the date of transfer has no bearing on the immediate capital gains tax liability of the transferor.

Position where consideration is paid by the transferee

6   Additional rules apply which affect the amount of the held over gain where actual consideration is paid to the transferor. Full holdover relief is only available if the actual consideration received does not exceed the transferor's allowable expenditure (TCGA 1992 s 38). If the actual consideration received exceeds the transferor's allowable expenditure on the asset, the holdover relief is restricted by that excess (TCGA 1992 ss 165(7), 260(5)).

7   Where consideration is paid, the transferee's acquisition cost will be equivalent to the sum of the transferor's allowable expenditure, the indexation allowance due to the date of disposal by the transferor and the gain immediately chargeable on the transferor.

Circumstances where in future market value at disposal need not be agreed with the Revenue

8   Subject to the following conditions, the Revenue will admit a claim for holdover relief without requiring a computation of the held over gain in any case where the transferor and transferee complete the second page of the claim form attached to the Help Sheet IR 295. In particular this requires –

–   a joint application by the transferor and the transferee,

–   provision of details concerning the asset and its history or alternatively

224

a calculation incorporating informally estimated valuations if necessary, and

–   a statement that both parties have satisfied themselves that the value of the asset at the date of transfer was in excess of the allowable expenditure plus indexation to that date,

The further conditions are that –

–   once a claim made on this basis has been accepted by the Revenue it may not be subsequently withdrawn,

–   if after acceptance by the Revenue it emerges that any information provided or statement made by either the transferor or transferee was incorrect or incomplete, in each case their capital gains tax position in relation to the asset will be computed in accordance with the relevant statutory provisions and assessments made as appropriate.

It should be noted that for years 1996–97 onwards all claims to holdover relief are to be made on the claim form attached to Help Sheet IR 295 or a copy of it.

9   Where, under the terms of this statement of practice, a claim is admitted without the held over gain being computed, this does not mean that the Revenue accepts as factually correct or will subsequently be bound by any information or statements given by any person, whether expressly or by implication, in connection with the claim. Neither the Revenue nor the claimants are bound in any way by any estimated values shown on the claim form or in any calculations.

Assets held on 31 March 1982

10   Unless actual consideration is given by the transferee, this practice will also apply to assets held by the transferor on 31 March 1982. It will only be necessary to agree a value at 31 March 1982 when the transferee disposes of the asset.

11   If the transferor has made an election under TCGA 1992 s 35(5), the transferee's acquisition cost of the asset will be equal to the 31 March 1982 value plus indexation up to the date of the transfer. If there is no election under TCGA 1992 s 35(5), the transferee's acquisition cost of the asset will be equal to the transferor's original cost plus indexation up to the date of the transfer or the 31 March 1982 value plus indexation up to the date of transfer – whichever is greater.

12   If the transferee has given some consideration for the asset it will be necessary to agree the 31 March 1982 value immediately. This is so that the excess over the allowable expenditure – which is chargeable to capital gains tax immediately – can be determined. However, the Revenue will still be prepared to accept a holdover relief claim without undertaking a valuation as at the date of transfer.

Circumstances in which a valuation may be required

13   There are certain cases where TCGA 1992 Sch 7 paras 5, 6 or 7 restrict the amount of the held over gain. These are cases where an asset has at some time during the transferor's ownership been used for non-business purposes, or has only been used in part for business purposes and cases involving shares etc, in a company which has non-business assets. This Statement of Practice cannot apply in any of these cases, because it is necessary to compute the chargeable gain before holdover relief. Otherwise the Revenue's expectation is, subject to the circumstances described in paras 8, 10–12 that it will rarely be necessary to determine the market value at the date of the gift. However, a valuation may become necessary as a result of the interaction of the held over gain with other capital gains tax reliefs. It is not expected that even in these cases will it be necessary to establish the market value immediately. Instead, it is more likely that a valuation will not be required before, for instance, a later disposal of the asset by the transferee. The following paragraphs cover the more common circumstances.

Retirement relief

14   Holdover relief is not available in the case of a disposal of an asset to the extent that any gain benefits from retirement relief (TCGA 1992 s 165(3)(a), (b); TCGA 1992 s 260(5) Sch 6). This means that holdover relief may be claimed if the market value at the date of transfer is at least equal to the sum of the transferor's allowable expenditure, indexation allowance to the date of disposal and the retirement relief due.

15   Unless requested by the claimants, the agreement of the market value of the asset will be deferred until either –

–   it is necessary to determine the quantum of the retirement relief due. Normally this will be when the transferor makes another disposal which attracts retirement relief, or

–   it is necessary to determine the transferee's cost of the asset.

Relief in respect of deferred charges on gains before 31 March 1982 (TCGA 1992 Sch 4)

16   In the case of an asset acquired before 31 March 1982 and transferred before 6 April 1988 it is necessary to compute any held over gain in order to give the benefit of the 50 per cent reduction available under TCGA 1992 Sch 4. To the extent that the market value of the asset at the date of transfer has not already been determined the Revenue is prepared to defer the need for a valuation until disposal by the transferee.

Time apportionment in the case of assets held on 6 April 1965

17 In the case of an asset held at 6 April 1965 chargeable gains and allowable losses arising on disposal are "time apportioned" so that only those accruing since 6 April 1965 are recognised for capital gains tax purposes. If holdover relief is claimed in relation to the gift of such an asset it is always necessary to agree a valuation at the date of transfer in order to apply time apportionment to the deferred gain. The Revenue are content to defer this valuation until the asset is disposed of by the transferee.

Application of statement of practice to existing holdover relief claims

18 In relation to existing holdover relief claims, valuation negotiations with the Revenue may have commenced, but not yet been completed. Taxpayers who want to take advantage of the practice in relation to such claims should write to the inspector of taxes to whom they were submitted.

First publication Revenue Press Release dated 26 October 1992.

First publication Revenue Press Release dated 26 October 1992.

SP 11/81 Additional redundancy payments

TA 1988 s 90 provides relief to an employer for certain redundancy payments made on or after 1 April 1980, which would otherwise have been treated as non-allowable because they were associated with the actual or notional discontinuance of the trade or business. In the Revenue view, the same principle for disallowing redundancy payments for tax purposes can apply where an identifiable part of a trade is discontinued.

In practice, s 90 will be regarded as applying to a partial, as to a complete, discontinuance where the redundancy payment would satisfy the test of TA 1988 s 74(1)(a) but for the fact that it is associated with a partial discontinuance.

First publication 6 November 1981.

SP 1/94 Non-statutory lump sum redundancy payments

1 ITEPA 2003 s 309(1), (2) provide that statutory redundancy payments shall be exempt from income tax as employment income, with the exception of any liability under s 401 of that Act.

2 Lump sum payments made under a non-statutory scheme, in addition to, or instead of statutory redundancy pay, will also be liable to income tax only under ITEPA 2003 s 401 provided they are genuinely made solely on account of redundancy as defined in the Employment Rights Act 1996. This will be so whether the scheme is a standing one which forms part of the terms on which the employees give their services or whether it is an ad hoc scheme devised to meet a specific situation such as the imminent closure of a particular factory.

3   However, payments made under a non-statutory scheme which are not genuinely made to compensate for loss of employment through redundancy may be liable to tax in full. In particular, payments which are, in reality, a form of terminal bonus will be chargeable to income tax as earnings under ITEPA 2003 s 62. Payments made for meeting production targets or doing extra work in the period leading up to redundancy are examples of such terminal bonuses. Payments conditional on continued service in the employment for a time will also represent terminal bonuses if calculated by reference to any additional period served following issue of the redundancy notice.

4   The Revenue is concerned to distinguish between payments under non-statutory schemes which are genuinely made to compensate for loss of employment through redundancy and payments which are made as a reward for services in the employment or more generally for having acted as or having been an employee. As arrangements for redundancy can often be complex and provide for a variety of payments, it follows that each scheme must be considered on its own facts. The Revenue's practice, in these circumstances, is to allow employers to submit proposed schemes to their inspectors of taxes for advance clearance.

5   An employer or any other person operating a redundancy scheme, who wishes to be satisfied that lump sum payments under a scheme will be accepted as liable to tax only under ITEPA 2003 s 401 should submit the full facts to the inspector for consideration. Applications for clearance should be made in writing and should be accompanied by the scheme document together with the text of any intended letter to employees which explains its terms.

First publication Revenue Press Release dated 17 February 1994.

Note: The Revenue's practice was revised following the decision of the House of Lords in *Mairs v Haughey* [1993] STC 569, and this statement supersedes Statement of Practice SP 1/81.

Checklist of items to be considered during the dissolution process

Set out below is a checklist of the items that need to be considered when proposing to dissolve the family company. In respect of many items the answer will simply be 'not applicable' but, it is suggested, by working through the checklist the great majority of problem areas will be anticipated and either avoided or accommodated.

Before working through the checklist the first action should be to set out a timetable. Not only will this concentrate the attention of both agent and client but would also, inevitably, set a target date by which the dissolution process is complete. In particular, having a timetable allows an assessment, for trading companies, of the impact of the loss of business asset taper relief and also allows a review to be undertaken to establish whether there are any areas of delay where that delay can be reduced to a minimum.

START AS SOON AS YOU CAN

Establishing those areas that can be dealt with before trading ceases should increase the efficiency with which these matters are dealt with. Most practitioners will begin to deal with the process only after the client company has ceased to trade but, by that time, the enthusiasm of the business proprietor will be less certain; but delay can potentially delay the dates on which the distributions are made so that more of any gain is subject to non-business CGT taper relief. It is suggested that in preparing the timetable a critical path analysis is prepared comparing those actions which require to be dealt with under the following categories:

- actions to be undertaken by the proprietor either before cessation of trade or immediately afterwards, together with any actions that are required to be taken to realise the assets at the appropriate times;

- actions to be taken by the professional adviser to include obtaining of any tax clearances, tax registrations and other related issues – this should include, for example, making sure that the accounts preparation for the final periods of trading are dealt with promptly; and

- those actions, which require a response from third party institutions, such as HMRC or Registrar of Companies.

Certainly if the aim of dissolution is to minimise the period of any gain that is subject to non-business taper relief, or more prosaically simply to ensure the shareholders get their cash as soon as possible, then a clear definition of responsibilities does help to concentrate, particularly, the mind of the company owner. Certainly, in my experience, when taper relief was not an influential issue in dissolving family companies, it was not unusual for proprietors to simply shut the business down and go away on holiday for an extended period. Equally it is not unusual for the professional advisers to park the cardboard box at the back of the office to be dealt with when more pressing matters had been resolved. As is clear from this publication the impact of non-business taper relief will seriously damage the distribution on liquidation by increasing the tax charges.

However, just as we continually stress to our clients, tax is not the only criteria that must be addressed so we must not allow the process to drift. Provided the management of the dissolution is dealt with efficiently then any desired taxation consequences should flow. Equally if the case is allowed to fester and matters are only dealt with as and when time is available then getting the cash to the shareholders promptly is unlikely to happen. Inevitably any desired taxation advantages will be lost in the organisational muddle. Whenever I have dealt with these arrangements I am generally on a fixed fee basis so the quicker matters can be resolved the more profitable is the transaction for the adviser. I have no incentive to delay matters, and as is equally clear the shareholders have no incentive to delay.

The checklist is a summary of actions that may or may not require attention. It is the nature of such checklists that they include items which may only be of relevance in a minority of cases. I find even so, that considering the points made often helps to improve the matters under consideration even if the particular point is discarded.

It is considered that the checklist should apply whether the dissolution is being dealt with under either the concession route or the more formal liquidation route. However as elsewhere in this publication the underlying assumption is of solvency. If matters are being dealt with by a licensed insolvency practitioner then greater care needs to be taken to ensure that all three parties to the arrangements are aware of the aims of the exercise and that unnecessary delay is avoided.

Included in each section are general observations to that section which are set out as italics.

TIMETABLE

- Establish a timetable for events to occur.

- Is the timetable realistic? Does it allow for third party delay or does it rely upon all parties dealing with matters promptly.

- Review the reliability of the timetable prior to commencement of the process both from experience of similar cases and from client knowledge that includes experience of compliance in the past.

- Review status of timetable on a regular basis and adjust whenever slippage occurs.

- Keep all interested parties aware of the status of the timetable, in particular the impact on the timing of both future events and payment of tax.

This should be established well before the company ceases to trade so that matters that can be dealt with now are dealt with now and do not delay any distribution to shareholders.

TAX PLANNING

- Make sure this is undertaken whilst the company is trading.

- Do not assume that a scheme works; you have to do the sums

- Consider all areas, not just the company's position but also the shareholders and any assets they may own outside the business.

- If a scheme is undertaken make sure that everyone knows what is happening and that any planning is not undone by shareholders doing their own thing.

- Make sure that the facts used to support the planning are based upon facts; review your files for earlier transactions and any agreement of value.

- In respect of any proposed purchase of own shares consider if application for HMRC clearance is required. If there is no value shift, which there should not be in dissolution since all shareholders should receive the same proportionate entitlement there may not be any need to obtain clearance.

- When any purchase of own shares has taken place, inform the HMRC office that deals with the company of the transaction.

- Wherever possible begin the process well before trading ceases. We generally know which clients have had enough so prime them to let you know when the point of no return is approaching.

HOW MUCH TO PAY OUT

- Prepare a pro forma balance sheet at the date trade ceases and from that prepare an estimated CGT computation.

- Consider whether the issued share capital is more than £5,000 so that the bona vacantia provisions may come into play.

- If the issued share capital is greater than £5,000 then organise a purchase of own shares to reduce issued capital below £5,000.

- Consider a cash flow forecast suggesting dates for interim distributions.

- Even if annual accounts do not have to be prepared for either tax or statutory purposes prepare updates of the pro forma so that interim payments are made as appropriate.

- Preserve all the interim pro forma balance sheets so that there is an audit trail.

- Prepare an appropriate file note to assess on a regular basis whether interim distributions can now be made.

Often the professional adviser will take control of payments in the dissolution period. Imagine the reaction of the client if he discovers whilst playing golf with his old bank manager that you have been sitting on funds for some time.

VALUE ADDED TAX

- Is the business to be deregistered?

  - Complete VAT 7

- Any assets at deregistration?

  - If taxable value exceeds £5,714 the declare output VAT on final return.

- If the business was operating the VAT cash basis, declare output VAT on recoverable value of debtors on final return.

- Complete final VAT return and ensure all input VAT on goods claimed back.

- Has the trade been sold?

  - Does the purchaser satisfy the TOGC requirements?

- If the assets sold include land or property where option to tax has been made, has purchaser opted to tax?

- If the assets sold include land or property does the vendor need to opt to tax to avoid input VAT clawback under the Capital Goods Scheme?

- If the assets sold include land or property, will any part be automatically standard rated because it relates to construction services previously supplied within three years before sale?

- If the assets sold include land or property will the purchaser own the asset in the same status?

- If the assets sold include land or property has option to tax been considered?

- If the business has been charged VAT on services after deregistration, complete VAT 427 and submit to HMRC with supporting VAT invoices.

Penalties from HMRC, even once the company has ceased to trade, will seriously impact upon the funds available to be distributed.

APPLICATION TO REGISTRAR

- Complete Form 652a and submit with the appropriate fee.

- Make sure the forms are signed by a majority of directors.

- File acknowledgement.

- If there is a change of mind and company is to continue file Form 652b.

Delay in submitting the forms can significantly delay distribution to shareholders.

REGISTRAR OF COMPANIES REQUIREMENTS

- Submit any accounts within the filing deadlines.

- If a purchase of own shares has been made, submit form G169 after payment of Stamp Duty due on payment.

- File Annual Returns required.

If penalties arise in the dissolution period who will be expected to pay these?

CLOSING DOWN THE BUSINESS

- Issue Form P45 to all employees.

- Notify insurers of the change in circumstances.

If there are assets on site but the premises are no longer attended on a regular basis this may impact upon the insurance conditions.

- Organise postal redirection.

- Notify all suppliers and arrange for them to send in final invoices and statements.

- Specify a final date where orders will be valid.

- Consider changing the registered office.

It is not unknown for employees to order goods whether for their own benefit or merely as mischief making in this period.

MONEY LAUNDERING

- Are there any unpaid liabilities that need to be paid over to the appropriate regulatory authorities?
  - Customer overpayments?
  - Unpaid VAT or Income Tax?

- Does the accountant/adviser need to make a report to NCIS for any retained amounts, which the company owners will not pay over.

- Care must be taken to avoid tipping off on the basis there may be other omissions and any discussion may put the client on guard.

- Many businesses will have arrangements whereby scrap and other waste materials are sold to local dealers for cash. Historically we know the amounts were not material from an audit perspective but consider what our response should be now.

- If we are dealing with disposals then full records must be maintained.

It is not unusual for accounts to include items that should have been resolved; where the proprietor should have contacted the appropriate authority to ensure that money has been paid to those who need to be paid because otherwise the retention of such monies amounts to stealing by finding.

UNINCORPORATED ASSOCIATIONS

- Make sure the decision to close the association down has been agreed at a general meeting.

- Consider writing to all members at their last know addresses to obtain written confirmation of agreement.

- Send a note showing the basis of distribution.

- Do not rely upon the authority of one or two members.

- Obtain receipts from all members.

Unincorporated associations are notorious for the bitter disputes that can arise. Make sure that everyone knows what is going on and has given their informed consent.

INHERITANCE TAX

- Are there any PETs either of shares or personal assets (but here we only need to consider the controlling shareholder) approaching the seven-year drop out?

- Are there any personally owned assets where a gift should be made prior to cessation of trade to allow CGT holdover even if this risks clawback at a later date? Once BPR is no longer available any gift may be a more expensive procedure.

- Is there any scope for making gifts where the loss to the estate is likely to be less than the value received on dissolution? Consider making gifts if this is a possibility.

- If the trade is to transfer to a newly established partnership or sole trader is the replacement asset rules satisfied?

Be aware of the impact of changing status on any IHT planning previously undertaken. Do not simply consider the current situation but review the statutory books to see what has happened over the previous seven years.

RESTARTING THE BUSINESS UNDER A NEW STATUS

- Establish a new PAYE scheme for employees. At the height of the new company formation frenzy some HMRC offices allowed the successor business to retain the old PAYE reference but this is now confirmed as incorrect.

- Obtain a new VAT registration number. Here it may be more acceptable to retain the old number using the VAT 169 procedure.

- Register as a new sole trader or partnership business using Form CWF 1, remembering that notification has to take place within three months of commencement to avoid a £100 penalty.

- If commencing as a company then again notification has to be made within three months of commencing to trade.

- Amend any business stationery to reflect the new status.

- Inform all suppliers and customers.

- Open a new business bank account.

Just because the actions taken are aimed at reducing the impact of red tape does not mean that there are no matters to be satisfied. A new business established by an existing client is still a new business and the administrative requirements must be satisfied.

SALE OF ASSETS

- Are there any assets where the sale will be long delayed with the consequence that the effect will be to delay distribution to shareholders? If so consider the possibility of allocating the asset to an individual shareholder in settlement of their entitlement.

- If the trade is to be continued as a partnership by the same individuals as are involved in the company, consider if a sale of assets is required in order to obtain a capital allowances advantage.

- Are there any assets the disposal of which will require special care, for example, in terms of pollution or other environmental issues?

- Does the company have legal ownership of all the assets? It is occasionally established that the formation of the company was not entirely satisfactory and there may still be assets in the names of directors or former partners.

- Is any asset being sold capable of independent operation? For example, is the company attempting to separate goodwill from the premises where the proper conclusion is that any goodwill is included in the value of property?

Anything that can go wrong to delay distribution to a shareholder is likely to go wrong. Clients are always more optimistic than agents so allow for delay in any timetable.

CORPORATION TAX ISSUES

- Review corporation tax computations for earlier years to see if there are any items of expenditure included in the profit and loss account that were disallowed as improvements where the expense should now be claimed through a capital gains tax computation.

- Consider whether any claim for terminal loss relief is appropriate and obtained.

- If there are disputes with HMRC concerning earlier years make sure that these are resolved promptly to avoid any Revenue objection to the dissolution process.

- Ensure the accounts and computations include full provision for all known items of expenditure. In particular be aware that post cessation expenditure cannot be deducted once the accounts for the final period are prepared and submitted.

- Make sure that all corporation tax returns are submitted on time.

- Pay any corporation tax due on time.

- Is there any ICTA 1988, s 419 tax to be recovered? Make sure the claim is made and if a loan is recovered against an interim distribution make sure this is clear on any distribution statement issued to the shareholder.

- Consider the date of sale, whilst liquidation or dissolution is in process, so that if relevant the lower rates of tax apply.

These are areas that need to be addressed. Some creditors do not bother to review the London Gazette but HMRC always do. If the company is being dissolved then sometimes it is possible to agree matters on a basis that would not be available if the company was ongoing.

COMPANIES ACT COMPLIANCE ISSUES

- If the dissolution process is likely to be extended make sure any annual returns are submitted to the Registrar of Companies on a timely basis.

- Similarly, complete accounts for all accounting reference periods and file with the Registrar of Companies within the appropriate time limits.

- Make sure the Registered Office of the company is an address that is regularly attended to ensure all statutory matters are dealt with. Consider changing the Registered Office to the office of a professional adviser.

- Make a diary note to review the company and its assets one month before the known dissolution date.

- Prepare a Form 652c notice of withdrawal in case this is required urgently when directors are unavailable.

There is a tendency to assume that compliance is less important once the decision to dissolve has been made but penalties are unacceptable at any time.

EMPLOYMENT ISSUES

- Make sure that all redundant employees receive their entitlement when the business closes down.

- Make sure that appropriate notice is given to employees of closing down to avoid any possibility of claims for unfair dismissal.

- Close down the PAYE scheme and submit to HMRC a Form P35 for the final period once all employment has ceased. However any scheme will need to continue whilst directors are in place and potentially continuing to receive salary and benefits.

- Make sure that Forms P11D and any other Revenue forms are submitted on time.

The proprietors may resent payment of redundancy but if any claim for unfair dismissal is successful because the directors failed to give adequate notice or consult with the employees then a payment under those circumstances will make redundancy seem a more than modest amount.

SHAREHOLDER/EMPLOYEE ISSUES

- If the shareholder/employee has a personal loan where interest relief is available make sure that interest is charged up to the date of cessation of trade before the company ceases trading.

- Make sure that the distributions from the company are used, in the first instance, to repay any borrowings to avoid interest that is not allowable.

- Calculate the impact upon capital gains tax taper relief for each shareholder and if the consequence of delay results in a significant increase in tax consider transfer to interest in possession settlements.

- If a shareholder wishes to make a gift of shares to family members in anticipation of dissolution make sure that the transfer is before cessation of trade, if holdover is required.

- Consider the consequences of loss of business taper relief on the recipient's part as against the availability of taper relief on the donor's part.

- If any holdover claim is needed to be made for gifts of shares make sure that they are submitted to HMRC within the statutory time limit of five years ten months from the end of the tax year in which the disposal took place

There can be an assumption that all we are doing is burying the business, and clients who were important to us when they were ongoing clients, now deserve second best. All clients should receive the best possible treatment because they may return; second best is likely to result in a firm being second choice in appointment for future work.

OTHER ISSUES

- If the trading name is to be retained and protected then consider forming a new dormant company with a name swap with the existing company. Make sure that all the forms are sent to the Registrar of Companies at the same time together with a letter of explanation.

- Review the accounting and other records of the company and arrange to shred any that are no longer required.

- If any records have to be stored then make arrangements with a storage company and make sure the fees are paid out before shareholder distribution.

- Make sure that any assets used by the company but which were always owned by a shareholder are transferred back to personal ownership. Where the dissolution is by a liquidator do this before they are appointed to avoid confusion and costs of retrieving from unwitting third party purchasers.

- Ensure all professional advisers invoice appropriately and before distributions are made.

- Retain a modest float, even when all known creditors have been paid because there will always be some who do not come forward. Many creditors assume, mistakenly, that any form of dissolution is insolvent and will simply not bother to make a claim.

The most important element here is to avoid any situation where money has to be returned to meet unexpected bills. Far better to pay out less in the early stages with an unexpected bonus at the end.

SHAREHOLDER CGT COMPUTATION ISSUES

- Make sure the correct proceeds are taken into account in the CGT computation. Ask to see the distribution statements so that the computations reflect the actual distribution not the cash distribution which may be net of monies owed to the company.

- Where interim distributions place review the likely level of future distributions to ensure that the value of 'B' used in the part disposal formula is reliable and based upon the current best estimate of future realisations.

- Review the timing of distributions particularly when close to 5 April. Remember delaying from 31 March to 10 April may gain another annual CGT exemption or 12 months' delay in tax payment.

- If there are several agents involved, consider agreeing that one firm will deal with HMRC negotiations. This should save costs.

- Keep the shareholders informed. If there is delay that was not envisaged then tell them, do not hide your head and hope it will be sorted before any one complains.

It is not unknown for clients to simply say this is the amount of cash I received so that is what my disposal proceeds should reflect.

FORMAL LIQUIDATION

- Involve the licensed insolvency practitioner in the initial discussions and obtain their input into the preliminary timetable.

- Request and obtain regular reports as to the financial progress.

- Agree an arrangement where copies of all financial documents are exchanged.

- Formalise the monthly/quarterly reporting to the directors/shareholders so that delay is identified early and can be put right.

- Agree that you, as accountant, will undertake most matters on behalf of the liquidator to avoid an extended decision-making process.

The more professionals that are involved in the chain the greater the chance there will be delay or the equally popular game of diverting blame onto someone else!

LIMITED LIABILITY PARTNERSHIPS

- Establish if any rolled-over or held-over gains will come back into charge.

- Ensure the permanent file includes a CGT history of all partnership assets.

- Prepare a CGT history of all partners' interests in the partnership assets.

The importance of a permanent file to contain this information cannot be stressed enough. It is the nature of partnerships that membership will change with greater rapidity than limited companies, so far more detailed information on CGT assets will be required.

STAMP DUTY AND STAMP DUTY LAND TAX

- Potentially only an issue if there is consideration where land and buildings are transferred to shareholders. (*Only likely to be encountered in rare circumstances*).

- If there is a purchase of own shares, to avoid the bona vacantia provisions, submit form G169 to HMRC with duty due.

- Once G169 received from HMRC file with the Registrar of Companies.

AND FINALLY

- Make sure all assets have been sold or distributed before application to the registrar is made.

- Ask all the directors and shareholders for written confirmation that all outstanding matters have been resolved.

- Make sure your bill is paid; if you are to be paid to deal with CGT issues for all shareholders, obtain payment in advance whilst there are funds in the company.

- Obtain authority to destroy accounting records as soon as permissible, and make sure that they are destroyed promptly.

- Give the shareholders the same treatment as any other client, not every dissolution is because the shareholders are retiring to 'tend their dahlias'.

No one else will want the responsibility of keeping the records but make sure your charges cover both storage and the costs of confidential shredding.

Index

[All references are to paragraph number and appendices]